HOLY BIBLE

THE
NEW TESTAMENT

KING JAMES VERSION

෴ PRESENTED ෴
TO

_____

_____

BY

_____

_____

ON

_____

THE NEW TESTAMENT
OF
OUR LORD AND SAVIOUR
JESUS CHRIST

RED LETTER EDITION

KING JAMES VERSION

Printed in China

Contents

HOLY BIBLE

THE
NEW TESTAMENT

THE GOSPEL ACCORDING TO

MATTHEW

1 The book of the generation of Jesus Christ, the son of David, the son of Abraham.

2 Abraham begat Isaac; and Isaac begat Jacob; and Jacob begat Judas and his brethren;

3 And Judas begat Phares and Zara of Thamar; and Phares begat Esrom; and Esrom begat Aram;

4 And Aram begat Aminadab; and Aminadab begat Naasson; and Naasson begat Salmon;

5 And Salmon begat Booz of Rachab; and Booz begat Obed of Ruth; and Obed begat Jesse;

6 And Jesse begat David the king; and David the king begat Solomon of her *that had been the wife* of Urias;

7 And Solomon begat Roboam; and Roboam begat Abia; and Abia begat Asa;

8 And Asa begat Josaphat; and Josaphat begat Joram; and Joram begat Ozias;

9 And Ozias begat Joatham; and Joatham begat Achaz; and Achaz begat Ezekias;

10 And Ezekias begat Manasses; and Manasses begat Amon; and Amon begat Josias;

11 And Josias begat Jechonias and his brethren, about the time they were carried away to Babylon:

12 And after they were brought to Babylon, Jechonias begat Salathiel; and Salathiel begat Zorobabel;

13 And Zorobabel begat Abiud; and Abiud begat Eliakim; and Eliakim begat Azor;

14 And Azor begat Sadoc; and Sadoc begat Achim; and Achim begat Eliud;

15 And Eliud begat Eleazar; and Eleazar begat Matthan; and Matthan begat Jacob;

16 And Jacob begat Joseph the husband of Mary, of whom was born Jesus, who is called Christ.

17 So all the generations from Abraham to David *are* fourteen generations; and from David until the carrying away into Babylon *are* fourteen generations; and from the carrying away into Babylon unto Christ *are* fourteen generations.

18 ¶ Now the birth of Jesus Christ was on this wise: When as his mother Mary was espoused to Joseph, before they came together, she was found with child of the Holy Ghost.

19 Then Joseph her husband, being a just *man*, and not willing to make her a publick example, was minded to put her away privily.

20 But while he thought on these things, behold, the angel of the Lord appeared unto him in a dream, saying, Joseph, thou son of David, fear not to take unto thee Mary thy wife: for that which is conceived in her is of the Holy Ghost.

21 And she shall bring forth a son, and thou shalt call his name JESUS: for he shall save his people from their sins.

22 Now all this was done, that it might be fulfilled which was spoken of the Lord by the prophet, saying,

23 Behold, a virgin shall be with child, and shall bring forth a son, and they shall call his name Emmanuel, which being interpreted is, God with us.

24 Then Joseph being raised from sleep did as the angel of the Lord had bidden him, and took unto him his wife:

25 And knew her not till she had brought forth her firstborn son: and he called his name JESUS.

2 Now when Jesus was born in Bethlehem of Judaea in the days of Herod the king, behold, there came wise men from the east to Jerusalem,

2 Saying, Where is he that is born King of the Jews? for we have seen his star in the east, and are come to worship him.

3 When Herod the king had heard *these things*, he was troubled, and all Jerusalem with him.

4 And when he had gathered all the chief priests and scribes of the people together, he demanded of them where Christ should be born.

5 And they said unto him, In Bethlehem of Judaea: for thus it is written by the prophet,

6 And thou Bethlehem, *in* the land of Juda, art not the least among the princes of Juda: for out of thee shall come a Governor, that shall rule my people Israel.

7 Then Herod, when he had privily called the wise men, enquired of them diligently what time the star appeared.

8 And he sent them to Bethlehem, and said, Go and search diligently for the young child; and when ye have found *him*, bring me word again, that I may come and worship him also.

9 When they had heard the king, they departed; and, lo, the star, which they saw in the east, went before them, till it came and stood over where the young child was.

10 When they saw the star, they rejoiced with exceeding great joy.

11 (And when they were come into the house, they saw the young child with Mary his mother, and fell down, and worshipped him: and when they had opened their treasures, they presented unto him gifts; gold, and frankincense and myrrh.

12 And being warned of God in a dream that they should not return to Herod, they departed into their own country another way.

13 And when they were departed, behold, the angel of the Lord appeareth to Joseph in a dream, saying, Arise, and take the young child and his mother, and flee into Egypt, and be thou there until I bring thee word: for Herod will seek the young child to destroy him.

14 When he arose, he took the young child and his mother by night, and departed into Egypt:

15 And was there until the death of Herod: that it might be fulfilled which was spoken of the Lord by the prophet, saying, Out of Egypt have I called my son.

16 ¶ Then Herod, when he saw that he was mocked of the wise men, was exceeding wroth, and sent forth, and slew all the children that were in Bethlehem, and in all the coasts thereof, from two years old and under, according to the time which he had diligently enquired of the wise men.

17 Then was fulfilled that which was spoken by Jeremy the prophet, saying,

18 In Rama was there a voice heard, lamentation, and weeping, and great mourning, Rachel weeping *for* her children, and would not be comforted, because they are not.

19 ¶ But when Herod was dead, behold, an angel of the Lord appeareth in a dream to Joseph in Egypt,

20 Saying, Arise, and take the young child and his mother, and go into the land of Israel: for they are dead which sought the young child's life.

21 And he arose, and took the young child and his mother, and came into the land of Israel.

22 But when he heard that Archelaus did reign in Judaea in the room of his father Herod, he was afraid to go thither: notwithstanding, being warned of God in a dream, he turned aside into the parts of Galilee:

23 And he came and dwelt in a city called Nazareth: that it might be fulfilled which was spoken by the prophets, He shall be called a Nazarene.

3 In those days came John the Baptist, preaching in the wilderness of Judaea,

2 And saying, Repent ye: for the kingdom of heaven is at hand.

3 For this is he that was spoken of by the prophet Esaias, saying, The voice of one crying in the wilderness, Prepare ye the way of the Lord, make his paths straight.

4 And the same John had his raiment of camel's hair, and a leathern girdle about his loins; and his meat was locusts and wild honey.

5 ¶ Then went out to him Jerusalem, and all Judaea, and all the region round about Jordan,

6 And were baptized of him in Jordan, confessing their sins.

7 ¶ But when he saw many of the Pharisees and Sadducees come to his baptism, he said unto them, O generation of vipers, who hath warned you to flee from the wrath to come?

8 Bring forth therefore fruits meet for repentance:

9 And think not to say within yourselves, We have Abraham to *our* father: for I say unto you, that God is able of these stones to raise up children unto Abraham.

10 And now also the axe is laid unto the root of the trees: therefore every tree which bringeth

3

not forth good fruit is hewn down, and cast into the fire.

11 I indeed baptize you with water unto repentance: but he that cometh after me is mightier than I, whose shoes I am not worthy to bear: he shall baptize you with the Holy Ghost, and *with* fire:

12 Whose fan *is* in his hand, and he will throughly purge his floor, and gather his wheat into the garner; but he will burn up the chaff with unquenchable fire.

13 ¶ Then cometh Jesus from Galilee to Jordan unto John, to be baptized of him.

14 But John forbad him, saying, I have need to be baptized of thee, and comest thou to me?

15 And Jesus answering said unto him, Suffer *it to be so* now: for thus it becometh us to fulfil all righteousness. Then he suffered him.

16 And Jesus, when he was baptized, went up straightway out of the water: and, lo, the heavens were opened unto him, and he saw the Spirit of God descending like a dove, and lighting upon him:

17 And lo a voice from heaven, saying, This is my beloved Son, in whom I am well pleased.

4 Then was Jesus led up of the spirit into the wilderness to be tempted of the devil.

2 And when he had fasted forty days and forty nights, he was afterward an hungred.

3 And when the tempter came to him, he said, If thou be the Son of God, command that these stones be made bread.

4 But he answered and said, It is written, Man shall not live by bread alone, but by every word that proceedeth out of the mouth of God.

5 Then the devil taketh him up into the holy city, and setteth him on a pinnacle of the temple.

6 And saith unto him, If thou be the Son of God, cast thyself down: for it is written, He shall give his angels charge concerning thee: and in *their* hands they shall bear thee up, lest at any time thou dash thy foot against a stone.

7 Jesus said unto him, It is written again, Thou shalt not tempt the Lord thy God.

8 Again, the devil taketh him up into an exceeding high mountain, and sheweth him all the kingdoms of the world, and the glory of them;

9 And saith unto him, All these things will I give thee, if thou wilt fall down and worship me.

10 Then saith Jesus unto him, Get thee hence, Satan: for it is written, Thou shalt worship the Lord thy God, and him only shalt thou serve.

11 Then the devil leaveth him, and, behold, angels came and ministered unto him.

12 ¶ Now when Jesus had heard that John was cast into prison, he departed into Galilee;

13 And leaving Nazareth, he came and dwelt in Capernaum, which is upon the sea coast, in the borders of Zabulon and

Nephthalim:

14 That it might be fulfilled which was spoken by Esaias the prophet, saying,

15 The land of Zabulon, and the land of Nephthalim, *by* the way of the sea, beyond Jordan, Galilee of the Gentiles;

16 The people which sat in darkness saw great light; and to them which sat in the region and shadow of death light is sprung up.

17 ¶ From that time Jesus began to preach, and to say, Repent: for the kingdom of heaven is at hand.

18 ¶ And Jesus, walking by the sea of Galilee, saw two brethren, Simon called Peter, and Andrew his brother, casting a net into the sea: for they were fishers.

19 And he saith unto them, Follow me, and I will make you fishers of men.

20 And they straightway left *their* nets, and followed him.

21 ¶ And going on from thence, he saw other two brethren, James *the son* of Zebedee, and John his brother, in a ship with Zebedee their father, mending their nets; and he called them.

22 And they immediately left the ship and their father, and followed him.

23 ¶ And Jesus went about all Galilee, teaching in their synagogues, and preaching the gospel of the kingdom, and healing all manner of sickness and all manner of disease among the people.

24 And his fame went through-

out all Syria: and they brought unto him all sick people that were taken with divers diseases and torments, and those which were possessed with devils, and those which were lunatick, and those that had the palsy; and he healed them.

25 And there followed him great multitudes of people from Galilee, and *from* Decapolis, and *from* Jerusalem, and *from* Judaea, and *from* beyond Jordan.

5 And seeing the multitudes, he went up into a mountain: and when he was set, his disciples came unto him:

2 And he opened his mouth, and taught them, saying,

3 Blessed *are* the poor in spirit: for theirs is the kingdom of heaven.

4 Blessed *are* they that mourn: for they shall be comforted.

5 Blessed *are* the meek: for they shall inherit the earth.

6 Blessed *are* they which do hunger and thirst after righteousness: for they shall be filled.

7 Blessed *are* the merciful: for they shall obtain mercy.

8 Blessed *are* the pure in heart: for they shall see God.

9 Blessed *are* the peacemakers: for they shall be called the children of God.

10 Blessed *are* they which are persecuted for righteousness' sake: for theirs is the kingdom of heaven.

11 Blessed are ye, when *men* shall revile you, and persecute *you*, and shall say all manner

5

of evil against you falsely, for my sake.

12 Rejoice, and be exceeding glad: for great *is* your reward in heaven: for so persecuted they the prophets which were before you.

13 ¶ Ye are the salt of the earth: but if the salt have lost his savour, wherewith shall it be salted? it is thenceforth good for nothing, but to be cast out, and to be trodden under foot of men.

14 ¶ Ye are the light of the world. A city that is set on an hill cannot be hid.

15 Neither do men light a candle, and put it under a bushel, but on a candlestick; and it giveth light unto all that are in the house.

16 Let your light so shine before men, that they may see your good works, and glorify your Father which is in heaven.

17 ¶ Think not that I am come to destroy the law, or the prophets: I am not come to destroy, but to fulfil.

18 For verily I say unto you, Till heaven and earth pass, one jot or one tittle shall in no wise pass from the law, till all be fulfilled.

19 Whosoever therefore shall break one of these least commandments, and shall teach men so, he shall be called the least in the kingdom of heaven: but whosoever shall do and teach *them*, the same shall be called great in the kingdom of heaven.

20 For I say unto you, That except your righteousness shall exceed *the righteousness* of the scribes and Pharisees, ye shall in no case enter into the kingdom of heaven.

21 ¶ Ye have heard that it was said by them of old time, Thou shalt not kill; and whosoever shall kill shall be in danger of the judgment:

22 But I say unto you, That whosoever is angry with his brother without a cause shall be in danger of the judgment: and whosoever shall say to his brother, Raca, shall be in danger of the council: but whosoever shall say, Thou fool, shall be in danger of hell fire.

23 Therefore if thou bring thy gift to the altar, and there rememberest that thy brother hath ought against thee;

24 Leave there thy gift before the altar, and go thy way; first be reconciled to thy brother, and then come and offer thy gift.

25 Agree with thine adversary quickly, whiles thou art in the way with him; lest at any time the adversary deliver thee to the judge, and the judge deliver thee to the officer, and thou be cast into prison.

26 Verily I say unto thee, Thou shalt by no means come out thence, till thou hast paid the uttermost farthing.

27 ¶ Ye have heard that it was said by them of old time, Thou shalt not commit adultery:

28 But I say unto you, That whosoever looketh on a woman to lust after her hath committed adultery with her already in his heart.

6

29 And if thy right eye offend thee, pluck it out, and cast *it* from thee: for it is profitable for thee that one of thy members should perish, and not *that* thy whole body should be cast into hell.

30 And if thy right hand offend thee, cut it off, and cast *it* from thee: for it is profitable for thee that one of thy members should perish, and not *that* thy whole body should be cast into hell.

31 It hath been said, Whosoever shall put away his wife, let him give her a writing of divorcement:

32 But I say unto you, That whosoever shall put away his wife, saving for the cause of fornication, causeth her to commit adultery: and whosoever shall marry her that is divorced committeth adultery.

33 ¶ Again, ye have heard that it hath been said by them of old time, Thou shalt not forswear thyself, but shalt perform unto the Lord thine oaths:

34 But I say unto you, Swear not at all; neither by heaven; for it is God's throne:

35 Nor by the earth; for it is his footstool: neither by Jerusalem; for it is the city of the great King.

36 Neither shalt thou swear by thy head, because thou canst not make one hair white or black.

37 But let your communication be, Yea, yea; Nay, nay: for whatsoever is more than these cometh of evil.

38 ¶ Ye have heard that it hath been said, An eye for an eye, and a tooth for a tooth:

39 But I say unto you, That ye resist not evil: but whosoever shall smite thee on thy right cheek, turn to him the other also.

40 And if any man will sue thee at the law, and take away thy coat, let him have *thy* cloak also.

41 And whosoever shall compel thee to go a mile, go with him twain.

42 Give to him that asketh thee, and from him that would borrow of thee turn not thou away.

43 ¶ Ye have heard that it hath been said, Thou shalt love thy neighbour, and hate thine enemy.

44 But I say unto you, Love your enemies, bless them that curse you, do good to them that hate you, and pray for them which despitefully use you, and persecute you;

45 That ye may be the children of your Father which is in heaven: for he maketh his sun to rise on the evil and on the good, and sendeth rain on the just and on the unjust.

46 For if ye love them which love you, what reward have ye? do not even the publicans the same?

47 And if ye salute your brethren only, what do ye more *than others*? do not even the publicans so?

48 Be ye therefore perfect, even as your Father which is in heaven is perfect.

6 Take heed that ye do not your alms before men, to be seen of them: otherwise ye have no reward of your Father which is in heaven.

2 Therefore when thou doest *thine* alms, do not sound a trumpet before thee, as the hypocrites do in the synagogues and in the streets, that they may have glory of men. Verily I say unto you, They have their reward.

3 But when thou doest alms, let not thy left hand know what thy right hand doeth:

4 That thine alms may be in secret: and thy Father which seeth in secret himself shall reward thee openly.

5 ¶ And when thou prayest, thou shalt not be as the hypocrites *are:* for they love to pray standing in the synagogues and in the corners of the streets, that they may be seen of men. Verily I say unto you, They have their reward.

6 But thou, when thou prayest, enter into thy closet, and when thou hast shut thy door, pray to thy Father which is in secret; and thy Father which seeth in secret shall reward thee openly.

7 But when ye pray, use not vain repetitions, as the heathen *do:* for they think that they shall be heard for their much speaking.

8 Be not ye therefore like unto them: for your Father knoweth what things ye have need of, before ye ask him.

9 ¶ After this manner therefore pray ye: Our Father which art in heaven, Hallowed be thy name.

10 Thy kingdom come, Thy will be done in earth, as *it is* in heaven.

11 Give us this day our daily bread.

12 And forgive us our debts, as we forgive our debtors.

13 And lead us not into temptation, but deliver us from evil: For thine is the kingdom, and the power, and the glory, for ever. Amen.

14 ¶ For if ye forgive men their trespasses, your heavenly Father will also forgive you:

15 But if ye forgive not men their trespasses, neither will your Father forgive your trespasses.

16 ¶ Moreover when ye fast, be not, as the hypocrites, of a sad countenance: for they disfigure their faces, that they may appear unto men to fast. Verily I say unto you, They have their reward.

17 But thou, when thou fastest, anoint thine head, and wash thy face;

18 That thou appear not unto men to fast, but unto thy Father which is in secret; and thy Father, which seeth in secret, shall reward thee openly.

19 ¶ Lay not up for yourselves treasures upon earth, where moth and rust doth corrupt, and where thieves break through and steal:

20 But lay up for yourselves treasures in heaven, where neither moth nor rust doth corrupt, and where thieves do not break through nor steal:

21 For where your treasure is, there will your heart be also.

22 The light of the Body is the

eye: if therefore thine eye be single, thy whole body shall be full of light.

23 But if thine eye be evil, thy whole body shall be full of darkness. If therefore the light that is in thee be darkness, how great *is* that darkness!

24 ₵ No man can serve two masters: for either he will hate the one, and love the other; or else he will hold to the one, and despise the other. Ye cannot serve God and mammon.

25 ₵ Therefore I say unto you, Take no thought for your life, what ye shall eat, or what ye shall drink; nor yet for your body, what ye shall put on. Is not the life more than meat, and the body than raiment?

26 Behold the fowls of the air: for they sow not, neither do they reap, nor gather into barns; yet your heavenly Father feedeth them. Are ye not much better than they?

27 Which of you by taking thought can add one cubit unto his stature?

28 And why take ye thought for raiment? Consider the lilies of the field, how they grow; they toil not, neither do they spin:

29 And yet I say unto you, That even Solomon in all his glory was not arrayed like one of these.

30 Wherefore, if God so clothe the grass of the field, which to day is, and to morrow is cast into the oven, *shall he* not much more *clothe* you, O ye of little faith?

31 Therefore take no thought, saying, What shall we eat? or,

What shall we drink? or, Wherewithal shall we be clothed?

32 (For after all these things do the Gentiles seek:) for your heavenly Father knoweth that ye have need of all these things.

33 ₵ But seek ye first the kingdom of God, and his righteousness; and all these things shall be added unto you.

34 Take therefore no thought for the morrow: for the morrow shall take thought for the things of itself. Sufficient unto the day *is* the evil thereof.

7 Judge not, that ye be not judged.

2 For with what judgment ye judge, ye shall be judged: and with what measure ye mete, it shall be measured to you again.

3 And why beholdest thou the mote that is in thy brother's eye, but considerest not the beam that is in thine own eye?

4 Or how wilt thou say to thy brother, Let me pull out the mote out of thine eye; and, behold, a beam *is* in thine own eye?

5 Thou hypocrite, first cast out the beam out of thine own eye; and then shalt thou see clearly to cast out the mote out of thy brother's eye.

6 ₵ Give not that which is holy unto the dogs, neither cast ye your pearls before swine, lest they trample them under their feet, and turn again and rend you.

7 ₵ Ask, and it shall be given you; seek, and ye shall find; knock, and it shall be opened unto you:

9

8 For every one that asketh receiveth; and he that seeketh findeth; and to him that knocketh it shall be opened.

9 Or what man is there of you, whom if his son ask bread, will he give him a stone?

10 Or if he ask a fish, will he give him a serpent?

11 If ye then, being evil, know how to give good gifts unto your children, how much more shall your Father which is in heaven give good things to them that ask him?

12 Therefore all things whatsoever ye would that men should do to you, do ye even so to them: for this is the law and the prophets.

13 ¶ Enter ye in at the strait gate: for wide *is* the gate, and broad *is* the way, that leadeth to destruction, and many there be which go in thereat:

14 Because strait *is* the gate, and narrow *is* the way, which leadeth unto life, and few there be that find it.

15 ¶ Beware of false prophets, which come to you in sheep's clothing, but inwardly they are ravening wolves.

16 Ye shall know them by their fruits. Do men gather grapes of thorns, or figs of thistles?

17 Even so every good tree bringeth forth good fruit; but a corrupt tree bringeth forth evil fruit.

18 A good tree cannot bring forth evil fruit, neither *can* a corrupt tree bring forth good fruit.

19 Every tree that bringeth not forth good fruit is hewn down, and cast into the fire.

20 Wherefore by their fruits ye shall know them.

21 ¶ Not every one that saith unto me, Lord, Lord, shall enter into the kingdom of heaven; but he that doeth the will of my Father which is in heaven.

22 Many will say to me in that day, Lord, Lord, have we not prophesied in thy name? and in thy name have cast out devils? and in thy name done many wonderful works?

23 And then will I profess unto them, I never knew you: depart from me, ye that work iniquity.

24 ¶ Therefore whosoever heareth these sayings of mine, and doeth them, I will liken him unto a wise man, which built his house upon a rock:

25 And the rain descended, and the floods came, and the winds blew, and beat upon that house; and it fell not: for it was founded upon a rock.

26 And every one that heareth these sayings of mine, and doeth them not, shall be likened unto a foolish man, which built his house upon the sand:

27 And the rain descended, and the floods came, and the winds blew, and beat upon that house; and it fell: and great was the fall of it.

28 And it came to pass, when Jesus had ended these sayings, the people were astonished at his doctrine:

29 For he taught them as *one*

having authority, and not as the scribes.

8 When he was come down from the mountain, great multitudes followed him.

2 And, behold, there came a leper and worshipped him, saying, Lord, if thou wilt, thou canst make me clean.

3 And Jesus put forth *his* hand, and touched him, saying, I will; be thou clean. And immediately his leprosy was cleansed.

4 And Jesus saith unto him, See thou tell no man; but go thy way, shew thyself to the priest, and offer the gift that Moses commanded, for a testimony unto them.

5 ¶ And when Jesus was entered into Capernaum, there came unto him a centurion, beseeching him,

6 And saying, Lord, my servant lieth at home sick of the palsy, grievously tormented.

7 And Jesus saith unto him, I will come and heal him.

8 The centurion answered and said, Lord, I am not worthy that thou shouldest come under my roof: but speak the word only, and my servant shall be healed.

9 For I am a man under authority, having soldiers under me: and I say to this *man*, Go, and he goeth; and to another, Come, and he cometh; and to my servant, Do this, and he doeth *it*.

10 When Jesus heard *it*, he marvelled, and said to them that followed, Verily I say unto you, I have not found so great faith, no, not in Israel.

11 And I say unto you, That many shall come from the east and west, and shall sit down with Abraham, and Isaac, and Jacob, in the kingdom of heaven.

12 But the children of the kingdom shall be cast out into outer darkness: there shall be weeping and gnashing of teeth.

13 And Jesus said unto the centurion, Go thy way; and as thou hast believed, *so* be it done unto thee. And his servant was healed in the selfsame hour.

14 ¶ And when Jesus was come into Peter's house, he saw his wife's mother laid, and sick of a fever.

15 And he touched her hand, and the fever left her: and she arose, and ministered unto them.

16 ¶ When the even was come, they brought unto him many that were possessed with devils: and he cast out the spirits with *his* word, and healed all that were sick:

17 That it might be fulfilled which was spoken by Esaias the prophet, saying, Himself took our infirmities, and bare *our* sicknesses.

18 ¶ Now when Jesus saw great multitudes about him, he gave commandment to depart unto the other side.

19 And a certain scribe came, and said unto him, Master, I will follow thee whithersoever thou goest.

20 And Jesus saith unto him, The foxes have holes, and the birds of the air *have* nests; but the Son of man hath not where to

lay *his* head.

21 And another of his disciples said unto him, Lord, suffer me first to go and bury my father.

22 But Jesus said unto him, Follow me; and let the dead bury their dead.

23 ¶ And when he was entered into a ship, his disciples followed him.

24 And, behold, there arose a great tempest in the sea, insomuch that the ship was covered with the waves: but he was asleep.

25 And his disciples came to *him*, and awoke him, saying, Lord, save us: we perish.

26 And he saith unto them, Why are ye fearful, O ye of little faith? Then he arose, and rebuked the winds and the sea; and there was a great calm.

27 But the men marvelled, saying, What manner of man is this, that even the winds and the sea obey him!

28 ¶ And when he was come to the other side into the country of the Gergesenes, there met him two possessed with devils, coming out of the tombs, exceeding fierce, so that no man might pass by that way.

29 And, behold, they cried out, saying, What have we to do with thee, Jesus, thou Son of God? art thou come hither to torment us before the time?

30 And there was a good way off from them an herd of many swine feeding.

31 ¶ So the devils besought him,

saying, If thou cast us out, suffer us to go away into the herd of swine.

32 And he said unto them, Go. And when they were come out, they went into the herd of swine: and, behold, the whole herd of swine ran violently down a steep place into the sea, and perished in the waters.

33 And they that kept them fled, and went their ways into the city, and told every thing, and what was befallen to the possessed of the devils.

34 And, behold, the whole city came out to meet Jesus: and when they saw him, they besought *him* that he would depart out of their coasts.

9 And he entered into a ship, and passed over, and came into his own city.

2 And, behold, they brought to him a man sick of the palsy, lying on a bed: and Jesus seeing their faith said unto the sick of the palsy; Son, be of good cheer; thy sins be forgiven thee.

3 And, behold, certain of the scribes said within themselves, This *man* blasphemeth.

4 And Jesus knowing their thoughts said, Wherefore think ye evil in your hearts?

5 For whether is easier, to say, *Thy* sins be forgiven thee; or to say, Arise, and walk?

6 But that ye may know that the Son of man hath power on earth to forgive sins, (then saith he to the sick of the palsy,) Arise, take up thy bed, and go unto thine house.

7 And he arose, and departed to his house.

8 But when the multitudes saw *it*, they marvelled, and glorified God, which had given such power unto men.

9 ¶ And as Jesus passed forth from thence, he saw a man, named Matthew, sitting at the receipt of custom: and he saith unto him, Follow me. And he arose, and followed him.

10 ¶ And it came to pass, as Jesus sat at meat in the house, behold, many publicans and sinners came and sat down with him and his disciples.

11 And when the Pharisees saw *it*, they said unto his disciples, Why eateth your Master with publicans and sinners?

12 But when Jesus heard *that*, he said unto them, They that be whole need not a physician, but they that are sick.

13 But go ye and learn what *that* meaneth, I will have mercy, and not sacrifice: for I am not come to call the righteous, but sinners to repentance.

14 ¶ Then came to him the disciples of John, saying, Why do we and the Pharisees fast oft, but thy disciples fast not?

15 And Jesus said unto them, Can the children of the bridechamber mourn, as long as the bridegroom is with them? but the days will come, when the bridegroom shall be taken from them, and then shall they fast.

16 No man putteth a piece of new cloth unto an old garment, for that which is put in to fill it up taketh from the garment, and the rent is made worse.

17 Neither do men put new wine into old bottles: else the bottles break, and the wine runneth out, and the bottles perish: but they put new wine into new bottles, and both are preserved.

18 ¶ While he spake these things unto them, behold, there came a certain ruler, and worshipped him, saying, My daughter is even now dead: but come and lay thy hand upon her, and she shall live.

19 And Jesus arose, and followed him, and *so did* his disciples.

20 ¶ And, behold, a woman, which was diseased with an issue of blood twelve years, came behind *him*, and touched the hem of his garment:

21 For she said within herself, If I may but touch his garment, I shall be whole.

22 But Jesus turned him about, and when he saw her, he said, Daughter, be of good comfort; thy faith hath made thee whole. And the woman was made whole from that hour.

23 And when Jesus came into the ruler's house, and saw the minstrels and the people making a noise,

24 He said unto them, Give place: for the maid is not dead, but sleepeth. And they laughed him to scorn.

25 But when the people were put forth, he went in, and took her by the hand, and the maid arose.

13

26 And the fame hereof went abroad into all that land.

27 ¶ And when Jesus departed thence, two blind men followed him, crying, and saying, **Thou** son of David, have mercy on us.

28 And when he was come into the house, the blind men came to him: and Jesus saith unto them, Believe ye that I am able to do this? They said unto him, Yea, Lord.

29 Then touched he their eyes, saying, According to your faith be it unto you.

30 And their eyes were opened; and Jesus straitly charged them, saying, See *that* no man know *it*.

31 But they, when they were departed, spread abroad his fame in all that country.

32 ¶ As they went out, behold, they brought to him a dumb man possessed with a devil.

33 And when the devil was cast out, the dumb spake: and the multitudes marvelled, saying, It was never so seen in Israel.

34 But the Pharisees said, He casteth out devils through the prince of the devils.

35 And Jesus went about all the cities and villages, teaching in their synagogues, and preaching the gospel of the kingdom, and healing every sickness and every disease among the people.

36 ¶ But when he saw the multitudes, he was moved with compassion on them, because they fainted, and were scattered abroad, as sheep having no shepherd.

37 Then saith he unto his disciples, The harvest truly *is* plenteous, but the labourers *are* few;

38 Pray ye therefore the Lord of the harvest, that he will send forth labourers into his harvest.

10 And when he had called unto *him* his twelve disciples, he gave them power *against* unclean spirits, to cast them out, and to heal all manner of sickness and all manner of disease.

2 Now the names of the twelve apostles are these; The first, Simon, who is called Peter, and Andrew his brother; James *the son* of Zebedee, and John his brother;

3 Philip, and Bartholomew; Thomas, and Matthew the publican; James *the son* of Alphaeus, and Lebbaeus, whose surname was Thaddaeus;

4 Simon the Canaanite, and Judas Iscariot, who also betrayed him.

5 These twelve Jesus sent forth, and commanded them, saying, Go not into the way of the Gentiles, and into *any* city of the Samaritans enter ye not:

6 But go rather to the lost sheep of the house of Israel.

7 And as ye go, preach, saying, The kingdom of heaven is at hand.

8 Heal the sick, cleanse the lepers, raise the dead, cast out devils: freely ye have received, freely give.

9 Provide neither gold, nor silver, nor brass in your purses,

14

10 Nor scrip for *your* journey, neither two coats, neither shoes, nor yet staves: for the workman is worthy of his meat.

11 And into whatsoever city or town ye shall enter, enquire who in it is worthy; and there abide till ye go thence.

12 And when ye come into an house, salute it.

13 And if the house be worthy, let your peace come upon it: but if it be not worthy, let your peace return to you.

14 And whosoever shall not receive you, nor hear your words, when ye depart out of that house or city, shake off the dust of your feet.

15 Verily I say unto you, It shall be more tolerable for the land of Sodom and Gomorrha in the day of judgment, than for that city.

16 ¶ Behold, I send you forth as sheep in the midst of wolves: be ye therefore wise as serpents, and harmless as doves.

17 But beware of men: for they will deliver you up to the councils, and they will scourge you in their synagogues;

18 And ye shall be brought before governors and kings for my sake, for a testimony against them and the Gentiles.

19 But when they deliver you up, take no thought how or what ye shall speak: for it shall be given you in that same hour what ye shall speak.

20 For it is not ye that speak, but the Spirit of *your* Father which speaketh in you.

21 And the brother shall del up the brother to death, and th father the child: and the childre shall rise up against *their* par ents, and cause them to be p to death.

22 And ye shall be hated of *men* for my name's sake: but that endureth to the end shall saved.

23 But when they persecute y in this city, flee ye into anoth for verily I say unto you, shall not have gone over the ies of Israel, till the Son of be come.

24 The disciple is not above master, nor the servant ab his lord.

25 It is enough for the dis that he be as his master, an servant as his lord. If they called the master of the Beelzebub, how much *shall they call* them of his h hold?

26 Fear them not therefor there is nothing covered, hid, shall not be revealed; and that shall not be known.

27 What I tell you in da *that* speak ye in light: and ye hear in the ear, *that* pre upon the housetops.

28 And fear not them kill the body, but are kill the soul: but rather f which is able to destroy b and body in hell.

29 Are not two sparro for a farthing? and one shall not fall on the grou out your Father.

30 But the very hairs

head are all numb...

31 Fear ye not th...re, ye are of more value th...any sparrows.

32 Whosoever th...ore shall confess me befor... him will I confess also befo... y Father which is in heaven.

33 But whosoever...all deny me before men, him...ill I also deny before my Fat... which is in heaven.

34 Think not that I... come to send peace on earth...ame not to send peace, but a s...rd.

35 For I am come to... a man at variance against his...ther, and the daughter against h... mother, and the daughter in la... against her mother in law.

36 And a man's foe...*shall be* they of his own househo...

37 He that loveth ...ther or mother more than me is...ot worthy of me: and he that lo...th son or daughter more than ... is not worthy of me.

38 And he that taketh ...not his cross, and followeth afte... me, is not worthy of me.

39 He that findeth his lif... shall lose it: and he that loseth ...is life for my sake shall find it.

40 ¶ He that receiveth you ...eceiveth me, and he that receiveth me receiveth him that sent me.

41 He that receiveth a p...ophet in the name of a prophet ...shall receive a prophet's reward... and he that receiveth a righteous ...man in the name of a righteous m...an's reward.

42 And whosoever shall give to drink unto one of these little ones a cup of cold *water* only in the name of a disciple, verily I say unto you, he shall in no wise lose his reward.

11 And it came to pass, when Jesus had made an end of commanding his twelve disciples, he departed thence to teach and to preach in their cities.

2 Now when John had heard in the prison the works of Christ, he sent two of his disciples,

3 And said unto him, Art thou he that should come, or do we look for another?

4 Jesus answered and said unto them, Go and shew John again those things which ye do hear and see:

5 The blind receive their sight, and the lame walk, the lepers are cleansed, and the deaf hear, the dead are raised up, and the poor have the gospel preached to them.

6 And blessed is *he*, whosoever shall not be offended in me.

7 ¶ And as they departed, Jesus began to say unto the multitudes concerning John, What went ye out into the wilderness to see? A reed shaken with the wind?

8 But what went ye out for to see? A man clothed in soft raiment? behold, they that wear soft *clothing* are in kings' houses.

9 But what went ye out for to see? A prophet? yea, I say unto you, and more than a prophet.

10 For this is *he*, of whom it is

written, Behold, I send my messenger before thy face, which shall prepare thy way before thee.

11 Verily I say unto you, Among them that are born of women there hath not risen a greater than John the Baptist: notwithstanding he that is least in the kingdom of heaven is greater than he.

12 And from the days of John the Baptist until now the kingdom of heaven suffereth violence, and the violent take it by force.

13 For all the prophets and the law prophesied until John.

14 And if ye will receive *it*, this is Elias, which was for to come.

15 He that hath ears to hear, let him hear.

16 ¶ But whereunto shall I liken this generation? It is like unto children sitting in the markets, and calling unto their fellows,

17 And saying, We have piped unto you, and ye have not danced; we have mourned unto you, and ye have not lamented.

18 For John came neither eating nor drinking, and they say, He hath a devil.

19 The Son of man came eating and drinking, and they say, Behold a man gluttonous, and a winebibber, a friend of publicans and sinners. But wisdom is justified of her children.

20 ¶ Then began he to upbraid the cities wherein most of his mighty works were done, because they repented not:

21 Woe unto thee, Chorazin! woe unto thee, Bethsaida! for if the mighty works, which were done in you, had been done in Tyre and Sidon, they would have repented long ago in sackcloth and ashes.

22 But I say unto you, It shall be more tolerable for Tyre and Sidon at the day of judgment, than for you.

23 And thou, Capernaum, which art exalted unto heaven, shalt be brought down to hell: for if the mighty works, which have been done in thee, had been done in Sodom, it would have remained until this day.

24 But I say unto you, That it shall be more tolerable for the land of Sodom in the day of judgment, than for thee.

25 ¶ At that time Jesus answered and said, I thank thee, O Father, Lord of heaven and earth, because thou hast hid these things from the wise and prudent, and hast revealed them unto babes.

26 Even so, Father: for so it seemed good in thy sight.

27 All things are delivered unto me of my Father: and no man knoweth the Son, but the Father; neither knoweth any man the Father, save the Son; and *he* to whomsoever the Son will reveal *him*.

28 ¶ Come unto me, all *ye* that labour and are heavy laden, and I will give you rest.

29 Take my yoke upon you, and learn of me; for I am meek and lowly in heart: and ye shall find rest unto your souls.

17

30 For my yoke *is* easy, and my burden is light.

12 At that time Jesus went on the sabbath day through the corn; and his disciples were an hungred, and began to pluck the ears of corn and to eat.

2 But when the Pharisees saw *it*, they said unto him, Behold, thy disciples do that which is not lawful to do upon the sabbath day.

3 But he said unto them, Have ye not read what David did, when he was an hungred, and they that were with him;

4 How he entered into the house of God, and did eat the shewbread, which was not lawful for him to eat, neither for them which were with him, but only for the priests?

5 Or have ye not read in the law, how that on the sabbath days the priests in the temple profane the sabbath, and are blameless?

6 But I say unto you, That in this place is *one* greater than the temple.

7 But if ye had known what *this* meaneth, I will have mercy, and not sacrifice, ye would not have condemned the guiltless.

8 For the Son of man is Lord even of the sabbath day.

9 And when he was departed thence, he went into their synagogue:

10 ℂ And, behold, there was a man which had *his* hand withered. And they asked him, saying, Is it lawful to heal on the

sabbath days? that they might accuse him?

11 And he said unto them, What man shall there be among you, that shall have one sheep, and if it fall into a pit on the sabbath day, will he not lay hold on it, and lift *it* out?

12 How much then is a man better than a sheep? Wherefore it is lawful to do well on the sabbath days.

13 Then saith he to the man, Stretch forth thine hand. And he stretched *it* forth; and it was restored whole, like as the other.

14 ℂ Then the Pharisees went out, and held a council against him, how they might destroy him.

15 But when Jesus knew *it*, he withdrew himself from thence: and great multitudes followed him, and he healed them all;

16 And charged them that they should not make him known:

17 That it might be fulfilled which was spoken by Esaias the prophet, saying,

18 Behold my servant, whom I have chosen; my beloved, in whom my soul is well pleased: I will put my spirit upon him, and he shall shew judgment to the Gentiles.

19 He shall not strive, nor cry; neither shall any man hear his voice in the streets.

20 A bruised reed shall he not break, and smoking flax shall he not quench, till he send forth judgment unto victory.

21 And in his name shall the Gentiles trust.

22 ¶ Then was brought unto him one possessed with a devil, blind, and dumb: and he healed him, insomuch that the blind and dumb both spake and saw.

23 And all the people were amazed, and said, Is not this the son of David?

24 But when the Pharisees heard *it*, they said, This *fellow* doth not cast out devils, but by Beelzebub the prince of the devils.

25 And Jesus knew their thoughts, and said unto them, Every kingdom divided against itself is brought to desolation; and every city or house divided against itself shall not stand:

26 And if Satan cast out Satan, he is divided against himself; how shall then his kingdom stand?

27 And if I by Beelzebub cast out devils, by whom do your children cast *them* out? therefore they shall be your judges.

28 But if I cast out devils by the Spirit of God, then the kingdom of God is come unto you.

29 Or else how can one enter into a strong man's house, and spoil his goods, except he first bind the strong man? and then he will spoil his house.

30 He that is not with me is against me; and he that gathereth not with me scattereth abroad.

31 ¶ Wherefore I say unto you, All manner of sin and blasphemy shall be forgiven unto men: but the blasphemy *against* the Holy Ghost shall not be forgiven unto men.

32 And whosoever speaketh a word against the Son of man, it shall be forgiven him: but whosoever speaketh against the Holy Ghost, it shall not be forgiven him, neither in this world, neither in the *world* to come.

33 Either make the tree good, and his fruit good; or else make the tree corrupt, and his fruit corrupt: for the tree is known by *his* fruit.

34 O generation of vipers, how can ye, being evil, speak good things? for out of the abundance of the heart the mouth speaketh.

35 A good man out of the good treasure of the heart bringeth forth good things: and an evil man out of the evil treasure bringeth forth evil things.

36 ¶ But I say unto you, That every idle word that men shall speak, they shall give account thereof in the day of judgment.

37 For by thy words thou shalt be justified, and by thy words thou shalt be condemned.

38 ¶ Then certain of the scribes and of the Pharisees answered, saying, Master, we would see a sign from thee.

39 But he answered and said unto them, An evil and adulterous generation seeketh after a sign; and there shall no sign be given to it, but the sign of the prophet Jonas:

40 For as Jonas was three days and three nights in the whale's belly; so shall the Son of man be three days and three nights in the heart of the earth.

41 The men of Nineveh shall rise in judgment with this gen-

19

eration, and shall condemn it: because they repented at the preaching of Jonas; and, behold, a greater than Jonas *is* here.

42 The queen of the south shall rise up in the judgment with this generation, and shall condemn it: for she came from the uttermost parts of the earth to hear the wisdom of Solomon; and, behold, a greater than Solomon *is* here.

43 When the unclean spirit is gone out of a man, he walketh through dry places, seeking rest, and findeth none.

44 Then he saith, I will return into my house from whence I came out; and when he is come, he findeth *it* empty, swept, and garnished.

45 Then goeth he, and taketh with himself seven other spirits more wicked than himself, and they enter in and dwell there: and the last *state* of that man is worse than the first. Even so shall it be also unto this wicked generation.

46 ¶ While he yet talked to the people, behold, *his* mother and his brethren stood without, desiring to speak with him.

47 Then one said unto him, Behold, thy mother and thy brethren stand without, desiring to speak with thee.

48 But he answered and said unto him that told him, Who is my mother? and who are my brethren?

49 And he stretched forth his hand toward his disciples, and said, Behold my mother and my brethren!

50 For whosoever shall do the will of my Father which is in heaven, the same is my brother, and sister, and mother.

13

The same day went Jesus out of the house, and sat by the sea side.

2 And great multitudes were gathered together unto him, so that he went into a ship, and sat; and the whole multitude stood on the shore.

3 And he spake many things unto them in parables, saying, Behold, a sower went forth to sow;

4 And when he sowed, some *seeds* fell by the way side, and the fowls came and devoured them up:

5 Some fell upon stony places, where they had not much earth: and forthwith they sprung up, because they had no deepness of earth:

6 And when the sun was up, they were scorched; and because they had no root, they withered away.

7 And some fell among thorns; and the thorns sprung up, and choked them:

8 But other fell into good ground, and brought forth fruit, some an hundredfold, some sixtyfold, some thirtyfold.

9 Who hath ears to hear, let him hear.

10 And the disciples came, and said unto him, Why speakest thou unto them in parables?

11 He answered and said unto them, Because it is given unto you to know the mysteries of the

kingdom of heaven, but to them it is not given.

12 For whosoever hath, to him shall be given, and he shall have more abundance: but whosoever hath not, from him shall be taken away even that he hath.

13 Therefore speak I to them in parables: because they seeing see not; and hearing they hear not, neither do they understand.

14 And in them is fulfilled the prophecy of Esaias, which saith, By hearing ye shall hear, and shall not understand; and seeing ye shall see, and shall not perceive:

15 For this people's heart is waxed gross, and *their* ears are dull of hearing, and their eyes they have closed; lest at any time they should see with *their* eyes and hear with *their* ears, and should understand with *their* heart, and should be converted, and I should heal them.

16 But blessed *are* your eyes, for they see: and your ears, for they hear.

17 For verily I say unto you, That many prophets and righteous *men* have desired to see *those things* which ye see, and have not seen *them*; and to hear *those things* which ye hear, and have not heard *them*.

18 ¶ Hear ye therefore the parable of the sower.

19 When any one heareth the word of the kingdom, and understandeth *it*, then cometh the wicked *one*, and catcheth away that which was sown in his heart. This is he which received seed by the way side.

20 But he that received the seed into stony places, the same is he that heareth the word, and anon with joy receiveth it;

21 Yet hath he not root in himself, but dureth for a while: for when tribulation or persecution ariseth because of the word, by and by he is offended.

22 He also that received seed among the thorns is he that heareth the word; and the care of this world, and the deceitfulness of riches, choke the word, and he becometh unfruitful.

23 But he that received seed into the good ground is he that heareth the word, and understandeth *it*; which also beareth fruit, and bringeth forth, some an hundredfold, some sixty, some thirty.

24 ¶ Another parable put he forth unto them, saying, The kingdom of heaven is likened unto a man which sowed good seed in his field:

25 But while men slept, his enemy came and sowed tares among the wheat, and went his way.

26 But when the blade was sprung up, and brought forth fruit, then appeared the tares also.

27 So the servants of the householder came and said unto him, Sir, didst not thou sow good seed in thy field? from whence then hath it tares?

28 He said unto them, An enemy hath done this. The servants said unto him, Wilt thou then that we go and gather them up?

29 But he said, Nay; lest while ye gather up the tares, ye root up also the wheat with them.

30 Let both grow together until the harvest: and in the time of harvest I will say to the reapers, Gather ye together first the tares, and bind them in bundles to burn them: but gather the wheat into my barn.

31 ℂ Another parable put he forth unto them, saying, The kingdom of heaven is like to a grain of mustard seed, which a man took, and sowed in his field:

32 Which indeed is the least of all seeds: but when it is grown, it is the greatest among herbs, and becometh a tree, so that the birds of the air come and lodge in the branches thereof.

33 ℂ Another parable spake he unto them; The kingdom of heaven is like unto leaven, which a woman took, and hid in three measures of meal, till the whole was leavened.

34 All these things spake Jesus unto the multitude in parables; and without a parable spake he not unto them:

35 That it might be fulfilled which was spoken by the prophet, saying, I will open my mouth in parables; I will utter things which have been kept secret from the foundation of the world.

36 Then Jesus sent the multitude away, and went into the house: and his disciples came unto him, saying, Declare unto us the parable of the tares of the field.

37 He answered and said unto them, He that soweth the good seed is the Son of man;

38 The field is the world; the good seed are the children of the kingdom; but the tares are the children of the wicked one;

39 The enemy that sowed them is the devil; the harvest is the end of the world; and the reapers are the angels.

40 As therefore the tares are gathered and burned in the fire; so shall it be in the end of this world.

41 The Son of man shall send forth his angels, and they shall gather out of his kingdom all things that offend, and them which do iniquity;

42 And shall cast them into a furnace of fire: there shall be wailing and gnashing of teeth.

43 Then shall the righteous shine forth as the sun in the kingdom of their Father. Who hath ears to hear, let him hear.

44 ℂ Again, the kingdom of heaven is like unto treasure hid in a field; the which when a man hath found, he hideth, and for joy thereof goeth and selleth all that he hath, and buyeth that field.

45 ℂ Again, the kingdom of heaven is like unto a merchant man, seeking goodly pearls:

46 Who, when he had found one pearl of great price, went and sold all that he had, and bought it.

47 ℂ Again, the kingdom of heaven is like unto a net, that was cast into the sea, and gathered of every kind:

48 Which, when it was full, they drew to shore, and sat down, and

gathered the good into vessels, but cast the bad away.

49 So shall it be at the end of the world: the angels shall come forth, and sever the wicked from among the just,

50 And shall cast them into the furnace of fire: there shall be wailing and gnashing of teeth.

51 Jesus saith unto them, Have ye understood all these things? They say unto him, Yea, Lord.

52 Then said he unto them, Therefore every scribe *which is* instructed unto the kingdom of heaven is like unto a man *that is* an householder, which bringeth forth out of his treasure *things* new and old.

53 ❧ And it came to pass, *that* when Jesus had finished these parables, he departed thence.

54 And when he was come into his own country, he taught them in their synagogue, insomuch that they were astonished, and said, Whence hath this *man* this wisdom, and *these* mighty works?

55 Is not this the carpenter's son? is not his mother called Mary? and his brethren, James, and Joses, and Simon, and Judas?

56 And his sisters, are they not all with us? Whence then hath this *man* all these things?

57 And they were offended in him. But Jesus said unto them, A prophet is not without honour, save in his own country, and in his own house.

58 And he did not many mighty works there because of their unbelief.

14 At that time Herod the tetrarch heard of the fame of Jesus,

2 And said unto his servants, This is John the Baptist; he is risen from the dead; and therefore mighty works do shew forth themselves in him.

3 ❧ For Herod had laid hold on John, and bound him, and put *him* in prison for Herodias' sake, his brother Philip's wife.

4 For John said unto him, It is not lawful for thee to have her.

5 And when he would have put him to death, he feared the multitude, because they counted him as a prophet.

6 But when Herod's birthday was kept, the daughter of Herodias danced before them, and pleased Herod.

7 Whereupon he promised with an oath to give her whatsoever she would ask.

8 And she, being before instructed of her mother, said, Give me here John Baptist's head in a charger.

9 And the king was sorry: nevertheless for the oath's sake, and them which sat with him at meat, he commanded *it* to be given *her.*

10 And he sent, and beheaded John in the prison.

11 And his head was brought in a charger, and given to the damsel: and she brought *it* to her mother.

12 And his disciples came, and

23

took up the body, and buried it, and went and told Jesus.

13 ¶ When Jesus heard *of it*, he departed thence by ship into a desert place apart: and when the people had heard *thereof*, they followed him on foot out of the cities.

14 And Jesus went forth, and saw a great multitude, and was moved with compassion toward them, and he healed their sick.

15 ¶ And when it was evening, his disciples came to him, saying, This is a desert place, and the time is now past; send the multitude away, that they may go into the villages, and buy themselves victuals.

16 But Jesus said unto them, They need not depart; give ye them to eat.

17 And they say unto him, We have here but five loaves, and two fishes.

18 He said, Bring them hither to me.

19 And he commanded the multitude to sit down on the grass, and took the five loaves, and the two fishes, and looking up to heaven, he blessed, and brake, and gave the loaves to *his* disciples, and the disciples to the multitude.

20 And they did all eat, and were filled: and they took up of the fragments that remained twelve baskets full.

21 And they that had eaten were about five thousand men, beside women and children.

22 ¶ And straightway Jesus con-

strained his disciples to get into a ship, and to go before him unto the other side, while he sent the multitudes away.

23 And when he had sent the multitudes away, he went up into a mountain apart to pray: and when the evening was come, he was there alone.

24 But the ship was now in the midst of the sea, tossed with waves: for the wind was contrary.

25 And in the fourth watch of the night Jesus went unto them, walking on the sea.

26 And when the disciples saw him walking on the sea, they were troubled, saying, It is a spirit; and they cried out for fear.

27 But straightway Jesus spake unto them, saying, Be of good cheer; it is I; be not afraid.

28 And Peter answered him and said, Lord, if it be thou, bid me come unto thee on the water.

29 And he said, Come. And when Peter was come down out of the ship, he walked on the water, to go to Jesus.

30 But when he saw the wind boisterous, he was afraid; and beginning to sink, he cried, saying, Lord, save me.

31 And immediately Jesus stretched forth *his* hand, and caught him, and said unto him, O thou of little faith, wherefore didst thou doubt?

32 And when they were come into the ship, the wind ceased.

33 Then they that were in the ship came and worshipped him,

saying, Of a truth thou art the Son of God.

34 ¶ And when they were gone over, they came into the land of Gennesaret.

35 And when the men of that place had knowledge of him, they sent out into all that country round about, and brought unto him all that were diseased;

36 And besought him that they might only touch the hem of his garment: and as many as touched were made perfectly whole.

15 Then came to Jesus scribes and Pharisees, which were of Jerusalem, saying,

2 Why do thy disciples transgress the tradition of the elders? for they wash not their hands when they eat bread.

3 But he answered and said unto them, Why do ye also transgress the commandment of God by your tradition?

4 For God commanded, saying, Honour thy father and mother: and, He that curseth father or mother, let him die the death.

5 But ye say, Whosoever shall say to *his* father or *his* mother, *It is* a gift, by whatsoever thou mightest be profited by me;

6 And honour not his father or his mother, *he shall be free.* Thus have ye made the commandment of God of none effect by your tradition.

7 Ye hypocrites, well did Esaias prophesy of you, saying,

8 This people draweth nigh unto me with their mouth, and honoureth me with *their* lips; but their heart is far from me.

9 But in vain they do worship me, teaching *for* doctrines the commandments of men.

10 ¶ And he called the multitude, and said unto them, Hear, and understand:

11 Not that which goeth into the mouth defileth a man; but that which cometh out of the mouth, this defileth a man.

12 Then came his disciples, and said unto him, Knowest thou that the Pharisees were offended, after they heard this saying?

13 But he answered and said, Every plant, which my heavenly Father hath not planted, shall be rooted up.

14 Let them alone: they be blind leaders of the blind. And if the blind lead the blind, both shall fall into the ditch.

15 Then answered Peter and said unto him, Declare unto us this parable.

16 And Jesus said, Are ye also yet without understanding?

17 Do not ye yet understand, that whatsoever entereth in at the mouth goeth into the belly, and is cast out into the draught?

18 But those things which proceed out of the mouth come forth from the heart; and they defile the man.

19 For out of the heart proceed evil thoughts, murders, adulteries, fornications, thefts, false witness, blasphemies:

20 These are *the things* which defile a man: but to eat with

unwashen hands defileth not a man.

21 ⟨ Then Jesus went thence, and departed into the coasts of Tyre and Sidon.

22 And, behold, a woman of Canaan came out of the same coasts, and cried unto him, saying, Have mercy on me, O Lord, *thou* Son of David; my daughter is grievously vexed with a devil.

23 But he answered her not a word. And his disciples came and besought him, saying, Send her away; for she crieth after us.

24 But he answered and said, I am not sent but unto the lost sheep of the house of Israel.

25 Then came she and worshipped him, saying, Lord, help me.

26 But he answered and said, It is not meet to take the children's bread, and to cast *it* to dogs.

27 And she said, Truth, Lord: yet the dogs eat of the crumbs which fall from their masters' table.

28 Then Jesus answered and said unto her, O woman, great *is* thy faith: be it unto thee even as thou wilt. And her daughter was made whole from that very hour.

29 And Jesus departed from thence, and came nigh unto the sea of Galilee; and went up into a mountain, and sat down there.

30 ⟨ And great multitudes came unto him, having with them *those that were* lame, blind, dumb, maimed, and many others, and cast them down at Jesus' feet; and he healed them:

31 Insomuch that the multitude wondered, when they saw the dumb to speak, the maimed to be whole, the lame to walk, and the blind to see: and they glorified the God of Israel.

32 ⟨ Then Jesus called his disciples *unto him*, and said, I have compassion on the multitude, because they continue with me now three days, and have nothing to eat: and I will not send them away fasting, lest they faint in the way.

33 And his disciples say unto him, Whence should we have so much bread in the wilderness, as to fill so great a multitude?

34 And Jesus saith unto them, How many loaves have ye? And they said, Seven, and a few little fishes.

35 And he commanded the multitude to sit down on the ground.

36 And he took the seven loaves and the fishes, and gave thanks, and brake *them*, and gave to his disciples, and the disciples to the multitude.

37 And they did all eat, and were filled: and they took up of the broken *meat* that was left seven baskets full.

38 And they that did eat were four thousand men, beside women and children.

39 And he sent away the multitude, and took ship, and came into the coasts of Magdala.

16 The Pharisees also with the Sadducees came, and tempting desired him that he would shew them a sign from heaven.

2 He answered and said unto them, When it is evening, ye say, *It will be* fair weather: for the sky is red.

3 And in the morning, *It will be* foul weather to day: for the sky is red and lowering. O ye hypocrites, ye can discern the face of the sky; but can ye not *discern* the signs of the times?

4 A wicked and adulterous generation seeketh after a sign; and there shall no sign be given unto it, but the sign of the prophet Jonas. And he left them, and departed.

5 And when his disciples were come to the other side, they had forgotten to take bread.

6 ¶ Then Jesus said unto them, Take heed and beware of the leaven of the Pharisees and of the Sadducees.

7 And they reasoned among themselves, saying, *It is* because we have taken no bread.

8 *Which* when Jesus perceived, he said unto them, O ye of little faith, why reason ye among yourselves, because ye have brought no bread?

9 Do ye not yet understand, neither remember the five loaves of the five thousand, and how many baskets ye took up?

10 Neither the seven loaves of the four thousand, and how many baskets ye took up?

11 How is it that ye do not understand that I spake *it* not to you concerning bread, that ye should beware of the leaven of the Pharisees and of the Sadducees?

12 Then understood they how that he bade *them* not beware of the leaven of bread, but of the doctrine of the Pharisees and of the Sadducees.

13 ¶ When Jesus came into the coasts of Caesarea Philippi, he asked his disciples, saying, Whom do men say that I the Son of man am?

14 And they said, Some *say that thou art* John the Baptist: some, Elias; and others, Jeremias, or one of the prophets.

15 He saith unto them, But whom say ye that I am?

16 And Simon Peter answered and said, Thou art the Christ, the Son of the living God.

17 And Jesus answered and said unto him, Blessed art thou, Simon Barj-ona: for flesh and blood hath not revealed *it* unto thee, but my Father which is in heaven.

18 And I say also unto thee, That thou art Peter, and upon this rock I will build my church; and the gates of hell shall not prevail against it.

19 And I will give unto thee the keys of the kingdom of heaven: and whatsoever thou shalt bind on earth shall be bound in heaven: and whatsoever thou shalt loose on earth shall be loosed in heaven.

20 Then charged he his disciples that they should tell no man that he was Jesus the Christ.

21 ¶ From that time forth began Jesus to shew unto his disciples, how that he must go unto Jerusalem, and suffer many things of the elders and chief priests and scribes, and be killed, and be

raised again the third day.

22 Then Peter took him, and began to rebuke him, saying, Be it far from thee, Lord: this shall not be unto thee.

23 But he turned, and said unto Peter, Get thee behind me, Satan: thou art an offence unto me: for thou savourest not the things that be of God, but those that be of men.

24 ¶ Then said Jesus unto his disciples, If any *man* will come after me, let him deny himself, and take up his cross, and follow me.

25 For whosoever will save his life shall lose it: and whosoever will lose his life for my sake shall find it.

26 For what is a man profited, if he shall gain the whole world, and lose his own soul? or what shall a man give in exchange for his soul?

27 For the Son of man shall come in the glory of his Father with his angels; and then he shall reward every man according to his works.

28 Verily I say unto you, There be some standing here, which shall not taste of death, till they see the Son of man coming in his kingdom.

17 And after six days Jesus taketh Peter, James, and John his brother, and bringeth them up into an high mountain apart,

2 And was transfigured before them: and his face did shine as the sun, and his raiment was white as the light.

3 And, behold, there appeared unto them Moses and Elias talking with him.

4 Then answered Peter, and said unto Jesus, Lord, it is good for us to be here: if thou wilt, let us make here three tabernacles; one for thee, and one for Moses, and one for Elias.

5 While he yet spake, behold, a bright cloud overshadowed them: and behold a voice out of the cloud, which said, This is my beloved Son, in whom I am well pleased; hear ye him.

6 And when the disciples heard *it*, they fell on their face, and were sore afraid.

7 And Jesus came and touched them, and said, Arise, and be not afraid.

8 And when they had lifted up their eyes, they saw no man, save Jesus only.

9 And as they came down from the mountain, Jesus charged them, saying, Tell the vision to no man, until the Son of man be risen again from the dead.

10 And his disciples asked him, saying, Why then say the scribes that Elias must first come?

11 And Jesus answered and said unto them, Elias truly shall first come, and restore all things.

12 But I say unto you, That Elias is come already, and they knew him not, but have done unto him whatsoever they listed. Likewise shall also the Son of man suffer of them.

13 Then the disciples understood that he spake unto them of John the Baptist.

28

14 ¶ And when they were come to the multitude, there came to him a *certain* man, kneeling down to him, and saying,

15 Lord, have mercy on my son: for he is lunatick, and sore vexed: for ofttimes he falleth into the fire, and oft into the water.

16 And I brought him to thy disciples, and they could not cure him.

17 Then Jesus answered and said, O faithless and perverse generation, how long shall I be with you? how long shall I suffer you? bring him hither to me.

18 And Jesus rebuked the devil; and he departed out of him: and the child was cured from that very hour.

19 Then came the disciples to Jesus apart, and said, Why could not we cast him out?

20 And Jesus said unto them, Because of your unbelief: for verily I say unto you, If ye have faith as a grain of mustard seed, ye shall say unto this mountain, Remove hence to yonder place; and it shall remove; and nothing shall be impossible unto you.

21 Howbeit this kind goeth not out but by prayer and fasting.

22 ¶ And while they abode in Galilee, Jesus said unto them, The Son of man shall be betrayed into the hands of men:

23 And they shall kill him, and the third day he shall be raised again. And they were exceeding sorry.

24 ¶ And when they were come to Capernaum, they that received

tribute *money* came to Peter, and said, Doth not your master pay tribute?

25 He saith, Yes. And when he was come into the house, Jesus prevented him, saying, What thinkest thou, Simon? of whom do the kings of the earth take custom or tribute? of their own children, or of strangers?

26 Peter saith unto him, Of strangers. Jesus saith unto him, Then are the children free.

27 Notwithstanding, lest we should offend them, go thou to the sea, and cast an hook, and take up the fish that first cometh up; and when thou hast opened his mouth, thou shalt find a piece of money: that take, and give unto them for me and thee.

18

At the same time came the disciples unto Jesus, saying, Who is the greatest in the kingdom of heaven?

2 And Jesus called a little child unto him, and set him in the midst of them,

3 And he said, Verily I say unto you, Except ye be converted, and become as little children, ye shall not enter into the kingdom of heaven.

4 Whosoever therefore shall humble himself as this little child, the same is greatest in the kingdom of heaven.

5 And whoso shall receive one such little child in my name receiveth me.

6 But whoso shall offend one of these little ones which believe in me, it were better for him that a

29

millstone were hanged about his neck, and *that* he were drowned in the depth of the sea.

7 ❧ Woe unto the world because of offences! for it must needs be that offences come; but woe to that man by whom the offence cometh!

8 Wherefore if thy hand or thy foot offend thee, cut them off, and cast *them* from thee: it is better for thee to enter into life halt or maimed, rather than having two hands or two feet to be cast into everlasting fire.

9 And if thine eye offend thee, pluck it out, and cast *it* from thee: it is better for thee to enter into life with one eye, rather than having two eyes to be cast into hell fire.

10 Take heed that ye despise not one of these little ones; for I say unto you, That in heaven their angels do always behold the face of my Father which is in heaven.

11 For the Son of man is come to save that which was lost.

12 How think ye? if a man have an hundred sheep, and one of them be gone astray, doth he not leave the ninety and nine, and goeth into the mountains, and seeketh that which is gone astray?

13 And if so be that he find it, verily I say unto you, he rejoiceth more of that *sheep*, than of the ninety and nine which went not astray.

14 Even so it is not the will of your Father which is in heaven, that one of these little ones should perish.

15 ❧ Moreover if thy brother shall trespass against thee, go and tell him his fault between thee and him alone: if he shall hear thee, thou hast gained thy brother.

16 But if he will not hear *thee*, *then* take with thee one or two more, that in the mouth of two or three witnesses every word may be established.

17 And if he shall neglect to hear them, tell *it* unto the church: but if he neglect to hear the church, let him be unto thee as an heathen man and a publican.

18 Verily I say unto you, Whatsoever ye shall bind on earth shall be bound in heaven: and whatsoever ye shall loose on earth shall be loosed in heaven.

19 Again I say unto you, That if two of you shall agree on earth as touching any thing that they shall ask, it shall be done for them of my Father which is in heaven.

20 For where two or three are gathered together in my name, there am I in the midst of them.

21 ❧ Then came Peter to him, and said, Lord, how oft shall my brother sin against me, and I forgive him? till seven times?

22 Jesus saith unto him, I say not unto thee, Until seven times: but, Until seventy times seven.

23 ❧ Therefore is the kingdom of heaven likened unto a certain king, which would take account of his servants.

24 And when he had begun to reckon, one was brought unto him, which owed him ten thousand talents.

25 But forasmuch as he had

not to pay, his lord commanded him to be sold, and his wife, and children, and all that he had, and payment to be made.

26 The servant therefore fell down, and worshipped him, saying, Lord, have patience with me, and I will pay thee all.

27 Then the lord of that servant was moved with compassion, and loosed him, and forgave him the debt.

28 But the same servant went out, and found one of his fellowservants, which owed him an hundred pence: and he laid hands on him, and took *him* by the throat, saying, Pay me that thou owest.

29 And his fellowservant fell down at his feet, and besought him, saying, Have patience with me, and I will pay thee all.

30 And he would not: but went and cast him into prison, till he should pay the debt.

31 So when his fellowservants saw what was done, they were very sorry, and came and told unto their lord all that was done.

32 Then his lord, after that he had called him, said unto him, O thou wicked servant, I forgave thee all that debt, because thou desiredst me:

33 Shouldest not thou also have had compassion on thy fellowservant, even as I had pity on thee?

34 And his lord was wroth, and delivered him to the tormentors, till he should pay all that was due unto him.

35 So likewise shall my heavenly Father do also unto you, if ye from your hearts forgive not every one his brother their trespasses.

19

And it came to pass, *that* when Jesus had finished these sayings, he departed from Galilee, and came into the coasts of Judaea beyond Jordan;

2 And great multitudes followed him; and he healed them there.

3 ¶ The Pharisees also came unto him, tempting him, and saying unto him, Is it lawful for a man to put away his wife for every cause?

4 And he answered and said unto them, Have ye not read, that he which made *them* at the beginning made them male and female,

5 And said, For this cause shall a man leave father and mother, and shall cleave to his wife: and they twain shall be one flesh?

6 Wherefore they are no more twain, but one flesh. What therefore God hath joined together, let not man put asunder.

7 They say unto him, Why did Moses then command to give a writing of divorcement, and to put her away?

8 He saith unto them, Moses because of the hardness of your hearts suffered you to put away your wives: but from the beginning it was not so.

9 And I say unto you, Whosoever shall put away his wife, except *it be* for fornication, and shall marry another, committeth

31

adultery: and whoso marrieth her which is put away doth commit adultery.

10 ¶ His disciples say unto him, If the case of the man be so with *his* wife, it is not good to marry.

11 But he said unto them, All *men* cannot receive this saying, save *they* to whom it is given.

12 For there are some eunuchs, which were so born from *their* mother's womb: and there are some eunuchs, which were made eunuchs of men: and there be eunuchs, which have made themselves eunuchs for the kingdom of heaven's sake. He that is able to receive *it*, let him receive *it*.

13 ¶ Then were there brought unto him little children, that he should put *his* hands on them, and pray: and the disciples rebuked them.

14 But Jesus said, Suffer little children, and forbid them not, to come unto me: for of such is the kingdom of heaven.

15 And he laid *his* hands on them, and departed thence.

16 ¶ And, behold, one came and said unto him, Good Master, what good thing shall I do, that I may have eternal life?

17 And he said unto him, Why callest thou me good? *there is* none good but one, *that is*, God: but if thou wilt enter into life, keep the commandments.

18 He saith unto him, Which? Jesus said, Thou shalt do no murder, Thou shalt not commit adultery, Thou shalt not steal, Thou shalt not bear false witness,

19 Honour thy father and *thy* mother: and, Thou shalt love thy neighbour as thyself.

20 The young man saith unto him, All these things have I kept from my youth up: what lack I yet?

21 Jesus said unto him, If thou wilt be perfect, go *and* sell that thou hast, and give to the poor, and thou shalt have treasure in heaven: and come *and* follow me.

22 But when the young man heard that saying, he went away sorrowful: for he had great possessions.

23 Then said Jesus unto his disciples, Verily I say unto you, That a rich man shall hardly enter into the kingdom of heaven.

24 And again I say unto you, It is easier for a camel to go through the eye of a needle, than for a rich man to enter into the kingdom of God.

25 When his disciples heard *it*, they were exceedingly amazed, saying, Who then can be saved?

26 But Jesus beheld *them*, and said unto them, With men this is impossible; but with God all things are possible.

27 ¶ Then answered Peter and said unto him, Behold, we have forsaken all, and followed thee; what shall we have therefore?

28 And Jesus said unto them, Verily I say unto you, That ye which have followed me, in the regeneration when the Son of man shall sit in the throne of his glory, ye also shall sit upon twelve thrones, judging the twelve tribes of Israel.

29 And every one that hath forsaken houses, or brethren, or sisters, or father, or mother, or wife, or children, or lands, for my name's sake, shall receive an hundredfold, and shall inherit everlasting life.

30 But many *that are* first shall be last; and the last *shall be* first.

20 For the kingdom of heaven is like unto a man *that is* an householder, which went out early in the morning to hire labourers into his vineyard.

2 And when he had agreed with the labourers for a penny a day, he sent them into his vineyard.

3 And he went out about the third hour, and saw others standing idle in the marketplace,

4 And said unto them; Go ye also into the vineyard, and whatsoever is right I will give you. And they went their way.

5 Again he went out about the sixth and ninth hour, and did likewise.

6 And about the eleventh hour he went out, and found others standing idle, and saith unto them, Why stand ye here all the day idle?

7 They say unto him, Because no man hath hired us. He saith unto them, Go ye also into the vineyard; and whatsoever is right, *that* shall ye receive.

8 So when even was come, the lord of the vineyard saith unto his steward, Call the labourers, and give them *their* hire, beginning from the last unto the first.

9 And when they came that *were* hired about the eleventh hour, they received every man a penny.

10 But when the first came, they supposed that they should have received more; and they likewise received every man a penny.

11 And when they had received *it*, they murmured against the goodman of the house,

12 Saying, These last have wrought *but* one hour, and thou hast made them equal unto us, which have borne the burden and heat of the day.

13 But he answered one of them, and said, Friend, I do thee no wrong: didst not thou agree with me for a penny?

14 Take *that* thine *is*, and go thy way: I will give unto this last, even as unto thee.

15 Is it not lawful for me to do what I will with mine own? Is thine eye evil, because I am good?

16 So the last shall be first, and the first last: for many be called, but few chosen.

17 ¶ And Jesus going up to Jerusalem took the twelve disciples apart in the way, and said unto them,

18 Behold, we go up to Jerusalem; and the Son of man shall be betrayed unto the chief priests and unto the scribes, and they shall condemn him to death,

19 And shall deliver him to the Gentiles to mock, and to scourge, and to crucify *him*: and the third day he shall rise again.

20 ¶ Then came to him the mother of Zebedee's children with her sons, worshipping *him*, and desiring a certain thing of him.

21 And he said unto her, What wilt thou? She saith unto him, Grant that these my two sons may sit, the one on thy right hand, and the other on the left, in thy kingdom.

22 But Jesus answered and said, Ye know not what ye ask. Are ye able to drink of the cup that I shall drink of, and to be baptized with the baptism that I am baptized with? They say unto him, We are able.

23 And he saith unto them, Ye shall drink indeed of my cup, and be baptized with the baptism that I am baptized with: but to sit on my right hand, and on my left, is not mine to give, but *it shall be given to them* for whom it is prepared of my Father.

24 And when the ten heard *it*, they were moved with indignation against the two brethren.

25 But Jesus called them *unto him*, and said, Ye know that the princes of the Gentiles exercise dominion over them, and they that are great exercise authority upon them.

26 But it shall not be so among you: but whosoever will be great among you, let him be your minister;

27 And whosoever will be chief among you, let him be your servant:

28 Even as the Son of man came not to be ministered unto, but to minister, and to give his life a ransom for many.

29 And as they departed from Jericho, a great multitude followed him.

30 ¶ And, behold, two blind men sitting by the way side, when they heard that Jesus passed by, cried out, saying, Have mercy on us, O Lord, *thou* son of David.

31 And the multitude rebuked them, because they should hold their peace: but they cried the more, saying, Have mercy on us, O Lord, *thou* Son of David.

32 And Jesus stood still, and called them, and said, What will ye that I shall do unto you?

33 They say unto him, Lord, that our eyes may be opened.

34 So Jesus had compassion *on them*, and touched their eyes: and immediately their eyes received sight, and they followed him.

21

And when they drew nigh unto Jerusalem, and were come to Bethphage, unto the mount of Olives, then sent Jesus two disciples,

2 Saying unto them, Go into the village over against you, and straightway ye shall find an ass tied, and a colt with her: loose *them*, and bring *them* unto me.

3 And if any *man* say ought unto you, ye shall say, The Lord hath need of them; and straightway he will send them.

4 All this was done, that it might be fulfilled which was spoken by the prophet, saying,

5 Tell ye the daughter of Sion, Behold, thy King cometh unto thee, meek, and sitting upon an

34

ass, and a colt the foal of an ass.

6 And the disciples went, and did as Jesus commanded them,

7 And brought the ass, and the colt, and put on them their clothes, and they set *him* thereon.

8 And a very great multitude spread their garments in the way; others cut down branches from the trees, and strawed *them* in the way.

9 And the multitudes that went before, and that followed, cried, saying, Hosanna to the son of David: Blessed *is* he that cometh in the name of the Lord; Hosanna in the highest.

10 And when he was come into Jerusalem, all the city was moved, saying, Who is this?

11 And the multitude said, This is Jesus the prophet of Nazareth of Galilee.

12 ¶ And Jesus went into the temple of God, and cast out all them that sold and bought in the temple, and overthrew the tables of the moneychangers, and the seats of them that sold doves,

13 And said unto them, It is written, My house shall be called the house of prayer; but ye have made it a den of thieves.

14 ¶ And the blind and the lame came to him in the temple; and he healed them.

15 And when the chief priests and scribes saw the wonderful things that he did, and the children crying in the temple, and saying, Hosanna to the Son of David; they were sore displeased,

16 And said unto him, Hearest thou what these say? And Jesus saith unto them, Yea; have ye never read, Out of the mouth of babes and sucklings thou hast perfected praise?

17 ¶ And he left him, and went out of the city into Bethany; and he lodged there.

18 Now in the morning as he returned into the city, he hungered.

19 And when he saw a fig tree in the way, he came to it, and found nothing thereon, but leaves only, and said unto it, Let no fruit grow on thee henceforward for ever. And presently the fig tree withered away.

20 And when the disciples saw *it*, they marvelled, saying, How soon is the fig tree withered away!

21 Jesus answered and said unto them, Verily I say unto you, If ye have faith, and doubt not, ye shall not only do this *which is done* to the fig tree, but also if ye shall say unto this mountain, Be thou removed, and be thou cast into the sea; it shall be done.

22 And all things, whatsoever ye shall ask in prayer, believing, ye shall receive.

23 ¶ And when he was come into the temple, the chief priests and the elders of the people came unto him as he was teaching, and said, By what authority doest thou these things? and who gave thee this authority?

24 And Jesus answered and said unto them, I also will ask you one thing, which if ye tell me, I in like wise will tell you by what

authority I do these things.

25 The baptism of John, whence was it? from heaven, or of men? And they reasoned with themselves, saying, If we shall say, From heaven; he will say unto us, Why did ye not then believe him?

26 But if we shall say, Of men; we fear the people; for all hold John as a prophet.

27 And they answered Jesus, and said, We cannot tell. And he said unto them, Neither tell I you by what authority I do these things.

28 ¶ But what think ye? A *certain* man had two sons; and he came to the first, and said, Son, go work to day in my vineyard.

29 He answered and said, I will not; but afterward he repented, and went.

30 And he came to the second, and said likewise. And he answered and said, I *go*, sir: and went not.

31 Whether of them twain did the will of *his* father? They say unto him, The first. Jesus saith unto them, Verily I say unto you, That the publicans and the harlots go into the kingdom of God before you.

32 For John came unto you in the way of righteousness, and ye believed him not; but the publicans and the harlots believed him: and ye, when ye had seen *it*, repented not afterward, that ye might believe him.

33 ¶ Hear another parable: There was a certain householder, which planted a vineyard, and hedged it round about, and digged a winepress in it, and built a tower, and let it out to husbandmen, and went into a far country:

34 And when the time of the fruit drew near, he sent his servants to the husbandmen, that they might receive the fruits of it.

35 And the husbandmen took his servants, and beat one, and killed another, and stoned another.

36 Again, he sent other servants more than the first: and they did unto them likewise.

37 But last of all he sent unto them his son, saying, They will reverence my son.

38 But when the husbandmen saw the son, they said among themselves, This is the heir; come, let us kill him, and let us seize on his inheritance.

39 And they caught him, and cast *him* out of the vineyard, and slew *him*.

40 When the lord therefore of the vineyard cometh, what will he do unto those husbandmen?

41 They say unto him, He will miserably destroy those wicked men, and will let out *his* vineyard unto other husbandmen, which shall render him the fruits in their seasons.

42 Jesus saith unto them, Did ye never read in the scriptures, The stone which the builders rejected, the same is become the head of the corner: this is the Lord's doing, and it is marvellous in our eyes?

43 Therefore say I unto you,

The kingdom of God shall be taken from you, and given to a nation bringing forth the fruits thereof.

44 And whosoever shall fall on this stone shall be broken: but on whomsoever it shall fall, it will grind him to powder.

45 And when the chief priests and Pharisees had heard his parables, they perceived that he spake of them.

46 But when they sought to lay hands on him, they feared the multitude, because they took him for a prophet.

22 And Jesus answered and spake unto them again by parables, and said,

2 The kingdom of heaven is like unto a certain king, which made a marriage for his son,

3 And sent forth his servants to call them that were bidden to the wedding: and they would not come.

4 Again, he sent forth other servants, saying, Tell them which are bidden, Behold, I have prepared my dinner: my oxen and *my* fatlings *are* killed, and all things *are* ready: come unto the marriage.

5 But they made light of *it*, and went their ways, one to his farm, another to his merchandise:

6 And the remnant took his servants, and intreated *them* spitefully, and slew *them*.

7 But when the king heard *thereof*, he was wroth: and he sent forth his armies, and destroyed those murderers, and burned up their city.

8 Then saith he to his servants, The wedding is ready, but they which were bidden were not worthy.

9 Go ye therefore into the highways, and as many as ye shall find, bid to the marriage.

10 So those servants went out into the highways, and gathered together all as many as they found, both bad and good: and the wedding was furnished with guests.

11 ¶ And when the king came in to see the guests, he saw there a man which had not on a wedding garment:

12 And he saith unto him, Friend, how camest thou in hither not having a wedding garment? And he was speechless.

13 Then said the king to the servants, Bind him hand and foot, and take him away, and cast *him* into outer darkness, there shall be weeping and gnashing of teeth.

14 For many are called, but few *are* chosen.

15 ¶ Then went the Pharisees, and took counsel how they might entangle him in *his* talk.

16 And they sent out unto him their disciples with the Herodians, saying, Master, we know that thou art true, and teachest the way of God in truth, neither carest thou for any *man*: for thou regardest not the person of men.

17 Tell us therefore, What thinkest thou? Is it lawful to give tribute unto Caesar, or not?

18 But Jesus perceived their

37

wickedness, and said, Why tempt ye me, *ye* hypocrites?

19 Shew me the tribute money. And they brought unto him a penny.

20 And he saith unto them, Whose *is* this image and superscription?

21 They say unto him, Caesar's. Then saith he unto them, Render therefore unto Caesar the things which are Caesar's; and unto God the things that are God's.

22 When they had heard *these words*, they marvelled, and left him, and went their way.

23 ¶The same day came to him the Sadducees, which say that there is no resurrection, and asked him,

24 Saying, Master, Moses said, If a man die, having no children, his brother shall marry his wife, and raise up seed unto his brother.

25 Now there were with us seven brethren: and the first, when he had married a wife, deceased, and, having no issue, left his wife unto his brother:

26 Likewise the second also, and the third, unto the seventh.

27 And last of all the woman died also.

28 Therefore in the resurrection whose wife shall she be of the seven? for they all had her.

29 Jesus answered and said unto them, Ye do err, not knowing the scriptures, nor the power of God.

30 For in the resurrection they neither marry, nor are given in marriage, but are as the angels of God in heaven.

31 But as touching the resurrection of the dead, have ye not read that which was spoken unto you by God, saying,

32 I am the God of Abraham, and the God of Isaac, and the God of Jacob? God is not the God of the dead, but of the living.

33 And when the multitude heard *this*, they were astonished at his doctrine.

34 ¶ But when the Pharisees had heard that he had put the Sadducees to silence, they were gathered together.

35 Then one of them, *which was* a lawyer, asked *him a question*, tempting him, and saying,

36 Master, which *is* the great commandment in the law?

37 Jesus said unto him, Thou shalt love the Lord thy God with all thy heart, and with all thy soul, and with all thy mind.

38 This is the first and great commandment.

39 And the second *is* like unto it, Thou shalt love thy neighbour as thyself.

40 On these two commandments hang all the law and the prophets.

41 ¶ While the Pharisees were gathered together, Jesus asked them,

42 Saying, What think ye of Christ? whose son is he? They say unto him, *The Son* of David.

43 He saith unto them, How then doth David in spirit call him Lord, saying,

44 The LORD said unto my Lord, Sit thou on my right hand, till I make thine enemies thy footstool?

45 If David then call him Lord, how is he his son?

46 And no man was able to answer him a word, neither durst any *man* from that day forth ask him any more *questions*.

23 Then spake Jesus to the multitude, and to his disciples,

2 Saying, The scribes and the Pharisees sit in Moses' seat:

3 All therefore whatsoever they bid you observe, *that* observe and do; but do not ye after their works: for they say, and do not.

4 For they bind heavy burdens and grievous to be borne, and lay *them* on men's shoulders; but they *themselves* will not move them with one of their fingers.

5 But all their works they do for to be seen of men: they make broad their phylacteries, and enlarge the borders of their garments,

6 And love the uppermost rooms at feasts, and the chief seats in the synagogues,

7 And greetings in the markets, and to be called of men, Rabbi, Rabbi.

8 But be not ye called Rabbi: for one is your Master, *even* Christ; and all ye are brethren.

9 And call no *man* your father upon the earth: for one is your Father, which is in heaven.

10 Neither be ye called masters: for one is your Master, *even* Christ.

11 But he that is greatest among you shall be your servant.

12 And whosoever shall exalt himself shall be abased; and he that shall humble himself shall be exalted.

13 ¶ But woe unto you, scribes and Pharisees, hypocrites! for ye shut up the kingdom of heaven against men: for ye neither go in *yourselves*, neither suffer ye them that are entering to go in.

14 Woe unto you, scribes and Pharisees, hypocrites! for ye devour widows' houses, and for a pretence make long prayer: therefore ye shall receive the greater damnation.

15 Woe unto you, scribes and Pharisees, hypocrites! for ye compass sea and land to make one proselyte; and when he is made, ye make him twofold more the child of hell than yourselves.

16 Woe unto you, *ye* blind guides, which say, Whosoever shall swear by the temple, it is nothing; but whosoever shall swear by the gold of the temple, he is a debtor!

17 *Ye* fools and blind: for whether is greater, the gold, or the temple that sanctifieth the gold?

18 And, Whosoever shall swear by the altar, it is nothing; but whosoever sweareth by the gift that is upon it, he is guilty.

19 *Ye* fools and blind: for whether is greater, the gift, or the altar that sanctifieth the gift?

20 Whoso therefore shall swear

by the altar, sweareth by it, and by all things thereon.

21 And whoso shall swear by the temple, sweareth by it, and by him that dwelleth therein.

22 And he that shall swear by heaven, sweareth by the throne of God, and by him that sitteth thereon.

23 Woe unto you, scribes and Pharisees, hypocrites! for ye pay tithe of mint and anise and cummin, and have omitted the weightier *matters* of the law, judgment, mercy, and faith: these ought ye to have done, and not to leave the other undone.

24 *Ye* blind guides, which strain at a gnat, and swallow a camel.

25 Woe unto you, scribes and Pharisees, hypocrites! for ye make clean the outside of the cup and of the platter, but within they are full of extortion and excess.

26 *Thou* blind Pharisee, cleanse first that *which is* within the cup and platter, that the outside of them may be clean also.

27 Woe unto you, scribes and Pharisees, hypocrites! for ye are like unto whited sepulchres, which indeed appear beautiful outward, but are within full of dead *men's* bones, and of all uncleanness.

28 Even so ye also outwardly appear righteous unto men, but within ye are full of hypocrisy and iniquity.

29 Woe unto you, scribes and Pharisees, hypocrites! because ye build the tombs of the prophets, and garnish the sepulchres of the righteous,

30 And say, If we had been in the days of our fathers, we would not have been partakers with them in the blood of the prophets.

31 Wherefore ye be witnesses unto yourselves, that ye are the children of them which killed the prophets.

32 Fill ye up then the measure of your fathers.

33 *Ye* serpents, *ye* generation of vipers, how can ye escape the damnation of hell?

34 ¶ Wherefore, behold, I send unto you prophets, and wise men, and scribes: and *some* of them ye shall kill and crucify; and *some* of them shall ye scourge in your synagogues, and persecute *them* from city to city:

35 That upon you may come all the righteous blood shed upon the earth, from the blood of righteous Abel unto the blood of Zacharias son of Barachias, whom ye slew between the temple and the altar.

36 Verily I say unto you, All these things shall come upon this generation.

37 O Jerusalem, Jerusalem, *thou* that killest the prophets, and stonest them which are sent unto thee, how often would I have gathered thy children together, even as a hen gathereth her chickens under *her* wings, and ye would not!

38 Behold, your house is left unto you desolate.

39 For I say unto you, Ye shall not see me henceforth, till ye shall say, Blessed *is* he that

cometh in the name of the Lord.

24 And Jesus went out, and departed from the temple: and his disciples came to *him* for to shew him the buildings of the temple.

2 And Jesus said unto them, See ye not all these things? verily I say unto you, There shall not be left here one stone upon another, that shall not be thrown down.

3 ¶ And as he sat upon the mount of Olives, the disciples came unto him privately, saying, Tell us, when shall these things be? and what *shall* be the sign of thy coming, and of the end of the world?

4 And Jesus answered and said unto them, Take heed that no man deceive you.

5 For many shall come in my name, saying, I am Christ; and shall deceive many.

6 And ye shall hear of wars and rumours of wars: see that ye be not troubled: for all *these things* must come to pass, but the end is not yet.

7 For nation shall rise against nation, and kingdom against kingdom: and there shall be famines, and pestilences, and earthquakes, in divers places.

8 All these *are* the beginning of sorrows.

9 Then shall they deliver you up to be afflicted, and shall kill you: and ye shall be hated of all nations for my name's sake.

10 And then shall many be offended, and shall betray one another, and shall hate one another.

11 And many false prophets shall rise, and shall deceive many.

12 And because iniquity shall abound, the love of many shall wax cold.

13 But he that shall endure unto the end, the same shall be saved.

14 And this gospel of the kingdom shall be preached in all the world for a witness unto all nations; and then shall the end come.

15 When ye therefore shall see the abomination of desolation, spoken of by Daniel the prophet, stand in the holy place, (whoso readeth, let him understand:)

16 Then let them which be in Judaea flee into the mountains:

17 Let him which is on the housetop not come down to take any thing out of his house:

18 Neither let him which is in the field return back to take his clothes.

19 And woe unto them that are with child, and to them that give suck in those days!

20 But pray ye that your flight be not in the winter, neither on the sabbath day:

21 For then shall be great tribulation, such as was not since the beginning of the world to this time, no, nor ever shall be.

22 And except those days should be shortened, there should no flesh be saved: but for the elect's sake those days shall be shortened.

23 Then if any man shall say unto you, Lo, here *is* Christ, or

there; believe *it* not.

24 For there shall arise false Christs, and false prophets, and shall shew great signs and wonders; insomuch that, if *it were* possible, they shall deceive the very elect.

25 Behold, I have told you before.

26 Wherefore if they shall say unto you, Behold, he is in the desert; go not forth: behold, *he is* in the secret chambers; believe *it* not.

27 For as the lightning cometh out of the east, and shineth even unto the west; so shall also the coming of the Son of man be.

28 For wheresoever the carcase is, there will the eagles be gathered together.

29 ¶ Immediately after the tribulation of those days shall the sun be darkened, and the moon shall not give her light, and the stars shall fall from heaven, and the powers of the heavens shall be shaken:

30 And then shall appear the sign of the Son of man in heaven: and then shall all the tribes of the earth mourn, and they shall see the Son of man coming in the clouds of heaven with power and great glory.

31 And he shall send his angels with a great sound of a trumpet, and they shall gather together his elect from the four winds, from one end of heaven to the other.

32 ¶ Now learn a parable of the fig tree; When his branch is yet tender, and putteth forth leaves, ye know that summer *is* nigh:

33 So likewise ye, when ye shall see all these things, know that it is near, *even* at the doors.

34 Verily I say unto you, This generation shall not pass, till all these things be fulfilled.

35 Heaven and earth shall pass away, but my words shall not pass away.

36 ¶ But of that day and hour knoweth no *man*, no, not the angels of heaven, but my Father only.

37 But as the days of Noe *were*, so shall also the coming of the Son of man be.

38 For as in the days that were before the flood they were eating and drinking, marrying and giving in marriage, until the day that Noe entered into the ark,

39 And knew not until the flood came, and took them all away; so shall also the coming of the Son of man be.

40 Then shall two be in the field; the one shall be taken, and the other left.

41 Two *women shall be* grinding at the mill; the one shall be taken, and the other left.

42 ¶ Watch therefore; for ye know not what hour your Lord doth come.

43 But know this, that if the goodman of the house had known in what watch the thief would come, he would have watched, and would not have suffered his house to be broken up.

44 Therefore be ye also ready: for in such an hour as ye think not the Son of man cometh.

45 Who then is a faithful and wise servant, whom his lord hath made ruler over his household, to give them meat in due season?

46 Blessed *is* that servant, whom his lord when he cometh shall find so doing.

47 Verily I say unto you, That he shall make him ruler over all his goods.

48 But and if that evil servant shall say in his heart, My lord delayeth his coming;

49 And shall begin to smite *his* fellowservants, and to eat and drink with the drunken;

50 The lord of that servant shall come in a day when he looketh not for *him*, and in an hour that he is not aware of,

51 And shall cut him asunder, and appoint *him* his portion with the hypocrites: there shall be weeping and gnashing of teeth.

25 Then shall the kingdom of heaven be likened unto ten virgins, which took their lamps, and went forth to meet the bridegroom.

2 And five of them were wise, and five *were* foolish.

3 They that *were* foolish took their lamps, and took no oil with them:

4 But the wise took oil in their vessels with their lamps.

5 While the bridegroom tarried, they all slumbered and slept.

6 And at midnight there was a cry made, Behold, the bridegroom cometh; go ye out to meet him.

7 Then all those virgins arose, and trimmed their lamps.

8 And the foolish said unto the wise, Give us of your oil; for our lamps are gone out.

9 But the wise answered, saying, *Not so*; lest there be not enough for us and you: but go ye rather to them that sell, and buy for yourselves.

10 And while they went to buy, the bridegroom came; and they that were ready went in with him to the marriage: and the door was shut.

11 Afterward came also the other virgins, saying, Lord, Lord, open to us.

12 But he answered and said, Verily I say unto you, I know you not.

13 Watch therefore, for ye know neither the day nor the hour wherein the Son of man cometh.

14 ¶ For *the kingdom of heaven is* as a man travelling into a far country, *who* called his own servants, and delivered unto them his goods.

15 And unto one he gave five talents, to another two, and to another one; to every man according to his several ability; and straightway took his journey.

16 Then he that had received the five talents went and traded with the same, and made *them* other five talents.

17 And likewise he that *had received* two, he also gained other two.

18 But he that had received one went and digged in the earth, and hid his lord's money.

43

19 After a long time the lord of those servants cometh, and reckoneth with them.

20 And so he that had received five talents came and brought other five talents, saying, Lord, thou deliveredst unto me five talents: behold, I have gained beside them five talents more.

21 His lord said unto him, Well done, *thou* good and faithful servant: thou hast been faithful over a few things, I will make thee ruler over many things: enter thou into the joy of thy lord.

22 He also that had received two talents came and said, Lord, thou deliveredst unto me two talents: behold, I have gained two other talents beside them.

23 His lord said unto him, Well done, good and faithful servant; thou hast been faithful over a few things, I will make thee ruler over many things: enter thou into the joy of thy lord.

24 Then he which had received the one talent came and said, Lord, I knew thee that thou art an hard man, reaping where thou hast not sown, and gathering where thou hast not strawed:

25 And I was afraid, and went and hid thy talent in the earth: lo, *there* thou hast *that* is thine.

26 His lord answered and said unto him, Thou wicked and slothful servant, thou knewest that I reap where I sowed not, and gather where I have not strawed:

27 Thou oughtest therefore to have put my money to the exchangers, and *then* at my coming

I should have received mine own with usury.

28 Take therefore the talent from him, and give *it* unto him which hath ten talents.

29 For unto every one that hath shall be given, and he shall have abundance: but from him that hath not shall be taken away even that which he hath.

30 And cast ye the unprofitable servant into outer darkness: there shall be weeping and gnashing of teeth.

31 ¶ When the Son of man shall come in his glory, and all the holy angels with him, then shall he sit upon the throne of his glory:

32 And before him shall be gathered all nations: and he shall separate them one from another, as a shepherd divideth *his* sheep from the goats:

33 And he shall set the sheep on his right hand, but the goats on the left.

34 Then shall the King say unto them on his right hand, Come, ye blessed of my Father, inherit the kingdom prepared for you from the foundation of the world:

35 For I was an hungred, and ye gave me meat: I was thirsty, and ye gave me drink: I was a stranger, and ye took me in:

36 Naked, and ye clothed me: I was sick, and ye visited me: I was in prison, and ye came unto me.

37 Then said the righteous answer him, saying, Lord, when saw we thee an hungred, and fed *thee*? or thirsty, and gave *thee* drink?

44

38 When saw we thee a stranger, and took thee in? or naked, and clothed thee?

39 Or when saw we thee sick, or in prison, and came unto thee?

40 And the King shall answer and say unto them, Verily I say unto you, Inasmuch as ye have done it unto one of the least of these my brethren, ye have done it unto me.

41 Then shall he say also unto them on the left hand, Depart from me, ye cursed, into everlasting fire, prepared for the devil and his angels:

42 For I was an hungred, and ye gave me no meat: I was thirsty, and ye gave me no drink:

43 I was a stranger, and ye took me not in: naked, and ye clothed me not: sick, and in prison, and ye visited me not.

44 Then shall they also answer him, saying, Lord, when saw we thee an hungred, or athirst, or a stranger, or naked, or sick, or in prison, and did not minister unto thee?

45 Then shall he answer them, saying, Verily I say unto you, Inasmuch as ye did it not to one of the least of these, ye did it not to me.

46 And these shall go away into everlasting punishment: but the righteous into life eternal.

26 And it came to pass, when Jesus had finished all these sayings, he said unto his disciples,

2 Ye know that after two days is the feast of the passover, and the Son of man is betrayed to be crucified.

3 Then assembled together the chief priests, and the scribes, and the elders of the people, unto the palace of the high priest, who was called Caiaphas,

4 And consulted that they might take Jesus by subtilty, and kill him.

5 But they said, Not on the feast day, lest there be an uproar among the people.

6 ¶ Now when Jesus was in Bethany, in the house of Simon the leper,

7 There came unto him a woman having an alabaster box of very precious ointment, and poured it on his head, as he sat at meat.

8 But when his disciples saw it, they had indignation, saying, To what purpose is this waste?

9 For this ointment might have been sold for much, and given to the poor.

10 When Jesus understood it, he said unto them, Why trouble ye the woman? for she hath wrought a good work upon me.

11 For ye have the poor always with you; but me ye have not always.

12 For in that she hath poured this ointment on my body, she did it for my burial.

13 Verily I say unto you, Wheresoever this gospel shall be preached in the whole world, there shall also this, that this woman hath done, be told for a

memorial of her.

14 ¶ Then one of the twelve, called Judas Iscariot, went unto the chief priests,

15 And said *unto them,* What will ye give me, and I will deliver him unto you? And they covenanted with him for thirty pieces of silver.

16 And from that time he sought opportunity to betray him.

17 ¶ Now the first *day* of the *feast of* unleavened bread the disciples came to Jesus, saying unto him, Where wilt thou that we prepare for thee to eat the passover?

18 And he said, Go into the city to such a man, and say unto him, The Master saith, My time is at hand; I will keep the passover at thy house with my disciples.

19 And the disciples did as Jesus had appointed them; and they made ready the passover.

20 Now when the even was come, he sat down with the twelve.

21 And as they did eat, he said, Verily I say unto you, that one of you shall betray me.

22 And they were exceeding sorrowful, and began every one of them to say unto him, Lord, is it I?

23 And he answered and said, He that dippeth *his* hand with me in the dish, the same shall betray me.

24 The Son of man goeth as it is written of him: but woe unto that man by whom the Son of man is betrayed! it had been good for that man if he had not

been born.

25 Then Judas, which betrayed him, answered and said, Master, is it I? He said unto him, Thou hast said.

26 ¶ And as they were eating, Jesus took bread, and blessed *it,* and brake *it,* and gave *it* to the disciples, and said, Take, eat; this is my body.

27 And he took the cup, and gave thanks, and gave *it* to them, saying, Drink ye all of it;

28 For this is my blood of the new testament, which is shed for many for the remission of sins.

29 But I say unto you, I will not drink henceforth of this fruit of the vine, until that day when I drink it new with you in my Father's kingdom.

30 ¶ And when they had sung an hymn, they went out into the mount of Olives.

31 Then saith Jesus unto them, All ye shall be offended because of me this night: for it is written, I will smite the shepherd, and the sheep of the flock shall be scattered abroad.

32 But after I am risen again, I will go before you into Galilee.

33 Peter answered and said unto him, Though all *men* shall be offended because of thee, *yet* will I never be offended.

34 Jesus said unto him, Verily I say unto thee, That this night, before the cock crow, thou shalt deny me thrice.

35 Peter said unto him, Though I should die with thee, yet will I not deny thee. Likewise also said

all the disciples.

36 ¶ Then cometh Jesus with them unto a place called Gethsemane, and saith unto the disciples, Sit ye here, while I go and pray yonder.

37 And he took with him Peter and the two sons of Zebedee, and began to be sorrowful and very heavy.

38 Then saith he unto them, My soul is exceeding sorrowful, even unto death: tarry ye here, and watch with me.

39 And he went a little farther, and fell on his face, and prayed, saying, O my Father, if it be possible, let this cup pass from me: nevertheless if this cup pass from me: nevertheless as I will, but as thou *wilt*.

40 And he cometh unto the disciples, and findeth them asleep, and saith unto Peter, What, could ye not watch with me one hour?

41 Watch and pray, that ye enter not into temptation: the spirit indeed *is* willing, but the flesh *is* weak.

42 He went away again the second time, and prayed, saying, O my Father, if this cup may not pass away from me, except I drink it, thy will be done.

43 And he came and found them asleep again: for their eyes were heavy.

44 And he left them, and went away again, and prayed the third time, saying the same words.

45 Then cometh he to his disciples, and saith unto them, Sleep on now, and take *your* rest: behold, the hour is at hand, and the Son of man is betrayed into the

hands of sinners.

46 Rise, let us be going: behold, he is at hand that doth betray me.

47 ¶ And while he yet spake, lo, Judas, one of the twelve, came, and with him a great multitude with swords and staves, from the chief priests and elders of the people.

48 Now he that betrayed him gave them a sign, saying, Whomsoever I shall kiss, that same is he: hold him fast.

49 And forthwith he came to Jesus, and said, Hail, master; and kissed him.

50 And Jesus said unto him, Friend, wherefore art thou come? Then came they, and laid hands on Jesus, and took him.

51 And, behold, one of them which were with Jesus stretched out *his* hand, and drew his sword, and struck a servant of the high priest's, and smote off his ear.

52 Then said Jesus unto him, Put up again thy sword into his place: for all they that take the sword shall perish with the sword.

53 Thinkest thou that I cannot now pray to my Father, and he shall presently give me more than twelve legions of angels?

54 But how then shall the scriptures be fulfilled, that thus it must be?

55 In that same hour said Jesus to the multitudes, Are ye come out as against a thief with swords and staves for to take me? I sat daily with you teaching in the temple, and ye laid no hold on

me.

56 ¶ But all this was done, that the scriptures of the prophets might be fulfilled. Then all the disciples forsook him, and fled.

57 ¶ And they that had laid hold on Jesus led *him* away to Caiaphas the high priest, where the scribes and the elders were assembled.

58 But Peter followed him afar off unto the high priest's palace, and went in, and sat with the servants, to see the end.

59 Now the chief priests, and elders, and all the council, sought false witness against Jesus, to put him to death;

60 But found none: yea, though many false witnesses came, *yet* found they none. At the last came two false witnesses,

61 And said, This *fellow* said, I am able to destroy the temple of God, and to build it in three days.

62 And the high priest arose, and said unto him, Answerest thou nothing? what *is it which* these witness against thee?

63 But Jesus held his peace. And the high priest answered and said unto him, I adjure thee by the living God, that thou tell us whether thou be the Christ, the Son of God.

64 Jesus saith unto him, Thou hast said: nevertheless I say unto you, Hereafter shall ye see the Son of man sitting on the right hand of power, and coming in the clouds of heaven.

65 Then the high priest rent his clothes, saying, He hath spoken blasphemy; what further need have we of witnesses? behold, now ye have heard his blasphemy.

66 What think ye? They answered and said, He is guilty of death.

67 Then did they spit in his face, and buffeted him; and others smote *him* with the palms of their hands,

68 Saying, Prophesy unto us, thou Christ, Who is he that smote thee?

69 ¶ Now Peter sat without in the palace: and a damsel came unto him, saying, Thou also wast with Jesus of Galilee.

70 But he denied before *them* all, saying, I know not what thou sayest.

71 And when he was gone out into the porch, another *maid* saw him, and said unto them that were there, This *fellow* was also with Jesus of Nazareth.

72 And again he denied with an oath, I do not know the man.

73 And after a while came unto *him* they that stood by, and said to Peter, Surely thou also art *one* of them; for thy speech bewrayeth thee.

74 Then began he to curse and to swear, *saying*, I know not the man. And immediately the cock crew.

75 And Peter remembered the word of Jesus, which said unto him, Before the cock crow, thou shalt deny me thrice. And he went out, and wept bitterly.

27 When the morning was come, all the chief priests and elders of the people took counsel against Jesus to put him to death:

2 And when they had bound him, they led *him* away, and delivered him to Pontius Pilate the governor.

3 ℂ Then Judas, which had betrayed him, when he saw that he was condemned, repented himself, and brought again the thirty pieces of silver to the chief priests and elders,

4 Saying, I have sinned in that I have betrayed the innocent blood. And they said, What *is that* to us? see thou *to that.*

5 And he cast down the pieces of silver in the temple, and departed, and went and hanged himself.

6 And the chief priests took the silver pieces, and said, It is not lawful for to put them into the treasury, because it is the price of blood.

7 And they took counsel, and bought with them the potter's field, to bury strangers in.

8 Wherefore that field was called, The field of blood, unto this day.

9 Then was fulfilled that which was spoken by Jeremy the prophet, saying, And they took the thirty pieces of silver, the price of him that was valued, whom they of the children of Israel did value;

10 And gave them for the potter's field, as the Lord appointed me.

11 ℂ And Jesus stood before the governor: and the governor asked him, saying, Art thou the King of the Jews? And Jesus said unto him, Thou sayest.

12 And when he was accused of the chief priests and elders, he answered nothing.

13 Then said Pilate unto him, Hearest thou not how many things they witness against thee?

14 And he answered him to never a word; insomuch that the governor marvelled greatly.

15 Now at *that* feast the governor was wont to release unto the people a prisoner, whom they would.

16 And they had then a notable prisoner, called Barabbas.

17 Therefore when they were gathered together, Pilate said unto them, Whom will ye that I release unto you? Barabbas, or Jesus which is called Christ?

18 For he knew that for envy they had delivered him.

19 ℂ When he was set down on the judgment seat, his wife sent unto him, saying, Have thou nothing to do with that just man: for I have suffered many things this day in a dream because of him.

20 But the chief priests and elders persuaded the multitude that they should ask Barabbas, and destroy Jesus.

21 The governor answered and said unto them, Whether of the twain will ye that I release unto you? They said, Barabbas.

22 Pilate saith unto them, What

shall I do then with Jesus which is called Christ? *They* all say unto him, Let him be crucified.

23 And the governor said, Why, what evil hath he done? But they cried out the more, saying, Let him be crucified.

24 ¶ When Pilate saw that he could prevail nothing, but *that* rather a tumult was made, he took water, and washed *his* hands before the multitude, saying, I am innocent of the blood of this just person: see ye *to it*.

25 Then answered all the people, and said, His blood *be* on us, and on our children.

26 ¶ Then released he Barabbas unto them: and when he had scourged Jesus, he delivered *him* to be crucified.

27 Then the soldiers of the governor took Jesus into the common hall, and gathered unto him the whole band *of soldiers*.

28 And they stripped him, and put on him a scarlet robe.

29 ¶ And when they had platted a crown of thorns, they put *it* upon his head, and a reed in his right hand: and they bowed the knee before him, and mocked him, saying, Hail, King of the Jews!

30 And they spit upon him, and took the reed, and smote him on the head.

31 And after that they had mocked him, they took the robe off from him, and put his own raiment on him, and led him away to crucify *him*.

32 And as they came out, they found a man of Cyrene, Simon

by name: him they compelled to bear his cross.

33 And when they were come unto a place called Golgotha, that is to say, a place of a skull,

34 ¶ They gave him vinegar to drink mingled with gall: and when he had tasted *thereof*, he would not drink.

35 And they crucified him, and parted his garments, casting lots: that it might be fulfilled which was spoken by the prophet, They parted my garments among them, and upon my vesture did they cast lots.

36 And sitting down they watched him there;

37 And set up over his head his accusation written, THIS IS JESUS THE KING OF THE JEWS.

38 Then were there two thieves crucified with him, one on the right hand, and another on the left.

39 ¶ And they that passed by reviled him, wagging their heads,

40 And saying, Thou that destroyest the temple, and buildest *it* in three days, save thyself. If thou be the Son of God, come down from the cross.

41 Likewise also the chief priests mocking *him*, with the scribes and elders, said,

42 He saved others; himself he cannot save. If he be the King of Israel, let him now come down from the cross, and we will believe him.

43 He trusted in God; let him deliver him now, if he will have

him: for he said, I am the Son of God.

44 The thieves also, which were crucified with him, cast the same in his teeth.

45 Now from the sixth hour there was darkness over all the land unto the ninth hour.

46 And about the ninth hour Jesus cried with a loud voice, saying, Eli, Eli, lama sabachthani? that is to say, My God, my God, why hast thou forsaken me?

47 Some of them that stood there, when they heard *that*, said, This *man* calleth for Elias.

48 And straightway one of them ran, and took a sponge, and filled *it* with vinegar, and put *it* on a reed, and gave him to drink.

49 The rest said, Let be, let us see whether Elias will come to save him.

50 ¶ Jesus, when he had cried again with a loud voice, yielded up the ghost.

51 And, behold, the veil of the temple was rent in twain from the top to the bottom; and the earth did quake, and the rocks rent;

52 And the graves were opened; and many bodies of the saints which slept arose,

53 And came out of the graves after his resurrection, and went into the holy city, and appeared unto many.

54 Now when the centurion, and they that were with him, watching Jesus, saw the earthquake, and those things that were done,

they feared greatly, saying, Truly this was the Son of God.

55 And many women were there beholding afar off, which followed Jesus from Galilee, ministering unto him:

56 Among which was Mary Magdalene, and Mary the mother of James and Joses, and the mother of Zebedee's children.

57 When the even was come, there came a rich man of Arimathaea, named Joseph, who also himself was Jesus' disciple:

58 He went to Pilate, and begged the body of Jesus. Then Pilate commanded the body to be delivered.

59 And when Joseph had taken the body, he wrapped it in a clean linen cloth,

60 And laid it in his own new tomb, which he had hewn out in the rock: and he rolled a great stone to the door of the sepulchre, and departed.

61 And there was Mary Magdalene, and the other Mary, sitting over against the sepulchre.

62 ¶ Now the next day, that followed the day of the preparation, the chief priests and Pharisees came together unto Pilate,

63 Saying, Sir, we remember that that deceiver said, while he was yet alive, After three days I will rise again.

64 Command therefore that the sepulchre be made sure until the third day, lest his disciples come by night, and steal him away, and say unto the people, He is risen

from the dead: so the last error shall be worse than the first.

65 Pilate said unto them, Ye have a watch: go your way, make *it* as sure as ye can.

66 So they went, and made the sepulchre sure, sealing the stone, and setting a watch.

28

In the end of the sabbath, as it began to dawn toward the first *day* of the week, came Mary Magdalene and the other Mary to see the sepulchre.

2 And, behold, there was a great earthquake: for the angel of the Lord descended from heaven, and came and rolled back the stone from the door, and sat upon it.

3 His countenance was like lightning, and his raiment white as snow:

4 And for fear of him the keepers did shake, and became as dead *men.*

5 And the angel answered and said unto the women, Fear not ye: for I know that ye seek Jesus, which was crucified.

6 He is not here: for he is risen, as he said. Come, see the place where the Lord lay.

7 And go quickly, and tell his disciples that he is risen from the dead; and, behold, he goeth before you into Galilee; there shall ye see him: lo, I have told you.

8 And they departed quickly from the sepulchre with fear and great joy; and did run to bring his disciples word.

9 ¶ And as they went to tell his disciples, behold, Jesus met them, saying, All hail. And they came and held him by the feet, and worshipped him.

10 Then said Jesus unto them, Be not afraid: go tell my brethren that they go into Galilee, and there shall they see me.

11 ¶ Now when they were going, behold, some of the watch came into the city, and shewed unto the chief priests all the things that were done.

12 And when they were assembled with the elders, and had taken counsel, they gave large money unto the soldiers,

13 Saying, Say ye, His disciples came by night, and stole him *away* while we slept.

14 And if this come to the governor's ears, we will persuade him, and secure you.

15 So they took the money, and did as they were taught: and this saying is commonly reported among the Jews until this day.

16 Then the eleven disciples went away into Galilee, into a mountain where Jesus had appointed them.

17 ¶ And when they saw him, they worshipped him: but some doubted.

18 And Jesus came and spake unto them, saying, All power is given unto me in heaven and in earth.

19 Go ye therefore, and teach all nations, baptizing them in the name of the Father, and of the Son, and of the Holy Ghost:

20 Teaching them to observe all

things whatsoever I have commanded you: and, lo, I am with you alway, *even* unto the end of the world. Amen.

THE GOSPEL ACCORDING

TO

MARK

1 The beginning of the gospel of Jesus Christ, the Son of God;

2 As it is written in the prophets, Behold, I send my messenger before thy face, which shall prepare thy way before thee.

3 The voice of one crying in the wilderness, Prepare ye the way of the Lord, make his paths straight.

4 John did baptize in the wilderness, and preach the baptism of repentance for the remission of sins.

5 And there went out unto him all the land of Judaea, and they of Jerusalem, and were all baptized of him in the river of Jordan, confessing their sins.

6 And John was clothed with camel's hair, and with a girdle of a skin about his loins; and he did eat locusts and wild honey;

7 And preached, saying, There cometh one mightier than I after me, the latchet of whose shoes I am not worthy to stoop down and unloose.

8 I indeed have baptized you with water: but he shall baptize you with the Holy Ghost.

9 ¶ And it came to pass in those days, that Jesus came from Nazareth of Galilee, and was baptized of John in Jordan.

10 And straightway coming up out of the water, he saw the heavens opened, and the Spirit like a dove descending upon him:

11 And there came a voice from heaven, *saying*, Thou art my beloved Son, in whom I am well pleased.

12 ¶ And immediately the Spirit driveth him into the wilderness.

13 And he was there in the wilderness forty days, tempted of Satan; and was with the wild beasts; and the angels ministered unto him.

14 ¶ Now after that John was put in prison, Jesus came into Galilee, preaching the gospel of the kingdom of God,

15 And saying, The time is fulfilled, and the kingdom of God is at hand: repent ye, and believe the gospel.

16 ¶ Now as he walked by the sea of Galilee, he saw Simon and Andrew his brother casting a net into the sea: for they were fishers.

17 And Jesus said unto them, Come ye after me, and I will make you to become fishers of men.

18 And straightway they forsook their nets, and followed him.

19 And when he had gone a little farther thence, he saw James the *son* of Zebedee, and John his brother, who also were in the ship mending their nets.

20 And straightway he called them: and they left their father Zebedee in the ship with the hired servants, and went after him.

21 ❡ And they went into Capernaum; and straightway on the sabbath day he entered into the synagogue, and taught.

22 And they were astonished at his doctrine: for he taught them as one that had authority, and not as the scribes.

23 And there was in their synagogue a man with an unclean spirit; and he cried out,

24 Saying, Let *us* alone; what have we to do with thee, thou Jesus of Nazareth? art thou come to destroy us? I know thee who thou art, the Holy One of God.

25 And Jesus rebuked him, saying, Hold thy peace, and come out of him.

26 And when the unclean spirit had torn him, and cried with a loud voice, he came out of him.

27 And they were all amazed, insomuch that they questioned among themselves, saying, What thing is this? what new doctrine *is* this? for with authority commandeth he even the unclean spirits, and they do obey him.

28 And immediately his fame spread abroad throughout all the region round about Galilee.

29 ❡ And forthwith, when they were come out of the synagogue, they entered into the house of Simon and Andrew, with James and John.

30 But Simon's wife's mother lay sick of a fever, and anon they tell him of her.

31 And he came and took her by the hand, and lifted her up; and immediately the fever left her, and she ministered unto them.

32 ❡ And at even, when the sun did set, they brought unto him all that were diseased, and them that were possessed with devils.

33 And all the city was gathered together at the door.

34 And he healed many that were sick of divers diseases, and cast out many devils; and suffered not the devils to speak, because they knew him.

35 ❡ And in the morning, rising up a great while before day, he went out, and departed into a solitary place, and there prayed.

36 And Simon and they that were with him followed after him.

37 And when they had found him, they said unto him, All *men* seek for thee.

38 And he said unto them, Let us go into the next towns, that I may preach there also: for therefore came I forth.

39 And he preached in their synagogues throughout all Galilee, and cast out devils.

40 ❡ And there came a leper to him, beseeching him, and kneel-

ing down to him, and saying unto him, If thou wilt, thou canst make me clean.

41 And Jesus, moved with compassion, put forth *his* hand, and touched him, and saith unto him, I will; be thou clean.

42 And as soon as he had spoken, immediately the leprosy departed from him, and he was cleansed.

43 And he straitly charged him, and forthwith sent him away;

44 And saith unto him, See thou say nothing to any man: but go thy way, shew thyself to the priest, and offer for thy cleansing those things which Moses commanded, for a testimony unto them.

45 But he went out, and began to publish *it* much, and to blaze abroad the matter, insomuch that Jesus could no more openly enter into the city, but was without in desert places: and they came to him from every quarter.

2 And again he entered into Capernaum after *some* days; and it was noised that he was in the house.

2 And straightway many were gathered together, insomuch that there was no room to receive *them*, no, not so much as about the door: and he preached the word unto them.

3 And they come unto him, bringing one sick of the palsy, which was borne of four.

4 And when they could not come nigh unto him for the press, they uncovered the roof where he

was: and when they had broken *it* up, they let down the bed wherein the sick of the palsy lay.

5 When Jesus saw their faith, he said unto the sick of the palsy, Son, thy sins be forgiven thee.

6 But there were certain of the scribes sitting there, and reasoning in their hearts,

7 Why doth this *man* thus speak blasphemies? who can forgive sins but God only?

8 And immediately when Jesus perceived in his spirit that they so reasoned within themselves, he said unto them, Why reason ye these things in your hearts?

9 Whether is it easier to say to the sick of the palsy, *Thy* sins be forgiven thee; or to say, Arise, and take up thy bed, and walk?

10 But that ye may know that the Son of man hath power on earth to forgive sins, (he saith to the sick of the palsy,)

11 I say unto thee, Arise, and take up thy bed, and go thy way into thine house.

12 And immediately he arose, took up the bed, and went forth before them all; insomuch that they were all amazed, and glorified God, saying, We never saw it on this fashion.

13 And he went forth again by the sea side; and all the multitude resorted unto him, and he taught them.

14 ¶ And as he passed by, he saw Levi the *son* of Alphaeus sitting at the receipt of custom, and said unto him, Follow me. And he arose and followed him.

15 ¶ And it came to pass, that, as Jesus sat at meat in his house, many publicans and sinners sat also together with Jesus and his disciples: for there were many, and they followed him.

16 And when the scribes and Pharisees saw him eat with publicans and sinners, said unto his disciples, How is it that he eateth and drinketh with publicans and sinners?

17 When Jesus heard *it*, he saith unto them, They that are whole have no need of the physician, but they that are sick: I came not to call the righteous, but sinners to repentance.

18 ¶ And the disciples of John and of the Pharisees used to fast: and they come and say unto him, Why do the disciples of John and of the Pharisees fast, but thy disciples fast not?

19 And Jesus said unto them, Can the children of the bridechamber fast, while the bridegroom is with them? as long as they have the bridegroom with them, they cannot fast.

20 But the days will come, when the bridegroom shall be taken away from them, and then shall they fast in those days.

21 No man also seweth a piece of new cloth on an old garment: else the new piece that filled it up taketh away from the old, and the rent is made worse.

22 And no man putteth new wine into old bottles: else the new wine doth burst the bottles, and the wine is spilled, and the bottles will be marred: but new wine must be put into new bottles.

23 ¶ And it came to pass, that he went through the corn fields on the sabbath day; and his disciples began, as they went, to pluck the ears of corn.

24 And the Pharisees said unto him, Behold, why do they on the sabbath day that which is not lawful?

25 And he said unto them, Have ye never read what David did, when he had need, and was an hungred, he, and they that were with him?

26 How he went into the house of God in the days of Abiathar the high priest, and did eat the shewbread, which is not lawful to eat but for the priests, and gave also to them which were with him?

27 ¶ And he said unto them, The sabbath was made for man, and not man for the sabbath:

28 Therefore the Son of man is Lord also of the sabbath.

3 And he entered again into the synagogue; and there was a man there which had a withered hand.

2 And they watched him, whether he would heal him on the sabbath day; that they might accuse him.

3 And he saith unto the man which had the withered hand, Stand forth.

4 And he saith unto them, Is it lawful to do good on the sabbath days, or to do evil? to save life, or to kill? But they held their

56

peace.

5 And when he had looked round about on them with anger, being grieved for the hardness of their hearts, he saith unto the man, Stretch forth thine hand. And he stretched *it* out: and his hand was restored whole as the other.

6 And the Pharisees went forth, and straightway took counsel with the Herodians against him, how they might destroy him.

7 But Jesus withdrew himself with his disciples to the sea: and a great multitude from Galilee followed him, and from Judaea,

8 And from Jerusalem, and from Idumaea, and *from* beyond Jordan; and they about Tyre and Sidon, a great multitude, when they had heard what great things he did, came unto him.

9 And he spake to his disciples, that a small ship should wait on him because of the multitude, lest they should throng him.

10 For he had healed many; insomuch that they pressed upon him for to touch him, as many as had plagues.

11 ¶ And unclean spirits, when they saw him, fell down before him, and cried, saying, Thou art the Son of God.

12 And he straitly charged them that they should not make him known.

13 ¶ And he goeth up into a mountain, and calleth *unto him* whom he would: and they came unto him.

14 And he ordained twelve, that they should be with him, and that he might send them forth to preach,

15 And to have power to heal sicknesses, and to cast out devils:

16 And Simon he surnamed Peter;

17 And James the *son* of Zebedee, and John the brother of James; and he surnamed them Boanerges, which is, The sons of thunder:

18 And Andrew, and Philip, and Bartholomew, and Matthew, and Thomas, and James the *son* of Alphaeus, and Thaddaeus, and Simon the Canaanite,

19 And Judas Iscariot, which also betrayed him: and they went into an house.

20 And the multitude cometh together again, so that they could not so much as eat bread.

21 And when his friends heard *of it,* they went out to lay hold on him: for they said, He is beside himself.

22 ¶ And the scribes which came down from Jerusalem said, He hath Beelzebub, and by the prince of the devils casteth he out devils.

23 And he called them *unto him,* and said unto them in parables, How can Satan cast out Satan?

24 And if a kingdom be divided against itself, that kingdom cannot stand.

25 And if a house be divided against itself, that house cannot stand.

26 And if Satan rise up against

himself, and be divided, he cannot stand, but hath an end.

27 No man can enter into a strong man's house, and spoil his goods, except he will first bind the strong man; and then he will spoil his house.

28 Verily I say unto you, All sins shall be forgiven unto the sons of men, and blasphemies wherewith soever they shall blaspheme:

29 But he that shall blaspheme against the Holy Ghost hath never forgiveness, but is in danger of eternal damnation:

30 Because they said, He hath an unclean spirit.

31 ¶ There came then his brethren and his mother, and, standing without, sent unto him, calling him.

32 And the multitude sat about him, and they said unto him, Behold, thy mother and thy brethren without seek for thee.

33 And he answered them, saying, Who is my mother, or my brethren?

34 And he looked round about on them which sat about him, and said, Behold my mother and my brethren!

35 For whosoever shall do the will of God, the same is my brother, and my sister, and mother.

4 And he began again to teach by the sea side: and there was gathered unto him a great multitude, so that he entered into a ship, and sat in the sea; and the whole multitude was by the sea on the land.

2 And he taught them many things by parables, and said unto them in his doctrine,

3 Hearken; Behold, there went out a sower to sow:

4 And it came to pass, as he sowed, some fell by the way side, and the fowls of the air came and devoured it up.

5 And some fell on stony ground, where it had not much earth; and immediately it sprang up, because it had no depth of earth:

6 But when the sun was up, it was scorched; and because it had no root, it withered away.

7 And some fell among thorns, and the thorns grew up, and choked it, and it yielded no fruit.

8 And other fell on good ground, and did yield fruit that sprang up and increased; and brought forth, some thirty, and some sixty, and some an hundred.

9 And he said unto them, He that hath ears to hear, let him hear.

10 And when he was alone, they that were about him with the twelve asked of him the parable.

11 And he said unto them, Unto you it is given to know the mystery of the kingdom of God: but unto them that are without, all *these* things are done in parables:

12 That seeing they may see, and not perceive; and hearing they may hear, and not understand; lest at any time they should be converted, and *their*

58

sins should be forgiven them.

13 And he said unto them, Know ye not this parable? and how then will ye know all parables?

14 ❡ The sower soweth the word.

15 And these are they by the way side, where the word is sown; but when they have heard, Satan cometh immediately, and taketh away the word that was sown in their hearts.

16 And these are they likewise which are sown on stony ground; who, when they have heard the word, immediately receive it with gladness;

17 And have no root in themselves, and so endure but for a time: afterward, when affliction or persecution ariseth for the word's sake, immediately they are offended.

18 And these are they which are sown among thorns; such as hear the word,

19 And the cares of this world, and the deceitfulness of riches, and the lusts of other things entering in, choke the word, and it becometh unfruitful.

20 And these are they which are sown on good ground; such as hear the word, and receive *it*, and bring forth fruit, some thirtyfold, some sixty, and some an hundred.

21 ❡ And he said unto them, Is a candle brought to be put under a bushel, or under a bed? and not to be set on a candlestick?

22 For there is nothing hid, which shall not be manifested; neither was any thing kept secret, but that it should come abroad.

23 If any man have ears to hear, let him hear.

24 And he said unto them, Take heed what ye hear: with what measure ye mete, it shall be measured to you: and unto you that hear shall more be given.

25 For he that hath, to him shall be given: and he that hath not, from him shall be taken even that which he hath.

26 ❡ And he said, So is the kingdom of God, as if a man should cast seed into the ground;

27 And should sleep, and rise night and day, and the seed should spring and grow up, he knoweth not how.

28 For the earth bringeth forth fruit of herself; first the blade, then the ear, after that the full corn in the ear.

29 But when the fruit is brought forth, immediately he putteth in the sickle, because the harvest is come.

30 ❡ And he said, Whereunto shall we liken the kingdom of God? or with what comparison shall we compare it?

31 *It is* like a grain of mustard seed, which, when it is sown in the earth, is less than all the seeds that be in the earth:

32 But when it is sown, it groweth up, and becometh greater than all herbs, and shooteth out great branches; so that the fowls of the air may lodge under the shadow of it.

33 And with many such parables spake he the word unto them, as they were able to hear *it*.

34 But without a parable spake he not unto them: and when they were alone, he expounded all things to his disciples.

35 ¶ And the same day, when the even was come, he saith unto them, Let us pass over unto the other side.

36 And when they had sent away the multitude, they took him even as he was in the ship. And there were also with him other little ships.

37 And there arose a great storm of wind, and the waves beat into the ship, so that it was now full.

38 And he was in the hinder part of the ship, asleep on a pillow: and they awake him, and say unto him, Master, carest thou not that we perish?

39 And he arose, and rebuked the wind, and said unto the sea, Peace, be still. And the wind ceased, and there was a great calm.

40 And he said unto them, Why are ye so fearful? how is it that ye have no faith?

41 And they feared exceedingly, and said one to another, What manner of man is this, that even the wind and the sea obey him?

5 And they came over unto the other side of the sea, into the country of the Gadarenes.

2 And when he was come out of the ship, immediately there met him out of the tombs a man with an unclean spirit,

3 Who had *his* dwelling among the tombs; and no man could bind him, no, not with chains:

4 Because that he had been often bound with fetters and chains, and the chains had been plucked asunder by him, and the fetters broken in pieces: neither could any *man* tame him.

5 And always, night and day, he was in the mountains, and in the tombs, crying, and cutting himself with stones.

6 But when he saw Jesus afar off, he ran and worshipped him,

7 And cried with a loud voice, and said, What have I to do with thee, Jesus, *thou* Son of the most high God? I adjure thee by God, that thou torment me not.

8 For he said unto him, Come out of the man, *thou* unclean spirit.

9 And he asked him, What *is* thy name? And he answered, saying, My name *is* Legion: for we are many.

10 And he besought him much that he would not send them away out of the country.

11 Now there was there nigh unto the mountains a great herd of swine feeding.

12 And all the devils besought him, saying, Send us into the swine, that we may enter into them.

13 And forthwith Jesus gave them leave. And the unclean spir its went out, and entered into the swine; and the herd ran violently down a steep place into the sea, (they were about two thousand;) and were choked in the sea.

14 And they that fed the swine fled, and told *it* in the city, and in the country. And they went out to see what it was that was done.

15 And they come to Jesus, and see him that was possessed with the devil, and had the legion, sitting, and clothed, and in his right mind: and they were afraid.

16 And they that saw *it* told them how it befell to him that was possessed with the devil, and *also* concerning the swine.

17 And they began to pray him to depart out of their coasts.

18 And when he was come into the ship, he that had been possessed with the devil prayed him that he might be with him.

19 Howbeit Jesus suffered him not, but saith unto him, Go home to thy friends, and tell them how great things the Lord hath done for thee, and hath had compassion on thee.

20 And he departed, and began to publish in Decapolis how great things Jesus had done for him: and all *men* did marvel.

21 And when Jesus was passed over again by ship unto the other side, much people gathered unto him: and he was nigh unto the sea.

22 And, behold, there cometh one of the rulers of the synagogue, Jairus by name; and when he saw him, he fell at his feet,

23 And besought him greatly, saying, My little daughter lieth at the point of death: *I pray thee*, come and lay thy hands on her, that she may be healed; and she shall live.

24 And *Jesus* went with him; and much people followed him, and thronged him.

25 And a certain woman, which had an issue of blood twelve years,

26 And had suffered many things of many physicians, and had spent all that she had, and was nothing bettered, but rather grew worse,

27 When she had heard of Jesus, came in the press behind, and touched his garment.

28 For she said, If I may touch but his clothes, I shall be whole.

29 And straightway the fountain of her blood was dried up; and she felt in *her* body that she was healed of that plague.

30 And Jesus, immediately knowing in himself that virtue had gone out of him, turned him about in the press, and said, Who touched my clothes?

31 And his disciples said unto him, Thou seest the multitude thronging thee, and sayest thou, Who touched me?

32 And he looked round about to see her that had done this thing.

33 But the woman fearing and trembling, knowing what was done in her, came and fell down before him, and told him all the truth.

34 And he said unto her, Daughter, thy faith hath made thee whole; go in peace, and be whole of thy plague.

35 While he yet spake, there came from the ruler of the syna-

gogue's *house certain* which said, Thy daughter is dead: why troublest thou the Master any further?

36 As soon as Jesus heard the word that was spoken, he saith unto the ruler of the synagogue, Be not afraid, only believe.

37 And he suffered no man to follow him, save Peter, and James, and John the brother of James.

38 And he cometh to the house of the ruler of the synagogue, and seeth the tumult, and them that wept and wailed greatly.

39 And when he was come in, he saith unto them, Why make ye this ado, and weep? the damsel is not dead, but sleepeth.

40 And they laughed him to scorn. But when he had put them all out, he taketh the father and the mother of the damsel, and them that were with him, and entereth in where the damsel was lying.

41 And he took the damsel by the hand, and said unto her, TALITHA CUMI; which is, being interpreted, Damsel, I say unto thee, arise.

42 And straightway the damsel arose, and walked; for she was *of the age* of twelve years. And they were astonished with a great astonishment.

43 And he charged them straitly that no man should know it; and commanded that something should be given her to eat.

6 And he went out from thence, and came into his own country; and his disciples follow him.

2 And when the sabbath day was come, he began to teach in the synagogue: and many hearing *him* were astonished, saying, From whence hath this *man* these things? and what wisdom *is* this which is given unto him, that even such mighty works are wrought by his hands?

3 Is not this the carpenter, the son of Mary, the brother of James, and Joses, and of Juda, and Simon? and are not his sisters here with us? And they were offended at him.

4 But Jesus said unto them, A prophet is not without honour, but in his own country, and among his own kin, and in his own house.

5 And he could there do no mighty work, save that he laid his hands upon a few sick folk, and healed *them*.

6 And he marvelled because of their unbelief. And he went round about the villages, teaching.

7 ¶ And he called *unto him* the twelve, and began to send them forth by two and two; and gave them power over unclean spirits;

8 And commanded them that they should take nothing for *their* journey, save a staff only; no scrip, no bread, no money in *their* purse:

9 But *be* shod with sandals; and not put on two coats.

10 And he said unto them, In what place soever ye enter into an house, there abide till ye depart from that place.

11 And whosoever shall not receive you, nor hear you, when ye depart thence, shake off the dust under your feet for a testimony against them. Verily I say unto you, It shall be more tolerable for Sodom and Gomorrha in the day of judgment, than for that city.

12 And they went out, and preached that men should repent.

13 And they cast out many devils, and anointed with oil many that were sick, and healed *them*.

14 And king Herod heard *of him;* (for his name was spread abroad:) and he said, That John the Baptist was risen from the dead, and therefore mighty works do shew forth themselves in him.

15 Others said, That it is Elias. And others said, That it is a prophet, or as one of the prophets.

16 But when Herod heard *thereof,* he said, It is John, whom I beheaded: he is risen from the dead.

17 ¶ For Herod himself had sent forth and laid hold upon John, and bound him in prison for Herodias' sake, his brother Philip's wife: for he had married her.

18 For John had said unto Herod, It is not lawful for thee to have thy brother's wife.

19 Therefore Herodias had a quarrel against him, and would have killed him; but she could not:

20 For Herod feared John, knowing that he was a just man and an holy, and observed him;

and when he heard him, he did many things, and heard him gladly.

21 And when a convenient day was come, that Herod on his birthday made a supper to his lords, high captains, and chief *estates* of Galilee;

22 And when the daughter of the said Herodias came in, and danced, and pleased Herod and them that sat with him, the king said unto the damsel, Ask of me whatsoever thou wilt, and I will give *it* thee.

23 And he sware unto her, Whatsoever thou shalt ask of me, I will give *it* thee, unto the half of my kingdom.

24 And she went forth, and said unto her mother, What shall I ask? And she said, The head of John the Baptist.

25 And she came in straightway with haste unto the king, and asked, saying, I will that thou give me by and by in a charger the head of John the Baptist.

26 And the king was exceeding sorry; *yet* for his oath's sake, and for their sakes which sat with him, he would not reject her.

27 And immediately the king sent an executioner, and commanded his head to be brought: and he went and beheaded him in the prison,

28 And brought his head in a charger, and gave it to the damsel: and the damsel gave it to her mother.

29 And when his disciples heard *of it,* they came and took up his corpse, and laid it in a tomb.

30 ¶ And the apostles gathered themselves together unto Jesus, and told him all things, both what they had done, and what they had taught.

31 And he said unto them, Come ye yourselves apart into a desert place, and rest a while: for there were many coming and going, and they had no leisure so much as to eat.

32 And they departed into a desert place by ship privately.

33 And the people saw them departing, and many knew him, and ran afoot thither out of all cities, and outwent them, and came together unto him.

34 And Jesus, when he came out, saw much people, and was moved with compassion toward them, because they were as sheep not having a shepherd: and he began to teach them many things.

35 ¶ And when the day was now far spent, his disciples came unto him, and said, This is a desert place, and now the time *is* far passed:

36 Send them away, that they may go into the country round about, and into the villages, and buy themselves bread: for they have nothing to eat.

37 He answered and said unto them, Give ye them to eat. And they say unto him, Shall we go and buy two hundred pennyworth of bread, and give them to eat?

38 He saith unto them, How many loaves have ye? go and see. And when they knew, they say, Five, and two fishes.

39 And he commanded them to make all sit down by companies upon the green grass.

40 And they sat down in ranks, by hundreds, and by fifties.

41 And when he had taken the five loaves and the two fishes, he looked up to heaven, and blessed, and brake the loaves, and gave *them* to his disciples to set before them; and the two fishes divided he among them all.

42 And they did all eat, and were filled.

43 And they took up twelve baskets full of the fragments, and of the fishes.

44 And they that did eat of the loaves were about five thousand men.

45 And straightway he constrained his disciples to get into the ship, and to go to the other side before unto Bethsaida, while he sent away the people.

46 And when he had sent them away, he departed into a mountain to pray.

47 ¶ And when even was come, the ship was in the midst of the sea, and he alone on the land.

48 And he saw them toiling in rowing; for the wind was contrary unto them: and about the fourth watch of the night he cometh unto them, walking upon the sea, and would have passed by them.

49 But when they saw him walking upon the sea, they supposed it had been a spirit, and cried out:

50 For they all saw him, and were troubled. And immediately he talked with them, and saith unto them, Be of good cheer: it is I; be not afraid.

51 And he went up unto them into the ship; and the wind ceased: and they were sore amazed in themselves beyond measure, and wondered.

52 For they considered not the *miracle* of the loaves: for their heart was hardened.

53 And when they had passed over, they came into the land of Gennesaret, and drew to the shore.

54 And when they were come out of the ship, straightway they knew him,

55 And ran through that whole region round about, and began to carry about in beds those that were sick, where they heard he was.

56 ¶ And whithersoever he entered, into villages, or cities, or country, they laid the sick in the streets, and besought him that they might touch if it were but the border of his garment: and as many as touched him were made whole.

7 Then came together unto him the Pharisees, and certain of the scribes, which came from Jerusalem.

2 And when they saw some of his disciples eat bread with defiled, that is to say, with unwashen, hands, they found fault.

3 For the Pharisees, and all the Jews, except they wash *their* hands oft, eat not, holding the

tradition of the elders.

4 And *when they come* from the market, except they wash, they eat not. And many other things there be, which they have received to hold, *as* the washing of cups, and pots, brasen vessels, and of tables.

5 Then the Pharisees and scribes asked him, Why walk not thy disciples according to the tradition of the elders, but eat bread with unwashen hands?

6 He answered and said unto them, Well hath Esaias prophesied of you hypocrites, as it is written, This people honoureth me with *their* lips, but their heart is far from me.

7 Howbeit in vain do they worship me, teaching *for* doctrines the commandments of men.

8 For laying aside the commandment of God, ye hold the tradition of men, *as* the washing of pots and cups: and many other such like things ye do.

9 And he said unto them, Full well ye reject the commandment of God, that ye may keep your own tradition.

10 For Moses said, Honour thy father and thy mother; and, Whoso curseth father or mother, let him die the death:

11 But ye say, If a man shall say to his father or mother, *It is* Corban, that is to say, a gift, by whatsoever thou mightest be profited by me; *he shall be free.*

12 And ye suffer him no more to do ought for his father or his mother;

13 Making the word of God of

none effect through your tradition, which ye have delivered: and many such like things do ye.

14 ¶ And when he had called all the people *unto him*, he said unto them, Hearken unto me every one *of you*, and understand:

15 There is nothing from without a man, that entering into him can defile him: but the things which come out of him, those are they that defile the man.

16 If any man have ears to hear, let him hear.

17 And when he was entered into the house from the people, his disciples asked him concerning the parable.

18 And he saith unto them, Are ye so without understanding also? Do ye not perceive, that whatsoever thing from without entereth into the man, *it* cannot defile him;

19 Because it entereth not into his heart, but into the belly, and goeth out into the draught, purging all meats?

20 And he said, That which cometh out of the man, that defileth the man.

21 For from within, out of the heart of men, proceed evil thoughts, adulteries, fornications, murders,

22 Thefts, covetousness, wickedness, deceit, lasciviousness, an evil eye, blasphemy, pride, foolishness:

23 All these evil things come from within, and defile the man.

24 ¶ And from thence he arose, and went into the borders of Tyre and Sidon, and entered into an house, and would have no man know *it*: but he could not be hid.

25 For a *certain* woman, whose young daughter had an unclean spirit, heard of him, and came and fell at his feet:

26 The woman was a Greek, a Syrophenician by nation; and she besought him that he would cast forth the devil out of her daughter.

27 But Jesus said unto her, Let the children first be filled: for it is not meet to take the children's bread, and to cast *it* unto the dogs.

28 And she answered and said unto him, Yes, Lord: yet the dogs under the table eat of the children's crumbs.

29 And he said unto her, For this saying go thy way; the devil is gone out of thy daughter.

30 And when she was come to her house, she found the devil gone out, and her daughter laid upon the bed.

31 ¶ And again, departing from the coasts of Tyre and Sidon, he came unto the sea of Galilee, through the midst of the coasts of Decapolis.

32 And they bring unto him one that was deaf, and had an impediment in his speech; and they beseech him to put his hand upon him.

33 And he took him aside from the multitude, and put his fingers into his ears, and he spit, and touched his tongue;

34 And looking up to heaven, he

sighed, and saith unto him, EPH-PHATHA, that is, Be opened.

35 And straightway his ears were opened, and the string of his tongue was loosed, and he spake plain.

36 And he charged them that they should tell no man: but the more he charged them, so much the more a great deal they published *it*,

37 And were beyond measure astonished, saying, He hath done all things well: he maketh both the deaf to hear, and the dumb to speak.

8 In those days the multitude being very great, and having nothing to eat, Jesus called his disciples *unto him*, and saith unto them,

2 I have compassion on the multitude, because they have now been with me three days, and have nothing to eat:

3 And if I send them away fasting to their own houses, they will faint by the way: for divers of them came from far.

4 And his disciples answered him, From whence can a man satisfy these *men* with bread here in the wilderness?

5 And he asked them, How many loaves have ye? And they said, Seven.

6 And he commanded the people to sit down on the ground: and he took the seven loaves, and gave thanks, and brake, and gave to his disciples to set before *them*; and they did set *them* before the people.

7 And they had a few small fishes: and he blessed, and commanded to set them also before *them*.

8 So they did eat, and were filled: and they took up of the broken *meat* that was left seven baskets.

9 And they that had eaten were about four thousand: and he sent them away.

10 ¶ And straightway he entered into a ship with his disciples, and came into the parts of Dalmanutha.

11 And the Pharisees came forth, and began to question with him, seeking of him a sign from heaven, tempting him.

12 And he sighed deeply in his spirit, and saith, Why doth this generation seek after a sign? verily I say unto you, There shall no sign be given unto this generation.

13 And he left them, and entering into the ship again departed to the other side.

14 ¶ Now *the disciples* had forgotten to take bread, neither had they in the ship with them more than one loaf.

15 And he charged them, saying, Take heed, beware of the leaven of the Pharisees, and *of* the leaven of Herod.

16 And they reasoned among themselves, saying, *It is* because we have no bread.

17 And when Jesus knew *it*, he saith unto them, Why reason ye, because ye have no bread? perceive ye not yet, neither un-

derstand? have ye your heart yet hardened?

18 Having eyes, see ye not? and having ears, hear ye not? and do ye not remember?

19 When I brake the five loaves among five thousand, how many baskets full of fragments took ye up? They say unto him, Twelve.

20 And when the seven among four thousand, how many baskets full of fragments took ye up? And they said, Seven.

21 And he said unto them, How is it that ye do not understand?

22 ¶ And he cometh to Bethsaida; and they bring a blind man unto him, and besought him to touch him.

23 And he took the blind man by the hand, and led him out of the town; and when he had spit on his eyes, and put his hands upon him, he asked him if he saw ought.

24 And he looked up, and said, I see men as trees, walking.

25 After that he put *his* hands again upon his eyes, and made him look up: and he was restored, and saw every man clearly.

26 And he sent him away to his house, saying, Neither go into the town, nor tell *it* to any in the town.

27 ¶ And Jesus went out, and his disciples, into the towns of Caesarea Philippi: and by the way he asked his disciples, saying unto them, Whom do men say that I am?

28 And they answered, John the Baptist; but some *say*, Elias; and others, One of the prophets.

29 And he saith unto them, But whom say ye that I am? And Peter answereth and saith unto him, Thou art the Christ.

30 And he charged them that they should tell no man of him.

31 And he began to teach them, that the Son of man must suffer many things, and be rejected of the elders, and *of* the chief priests, and scribes, and be killed, and after three days rise again.

32 And he spake that saying openly. And Peter took him, and began to rebuke him.

33 But when he had turned about and looked on his disciples, he rebuked Peter, saying, Get thee behind me, Satan: for thou savourest not the things that be of God, but the things that be of men.

34 ¶ And when he had called the people *unto him* with his disciples also, he said unto them, Whosoever will come after me, let him deny himself, and take up his cross, and follow me.

35 For whosoever will save his life shall lose it; but whosoever shall lose his life for my sake and the gospel's, the same shall save it.

36 For what shall it profit a man, if he shall gain the whole world, and lose his own soul?

37 Or what shall a man give in exchange for his soul?

38 Whosoever therefore shall be ashamed of me and of my words in this adulterous and sinful generation; of him also shall the Son of man be ashamed, when he

cometh in the glory of his Father with the holy angels.

9 And he said unto them, Verily I say unto you, That there be some of them that stand here, which shall not taste of death, till they have seen the kingdom of God come with power.

2 ¶ And after six days Jesus taketh *with him* Peter, and James, and John, and leadeth them up into an high mountain by themselves: and he was transfigured before them.

3 And his raiment became shining, exceeding white as snow; so as no fuller on earth can white them.

4 And there appeared unto them Elias with Moses: and they were talking with Jesus.

5 And Peter answered and said to Jesus, Master, it is good for us to be here: and let us make three tabernacles; one for thee, and one for Moses, and one for Elias.

6 For he wist not what to say; for they were sore afraid.

7 And there was a cloud that overshadowed them: and a voice came out of the cloud, saying, This is my beloved Son: hear him.

8 And suddenly, when they had looked round about, they saw no man any more, save Jesus only with themselves.

9 And as they came down from the mountain, he charged them that they should tell no man what things they had seen, till the Son of man were risen from the dead.

10 And they kept that saying with themselves, questioning one with another what the rising from the dead should mean.

11 ¶ And they asked him, saying, Why say the scribes that Elias must first come?

12 And he answered and told them, Elias verily cometh first, and restoreth all things; and how it is written of the Son of man, that he must suffer many things, and be set at nought.

13 But I say unto you, That Elias is indeed come, and they have done unto him whatsoever they listed, as it is written of him.

14 ¶ And when he came to *his* disciples, he saw a great multitude about them, and the scribes questioning with them.

15 And straightway all the people, when they beheld him, were greatly amazed, and running to *him* saluted him.

16 And he asked the scribes, What question ye with them?

17 And one of the multitude answered and said, Master, I have brought unto thee my son, which hath a dumb spirit;

18 And wheresoever he taketh him, he teareth him: and he foameth, and gnasheth with his teeth, and pineth away: and I spake to thy disciples that they should cast him out; and they could not.

19 He answered him, and saith, O faithless generation, how long shall I be with you? how long shall I suffer you? bring him unto me.

20 And they brought him unto

him: and when he saw him, straightway the spirit tare him; and he fell on the ground, and wallowed foaming.

21 And he asked his father, How long is it ago since this came unto him? And he said, Of a child.

22 And ofttimes it hath cast him into the fire, and into the waters, to destroy him: but if thou canst do any thing, have compassion on us, and help us.

23 Jesus said unto him, If thou canst believe, all things *are* possible to him that believeth.

24 And straightway the father of the child cried out, and said with tears, Lord, I believe; help thou mine unbelief.

25 When Jesus saw that the people came running together, he rebuked the foul spirit, saying unto him, *Thou* dumb and deaf spirit, I charge thee, come out of him, and enter no more into him.

26 And *the spirit* cried, and rent him sore, and came out of him: and he was as one dead; insomuch that many said, He is dead.

27 But Jesus took him by the hand, and lifted him up; and he arose.

28 And when he was come into the house, his disciples asked him privately, Why could not we cast him out?

29 And he said unto them, This kind can come forth by nothing, but by prayer and fasting.

30 ¶ And they departed thence, and passed through Galilee;

and he would not that any man should know *it*.

31 For he taught his disciples, and said unto them, The Son of man is delivered into the hands of men, and they shall kill him; and after that he is killed, he shall rise the third day.

32 But they understood not that saying, and were afraid to ask him.

33 ¶ And he came to Capernaum: and being in the house he asked them, What was it that ye disputed among yourselves by the way?

34 But they held their peace: for by the way they had disputed among themselves, who *should be* the greatest.

35 And he sat down, and called the twelve, and saith unto them, If any man desire to be first, *the same* shall be last of all, and servant of all.

36 And he took a child, and set him in the midst of them: and when he had taken him in his arms, he said unto them,

37 Whosoever shall receive one of such children in my name, receiveth me: and whosoever shall receive me, receiveth not me, but him that sent me.

38 ¶ And John answered him, saying, Master, we saw one casting out devils in thy name, and he followeth not us: and we forbad him, because he followeth not us.

39 But Jesus said, Forbid him not: for there is no man which shall do a miracle in my name, that can lightly speak evil of me.

40 For he that is not against us is on our part.

41 For whosoever shall give you a cup of water to drink in my name, because ye belong to Christ, verily I say unto you, he shall not lose his reward.

42 And whosoever shall offend one of *these* little ones that believe in me, it is better for him that a millstone were hanged about his neck, and he were cast into the sea.

43 And if thy hand offend thee, cut it off: it is better for thee to enter into life maimed, than having two hands to go into hell, into the fire that never shall be quenched:

44 Where their worm dieth not, and the fire is not quenched.

45 And if thy foot offend thee, cut it off: it is better for thee to enter halt into life, than having two feet to be cast into hell, into the fire that never shall be quenched:

46 Where their worm dieth not, and the fire is not quenched.

47 And if thine eye offend thee, pluck it out: it is better for thee to enter into the kingdom of God with one eye, than having two eyes to be cast into hell fire:

48 Where their worm dieth not, and the fire is not quenched.

49 For every one shall be salted with fire, and every sacrifice shall be salted with salt.

50 Salt *is* good: but if the salt have lost his saltness, wherewith will ye season it? Have salt in yourselves, and have peace one with another.

10 And he arose from thence, and cometh into the coasts of Judaea by the farther side of Jordan: and the people resort unto him again; and, as he was wont, he taught them again.

2 ❡ And the Pharisees came to him, and asked him, Is it lawful for a man to put away *his* wife? tempting him.

3 And he answered and said unto them, What did Moses command you?

4 And they said, Moses suffered to write a bill of divorcement, and to put *her* away.

5 And Jesus answered and said unto them, For the hardness of your heart he wrote you this precept.

6 But from the beginning of the creation God made them male and female.

7 For this cause shall a man leave his father and mother, and cleave to his wife;

8 And they twain shall be one flesh: so then they are no more twain, but one flesh.

9 What therefore God hath joined together, let not man put asunder.

10 And in the house his disciples asked him again of the same *matter.*

11 And he saith unto them, Whosoever shall put away his wife, and marry another, committeth adultery against her.

12 And if a woman shall put away her husband, and be mar-

ried to another, she committeth adultery.

13 ¶ And they brought young children to him, that he should touch them: and *his* disciples rebuked those that brought *them*.

14 But when Jesus saw *it*, he was much displeased, and said unto them, Suffer the little children to come unto me, and forbid them not: for of such is the kingdom of God.

15 Verily I say unto you, Whosoever shall not receive the kingdom of God as a little child, he shall not enter therein.

16 And he took them up in his arms, put *his* hands upon them, and blessed them.

17 ¶ And when he was gone forth into the way, there came one running, and kneeled to him, and asked him, Good Master, what shall I do that I may inherit eternal life?

18 And Jesus said unto him, Why callest thou me good? *there* is none good but one, *that is*, God.

19 Thou knowest the commandments, Do not commit adultery, Do not kill, Do not steal, Do not bear false witness, Defraud not, Honour thy father and mother.

20 And he answered and said unto him, Master, all these have I observed from my youth.

21 Then Jesus beholding him loved him, and said unto him, One thing thou lackest: go thy way, sell whatsoever thou hast, and give to the poor, and thou shalt have treasure in heaven: and come, take up the cross, and follow me.

22 And he was sad at that saying, and went away grieved: for he had great possessions.

23 ¶ And Jesus looked round about, and saith unto his disciples, How hardly shall they that have riches enter into the kingdom of God!

24 And the disciples were astonished at his words. But Jesus answereth again, and saith unto them, Children, how hard is it for them that trust in riches to enter into the kingdom of God!

25 It is easier for a camel to go through the eye of a needle, than for a rich man to enter into the kingdom of God.

26 And they were astonished out of measure, saying among themselves, Who then can be saved?

27 And Jesus looking upon them saith, With men *it* is impossible, but not with God: for with God all things are possible.

28 ¶ Then Peter began to say unto him, Lo, we have left all, and have followed thee.

29 And Jesus answered and said, Verily I say unto you, There is no man that hath left house, or brethren, or sisters, or father, or mother, or wife, or children, or lands, for my sake, and the gospel's,

30 But he shall receive an hundredfold now in this time, houses, and brethren, and sisters, and mothers, and children, and lands, with persecutions; and in the world to come eternal life.

31 But many *that are* first shall

be last; and the last first.

32 ¶ And they were in the way going up to Jerusalem; and Jesus went before them: and they were amazed; and as they followed, they were afraid. And he took again the twelve, and began to tell them what things should happen unto him,

33 Saying, Behold, we go up to Jerusalem; and the Son of man shall be delivered unto the chief priests, and unto the scribes; and they shall condemn him to death, and shall deliver him to the Gentiles:

34 And they shall mock him, and shall scourge him, and shall spit upon him, and shall kill him: and the third day he shall rise again.

35 ¶ And James and John, the sons of Zebedee, come unto him, saying, Master, we would that thou shouldest do for us whatsoever we shall desire.

36 And he said unto them, What would ye that I should do for you?

37 They said unto him, Grant unto us that we may sit, one on thy right hand, and the other on thy left hand, in thy glory.

38 But Jesus said unto them, Ye know not what ye ask: can ye drink of the cup that I drink of? and be baptized with the baptism that I am baptized with?

39 And they said unto him, We can. And Jesus said unto them, Ye shall indeed drink of the cup that I drink of; and with the baptism that I am baptized withal shall ye be baptized:

40 But to sit on my right hand and on my left hand is not mine to give; *but it shall be given to them* for whom it is prepared.

41 And when the ten heard *it*, they began to be much displeased with James and John.

42 But Jesus called them to *him*, and saith unto them, Ye know that they which are accounted to rule over the Gentiles exercise lordship over them; and their great ones exercise authority upon them.

43 But so shall it not be among you: but whosoever will be great among you, shall be your minister:

44 And whosoever of you will be the chiefest, shall be servant of all.

45 For even the Son of man came not to be ministered unto, but to minister, and to give his life a ransom for many.

46 ¶ And they came to Jericho: and as he went out of Jericho with his disciples and a great number of people, blind Bartimaeus, the son of Timaeus, sat by the highway side begging.

47 And when he heard that it was Jesus of Nazareth, he began to cry out, and say, Jesus, *thou* son of David, have mercy on me.

48 And many charged him that he should hold his peace: but he cried the more a great deal, *Thou* son of David, have mercy on me.

49 And Jesus stood still, and commanded him to be called. And they call the blind man, say-

73

ing unto him, Be of good comfort, rise; he calleth thee.

50 And he, casting away his garment, rose, and came to Jesus.

51 And Jesus answered and said unto him, What wilt thou that I should do unto thee? The blind man said unto him, Lord, that I might receive my sight.

52 And Jesus said unto him, Go thy way; thy faith hath made thee whole. And immediately he received his sight, and followed Jesus in the way.

11

And when they came nigh to Jerusalem, unto Bethphage and Bethany, at the mount of Olives, he sendeth forth two of his disciples,

2 And saith unto them, Go your way into the village over against you: and as soon as ye be entered into it, ye shall find a colt tied, whereon never man sat; loose him, and bring *him*.

3 And if any man say unto you, Why do ye this? say ye that the Lord hath need of him; and straightway he will send him hither.

4 And they went their way, and found the colt tied by the door without in a place where two ways met; and they loose him.

5 And certain of them that stood there said unto them, What do ye, loosing the colt?

6 And they said unto them even as Jesus had commanded: and they let them go.

7 And they brought the colt to Jesus, and cast their garments on him; and he sat upon him.

8 And many spread their garments in the way: and others cut down branches off the trees, and strawed them in the way.

9 And they that went before, and they that followed, cried, saying, Hosanna; Blessed *is* he that cometh in the name of the Lord:

10 Blessed *be* the kingdom of our father David, that cometh in the name of the Lord: Hosanna in the highest.

11 And Jesus entered into Jerusalem, and into the temple: and when he had looked round about upon all things, and now the eventide was come, he went out unto Bethany with the twelve.

12 ¶ And on the morrow, when they were come from Bethany, he was hungry:

13 And seeing a fig tree afar off having leaves, he came, if haply he might find any thing thereon: and when he came to it, he found nothing but leaves; for the time of figs was not *yet*.

14 And Jesus answered and said unto it, No man eat fruit of thee hereafter for ever. And his disciples heard *it*.

15 ¶ And they come to Jerusalem: and Jesus went into the temple, and began to cast out them that sold and bought in the temple, and overthrew the tables of the moneychangers, and the seats of them that sold doves;

16 And would not suffer that any man should carry *any* vessel through the temple.

17 And he taught, saying unto them, Is it not written, My house

shall be called of all nations the house of prayer? but ye have made it a den of thieves.

18 And the scribes and chief priests heard *it*, and sought how they might destroy him: for they feared him, because all the people was astonished at his doctrine.

19 And when even was come, he went out of the city.

20 ¶ And in the morning, as they passed by, they saw the fig tree dried up from the roots.

21 And Peter calling to remembrance saith unto him, Master, behold, the fig tree which thou cursedst is withered away.

22 And Jesus answering saith unto them, Have faith in God.

23 For verily I say unto you, That whosoever shall say unto this mountain, Be thou removed, and be thou cast into the sea; and shall not doubt in his heart, but shall believe that those things which he saith shall come to pass; he shall have whatsoever he saith.

24 Therefore I say unto you, What things soever ye desire, when ye pray, believe that ye receive *them*, and ye shall have *them*.

25 ¶ And when ye stand praying, forgive, if ye have ought against any: that your Father also which is in heaven may forgive you your trespasses.

26 But if ye do not forgive, neither will your Father which is in heaven forgive your trespasses.

27 ¶ And they come again to Jerusalem: and as he was walking in the temple, there come to him the chief priests, and the scribes, and the elders,

28 And say unto him, By what authority doest thou these things? and who gave thee this authority to do these things?

29 And Jesus answered and said unto them, I will also ask of you one question, and answer me, and I will tell you by what authority I do these things.

30 The baptism of John, was *it* from heaven, or of men? answer me.

31 And they reasoned with themselves, saying, If we shall say, From heaven; he will say, Why then did ye not believe him?

32 But if we shall say, Of men; they feared the people: for all *men* counted John, that he was a prophet indeed.

33 And they answered and said unto Jesus, We cannot tell. And Jesus answering saith unto them, Neither do I tell you by what authority I do these things.

12 And he began to speak unto them by parables. A *certain* man planted a vineyard, and set an hedge about *it*, and digged a *place for* the winefat, and built a tower, and let it out to husbandmen, and went into a far country.

2 And at the season he sent to the husbandmen a servant, that he might receive from the husbandmen of the fruit of the vineyard.

3 And they caught *him*, and

beat him, and sent *him* away empty.

4 And again he sent unto them another servant; and at him they cast stones, and wounded *him* in the head, and sent *him* away shamefully handled.

5 And again he sent another; and him they killed, and many others; beating some, and killing some.

6 Having yet therefore one son, his wellbeloved, he sent him also last unto them, saying, They will reverence my son.

7 But those husbandmen said among themselves, This is the heir; come, let us kill him, and the inheritance shall be ours.

8 And they took him, and killed *him*, and cast *him* out of the vineyard.

9 What shall therefore the lord of the vineyard do? he will come and destroy the husbandmen, and will give the vineyard unto others.

10 And have ye not read this scripture; The stone which the builders rejected is become the head of the corner:

11 This was the Lord's doing, and it is marvellous in our eyes?

12 And they sought to lay hold on him, but feared the people: for they knew that he had spoken the parable against them: and they left him, and went their way.

13 ¶ And they send unto him certain of the Pharisees and of the Herodians, to catch him in *his* words.

14 And when they were come,

they say unto him, Master, we know that thou art true, and carest for no man: for thou regardest not the person of men, but teachest the way of God in truth: Is it lawful to give tribute to Caesar, or not?

15 Shall we give, or shall we not give? But he, knowing their hypocrisy, said unto them, Why tempt ye me? bring me a penny, that I may see *it*.

16 And they brought *it*. And he saith unto them, Whose *is* this image and superscription? And they said unto him, Caesar's.

17 And Jesus answering said unto them, Render to Caesar the things that are Caesar's, and to God the things that are God's. And they marvelled at him.

18 ¶ Then come unto him the Sadducees, which say there is no resurrection; and they asked him, saying,

19 Master, Moses wrote unto us, If a man's brother die, and leave *his* wife *behind him*, and leave no children, that his brother should take his wife, and raise up seed unto his brother.

20 Now there were seven brethren: and the first took a wife, and dying left no seed.

21 And the second took her, and died, neither left he any seed: and the third likewise.

22 And the seven had her, and left no seed: last of all the woman died also.

23 In the resurrection therefore, when they shall rise, whose wife shall she be of them? for the seven had her to wife.

24 And Jesus answering said unto them, Do ye not therefore err, because ye know not the Scriptures, neither the power of God?

25 For when they shall rise from the dead, they neither marry, nor are given in marriage; but are as the angels which are in heaven.

26 And as touching the dead, that they rise: have ye not read in the book of Moses, how in the bush God spake unto him, saying, I am the God of Abraham, and the God of Isaac, and the God of Jacob?

27 He is not the God of the dead, but the God of the living: ye therefore do greatly err.

28 ¶ And one of the scribes came, and having heard them reasoning together, and perceiving that he had answered them well, asked him, Which is the first commandment of all?

29 And Jesus answered him, The first of all the commandments is, Hear, O Israel; The Lord our God is one Lord:

30 And thou shalt love the Lord thy God with all thy heart, and with all thy soul, and with all thy mind, and with all thy strength: this is the first commandment.

31 And the second is like, namely this, Thou shalt love thy neighbour as thyself. There is none other commandment greater than these.

32 And the scribe said unto him, Well, Master, thou hast said the truth: for there is one God; and there is none other but he:

33 And to love him with all the heart, and with all the understanding, and with all the soul, and with all the strength, and to love his neighbour as himself, is more than all whole burnt offerings and sacrifices.

34 And when Jesus saw that he answered discreetly, he said unto him, Thou art not far from the kingdom of God. And no man after that durst ask him any question.

35 ¶ And Jesus answered and said, while he taught in the temple, How say the scribes that Christ is the son of David?

36 For David himself said by the Holy Ghost, The LORD said to my Lord, Sit thou on my right hand, till I make thine enemies thy footstool.

37 David therefore himself calleth him Lord; and whence is he then his son? And the common people heard him gladly.

38 ¶ And he said unto them in his doctrine, Beware of the scribes, which love to go in long clothing, and love salutations in the marketplaces,

39 And the chief seats in the synagogues, and the uppermost rooms at feasts:

40 Which devour widows' houses, and for a pretence make long prayers: these shall receive greater damnation.

41 ¶ And Jesus sat over against the treasury, and beheld how the people cast money into the treasury: and many that were rich cast in much.

42 And there came a certain poor widow, and she threw in

two mites, which make a farthing.

43 And he called *unto him* his disciples, and saith unto them, Verily I say unto you, That this poor widow hath cast more in, than all they which have cast into the treasury:

44 For all *they* did cast in of their abundance; but she of her want did cast in all that she had, *even* all her living.

13 And as he went out of the temple, one of his disciples saith unto him, Master, see what manner of stones and what buildings *are* here!

2 And Jesus answering said unto him, Seest thou these great buildings? there shall not be left one stone upon another, that shall not be thrown down.

3 And as he sat upon the mount of Olives over against the temple, Peter and James and John and Andrew asked him privately,

4 Tell us, when shall these things be? and what *shall* be the sign when all these things shall be fulfilled?

5 And Jesus answering them began to say, Take heed lest any *man* deceive you:

6 For many shall come in my name, saying, I am *Christ*; and shall deceive many.

7 And when ye shall hear of wars and rumours of wars, be ye not troubled: for *such things* must needs be; but the end *shall* not be yet.

8 For nation shall rise against nation, and kingdom against kingdom: and there shall be earthquakes in divers places, and there shall be famines and troubles: these *are* the beginnings of sorrows.

9 ¶ But take heed to yourselves: for they shall deliver you up to councils; and in the synagogues ye shall be beaten: and ye shall be brought before rulers and kings for my sake, for a testimony against them.

10 And the gospel must first be published among all nations.

11 But when they shall lead *you*, and deliver you up, take no thought beforehand what ye shall speak, neither do ye premeditate: but whatsoever shall be given you in that hour, that speak ye: for it is not ye that speak, but the Holy Ghost.

12 Now the brother shall betray the brother to death, and the father the son; and children shall rise up against *their* parents, and shall cause them to be put to death.

13 And ye shall be hated of all *men* for my name's sake: but he that shall endure unto the end, the same shall be saved.

14 ¶ But when ye shall see the abomination of desolation, spoken of by Daniel the prophet, standing where it ought not, (let him that readeth understand,) then let them that be in Judaea flee to the mountains:

15 And let him that is on the housetop not go down into the house, neither enter *therein*, to take any thing out of his house:

16 And let him that is in the field not turn back again for to

17 But woe to them that are with child, and to them that give suck in those days!

18 And pray ye that your flight be not in the winter.

19 For in those days shall be affliction, such as was not from the beginning of the creation which God created unto this time, neither shall be.

20 And except that the Lord had shortened those days, no flesh should be saved: but for the elect's sake, whom he hath chosen, he hath shortened the days.

21 And then if any man shall say to you, Lo, here is Christ; or, lo, he is there; believe him not:

22 For false Christs and false prophets shall rise, and shall shew signs and wonders, to seduce, if it were possible, even the elect.

23 But take ye heed: behold, I have foretold you all things.

24 ¶ But in those days, after that tribulation, the sun shall be darkened, and the moon shall not give her light,

25 And the stars of heaven shall fall, and the powers that are in heaven shall be shaken.

26 And then shall they see the Son of man coming in the clouds with great power and glory.

27 And then shall he send his angels, and shall gather together his elect from the four winds, from the uttermost part of the earth to the uttermost part of heaven.

28 ¶ Now learn a parable of the fig tree; When her branch is yet tender, and putteth forth leaves, ye know that summer is near:

29 So ye in like manner, when ye shall see these things come to pass, know that it is nigh, even at the doors.

30 Verily I say unto you, that this generation shall not pass, till all these things be done.

31 ¶ Heaven and earth shall pass away: but my words shall not pass away.

32 ¶ But of that day and that hour knoweth no man, no, not the angels which are in heaven, neither the Son, but the Father.

33 Take ye heed, watch and pray: for ye know not when the time is.

34 For the Son of man is as a man taking a far journey, who left his house, and gave authority to his servants, and to every man his work, and commanded the porter to watch.

35 Watch ye therefore: for ye know not when the master of the house cometh, at even, or at midnight, or at the cockcrowing, or in the morning:

36 Lest coming suddenly he find you sleeping.

37 And what I say unto you I say unto all, Watch.

14 After two days was the feast of the passover, and of unleavened bread: and the chief priests and the scribes sought how they might take him by craft, and put him to death.

2 But they said, Not on the feast day, lest there be an uproar of the

people.

3 ¶ And being in Bethany in the house of Simon the leper, as he sat at meat, there came a woman having an alabaster box of ointment of spikenard very precious; and she brake the box, and poured *it* on his head.

4 And there were some that had indignation within themselves, and said, Why was this waste of the ointment made?

5 For it might have been sold for more than three hundred pence, and have been given to the poor. And they murmured against her.

6 And Jesus said, Let her alone; why trouble ye her? she hath wrought a good work on me.

7 For ye have the poor with you always, and whensoever ye will ye may do them good: but me ye have not always.

8 She hath done what she could: she is come aforehand to anoint my body to the burying.

9 Verily I say unto you, Wheresoever this gospel shall be preached throughout the whole world, *this* also that she hath done shall be spoken of for a memorial of her.

10 ¶ And Judas Iscariot, one of the twelve, went unto the chief priests, to betray him unto them.

11 And when they heard *it*, they were glad, and promised to give him money. And he sought how he might conveniently betray him.

12 ¶ And the first day of unleavened bread, when they killed the passover, his disciples said unto him, Where wilt thou that we go and prepare that thou mayest eat the passover?

13 And he sendeth forth two of his disciples, and saith unto them, Go ye into the city, and there shall meet you a man bearing a pitcher of water: follow him.

14 And wheresoever he shall go in, say ye to the goodman of the house, The Master saith, Where is the guestchamber, where I shall eat the passover with my disciples?

15 And he will shew you a large upper room furnished *and* prepared: there make ready for us.

16 And his disciples went forth, and came into the city, and found as he had said unto them: and they made ready the passover.

17 And in the evening he cometh with the twelve.

18 And as they sat and did eat, Jesus said, Verily I say unto you, One of you which eateth with me shall betray me.

19 And they began to be sorrowful, and to say unto him one by one, *Is* it I? and another *said, Is* it I?

20 And he answered and said unto them, *It is* one of the twelve, that dippeth with me in the dish.

21 The Son of man indeed goeth, as it is written of him: but woe to that man by whom the Son of man is betrayed! good were it for that man if he had never been born.

22 ¶ And as they did eat, Jesus took bread, and blessed, and

brake *it*, and gave to them, and said, Take, eat: this is my body.

23 And he took the cup, and when he had given thanks, he gave *it* to them: and they all drank of it.

24 And he said unto them, This is my blood of the new testament, which is shed for many.

25 Verily I say unto you, I will drink no more of the fruit of the vine, until that day that I drink it new in the kingdom of God.

26 ¶ And when they had sung an hymn, they went out into the mount of Olives.

27 And Jesus saith unto them, All ye shall be offended because of me this night: for it is written, I will smite the shepherd, and the sheep shall be scattered.

28 But after that I am risen, I will go before you into Galilee.

29 But Peter said unto him, Although all shall be offended, yet *will* not I.

30 And Jesus saith unto him, Verily I say unto thee, That this day, *even* in this night, before the cock crow twice, thou shalt deny me thrice.

31 But he spake the more vehemently, If I should die with thee, I will not deny thee in any wise. Likewise also said they all.

32 ¶ And they came to a place which was named Gethsemane: and he saith to his disciples, Sit ye here, while I shall pray.

33 And he taketh with him Peter and James and John, and began to be sore amazed, and to be very heavy;

34 And saith unto them, My soul is exceeding sorrowful unto death: tarry ye here, and watch.

35 And he went forward a little, and fell on the ground, and prayed that, if it were possible, the hour might pass from him.

36 And he said, Abba, Father, all things *are* possible unto thee; take away this cup from me: nevertheless not what I will, but what thou wilt.

37 And he cometh, and findeth them sleeping, and saith unto Peter, Simon, sleepest thou? couldest not thou watch one hour?

38 Watch ye and pray, lest ye enter into temptation. The spirit truly *is* ready, but the flesh *is* weak.

39 And again he went away, and prayed, and spake the same words.

40 And when he returned, he found them asleep again, (for their eyes were heavy,) neither wist they what to answer him.

41 And he cometh the third time, and saith unto them, Sleep on now, and take *your* rest: it is enough, the hour is come; behold, the Son of man is betrayed into the hands of sinners.

42 Rise up, let us go; lo, he that betrayeth me is at hand.

43 ¶ And immediately, while he yet spake, cometh Judas, one of the twelve, and with him a great multitude with swords and staves, from the chief priests and the scribes and the elders.

44 And he that betrayed him had given them a token, saying,

Whomsoever I shall kiss, that same is he; take him, and lead *him* away safely.

45 And as soon as he was come, he goeth straightway to him, and saith, Master, master; and kissed him.

46 ¶ And they laid their hands on him, and took him.

47 And one of them that stood by drew a sword, and smote a servant of the high priest, and cut off his ear.

48 And Jesus answered and said unto them, Are ye come out, as against a thief, with swords and *with* staves to take me?

49 I was daily with you in the temple teaching, and ye took me not: but the scriptures must be fulfilled.

50 And they all forsook him, and fled.

51 And there followed him a certain young man, having a linen cloth cast about *his* naked *body*; and the young men laid hold on him:

52 And he left the linen cloth, and fled from them naked.

53 ¶ And they led Jesus away to the high priest: and with him were assembled all the chief priests and the elders and the scribes.

54 And Peter followed him afar off, even into the palace of the high priest: and he sat with the servants, and warmed himself at the fire.

55 And the chief priests and all the council sought for witness against Jesus to put him to death;

and found none.

56 For many bare false witness against him, but their witness agreed not together.

57 And there arose certain, and bare false witness against him, saying,

58 We heard him say, I will destroy this temple that is made with hands, and within three days I will build another made without hands.

59 But neither so did their witness agree together.

60 And the high priest stood up in the midst, and asked Jesus, saying, Answerest thou nothing? what *is it which* these witness against thee?

61 But he held his peace, and answered nothing. Again the high priest asked him, and said unto him, Art thou the Christ, the Son of the Blessed?

62 And Jesus said, I am: and ye shall see the Son of man sitting on the right hand of power, and coming in the clouds of heaven.

63 Then the high priest rent his clothes, and saith, What need we any further witnesses?

64 Ye have heard the blasphemy: what think ye? And they all condemned him to be guilty of death.

65 And some began to spit on him, and to cover his face, and to buffet him, and to say unto him, Prophesy: and the servants did strike him with the palms of their hands.

66 ¶ And as Peter was beneath in the palace, there cometh one of

the maids of the high priest:

67 And when she saw Peter warming himself, she looked upon him, and said, And thou also wast with Jesus of Nazareth.

68 But he denied, saying, I know not, neither understand I what thou sayest. And he went out into the porch; and the cock crew.

69 And a maid saw him again, and began to say to them that stood by, This is *one* of them.

70 And he denied it again. And a little after, they that stood by said again to Peter, Surely thou art *one* of them: for thou art a Galilaean, and thy speech agreeth *thereto*.

71 But he began to curse and to swear, *saying*, I know not this man of whom ye speak.

72 And the second time the cock crew. And Peter called to mind the word that Jesus said unto him, Before the cock crow twice, thou shalt deny me thrice. And when he thought thereon, he wept.

15 And straightway in the morning the chief priests held a consultation with the elders and scribes and the whole council, and bound Jesus, and carried *him* away, and delivered *him* to Pilate.

2 And Pilate asked him, Art thou the King of the Jews? And he answering said unto him, Thou sayest *it*.

3 And the chief priests accused him of many things: but he answered nothing.

4 And Pilate asked him again, saying, Answerest thou nothing? behold how many things they witness against thee.

5 But Jesus yet answered nothing; so that Pilate marvelled.

6 Now at *that* feast he released unto them one prisoner, whomsoever they desired.

7 ¶ And there was *one* named Barabbas, *which* lay bound with them that had made insurrection with him, who had committed murder in the insurrection.

8 And the multitude crying aloud began to desire *him to do* as he had ever done unto them.

9 But Pilate answered them, saying, Will ye that I release unto you the King of the Jews?

10 For he knew that the chief priests had delivered him for envy.

11 But the chief priests moved the people, that he should rather release Barabbas unto them.

12 And Pilate answered and said again unto them, What will ye then that I shall do *unto him* whom ye call the King of the Jews?

13 And they cried out again, Crucify him.

14 Then Pilate said unto them, Why, what evil hath he done? And they cried out the more exceedingly, Crucify him.

15 And *so* Pilate, willing to content the people, released Barabbas unto them, and delivered Jesus, when he had scourged *him*, to be crucified.

16 ¶ And the soldiers led him away into the hall, called Praetorium; and they call together the whole band.

17 And they clothed him with purple, and platted a crown of thorns, and put it about his *head*,

18 And began to salute him, Hail, King of the Jews!

19 And they smote him on the head with a reed, and did spit upon him, and bowing *their* knees worshipped him.

20 And when they had mocked him, they took off the purple from him, and put his own clothes on him, and led him out to crucify him.

21 And they compel one Simon a Cyrenian, who passed by, coming out of the country, the father of Alexander and Rufus, to bear his cross.

22 And they bring him unto the place Golgotha, which is, being interpreted, The place of a skull.

23 And they gave him to drink wine mingled with myrrh: but he received *it* not.

24 And when they had crucified him, they parted his garments, casting lots upon them, what every man should take.

25 And it was the third hour, and they crucified him.

26 And the superscription of his accusation was written over, THE KING OF THE JEWS.

27 And with him they crucify two thieves; the one on his right hand, and the other on his left.

28 And the scripture was fulfilled, which saith, And he was numbered with the transgressors.

29 And they that passed by railed on him, wagging their heads, and saying, Ah, thou that destroyest the temple, and buildest *it* in three days,

30 Save thyself, and come down from the cross.

31 Likewise also the chief priests mocking said among themselves with the scribes, He saved others; himself he cannot save.

32 Let Christ the King of Israel descend now from the cross, that we may see and believe. And they that were crucified with him reviled him.

33 And when the sixth hour was come, there was darkness over the whole land until the ninth hour.

34 And at the ninth hour Jesus cried with a loud voice, saying, Eloi, Eloi, lama sabachthani? which is, being interpreted, My God, my God, why hast thou forsaken me?

35 And some of them that stood by, when they heard *it*, said, Behold, he calleth Elias.

36 And one ran and filled a spunge full of vinegar, and put *it* on a reed, and gave him to drink, saying, Let alone; let us see whether Elias will come to take him down.

37 And Jesus cried with a loud voice, and gave up the ghost.

38 And the veil of the temple was rent in twain from the top to the bottom.

39 ¶ And when the centurion,

which stood over against him, saw that he so cried out, and gave up the ghost, he said, Truly this man was the Son of God.

40 There were also women looking on afar off: among whom was Mary Magdalene, and Mary the mother of James the less and of Joses, and Salome;

41 (Who also, when he was in Galilee, followed him, and ministered unto him;) and many other women which came up with him unto Jerusalem.

42 ¶ And now when the even was come, because it was the preparation, that is, the day before the sabbath,

43 Joseph of Arimathaea, an honourable counsellor, which also waited for the kingdom of God, came, and went in boldly unto Pilate, and craved the body of Jesus.

44 And Pilate marvelled if he were already dead: and calling unto him the centurion, he asked him whether he had been any while dead.

45 And when he knew *it* of the centurion, he gave the body to Joseph.

46 And he bought fine linen, and took him down, and wrapped him in the linen, and laid him in a sepulchre which was hewn out of a rock, and rolled a stone unto the door of the sepulchre.

47 And Mary Magdalene and Mary *the mother* of Joses beheld where he was laid.

16 And when the sabbath was past, Mary Magdalene, and Mary the *mother* of James, and Salome, had bought sweet spices, that they might come and anoint him.

2 And very early in the morning the first *day* of the week, they came unto the sepulchre at the rising of the sun.

3 And they said among themselves, Who shall roll us away the stone from the door of the sepulchre?

4 And when they looked, they saw that the stone was rolled away: for it was very great.

5 And entering into the sepulchre, they saw a young man sitting on the right side, clothed in a long white garment; and they were affrighted.

6 And he saith unto them, Be not affrighted: Ye seek Jesus of Nazareth, which was crucified: he is risen; he is not here: behold the place where they laid him.

7 But go your way, tell his disciples and Peter that he goeth before you into Galilee: there shall ye see him, as he said unto you.

8 And they went out quickly, and fled from the sepulchre; for they trembled and were amazed: neither said they any thing to any *man*; for they were afraid.

9 ¶ Now when *Jesus* was risen early the first *day* of the week, he appeared first to Mary Magdalene, out of whom he had cast seven devils.

10 *And* she went and told them that had been with him, as they mourned and wept.

11 And they, when they had heard that he was alive, and had

been seen of her, believed not.

12 ¶ After that he appeared in another form unto two of them, as they walked, and went into the country.

13 And they went and told *it* unto the residue: neither believed they them.

14 ¶ Afterward he appeared unto the eleven as they sat at meat, and upbraided them with their unbelief and hardness of heart, because they believed not them which had seen him after he was risen.

15 ¶ And he said unto them, Go ye into all the world, and preach the gospel to every creature.

16 He that believeth and is bap-tized shall be saved; but he that believeth not shall be damned.

17 And these signs shall follow them that believe; In my name shall they cast out devils; they shall speak with new tongues;

18 They shall take up serpents; and if they drink any deadly thing, it shall not hurt them; they shall lay hands on the sick, and they shall recover.

19 ¶ So then after the Lord had spoken unto them, he was received up into heaven, and sat on the right hand of God.

20 And they went forth, and preached every where, the Lord working with *them*, and confirming the word with signs following. Amen.

THE GOSPEL ACCORDING
TO
LUKE

1 Forasmuch as many have taken in hand to set forth in order a declaration of those things which are most surely believed among us,

2 Even as they delivered them unto us, which from the beginning were eyewitnesses, and ministers of the word;

3 It seemed good to me also, having had perfect understanding of all things from the very first, to write unto thee in order, most excellent Theophilus,

4 That thou mightest know the certainty of those things, wherein thou hast been instructed.

5 ¶ There was in the days of Herod, the king of Judaea, a certain priest named Zacharias, of the course of Abia: and his wife *was* of the daughters of Aaron, and her name *was* Elisabeth.

6 And they were both righteous before God, walking in all the commandments and ordinances of the Lord blameless.

7 And they had no child, because that Elisabeth was barren, and they both were *now* well stricken in years.

8 And it came to pass, that while he executed the priest's office before God in the order of

his course,

9 According to the custom of the priest's office, his lot was to burn incense when he went into the temple of the Lord.

10 And the whole multitude of the people were praying without at the time of incense.

11 And there appeared unto him an angel of the Lord standing on the right side of the altar of incense.

12 And when Zacharias saw *him*, he was troubled, and fear fell upon him.

13 But the angel said unto him, Fear not, Zacharias: for thy prayer is heard; and thy wife Elisabeth shall bear thee a son, and thou shalt call his name John.

14 And thou shalt have joy and gladness; and many shall rejoice at his birth.

15 For he shall be great in the sight of the Lord, and shall drink neither wine nor strong drink; and he shall be filled with the Holy Ghost, even from his mother's womb.

16 And many of the children of Israel shall he turn to the Lord their God.

17 And he shall go before him in the spirit and power of Elias, to turn the hearts of the fathers to the children, and the disobedient to the wisdom of the just; to make ready a people prepared for the Lord.

18 And Zacharias said unto the angel, Whereby shall I know this? for I am an old man, and my wife well stricken in years.

19 And the angel answering said unto him, I am Gabriel, that stand in the presence of God; and am sent to speak unto thee, and to shew thee these glad tidings.

20 And, behold, thou shalt be dumb, and not able to speak, until the day that these things shall be performed, because thou believest not my words, which shall be fulfilled in their season.

21 And the people waited for Zacharias, and marvelled that he tarried so long in the temple.

22 And when he came out, he could not speak unto them: and they perceived that he had seen a vision in the temple: for he beckoned unto them, and remained speechless.

23 And it came to pass, that, as soon as the days of his ministration were accomplished, he departed to his own house.

24 And after those days his wife Elisabeth conceived, and hid herself five months, saying,

25 Thus hath the Lord dealt with me in the days wherein he looked on *me*, to take away my reproach among men.

26 ¶ And in the sixth month the angel Gabriel was sent from God unto a city of Galilee, named Nazareth,

27 To a virgin espoused to a man whose name was Joseph, of the house of David; and the virgin's name *was* Mary.

28 And the angel came in unto her, and said, Hail, *thou that art* highly favoured, the Lord *is* with

thee: blessed *art* thou among women.

29 And when she saw *him* she was troubled at his saying, and cast in her mind what manner of salutation this should be.

30 And the angel said unto her, Fear not, Mary: for thou hast found favour with God.

31 And, behold, thou shalt conceive in thy womb, and bring forth a son, and shalt call his name JESUS.

32 He shall be great, and shall be called the Son of the Highest: and the Lord God shall give unto him the throne of his father David:

33 And he shall reign over the house of Jacob for ever; and of his kingdom there shall be no end.

34 Then said Mary unto the angel, How shall this be, seeing I know not a man?

35 And the angel answered and said unto her, The Holy Ghost shall come upon thee, and the power of the Highest shall overshadow thee: therefore also that holy thing which shall be born of thee shall be called the Son of God.

36 And, behold, thy cousin Elisabeth, she hath also conceived a son in her old age: and this is the sixth month with her, who was called barren.

37 For with God nothing shall be impossible.

38 And Mary said, Behold the handmaid of the Lord; be it unto me according to thy word. And the angel departed from her.

39 ¶ And Mary arose in those days, and went into the hill country with haste, into a city of Juda;

40 And entered into the house of Zacharias, and saluted Elisabeth.

41 And it came to pass, that, when Elisabeth heard the salutation of Mary, the babe leaped in her womb; and Elisabeth was filled with the Holy Ghost:

42 And she spake out with a loud voice, and said, Blessed *art* thou among women, and blessed *is* the fruit of thy womb.

43 And whence *is* this to me, that the mother of my Lord should come to me?

44 For, lo, as soon as the voice of thy salutation sounded in mine ears, the babe leaped in my womb for joy.

45 And blessed *is* she that believed: for there shall be a performance of those things which were told her from the Lord.

46 And Mary said, My soul doth magnify the Lord,

47 And my spirit hath rejoiced in God my Saviour.

48 For he hath regarded the low estate of his handmaiden: for, behold, from henceforth all generations shall call me blessed.

49 For he that is mighty hath done to me great things; and holy *is* his name.

50 And his mercy *is* on them that fear him from generation to generation.

51 He hath shewed strength

with his arm; he hath scattered the proud in the imagination of their hearts.

52 He hath put down the mighty from *their* seats, and exalted them of low degree.

53 He hath filled the hungry with good things; and the rich he hath sent empty away.

54 He hath holpen his servant Israel, in remembrance of *his* mercy;

55 As he spake to our fathers, to Abraham, and to his seed for ever.

56 And Mary abode with her about three months, and returned to her own house.

57 ¶ Now Elisabeth's full time came that she should be delivered; and she brought forth a son.

58 And her neighbours and her cousins heard how the Lord had shewed great mercy upon her; and they rejoiced with her.

59 And it came to pass, that on the eighth day they came to circumcise the child; and they called him Zacharias, after the name of his father.

60 And his mother answered and said, Not so; but he shall be called John.

61 And they said unto her, There is none of thy kindred that is called by this name.

62 And they made signs to his father, how he would have him called.

63 And he asked for a writing table, and wrote, saying, His name is John. And they mar-

velled all.

64 ¶ And his mouth was opened immediately, and his tongue *loosed*, and he spake, and praised God.

65 And fear came on all that dwelt round about them: and all these sayings were noised abroad throughout all the hill country of Judaea.

66 And all they that heard *them* laid *them* up in their hearts, saying, What manner of child shall this be! And the hand of the Lord was with him.

67 ¶ And his father Zacharias was filled with the Holy Ghost, and prophesied, saying,

68 Blessed *be* the Lord God of Israel; for he hath visited and redeemed his people,

69 And hath raised up an horn of salvation for us in the house of his servant David;

70 As he spake by the mouth of his holy prophets, which have been since the world began:

71 That we should be saved from our enemies, and from the hand of all that hate us;

72 To perform the mercy *promised* to our fathers, and to remember his holy covenant;

73 The oath which he sware to our father Abraham,

74 That he would grant unto us, that we being delivered out of the hand of our enemies might serve him without fear,

75 In holiness and righteousness before him, all the days of our life.

76 And thou, child, shalt be

called the prophet of the Highest: for thou shalt go before the face of the Lord to prepare his ways;

77 To give knowledge of salvation unto his people by the remission of their sins,

78 Through the tender mercy of our God; whereby the dayspring from on high hath visited us,

79 To give light to them that sit in darkness and *in* the shadow of death, to guide our feet into the way of peace.

80 And the child grew, and waxed strong in spirit, and was in the deserts till the day of his shewing unto Israel.

2 And it came to pass in those days, that there went out a decree from Caesar Augustus, that all the world should be taxed.

2 (*And* this taxing was first made when Cyrenius was governor of Syria.)

3 And all went to be taxed, every one into his own city.

4 And Joseph also went up from Galilee, out of the city of Nazareth, into Judaea, unto the city of David, which is called Bethlehem; (because he was of the house and lineage of David:)

5 To be taxed with Mary his espoused wife, being great with child.

6 ¶ And so it was, that, while they were there, the days were accomplished that she should be delivered.

7 And she brought forth her firstborn son, and wrapped him in swaddling clothes, and laid him in a manger; because there was no room for them in the inn.

8 ¶ And there were in the same country shepherds abiding in the field, keeping watch over their flock by night.

9 And, lo, the angel of the Lord came upon them, and the glory of the Lord shone round about them: and they were sore afraid.

10 And the angel said unto them, Fear not: for, behold, I bring you good tidings of great joy, which shall be to all people.

11 For unto you is born this day in the city of David a Saviour, which is Christ the Lord.

12 And this **shall be** a sign unto you; Ye shall find the babe wrapped in swaddling clothes, lying in a manger.

13 ¶ And suddenly there was with the angel a multitude of the heavenly host praising God, and saying,

14 Glory to God in the highest, and on earth peace, good will toward men.

15 And it came to pass, as the angels were gone away from them into heaven, the shepherds said one to another, Let us now go even unto Bethlehem, and see this thing which is come to pass, which the Lord hath made known unto us.

16 And they came with haste, and found Mary, and Joseph, and the babe lying in a manger.

17 And when they had seen *it*, they made known abroad the saying which was told them concerning this child.

18 And all they that heard *it* wondered at those things which were told them by the shepherds.

19 But Mary kept all these things, and pondered *them* in her heart.

20 And the shepherds returned, glorifying and praising God for all the things that they had heard and seen, as it was told unto them.

21 ¶ And when eight days were accomplished for the circumcising of the child, his name was called JESUS, which was so named of the angel before he was conceived in the womb.

22 And when the days of her purification according to the law of Moses were accomplished, they brought him to Jerusalem, to present *him* to the Lord;

23 (As it is written in the law of the Lord, Every male that openeth the womb shall be called holy to the Lord;)

24 And to offer a sacrifice according to that which is said in the law of the Lord, A pair of turtledoves, or two young pigeons.

25 And, behold, there was a man in Jerusalem, whose name *was* Simeon; and the same man *was* just and devout, waiting for the consolation of Israel: and the Holy Ghost was upon him.

26 And it was revealed unto him by the Holy Ghost, that he should not see death, before he had seen the Lord's Christ.

27 And he came by the Spirit into the temple: and when the parents brought in the child Jesus, to do for him after the custom of the law,

28 ¶ Then took he him up in his arms, and blessed God, and said,

29 Lord, now lettest thou thy servant depart in peace, according to thy word:

30 For mine eyes have seen thy salvation,

31 Which thou hast prepared before the face of all people;

32 A light to lighten the Gentiles, and the glory of thy people Israel.

33 And Joseph and his mother marvelled at those things which were spoken of him.

34 And Simeon blessed them, and said unto Mary his mother, Behold, this *child* is set for the fall and rising again of many in Israel; and for a sign which shall be spoken against;

35 (Yea, a sword shall pierce through thy own soul also,) that the thoughts of many hearts may be revealed.

36 ¶ And there was one Anna, a prophetess, the daughter of Phanuel, of the tribe of Aser: she was of a great age, and had lived with an husband seven years from her virginity;

37 And she *was* a widow of about fourscore and four years, which departed not from the temple, but served *God* with fastings and prayers night and day.

38 And she coming in that instant gave thanks likewise unto the Lord, and spake of him to all them that looked for redemption in Jerusalem.

39 And when they had per-

formed all things according to the law of the Lord, they returned into Galilee, to their own city Nazareth.

40 ¶ And the child grew, and waxed strong in spirit, filled with wisdom: and the grace of God was upon him.

41 ¶ Now his parents went to Jerusalem every year at the feast of the passover.

42 And when he was twelve years old, they went up to Jerusalem after the custom of the feast.

43 And when they had fulfilled the days, as they returned, the child Jesus tarried behind in Jerusalem; and Joseph and his mother knew not of it.

44 But they, supposing him to have been in the company, went a day's journey; and they sought him among *their* kinsfolk and acquaintance.

45 And when they found him not, they turned back again to Jerusalem, seeking him.

46 And it came to pass, that after three days they found him in the temple, sitting in the midst of the doctors, both hearing them, and asking them questions.

47 And all that heard him were astonished at his understanding and answers.

48 And when they saw him, they were amazed: and his mother said unto him, Son, why hast thou thus dealt with us? behold, thy father and I have sought thee sorrowing.

49 And he said unto them, How is it that ye sought me? wist ye not that I must be about my Father's business?

50 And they understood not the saying which he spake unto them.

51 And he went down with them, and came to Nazareth, and was subject unto them: but his mother kept all these sayings in her heart.

52 And Jesus increased in wisdom and stature, and in favour with God and man.

3 Now in the fifteenth year of the reign of Tiberius Caesar, Pontius Pilate being governor of Judaea, and Herod being tetrarch of Galilee, and his brother Philip tetrarch of Ituraea and of the region of Trachonitis, and Lysanias the tetrarch of Abilene,

2 Annas and Caiaphas being the high priests, the word of God came unto John the son of Zacharias in the wilderness.

3 And he came into all the country about Jordan, preaching the baptism of repentance for the remission of sins;

4 As it is written in the book of the words of Esaias the prophet, saying, The voice of one crying in the wilderness, Prepare ye the way of the Lord, make his paths straight.

5 Every valley shall be filled, and every mountain and hill shall be brought low; and the crooked shall be made straight, and the rough ways *shall be* made smooth;

6 And all flesh shall see the salvation of God.

7 Then said he to the multitude that came forth to be baptized of him, O generation of vipers, who hath warned you to flee from the wrath to come?

8 Bring forth therefore fruits worthy of repentance, and begin not to say within yourselves, We have Abraham to *our* father: for I say unto you, That God is able of these stones to raise up children unto Abraham.

9 And now also the axe is laid unto the root of the trees: every tree therefore which bringeth not forth good fruit is hewn down, and cast into the fire.

10 And the people asked him, saying, What shall we do then?

11 He answereth and saith unto them, He that hath two coats, let him impart to him that hath none; and he that hath meat, let him do likewise.

12 Then came also publicans to be baptized, and said unto him, Master, what shall we do?

13 And he said unto them, Exact no more than that which is appointed you.

14 And the soldiers likewise demanded of him, saying, And what shall we do? And he said unto them, Do violence to no man, neither accuse *any* falsely; and be content with your wages.

15 ¶ And as the people were in expectation, and all men mused in their hearts of John, whether he were the Christ, or not;

16 John answered, saying unto *them* all, I indeed baptize you with water; but one mightier than I cometh, the latchet of whose shoes I am not worthy to unloose: he shall baptize you with the Holy Ghost and with fire:

17 Whose fan *is* in his hand, and he will throughly purge his floor, and will gather the wheat into his garner; but the chaff he will burn with fire unquenchable.

18 And many other things in his exhortation preached he unto the people.

19 ¶ But Herod the tetrarch, being reproved by him for Herodias his brother Philip's wife, and for all the evils which Herod had done,

20 Added yet this above all, that he shut up John in prison.

21 ¶ Now when all the people were baptized, it came to pass, that Jesus also being baptized, and praying, the heaven was opened,

22 And the Holy Ghost descended in a bodily shape like a dove upon him, and a voice came from heaven, which said, Thou art my beloved Son; in thee I am well pleased.

23 And Jesus himself began to be about thirty years of age, being (as was supposed) the son of Joseph, which was *the son* of Heli,

24 Which was *the son* of Matthat, which was *the son* of Levi, which was *the son* of Melchi, which was *the son* of Janna, which was *the son* of Joseph,

25 Which was *the son* of Mattathias, which was *the son* of Amos, which was *the son* of Naum, which was *the son* of Esli, which was *the son* of Nagge,

26 Which was *the son* of Maath, which was *the son* of Mattathias, which was *the son* of Semei, which was *the son* of Joseph, which was *the son* of Juda,

27 Which was *the son* of Joanna, which was *the son* of Rhesa, which was *the son* of Zorobabel, which was *the son* of Salathiel, which was *the son* of Neri,

28 Which was *the son* of Melchi, which was *the son* of Addi, which was *the son* of Cosam, which was *the son* of Elmodam, which was *the son* of Er,

29 Which was *the son* of Jose, which was *the son* of Eliezer, which was *the son* of Jorim, which was *the son* of Matthat, which was *the son* of Levi,

30 Which was *the son* of Simeon, which was *the son* of Juda, which was *the son* of Joseph, which was *the son* of Jonan, which was *the son* of Eliakim,

31 Which was *the son* of Melea, which was *the son* of Menan, which was *the son* of Mattatha, which was *the son* of Nathan, which was *the son* of David,

32 Which was *the son* of Jesse, which was *the son* of Obed, which was *the son* of Booz, which was *the son* of Salmon, which was *the son* of Naasson,

33 Which was *the son* of Aminadab, which was *the son* of Aram, which was *the son* of Esrom, which was *the son* of Phares, which was *the son* of Juda,

34 Which was *the son* of Jacob, which was *the son* of Isaac,

which was *the son* of Abraham, which was *the son* of Thara, which was *the son* of Nachor,

35 Which was *the son* of Saruch, which was *the son* of Ragau, which was *the son* of Phalec, which was *the son* of Heber, which was *the son* of Sala,

36 Which was *the son* of Cainan, which was *the son* of Arphaxad, which was *the son* of Sem, which was *the son* of Noe, which was *the son* of Lamech,

37 Which was *the son* of Mathusala, which was *the son* of Enoch, which was *the son* of Jared, which was *the son* of Maleleel, which was *the son* of Cainan,

38 Which was *the son* of Enos, which was *the son* of Seth, which was *the son* of Adam, which was *the son* of God.

4 And Jesus being full of the Holy Ghost returned from Jordan, and was led by the Spirit into the wilderness,

2 Being forty days tempted of the devil. And in those days he did eat nothing: and when they were ended, he afterward hungered.

3 And the devil said unto him, If thou be the Son of God, command this stone that it be made bread.

4 And Jesus answered him, saying, It is written, That man shall not live by bread alone, but by every word of God.

5 And the devil, taking him up into an high mountain, shewed unto him all the kingdoms of the

world in a moment of time.

6 And the devil said unto him, All this power will I give thee, and the glory of them: for that is delivered unto me; and to whomsoever I will I give it.

7 If thou therefore wilt worship me, all shall be thine.

8 And Jesus answered and said unto him, Get thee behind me, Satan: for it is written, Thou shalt worship the Lord thy God, and him only shalt thou serve.

9 And he brought him to Jerusalem, and set him on a pinnacle of the temple, and said unto him, If thou be the Son of God, cast thyself down from hence:

10 For it is written, He shall give his angels charge over thee, to keep thee:

11 And in *their* hands they shall bear thee up, lest at any time thou dash thy foot against a stone.

12 And Jesus answering said unto him, It is said, Thou shalt not tempt the Lord thy God.

13 And when the devil had ended all the temptation, he departed from him for a season.

14 ¶ And Jesus returned in the power of the Spirit into Galilee: and there went out a fame of him through all the region round about.

15 And he taught in their synagogues, being glorified of all.

16 ¶ And he came to Nazareth, where he had been brought up: and, as his custom was, he went into the synagogue on the sabbath day, and stood up for to read.

17 And there was delivered unto him the book of the prophet Esaias. And when he had opened the book, he found the place where it was written,

18 The Spirit of the Lord *is* upon me, because he hath anointed me to preach the gospel to the poor; he hath sent me to heal the brokenhearted, to preach deliverance to the captives, and recovering of sight to the blind, to set at liberty them that are bruised,

19 To preach the acceptable year of the Lord.

20 And he closed the book, and he gave *it* again to the minister, and sat down. And the eyes of all them that were in the synagogue were fastened on him.

21 And he began to say unto them, This day is this scripture fulfilled in your ears.

22 And all bare him witness, and wondered at the gracious words which proceeded out of his mouth. And they said, Is not this Joseph's son?

23 And he said unto them, Ye will surely say unto me this proverb, Physician, heal thyself: whatsoever we have heard done in Capernaum, do also here in thy country.

24 And he said, Verily I say unto you, No prophet is accepted in his own country.

25 But I tell you of a truth, many widows were in Israel in the days of Elias, when the heaven was shut up three years and six months, when great famine was throughout all the land;

26 But unto none of them was

Elias sent, save unto Sarepta, *a city* of Sidon, unto a woman *that was* a widow.

27 And many lepers were in Israel in the time of Eliseus the prophet; and none of them was cleansed, saving Naaman the Syrian.

28 And all they in the synagogue, when they heard these things, were filled with wrath,

29 And rose up, and thrust him out of the city, and led him unto the brow of the hill whereon their city was built, that they might cast him down headlong.

30 But he passing through the midst of them went his way,

31 ¶ And came down to Capernaum, a city of Galilee, and taught them on the sabbath days.

32 And they were astonished at his doctrine: for his word was with power.

33 ¶ And in the synagogue there was a man, which had a spirit of an unclean devil, and cried out with a loud voice,

34 Saying, Let *us* alone; what have we to do with thee, *thou* Jesus of Nazareth? art thou come to destroy us? I know thee who thou art; the Holy One of God.

35 And Jesus rebuked him, saying, Hold thy peace, and come out of him. And when the devil had thrown him in the midst, he came out of him, and hurt him not.

36 And they were all amazed, and spake among themselves, saying, What a word *is* this! for with authority and power he commandeth the unclean spirits, and they come out.

37 And the fame of him went out into every place of the country round about.

38 ¶ And he arose out of the synagogue, and entered into Simon's house. And Simon's wife's mother was taken with a great fever; and they besought him for her.

39 And he stood over her, and rebuked the fever; and it left her: and immediately she arose and ministered unto them.

40 ¶ Now when the sun was setting, all they that had any sick with divers diseases brought them unto him; and he laid his hands on every one of them, and healed them.

41 And devils also came out of many, crying out, and saying, Thou art Christ the Son of God. And he rebuking *them* suffered them not to speak: for they knew that he was Christ.

42 And when it was day, he departed and went into a desert place: and the people sought him, and came unto him, and stayed him, that he should not depart from them.

43 And he said unto them, I must preach the kingdom of God to other cities also: for therefore am I sent.

44 And he preached in the synagogues of Galilee.

5 And it came to pass, that, as the people pressed upon him to hear the word of God, he stood by the lake of Gennesaret,

2 And saw two ships standing

by the lake: but the fishermen were gone out of them, and were washing *their* nets.

3 And he entered into one of the ships, which was Simon's, and prayed him that he would thrust out a little from the land. And he sat down, and taught the people out of the ship.

4 ¶ Now when he had left speaking, he said unto Simon, Launch out into the deep, and let down your nets for a draught.

5 And Simon answering said unto him, Master, we have toiled all the night, and have taken nothing: nevertheless at thy word I will let down the net.

6 And when they had this done, they inclosed a great multitude of fishes: and their net brake.

7 And they beckoned unto *their* partners, which were in the other ship, that they should come and help them. And they came, and filled both the ships, so that they began to sink.

8 When Simon Peter saw *it*, he fell down at Jesus' knees, saying, Depart from me; for I am a sinful man, O Lord.

9 For he was astonished, and all that were with him, at the draught of the fishes which they had taken:

10 And so *was* also James, and John, the sons of Zebedee, which were partners with Simon. And Jesus said unto Simon, Fear not; from henceforth thou shalt catch men.

11 And when they had brought their ships to land, they forsook all, and followed him.

12 ¶ And it came to pass, when he was in a certain city, behold a man full of leprosy: who seeing Jesus fell on *his* face, and besought him, saying, Lord, if thou wilt, thou canst make me clean.

13 And he put forth *his* hand, and touched him, saying, I will: be thou clean. And immediately the leprosy departed from him.

14 And he charged him to tell no man: but go, and shew thyself to the priest, and offer for thy cleansing, according as Moses commanded, for a testimony unto them.

15 But so much the more went there a fame abroad of him: and great multitudes came together to hear, and to be healed by him of their infirmities.

16 ¶ And he withdrew himself into the wilderness, and prayed.

17 And it came to pass on a certain day, as he was teaching, that there were Pharisees and doctors of the law sitting by, which were come out of every town of Galilee, and Judaea, and Jerusalem: and the power of the Lord was *present* to heal them.

18 ¶ And, behold, men brought in a bed a man which was taken with a palsy: and they sought *means* to bring him in, and to lay *him* before him.

19 And when they could not find by what *way* they might bring him in because of the multitude, they went upon the housetop, and let him down through the tiling with *his* couch into the midst before Jesus.

20 And when he saw their faith,

he said unto him, Man, thy sins are forgiven thee.

21 And the scribes and the Pharisees began to reason, saying, Who is this which speaketh blasphemies? Who can forgive sins, but God alone?

22 But when Jesus perceived their thoughts, he answering said unto them, What reason ye in your hearts?

23 Whether is easier, to say, Thy sins be forgiven thee; or to say, Rise up and walk?

24 But that ye may know that the Son of man hath power upon earth to forgive sins, (he said unto the sick of the palsy,) I say unto thee, Arise, and take up thy couch, and go into thine house.

25 And immediately he rose up before them, and took up that whereon he lay, and departed to his own house, glorifying God.

26 And they were all amazed, and they glorified God, and were filled with fear, saying, We have seen strange things to day.

27 ¶ And after these things he went forth, and saw a publican, named Levi, sitting at the receipt of custom: and he said unto him, Follow me.

28 And he left all, rose up, and followed him.

29 ¶ And Levi made him a great feast in his own house: and there was a great company of publicans and of others that sat down with them.

30 But their scribes and Pharisees murmured against his disciples, saying, Why do ye eat and drink with publicans and sinners?

31 And Jesus answering said unto them, They that are whole need not a physician; but they that are sick.

32 I came not to call the righteous, but sinners to repentance.

33 ¶ And they said unto him, Why do the disciples of John fast often, and make prayers, and likewise *the disciples* of the Pharisees; but thine eat and drink?

34 And he said unto them, Can ye make the children of the bridechamber fast, while the bridegroom is with them?

35 But the days will come, when the bridegroom shall be taken away from them, and then shall they fast in those days.

36 ¶ And he spake also a parable unto them; No man putteth a piece of a new garment upon an old; if otherwise, then both the new maketh a rent, and the piece that was *taken* out of the new agreeth not with the old.

37 And no man putteth new wine into old bottles; else the new wine will burst the bottles, and be spilled, and the bottles shall perish.

38 But new wine must be put into new bottles; and both are preserved.

39 No man also having drunk old *wine* straightway desireth new: for he saith, The old is better.

6 And it came to pass on the second sabbath after the

first, that he went through the corn fields; and his disciples plucked the ears of corn, and did eat, rubbing *them* in *their* hands.

2 And certain of the Pharisees said unto them, Why do ye that which is not lawful to do on the sabbath days?

3 And Jesus answering them said, Have ye not read so much as this, what David did, when himself was an hungred, and they which were with him;

4 How he went into the house of God, and did take and eat the shewbread, and gave also to them that were with him; which it is not lawful to eat but for the priests alone?

5 And he said unto them, That the Son of man is Lord also of the sabbath.

6 ¢ And it came to pass also on another sabbath, that he entered into the synagogue and taught: and there was a man whose right hand was withered.

7 And the scribes and Pharisees watched him, whether he would heal on the sabbath day; that they might find an accusation against him.

8 But he knew their thoughts, and said to the man which had the withered hand, Rise up, and stand forth in the midst. And he arose and stood forth.

9 Then said Jesus unto them, I will ask you one thing; Is it lawful on the sabbath days to do good, or to do evil? to save life, or to destroy *it?*

10 And looking round about upon them all, he said unto the man, Stretch forth thy hand. And he did so: and his hand was restored whole as the other.

11 And they were filled with madness; and communed one with another what they might do to Jesus.

12 And it came to pass in those days, that he went out into a mountain to pray, and continued all night in prayer to God.

13 ¢ And when it was day, he called *unto him* his disciples: and of them he chose twelve, whom also he named apostles;

14 Simon, (whom he also named Peter,) and Andrew his brother, James and John, Philip and Bartholomew,

15 Matthew and Thomas, James the *son* of Alphaeus, and Simon called Zelotes,

16 And Judas *the brother* of James, and Judas Iscariot, which also was the traitor.

17 ¢ And he came down with them, and stood in the plain, and the company of his disciples, and a great multitude of people out of all Judaea and Jerusalem, and from the sea coast of Tyre and Sidon, which came to hear him, and to be healed of their diseases;

18 And they that were vexed with unclean spirits: and they were healed.

19 And the whole multitude sought to touch him: for there went virtue out of him, and healed *them* all.

20 ¢ And he lifted up his eyes on his disciples, and said, Blessed

99

be ye poor: for yours is the kingdom of God.

21 Blessed *are* ye that hunger now: for ye shall be filled. Blessed *are* ye that weep now: for ye shall laugh.

22 Blessed are ye, when men shall hate you, and when they shall separate you *from their company*, and shall reproach *you*, and cast out your name as evil, for the Son of man's sake.

23 Rejoice ye in that day, and leap for joy: for, behold, your reward *is* great in heaven: for in the like manner did their fathers unto the prophets.

24 But woe unto you that are rich! for ye have received your consolation.

25 Woe unto you that are full! for ye shall hunger. Woe unto you that laugh now! for ye shall mourn and weep.

26 Woe unto you, when all men shall speak well of you! for so did their fathers to the false prophets.

27 ¶ But I say unto you which hear, Love your enemies, do good to them which hate you,

28 Bless them that curse you, and pray for them which despitefully use you.

29 And unto him that smiteth thee on the *one* cheek offer also the other; and him that taketh away thy cloak forbid not *to take* thy coat also.

30 Give to every man that asketh of thee; and of him that taketh away thy goods ask *them* not again.

31 And as ye would that men should do to you, do ye also to them likewise.

32 For if ye love them which love you, what thank have ye? for sinners also love those that love them.

33 And if ye do good to them which do good to you, what thank have ye? for sinners also do even the same.

34 And if ye lend *to them* of whom ye hope to receive, what thank have ye? for sinners also lend to sinners, to receive as much again.

35 But love ye your enemies, and do good, and lend, hoping for nothing again; and your reward shall be great, and ye shall be the children of the Highest: for he is kind unto the unthankful and *to* the evil.

36 Be ye therefore merciful, as your Father also is merciful.

37 Judge not, and ye shall not be judged: condemn not, and ye shall not be condemned: forgive, and ye shall be forgiven:

38 Give, and it shall be given unto you; good measure, pressed down, and shaken together, and running over, shall men give into your bosom. For with the same measure that ye mete withal it shall be measured to you again.

39 ¶ And he spake a parable unto them, Can the blind lead the blind? shall they not both fall into the ditch?

40 The disciple is not above his master: but every one that is perfect shall be as his master.

41 ❡ And why beholdest thou the mote that is in thy brother's eye, but perceivest not the beam that is in thine own eye?

42 Either how canst thou say to thy brother, Brother, let me pull out the mote that is in thine eye, when thou thyself beholdest not the beam that is in thine own eye? Thou hypocrite, cast out first the beam out of thine own eye, and then shalt thou see clearly to pull out the mote that is in thy brother's eye.

43 For a good tree bringeth not forth corrupt fruit; neither doth a corrupt tree bring forth good fruit.

44 For every tree is known by his own fruit. For of thorns men do not gather figs, nor of a bramble bush gather they grapes.

45 A good man out of the good treasure of his heart bringeth forth that which is good; and an evil man out of the evil treasure of his heart bringeth forth that which is evil: for of the abundance of the heart his mouth speaketh.

46 ❡ And why call ye me, Lord, Lord, and do not the things which I say?

47 Whosoever cometh to me, and heareth my sayings, and doeth them, I will shew you to whom he is like:

48 He is like a man which built an house, and digged deep, and laid the foundation on a rock: and when the flood arose, the stream beat vehemently upon that house, and could not shake it: for it was founded upon a rock.

49 But he that heareth, and doeth not, is like a man that without a foundation built an house upon the earth; against which the stream did beat vehemently, and immediately it fell; and the ruin of that house was great.

7 Now when he had ended all his sayings in the audience of the people, he entered into Capernaum.

2 And a certain centurion's servant, who was dear unto him, was sick, and ready to die.

3 And when he heard of Jesus, he sent unto him the elders of the Jews, beseeching him that he would come and heal his servant.

4 And when they came to Jesus, they besought him instantly, saying, That he was worthy for whom he should do this:

5 For he loveth our nation, and he hath built us a synagogue.

6 Then Jesus went with them. And when he was now not far from the house, the centurion sent friends to him, saying unto him, Lord, trouble not thyself: for I am not worthy that thou shouldest enter under my roof:

7 Wherefore neither thought I myself worthy to come unto thee: but say in a word, and my servant shall be healed.

8 For I also am a man set under authority, having under me soldiers, and I say unto one, Go, and he goeth; and to another, Come, and he cometh; and to my servant, Do this, and he doeth it.

9 When Jesus heard these

things, he marvelled at him, and turned him about, and said unto the people that followed him, I say unto you, I have not found so great faith, no, not in Israel.

10 And they that were sent, returning to the house, found the servant whole that had been sick.

11 ¶ And it came to pass the day after, that he went into a city called Nain; and many of his disciples went with him, and much people.

12 Now when he came nigh to the gate of the city, behold, there was a dead man carried out, the only son of his mother, and she was a widow: and much people of the city was with her.

13 And when the Lord saw her, he had compassion on her, and said unto her, Weep not.

14 And he came and touched the bier: and they that bare *him* stood still. And he said, Young man, I say unto thee, Arise.

15 And he that was dead sat up, and began to speak. And he delivered him to his mother.

16 And there came a fear on all: and they glorified God, saying, That a great prophet is risen up among us; and, That God hath visited his people.

17 And this rumour of him went forth throughout all Judaea, and throughout all the region round about.

18 And the disciples of John shewed him of all these things.

19 ¶ And John calling *unto him* two of his disciples sent *them*

to Jesus, saying, Art thou he that should come? or look we for another?

20 When the men were come unto him, they said, John Baptist hath sent us unto thee, saying, Art thou he that should come? or look we for another?

21 And in that same hour he cured many of *their* infirmities and plagues, and of evil spirits; and unto many *that were* blind he gave sight.

22 Then Jesus answering said unto them, Go your way, and tell John what things ye have seen and heard; how that the blind see, the lame walk, the lepers are cleansed, the deaf hear, the dead are raised, to the poor the gospel is preached.

23 And blessed is *he*, whosoever shall not be offended in me.

24 ¶ And when the messengers of John were departed, he began to speak unto the people concerning John, What went ye out into the wilderness for to see? A reed shaken with the wind?

25 But what went ye out for to see? A man clothed in soft raiment? Behold, they which are gorgeously apparelled, and live delicately, are in kings' courts.

26 But what went ye out for to see? A prophet? Yea, I say unto you, and much more than a prophet.

27 This is *he*, of whom it is written, Behold, I send my messenger before thy face, which shall prepare thy way before thee.

28 For I say unto you, Among those that are born of women

there is not a greater prophet than John the Baptist: but he that is least in the kingdom of God is greater than he.

29 And all the people that heard *him*, and the publicans, justified God, being baptized with the baptism of John.

30 But the Pharisees and lawyers rejected the counsel of God against themselves, being not baptized of him.

31 (And the Lord said, Whereunto then shall I liken the men of this generation? and to what are they like?

32 They are like unto children sitting in the marketplace, and calling one to another, and saying, We have piped unto you, and ye have not danced; we have mourned to you, and ye have not wept.

33 For John the Baptist came neither eating bread nor drinking wine; and ye say, He hath a devil.

34 The Son of man is come eating and drinking; and ye say, Behold a gluttonous man, and a winebibber, a friend of publicans and sinners!

35 But wisdom is justified of all her children.

36 (And one of the Pharisees desired him that he would eat with him. And he went into the Pharisee's house, and sat down to meat.

37 And, behold, a woman in the city, which was a sinner, when she knew that *Jesus* sat at meat in the Pharisee's house, brought an alabaster box of ointment,

38 And stood at his feet behind *him* weeping, and began to wash his feet with tears, and did wipe *them* with the hairs of her head, and kissed his feet, and anointed *them* with the ointment.

39 Now when the Pharisee which had bidden him saw *it*, he spake within himself, saying, This man, if he were a prophet, would have known who and what manner of woman *this is* that toucheth him: for she is a sinner.

40 And Jesus answering said unto him, Simon, I have somewhat to say unto thee. And he saith, Master, say on.

41 (There was a certain creditor which had two debtors: the one owed five hundred pence, and the other fifty.

42 And when they had nothing to pay, he frankly forgave them both. Tell me therefore, which of them will love him most?

43 Simon answered and said, I suppose that *he*, to whom he forgave most. And he said unto him, Thou hast rightly judged.

44 (And he turned to the woman, and said unto Simon, Seest thou this woman? I entered into thine house, thou gavest me no water for my feet: but she hath washed my feet with tears, and wiped *them* with the hairs of her head.

45 Thou gavest me no kiss: but this woman since the time I came in hath not ceased to kiss my feet.

46 My head with oil thou didst not anoint: but this woman hath anointed my feet with ointment.

103

47 Wherefore I say unto thee, Her sins, which are many, are forgiven; for she loved much: but to whom little is forgiven, *the same* loveth little.

48 And he said unto her, Thy sins are forgiven.

49 And they that sat at meat with him began to say within themselves, Who is this that forgiveth sins also?

50 And he said to the woman, Thy faith hath saved thee; go in peace.

8 And it came to pass afterward, that he went throughout every city and village, preaching and shewing the glad tidings of the kingdom of God: and the twelve *were* with him,

2 And certain women, which had been healed of evil spirits and infirmities, Mary called Magdalene, out of whom went seven devils,

3 And Joanna the wife of Chuza Herod's steward, and Susanna, and many others, which ministered unto him of their substance.

4 ¶ And when much people were gathered together, and were come to him out of every city, he spake by a parable:

5 A sower went out to sow his seed: and as he sowed, some fell by the way side; and it was trodden down, and the fowls of the air devoured it.

6 And some fell upon a rock; and as soon as it was sprung up, it withered away, because it lacked moisture.

7 And some fell among thorns; and the thorns sprang up with it, and choked it.

8 And other fell on good ground, and sprang up, and bare fruit an hundredfold. And when he had said these things, he cried, He that hath ears to hear, let him hear.

9 And his disciples asked him, saying, What might this parable be?

10 And he said, Unto you it is given to know the mysteries of the kingdom of God: but to others in parables; that seeing they might not see, and hearing they might not understand.

11 Now the parable is this: The seed is the word of God.

12 Those by the way side are they that hear; then cometh the devil, and taketh away the word out of their hearts, lest they should believe and be saved.

13 They on the rock *are they*, which, when they hear, receive the word with joy; and these have no root, which for a while believe, and in time of temptation fall away.

14 And that which fell among thorns are they, which, when they have heard, go forth, and are choked with cares and riches and pleasures of *this* life, and bring no fruit to perfection.

15 But that on the good ground are they, which in an honest and good heart, having heard the word, keep *it*, and bring forth fruit with patience.

16 ¶ No man, when he hath lighted a candle, covereth it with

a vessel, or putteth *it* under a bed; but setteth *it* on a candlestick, that they which enter in may see the light.

17 For nothing is secret, that shall not be made manifest; neither *any* thing hid, that shall not be known and come abroad.

18 Take heed therefore how ye hear: for whosoever hath, to him shall be given; and whosoever hath not, from him shall be taken even that which he seemeth to have.

19 ¶ Then came to him *his* mother and his brethren, and could not come at him for the press.

20 And it was told him *by certain* which said, Thy mother and thy brethren stand without, desiring to see thee.

21 And he answered and said unto them, My mother and my brethren are these which hear the word of God, and do it.

22 ¶ Now it came to pass on a certain day, that he went into a ship with his disciples: and he said unto them, Let us go over unto the other side of the lake. And they launched forth.

23 But as they sailed he fell asleep: and there came down a storm of wind on the lake; and they were filled *with water*, and were in jeopardy.

24 And they came to him, and awoke him, saying, Master, master, we perish. Then he arose, and rebuked the wind and the raging of the water: and they ceased, and there was a calm.

25 And he said unto them, Where is your faith? And they being afraid wondered, saying one to another, What manner of man is this! for he commandeth even the winds and water, and they obey him.

26 ¶ And they arrived at the country of the Gadarenes, which is over against Galilee.

27 And when he went forth to land, there met him out of the city a certain man, which had devils long time, and ware no clothes, neither abode in *any* house, but in the tombs.

28 When he saw Jesus, he cried out, and fell down before him, and with a loud voice said, What have I to do with thee, Jesus, *thou* Son of God most high? I beseech thee, torment me not.

29 (For he had commanded the unclean spirit to come out of the man. For oftentimes it had caught him: and he was kept bound with chains and in fetters; and he brake the bands, and was driven of the devil into the wilderness.)

30 And Jesus asked him, saying, What is thy name? And he said, Legion: because many devils were entered into him.

31 And they besought him that he would not command them to go out into the deep.

32 And there was there an herd of many swine feeding on the mountain: and they besought him that he would suffer them to enter into them. And he suffered them.

33 Then went the devils out of the man, and entered into the swine: and the herd ran violently

down a steep place into the lake, and were choked.

34 When they that fed *them* saw what was done, they fled, and went and told *it* in the city and in the country.

35 Then they went out to see what was done; and came to Jesus, and found the man, out of whom the devils were departed, sitting at the feet of Jesus, clothed, and in his right mind: and they were afraid.

36 They also which saw *it* told them by what means he that was possessed of the devils was healed.

37 ¶ Then the whole multitude of the country of the Gadarenes round about besought him to depart from them; for they were taken with great fear: and he went up into the ship, and returned back again.

38 Now the man out of whom the devils were departed besought him that he might be with him: but Jesus sent him away, saying,

39 Return to thine own house, and shew how great things God hath done unto thee. And he went his way, and published throughout the whole city how great things Jesus had done unto him.

40 And it came to pass, that, when Jesus was returned, the people *gladly* received him: for they were all waiting for him.

41 ¶ And, behold, there came a man named Jairus, and he was a ruler of the synagogue: and he fell down at Jesus' feet, and besought him that he would come into his house:

42 For he had one only daughter, about twelve years of age, and she lay a dying. But as he went the people thronged him.

43 ¶ And a woman having an issue of blood twelve years, which had spent all her living upon physicians, neither could be healed of any,

44 Came behind *him*, and touched the border of his garment: and immediately her issue of blood stanched.

45 And Jesus said, Who touched me? When all denied, Peter and they that were with him said, Master, the multitude throng thee and press *thee*, and sayest thou, Who touched me?

46 And Jesus said, Somebody hath touched me: for I perceive that virtue is gone out of me.

47 And when the woman saw that she was not hid, she came trembling, and falling down before him, she declared unto him before all the people for what cause she had touched him, and how she was healed immediately.

48 And he said unto her, Daughter, be of good comfort: thy faith hath made thee whole; go in peace.

49 ¶ While he yet spake, there cometh one from the ruler of the synagogue's *house*, saying to him, Thy daughter is dead; trouble not the Master.

50 But when Jesus heard *it*, he answered her, saying, Fear not: believe only, and she shall be made whole.

106

51 And when he came into the house, he suffered no man to go in, save Peter, and James, and John, and the father and the mother of the maiden.

52 And they all wept, and bewailed her: but he said, Weep not; she is not dead, but sleepeth.

53 And they laughed him to scorn, knowing that she was dead.

54 And he put them all out, and took her by the hand, and called, saying, Maid, arise.

55 And her spirit came again, and she arose straightway: and he commanded to give her meat.

56 And her parents were astonished: but he charged them that they should tell no man what was done.

9

Then he called his twelve disciples together, and gave them power and authority over all devils, and to cure diseases.

2 And he sent them to preach the kingdom of God, and to heal the sick.

3 And he said unto them, Take nothing for *your* journey, neither staves, nor scrip, neither bread, neither money; neither have two coats apiece.

4 And whatsoever house ye enter into, there abide, and thence depart.

5 And whosoever will not receive you, when ye go out of that city, shake off the very dust from your feet for a testimony against them.

6 And they departed, and went through the towns, preaching the gospel, and healing every where.

7 ¶ Now Herod the tetrarch heard of all that was done by him: and he was perplexed, because that it was said of some, that John was risen from the dead;

8 And of some, that Elias had appeared; and of others, that one of the old prophets was risen again.

9 And Herod said, John have I beheaded: but who is this, of whom I hear such things? And he desired to see him.

10 ¶ And the apostles, when they were returned, told him all that they had done. And he took them, and went aside privately into a desert place belonging to the city called Bethsaida.

11 And the people, when they knew *it*, followed him: and he received them, and spake unto them of the kingdom of God, and healed them that had need of healing.

12 And when the day began to wear away, then came the twelve, and said unto him, Send the multitude away, that they may go into the towns and country round about, and lodge, and get victuals: for we are here in a desert place.

13 But he said unto them, Give ye them to eat. And they said, We have no more but five loaves and two fishes; except we should go and buy meat for all this people.

14 For they were about five thousand men. And he said to his disciples, Make them sit down by fifties in a company.

15 And they did so, and made

them all sit down.

16 Then he took the five loaves and the two fishes, and looking up to heaven, he blessed them, and brake, and gave to the disciples to set before the multitude.

17 And they did eat, and were all filled: and there was taken up of fragments that remained to them twelve baskets.

18 ¶ And it came to pass, as he was alone praying, his disciples were with him: and he asked them, saying, Whom say the people that I am?

19 They answering said, John the Baptist; but some say, Elias; and others say, that one of the old prophets is risen again.

20 He said unto them, But whom say ye that I am? Peter answering said, The Christ of God.

21 And he straitly charged them, and commanded them to tell no man that thing;

22 Saying, The Son of man must suffer many things, and be rejected of the elders and chief priests and scribes, and be slain, and be raised the third day.

23 ¶ And he said to them all, If any man will come after me, let him deny himself, and take up his cross daily, and follow me.

24 For whosoever will save his life shall lose it: but whosoever will lose his life for my sake, the same shall save it.

25 For what is a man advantaged, if he gain the whole world, and lose himself, or be cast away?

26 For whosoever shall be ashamed of me and of my words, of him shall the Son of man be ashamed, when he shall come in his own glory, and in his Father's, and of the holy angels.

27 But I tell you of a truth, there be some standing here, which shall not taste of death, till they see the kingdom of God.

28 ¶ And it came to pass about an eight days after these sayings, he took Peter and John and James, and went up into a mountain to pray.

29 And as he prayed, the fashion of his countenance was altered, and his raiment was white and glistering.

30 And, behold, there talked with him two men, which were Moses and Elias:

31 Who appeared in glory, and spake of his decease which he should accomplish at Jerusalem.

32 But Peter and they that were with him were heavy with sleep: and when they were awake, they saw his glory, and the two men that stood with him.

33 And it came to pass, as they departed from him, Peter said unto Jesus, Master, it is good for us to be here: and let us make three tabernacles; one for thee, and one for Moses, and one for Elias: not knowing what he said.

34 While he thus spake, there came a cloud, and overshadowed them: and they feared as they entered into the cloud.

35 And there came a voice out of the cloud, saying, This is my beloved Son: hear him.

36 And when the voice was past, Jesus was found alone. And they kept *it* close, and told no man in those days any of those things which they had seen.

37 ¶ And it came to pass, that on the next day, when they were come down from the hill, much people met him.

38 And, behold, a man of the company cried out, saying, Master, I beseech thee, look upon my son: for he is mine only child.

39 And, lo, a spirit taketh him, and he suddenly crieth out; and it teareth him that he foameth again, and bruising him hardly departeth from him.

40 And I besought thy disciples to cast him out; and they could not.

41 And Jesus answering said, O faithless and perverse generation, how long shall I be with you, and suffer you? Bring thy son hither.

42 And as he was yet a coming, the devil threw him down, and tare *him*. And Jesus rebuked the unclean spirit, and healed the child, and delivered him again to his father.

43 ¶ And they were all amazed at the mighty power of God. But while they wondered every one at all things which Jesus did, he said unto his disciples,

44 Let these sayings sink down into your ears: for the Son of man shall be delivered into the hands of men.

45 But they understood not this saying, and it was hid from them, that they perceived it not: and they feared to ask him of that saying.

46 ¶ Then there arose a reasoning among them, which of them should be greatest.

47 And Jesus, perceiving the thought of their heart, took a child, and set him by him,

48 And said unto them, Whosoever shall receive this child in my name receiveth me: and whosoever shall receive me receiveth him that sent me: for he that is least among you all, the same shall be great.

49 ¶ And John answered and said, Master, we saw one casting out devils in thy name; and we forbad him, because he followeth not with us.

50 And Jesus said unto him, Forbid *him* not: for he that is not against us is for us.

51 ¶ And it came to pass, when the time was come that he should be received up, he stedfastly set his face to go to Jerusalem,

52 And sent messengers before his face: and they went, and entered into a village of the Samaritans, to make ready for him.

53 And they did not receive him, because his face was as though he would go to Jerusalem.

54 And when his disciples James and John saw *this*, they said, Lord, wilt thou that we command fire to come down from heaven, and consume them, even as Elias did?

55 But he turned, and rebuked them, and said, Ye know not what manner of spirit ye are of.

56 For the Son of man is not come to destroy men's lives, but to save *them.* And they went to another village.

57 ¶ And it came to pass, that, as they went in the way, a certain *man* said unto him, Lord, I will follow thee whithersoever thou goest.

58 And Jesus said unto him, Foxes have holes, and birds of the air *have* nests; but the Son of man hath not where to lay *his* head.

59 And he said unto another, Follow me. But he said, Lord, suffer me first to go and bury my father.

60 Jesus said unto him, Let the dead bury their dead: but go thou and preach the kingdom of God.

61 And another also said, Lord, I will follow thee; but let me first go bid them farewell, which are at home at my house.

62 And Jesus said unto him, No man, having put his hand to the plough, and looking back, is fit for the kingdom of God.

10

After these things the Lord appointed other seventy also, and sent them two and two before his face into every city and place, whither he himself would come.

2 Therefore said he unto them, The harvest truly *is* great, but the labourers *are* few: pray ye therefore the Lord of the harvest, that he would send forth labourers into his harvest.

3 Go your ways: behold, I send you forth as lambs among wolves.

4 Carry neither purse, nor scrip, nor shoes: and salute no man by the way.

5 And into whatsoever house ye enter, first say, Peace *be* to this house.

6 And if the son of peace be there, your peace shall rest upon it: if not, it shall turn to you again.

7 And in the same house remain, eating and drinking such things as they give: for the labourer is worthy of his hire. Go not from house to house.

8 And into whatsoever city ye enter, and they receive you, eat such things as are set before you:

9 And heal the sick that are therein, and say unto them, The kingdom of God is come nigh unto you.

10 ¶ But into whatsoever city ye enter, and they receive you not, go your ways out into the streets of the same, and say,

11 Even the very dust of your city, which cleaveth on us, we do wipe off against you: notwithstanding *be* ye sure of this, that the kingdom of God is come nigh unto you.

12 But I say unto you, that it shall be more tolerable in that day for Sodom, than for that city.

13 ¶ Woe unto thee, Chorazin! woe unto thee, Bethsaida! for if the mighty works had been done in Tyre and Sidon, which have been done in you, they had a

great while ago repented, sitting in sackcloth and ashes.

14 But it shall be more tolerable for Tyre and Sidon at the judgment, than for you.

15 And thou, Capernaum, which art exalted to heaven, shalt be thrust down to hell.

16 He that heareth you heareth me; and he that despiseth you despiseth me; and he that despiseth me despiseth him that sent me.

17 ¶ And the seventy returned again with joy, saying, Lord, even the devils are subject unto us through thy name.

18 And he said unto them, I beheld Satan as lightning fall from heaven.

19 Behold, I give unto you power to tread on serpents and scorpions, and over all the power of the enemy: and nothing shall by any means hurt you.

20 Notwithstanding in this rejoice not, that the spirits are subject unto you; but rather rejoice, because your names are written in heaven.

21 ¶ In that hour Jesus rejoiced in spirit, and said, I thank thee, O Father, Lord of heaven and earth, that thou hast hid these things from the wise and prudent, and hast revealed them unto babes: even so, Father; for so it seemed good in thy sight.

22 All things are delivered to me of my Father: and no man knoweth who the Son is, but the Father; and who the Father is, but the Son, and he to whom the Son will reveal him.

23 ¶ And he turned him unto his disciples, and said privately, Blessed are the eyes which see the things that ye see:

24 For I tell you, that many prophets and kings have desired to see those things which ye see, and have not seen them; and to hear those things which ye hear, and have not heard them.

25 ¶ And, behold, a certain lawyer stood up, and tempted him, saying, Master, what shall I do to inherit eternal life?

26 He said unto him, What is written in the law? how readest thou?

27 And he answering said, Thou shalt love the Lord thy God with all thy heart, and with all thy soul, and with all thy strength, and with all thy mind; and thy neighbour as thyself.

28 And he said unto him, Thou hast answered right: this do, and thou shalt live.

29 But he, willing to justify himself, said unto Jesus, And who is my neighbour?

30 And Jesus answering said, A certain man went down from Jerusalem to Jericho, and fell among thieves, which stripped him of his raiment, and wounded him, and departed, leaving him half dead.

31 And by chance there came down a certain priest that way: and when he saw him, he passed by on the other side.

32 And likewise a Levite, when he was at the place, came and looked on him, and passed by on the other side.

33 But a certain Samaritan, as he journeyed, came where he was: and when he saw him, he had compassion *on him*,

34 And went to *him*, and bound up his wounds, pouring in oil and wine, and set him on his own beast, and brought him to an inn, and took care of him.

35 And on the morrow when he departed, he took out two pence, and gave *them* to the host, and said unto him, Take care of him; and whatsoever thou spendest more, when I come again, I will repay thee.

36 Which now of these three, thinkest thou, was neighbour unto him that fell among the thieves?

37 And he said, He that shewed mercy on him. Then said Jesus unto him, Go, and do thou likewise.

38 ¶ Now it came to pass, as they went, that he entered into a certain village: and a certain woman named Martha received him into her house.

39 And she had a sister called Mary, which also sat at Jesus' feet, and heard his word.

40 But Martha was cumbered about much serving, and came to him, and said, Lord, dost thou not care that my sister hath left me to serve alone? bid her therefore that she help me.

41 And Jesus answered and said unto her, Martha, Martha, thou art careful and troubled about many things:

42 But one thing is needful: and Mary hath chosen that good part, which shall not be taken away from her.

11

And it came to pass, that, as he was praying in a certain place, when he ceased, one of his disciples said unto him, Lord, teach us to pray, as John also taught his disciples.

2 And he said unto them, When ye pray, say, Our Father which art in heaven, Hallowed be thy name. Thy kingdom come. Thy will be done, as in heaven, so in earth.

3 Give us day by day our daily bread.

4 And forgive us our sins; for we also forgive every one that is indebted to us. And lead us not into temptation; but deliver us from evil.

5 ¶ And he said unto them, Which of you shall have a friend, and shall go unto him at midnight, and say unto him, Friend, lend me three loaves;

6 For a friend of mine in his journey is come to me, and I have nothing to set before him?

7 And he from within shall answer and say, Trouble me not: the door is now shut, and my children are with me in bed; I cannot rise and give thee.

8 I say unto you, Though he will not rise and give him, because he is his friend, yet because of his importunity he will rise and give him as many as he needeth.

9 And I say unto you, Ask, and it shall be given you; seek, and ye shall find; knock, and it shall be opened unto you.

10 For every one that asketh receiveth; and he that seeketh findeth; and to him that knocketh it shall be opened.

11 If a son shall ask bread of any of you that is a father, will he give him a stone? or if *he ask* a fish, will he for a fish give him a serpent?

12 Or if he shall ask an egg, will he offer him a scorpion?

13 If ye then, being evil, know how to give good gifts unto your children: how much more shall *your* heavenly Father give the Holy Spirit to them that ask him?

14 ¶ And he was casting out a devil, and it was dumb. And it came to pass, when the devil was gone out, the dumb spake; and the people wondered.

15 But some of them said, He casteth out devils through Beelzebub the chief of the devils.

16 And others, tempting *him*, sought of him a sign from heaven.

17 ¶ But he, knowing their thoughts, said unto them, Every kingdom divided against itself is brought to desolation; and a house *divided* against a house falleth.

18 If Satan also be divided against himself, how shall his kingdom stand? because ye say that I cast out devils through Beelzebub.

19 And if I by Beelzebub cast out devils, by whom do your sons cast *them* out? therefore shall they be your judges.

20 But if I with the finger of God cast out devils, no doubt the kingdom of God is come upon you.

21 When a strong man armed keepeth his palace, his goods are in peace:

22 But when a stronger than he shall come upon him, and overcome him, he taketh from him all his armour wherein he trusted, and divideth his spoils.

23 He that is not with me is against me: and he that gathereth not with me scattereth.

24 When the unclean spirit is gone out of a man, he walketh through dry places, seeking rest; and finding none, he saith, I will return unto my house whence I came out.

25 And when he cometh, he findeth *it* swept and garnished.

26 Then goeth he, and taketh *to him* seven other spirits more wicked than himself; and they enter in, and dwell there: and the last *state* of that man is worse than the first.

27 ¶ And it came to pass, as he spake these things, a certain woman of the company lifted up her voice, and said unto him, Blessed *is* the womb that bare thee, and the paps which thou hast sucked.

28 But he said, Yea rather, blessed *are* they that hear the word of God, and keep it.

29 ¶ And when the people were gathered thick together, he began to say, This is an evil generation: they seek a sign; and there shall no sign be given it, but the sign of Jonas the prophet.

30 For as Jonas was a sign unto the Ninevites, so shall also the Son of man be to this generation.

31 The queen of the south shall rise up in the judgment with the men of this generation, and condemn them: for she came from the utmost parts of the earth to hear the wisdom of Solomon; and, behold, a greater than Solomon *is* here.

32 The men of Nineve shall rise up in the judgment with this generation, and shall condemn it: for they repented at the preaching of Jonas; and, behold, a greater than Jonas *is* here.

33 ¶ No man, when he hath lighted a candle, putteth *it* in a secret place, neither under a bushel, but on a candlestick, that they which come in may see the light.

34 The light of the body is the eye: therefore when thine eye is single, thy whole body also is full of light; but when *thine eye* is evil, thy body also is full of darkness.

35 Take heed therefore that the light which is in thee be not darkness.

36 If thy whole body therefore *be* full of light, having no part dark, the whole shall be full of light, as when the bright shining of a candle doth give thee light.

37 ¶ And as he spake, a certain Pharisee besought him to dine with him: and he went in, and sat down to meat.

38 And when the Pharisee saw *it*, he marvelled that he had not first washed before dinner.

39 And the Lord said unto him, Now do ye Pharisees make clean the outside of the cup and the platter; but your inward part is full of ravening and wickedness.

40 *Ye* fools, did not he that made that which is without make that which is within also?

41 But rather give alms of such things as ye have; and, behold, all things are clean unto you.

42 But woe unto you, Pharisees! for ye tithe mint and rue and all manner of herbs, and pass over judgment and the love of God: these ought ye to have done, and not to leave the other undone.

43 Woe unto you, Pharisees! for ye love the uppermost seats in the synagogues, and greetings in the markets.

44 Woe unto you, scribes and Pharisees, hypocrites! for ye are as graves which appear not, and the men that walk over *them* are not aware of *them*.

45 ¶ Then answered one of the lawyers, and said unto him, Master, thus saying thou reproachest us also.

46 And he said, Woe unto you also, *ye* lawyers! for ye lade men with burdens grievous to be borne, and ye yourselves touch not the burdens with one of your fingers.

47 Woe unto you! for ye build the sepulchres of the prophets, and your fathers killed them.

48 Truly ye bear witness that ye allow the deeds of your fathers: for they indeed killed them, and ye build their sepulchres.

49 Therefore also said the wis-

dom of God, I will send them prophets and apostles, and *some* of them they shall slay and persecute:

50 That the blood of all the prophets, which was shed from the foundation of the world, may be required of this generation;

51 From the blood of Abel unto the blood of Zacharias, which perished between the altar and the temple: verily I say unto you, It shall be required of this generation.

52 Woe unto you, lawyers! for ye have taken away the key of knowledge: ye entered not in yourselves, and them that were entering in ye hindered.

53 And as he said these things unto them, the scribes and the Pharisees began to urge *him* vehemently, and to provoke him to speak of many things:

54 Laying wait for him, and seeking to catch something out of his mouth, that they might accuse him.

12 In the mean time, when there were gathered together an innumerable multitude of people, insomuch that they trode one upon another, he began to say unto his disciples first of all, Beware ye of the leaven of the Pharisees, which is hypocrisy.

2 For there is nothing covered, that shall not be revealed; neither hid, that shall not be known.

3 Therefore whatsoever ye have spoken in darkness shall be heard in the light; and that which ye have spoken in the ear in clos-

ets shall be proclaimed upon the housetops.

4 ¶ And I say unto you my friends, Be not afraid of them that kill the body, and after that have no more that they can do.

5 But I will forewarn you whom ye shall fear: Fear him, which after he hath killed hath power to cast into hell; yea, I say unto you, Fear him.

6 Are not five sparrows sold for two farthings, and not one of them is forgotten before God?

7 But even the very hairs of your head are all numbered. Fear not therefore: ye are of more value than many sparrows.

8 Also I say unto you, Whosoever shall confess me before men, him shall the Son of man also confess before the angels of God:

9 But he that denieth me before men shall be denied before the angels of God.

10 And whosoever shall speak a word against the Son of man, it shall be forgiven him: but unto him that blasphemeth against the Holy Ghost it shall not be forgiven.

11 And when they bring you unto the synagogues, and *unto* magistrates, and powers, take ye no thought how or what thing ye shall answer, or what ye shall say:

12 For the Holy Ghost shall teach you in the same hour what ye ought to say.

13 ¶ And one of the company said unto him, Master, speak to my brother, that he divide the

115

inheritance with me.

14 And he said to him, Man, who made me a judge or a divider over you?

15 And he said unto them, Take heed, and beware of covetousness: for a man's life consisteth not in the abundance of the things which he possesseth.

16 ❧ And he spake a parable unto them, saying, The ground of a certain rich man brought forth plentifully:

17 And he thought within himself, saying, What shall I do, because I have no room where to bestow my fruits?

18 And he said, This will I do: I will pull down my barns, and build greater; and there will I bestow all my fruits and my goods.

19 And I will say to my soul, Soul, thou hast much goods laid up for many years; take thine ease, eat, drink, *and* be merry.

20 But God said unto him, *Thou* fool, this night thy soul shall be required of thee: then whose shall those things be, which thou hast provided?

21 So *is* he that layeth up treasure for himself, and is not rich toward God.

22 ❧ And he said unto his disciples, Therefore I say unto you, Take no thought for your life, what ye shall eat; neither for the body, what ye shall put on.

23 The life is more than meat, and the body *is* more than raiment.

24 Consider the ravens: for they neither sow nor reap; which nei-

ther have storehouse nor barn; and God feedeth them: how much more are ye better than the fowls?

25 And which of you with taking thought can add to his stature one cubit?

26 If ye then be not able to do that thing which is least, why take ye thought for the rest?

27 Consider the lilies how they grow: they toil not, they spin not; and yet I say unto you, that Solomon in all his glory was not arrayed like one of these.

28 If then God so clothe the grass, which is to day in the field, and to morrow is cast into the oven; how much more *will he clothe* you, O ye of little faith?

29 And seek not ye what ye shall eat, or what ye shall drink, neither be ye of doubtful mind.

30 For all these things do the nations of the world seek after: and your Father knoweth that ye have need of these things.

31 ❧ But rather seek ye the kingdom of God, and all these things shall be added unto you.

32 Fear not, little flock; for it is your Father's good pleasure to give you the kingdom.

33 Sell that ye have, and give alms; provide yourselves bags which wax not old, a treasure in the heavens that faileth not, where no thief approacheth, neither moth corrupteth.

34 For where your treasure is, there will your heart be also.

35 Let your loins be girded about, and *your* lights burning;

116

³⁶ And ye yourselves like unto men that wait for their lord, when he will return from the wedding; that when he cometh and knocketh, they may open unto him immediately.

³⁷ Blessed *are* those servants, whom the lord when he cometh shall find watching: verily I say unto you, that he shall gird himself, and make them to sit down to meat, and will come forth and serve them.

³⁸ And if he shall come in the second watch, or come in the third watch, and find *them* so, blessed are those servants.

³⁹ And this know, that if the goodman of the house had known what hour the thief would come, he would have watched, and not have suffered his house to be broken through.

⁴⁰ Be ye therefore ready also: for the Son of man cometh at an hour when ye think not.

⁴¹ ❛ Then Peter said unto him, Lord, speakest thou this parable unto us, or even to all?

⁴² And the Lord said, Who then is that faithful and wise steward, whom *his* lord shall make ruler over his household, to give *them their* portion of meat in due season?

⁴³ Blessed *is* that servant, whom his lord when he cometh shall find so doing.

⁴⁴ Of a truth I say unto you, that he will make him ruler over all that he hath.

⁴⁵ But and if that servant say in his heart, My lord delayeth his coming; and shall begin to beat the menservants and maidens, and to eat and drink, and to be drunken;

⁴⁶ The lord of that servant will come in a day when he looketh not for *him*, and at an hour when he is not aware, and will cut him in sunder and will appoint him his portion with the unbelievers.

⁴⁷ And that servant, which knew his lord's will, and prepared not *himself*, neither did according to his will, shall be beaten with many *stripes*.

⁴⁸ But he that knew not, and did commit things worthy of stripes, shall be beaten with few *stripes*. For unto whomsoever much is given, of him shall be much required: and to whom men have committed much, of him they will ask the more.

⁴⁹ ❛ I am come to send fire on the earth; and what will I, if it be already kindled?

⁵⁰ But I have a baptism to be baptized with; and how am I straitened till it be accomplished?

⁵¹ Suppose ye that I am come to give peace on earth? I tell you, Nay; but rather division:

⁵² For from henceforth there shall be five in one house divided, three against two, and two against three.

⁵³ The father shall be divided against the son, and the son against the father; the mother against the daughter, and the daughter against the mother; the mother in law against her daughter in law, and the daughter in law against her mother in law.

54 ¶ And he said also to the people, When ye see a cloud rise out of the west, straightway ye say, There cometh a shower; and so it is.

55 And when ye see the south wind blow, ye say, There will be heat; and it cometh to pass.

56 Ye hypocrites, ye can discern the face of the sky and of the earth; but how is it that ye do not discern this time?

57 Yea, and why even of yourselves judge ye not what is right?

58 ¶ When thou goest with thine adversary to the magistrate, as thou art in the way, give diligence that thou mayest be delivered from him; lest he hale thee to the judge, and the judge deliver thee to the officer, and the officer cast thee into prison.

59 I tell thee, thou shalt not depart thence, till thou hast paid the very last mite.

13 There were present at that season some that told him of the Galilaeans, whose blood Pilate had mingled with their sacrifices.

2 And Jesus answering said unto them, Suppose ye that these Galilaeans were sinners above all the Galilaeans, because they suffered such things?

3 I tell you, Nay: but, except ye repent, ye shall all likewise perish.

4 Or those eighteen, upon whom the tower in Siloam fell, and slew them, think ye that they were sinners above all men that dwelt in Jerusalem?

5 I tell you, Nay: but, except ye repent, ye shall all likewise perish.

6 ¶ He spake also this parable; A certain man had a fig tree planted in his vineyard; and he came and sought fruit thereon, and found none.

7 Then said he unto the dresser of his vineyard, Behold, these three years I come seeking fruit on this fig tree, and find none: cut it down; why cumbereth it the ground?

8 And he answering said unto him, Lord, let it alone this year also, till I shall dig about it, and dung it:

9 And if it bear fruit, well: and if not, then after that thou shalt cut it down.

10 And he was teaching in one of the synagogues on the sabbath.

11 ¶ And, behold, there was a woman which had a spirit of infirmity eighteen years, and was bowed together, and could in no wise lift up herself.

12 And when Jesus saw her, he called her to him, and said unto her, Woman, thou art loosed from thine infirmity.

13 And he laid his hands on her: and immediately she was made straight, and glorified God.

14 And the ruler of the synagogue answered with indignation, because that Jesus had healed on the sabbath day, and said unto the people, There are six days in which men ought to

work: in them therefore come and be healed, and not on the sabbath day.

15 The Lord then answered him, and said, *Thou* hypocrite, doth not each one of you on the sabbath loose his ox or *his* ass from the stall, and lead *him* away to watering?

16 And ought not this woman, being a daughter of Abraham, whom Satan hath bound, lo, these eighteen years, be loosed from this bond on the sabbath day?

17 And when he had said these things, all his adversaries were ashamed: and all the people rejoiced for all the glorious things that were done by him.

18 ¶ Then said he, Unto what is the kingdom of God like? and whereunto shall I resemble it?

19 It is like a grain of mustard seed, which a man took, and cast into his garden; and it grew, and waxed a great tree; and the fowls of the air lodged in the branches of it.

20 ¶ And again he said, Whereunto shall I liken the kingdom of God?

21 It is like leaven, which a woman took and hid in three measures of meal, till the whole was leavened.

22 ¶ And he went through the cities and villages, teaching, and journeying toward Jerusalem.

23 Then said one unto him, Lord, are there few that be saved? And he said unto them,

24 ¶ Strive to enter in at the strait gate: for many, I say unto you, will seek to enter in, and shall not be able.

25 When once the master of the house is risen up, and hath shut to the door, and ye begin to stand without, and to knock at the door, saying, Lord, Lord, open unto us; and he shall answer and say unto you, I know you not whence ye are:

26 Then shall ye begin to say, We have eaten and drunk in thy presence, and thou hast taught in our streets.

27 But he shall say, I tell you, I know you not whence ye are; depart from me, all *ye* workers of iniquity.

28 There shall be weeping and gnashing of teeth, when ye shall see Abraham, and Isaac, and Jacob, and all the prophets, in the kingdom of God, and you *yourselves* thrust out.

29 And they shall come from the east, and *from* the west, and from the north, and *from* the south, and shall sit down in the kingdom of God.

30 And, behold, there are last which shall be first, and there are first which shall be last.

31 ¶ The same day there came certain of the Pharisees, saying unto him, Get thee out, and depart hence: for Herod will kill thee.

32 And he said unto them, Go ye, and tell that fox, Behold, I cast out devils, and I do cures to day and to morrow, and the third *day* I shall be perfected.

33 ¶ Nevertheless I must walk to day, and to morrow, and the *day*

following: for it cannot be that a prophet perish out of Jerusalem.

34 O Jerusalem, Jerusalem, which killest the prophets, and stonest them that are sent unto thee; how often would I have gathered thy children together, as a hen *doth gather* her brood under *her* wings, and ye would not!

35 Behold, your house is left unto you desolate: and verily I say unto you, Ye shall not see me, until *the time* come when ye shall say, Blessed *is* he that cometh in the name of the Lord.

14 And it came to pass, as he went into the house of one of the chief Pharisees to eat bread on the sabbath day, that they watched him.

2 And, behold, there was a certain man before him which had the dropsy.

3 And Jesus answering spake unto the lawyers and Pharisees, saying, Is it lawful to heal on the sabbath day?

4 And they held their peace. And he took *him*, and healed him, and let him go;

5 And answered them, saying, Which of you shall have an ass or an ox fallen into a pit, and will not straightway pull him out on the sabbath day?

6 And they could not answer him again to these things.

7 ¶ And he put forth a parable to those which were bidden, when he marked how they chose out the chief rooms; saying unto them.

8 When thou art bidden of any *man* to a wedding, sit not down in the highest room; lest a more honourable man than thou be bidden of him;

9 And he that bade thee and him come and say to thee, Give this man place; and thou begin with shame to take the lowest room.

10 But when thou art bidden, go and sit down in the lowest room; that when he that bade thee cometh, he may say unto thee, Friend, go up higher: then shalt thou have worship in the presence of them that sit at meat with thee.

11 For whosoever exalteth himself shall be abased; and he that humbleth himself shall be exalted.

12 ¶ Then said he also to him that bade him, When thou makest a dinner or a supper, call not thy friends, nor thy brethren, neither thy kinsmen, nor *thy* rich neighbours; lest they also bid thee again, and a recompence be made thee.

13 But when thou makest a feast, call the poor, the maimed, the lame, the blind:

14 And thou shalt be blessed; for they cannot recompense thee: for thou shalt be recompensed at the resurrection of the just.

15 ¶ And when one of them that sat at meat with him heard these things, he said unto him, Blessed *is* he that shall eat bread in the kingdom of God.

16 Then said he unto him, A certain man made a great supper, and bade many:

17 And sent his servant at supper time to say to them that were bidden, Come; for all things are now ready.

18 And they all with one *consent* began to make excuse. The first said unto him, I have bought a piece of ground, and I must needs go and see it: I pray thee have me excused.

19 And another said, I have bought five yoke of oxen, and I go to prove them: I pray thee have me excused.

20 And another said, I have married a wife, and therefore I cannot come.

21 So that servant came, and shewed his lord these things. Then the master of the house being angry said to his servant, Go out quickly into the streets and lanes of the city, and bring in hither the poor, and the maimed, and the halt, and the blind.

22 And the servant said, Lord, it is done as thou hast commanded, and yet there is room.

23 And the lord said unto the servant, Go out into the highways and hedges, and compel *them* to come in, that my house may be filled.

24 For I say unto you, That none of those men which were bidden shall taste of my supper.

25 ¶ And there went great multitudes with him: and he turned, and said unto them,

26 If any *man* come to me, and hate not his father, and mother, and wife, and children, and brethren, and sisters, yea, and his own life also, he cannot be my disciple.

27 And whosoever doth not bear his cross, and come after me, cannot be my disciple.

28 For which of you, intending to build a tower, sitteth not down first, and counteth the cost, whether he have *sufficient* to finish *it*?

29 Lest haply, after he hath laid the foundation, and is not able to finish *it*, all that behold *it* begin to mock him,

30 Saying, This man began to build, and was not able to finish.

31 Or what king, going to make war against another king, sitteth not down first, and consulteth whether he be able with ten thousand to meet him that cometh against him with twenty thousand?

32 Or else, while the other is yet a great way off, he sendeth an ambassage, and desireth conditions of peace.

33 So likewise, whosoever he be of you that forsaketh not all that he hath, he cannot be my disciple.

34 ¶ Salt *is* good: but if the salt have lost his savour, wherewith shall it be seasoned?

35 It is neither fit for the land, nor yet for the dunghill; *but* men cast it out. He that hath ears to hear, let him hear.

15

Then drew near unto him all the publicans and sinners for to hear him.

2 And the Pharisees and scribes murmured, saying, This man receiveth sinners, and eateth with

them.

3 ¶ And he spake this parable unto them, saying,

4 What man of you, having an hundred sheep, if he lose one of them, doth not leave the ninety and nine in the wilderness, and go after that which is lost, until he find it?

5 And when he hath found *it*, he layeth *it* on his shoulders, rejoicing.

6 And when he cometh home, he calleth together *his* friends and neighbours, saying unto them, Rejoice with me; for I have found my sheep which was lost.

7 I say unto you, that likewise joy shall be in heaven over one sinner that repenteth, more than over ninety and nine just persons, which need no repentance.

8 ¶ Either what woman having ten pieces of silver, if she lose one piece, doth not light a candle, and sweep the house, and seek diligently till she find *it*?

9 And when she hath found *it*, she calleth *her* friends and *her* neighbours together, saying, Rejoice with me; for I have found the piece which I had lost.

10 Likewise, I say unto you, there is joy in the presence of the angels of God over one sinner that repenteth.

11 ¶ And he said, A certain man had two sons:

12 And the younger of them said to *his* father, Father, give me the portion of goods that falleth *to* me. And he divided unto them *his* living.

13 And not many days after the younger son gathered all together, and took his journey into a far country, and there wasted his substance with riotous living.

14 And when he had spent all, there arose a mighty famine in that land; and he began to be in want.

15 And he went and joined himself to a citizen of that country; and he sent him into his fields to feed swine.

16 And he would fain have filled his belly with the husks that the swine did eat: and no man gave unto him.

17 And when he came to himself, he said, How many hired servants of my father's have bread enough and to spare, and I perish with hunger!

18 I will arise and go to my father, and will say unto him, Father, I have sinned against heaven, and before thee,

19 And am no more worthy to be called thy son: make me as one of thy hired servants.

20 And he arose, and came to his father. But when he was yet a great way off, his father saw him, and had compassion, and ran, and fell on his neck, and kissed him.

21 And the son said unto him, Father, I have sinned against heaven, and in thy sight, and am no more worthy to be called thy son.

22 But the father said to his servants, Bring forth the best robe, and put *it* on him; and put a ring on his hand, and shoes on *his* feet:

23 And bring hither the fatted calf, and kill *it*; and let us eat, and be merry:

24 For this my son was dead, and is alive again; he was lost, and is found. And they began to be merry.

25 Now his elder son was in the field: and as he came and drew nigh to the house, he heard musick and dancing.

26 And he called one of the servants, and asked what these things meant.

27 And he said unto him, Thy brother is come; and thy father hath killed the fatted calf, because he hath received him safe and sound.

28 And he was angry, and would not go in: therefore came his father out, and intreated him.

29 And he answering said to *his* father, Lo, these many years do I serve thee, neither transgressed I at any time thy commandment: and yet thou never gavest me a kid, that I might make merry with my friends:

30 But as soon as this thy son was come, which hath devoured thy living with harlots, thou hast killed for him the fatted calf.

31 And he said unto him, Son, thou art ever with me, and all that I have is thine.

32 It was meet that we should make merry, and be glad: for this thy brother was dead, and is alive again; and was lost, and is found.

16 And he said also unto his disciples, There was a certain rich man, which had a steward; and the same was accused unto him that he had wasted his goods.

2 And he called him, and said unto him, How is it that I hear this of thee? give an account of thy stewardship; for thou mayest be no longer steward.

3 Then the steward said within himself, What shall I do? for my lord taketh away from me the stewardship: I cannot dig; to beg I am ashamed.

4 I am resolved what to do, that, when I am put out of the stewardship, they may receive me into their houses.

5 So he called every one of his lord's debtors *unto him*, and said unto the first, How much owest thou unto my lord?

6 And he said, An hundred measures of oil. And he said unto him, Take thy bill, and sit down quickly, and write fifty.

7 Then said he to another, And how much owest thou? And he said, An hundred measures of wheat. And he said unto him, Take thy bill, and write fourscore.

8 And the lord commended the unjust steward, because he had done wisely: for the children of this world are in their generation wiser than the children of light.

9 And I say unto you, Make to yourselves friends of the mammon of unrighteousness; that, when ye fail, they may receive you into everlasting habitations.

10 He that is faithful in that which is least is faithful also in

123

much: and he that is unjust in the least is unjust also in much.

11 If therefore ye have not been faithful in the unrighteous mammon, who will commit to your trust the true *riches*?

12 And if ye have not been faithful in that which is another man's, who shall give you that which is your own?

13 ¶ No servant can serve two masters: for either he will hate the one, and love the other; or else he will hold to the one, and despise the other. Ye cannot serve God and mammon.

14 And the Pharisees also, who were covetous, heard all these things: and they derided him.

15 And he said unto them, Ye are they which justify yourselves before men; but God knoweth your hearts: for that which is highly esteemed among men is abomination in the sight of God.

16 The law and the prophets *were* until John: since that time the kingdom of God is preached, and every man presseth into it.

17 And it is easier for heaven and earth to pass, than one tittle of the law to fail.

18 ¶ Whosoever putteth away his wife, and marrieth another, committeth adultery: and whosoever marrieth her that is put away from *her* husband committeth adultery.

19 ¶ There was a certain rich man, which was clothed in purple and fine linen, and fared sumptuously every day:

20 And there was a certain beggar named Lazarus, which was laid at his gate, full of sores,

21 And desiring to be fed with the crumbs which fell from the rich man's table: moreover the dogs came and licked his sores.

22 And it came to pass, that the beggar died, and was carried by the angels into Abraham's bosom: the rich man also died, and was buried;

23 And in hell he lift up his eyes, being in torments, and seeth Abraham afar off, and Lazarus in his bosom.

24 And he cried and said, Father Abraham, have mercy on me, and send Lazarus, that he may dip the tip of his finger in water, and cool my tongue; for I am tormented in this flame.

25 But Abraham said, Son, remember that thou in thy lifetime receivedst thy good things, and likewise Lazarus evil things: but now he is comforted, and thou art tormented.

26 And beside all this, between us and you there is a great gulf fixed: so that they which would pass from hence to you cannot; neither can they pass to us, that *would come* from thence.

27 Then he said, I pray thee therefore, father, that thou wouldest send him to my father's house:

28 For I have five brethren; that he may testify unto them, lest they also come into this place of torment.

29 Abraham saith unto him, They have Moses and the prophets; let them hear them.

30 And he said, Nay, father Abraham: but if one went unto them from the dead, they will repent.

31 And he said unto him, If they hear not Moses and the prophets, neither will they be persuaded, though one rose from the dead.

17 Then said he unto the disciples, It is impossible but that offences will come: but woe *unto him*, through whom they come!

2 It were better for him that a millstone were hanged about his neck, and he cast into the sea, than that he should offend one of these little ones.

3 ℂ Take heed to yourselves: If thy brother trespass against thee, rebuke him; and if he repent, forgive him.

4 And if he trespass against thee seven times in a day, and seven times in a day turn again to thee, saying, I repent; thou shalt forgive him.

5 ℂ And the apostles said unto the Lord, Increase our faith.

6 And the Lord said, If ye had faith as a grain of mustard seed, ye might say unto this sycamine tree, Be thou plucked up by the root, and be thou planted in the sea; and it should obey you.

7 ℂ But which of you, having a servant plowing or feeding cattle, will say unto him by and by, when he is come from the field, Go and sit down to meat?

8 And will not rather say unto him, Make ready wherewith I may sup, and gird thyself, and serve me, till I have eaten and drunken; and afterward thou shalt eat and drink?

9 Doth he thank that servant because he did the things that were commanded him? I trow not.

10 So likewise ye, when ye shall have done all those things which are commanded you, say, We are unprofitable servants: we have done that which was our duty to do.

11 ℂ And it came to pass, as he went to Jerusalem, that he passed through the midst of Samaria and Galilee.

12 And as he entered into a certain village, there met him ten men that were lepers, which stood afar off:

13 And they lifted up *their* voices, and said, Jesus, Master, have mercy on us.

14 And when he saw *them*, he said unto them, Go shew yourselves unto the priests. And it came to pass, that, as they went, they were cleansed.

15 And one of them, when he saw that he was healed, turned back, and with a loud voice glorified God,

16 And fell down on *his* face at his feet, giving him thanks: and he was a Samaritan.

17 And Jesus answering said, Were there not ten cleansed? but where *are* the nine?

18 There are not found that returned to give glory to God, save this stranger.

19 And he said unto him, Arise, go thy way: thy faith hath made

thee whole.

20 ¶ And when he was demanded of the Pharisees, when the kingdom of God should come, he answered them and said, The kingdom of God cometh not with observation:

21 Neither shall they say, Lo here! or, lo there! for, behold, the kingdom of God is within you.

22 ¶ And he said unto the disciples, The days will come, when ye shall desire to see one of the days of the Son of man, and ye shall not see *it*.

23 And they shall say to you, See here; or, see there: go not after *them*, nor follow *them*.

24 For as the lightning, that lighteneth out of the one *part* under heaven, shineth unto the other *part* under heaven; so shall also the Son of man be in his day.

25 But first must he suffer many things, and be rejected of this generation.

26 And as it was in the days of Noe, so shall it be also in the days of the Son of man.

27 They did eat, they drank, they married wives, they were given in marriage, until the day that Noe entered into the ark, and the flood came, and destroyed them all.

28 Likewise also as it was in the days of Lot; they did eat, they drank, they bought, they sold, they planted, they builded;

29 But the same day that Lot went out of Sodom it rained fire and brimstone from heaven, and destroyed *them* all.

30 Even thus shall it be in the day when the Son of man is revealed.

31 In that day, he which shall be upon the housetop, and his stuff in the house, let him not come down to take it away: and he that is in the field, let him likewise not return back.

32 Remember Lot's wife.

33 Whosoever shall seek to save his life shall lose it; and whosoever shall lose his life shall preserve it.

34 I tell you, in that night there shall be two *men* in one bed; the one shall be taken, and the other shall be left.

35 Two *women* shall be grinding together; the one shall be taken, and the other left.

36 Two *men* shall be in the field; the one shall be taken, and the other left.

37 And they answered and said unto him, Where, Lord? And he said unto them, Wheresoever the body *is*, thither will the eagles be gathered together.

18

And he spake a parable unto them *to this end*, that men ought always to pray, and not to faint;

2 Saying, There was in a city a judge, which feared not God, neither regarded man:

3 And there was a widow in that city; and she came unto him, saying, Avenge me of mine adversary.

4 And he would not for a while: but afterward he said within him-

self, Though I fear not God, nor regard man;

5 Yet because this widow troubleth me, I will avenge her, lest by her continual coming she weary me.

6 And the Lord said, Hear what the unjust judge saith.

7 And shall not God avenge his own elect, which cry day and night unto him, though he bear long with them?

8 I tell you that he will avenge them speedily. Nevertheless when the Son of man cometh, shall he find faith on the earth?

9 ¶ And he spake this parable unto certain which trusted in themselves that they were righteous, and despised others:

10 Two men went up into the temple to pray; the one a Pharisee, and the other a publican.

11 The Pharisee stood and prayed thus with himself, God, I thank thee, that I am not as other men *are*, extortioners, unjust, adulterers, or even as this publican.

12 I fast twice in the week, I give tithes of all that I possess.

13 And the publican, standing afar off, would not lift up so much as *his* eyes unto heaven, but smote upon his breast, saying, God be merciful to me a sinner.

14 I tell you, this man went down to his house justified *rather* than the other: for every one that exalteth himself shall be abased; and he that humbleth himself shall be exalted.

15 ¶ And they brought unto him also infants, that he would touch them: but when *his* disciples saw *it*, they rebuked them.

16 But Jesus called them *unto him*, and said, Suffer little children to come unto me, and forbid them not: for of such is the kingdom of God.

17 Verily I say unto you, Whosoever shall not receive the kingdom of God as a little child shall in no wise enter therein.

18 ¶ And a certain ruler asked him, saying, Good Master, what shall I do to inherit eternal life?

19 And Jesus said unto him, Why callest thou me good? none *is* good, save one, *that is*, God.

20 Thou knowest the commandments, Do not commit adultery, Do not kill, Do not steal, Do not bear false witness, Honour thy father and thy mother.

21 And he said, All these have I kept from my youth up.

22 Now when Jesus heard these things, he said unto him, Yet lackest thou one thing: sell all that thou hast, and distribute unto the poor, and thou shalt have treasure in heaven: and come, follow me.

23 And when he heard this, he was very sorrowful: for he was very rich.

24 And when Jesus saw that he was very sorrowful, he said, How hardly shall they that have riches enter into the kingdom of God!

25 For it is easier for a camel to go through a needle's eye, than

for a rich man to enter into the kingdom of God.

26 And they that heard *it* said, Who then can be saved?

27 And he said, The things which are impossible with men are possible with God.

28 ¶ Then Peter said, Lo, we have left all, and followed thee.

29 And he said unto them, Verily I say unto you, There is no man that hath left house, or parents, or brethren, or wife, or children, for the kingdom of God's sake,

30 Who shall not receive manifold more in this present time, and in the world to come life everlasting.

31 ¶ Then he took *unto him* the twelve, and said unto them, Behold, we go up to Jerusalem, and all things that are written by the prophets concerning the Son of man shall be accomplished.

32 For he shall be delivered unto the Gentiles, and shall be mocked, and spitefully entreated, and spitted on:

33 And they shall scourge *him*, and put him to death: and the third day he shall rise again.

34 And they understood none of these things: and this saying was hid from them, neither knew they the things which were spoken.

35 ¶ And it came to pass, that as he was come nigh unto Jericho, a certain blind man sat by the way side begging:

36 And hearing the multitude pass by, he asked what it meant.

37 And they told him, that Jesus of Nazareth passeth by.

38 And he cried, saying, Jesus, *thou* son of David, have mercy on me.

39 And they which went before rebuked him, that he should hold his peace: but he cried so much the more, *Thou* Son of David, have mercy on me.

40 And Jesus stood, and commanded him to be brought unto him: and when he was come near, he asked him,

41 Saying, What wilt thou that I shall do unto thee? And he said, Lord, that I may receive my sight.

42 And Jesus said unto him, Receive thy sight: thy faith hath saved thee.

43 And immediately he received his sight, and followed him, glorifying God: and all the people, when they saw *it*, gave praise unto God.

19 And *Jesus* entered and passed through Jericho.

2 ¶ And, behold, *there was* a man named Zacchaeus, which was the chief among the publicans, and he was rich.

3 And he sought to see Jesus who he was; and could not for the press, because he was little of stature.

4 And he ran before, and climbed up into a sycomore tree to see him: for he was to pass that *way*.

5 And when Jesus came to the place, he looked up, and saw him, and said unto him, Zacchaeus, make haste, and come down; for to day I must abide at

thy house.

6 And he made haste, and came down, and received him joyfully.

7 And when they saw it, they all murmured, saying, That he was gone to be guest with a man that is a sinner.

8 And Zacchaeus stood, and said unto the Lord: Behold, Lord, the half of my goods I give to the poor; and if I have taken any thing from any man by false accusation, I restore him fourfold.

9 And Jesus said unto him, This day is salvation come to this house, forsomuch as he also is a son of Abraham.

10 For the Son of man is come to seek and to save that which was lost.

11 ¶ And as they heard these things, he added and spake a parable, because he was nigh to Jerusalem, and because they thought that the kingdom of God should immediately appear.

12 He said therefore, A certain nobleman went into a far country to receive for himself a kingdom, and to return.

13 And he called his ten servants, and delivered them ten pounds, and said unto them, Occupy till I come.

14 But his citizens hated him, and sent a message after him, saying, We will not have this man to reign over us.

15 And it came to pass, that when he was returned, having received the kingdom, then he commanded these servants to be called unto him, to whom he had given the money, that he might know how much every man had gained by trading.

16 Then came the first, saying, Lord, thy pound hath gained ten pounds.

17 And he said unto him, Well, thou good servant: because thou hast been faithful in a very little, have thou authority over ten cities.

18 And the second came, saying, Lord, thy pound hath gained five pounds.

19 And he said likewise to him, Be thou also over five cities.

20 And another came, saying, Lord, behold, here is thy pound, which I have kept laid up in a napkin:

21 For I feared thee, because thou art an austere man: thou takest up that thou layedst not down, and reapest that thou didst not sow.

22 And he saith unto him, Out of thine own mouth will I judge thee, thou wicked servant. Thou knewest that I was an austere man, taking up that I laid not down, and reaping that I did not sow:

23 Wherefore then gavest not thou my money into the bank, that at my coming I might have required mine own with usury?

24 And he said unto them that stood by, Take from him the pound, and give it to him that hath ten pounds.

25 (And they said unto him, Lord, he hath ten pounds.)

26 For I say unto you, That unto

every one which hath shall be given; and from him that hath not, even that he hath shall be taken away from him.

27 But those mine enemies, which would not that I should reign over them, bring hither, and slay *them* before me.

28 ¶ And when he had thus spoken, he went before, ascending up to Jerusalem.

29 And it came to pass, when he was come nigh to Bethphage and Bethany, at the mount called *the mount* of Olives, he sent two of his disciples,

30 Saying, Go ye into the village over against *you*; in the which at your entering ye shall find a colt tied, whereon yet never man sat: loose him, and bring *him* hither.

31 And if any man ask *you*, Why do ye loose *him*? thus shall ye say unto him, Because the Lord hath need of him.

32 And they that were sent went their way, and found even as he had said unto them.

33 And as they were loosing the colt, the owners thereof said unto them, Why loose ye the colt?

34 And they said, The Lord hath need of him.

35 And they brought him to Jesus: and they cast their garments upon the colt, and they set Jesus thereon.

36 And as he went, they spread their clothes in the way.

37 And when he was come nigh, even now at the descent of the mount of Olives, the whole multitude of the disciples began to rejoice and praise God with a loud voice for all the mighty works that they had seen;

38 Saying, Blessed *be* the King that cometh in the name of the Lord: peace in heaven, and glory in the highest.

39 And some of the Pharisees from among the multitude said unto him, Master, rebuke thy disciples.

40 And he answered and said unto them, I tell you, that, if these should hold their peace, the stones would immediately cry out.

41 ¶ And when he was come near, he beheld the city, and wept over it,

42 Saying, If thou hadst known, even thou, at least in this thy day, the things *which belong* unto thy peace! but now they are hid from thine eyes.

43 For the days shall come upon thee, that thine enemies shall cast a trench about thee, and compass thee round, and keep thee in on every side,

44 And shall lay thee even with the ground, and thy children within thee; and they shall not leave in thee one stone upon another; because thou knewest not the time of thy visitation.

45 ¶ And he went into the temple, and began to cast out them that sold therein, and them that bought;

46 Saying unto them, It is written, My house is the house of prayer: but ye have made it a den of thieves.

47 ¶ And he taught daily in the temple. But the chief priests and the scribes and the chief of the people sought to destroy him,

48 And could not find what they might do: for all the people were very attentive to hear him.

20 And it came to pass, *that* on one of those days, as he taught the people in the temple, and preached the gospel, the chief priests and the scribes came upon *him* with the elders,

2 And spake unto him, saying, Tell us, by what authority doest thou these things? or who is he that gave thee this authority?

3 And he answered and said unto them, I will also ask you one thing; and answer me:

4 The baptism of John, was it from heaven, or of men?

5 And they reasoned with themselves, saying, If we shall say, From heaven; he will say, Why then believed ye him not?

6 But and if we say, Of men; all the people will stone us: for they be persuaded that John was a prophet.

7 And they answered, that they could not tell whence *it was.*

8 And Jesus said unto them, Neither tell I you by what authority I do these things.

9 ¶ Then began he to speak to the people this parable; A certain man planted a vineyard, and let it forth to husbandmen, and went into a far country for a long time.

10 And at the season he sent a servant to the husbandmen, that they should give him of the fruit of the vineyard: but the husbandmen beat him, and sent *him* away empty.

11 And again he sent another servant: and they beat him also, and entreated *him* shamefully, and sent *him* away empty.

12 And again he sent a third: and they wounded him also, and cast *him* out.

13 Then said the lord of the vineyard, What shall I do? I will send my beloved son: it may be they will reverence *him* when they see him.

14 But when the husbandmen saw him, they reasoned among themselves, saying, This is the heir: come, let us kill him, that the inheritance may be ours.

15 So they cast him out of the vineyard, and killed *him*. What therefore shall the lord of the vineyard do unto them?

16 He shall come and destroy these husbandmen, and shall give the vineyard to others. And when they heard *it,* they said, God forbid.

17 And he beheld them, and said, What is this then that is written, The stone which the builders rejected, the same is become the head of the corner?

18 Whosoever shall fall upon that stone shall be broken; but on whomsoever it shall fall, it will grind him to powder.

19 ¶ And the chief priests and the scribes the same hour sought to lay hands on him; and they feared the people: for they per-

ceived that he had spoken this parable against them.

20 And they watched *him*, and sent forth spies, which should feign themselves just men, that they might take hold of his words, that so they might deliver him unto the power and authority of the governor.

21 And they asked him, saying, Master, we know that thou sayest and teachest rightly, neither acceptest thou the person *of any*, but teachest the way of God truly:

22 Is it lawful for us to give tribute unto Caesar, or no?

23 But he perceived their craftiness, and said unto them, Why tempt ye me?

24 Shew me a penny. Whose image and superscription hath it? They answered and said, Caesar's.

25 And he said unto them, Render therefore unto Caesar the things which be Caesar's, and unto God the things which be God's.

26 And they could not take hold of his words before the people: and they marvelled at his answer, and held their peace.

27 ❧ Then came to *him* certain of the Sadducees, which deny that there is any resurrection; and they asked him,

28 Saying, Master, Moses wrote unto us, If any man's brother die, having a wife, and he die without children, that his brother should take his wife, and raise up seed unto his brother.

29 There were therefore seven

brethren: and the first took a wife, and died without children.

30 And the second took her to wife, and he died childless.

31 And the third took her; and in like manner the seven also: and they left no children, and died.

32 Last of all the woman died also.

33 Therefore in the resurrection whose wife of them is she? for seven had her to wife.

34 And Jesus answering said unto them, The children of this world marry, and are given in marriage:

35 But they which shall be accounted worthy to obtain that world, and the resurrection from the dead, neither marry, nor are given in marriage:

36 Neither can they die any more: for they are equal unto the angels; and are the children of God, being the children of the resurrection.

37 Now that the dead are raised, even Moses shewed at the bush, when he calleth the Lord the God of Abraham, and the God of Isaac, and the God of Jacob.

38 For he is not a God of the dead, but of the living: for all live unto him.

39 ❧ Then certain of the scribes answering said, Master, thou hast well said.

40 And after that they durst not ask him any *question at all*.

41 And he said unto them, How say they that Christ is David's son?

42 And David himself saith in the book of Psalms, The LORD said unto my Lord, Sit thou on my right hand,

43 Till I make thine enemies thy footstool.

44 David therefore calleth him Lord, how is he then his son?

45 ¶ Then in the audience of all the people he said unto his disciples,

46 Beware of the scribes, which desire to walk in long robes, and love greetings in the markets, and the highest seats in the synagogues, and the chief rooms at feasts;

47 Which devour widows' houses, and for a shew make long prayers: the same shall receive greater damnation.

21 And he looked up, and saw the rich men casting their gifts into the treasury.

2 And he saw also a certain poor widow casting in thither two mites.

3 And he said, Of a truth I say unto you, that this poor widow hath cast in more than they all:

4 For all these have of their abundance cast in unto the offerings of God: but she of her penury hath cast in all the living that she had.

5 ¶ And as some spake of the temple, how it was adorned with goodly stones and gifts, he said,

6 As for these things which ye behold, the days will come, in the which there shall not be left one stone upon another, that shall not be thrown down.

7 And they asked him, saying, Master, but when shall these things be? and what sign will there be when these things shall come to pass?

8 And he said, Take heed that ye be not deceived: for many shall come in my name, saying, I am Christ; and the time draweth near: go ye not therefore after them.

9 But when ye shall hear of wars and commotions, be not terrified: for these things must first come to pass; but the end is not by and by.

10 Then said he unto them, Nation shall rise against nation, and kingdom against kingdom:

11 And great earthquakes shall be in divers places, and famines, and pestilences; and fearful sights and great signs shall there be from heaven.

12 But before all these, they shall lay their hands on you, and persecute you, delivering you up to the synagogues, and into prisons, being brought before kings and rulers for my name's sake.

13 And it shall turn to you for a testimony.

14 Settle it therefore in your hearts, not to meditate before what ye shall answer:

15 For I will give you a mouth and wisdom, which all your adversaries shall not be able to gainsay nor resist.

16 And ye shall be betrayed both by parents, and brethren, and kinsfolks, and friends; and some of you shall they cause to be put to death.

17 And ye shall be hated of all *men* for my name's sake.

18 But there shall not an hair of your head perish.

19 In your patience possess ye your souls.

20 And when ye shall see Jerusalem compassed with armies, then know that the desolation thereof is nigh.

21 Then let them which are in Judaea flee to the mountains; and let them which are in the midst of it depart out; and let not them that are in the countries enter thereinto.

22 For these be the days of vengeance, that all things which are written may be fulfilled.

23 But woe unto them that are with child, and to them that give suck, in those days! for there shall be great distress in the land, and wrath upon this people.

24 And they shall fall by the edge of the sword, and shall be led away captive into all nations: and Jerusalem shall be trodden down of the Gentiles, until the times of the Gentiles be fulfilled.

25 ¶ And there shall be signs in the sun, and in the moon, and in the stars; and upon the earth distress of nations, with perplexity; the sea and the waves roaring;

26 Men's hearts failing them for fear, and for looking after those things which are coming on the earth: for the powers of heaven shall be shaken.

27 And then shall they see the Son of man coming in a cloud with power and great glory.

28 And when these things begin to come to pass, then look up, and lift up your heads; for your redemption draweth nigh.

29 ¶ And he spake to them a parable; Behold the fig tree, and all the trees;

30 When they now shoot forth, ye see and know of your own selves that summer is now nigh at hand.

31 So likewise ye, when ye see these things come to pass, know ye that the kingdom of God is nigh at hand.

32 Verily I say unto you, This generation shall not pass away, till all be fulfilled.

33 Heaven and earth shall pass away: but my words shall not pass away.

34 ¶ And take heed to yourselves, lest at any time your hearts be overcharged with surfeiting, and drunkenness, and cares of this life, and *so* that day come upon you unawares.

35 For as a snare shall it come on all them that dwell on the face of the whole earth.

36 Watch ye therefore, and pray always, that ye may be accounted worthy to escape all these things that shall come to pass, and to stand before the Son of man.

37 And in the day time he was teaching in the temple; and at night he went out, and abode in the mount that is called *the mount* of Olives.

38 And all the people came early in the morning to him in the temple, for to hear him.

22 Now the feast of unleavened bread drew nigh, which is called the Passover.

2 And the chief priests and scribes sought how they might kill him; for they feared the people.

3 ¶ Then entered Satan into Judas surnamed Iscariot, being of the number of the twelve.

4 And he went his way, and communed with the chief priests and captains, how he might betray him unto them.

5 And they were glad, and covenanted to give him money.

6 And he promised, and sought opportunity to betray him unto them in the absence of the multitude.

7 ¶ Then came the day of unleavened bread, when the passover must be killed.

8 And he sent Peter and John, saying, Go and prepare us the passover, that we may eat.

9 And they said unto him, Where wilt thou that we prepare?

10 And he said unto them, Behold, when ye are entered into the city, there shall a man meet you, bearing a pitcher of water; follow him into the house where he entereth in.

11 And ye shall say unto the goodman of the house, The Master saith unto thee, Where is the guestchamber, where I shall eat the passover with my disciples?

12 And he shall shew you a large upper room furnished: there make ready.

13 And they went, and found as he had said unto them: and they made ready the passover.

14 ¶ And when the hour was come, he sat down, and the twelve apostles with him.

15 And he said unto them, With desire I have desired to eat this passover with you before I suffer:

16 For I say unto you, I will not any more eat thereof, until it be fulfilled in the kingdom of God.

17 And he took the cup, and gave thanks, and said, Take this, and divide *it* among yourselves:

18 For I say unto you, I will not drink of the fruit of the vine, until the kingdom of God shall come.

19 ¶ And he took bread, and gave thanks, and brake *it*, and gave unto them, saying, This is my body which is given for you: this do in remembrance of me.

20 Likewise also the cup after supper, saying, This cup *is* the new testament in my blood, which is shed for you.

21 ¶ But, behold, the hand of him that betrayeth me *is* with me on the table.

22 And truly the Son of man goeth, as it was determined: but woe unto that man by whom he is betrayed!

23 And they began to enquire among themselves, which of them it was that should do this thing.

24 ¶ And there was also a strife among them, which of them should be accounted the great-

est.

25 And he said unto them, The kings of the Gentiles exercise lordship over them; and they that exercise authority upon them are called benefactors.

26 But ye *shall* not *be* so: but he that is greatest among you, let him be as the younger; and he that is chief, as he that doth serve.

27 For whether *is* greater, he that sitteth at meat, or he that serveth? *is* not he that sitteth at meat? but I am among you as he that serveth.

28 Ye are they which have continued with me in my temptations.

29 And I appoint unto you a kingdom, as my Father hath appointed unto me;

30 That ye may eat and drink at my table in my kingdom, and sit on thrones judging the twelve tribes of Israel.

31 ¶ And the Lord said, Simon, Simon, behold, Satan hath desired *to have* you, that he may sift *you* as wheat:

32 But I have prayed for thee, that thy faith fail not: and when thou art converted, strengthen thy brethren.

33 And he said unto him, Lord, I am ready to go with thee, both into prison, and to death.

34 And he said, I tell thee, Peter, the cock shall not crow this day, before that thou shalt thrice deny that thou knowest me.

35 ¶ And he said unto them, When I sent you without purse, and scrip, and shoes, lacked ye any thing? And they said, Nothing.

36 Then said he unto them, But now, he that hath a purse, let him take *it*, and likewise *his* scrip: and he that hath no sword, let him sell his garment, and buy one.

37 For I say unto you, that this that is written must yet be accomplished in me, And he was reckoned among the transgressors: for the things concerning me have an end.

38 And they said, Lord, behold, here *are* two swords. And he said unto them, It is enough.

39 ¶ And he came out, and went, as he was wont, to the mount of Olives; and his disciples also followed him.

40 And when he was at the place, he said unto them, Pray that ye enter not into temptation.

41 And he was withdrawn from them about a stone's cast, and kneeled down, and prayed,

42 Saying, Father, if thou be willing, remove this cup from me: nevertheless not my will, but thine, be done.

43 And there appeared an angel unto him from heaven, strengthening him.

44 And being in an agony he prayed more earnestly: and his sweat was as it were great drops of blood falling down to the ground.

45 And when he rose up from prayer, and was come to his disciples, he found them sleeping

for sorrow,

46 And said unto them, Why sleep ye? rise and pray, lest ye enter into temptation.

47 ¶ And while he yet spake, behold a multitude, and he that was called Judas, one of the twelve, went before them, and drew near unto Jesus to kiss him.

48 But Jesus said unto him, Judas, betrayest thou the Son of man with a kiss?

49 When they which were about him saw what would follow, they said unto him, Lord, shall we smite with the sword?

50 ¶ And one of them smote the servant of the high priest, and cut off his right ear.

51 And Jesus answered and said, Suffer ye thus far. And he touched his ear, and healed him.

52 Then Jesus said unto the chief priests, and captains of the temple, and the elders, which were come to him, Be ye come out, as against a thief, with swords and staves?

53 When I was daily with you in the temple, ye stretched forth no hands against me: but this is your hour, and the power of darkness.

54 ¶ Then took they him, and led him, and brought him into the high priest's house. And Peter followed afar off.

55 ¶ And when they had kindled a fire in the midst of the hall, and were set down together, Peter sat down among them.

56 But a certain maid beheld him as he sat by the fire, and earnestly looked upon him, and said,

This man was also with him.

57 And he denied him, saying, Woman, I know him not.

58 And after a little while another saw him, and said, Thou art also of them. And Peter said, Man, I am not.

59 And about the space of one hour after another confidently affirmed, saying, Of a truth this *fellow* also was with him; for he is a Galilaean.

60 And Peter said, Man, I know not what thou sayest. And immediately, while he yet spake, the cock crew.

61 And the Lord turned, and looked upon Peter. And Peter remembered the word of the Lord, how he had said unto him, Before the cock crow, thou shalt deny me thrice.

62 And Peter went out, and wept bitterly.

63 ¶ And the men that held Jesus mocked him, and smote *him.*

64 And when they had blindfolded him, they struck him on the face, and asked him, saying, Prophesy, who is it that smote thee?

65 And many other things blasphemously spake they against him.

66 ¶ And as soon as it was day, the elders of the people and the chief priests and the scribes came together, and led him into their council, saying,

67 Art thou the Christ? tell us. And he said unto them, If I tell you, ye will not believe:

68 And if I also ask *you,* ye will

not answer me, nor let *me* go.

69 Hereafter shall the Son of man sit on the right hand of the power of God.

70 Then said they all, Art thou then the Son of God? And he said unto them, Ye say that I am.

71 And they said, What need we any further witness? for we ourselves have heard of his own mouth.

23

And the whole multitude of them arose, and led him unto Pilate.

2 And they began to accuse him, saying, We found this *fellow* perverting the nation, and forbidding to give tribute to Caesar, saying that he himself is Christ a King.

3 And Pilate asked him, saying, Art thou the King of the Jews? And he answered him and said, Thou sayest *it*.

4 Then said Pilate to the chief priests and *to* the people, I find no fault in this man.

5 And they were the more fierce, saying, He stirreth up the people, teaching throughout all Jewry, beginning from Galilee to this place.

6 When Pilate heard of Galilee, he asked whether the man were a Galilaean.

7 And as soon as he knew that he belonged unto Herod's jurisdiction, he sent him to Herod, who himself also was at Jerusalem at that time.

8 ⊄ And when Herod saw Jesus, he was exceeding glad: for he was desirous to see him of a long

season, because he had heard many things of him; and he hoped to have seen some miracle done by him.

9 Then he questioned with him in many words; but he answered him nothing.

10 ⊄ And the chief priests and scribes stood and vehemently accused him.

11 And Herod with his men of war set him at nought, and mocked *him*, and arrayed him in a gorgeous robe, and sent him again to Pilate.

12 ⊄ And the same day Pilate and Herod were made friends together: for before they were at enmity between themselves.

13 ⊄ And Pilate, when he had called together the chief priests and the rulers and the people,

14 Said unto them, Ye have brought this man unto me, as one that perverteth the people: and, behold, I, having examined *him* before you, have found no fault in this man touching those things whereof ye accuse him:

15 No, nor yet Herod: for I sent you to him; and, lo, nothing worthy of death is done unto him.

16 I will therefore chastise him, and release *him*.

17 (For of necessity he must release one unto them at the feast.)

18 And they cried out all at once, saying, Away with this *man*, and release unto us Barabbas:

19 (Who for a certain sedition made in the city, and for murder, was cast into prison.)

20 Pilate therefore, willing to

release Jesus, spake again to them.

21 But they cried, saying, Crucify *him*, crucify him.

22 And he said unto them the third time, Why, what evil hath he done? I have found no cause of death in him: I will therefore chastise him, and let him go.

23 And they were instant with loud voices, requiring that he might be crucified. And the voices of them and of the chief priests prevailed.

24 And Pilate gave sentence that it should be as they required.

25 And he released unto them him that for sedition and murder was cast into prison, whom they had desired; but, he delivered Jesus to their will.

26 And as they led him away, they laid hold upon one Simon, a Cyrenian, coming out of the country, and on him they laid the cross, that he might bear *it* after Jesus.

27 ¶ And there followed him a great company of people, and of women, which also bewailed and lamented him.

28 But Jesus turning unto them said, Daughters of Jerusalem, weep not for me, but weep for yourselves, and for your children.

29 For, behold, the days are coming, in the which they shall say, Blessed *are* the barren, and the wombs that never bare, and the paps which never gave suck.

30 Then shall they begin to say to the mountains, Fall on us; and to the hills, Cover us.

31 For if they do these things in a green tree, what shall be done in the dry?

32 And there were also two other, malefactors, led with him to be put to death.

33 ¶ And when they were come to the place, which is called Calvary, there they crucified him, and the malefactors, one on the right hand, and the other on the left.

34 ¶ Then said Jesus, Father, forgive them; for they know not what they do. And they parted his raiment, and cast lots.

35 ¶ And the people stood beholding. And the rulers also with them derided *him*, saying, He saved others; let him save himself, if he be Christ, the chosen of God.

36 And the soldiers also mocked him, coming to him, and offering him vinegar,

37 And saying, If thou be the king of the Jews, save thyself.

38 And a superscription was written over him in letters of Greek, and Latin, and Hebrew, THIS IS THE KING OF THE JEWS.

39 ¶ And one of the malefactors which were hanged railed on him, saying, If thou be Christ, save thyself and us.

40 But the other answering rebuked him, saying, Dost not thou fear God, seeing thou art in the same condemnation?

41 And we indeed justly; for we receive the due reward of our deeds: but this man hath done

nothing amiss.

42 And he said unto Jesus, Lord, remember me when thou comest into thy kingdom.

43 And Jesus said unto him, Verily I say unto thee, To day shalt thou be with me in paradise.

44 And it was about the sixth hour, and there was a darkness over all the earth until the ninth hour.

45 And the sun was darkened, and the vail of the temple was rent in the midst.

46 ¶ And when Jesus had cried with a loud voice, he said, Father, into thy hands I commend my spirit: and having said thus, he gave up the ghost.

47 Now when the centurion saw what was done, he glorified God, saying, Certainly this was a righteous man.

48 And all the people that came together to that sight, beholding the things which were done, smote their breasts, and returned.

49 And all his acquaintance, and the women that followed him from Galilee, stood afar off, beholding these things.

50 ¶ And, behold, *there was* a man named Joseph, a counseller; *and he was* a good man, and a just:

51 (The same had not consented to the counsel and deed of them;) *he was* of Arimathaea, a city of the Jews: who also himself waited for the kingdom of God.

52 This *man* went unto Pilate, and begged the body of Jesus.

53 And he took it down, and wrapped it in linen, and laid it in a sepulchre that was hewn in stone, wherein never man before was laid.

54 And that day was the preparation, and the sabbath drew on.

55 And the women also, which came with him from Galilee, followed after, and beheld the sepulchre, and how his body was laid.

56 And they returned, and prepared spices and ointments; and rested the sabbath day according to the commandment.

24

Now upon the first *day* of the week, very early in the morning, they came unto the sepulchre, bringing the spices which they had prepared, and certain *others* with them.

2 And they found the stone rolled away from the sepulchre.

3 And they entered in, and found not the body of the Lord Jesus.

4 And it came to pass, as they were much perplexed thereabout, behold, two men stood by them in shining garments:

5 And as they were afraid, and bowed down *their* faces to the earth, they said unto them, Why seek ye the living among the dead?

6 He is not here, but is risen: remember how he spake unto you when he was yet in Galilee,

7 Saying, The Son of man must be delivered into the hands of sinful men, and be crucified, and

the third day rise again.

8 And they remembered his words,

9 And returned from the sepulchre, and told all these things unto the eleven, and to all the rest.

10 It was Mary Magdalene and Joanna, and Mary *the mother* of James, and other *women that were* with them, which told these things unto the apostles.

11 And their words seemed to them as idle tales, and they believed them not.

12 Then arose Peter, and ran unto the sepulchre; and stooping down, he beheld the linen clothes laid by themselves, and departed, wondering in himself at that which was come to pass.

13 ¶ And, behold, two of them went that same day to a village called Emmaus, which was from Jerusalem *about* threescore furlongs.

14 And they talked together of all these things which had happened.

15 And it came to pass, that, while they communed *together* and reasoned, Jesus himself drew near, and went with them.

16 But their eyes were holden that they should not know him.

17 And he said unto them, What manner of communications *are* these that ye have one to another, as ye walk, and are sad?

18 And the one of them, whose name was Cleopas, answering said unto him, Art thou only a stranger in Jerusalem, and hast

not known the things which are come to pass there in these days?

19 And he said unto them, What things? And they said unto him, Concerning Jesus of Nazareth, which was a prophet mighty in deed and word before God and all the people:

20 And how the chief priests and our rulers delivered him to be condemned to death, and have crucified him.

21 But we trusted that it had been he which should have redeemed Israel: and beside all this, to day is the third day since these things were done.

22 Yea, and certain women also of our company made us astonished, which were early at the sepulchre;

23 And when they found not his body, they came, saying, that they had also seen a vision of angels, which said that he was alive.

24 And certain of them which were with us went to the sepulchre, and found *it* even so as the women had said: but him they saw not.

25 Then he said unto them, O fools, and slow of heart to believe all that the prophets have spoken:

26 Ought not Christ to have suffered these things, and to enter into his glory?

27 And beginning at Moses and all the prophets, he expounded unto them in all the scriptures the things concerning himself.

28 And they drew nigh unto the village, whither they went: and he made as though he would have gone further.

29 But they constrained him, saying, Abide with us: for it is toward evening, and the day is far spent. And he went in to tarry with them.

30 And it came to pass, as he sat at meat with them, he took bread, and blessed *it*, and brake, and gave to them.

31 And their eyes were opened, and they knew him; and he vanished out of their sight.

32 And they said one to another, Did not our heart burn within us, while he talked with us by the way, and while he opened to us the scriptures?

33 And they rose up the same hour, and returned to Jerusalem, and found the eleven gathered together, and them that were with them,

34 Saying, The Lord is risen indeed, and hath appeared to Simon.

35 And they told what things *were done* in the way, and how he was known of them in breaking of bread.

36 ¶ And as they thus spake, Jesus himself stood in the midst of them, and saith unto them, Peace *be* unto you.

37 But they were terrified and affrighted, and supposed that they had seen a spirit.

38 And he said unto them, Why are ye troubled? and why do thoughts arise in your hearts?

39 Behold my hands and my feet, that it is I myself: handle me, and see; for a spirit hath not flesh and bones, as ye see me have.

40 And when he had thus spoken, he shewed them *his* hands and *his* feet.

41 And while they yet believed not for joy, and wondered, he said unto them, Have ye here any meat?

42 And they gave him a piece of a broiled fish, and of an honeycomb.

43 And he took *it*, and did eat before them.

44 And he said unto them, These *are* the words which I spake unto you, while I was yet with you, that all things must be fulfilled, which were written in the law of Moses, and *in* the prophets, and *in* the psalms, concerning me.

45 ¶ Then opened he their understanding, that they might understand the scriptures,

46 And said unto them, Thus it is written, and thus it behoved Christ to suffer, and to rise from the dead the third day:

47 And that repentance and remission of sins should be preached in his name among all nations, beginning at Jerusalem.

48 And ye are witnesses of these things.

49 ¶ And, behold, I send the promise of my Father upon you: but tarry ye in the city of Jerusalem, until ye be endued with power from on high.

50 ¶ And he led them out as far as

to Bethany, and he lifted up his hands, and blessed them.

51 And it came to pass, while he blessed them, he was parted from them, and carried up into heaven.

52 And they worshipped him, and returned to Jerusalem with great joy:

53 And were continually in the temple, praising and blessing God. Amen.

THE GOSPEL ACCORDING

TO

JOHN

1 In the beginning was the Word, and the Word was with God, and the Word was God.

2 The same was in the beginning with God.

3 All things were made by him; and without him was not any thing made that was made.

4 In him was life; and the life was the light of men.

5 And the light shineth in darkness; and the darkness comprehended it not.

6 ¶ There was a man sent from God, whose name *was* John.

7 The same came for a witness, to bear witness of the Light, that all *men* through him might believe.

8 He was not that Light, but *was sent* to bear witness of that Light.

9 ¶ *That* was the true Light, which lighteth every man that cometh into the world.

10 He was in the world, and the world was made by him, and the world knew him not.

11 ¶ He came unto his own, and his own received him not.

12 But as many as received him, to them gave he power to become the sons of God, *even* to them that believe on his name:

13 Which were born, not of blood, nor of the will of the flesh, nor of the will of man, but of God.

14 And the Word was made flesh, and dwelt among us, (and we beheld his glory, the glory as of the only begotten of the Father,) full of grace and truth.

15 ¶ John bare witness of him, and cried, saying, This was he of whom I spake, He that cometh after me is preferred before me: for he was before me.

16 And of his fulness have all we received, and grace for grace.

17 For the law was given by Moses, *but* grace and truth came by Jesus Christ.

18 No man hath seen God at any time; the only begotten Son, which is in the bosom of the Father, he hath declared *him*.

19 ¶ And this is the record of John, when the Jews sent priests

and Levites from Jerusalem to ask him, Who art thou?

20 And he confessed, and denied not; but confessed, I am not the Christ.

21 And they asked him, What then? Art thou Elias? And he saith, I am not. Art thou that prophet? And he answered, No.

22 Then said they unto him, Who art thou? that we may give an answer to them that sent us. What sayest thou of thyself?

23 He said, I *am* the voice of one crying in the wilderness, Make straight the way of the Lord, as said the prophet Esaias.

24 And they which were sent were of the Pharisees.

25 And they asked him, and said unto him, Why baptizest thou then, if thou be not that Christ, nor Elias, neither that prophet?

26 John answered them, saying, I baptize with water: but there standeth one among you, whom ye know not;

27 He it is, who coming after me is preferred before me, whose shoe's latchet I am not worthy to unloose.

28 These things were done in Bethabara beyond Jordan, where John was baptizing.

29 ¶ The next day John seeth Jesus coming unto him, and saith, Behold the Lamb of God, which taketh away the sin of the world.

30 This is he of whom I said, After me cometh a man which is preferred before me: for he was before me.

31 And I knew him not: but that he should be made manifest to Israel, therefore am I come baptizing with water.

32 And John bare record, saying, I saw the Spirit descending from heaven like a dove, and it abode upon him.

33 And I knew him not: but he that sent me to baptize with water, the same said unto me, Upon whom thou shalt see the Spirit descending, and remaining on him, the same is he which baptizeth with the Holy Ghost.

34 And I saw, and bare record that this is the Son of God.

35 ¶ Again the next day after John stood, and two of his disciples;

36 And looking upon Jesus as he walked, he saith, Behold the Lamb of God!

37 And the two disciples heard him speak, and they followed Jesus.

38 Then Jesus turned, and saw them following, and saith unto them, What seek ye? They said unto him, Rabbi, (which is to say, being interpreted, Master,) where dwellest thou?

39 He saith unto them, Come and see. They came and saw where he dwelt, and abode with him that day: for it was about the tenth hour.

40 One of the two which heard John *speak*, and followed him, was Andrew, Simon Peter's brother.

41 He first findeth his own brother Simon, and saith unto him, We have found the Messias, which is, being interpreted,

the Christ.

42 And he brought him to Jesus. And when Jesus beheld him, he said, Thou art Simon the son of Jona: thou shalt be called Cephas, which is by interpretation, A stone.

43 ℂ The day following Jesus would go forth into Galilee, and findeth Philip, and saith unto him, Follow me.

44 Now Philip was of Bethsaida, the city of Andrew and Peter.

45 Philip findeth Nathanael, and saith unto him, We have found him, of whom Moses in the law, and the prophets, did write, Jesus of Nazareth, the son of Joseph.

46 And Nathanael said unto him, Can there any good thing come out of Nazareth? Philip saith unto him, Come and see.

47 Jesus saw Nathanael coming to him, and saith of him, Behold an Israelite indeed, in whom is no guile!

48 Nathanael saith unto him, Whence knowest thou me? Jesus answered and said unto him, Before that Philip called thee, when thou wast under the fig tree, I saw thee.

49 Nathanael answered and saith unto him, Rabbi, thou art the Son of God; thou art the King of Israel.

50 Jesus answered and said unto him, Because I said unto thee, I saw thee under the fig tree, believest thou? thou shalt see greater things than these.

51 And he saith unto him, Verily, verily, I say unto you, Here-after ye shall see heaven open, and the angels of God ascending and descending upon the Son of man.

2 And the third day there was a marriage in Cana of Galilee; and the mother of Jesus was there:

2 And both Jesus was called, and his disciples, to the marriage.

3 And when they wanted wine, the mother of Jesus saith unto him, They have no wine.

4 Jesus saith unto her, Woman, what have I to do with thee? mine hour is not yet come.

5 His mother saith unto the servants, Whatsoever he saith unto you, do it.

6 And there were set there six waterpots of stone, after the manner of the purifying of the Jews, containing two or three firkins apiece.

7 Jesus saith unto them, Fill the waterpots with water. And they filled them up to the brim.

8 And he saith unto them, Draw out now, and bear unto the governor of the feast. And they bare it.

9 When the ruler of the feast had tasted the water that was made wine, and knew not whence it was: (but the servants which drew the water knew;) the governor of the feast called the bridegroom,

10 And saith unto him, Every man at the beginning doth set forth good wine; and when men have well drunk, then that which is worse: but thou hast kept the

good wine until now.

11 This beginning of miracles did Jesus in Cana of Galilee, and manifested forth his glory; and his disciples believed on him.

12 ¶ After this he went down to Capernaum, he, and his mother, and his brethren, and his disciples: and they continued there not many days.

13 ¶ And the Jews' passover was at hand, and Jesus went up to Jerusalem.

14 And found in the temple those that sold oxen and sheep and doves, and the changers of money sitting:

15 And when he had made a scourge of small cords, he drove them all out of the temple, and the sheep, and the oxen; and poured out the changers' money, and overthrew the tables;

16 And said unto them that sold doves, Take these things hence; make not my Father's house an house of merchandise.

17 And his disciples remembered that it was written, The zeal of thine house hath eaten me up.

18 ¶ Then answered the Jews and said unto him, What sign shewest thou unto us, seeing that thou doest these things?

19 Jesus answered and said unto them, Destroy this temple, and in three days I will raise it up.

20 Then said the Jews, Forty and six years was this temple in building, and wilt thou rear it up in three days?

21 But he spake of the temple of his body.

22 When therefore he was risen from the dead, his disciples remembered that he had said this unto them; and they believed the scripture, and the word which Jesus had said.

23 ¶ Now when he was in Jerusalem at the passover, in the feast day, many believed in his name, when they saw the miracles which he did.

24 But Jesus did not commit himself unto them, because he knew all men,

25 And needed not that any should testify of man: for he knew what was in man.

3 There was a man of the Pharisees, named Nicodemus, a ruler of the Jews:

2 The same came to Jesus by night, and said unto him, Rabbi, we know that thou art a teacher come from God: for no man can do these miracles that thou doest, except God be with him.

3 Jesus answered and said unto him, Verily, verily, I say unto thee, Except a man be born again, he cannot see the kingdom of God.

4 Nicodemus saith unto him, How can a man be born when he is old? can he enter the second time into his mother's womb, and be born?

5 Jesus answered, Verily, verily, I say unto thee, Except a man be born of water and of the Spirit, he cannot enter into the kingdom of God.

6 That which is born of the flesh

is flesh; and that which is born of the Spirit is spirit.

7 Marvel not that I said unto thee, Ye must be born again.

8 The wind bloweth where it listeth, and thou hearest the sound thereof, but canst not tell whence it cometh, and whither it goeth: so is every one that is born of the Spirit.

9 Nicodemus answered and said unto him, How can these things be?

10 Jesus answered and said unto him, Art thou a master of Israel, and knowest not these things?

11 Verily, verily, I say unto thee, We speak that we do know, and testify that we have seen; and ye receive not our witness.

12 If I have told you earthly things, and ye believe not, how shall ye believe, if I tell you *of* heavenly things?

13 And no man hath ascended up to heaven, but he that came down from heaven, *even* the Son of man which is in heaven.

14 ℂ And as Moses lifted up the serpent in the wilderness, even so must the Son of man be lifted up:

15 That whosoever believeth in him should not perish, but have eternal life.

16 ℂ For God so loved the world, that he gave his only begotten Son, that whosoever believeth in him should not perish, but have everlasting life.

17 For God sent not his Son into the world to condemn the world; but that the world through him might be saved.

18 ℂ He that believeth on him is not condemned: but he that believeth not is condemned already, because he hath not believed in the name of the only begotten Son of God.

19 And this is the condemnation, that light is come into the world, and men loved darkness rather than light, because their deeds were evil.

20 For every one that doeth evil hateth the light, neither cometh to the light, lest his deeds should be reproved.

21 But he that doeth truth cometh to the light, that his deeds may be made manifest, that they are wrought in God.

22 ℂ After these things came Jesus and his disciples into the land of Judaea; and there he tarried with them, and baptized.

23 ℂ And John also was baptizing in Aenon near to Salim, because there was much water there: and they came, and were baptized.

24 For John was not yet cast into prison.

25 ℂ Then there arose a question between *some* of John's disciples and the Jews about purifying.

26 And they came unto John, and said unto him, Rabbi, he that was with thee beyond Jordan, to whom thou barest witness, behold, the same baptizeth, and all *men* come to him.

27 John answered and said, A man can receive nothing, except it be given him from heaven.

28 Ye yourselves bear me wit-

ness, that I said, I am not the Christ, but that I am sent before him.

29 He that hath the bride is the bridegroom: but the friend of the bridegroom, which standeth and heareth him, rejoiceth greatly because of the bridegroom's voice: this my joy therefore is fulfilled.

30 He must increase, but I *must* decrease.

31 He that cometh from above is above all: he that is of the earth is earthly, and speaketh of the earth: he that cometh from heaven is above all.

32 And what he hath seen and heard, that he testifieth; and no man receiveth his testimony.

33 He that hath received his testimony hath set to his seal that God is true.

34 For he whom God hath sent speaketh the words of God: for God giveth not the Spirit by measure *unto him.*

35 The Father loveth the Son, and hath given all things into his hand.

36 He that believeth on the Son hath everlasting life: and he that believeth not the Son shall not see life; but the wrath of God abideth on him.

4 When therefore the Lord knew how the Pharisees had heard that Jesus made and baptized more disciples than John,

2 (Though Jesus himself baptized not, but his disciples,)

3 He left Judaea, and departed again into Galilee.

4 And he must needs go through Samaria.

5 Then cometh he to a city of Samaria, which is called Sychar, near to the parcel of ground that Jacob gave to his son Joseph.

6 Now Jacob's well was there. Jesus therefore, being wearied with *his* journey, sat thus on the well: *and* it was about the sixth hour.

7 There cometh a woman of Samaria to draw water: Jesus saith unto her, Give me to drink.

8 (For his disciples were gone away unto the city to buy meat.)

9 Then saith the woman of Samaria unto him, How is it that thou, being a Jew, askest drink of me, which am a woman of Samaria? for the Jews have no dealings with the Samaritans.

10 Jesus answered and said unto her, If thou knewest the gift of God, and who it is that saith to thee, Give me to drink; thou wouldest have asked of him, and he would have given thee living water.

11 The woman saith unto him, Sir, thou hast nothing to draw with, and the well is deep: from whence then hast thou that living water?

12 Art thou greater than our father Jacob, which gave us the well, and drank thereof himself, and his children, and his cattle?

13 Jesus answered and said unto her, Whosoever drinketh of this water shall thirst again:

14 But whosoever drinketh of the water that I shall give him

shall never thirst; but the water that I shall give him shall be in him a well of water springing up into everlasting life.

15 The woman saith unto him, Sir, give me this water, that I thirst not, neither come hither to draw.

16 Jesus saith unto her, Go, call thy husband, and come hither.

17 The woman answered and said, I have no husband. Jesus said unto her, Thou hast well said, I have no husband:

18 For thou hast had five husbands; and he whom thou now hast is not thy husband: in that saidst thou truly.

19 The woman saith unto him, Sir, I perceive that thou art a prophet.

20 Our fathers worshipped in this mountain; and ye say, that in Jerusalem is the place where men ought to worship.

21 Jesus saith unto her, Woman, believe me, the hour cometh, when ye shall neither in this mountain, nor yet at Jerusalem, worship the Father.

22 Ye worship ye know not what: we know what we worship: for salvation is of the Jews.

23 But the hour cometh, and now is, when the true worshippers shall worship the Father in spirit and in truth: for the Father seeketh such to worship him.

24 God is a Spirit: and they that worship him must worship him in spirit and in truth.

25 The woman saith unto him, I know that Messias cometh, which is called Christ: when he is come, he will tell us all things.

26 Jesus saith unto her, I that speak unto thee am he.

27 ¶ And upon this came his disciples, and marvelled that he talked with the woman: yet no man said, What seekest thou? or, Why talkest thou with her?

28 The woman then left her waterpot, and went her way into the city, and saith to the men,

29 Come, see a man, which told me all things that ever I did: is not this the Christ?

30 Then they went out of the city, and came unto him.

31 ¶ In the mean while his disciples prayed him, saying, Master, eat.

32 But he said unto them, I have meat to eat that ye know not of.

33 Therefore said the disciples one to another, Hath any man brought him ought to eat?

34 Jesus saith unto them, My meat is to do the will of him that sent me, and to finish his work.

35 Say not ye, There are yet four months, and then cometh harvest? behold, I say unto you, Lift up your eyes, and look on the fields; for they are white already to harvest.

36 And he that reapeth receiveth wages, and gathereth fruit unto life eternal: that both he that soweth and he that reapeth may rejoice together.

37 And herein is that saying true, One soweth, and another reapeth.

38 I sent you to reap that

whereon ye bestowed no labour: other men laboured, and ye are entered into their labours.

39 ¶ And many of the Samaritans of that city believed on him for the saying of the woman, which testified, He told me all that ever I did.

40 So when the Samaritans were come unto him, they besought him that he would tarry with them: and he abode there two days.

41 And many more believed because of his own word;

42 And said unto the woman, Now we believe, not because of thy saying: for we have heard *him* ourselves, and know that this is indeed the Christ, the Saviour of the world.

43 ¶ Now after two days he departed thence, and went into Galilee.

44 For Jesus himself testified, that a prophet hath no honour in his own country.

45 Then when he was come into Galilee, the Galilaeans received him, having seen all the things that he did at Jerusalem at the feast: for they also went unto the feast.

46 So Jesus came again into Cana of Galilee, where he made the water wine. And there was a certain nobleman, whose son was sick at Capernaum.

47 When he heard that Jesus was come out of Judaea into Galilee, he went unto him, and besought him that he would come down, and heal his son: for he was at the point of death.

48 Then said Jesus unto him, Except ye see signs and wonders, ye will not believe.

49 The nobleman saith unto him, Sir, come down ere my child die.

50 Jesus saith unto him, Go thy way; thy son liveth. And the man believed the word that Jesus had spoken unto him, and he went his way.

51 And as he was now going down, his servants met him, and told *him*, saying, Thy son liveth.

52 Then inquired he of them the hour when he began to amend. And they said unto him, Yesterday at the seventh hour the fever left him.

53 So the father knew that *it was* at the same hour, in the which Jesus said unto him, Thy son liveth: and himself believed, and his whole house.

54 This *is* again the second miracle *that* Jesus did, when he was come out of Judaea into Galilee.

5 After this there was a feast of the Jews; and Jesus went up to Jerusalem.

2 Now there is at Jerusalem by the sheep *market* a pool, which is called in the Hebrew tongue Bethesda, having five porches.

3 In these lay a great multitude of impotent folk, of blind, halt, withered, waiting for the moving of the water.

4 For an angel went down at a certain season into the pool, and troubled the water: whosoever then first after the troubling of the water stepped in was made

whole of whatsoever disease he had.

5 And a certain man was there, which had an infirmity thirty and eight years.

6 When Jesus saw him lie, and knew that he had been now a long time *in that case,* he saith unto him, Wilt thou be made whole?

7 The impotent man answered him, Sir, I have no man, when the water is troubled, to put me into the pool: but while I am coming, another steppeth down before me.

8 Jesus saith unto him, Rise, take up thy bed, and walk.

9 And immediately the man was made whole, and took up his bed, and walked: and on the same day was the sabbath.

10 ¶ The Jews therefore said unto him that was cured, It is the sabbath day: it is not lawful for thee to carry *thy* bed.

11 He answered them, He that made me whole, the same said unto me, Take up thy bed, and walk.

12 Then asked they him, What man is that which said unto thee, Take up thy bed, and walk?

13 And he that was healed wist not who it was: for Jesus had conveyed himself away, a multitude being in *that* place.

14 Afterward Jesus findeth him in the temple, and said unto him, Behold, thou art made whole: sin no more, lest a worse thing come unto thee.

15 The man departed, and told the Jews that it was Jesus, which had made him whole.

16 And therefore did the Jews persecute Jesus, and sought to slay him, because he had done these things on the sabbath day.

17 ¶ But Jesus answered them, My Father worketh hitherto, and I work.

18 Therefore the Jews sought the more to kill him, because he not only had broken the sabbath, but said also that God was his Father, making himself equal with God.

19 Then answered Jesus and said unto them, Verily, verily, I say unto you, The Son can do nothing of himself, but what he seeth the Father do: for what things soever he doeth, these also doeth the Son likewise.

20 For the Father loveth the Son, and sheweth him all things that himself doeth: and he will shew him greater works than these, that ye may marvel.

21 For as the Father raiseth up the dead, and quickeneth *them;* even so the Son quickeneth whom he will.

22 For the Father judgeth no man, but hath committed all judgment unto the Son:

23 That all *men* should honour the Son, even as they honour the Father. He that honoureth not the Son honoureth not the Father which hath sent him.

24 Verily, verily, I say unto you, He that heareth my word, and believeth on him that sent me, hath everlasting life, and shall not come into condemnation; but is

passed from death unto life.

25 Verily, verily, I say unto you, The hour is coming, and now is, when the dead shall hear the voice of the Son of God: and they that hear shall live.

26 For as the Father hath life in himself; so hath he given to the Son to have life in himself;

27 And hath given him authority to execute judgment also, because he is the Son of man.

28 Marvel not at this: for the hour is coming, in the which all that are in the graves shall hear his voice,

29 And shall come forth; they that have done good, unto the resurrection of life; and they that have done evil, unto the resurrection of damnation.

30 I can of mine own self do nothing: as I hear, I judge: and my judgment is just; because I seek not mine own will, but the will of the Father which hath sent me.

31 If I bear witness of myself, my witness is not true.

32 ¶ There is another that beareth witness of me; and I know that the witness which he witnesseth of me is true.

33 Ye sent unto John, and he bare witness unto the truth.

34 But I receive not testimony from man: but these things I say, that ye might be saved.

35 He was a burning and a shining light: and ye were willing for a season to rejoice in his light.

36 ¶ But I have greater witness than *that* of John: for the works which the Father hath given me to finish, the same works that I do, bear witness of me, that the Father hath sent me.

37 ¶ And the Father himself, which hath sent me, hath borne witness of me. Ye have neither heard his voice at any time, nor seen his shape.

38 And ye have not his word abiding in you: for whom he hath sent, him ye believe not.

39 ¶ Search the scriptures; for in them ye think ye have eternal life: and they are they which testify of me.

40 And ye will not come to me, that ye might have life.

41 I receive not honour from men.

42 But I know you, that ye have not the love of God in you.

43 I am come in my Father's name, and ye receive me not: if another shall come in his own name, him ye will receive.

44 How can ye believe, which receive honour one of another, and seek not the honour which *cometh* from God only?

45 Do not think that I will accuse you to the Father: there is *one* that accuseth you, *even* Moses, in whom ye trust.

46 For had ye believed Moses, ye would have believed me: for he wrote of me.

47 But if ye believe not his writings, how shall ye believe my words?

6 After these things Jesus went over the sea of Galilee, which is *the sea of* Tiberias.

2 And a great multitude followed him, because they saw his miracles which he did on them that were diseased.

3 And Jesus went up into a mountain, and there he sat with his disciples.

4 And the passover, a feast of the Jews, was nigh.

5 ¶ When Jesus then lifted up *his* eyes, and saw a great company come unto him, he saith unto Philip, Whence shall we buy bread, that these may eat?

6 And this he said to prove him: for he himself knew what he would do.

7 Philip answered him, Two hundred pennyworth of bread is not sufficient for them, that every one of them may take a little.

8 One of his disciples, Andrew, Simon Peter's brother, saith unto him,

9 There is a lad here, which hath five barley loaves, and two small fishes: but what are they among so many?

10 And Jesus said, Make the men sit down. Now there was much grass in the place. So the men sat down, in number about five thousand.

11 And Jesus took the loaves; and when he had given thanks, he distributed to the disciples, and the disciples to them that were set down; and likewise of the fishes as much as they would.

12 When they were filled, he said unto his disciples, Gather up the fragments that remain, that nothing be lost.

13 Therefore they gathered *them* together, and filled twelve baskets with the fragments of the five barley loaves, which remained over and above unto them that had eaten.

14 Then those men, when they had seen the miracle that Jesus did, said, This is of a truth that prophet that should come into the world.

15 ¶ When Jesus therefore perceived that they would come and take him by force, to make him a king, he departed again into a mountain himself alone.

16 And when even was *now* come, his disciples went down unto the sea,

17 And entered into a ship, and went over the sea toward Capernaum. And it was now dark, and Jesus was not come to them.

18 And the sea arose by reason of a great wind that blew.

19 So when they had rowed about five and twenty or thirty furlongs, they see Jesus walking on the sea, and drawing nigh unto the ship: and they were afraid.

20 But he saith unto them, It is I; be not afraid.

21 Then they willingly received him into the ship: and immediately the ship was at the land whither they went.

22 ¶ The day following, when the people which stood on the other side of the sea saw that there was none other boat there, save that one whereinto his disciples were entered, and that Jesus went not with his disciples into the boat, but *that* his disciples were gone

153

away alone;

23 (Howbeit there came other boats from Tiberias nigh unto the place where they did eat bread, after that the Lord had given thanks:)

24 When the people therefore saw that Jesus was not there, neither his disciples, they also took shipping, and came to Capernaum, seeking for Jesus.

25 And when they had found him on the other side of the sea, they said unto him, Rabbi, when camest thou hither?

26 Jesus answered them and said, Verily, verily, I say unto you, Ye seek me, not because ye saw the miracles, but because ye did eat of the loaves, and were filled.

27 Labour not for the meat which perisheth, but for that meat which endureth unto everlasting life, which the Son of man shall give unto you: for him hath God the Father sealed.

28 Then said they unto him, What shall we do, that we might work the works of God?

29 Jesus answered and said unto them, This is the work of God, that ye believe on him whom he hath sent.

30 They said therefore unto him, What sign shewest thou then, that we may see, and believe thee? what dost thou work?

31 Our fathers did eat manna in the desert; as it is written, He gave them bread from heaven to eat.

32 Then said Jesus unto them,

Verily, verily, I say unto you, Moses gave you not that bread from heaven; but my Father giveth you the true bread from heaven.

33 For the bread of God is he which cometh down from heaven, and giveth life unto the world.

34 Then said they unto him, Lord, evermore give us this bread.

35 And Jesus said unto them, I am the bread of life: he that cometh to me shall never hunger; and he that believeth on me shall never thirst.

36 But I said unto you, That ye also have seen me, and believe not.

37 All that the Father giveth me shall come to me; and him that cometh to me I will in no wise cast out.

38 For I came down from heaven, not to do mine own will, but the will of him that sent me.

39 And this is the Father's will which hath sent me, that of all which he hath given me I should lose nothing, but should raise it up again at the last day.

40 And this is the will of him that sent me, that every one which seeth the Son, and believeth on him, may have everlasting life: and I will raise him up at the last day.

41 The Jews then murmured at him, because he said, I am the bread which came down from heaven.

42 And they said, Is not this

Jesus, the son of Joseph, whose father and mother we know? how is it then that he saith, I came down from heaven?

43 Jesus therefore answered and said unto them, Murmur not among yourselves.

44 No man can come to me, except the Father which hath sent me draw him: and I will raise him up at the last day.

45 It is written in the prophets, And they shall be all taught of God. Every man therefore that hath heard, and hath learned of the Father, cometh unto me.

46 Not that any man hath seen the Father, save he which is of God, he hath seen the Father.

47 Verily, verily, I say unto you, He that believeth on me hath everlasting life.

48 I am that bread of life.

49 Your fathers did eat manna in the wilderness, and are dead.

50 This is the bread which cometh down from heaven, that a man may eat thereof, and not die.

51 I am the living bread which came down from heaven: if any man eat of this bread, he shall live for ever: and the bread that I will give is my flesh, which I will give for the life of the world.

52 The Jews therefore strove among themselves, saying, How can this man give us *his* flesh to eat?

53 Then Jesus said unto them, Verily, verily, I say unto you, Except ye eat the flesh of the Son of man, and drink his blood, ye have no life in you.

54 Whoso eateth my flesh, and drinketh my blood, hath eternal life; and I will raise him up at the last day.

55 For my flesh is meat indeed, and my blood is drink indeed.

56 He that eateth my flesh, and drinketh my blood, dwelleth in me, and I in him.

57 As the living Father hath sent me, and I live by the Father: so he that eateth me, even he shall live by me.

58 This is that bread which came down from heaven: not as your fathers did eat manna, and are dead: he that eateth of this bread shall live for ever.

59 These things said he in the synagogue, as he taught in Capernaum.

60 Many therefore of his disciples, when they had heard *this,* said, This is an hard saying; who can hear it?

61 When Jesus knew in himself that his disciples murmured at it, he said unto them, Doth this offend you?

62 *What* and if ye shall see the Son of man ascend up where he was before?

63 It is the spirit that quickeneth; the flesh profiteth nothing: the words that I speak unto you, *they* are spirit, and *they* are life.

64 But there are some of you that believe not. For Jesus knew from the beginning who they were that believed not, and who should betray him.

65 And he said, Therefore said I

155

unto you, that no man can come unto me, except it were given unto him of my Father.

66 ¶ From that *time* many of his disciples went back, and walked no more with him.

67 Then said Jesus unto the twelve, Will ye also go away?

68 ¶ Then Simon Peter answered him, Lord, to whom shall we go? thou hast the words of eternal life.

69 And we believe and are sure that thou art that Christ, the Son of the living God.

70 ¶ Jesus answered them, Have not I chosen you twelve, and one of you is a devil?

71 He spake of Judas Iscariot *the son* of Simon: for he it was that should betray him, being one of the twelve.

7 After these things Jesus walked in Galilee: for he would not walk in Jewry, because the Jews sought to kill him.

2 Now the Jew's feast of tabernacles was at hand.

3 His brethren therefore said unto him, Depart hence, and go into Judaea, that thy disciples also may see the works that thou doest.

4 For *there is* no man *that* doeth any thing in secret, and he himself seeketh to be known openly. If thou do these things, shew thyself to the world.

5 For neither did his brethren believe in him.

6 Then Jesus said unto them, My time is not yet come: but your time is alway ready.

7 The world cannot hate you; but me it hateth, because I testify of it, that the works thereof are evil.

8 Go ye up unto this feast: I go not up yet unto this feast; for my time is not yet full come.

9 When he had said these words unto them, he abode *still* in Galilee.

10 ¶ But when his brethren were gone up, then went he also up unto the feast, not openly, but as it were in secret.

11 Then the Jews sought him at the feast, and said, Where is he?

12 And there was much murmuring among the people concerning him: for some said, He is a good man: others said, Nay; but he deceiveth the people.

13 Howbeit no man spake openly of him for fear of the Jews.

14 ¶ Now about the midst of the feast Jesus went up into the temple, and taught.

15 And the Jews marvelled, saying, How knoweth this man letters, having never learned?

16 Jesus answered them, and said, My doctrine is not mine, but his that sent me.

17 If any man will do his will, he shall know of the doctrine, whether it be of God, or *whether* I speak of myself.

18 He that speaketh of himself seeketh his own glory: but he that seeketh his glory that sent him, the same is true, and no unrighteousness is in him.

19 Did not Moses give you the law, and yet none of you keepeth

the law? Why go ye about to kill me?

20 The people answered and said, Thou hast a devil: who goeth about to kill thee?

21 Jesus answered and said unto them, I have done one work, and ye all marvel.

22 Moses therefore gave unto you circumcision; (not because it is of Moses, but of the fathers;) and ye on the sabbath day circumcise a man.

23 If a man on the sabbath day receive circumcision, that the law of Moses should not be broken; are ye angry at me, because I have made a man every whit whole on the sabbath day?

24 Judge not according to the appearance, but judge righteous judgment.

25 Then said some of them of Jerusalem, Is not this he, whom they seek to kill?

26 But, lo, he speaketh boldly, and they say nothing unto him. Do the rulers know indeed that this is the very Christ?

27 Howbeit we know this man whence he is: but when Christ cometh, no man knoweth whence he is.

28 Then cried Jesus in the temple as he taught, saying, Ye both know me, and ye know whence I am: and I am not come of myself, but he that sent me is true, whom ye know not.

29 But I know him: for I am from him, and he hath sent me.

30 Then they sought to take him: but no man laid hands on him, because his hour was not yet come.

31 And many of the people believed on him, and said, When Christ cometh, will he do more miracles than these which this *man* hath done?

32 ❡ The Pharisees heard that the people murmured such things concerning him; and the Pharisees and the chief priests sent officers to take him.

33 Then said Jesus unto them, Yet a little while am I with you, and *then* I go unto him that sent me.

34 Ye shall seek me, and shall not find *me*: and where I am, *thither* ye cannot come.

35 Then said the Jews among themselves, Whither will he go, that we shall not find him? will he go unto the dispersed among the Gentiles, and teach the Gentiles?

36 What *manner of* saying is this that he said, Ye shall seek me, and shall not find *me*: and where I am, *thither* ye cannot come?

37 In the last day, that great *day* of the feast, Jesus stood and cried, saying, If any man thirst, let him come unto me, and drink.

38 He that believeth on me, as the scripture hath said, out of his belly shall flow rivers of living water.

39 (But this spake he of the Spirit, which they that believe on him should receive: for the Holy Ghost was not yet *given*; because that Jesus was not yet glorified.)

40 ❡ Many of the people there-

JOHN 7:41

fore, when they heard this saying, said, Of a truth this is the Prophet.

41 Others said, This is the Christ. But some said, Shall Christ come out of Galilee?

42 Hath not the scripture said, That Christ cometh of the seed of David, and out of the town of Bethlehem, where David was?

43 So there was a division among the people because of him.

44 And some of them would have taken him; but no man laid hands on him.

45 ¶ Then came the officers to the chief priests and Pharisees; and they said unto them, Why have ye not brought him?

46 The officers answered, Never man spake like this man.

47 Then answered them the Pharisees, Are ye also deceived?

48 Have any of the rulers or of the Pharisees believed on him?

49 But this people who knoweth not the law are cursed.

50 Nicodemus saith unto them, (he that came to Jesus by night, being one of them,)

51 Doth our law judge *any* man, before it hear him, and know what he doeth?

52 They answered and said unto him, Art thou also of Galilee? Search, and look: for out of Galilee ariseth no prophet.

53 And every man went unto his own house.

8 Jesus went unto the mount of Olives.

2 And early in the morning he came again into the temple, and all the people came unto him; and he sat down, and taught them.

3 And the scribes and Pharisees brought unto him a woman taken in adultery; and when they had set her in the midst,

4 They say unto him, Master, this woman was taken in adultery, in the very act.

5 Now Moses in the law commanded us, that such should be stoned: but what sayest thou?

6 This they said, tempting him, that they might have to accuse him. But Jesus stooped down, and with *his* finger wrote on the ground, *as though he heard them not.*

7 So when they continued asking him, he lifted up himself, and said unto them, He that is without sin among you, let him first cast a stone at her.

8 And again he stooped down, and wrote on the ground.

9 And they which heard *it*, being convicted by *their* own conscience, went out one by one, beginning at the eldest, *even* unto the last: and Jesus was left alone, and the woman standing in the midst.

10 When Jesus had lifted up himself, and saw none but the woman, he said unto her, Woman, where are those thine accusers? hath no man condemned thee?

11 She said, No man, Lord. And Jesus said unto her, Neither do I condemn thee: go, and sin no

more.

12 ¶ Then spake Jesus again unto them, saying, I am the light of the world: he that followeth me shall not walk in darkness, but shall have the light of life.

13 The Pharisees therefore said unto him, Thou bearest record of thyself; thy record is not true.

14 Jesus answered and said unto them, Though I bear record of myself, yet my record is true: for I know whence I came, and whither I go; but ye cannot tell whence I come, and whither I go.

15 Ye judge after the flesh; I judge no man.

16 And yet if I judge, my judgment is true: for I am not alone, but I and the Father that sent me.

17 It is also written in your law, that the testimony of two men is true.

18 I am one that bear witness of myself, and the Father that sent me beareth witness of me.

19 Then said they unto him, Where is thy Father? Jesus answered, Ye neither know me, nor my Father: if ye had known me, ye should have known my Father also.

20 These words spake Jesus in the treasury, as he taught in the temple: and no man laid hands on him; for his hour was not yet come.

21 Then said Jesus again unto them, I go my way, and ye shall seek me, and shall die in your sins: whither I go, ye cannot come.

22 Then said the Jews, Will he kill himself? because he saith, Whither I go, ye cannot come.

23 And he said unto them, Ye are from beneath; I am from above: ye are of this world; I am not of this world.

24 I said therefore unto you, that ye shall die in your sins: for if ye believe not that I am he, ye shall die in your sins.

25 Then said they unto him, Who art thou? And Jesus saith unto them, Even the same that I said unto you from the beginning.

26 I have many things to say and to judge of you: but he that sent me is true; and I speak to the world those things which I have heard of him.

27 They understood not that he spake to them of the Father.

28 Then said Jesus unto them, When ye have lifted up the Son of man, then shall ye know that I am he, and that I do nothing of myself; but as my Father hath taught me, I speak these things.

29 And he that sent me is with me: the Father hath not left me alone; for I do always those things that please him.

30 As he spake these words, many believed on him.

31 Then said Jesus to those Jews which believed on him, If ye continue in my word, then are ye my disciples indeed;

32 And ye shall know the truth, and the truth shall make you free.

33 ¶ They answered him, We be

Abraham's seed, and were never in bondage to any man: how sayest thou, Ye shall be made free?

34 Jesus answered them, Verily, verily, I say unto you, Whosoever committeth sin is the servant of sin.

35 And the servant abideth not in the house for ever: *but* the Son abideth ever.

36 If the Son therefore shall make you free, ye shall be free indeed.

37 I know that ye are Abraham's seed; but ye seek to kill me, because my word hath no place in you.

38 I speak that which I have seen with my Father: and ye do that which ye have seen with your father.

39 They answered and said unto him, Abraham is our father. Jesus saith unto them, If ye were Abraham's children, ye would do the works of Abraham.

40 But now ye seek to kill me, a man that hath told you the truth, which I have heard of God: this did not Abraham.

41 Ye do the deeds of your father. Then said they to him, We be not born of fornication; we have one Father, *even* God.

42 Jesus said unto them, If God were your Father, ye would love me: for I proceeded forth and came from God; neither came I of myself, but he sent me.

43 Why do ye not understand my speech? *even* because ye cannot hear my word.

44 Ye are of *your* father the dev-

il, and the lusts of your father ye will do. He was a murderer from the beginning, and abode not in the truth, because there is no truth in him. When he speaketh a lie, he speaketh of his own: for he is a liar, and the father of it.

45 And because I tell *you* the truth, ye believe me not.

46 Which of you convinceth me of sin? And if I say the truth, why do ye not believe me?

47 He that is of God heareth God's words: ye therefore hear *them* not, because ye are not of God.

48 Then answered the Jews, and said unto him, Say we not well that thou art a Samaritan, and hast a devil?

49 Jesus answered, I have not a devil; but I honour my Father, and ye do dishonour me.

50 And I seek not mine own glory: there is one that seeketh and judgeth.

51 Verily, verily, I say unto you, If a man keep my saying, he shall never see death.

52 Then said the Jews unto him, Now we know that thou hast a devil. Abraham is dead, and the prophets; and thou sayest, If a man keep my saying, he shall never taste of death.

53 Art thou greater than our father Abraham, which is dead? and the prophets are dead: whom makest thou thyself?

54 Jesus answered, If I honour myself, my honour is nothing: it is my Father that honoureth me; of whom ye say, that he is

your God:

55 Yet ye have not known him; but I know him: and if I should say, I know him not, I shall be a liar like unto you: but I know him, and keep his saying.

56 Your father Abraham rejoiced to see my day: and he saw *it*, and was glad.

57 Then said the Jews unto him, Thou art not yet fifty years old, and hast thou seen Abraham?

58 Jesus said unto them, Verily, verily, I say unto you, Before Abraham was, I am.

59 ¶ Then took they up stones to cast at him: but Jesus hid himself, and went out of the temple, going through the midst of them, and so passed by.

9 And as *Jesus* passed by, he saw a man which was blind from *his* birth.

2 And his disciples asked him, saying, Master, who did sin, this man, or his parents, that he was born blind?

3 Jesus answered, Neither hath this man sinned, nor his parents: but that the works of God should be made manifest in him.

4 I must work the works of him that sent me, while it is day: the night cometh, when no man can work.

5 As long as I am in the world, I am the light of the world.

6 When he had thus spoken, he spat on the ground, and made clay of the spittle, and he anointed the eyes of the blind man with the clay,

7 And said unto him, Go, wash in the pool of Siloam, (which is by interpretation, Sent.) He went his way therefore, and washed, and came seeing.

8 ¶ The neighbours therefore, and they which before had seen him that he was blind, said, Is not this he that sat and begged?

9 Some said, This is he: others *said*, He is like him: *but* he said, I am *he*.

10 Therefore said they unto him, How were thine eyes opened?

11 He answered and said, A man that is called Jesus made clay, and anointed mine eyes, and said unto me, Go to the pool of Siloam, and wash: and I went and washed, and I received sight.

12 Then said they unto him, Where is he? He said, I know not.

13 ¶ They brought to the Pharisees him that aforetime was blind.

14 And it was the sabbath day when Jesus made the clay, and opened his eyes.

15 Then again the Pharisees also asked him how he had received his sight. He said unto them, He put clay upon mine eyes, and I washed, and do see.

16 Therefore said some of the Pharisees, This man is not of God, because he keepeth not the sabbath day. Others said, How can a man that is a sinner do such miracles? And there was a division among them.

17 They say unto the blind man again, What sayest thou of him, that he hath opened thine eyes?

He said, He is a prophet.

18 But the Jews did not believe concerning him, that he had been blind, and received his sight, until they called the parents of him that had received his sight.

19 And they asked them, saying, Is this your son, who ye say was born blind? how then doth he now see?

20 His parents answered them and said, We know that this is our son, and that he was born blind:

21 But by what means he now seeth, we know not; or who hath opened his eyes, we know not: he is of age; ask him: he shall speak for himself.

22 These *words* spake his parents, because they feared the Jews: for the Jews had agreed already, that if any man did confess that he was Christ, he should be put out of the synagogue.

23 Therefore said his parents, He is of age; ask him.

24 Then again called they the man that was blind, and said unto him, Give God the praise: we know that this man is a sinner.

25 He answered and said, Whether he be a sinner *or no*, I know not: one thing I know, that, whereas I was blind, now I see.

26 Then said they to him again, What did he to thee? how opened he thine eyes?

27 He answered them, I have told you already, and ye did not hear: wherefore would ye hear *it* again? will ye also be his disciples?

28 Then they reviled him, and said, Thou art his disciple; but we are Moses' disciples.

29 We know that God spake unto Moses: *as for* this *fellow*, we know not from whence he is.

30 The man answered and said unto them, Why herein is a marvellous thing, that ye know not from whence he is, and *yet* he hath opened mine eyes.

31 Now we know that God heareth not sinners: but if any man be a worshipper of God, and doeth his will, him he heareth.

32 Since the world began was it not heard that any man opened the eyes of one that was born blind.

33 If this man were not of God, he could do nothing.

34 They answered and said unto him, Thou wast altogether born in sins, and dost thou teach us? And they cast him out.

35 ¶ Jesus heard that they had cast him out; and when he had found him, he said unto him, Dost thou believe on the Son of God?

36 He answered and said, Who is he, Lord, that I might believe on him?

37 And Jesus said unto him, Thou hast both seen him, and it is he that talketh with thee.

38 And he said, Lord, I believe. And he worshipped him.

39 ¶ And Jesus said, For judgment I am come into this world, that they which see not might see; and that they which see might be made blind.

40 And *some* of the Pharisees which were with him heard these

words, and said unto him, Are we blind also?

41 Jesus said unto them, If ye were blind, ye should have no sin: but now ye say, We see; therefore your sin remaineth.

10

Verily, verily, I say unto you, He that entereth not by the door into the sheepfold, but climbeth up some other way, the same is a thief and a robber.

2 But he that entereth in by the door is the shepherd of the sheep.

3 To him the porter openeth; and the sheep hear his voice: and he calleth his own sheep by name, and leadeth them out.

4 And when he putteth forth his own sheep, he goeth before them, and the sheep follow him: for they know his voice.

5 And a stranger will they not follow, but will flee from him: for they know not the voice of strangers.

6 This parable spake Jesus unto them: but they understood not what things they were which he spake unto them.

7 Then said Jesus unto them again, Verily, verily, I say unto you, I am the door of the sheep.

8 All that ever came before me are thieves and robbers: but the sheep did not hear them.

9 I am the door: by me if any man enter in, he shall be saved, and shall go in and out, and find pasture.

10 The thief cometh not, but for to steal, and to kill, and to destroy: I am come that they might have life, and that they might have *it* more abundantly.

11 I am the good shepherd: the good shepherd giveth his life for the sheep.

12 But he that is an hireling, and not the shepherd, whose own the sheep are not, seeth the wolf coming, and leaveth the sheep, and fleeth: and the wolf catcheth them, and scattereth the sheep.

13 The hireling fleeth, because he is an hireling, and careth not for the sheep.

14 I am the good shepherd, and know my *sheep*, and am known of mine.

15 As the Father knoweth me, even so know I the Father: and I lay down my life for the sheep.

16 And other sheep I have, which are not of this fold: them also I must bring, and they shall hear my voice; and there shall be one fold, *and* one shepherd.

17 Therefore doth my Father love me, because I lay down my life, that I might take it again.

18 ¶ No man taketh it from me, but I lay it down of myself. I have power to lay it down, and I have power to take it again. This commandment have I received of my Father.

19 There was a division therefore again among the Jews for these sayings.

20 And many of them said, He hath a devil, and is mad; why hear ye him?

21 Others said, These are not the words of him that hath a

devil. Can a devil open the eyes of the blind?

22 ¢ And it was at Jerusalem the feast of the dedication, and it was winter.

23 And Jesus walked in the temple in Solomon's porch.

24 Then came the Jews round about him, and said unto him, How long dost thou make us to doubt? If thou be the Christ, tell us plainly.

25 Jesus answered them, I told you, and ye believed not: the works that I do in my Father's name, they bear witness of me.

26 But ye believe not, because ye are not of my sheep, as I said unto you.

27 My sheep hear my voice, and I know them, and they follow me:

28 And I give unto them eternal life; and they shall never perish, neither shall any *man* pluck them out of my hand.

29 My Father, which gave *them* me, is greater than all; and no *man* is able to pluck *them* out of my Father's hand.

30 I and *my* Father are one.

31 Then the Jews took up stones again to stone him.

32 Jesus answered them, Many good works have I shewed you from my Father; for which of those works do ye stone me?

33 The Jews answered him, saying, For a good work we stone thee not; but for blasphemy; and because that thou, being a man, makest thyself God.

34 Jesus answered them, Is it not written in your law, I said, Ye are gods?

35 If he called them gods, unto whom the word of God came, and the scripture cannot be broken;

36 Say ye of him, whom the Father hath sanctified, and sent into the world, Thou blasphemest; because I said, I am the Son of God?

37 If I do not the works of my Father, believe me not.

38 But if I do, though ye believe not me, believe the works: that ye may know, and believe, that the Father *is* in me, and I in him.

39 Therefore they sought again to take him: but he escaped out of their hand,

40 And went away again beyond Jordan into the place where John at first baptized; and there he abode.

41 And many resorted unto him, and said, John did no miracle: but all things that John spake of this man were true.

42 And many believed on him there.

11 Now a certain *man* was sick, *named* Lazarus, of Bethany, the town of Mary and her sister Martha.

2 (It was *that* Mary which anointed the Lord with ointment, and wiped his feet with her hair, whose brother Lazarus was sick.)

3 Therefore his sisters sent unto him, saying, Lord, behold, he whom thou lovest is sick.

4 When Jesus heard *that*, he

said, This sickness is not unto death, but for the glory of God, that the Son of God might be glorified thereby.

5 Now Jesus loved Martha, and her sister, and Lazarus.

6 When he had heard therefore that he was sick, he abode two days still in the same place where he was.

7 Then after that saith he to *his* disciples, Let us go into Judaea again.

8 *His* disciples say unto him, Master, the Jews of late sought to stone thee; and goest thou thither again?

9 Jesus answered, Are there not twelve hours in the day? If any man walk in the day, he stumbleth not, because he seeth the light of this world.

10 But if a man walk in the night, he stumbleth, because there is no light in him.

11 These things said he: and after that he saith unto them, Our friend Lazarus sleepeth; but I go, that I may awake him out of sleep.

12 Then said his disciples, Lord, if he sleep, he shall do well.

13 Howbeit Jesus spake of his death: but they thought that he had spoken of taking of rest in sleep.

14 Then said Jesus unto them plainly, Lazarus is dead.

15 And I am glad for your sakes that I was not there, to the intent ye may believe; nevertheless let us go unto him.

16 Then said Thomas, which is called Didymus, unto his fellowdisciples, Let us also go, that we may die with him.

17 Then when Jesus came, he found that he had *lain* in the grave four days already.

18 Now Bethany was nigh unto Jerusalem, about fifteen furlongs off:

19 And many of the Jews came to Martha and Mary, to comfort them concerning their brother.

20 Then Martha, as soon as she heard that Jesus was coming, went and met him: but Mary sat *still* in the house.

21 Then said Martha unto Jesus, Lord, if thou hadst been here, my brother had not died.

22 But I know, that even now, whatsoever thou wilt ask of God, God will give *it* thee.

23 Jesus saith unto her, Thy brother shall rise again.

24 Martha saith unto him, I know that he shall rise again in the resurrection at the last day.

25 Jesus said unto her, I am the resurrection, and the life: he that believeth in me, though he were dead, yet shall he live:

26 And whosoever liveth and believeth in me shall never die. Believest thou this?

27 She saith unto him, Yea, Lord: I believe that thou art the Christ, the Son of God, which should come into the world.

28 And when she had so said, she went her way, and called Mary her sister secretly, saying, The Master is come, and calleth for thee.

29 As soon as she heard *that,* she arose quickly, and came unto him.

30 Now Jesus was not yet come into the town, but was in that place where Martha met him.

31 The Jews then which were with her in the house, and comforted her, when they saw Mary, that she rose up hastily and went out, followed her, saying, She goeth unto the grave to weep there.

32 Then when Mary was come where Jesus was, and saw him, she fell down at his feet, saying unto him, Lord, if thou hadst been here, my brother had not died.

33 When Jesus therefore saw her weeping, and the Jews also weeping which came with her, he groaned in the spirit, and was troubled.

34 And said, Where have ye laid him? They said unto him, Lord, come and see.

35 Jesus wept.

36 Then said the Jews, Behold how he loved him!

37 And some of them said, Could not this man, which opened the eyes of the blind, have caused that even this man should not have died?

38 Jesus therefore again groaning in himself cometh to the grave. It was a cave, and a stone lay upon it.

39 Jesus said, Take ye away the stone. Martha, the sister of him that was dead, saith unto him, Lord, by this time he stinketh: for he hath been *dead* four days.

40 Jesus saith unto her, Said I not unto thee, that, if thou wouldest believe, thou shouldest see the glory of God?

41 Then they took away the stone *from the place* where the dead was laid. And Jesus lifted up *his* eyes, and said, Father, I thank thee that thou hast heard me.

42 And I knew that thou hearest me always: but because of the people which stand by I said *it,* that they may believe that thou hast sent me.

43 And when he thus had spoken, he cried with a loud voice, Lazarus, come forth.

44 And he that was dead came forth, bound hand and foot with graveclothes: and his face was bound about with a napkin. Jesus saith unto them, Loose him, and let him go.

45 Then many of the Jews which came to Mary, and had seen the things which Jesus did, believed on him.

46 ¶ But some of them went their ways to the Pharisees, and told them what things Jesus had done.

47 Then gathered the chief priests and the Pharisees a council, and said, What do we? for this man doeth many miracles.

48 If we let him thus alone, all *men* will believe on him: and the Romans shall come and take away both our place and nation.

49 And one of them, *named* Caiaphas, being the high priest

that same year, said unto them, Ye know nothing at all,

50 Nor consider that it is expedient for us, that one man should die for the people, and that the whole nation perish not.

51 And this spake he not of himself: but being high priest that year, he prophesied that Jesus should die for that nation;

52 And not for that nation only, but that also he should gather together in one the children of God that were scattered abroad.

53 Then from that day forth they took counsel together for to put him to death.

54 Jesus therefore walked no more openly among the Jews; but went thence unto a country near to the wilderness, into a city called Ephraim, and there continued with his disciples.

55 ¶ And the Jews' passover was nigh at hand: and many went out of the country up to Jerusalem before the passover, to purify themselves.

56 Then sought they for Jesus, and spake among themselves, as they stood in the temple, What think ye, that he will not come to the feast?

57 Now both the chief priests and the Pharisees had given a commandment, that, if any man knew where he were, he should shew *it*, that they might take him.

12 Then Jesus six days before the passover came to Bethany, where Lazarus was which had been dead, whom he

raised from the dead.

2 There they made him a supper; and Martha served: but Lazarus was one of them that sat at the table with him.

3 Then took Mary a pound of ointment of spikenard, very costly, and anointed the feet of Jesus, and wiped his feet with her hair: and the house was filled with the odour of the ointment.

4 Then saith one of his disciples, Judas Iscariot, Simon's *son*, which should betray him,

5 Why was not this ointment sold for three hundred pence, and given to the poor?

6 This he said, not that he cared for the poor; but because he was a thief, and had the bag, and bare what was put therein.

7 Then said Jesus, Let her alone: against the day of my burying hath she kept this.

8 For the poor always ye have with you; but me ye have not always.

9 Much people of the Jews therefore knew that he was there: and they came not for Jesus' sake only, but that they might see Lazarus also, whom he had raised from the dead.

10 ¶ But the chief priests consulted that they might put Lazarus also to death;

11 Because that by reason of him many of the Jews went away, and believed on Jesus.

12 ¶ On the next day much people that were come to the feast, when they heard that Jesus was coming to Jerusalem,

13 Took branches of palm trees, and went forth to meet him, and cried, Hosanna: Blessed *is* the King of Israel that cometh in the name of the Lord.

14 And Jesus, when he had found a young ass, sat thereon; as it is written,

15 Fear not, daughter of Sion: behold, thy King cometh, sitting on an ass's colt.

16 These things understood not his disciples at the first: but when Jesus was glorified, then remembered they that these things were written of him, and *that* they had done these things unto him.

17 The people therefore that was with him when he called Lazarus out of his grave, and raised him from the dead, bare record.

18 For this cause the people also met him, for that they heard that he had done this miracle.

19 The Pharisees therefore said among themselves, Perceive ye how ye prevail nothing? behold, the world is gone after him.

20 ¶ And there were certain Greeks among them that came up to worship at the feast:

21 The same came therefore to Philip, which was of Bethsaida of Galilee, and desired him, saying, Sir, we would see Jesus.

22 Philip cometh and telleth Andrew: and again Andrew and Philip tell Jesus.

23 ¶ And Jesus answered them, saying, The hour is come, that the Son of man should be glorified.

24 Verily, verily, I say unto you,

Except a corn of wheat fall into the ground and die, it abideth alone: but if it die, it bringeth forth much fruit.

25 He that loveth his life shall lose it; and he that hateth his life in this world shall keep it unto life eternal.

26 If any man serve me, let him follow me; and where I am, there shall also my servant be: if any man serve me, him will *my* Father honour.

27 Now is my soul troubled; and what shall I say? Father, save me from this hour: but for this cause came I unto this hour.

28 Father, glorify thy name. Then came there a voice from heaven, *saying,* I have both glorified *it,* and will glorify *it* again.

29 The people therefore, that stood by, and heard *it,* said that it thundered: others said, An angel spake to him.

30 Jesus answered and said, This voice came not because of me, but for your sakes.

31 Now is the judgment of this world: now shall the prince of this world be cast out.

32 And I, if I be lifted up from the earth, will draw all *men* unto me.

33 This he said, signifying what death he should die.

34 The people answered him, We have heard out of the law that Christ abideth for ever: and how sayest thou, The Son of man must be lifted up? who is this Son of man?

35 Then Jesus said unto them,

Yet a little while is the light with you. Walk while ye have the light, lest darkness come upon you: for he that walketh in darkness knoweth not whither he goeth.

36 While ye have light, believe in the light, that ye may be the children of light. These things spake Jesus, and departed, and did hide himself from them.

37 ¶ But though he had done so many miracles before them, yet they believed not on him:

38 That the saying of Esaias the prophet might be fulfilled, which he spake, Lord, who hath believed our report? and to whom hath the arm of the Lord been revealed?

39 Therefore they could not believe, because that Esaias said again,

40 He hath blinded their eyes, and hardened their heart; that they should not see with *their* eyes, nor understand with *their* heart, and be converted, and I should heal them.

41 These things said Esaias, when he saw his glory, and spake of him.

42 ¶ Nevertheless among the chief rulers also many believed on him; but because of the Pharisees they did not confess *him*, lest they should be put out of the synagogue:

43 For they loved the praise of men more than the praise of God.

44 ¶ Jesus cried and said, He that believeth on me, believeth not on me, but on him that sent me.

45 And he that seeth me seeth him that sent me.

46 I am come a light into the world, that whosoever believeth on me should not abide in darkness.

47 And if any man hear my words, and believe not, I judge him not: for I came not to judge the world, but to save the world.

48 He that rejecteth me, and receiveth not my words, hath one that judgeth him: the word that I have spoken, the same shall judge him in the last day.

49 For I have not spoken of myself; but the Father which sent me, he gave me a commandment, what I should say, and what I should speak.

50 And I know that his commandment is life everlasting: whatsoever I speak therefore, even as the Father said unto me, so I speak.

13

Now before the feast of the passover, when Jesus knew that his hour was come that he should depart out of this world unto the Father, having loved his own which were in the world, he loved them unto the end.

2 And supper being ended, the devil having now put into the heart of Judas Iscariot, Simon's *son*, to betray him;

3 Jesus knowing that the Father had given all things into his hands, and that he was come from God, and went to God;

4 He riseth from supper, and laid aside his garments; and took

169

a towel, and girded himself.

5 After that he poureth water into a bason, and began to wash the disciples' feet, and to wipe *them* with the towel wherewith he was girded.

6 Then cometh he to Simon Peter: and Peter saith unto him, Lord, dost thou wash my feet?

7 Jesus answered and said unto him, What I do thou knowest not now; but thou shalt know hereafter.

8 Peter saith unto him, Thou shalt never wash my feet. Jesus answered him, If I wash thee not, thou hast no part with me.

9 Simon Peter saith unto him, Lord, not my feet only, but also *my* hands and *my* head.

10 Jesus saith to him, He that is washed needeth not save to wash *his* feet, but is clean every whit: and ye are clean, but not all.

11 For he knew who should betray him; therefore said he, Ye are not all clean.

12 So after he had washed their feet, and had taken his garments, and was set down again, he said unto them, Know ye what I have done to you?

13 Ye call me Master and Lord: and ye say well; for *so* I am.

14 If I then, *your* Lord and Master, have washed your feet; ye also ought to wash one another's feet.

15 For I have given you an example, that ye should do as I have done to you.

16 Verily, verily, I say unto you, The servant is not greater than his lord; neither he that is sent greater than he that sent him.

17 If ye know these things, happy are ye if ye do them.

18 ¶ I speak not of you all: I know whom I have chosen: but that the scripture may be fulfilled, He that eateth bread with me hath lifted up his heel against me.

19 Now I tell you before it come, that, when it is come to pass, ye may believe that I am *he.*

20 Verily, verily, I say unto you, He that receiveth whomsoever I send receiveth me; and he that receiveth me receiveth him that sent me.

21 When Jesus had thus said, he was troubled in spirit, and testified, and said, Verily, verily, I say unto you, that one of you shall betray me.

22 Then the disciples looked one on another, doubting of whom he spake.

23 Now there was leaning on Jesus' bosom one of his disciples, whom Jesus loved.

24 Simon Peter therefore beckoned to him, that he should ask who it should be of whom he spake.

25 He then lying on Jesus' breast saith unto him, Lord, who is it?

26 Jesus answered, He it is, to whom I shall give a sop, when I have dipped *it.* And when he had dipped the sop, he gave *it* to Judas Iscariot, *the son* of Simon.

27 And after the sop Satan entered into him. Then said Jesus unto him, That thou doest, do

quickly.

28 Now no man at the table knew for what intent he spake this unto him.

29 For some *of them* thought, because Judas had the bag, that Jesus had said unto him, Buy *those things* that we have need of against the feast; or, that he should give something to the poor.

30 He then having received the sop went immediately out: and it was night.

31 ¶ Therefore, when he was gone out, Jesus said, Now is the Son of man glorified, and God is glorified in him.

32 If God be glorified in him, God shall also glorify him in himself, and shall straightway glorify him.

33 Little children, yet a little while I am with you. Ye shall seek me: and as I said unto the Jews, Whither I go, ye cannot come; so now I say to you.

34 A new commandment I give unto you, That ye love one another; as I have loved you, that ye also love one another.

35 By this shall all *men* know that ye are my disciples, if ye have love one to another.

36 ¶ Simon Peter said unto him, Lord, whither goest thou? Jesus answered him, Whither I go, thou canst not follow me now; but thou shalt follow me afterwards.

37 Peter said unto him, Lord, why cannot I follow thee now? I will lay down my life for thy sake.

38 Jesus answered him, Wilt thou lay down thy life for my sake? Verily, verily, I say unto thee, The cock shall not crow, till thou hast denied me thrice.

14 Let not your heart be troubled: ye believe in God, believe also in me.

2 In my Father's house are many mansions: if *it were* not *so,* I would have told you. I go to prepare a place for you.

3 And if I go and prepare a place for you, I will come again, and receive you unto myself; that where I am, *there* ye may be also.

4 And whither I go ye know, and the way ye know.

5 Thomas saith unto him, Lord, we know not whither thou goest; and how can we know the way?

6 ¶ Jesus saith unto him, I am the way, the truth, and the life: no man cometh unto the Father, but by me.

7 If ye had known me, ye should have known my Father also: and from henceforth ye know him, and have seen him.

8 Philip saith unto him, Lord, shew us the Father, and it sufficeth us.

9 Jesus saith unto him, Have I been so long time with you, and yet hast thou not known me, Philip? he that hath seen me hath seen the Father; and how sayest thou *then,* Shew us the Father?

10 Believest thou not that I am in the Father, and the Father in me? the words that I speak unto

you I speak not of myself: but the Father that dwelleth in me, he doeth the works.

11 Believe me that I *am* in the Father, and the Father in me: or else believe me for the very works' sake.

12 Verily, verily, I say unto you, He that believeth on me, the works that I do shall he do also; and greater *works* than these shall he do; because I go unto my Father.

13 ¶ And whatsoever ye shall ask in my name, that will I do, that the Father may be glorified in the Son.

14 If ye shall ask any thing in my name, I will do *it.*

15 ¶ If ye love me, keep my commandments.

16 And I will pray the Father, and he shall give you another Comforter, that he may abide with you for ever;

17 *Even* the Spirit of truth; whom the world cannot receive, because it seeth him not, neither knoweth him: but ye know him; for he dwelleth with you, and shall be in you.

18 I will not leave you comfortless: I will come to you.

19 Yet a little while, and the world seeth me no more; but ye see me: because I live, ye shall live also.

20 At that day ye shall know that I *am* in my Father, and ye in me, and I in you.

21 He that hath my commandments, and keepeth them, he it is that loveth me: and he that loveth

me shall be loved of my Father, and I will love him, and will manifest myself to him.

22 Judas saith unto him, not Iscariot, Lord, how is it that thou wilt manifest thyself unto us, and not unto the world?

23 Jesus answered and said unto him, If a man love me, he will keep my words: and my Father will love him, and we will come unto him, and make our abode with him.

24 He that loveth me not keepeth not my sayings: and the word which ye hear is not mine, but the Father's which sent me.

25 These things have I spoken unto you, being *yet* present with you.

26 But the Comforter, *which is* the Holy Ghost, whom the Father will send in my name, he shall teach you all things, and bring all things to your remembrance, whatsoever I have said unto you.

27 ¶ Peace I leave with you, my peace I give unto you: not as the world giveth, give I unto you. Let not your heart be troubled, neither let it be afraid.

28 Ye have heard how I said unto you, I go away, and come *again* unto you. If ye loved me, ye would rejoice, because I said, I go unto the Father: for my Father is greater than I.

29 And now I have told you before it come to pass, that, when it is come to pass, ye might believe.

30 Hereafter I will not talk much with you: for the prince of this world cometh, and hath

nothing in me.

31 But that the world may know that I love the Father; and as the Father gave me commandment, even so I do. Arise, let us go hence.

15 I am the true vine, and my Father is the husbandman.

2 Every branch in me that beareth not fruit he taketh away: and every *branch* that beareth fruit, he purgeth it, that it may bring forth more fruit.

3 Now ye are clean through the word which I have spoken unto you.

4 Abide in me, and I in you. As the branch cannot bear fruit of itself, except it abide in the vine; no more can ye, except ye abide in me.

5 I am the vine, ye *are* the branches: He that abideth in me, and I in him, the same bringeth forth much fruit; for without me ye can do nothing.

6 If a man abide not in me, he is cast forth as a branch, and is withered; and men gather them, and cast *them* into the fire, and they are burned.

7 If ye abide in me, and my words abide in you, ye shall ask what ye will, and it shall be done unto you.

8 Herein is my Father glorified, that ye bear much fruit; so shall ye be my disciples.

9 As the Father hath loved me, so have I loved you: continue ye in my love.

10 If ye keep my commandments, ye shall abide in my love; even as I have kept my Father's commandments, and abide in his love.

11 These things have I spoken unto you, that my joy might remain in you, and *that* your joy might be full.

12 This is my commandment, That ye love one another, as I have loved you.

13 Greater love hath no man than this, that a man lay down his life for his friends.

14 Ye are my friends, if ye do whatsoever I command you.

15 Henceforth I call you not servants; for the servant knoweth not what his lord doeth: but I have called you friends; for all things that I have heard of my Father I have made known unto you.

16 Ye have not chosen me, but I have chosen you, and ordained you, that ye should go and bring forth fruit, and *that* your fruit should remain: that whatsoever ye shall ask of the Father in my name, he may give it you.

17 These things I command you, that ye love one another.

18 ❡ If the world hate you, ye know that it hated me before *it hated* you.

19 If ye were of the world, the world would love his own: but because ye are not of the world, but I have chosen you out of the world, therefore the world hateth you.

20 Remember the word that I said unto you, The servant is

not greater than his lord. If they have persecuted me, they will also persecute you; if they have kept my saying, they will keep yours also.

21 But all these things will they do unto you for my name's sake, because they know not him that sent me.

22 If I had not come and spoken unto them, they had not had sin: but now they have no cloke for their sin.

23 He that hateth me hateth my Father also.

24 If I had not done among them the works which none other man did, they had not had sin: but now have they both seen and hated both me and my Father.

25 But *this cometh to pass*, that the word might be fulfilled that is written in their law, They hated me without a cause.

26 But when the Comforter is come, whom I will send unto you from the Father, *even* the Spirit of truth, which proceedeth from the Father, he shall testify of me:

27 And ye also shall bear witness, because ye have been with me from the beginning.

16

These things have I spoken unto you, that ye should not be offended.

2 They shall put you out of the synagogues: yea, the time cometh, that whosoever killeth you will think that he doeth God service.

3 And these things will they do unto you, because they have not known the Father, nor me.

4 But these things have I told you, that when the time shall come, ye may remember that I told you of them. And these things I said not unto you at the beginning, because I was with you.

5 But now I go my way to him that sent me; and none of you asketh me, Whither goest thou?

6 But because I have said these things unto you, sorrow hath filled your heart.

7 Nevertheless I tell you the truth; It is expedient for you that I go away: for if I go not away, the Comforter will not come unto you; but if I depart, I will send him unto you.

8 And when he is come, he will reprove the world of sin, and of righteousness, and of judgment:

9 Of sin, because they believe not on me;

10 Of righteousness, because I go to my Father, and ye see me no more;

11 Of judgment, because the prince of this world is judged.

12 I have yet many things to say unto you, but ye cannot bear them now.

13 Howbeit when he, the Spirit of truth, is come, he will guide you into all truth: for he shall not speak of himself; but whatsoever he shall hear, *that* shall he speak: and he will shew you things to come.

14 He shall glorify me: for he shall receive of mine, and shall shew *it* unto you.

15 All things that the Father

hath are mine: therefore said I, that he shall take of mine, and shall shew *it* unto you.

16 A little while, and ye shall not see me: and again, a little while, and ye shall not see me, because I go to the Father.

17 Then said *some* of his disciples among themselves, What is this that he saith unto us, A little while, and ye shall not see me: and again, a little while, and ye shall see me: and, Because I go to the Father?

18 They said therefore, What is this that he saith, A little while? we cannot tell what he saith.

19 Now Jesus knew that they were desirous to ask him, and said unto them, Do ye enquire among yourselves of that I said, A little while, and ye shall not see me: and again, a little while, and ye shall see me?

20 Verily, verily, I say unto you, That ye shall weep and lament, but the world shall rejoice: and ye shall be sorrowful, but your sorrow shall be turned into joy.

21 A woman when she is in travail hath sorrow, because her hour is come: but as soon as she is delivered of the child, she remembereth no more the anguish, for joy that a man is born into the world.

22 And ye now therefore have sorrow: but I will see you again, and your heart shall rejoice, and your joy no man taketh from you.

23 ¶ And in that day ye shall ask me nothing. Verily, verily, I say unto you, Whatsoever ye shall ask the Father in my name, he will give *it* you.

24 Hitherto have ye asked nothing in my name: ask, and ye shall receive, that your joy may be full.

25 These things have I spoken unto you in proverbs: but the time cometh, when I shall no more speak unto you in proverbs, but I shall shew you plainly of the Father.

26 At that day ye shall ask in my name: and I say not unto you, that I will pray the Father for you:

27 For the Father himself loveth you, because ye have loved me, and have believed that I came out from God.

28 I came forth from the Father, and am come into the world: again, I leave the world, and go to the Father.

29 ¶ His disciples said unto him, Lo, now speakest thou plainly, and speakest no proverb.

30 Now are we sure that thou knowest all things, and needest not that any man should ask thee: by this we believe that thou camest forth from God.

31 Jesus answered them, Do ye now believe?

32 Behold, the hour cometh, yea, is now come, that ye shall be scattered, every man to his own, and shall leave me alone: and yet I am not alone, because the Father is with me.

33 These things have I spoken unto you, that in me ye might have peace. In the world ye

shall have tribulation: but be of good cheer; I have overcome the world.

17 These words spake Jesus, and lifted up his eyes to heaven, and said, Father, the hour is come; glorify thy Son, that thy Son also may glorify thee:

2 As thou hast given him power over all flesh, that he should give eternal life to as many as thou hast given him.

3 And this is life eternal, that they might know thee the only true God, and Jesus Christ, whom thou hast sent.

4 I have glorified thee on the earth: I have finished the work which thou gavest me to do.

5 And now, O Father, glorify thou me with thine own self with the glory which I had with thee before the world was.

6 ❡ I have manifested thy name unto the men which thou gavest me out of the world: thine they were, and thou gavest them me; and they have kept thy word.

7 Now they have known that all things whatsoever thou hast given me are of thee.

8 For I have given unto them the words which thou gavest me; and they have received *them*, and have known surely that I came out from thee, and they have believed that thou didst send me.

9 I pray for them: I pray not for the world, but for them which thou hast given me; for they are thine.

10 And all mine are thine, and thine are mine; and I am glorified in them.

11 And now I am no more in the world, but these are in the world, and I come to thee. Holy Father, keep through thine own name those whom thou hast given me, that they may be one, as we *are*.

12 While I was with them in the world, I kept them in thy name: those that thou gavest me I have kept, and none of them is lost, but the son of perdition; that the scripture might be fulfilled.

13 And now come I to thee; and these things I speak in the world, that they might have my joy fulfilled in themselves.

14 I have given them thy word; and the world hath hated them, because they are not of the world, even as I am not of the world.

15 I pray not that thou shouldest take them out of the world, but that thou shouldest keep them from the evil.

16 They are not of the world, even as I am not of the world.

17 Sanctify them through thy truth: thy word is truth.

18 As thou hast sent me into the world, even so have I also sent them into the world.

19 And for their sakes I sanctify myself, that they also might be sanctified through the truth.

20 ❡ Neither pray I for these alone, but for them also which shall believe on me through their word;

21 That they all may be one; as thou, Father, *art* in me, and I in

thee, that they also may be one in us: that the world may believe that thou hast sent me.

22 And the glory which thou gavest me I have given them; that they may be one, even as we are one:

23 I in them, and thou in me, that they may be made perfect in one; and that the world may know that thou hast sent me, and hast loved them, as thou hast loved me.

24 Father, I will that they also, whom thou hast given me, be with me where I am; that they may behold my glory, which thou hast given me: for thou lovedst me before the foundation of the world.

25 O righteous Father, the world hath not known thee: but I have known thee, and these have known that thou hast sent me.

26 And I have declared unto them thy name, and will declare *it*: that the love wherewith thou hast loved me may be in them, and I in them.

18 When Jesus had spoken these words, he went forth with his disciples over the brook Cedron, where was a garden, into the which he entered, and his disciples.

2 And Judas also, which betrayed him, knew the place: for Jesus ofttimes resorted thither with his disciples.

3 Judas then, having received a band of *men* and officers from the chief priests and Pharisees, cometh thither with lanterns and torches and weapons.

4 Jesus therefore, knowing all things that should come upon him, went forth, and said unto them, Whom seek ye?

5 They answered him, Jesus of Nazareth. Jesus saith unto them, I am *he*. And Judas also, which betrayed him, stood with them.

6 As soon then as he had said unto them, I am *he*, they went backward, and fell to the ground.

7 Then asked he them again, Whom seek ye? And they said, Jesus of Nazareth.

8 Jesus answered, I have told you that I am *he*: if therefore ye seek me, let these go their way:

9 That the saying might be fulfilled, which he spake, Of them which thou gavest me have I lost none.

10 Then Simon Peter having a sword drew it, and smote the high priest's servant, and cut off his right ear. The servant's name was Malchus.

11 Then said Jesus unto Peter, Put up thy sword into the sheath: the cup which my Father hath given me, shall I not drink it?

12 Then the band and the captain and officers of the Jews took Jesus, and bound him,

13 And led him away to Annas first; for he was father in law to Caiaphas, which was the high priest that same year.

14 Now Caiaphas was he, which gave counsel to the Jews, that it was expedient that one man should die for the people.

15 ¶ And Simon Peter followed

Jesus, and *so did* another disciple: that disciple was known unto the high priest, and went in with Jesus into the palace of the high priest.

16 But Peter stood at the door without. Then went out that other disciple, which was known unto the high priest, and spake unto her that kept the door, and brought in Peter.

17 Then saith the damsel that kept the door unto Peter, Art not thou also *one* of this man's disciples? He saith, I am not.

18 And the servants and officers stood there, who had made a fire of coals; for it was cold; and they warmed themselves: and Peter stood with them, and warmed himself.

19 ¶ The high priest then asked Jesus of his disciples, and of his doctrine.

20 Jesus answered him, I spake openly to the world; I ever taught in the synagogue, and in the temple, whither the Jews always resort; and in secret have I said nothing.

21 Why askest thou me? ask them which heard me, what I have said unto them: behold, they know what I said.

22 And when he had thus spoken, one of the officers which stood by struck Jesus with the palm of his hand, saying, Answerest thou the high priest so?

23 Jesus answered him, If I have spoken evil, bear witness of the evil: but if well, why smitest thou me?

24 Now Annas had sent him bound unto Caiaphas the high priest.

25 ¶ And Simon Peter stood and warmed himself. They said therefore unto him, Art not thou also *one* of his disciples? He denied *it*, and said, I am not.

26 One of the servants of the high priest, being *his* kinsman whose ear Peter cut off, saith, Did not I see thee in the garden with him ?

27 Peter then denied again: and immediately the cock crew.

28 ¶ Then led they Jesus from Caiaphas unto the hall of judgment: and it was early; and they themselves went not into the judgment hall, lest they should be defiled; but that they might eat the passover.

29 Pilate then went out unto them, and said, What accusation bring ye against this man?

30 They answered and said unto him, If he were not a malefactor, we would not have delivered him up unto thee.

31 Then said Pilate unto them, Take ye him, and judge him according to your law. The Jews therefore said unto him, It is not lawful for us to put any man to death:

32 That the saying of Jesus might be fulfilled, which he spake, signifying what death he should die.

33 Then Pilate entered into the judgment hall again, and called Jesus, and said unto him, Art thou the King of the Jews?

34 Jesus answered him, Sayest thou this thing of thyself, or did

others tell it thee of me?

35 Pilate answered, Am I a Jew? Thine own nation and the chief priests have delivered thee unto me: what hast thou done?

36 Jesus answered, My kingdom is not of this world: if my kingdom were of this world, then would my servants fight, that I should not be delivered to the Jews: but now is my kingdom not from hence.

37 Pilate therefore said unto him, Art thou a king then? Jesus answered, Thou sayest that I am a king. To this end was I born, and for this cause came I into the world, that I should bear witness unto the truth. Every one that is of the truth heareth my voice.

38 Pilate saith unto him, What is truth? And when he had said this, he went out again unto the Jews, and saith unto them, I find in him no fault *at all*.

39 But ye have a custom, that I should release unto you one at the passover: will ye therefore that I release unto you the King of the Jews?

40 Then cried they all again, saying, Not this man, but Barabbas. Now Barabbas was a robber.

19 Then Pilate therefore took Jesus, and scourged *him*.

2 And the soldiers platted a crown of thorns, and put *it* on his head, and they put on him a purple robe,

3 And said, Hail, King of the Jews! and they smote him with their hands.

4 Pilate therefore went forth again, and saith unto them, Behold, I bring him forth to you, that ye may know that I find no fault in him.

5 Then came Jesus forth, wearing the crown of thorns, and the purple robe. And *Pilate* saith unto them, Behold the man!

6 When the chief priests therefore and officers saw him, they cried out, saying, Crucify *him*, crucify *him*. Pilate saith unto them, Take ye him, and crucify *him*: for I find no fault in him.

7 The Jews answered him, We have a law, and by our law he ought to die, because he made himself the Son of God.

8 When Pilate therefore heard that saying, he was the more afraid;

9 And went again into the judgment hall, and saith unto Jesus, Whence art thou? But Jesus gave him no answer.

10 Then saith Pilate unto him, Speakest thou not unto me? knowest thou not that I have power to crucify thee, and have power to release thee?

11 Jesus answered, Thou couldest have no power *at all* against me, except it were given thee from above: therefore he that delivered me unto thee hath the greater sin.

12 And from thenceforth Pilate sought to release him: but the Jews cried out, saying, If thou let this man go, thou art not Caesar's friend: whosoever maketh himself a king speaketh against

Caesar.

13 ¶ When Pilate therefore heard that saying, he brought Jesus forth, and sat down in the judgment seat in a place that is called the Pavement, but in the Hebrew, Gabbatha.

14 And it was the preparation of the passover, and about the sixth hour: and he saith unto the Jews, Behold your King!

15 But they cried out, Away with *him*, away with *him*, crucify him. Pilate saith unto them, Shall I crucify your King? The chief priests answered, We have no king but Caesar.

16 Then delivered he him therefore unto them to be crucified. And they took Jesus, and led *him* away.

17 And he bearing his cross went forth into a place called *the place* of a skull, which is called in the Hebrew Golgotha:

18 Where they crucified him, and two other with him, on either side one, and Jesus in the midst.

19 And Pilate wrote a title, and put *it* on the cross. And the writing was JESUS OF NAZARETH THE KING OF THE JEWS.

20 This title then read many of the Jews: for the place where Jesus was crucified was nigh to the city: and it was written in Hebrew, and Greek, and Latin.

21 Then said the chief priests of the Jews to Pilate, Write not, The King of the Jews; but that he said, I am King of the Jews.

22 Pilate answered, What I have written I have written.

23 ¶ Then the soldiers, when they had crucified Jesus, took his garments, and made four parts, to every soldier a part; and also *his* coat: now the coat was without seam, woven from the top throughout.

24 They said therefore among themselves, Let us not rend it, but cast lots for it, whose it shall be: that the scripture might be fulfilled, which saith, They parted my raiment among them, and for my vesture they did cast lots. These things therefore the soldiers did.

25 Now there stood by the cross of Jesus his mother, and his mother's sister, Mary the *wife* of Cleophas, and Mary Magdalene.

26 When Jesus therefore saw his mother, and the disciple standing by, whom he loved, he saith unto his mother, Woman, behold thy son!

27 Then saith he to the disciple, Behold thy mother! And from that hour that disciple took her unto his own *home*.

28 ¶ After this, Jesus knowing that all things were now accomplished, that the scripture might be fulfilled, saith, I thirst.

29 Now there was set a vessel full of vinegar: and they filled a spunge with vinegar, and put *it* upon hyssop, and put *it* to his mouth.

30 ¶ When Jesus therefore had received the vinegar, he said, It is finished: and he bowed his head, and gave up the ghost.

31 The Jews therefore, because it was the preparation, that the

bodies should not remain upon the cross on the sabbath day, (for that sabbath day was an high day,) besought Pilate that their legs might be broken, and *that* they might be taken away.

32 Then came the soldiers, and brake the legs of the first, and of the other which was crucified with him.

33 But when they came to Jesus, and saw that he was dead already, they brake not his legs:

34 But one of the soldiers with a spear pierced his side, and forthwith came there out blood and water.

35 And he that saw *it* bare record, and his record is true: and he knoweth that he saith true, that ye might believe.

36 For these things were done, that the scripture should be fulfilled, A bone of him shall not be broken.

37 And again another scripture saith, They shall look on him whom they pierced.

38 And after this Joseph of Arimathaea, being a disciple of Jesus, but secretly for fear of the Jews, besought Pilate that he might take away the body of Jesus: and Pilate gave *him* leave. He came therefore, and took the body of Jesus.

39 And there came also Nicodemus, which at the first came to Jesus by night, and brought a mixture of myrrh and aloes, about an hundred pound *weight*.

40 Then took they the body of Jesus, and wound it in linen clothes with the spices, as the manner of the Jews is to bury.

41 Now in the place where he was crucified there was a garden; and in the garden a new sepulchre, wherein was never man yet laid.

42 There laid they Jesus therefore because of the Jews' preparation *day*; for the sepulchre was nigh at hand.

20

The first *day* of the week cometh Mary Magdalene early, when it was yet dark, unto the sepulchre, and seeth the stone taken away from the sepulchre.

2 Then she runneth, and cometh to Simon Peter, and to the other disciple, whom Jesus loved, and saith unto them, They have taken away the Lord out of the sepulchre, and we know not where they have laid him.

3 Peter therefore went forth, and that other disciple, and came to the sepulchre.

4 So they ran both together: and the other disciple did outrun Peter, and came first to the sepulchre.

5 And he stooping down, *and looking in*, saw the linen clothes lying; yet went he not in.

6 Then cometh Simon Peter following him, and went into the sepulchre, and seeth the linen clothes lie,

7 And the napkin, that was about his head, not lying with the linen clothes, but wrapped together in a place by itself.

8 Then went in also that other disciple, which came first to

181

the sepulchre, and he saw, and believed.

9 For as yet they knew not the scripture, that he must rise again from the dead.

10 Then the disciples went away again unto their own home.

11 ¶ But Mary stood without at the sepulchre weeping: and as she wept, she stooped down, *and looked* into the sepulchre.

12 And seeth two angels in white sitting, the one at the head, and the other at the feet, where the body of Jesus had lain.

13 And they say unto her, Woman, why weepest thou? She saith unto them, Because they have taken away my Lord, and I know not where they have laid him.

14 And when she had thus said, she turned herself back, and saw Jesus standing, and knew not that it was Jesus.

15 Jesus saith unto her, Woman, why weepest thou? whom seekest thou? She, supposing him to be the gardener, saith unto him, Sir, if thou have borne him hence, tell me where thou hast laid him, and I will take him away.

16 Jesus saith unto her, Mary. She turned herself, and saith unto him, Rabboni; which is to say, Master.

17 Jesus saith unto her, Touch me not; for I am not yet ascended to my Father: but go to my brethren, and say unto them, I ascend unto my Father, and your Father; and *to* my God, and your God.

18 Mary Magdalene came and told the disciples that she had seen the Lord, and *that* he had spoken these things unto her.

19 ¶Then the same day at evening, being the first *day* of the week, when the doors were shut where the disciples were assembled for fear of the Jews, came Jesus and stood in the midst, and saith unto them, Peace *be* unto you.

20 And when he had so said, he shewed unto them *his* hands and his side. Then were the disciples glad, when they saw the Lord.

21 Then said Jesus to them again, Peace *be* unto you: as *my* Father hath sent me, even so send I you.

22 And when he had said this, he breathed on *them,* and saith unto them, Receive ye the Holy Ghost:

23 Whose soever sins ye remit, they are remitted unto them; *and* whose soever *sins* ye retain, they are retained.

24 ¶ But Thomas, one of the twelve, called Didymus, was not with them when Jesus came.

25 The other disciples therefore said unto him, We have seen the Lord. But he said unto them, Except I shall see in his hands the print of the nails, and put my finger into the print of the nails, and thrust my hand into his side, I will not believe.

26 And after eight days again his disciples were within, and Thomas with them: *then* came Jesus, the doors being shut, and stood in the midst, and said, Peace *be* unto you.

27 Then saith he to Thomas,

Reach hither thy finger, and behold my hands; and reach hither thy hand, and thrust *it* into my side: and be not faithless, but believing.

28 And Thomas answered and said unto him, My Lord and my God.

29 Jesus saith unto him, Thomas, because thou hast seen me, thou hast believed: blessed *are* they that have not seen, and *yet* have believed.

30 And many other signs truly did Jesus in the presence of his disciples, which are not written in this book:

31 But these are written, that ye might believe that Jesus is the Christ, the Son of God; and that believing ye might have life through his name.

21 After these things Jesus shewed himself again to the disciples at the sea of Tiberias; and on this wise shewed he *himself.*

2 There were together Simon Peter, and Thomas called Didymus, and Nathanael of Cana in Galilee, and the *sons* of Zebedee, and two other of his disciples.

3 Simon Peter saith unto them, I go a fishing. They say unto him, We also go with thee. They went forth, and entered into a ship immediately; and that night they caught nothing.

4 But when the morning was now come, Jesus stood on the shore: but the disciples knew not that it was Jesus.

5 Then Jesus saith unto them,

Children, have ye any meat? They answered him, No.

6 And he said unto them, Cast the net on the right side of the ship, and ye shall find. They cast therefore, and now they were not able to draw it for the multitude of fishes.

7 Therefore that disciple whom Jesus loved saith unto Peter, It is the Lord. Now when Simon Peter heard that it was the Lord, he girt *his* fisher's coat *unto him,* (for he was naked,) and did cast himself into the sea.

8 And the other disciples came in a little ship: (for they were not far from land, but as it were two hundred cubits,) dragging the net with fishes.

9 As soon then as they were come to land, they saw a fire of coals there, and fish laid thereon, and bread.

10 Jesus saith unto them, Bring of the fish which ye have now caught.

11 Simon Peter went up, and drew the net to land full of great fishes, an hundred and fifty and three: and for all there were so many, yet was not the net broken.

12 Jesus saith unto them, Come *and* dine. And none of the disciples durst ask him, Who art thou? knowing that it was the Lord.

13 Jesus then cometh, and taketh bread, and giveth them, and fish likewise.

14 ¶ This is now the third time that Jesus shewed himself to his disciples, after that he was risen from the dead.

15 So when they had dined, Jesus saith to Simon Peter, Simon, *son* of Jonas, lovest thou me more than these? He saith unto him, Yea, Lord; thou knowest that I love thee. He saith unto him, Feed my lambs.

16 He saith to him again the second time, Simon, *son* of Jonas, lovest thou me? He saith unto him, Yea, Lord; thou knowest that I love thee. He saith unto him, Feed my sheep.

17 He saith unto him the third time, Simon, *son* of Jonas, lovest thou me? Peter was grieved because he said unto him the third time, Lovest thou me? And he said unto him, Lord, thou knowest all things; thou knowest that I love thee. Jesus saith unto him, Feed my sheep.

18 Verily, verily, I say unto thee, When thou wast young, thou girdedst thyself, and walkedst whither thou wouldest: but when thou shalt be old, thou shalt stretch forth thy hands, and another shall gird thee, and carry *thee* whither thou wouldest not.

19 This spake he, signifying by what death he should glorify God. And when he had spoken this, he saith unto him, Follow me.

20 Then Peter, turning about, seeth the disciple whom Jesus loved following; which also leaned on his breast at supper, and said, Lord, which is he that betrayeth thee?

21 Peter seeing him saith to Jesus, Lord, and what *shall* this man *do*?

22 Jesus saith unto him, If I will that he tarry till I come, what *is that* to thee? follow thou me.

23 Then went this saying abroad among the brethren, that that disciple should not die: yet Jesus said not unto him, He shall not die; but, If I will that he tarry till I come, what *is that* to thee?

24 This is the disciple which testifieth of these things, and wrote these things: and we know that his testimony is true.

25 And there are also many other things which Jesus did, the which, if they should be written every one, I suppose that even the world itself could not contain the books that should be written. Amen.

THE ACTS
OF THE APOSTLES

1 The former treatise have I made, O Theophilus, of all that Jesus began both to do and teach,

2 Until the day in which he was taken up, after that he through the Holy Ghost had given commandments unto the apostles whom he had chosen:

3 To whom also he shewed himself alive after his passion by many infallible proofs, be-

ing seen of them forty days, and speaking of the things pertaining to the kingdom of God:

4 And, being assembled together with **them**, commanded them that they should not depart from Jerusalem, but wait for the promise of the Father, which, *saith he*, ye have heard of me.

5 For John truly baptized with water; but ye shall be baptized with the Holy Ghost not many days hence.

6 When they therefore were come together, they asked of him, saying, Lord, wilt thou at this time restore again the kingdom to Israel?

7 And he said unto them, It is not for you to know the times or the seasons, which the Father hath put in his own power.

8 But ye shall receive power, after that the Holy Ghost is come upon you: and ye shall be witnesses unto me both in Jerusalem, and in all Judaea, and in Samaria, and unto the uttermost part of the earth.

9 And when he had spoken these things, while they beheld, he was taken up; and a cloud received him out of their sight.

10 And while they looked stedfastly toward heaven as he went up, behold, two men stood by them in white apparel;

11 Which also said, Ye men of Galilee, why stand ye gazing up into heaven? this same Jesus, which is taken up from you into heaven, shall so come in like manner as ye have seen him go into heaven.

12 ❡ Then returned they unto Jerusalem from the mount called Olivet, which is from Jerusalem a sabbath day's journey.

13 And when they were come in, they went up into an upper room, where abode both Peter, and James, and John, and Andrew, Philip, and Thomas, Bartholomew, and Matthew, James *the son* of Alphaeus, and Simon Zelotes, and Judas *the brother* of James.

14 These all continued with one accord in prayer and supplication, with the women, and Mary the mother of Jesus, and with his brethren.

15 ❡ And in those days Peter stood up in the midst of the disciples, and said, (the number of names together were about an hundred and twenty,)

16 Men *and* brethren, this scripture must needs have been fulfilled, which the Holy Ghost by the mouth of David spake before concerning Judas, which was guide to them that took Jesus.

17 For he was numbered with us, and had obtained part of this ministry.

18 Now this man purchased a field with the reward of iniquity; and falling headlong, he burst asunder in the midst, and all his bowels gushed out.

19 And it was known unto all the dwellers at Jerusalem; insomuch as that field is called in their proper tongue, Aceldama, that is to say, The field of blood.

20 For it is written in the book of Psalms, Let his habitation be

desolate, and let no man dwell therein: and his bishoprick let another take.

21 Wherefore of these men which have companied with us all the time that the Lord Jesus went in and out among us,

22 Beginning from the baptism of John, unto that same day that he was taken up from us, must one be ordained to be a witness with us of his resurrection.

23 And they appointed two, Joseph called Barsabas, who was surnamed Justus, and Matthias.

24 And they prayed, and said, Thou, Lord, which knowest the hearts of all **men**, shew whether of these two thou hast chosen,

25 That he may take part of this ministry and apostleship, from which Judas by transgression fell, that he might go to his own place.

26 And they gave forth their lots; and the lot fell upon Matthias; and he was numbered with the eleven apostles.

2

And when the day of Pentecost was fully come, they were all with one accord in one place.

2 And suddenly there came a sound from heaven as of a rushing mighty wind, and it filled all the house where they were sitting.

3 And there appeared unto them cloven tongues like as of fire, and it sat upon each of them.

4 And they were all filled with the Holy Ghost, and began to speak with other tongues, as the Spirit gave them utterance.

5 And there were dwelling at Jerusalem Jews, devout men, out of every nation under heaven.

6 Now when this was noised abroad, the multitude came together, and were confounded, because that every man heard them speak in his own language.

7 And they were all amazed and marvelled, saying one to another, Behold, are not all these which speak Galilaeans?

8 And how hear we every man in our own tongue, wherein we were born?

9 Parthians, and Medes, and Elamites, and the dwellers in Mesopotamia, and in Judaea, and Cappadocia, in Pontus, and Asia,

10 Phrygia, and Pamphylia, in Egypt, and in the parts of Libya about Cyrene, and strangers of Rome, Jews and proselytes,

11 Cretes and Arabians, we do hear them speak in our tongues the wonderful works of God.

12 And they were all amazed, and were in doubt, saying one to another, What meaneth this?

13 Others mocking said, These men are full of new wine.

14 ¶ But Peter, standing up with the eleven, lifted up his voice, and said unto them, Ye men of Judaea, and all **ye** that dwell at Jerusalem, be this known unto you, and hearken to my words:

15 For these are not drunken, as ye suppose, seeing it is *but* the third hour of the day.

16 But this is that which was spoken by the prophet Joel;

17 And it shall come to pass in the last days, saith God, I will pour out of my Spirit upon all flesh: and your sons and your daughters shall prophesy, and your young men shall see visions, and your old men shall dream dreams:

18 And on my servants and on my handmaidens I will pour out in those days of my Spirit; and they shall prophesy:

19 And I will shew wonders in heaven above, and signs in the earth beneath; blood, and fire, and vapour of smoke:

20 The sun shall be turned into darkness, and the moon into blood, before the great and notable day of the Lord come:

21 And it shall come to pass, *that* whosoever shall call on the name of the Lord shall be saved.

22 Ye men of Israel, hear these words; Jesus of Nazareth, a man approved of God among you by miracles and wonders and signs, which God did by him in the midst of you, as ye yourselves also know:

23 Him, being delivered by the determinate counsel and foreknowledge of God, ye have taken, and by wicked hands have crucified and slain:

24 Whom God hath raised up, having loosed the pains of death: because it was not possible that he should be holden of it.

25 For David speaketh concerning him, I foresaw the Lord always before my face, for he is on my right hand, that I should not be moved:

26 Therefore did my heart rejoice, and my tongue was glad; moreover also my flesh shall rest in hope:

27 Because thou wilt not leave my soul in hell, neither wilt thou suffer thine Holy One to see corruption.

28 Thou hast made known to me the ways of life; thou shalt make me full of joy with thy countenance.

29 Men *and* brethren, let me freely speak unto you of the patriarch David, that he is both dead and buried, and his sepulchre is with us unto this day.

30 Therefore being a prophet, and knowing that God had sworn with an oath to him, that of the fruit of his loins, according to the flesh, he would raise up Christ to sit on his throne;

31 He seeing this before spake of the resurrection of Christ, that his soul was not left in hell, neither his flesh did see corruption.

32 This Jesus hath God raised up, whereof we all are witnesses.

33 Therefore being by the right hand of God exalted, and having received of the Father the promise of the Holy Ghost, he hath shed forth this, which ye now see and hear.

34 For David is not ascended into the heavens: but he saith himself, The LORD said unto my Lord, Sit thou on my right hand,

35 Until I make thy foes thy footstool.

36 Therefore let all the house of Israel know assuredly, that

God hath made that same Jesus, whom ye have crucified, both Lord and Christ.

37 ¶ Now when they heard *this*, they were pricked in their heart, and said unto Peter and to the rest of the apostles, Men *and* brethren, what shall we do?

38 Then Peter said unto them, Repent, and be baptized every one of you in the name of Jesus Christ for the remission of sins, and ye shall receive the gift of the Holy Ghost.

39 For the promise is unto you, and to your children, and to all that are afar off, *even* as many as the Lord our God shall call.

40 And with many other words did he testify and exhort, saying, Save yourselves from this untoward generation.

41 ¶ Then they that gladly received his word were baptized: and the same day there were added *unto them* about three thousand souls.

42 And they continued stedfastly in the apostles' doctrine and fellowship, and in breaking of bread, and in prayers.

43 And fear came upon every soul; and many wonders and signs were done by the apostles.

44 And all that believed were together, and had all things common;

45 And sold their possessions and goods, and parted them to all *men*, as every man had need.

46 And they, continuing daily with one accord in the temple, and breaking bread from house to house, did eat their meat with gladness and singleness of heart,

47 Praising God, and having favour with all the people. And the Lord added to the church daily such as should be saved.

3 Now Peter and John went up together into the temple at the hour of prayer, *being* the ninth *hour*.

2 And a certain man lame from his mother's womb was carried, whom they laid daily at the gate of the temple which is called Beautiful, to ask alms of them that entered into the temple;

3 Who seeing Peter and John about to go into the temple asked an alms.

4 And Peter, fastening his eyes upon him with John, said, Look on us.

5 And he gave heed unto them, expecting to receive something of them.

6 Then Peter said, Silver and gold have I none; but such as I have give I thee: In the name of Jesus Christ of Nazareth rise up and walk.

7 And he took him by the right hand, and lifted *him* up: and immediately his feet and ankle bones received strength.

8 And he leaping up stood, and walked, and entered with them into the temple, walking, and leaping, and praising God.

9 And all the people saw him walking and praising God:

10 And they knew that it was he which sat for alms at the Beautiful gate of the temple: and they

were filled with wonder and amazement at that which had happened unto him.

11 And as the lame man which was healed held Peter and John, all the people ran together unto them in the porch that is called Solomon's, greatly wondering.

12 ⟨ And when Peter saw it, he answered unto the people, Ye men of Israel, why marvel ye at this? or why look ye so earnestly on us, as though we by our own power or holiness we had made this man to walk?

13 The God of Abraham, and of Isaac, and of Jacob, the God of our fathers, hath glorified his Son Jesus; whom ye delivered up, and denied him in the presence of Pilate, when he was determined to let him go.

14 But ye denied the Holy One and the Just, and desired a murderer to be granted unto you;

15 And killed the Prince of life, whom God hath raised from the dead; whereof we are witnesses.

16 And his name through faith in his name hath made this man strong, whom ye see and know: yea, the faith which is by him hath given him this perfect soundness in the presence of you all.

17 And now, brethren, I wot that through ignorance ye did *it*, as *did* also your rulers.

18 But those things, which God before had shewed by the mouth of all his prophets, that Christ should suffer, he hath so fulfilled.

19 ⟨ Repent ye therefore, and be

converted, that your sins may be blotted out, when the times of refreshing shall come from the presence of the Lord;

20 And he shall send Jesus Christ, which before was preached unto you:

21 Whom the heaven must receive until the times of restitution of all things, which God hath spoken by the mouth of all his holy prophets since the world began.

22 For Moses truly said unto the fathers, A prophet shall the Lord your God raise up unto you of your brethren, like unto me; him shall ye hear in all things whatsoever he shall say unto you.

23 And it shall come to pass, *that* every soul, which will not hear that prophet, shall be destroyed from among the people.

24 Yea, and all the prophets from Samuel and those that follow after, as many as have spoken, have likewise foretold of these days.

25 Ye are the children of the prophets, and of the covenant which God made with our fathers, saying unto Abraham, And in thy seed shall all the kindreds of the earth be blessed.

26 Unto you first God, having raised up his Son Jesus, sent him to bless you, in turning away every one of you from his iniquities.

4 And as they spake unto the people, the priests, and the captain of the temple, and the Sadducees, came upon them,

2 Being grieved that they taught the people, and preached through Jesus the resurrection from the dead.

3 And they laid hands on them, and put *them* in hold until the next day: for it was now eventide.

4 Howbeit many of them which heard the word believed; and the number of the men was about five thousand.

5 ¶ And it came to pass on the morrow, that their rulers, and elders, and scribes,

6 And Annas the high priest, and Caiaphas, and John, and Alexander, and as many as were of the kindred of the high priest, were gathered together at Jerusalem.

7 And when they had set them in the midst, they asked, By what power, or by what name, have ye done this?

8 Then Peter, filled with the Holy Ghost, said unto them, Ye rulers of the people, and elders of Israel,

9 If we this day be examined of the good deed done to the impotent man, by what means he is made whole;

10 Be it known unto you all, and to all the people of Israel, that by the name of Jesus Christ of Nazareth, whom ye crucified, whom God raised from the dead, *even* by him doth this man stand here before you whole.

11 This is the stone which was set at nought of you builders, which is become the head of the corner.

12 Neither is there salvation in any other: for there is none other name under heaven given among men, whereby we must be saved.

13 ¶ Now when they saw the boldness of Peter and John, and perceived that they were unlearned and ignorant men, they marvelled; and they took knowledge of them, that they had been with Jesus.

14 And beholding the man which was healed standing with them, they could say nothing against it.

15 But when they had commanded them to go aside out of the council, they conferred among themselves,

16 Saying, What shall we do to these men? for that indeed a notable miracle hath been done by them *is* manifest to all them that dwell in Jerusalem; and we cannot deny *it*.

17 But that it spread no further among the people, let us straitly threaten them, that they speak henceforth to no man in this name.

18 And they called them, and commanded them not to speak at all nor teach in the name of Jesus.

19 But Peter and John answered and said unto them, Whether it be right in the sight of God to hearken unto you more than unto God, judge ye.

20 For we cannot but speak the things which we have seen and heard.

21 So when they had further

threatened them, they let them go, finding nothing how they might punish them, because of the people: for all men glorified God for that which was done.

22 ¶ For the man was above forty years old, on whom this miracle of healing was shewed.

23 And being let go, they went to their own company, and reported all that the chief priests and elders had said unto them.

24 And when they heard that, they lifted up their voice to God with one accord, and said, Lord, thou *art* God, which hast made heaven, and earth, and the sea, and all that in them is:

25 Who by the mouth of thy servant David hast said, Why did the heathen rage, and the people imagine vain things?

26 The kings of the earth stood up, and the rulers were gathered together against the Lord, and against his Christ.

27 For of a truth against thy holy child Jesus, whom thou hast anointed, both Herod, and Pontius Pilate, with the Gentiles, and the people of Israel, were gathered together,

28 For to do whatsoever thy hand and thy counsel determined before to be done.

29 And now, Lord, behold their threatenings: and grant unto thy servants, that with all boldness they may speak thy word,

30 By stretching forth thine hand to heal; and that signs and wonders may be done by the name of thy holy child Jesus.

31 ¶ And when they had prayed, the place was shaken where they were assembled together; and they were all filled with the Holy Ghost, and they spake the word of God with boldness.

32 And the multitude of them that believed were of one heart and of one soul: neither said any *of them* that ought of the things which he possessed was his own; but they had all things common.

33 And with great power gave the apostles witness of the resurrection of the Lord Jesus: and great grace was upon them all.

34 Neither was there any among them that lacked: for as many as were possessors of lands or houses sold them, and brought the prices of the things that were sold,

35 And laid *them* down at the apostles' feet: and distribution was made unto every man according as he had need.

36 And Joses, who by the apostles was surnamed Barnabas, (which is, being interpreted, The son of consolation,) a Levite, *and* of the country of Cyprus,

37 Having land, sold *it*, and brought the money, and laid *it* at the apostles' feet.

5 But a certain man named Ananias, with Sapphira his wife, sold a possession,

2 And kept back *part* of the price, his wife also being privy *to it*, and brought a certain part, and laid *it* at the apostles' feet.

3 But Peter said, Ananias, why hath Satan filled thine heart to

lie to the Holy Ghost, and to keep back *part* of the price of the land?

4 Whiles it remained, was it not thine own? and after it was sold, was it not in thine own power? why hast thou conceived this thing in thine heart? thou hast not lied unto men, but unto God.

5 And Ananias hearing these words fell down, and gave up the ghost: and great fear came on all them that heard these things.

6 And the young men arose, wound him up, and carried *him* out, and buried *him*.

7 And it was about the space of three hours after, when his wife, not knowing what was done, came in.

8 And Peter answered unto her, Tell me whether ye sold the land for so much? And she said, Yea, for so much.

9 Then Peter said unto her, How is it that ye have agreed together to tempt the Spirit of the Lord? behold, the feet of them which have buried thy husband *are* at the door, and shall carry thee out.

10 Then fell she down straightway at his feet, and yielded up the ghost: and the young men came in, and found her dead, and, carrying *her* forth, buried *her* by her husband.

11 And great fear came upon all the church, and upon as many as heard these things.

12 ¶ And by the hands of the apostles were many signs and wonders wrought among the people; (and they were all with one accord in Solomon's porch.

13 And of the rest durst no man join himself to them: but the people magnified them.

14 And believers were the more added to the Lord, multitudes both of men and women.)

15 Insomuch that they brought forth the sick into the streets, and laid *them* on beds and couches, that at the least the shadow of Peter passing by might overshadow some of them.

16 There came also a multitude *out* of the cities round about unto Jerusalem, bringing sick folks, and them which were vexed with unclean spirits: and they were healed every one.

17 ¶ Then the high priest rose up, and all they that were with him, (which is the sect of the Sadducees,) and were filled with indignation,

18 ¶ And laid their hands on the apostles, and put them in the common prison.

19 But the angel of the Lord by night opened the prison doors, and brought them forth, and said,

20 Go, stand and speak in the temple to the people all the words of this life.

21 And when they heard *that*, they entered into the temple early in the morning, and taught. But the high priest came, and they that were with him, and called the council together, and all the senate of the children of Israel, and sent to the prison to have them brought.

22 But when the officers came,

and found them not in the prison, they returned and told,

23 Saying, The prison truly found we shut with all safety, and the keepers standing without before the doors: but when we had opened, we found no man within.

24 Now when the high priest and the captain of the temple and the chief priests heard these things, they doubted of them whereunto this would grow.

25 ¶ Then came one and told them, saying, Behold, the men whom ye put in prison are standing in the temple, and teaching the people.

26 Then went the captain with the officers, and brought them without violence: for they feared the people, lest they should have been stoned.

27 And when they had brought them, they set *them* before the council: and the high priest asked them,

28 Saying, Did not we straitly command you that ye should not teach in this name? and, behold, ye have filled Jerusalem with your doctrine, and intend to bring this man's blood upon us.

29 ¶ Then Peter and the *other* apostles answered and said, We ought to obey God rather than men.

30 The God of our fathers raised up Jesus, whom ye slew and hanged on a tree.

31 Him hath God exalted with his right hand *to be* a Prince and a Saviour, for to give repentance to Israel, and forgiveness of sins.

32 ¶ And we are his witnesses of these things; and *so is* also the Holy Ghost, whom God hath given to them that obey him.

33 When they heard *that*, they were cut to *the* heart, and took counsel to slay them.

34 Then stood there up one in the council, a Pharisee, named Gamaliel, a doctor of the law, had in reputation among all the people, and commanded to put the apostles forth a little space;

35 And said unto them, Ye men of Israel, take heed to yourselves what ye intend to do as touching these men.

36 For before these days rose up Theudas, boasting himself to be somebody; to whom a number of men, about four hundred, joined themselves: who was slain; and all, as many as obeyed him, were scattered, and brought to nought.

37 After this man rose up Judas of Galilee in the days of the taxing, and drew away much people after him: he also perished; and all, *even* as many as obeyed him, were dispersed.

38 And now I say unto you, Refrain from these men, and let them alone: for if this counsel or this work be of men, it will come to nought:

39 But if it be of God, ye cannot overthrow it; lest haply ye be found even to fight against God.

40 And to him they agreed: and when they had called the apostles, and beaten them, they commanded that they should not speak in the name of Jesus, and let them go.

41 ¶ And they departed from the presence of the council, rejoicing that they were counted worthy to suffer shame for his name.

42 And daily in the temple, and in every house, they ceased not to teach and preach Jesus Christ.

6 And in those days, when the number of the disciples was multiplied, there arose a murmuring of the Grecians against the Hebrews, because their widows were neglected in the daily ministration.

2 Then the twelve called the multitude of the disciples *unto them*, and said, It is not reason that we should leave the word of God, and serve tables.

3 Wherefore, brethren, look ye out among you seven men of honest report, full of the Holy Ghost and wisdom, whom we may appoint over this business.

4 But we will give ourselves continually to prayer, and to the ministry of the word.

5 ¶ And the saying pleased the whole multitude: and they chose Stephen, a man full of faith and of the Holy Ghost, and Philip, and Prochorus, and Nicanor, and Timon, and Parmenas, and Nicolas a proselyte of Antioch:

6 Whom they set before the apostles: and when they had prayed, they laid *their* hands on them.

7 And the word of God increased; and the number of the disciples multiplied in Jerusalem greatly; and a great company of the priests were obedient to the faith.

8 And Stephen, full of faith and power, did great wonders and miracles among the people.

9 ¶ Then there arose certain of the synagogue, which is called *the synagogue* of the Libertines, and Cyrenians, and Alexandrians, and of them of Cilicia and of Asia, disputing with Stephen.

10 And they were not able to resist the wisdom and the spirit by which he spake.

11 Then they suborned men, which said, We have heard him speak blasphemous words against Moses, and *against* God.

12 And they stirred up the people, and the elders, and the scribes, and came upon *him*, and caught him, and brought *him* to the council,

13 And set up false witnesses, which said, This man ceaseth not to speak blasphemous words against this holy place, and the law:

14 For we have heard him say, that this Jesus of Nazareth shall destroy this place, and shall change the customs which Moses delivered us.

15 And all that sat in the council, looking stedfastly on him, saw his face as it had been the face of an angel.

7 Then said the high priest, Are these things so?

2 And he said, Men, brethren, and fathers, hearken; The God of glory appeared unto our father Abraham, when he was in Mesopotamia, before he dwelt in Charran,

3 And said unto him, Get thee out of thy country, and from thy kindred, and come into the land which I shall shew thee.

4 Then came he out of the land of the Chaldaeans, and dwelt in Charran: and from thence, when his father was dead, he removed him into this land, wherein ye now dwell.

5 And he gave him none inheritance in it, no, not *so much as* to set his foot on: yet he promised that he would give it to him for a possession, and to his seed after him, when *as yet* he had no child.

6 And God spake on this wise, That his seed should sojourn in a strange land; and that they should bring them into bondage, and entreat *them* evil four hundred years.

7 And the nation to whom they shall be in bondage will I judge, said God: and after that shall they come forth, and serve me in this place.

8 And he gave him the covenant of circumcision: and so *Abraham* begat Isaac, and circumcised him the eighth day; and Isaac *begat* Jacob; and Jacob *begat* the twelve patriarchs.

9 And the patriarchs, moved with envy, sold Joseph into Egypt: but God was with him,

10 And delivered him out of all his afflictions, and gave him favour and wisdom in the sight of Pharaoh king of Egypt; and he made him governor over Egypt and all his house.

11 Now there came a dearth over all the land of Egypt and Chanaan, and great affliction: and our fathers found no sustenance.

12 But when Jacob heard that there was corn in Egypt, he sent out our fathers first.

13 And at the second *time* Joseph was made known to his brethren; and Joseph's kindred was made known unto Pharaoh.

14 Then sent Joseph, and called his father Jacob to *him*, and all his kindred, threescore and fifteen souls.

15 So Jacob went down into Egypt, and died, he, and our fathers,

16 And were carried over into Sychem, and laid in the sepulchre that Abraham bought for a sum of money of the sons of Emmor *the father* of Sychem.

17 But when the time of the promise drew nigh, which God had sworn to Abraham, the people grew and multiplied in Egypt,

18 Till another king arose, which knew not Joseph.

19 The same dealt subtilly with our kindred, and evil entreated our fathers, so that they cast out their young children, to the end they might not live.

20 In which time Moses was born, and was exceeding fair, and nourished up in his father's house three months:

21 And when he was cast out, Pharaoh's daughter took him up, and nourished him for her own son.

22 And Moses was learned in all the wisdom of the Egyptians, and was mighty in words and in deeds.

23 And when he was full forty years old, it came into his heart to visit his brethren the children of Israel.

24 And seeing one *of them* suffer wrong, he defended *him*, and avenged him that was oppressed, and smote the Egyptian:

25 For he supposed his brethren would have understood how that God by his hand would deliver them: but they understood not.

26 And the next day he shewed himself unto them as they strove, and would have set them at one again, saying, Sirs, ye are brethren; why do ye wrong one to another?

27 But he that did his neighbour wrong thrust him away, saying, Who made thee a ruler and a judge over us?

28 Wilt thou kill me, as thou diddest the Egyptian yesterday?

29 Then fled Moses at this saying, and was a stranger in the land of Madian, where he begat two sons.

30 And when forty years were expired, there appeared to him in the wilderness of mount Sina an angel of the Lord in a flame of fire in a bush.

31 When Moses saw *it*, he wondered at the sight: and as he drew near to behold *it*, the voice of the Lord came unto him,

32 *Saying*, I am the God of thy fathers, the God of Abraham, and the God of Isaac, and the God of Jacob. Then Moses trembled, and durst not behold.

33 Then said the Lord to him, Put off thy shoes from thy feet: for the place where thou standest is holy ground.

34 I have seen, I have seen the affliction of my people which is in Egypt, and I have heard their groaning, and am come down to deliver them. And now come, I will send thee into Egypt.

35 This Moses whom they refused, saying, Who made thee a ruler and a judge? the same did God send *to be* a ruler and a deliverer by the hand of the angel which appeared to him in the bush.

36 ¶ He brought them out, after that he had shewed wonders and signs in the land of Egypt, and in the Red sea, and in the wilderness forty years.

37 This is that Moses, which said unto the children of Israel, A prophet shall the Lord your God raise up unto you of your brethren, like unto me; him shall ye hear.

38 This is he, that was in the church in the wilderness with the angel which spake to him in the mount Sina, and *with* our fathers: who received the lively oracles to give unto us:

39 To whom our fathers would not obey, but thrust *him* from them, and in their hearts turned back again into Egypt,

40 Saying unto Aaron, Make us gods to go before us: for *as for* this Moses, which brought us out

of the land of Egypt, we wot not what is become of him.

41 And they made a calf in those days, and offered sacrifice unto the idol, and rejoiced in the works of their own hands.

42 Then God turned, and gave them up to worship the host of heaven; as it is written in the book of the prophets, O ye house of Israel, have ye offered to me slain beasts and sacrifices *by the space of* forty years in the wilderness?

43 Yea, ye took up the tabernacle of Moloch, and the star of your god Remphan, figures which ye made to worship them: and I will carry you away beyond Babylon.

44 Our fathers had the tabernacle of witness in the wilderness, as he had appointed, speaking unto Moses, that he should make it according to the fashion that he had seen.

45 Which also our fathers that came after brought in with Jesus into the possession of the Gentiles, whom God drave out before the face of our fathers, unto the days of David;

46 Who found favour before God, and desired to find a tabernacle for the God of Jacob.

47 But Solomon built him an house.

48 Howbeit the most High dwelleth not in temples made with hands; as saith the prophet,

49 Heaven *is* my throne, and earth *is* my footstool: what house will ye build me? saith the Lord: or what *is* the place of my rest?

50 Hath not my hand made all these things?

51 ¶ Ye stiffnecked and uncircumcised in heart and ears, ye do always resist the Holy Ghost: as your fathers *did*, so *do* ye.

52 Which of the prophets have not your fathers persecuted? and they have slain them which shewed before of the coming of the Just One; of whom ye have been now the betrayers and murderers:

53 Who have received the law by the disposition of angels, and have not kept *it*.

54 ¶ When they heard these things, they were cut to the heart, and they gnashed on him with *their* teeth.

55 But he, being full of the Holy Ghost, looked up stedfastly into heaven, and saw the glory of God, and Jesus standing on the right hand of God,

56 And said, Behold, I see the heavens opened, and the Son of man standing on the right hand of God.

57 Then they cried out with a loud voice, and stopped their ears, and ran upon him with one accord,

58 And cast *him* out of the city, and stoned *him*: and the witnesses laid down their clothes at a young man's feet, whose name was Saul.

59 And they stoned Stephen, calling upon *God*, and saying, Lord Jesus, receive my spirit.

60 And he kneeled down, and cried with a loud voice, Lord,

lay not this sin to their charge. And when he had said this, he fell asleep.

8 And Saul was consenting unto his death. And at that time there was a great persecution against the church which was at Jerusalem; and they were all scattered abroad throughout the regions of Judaea and Samaria, except the apostles.

2 And devout men carried Stephen *to his burial*, and made great lamentation over him.

3 As for Saul, he made havock of the church, entering into every house, and haling men and women committed *them* to prison.

4 ¶ Therefore they that were scattered abroad went every where preaching the word.

5 ¶ Then Philip went down to the city of Samaria, and preached Christ unto them.

6 And the people with one accord gave heed unto those things which Philip spake, hearing and seeing the miracles which he did.

7 For unclean spirits, crying with loud voice, came out of many that were possessed *with them*: and many taken with palsies, and that were lame, were healed.

8 And there was great joy in that city.

9 ¶ But there was a certain man, called Simon, which beforetime in the same city used sorcery, and bewitched the people of Samaria, giving out that himself was some great one:

10 To whom they all gave heed, from the least to the greatest, saying, This man is the great power of God.

11 And to him they had regard, because that of long time he had bewitched them with sorceries.

12 But when they believed Philip preaching the things concerning the kingdom of God, and the name of Jesus Christ, they were baptized, both men and women.

13 Then Simon himself believed also: and when he was baptized, he continued with Philip, and wondered, beholding the miracles and signs which were done.

14 Now when the apostles which were at Jerusalem heard that Samaria had received the word of God, they sent unto them Peter and John:

15 Who, when they were come down, prayed for them, that they might receive the Holy Ghost:

16 (For as yet he was fallen upon none of them: only they were baptized in the name of the Lord Jesus.)

17 Then laid they *their* hands on them, and they received the Holy Ghost.

18 And when Simon saw that through laying on of the apostles' hands the Holy Ghost was given, he offered them money,

19 Saying, Give me also this power, that on whomsoever I lay hands, he may receive the Holy Ghost.

20 But Peter said unto him, Thy money perish with thee, because

thou hast thought that the gift of God may be purchased with money.

21 Thou hast neither part nor lot in this matter: for thy heart is not right in the sight of God.

22 Repent therefore of this thy wickedness, and pray God, if perhaps the thought of thine heart may be forgiven thee.

23 For I perceive that thou art in the gall of bitterness, and *in* the bond of iniquity.

24 Then answered Simon, and said, Pray ye to the Lord for me, that none of these things which ye have spoken come upon me.

25 And they, when they had testified and preached the word of the Lord, returned to Jerusalem, and preached the gospel in many villages of the Samaritans.

26 ¶ And the angel of the Lord spake unto Philip, saying, Arise, and go toward the south unto the way that goeth down from Jerusalem unto Gaza, which is desert.

27 And he arose and went: and, behold, a man of Ethiopia, an eunuch of great authority under Candace queen of the Ethiopians, who had the charge of all her treasure, and had come to Jerusalem for to worship,

28 Was returning, and sitting in his chariot read Esaias the prophet.

29 Then the Spirit said unto Philip, Go near, and join thyself to this chariot.

30 And Philip ran thither to *him*, and heard him read the prophet

Esaias, and said, Understandest thou what thou readest?

31 And he said, How can I, except some man should guide me? And he desired Philip that he would come up and sit with him.

32 The place of the scripture which he read was this, He was led as a sheep to the slaughter; and like a lamb dumb before his shearer, so opened he not his mouth:

33 In his humiliation his judgment was taken away: and who shall declare his generation? for his life is taken from the earth.

34 And the eunuch answered Philip, and said, I pray thee, of whom speaketh the prophet this? of himself, or of some other man?

35 ¶ Then Philip opened his mouth, and began at the same scripture, and preached unto him Jesus.

36 And as they went on *their* way, they came unto a certain water: and the eunuch said, See, *here is* water; what doth hinder me to be baptized?

37 And Philip said, If thou believest with all thine heart, thou mayest. And he answered and said, I believe that Jesus Christ is the Son of God.

38 And he commanded the chariot to stand still: and they went down both into the water, both Philip and the eunuch; and he baptized him.

39 And when they were come up out of the water, the Spirit of the Lord caught away Philip, that the eunuch saw him no more: and

he went on his way rejoicing.

40 But Philip was found at Azotus: and passing through he preached in all the cities, till he came to Caesarea.

9 And Saul, yet breathing out threatenings and slaughter against the disciples of the Lord, went unto the high priest,

2 And desired of him letters to Damascus to the synagogues, that if he found any of this way, whether they were men or women, he might bring them bound unto Jerusalem.

3 And as he journeyed, he came near Damascus: and suddenly there shined round about him a light from heaven:

4 And he fell to the earth, and heard a voice saying unto him, Saul, Saul, why persecutest thou me?

5 And he said, Who art thou, Lord? And the Lord said, I am Jesus whom thou persecutest: *it is* hard for thee to kick against the pricks.

6 And he trembling and astonished said, Lord, what wilt thou have me to do? And the Lord *said* unto him, Arise, and go into the city, and it shall be told thee what thou must do.

7 And the men which journeyed with him stood speechless, hearing a voice, but seeing no man.

8 And Saul arose from the earth; and when his eyes were opened, he saw no man: but they led him by the hand, and brought *him* into Damascus.

9 And he was three days without sight, and neither did eat nor drink.

10 ¶ And there was a certain disciple at Damascus, named Ananias; and to him said the Lord in a vision, Ananias. And he said, Behold, I *am here*, Lord.

11 And the Lord *said* unto him, Arise, and go into the street which is called Straight, and enquire in the house of Judas for *one* called Saul, of Tarsus: for, behold, he prayeth,

12 And hath seen in a vision a man named Ananias coming in, and putting *his* hand on him, that he might receive his sight.

13 Then Ananias answered, Lord, I have heard by many of this man, how much evil he hath done to thy saints at Jerusalem:

14 And here he hath authority from the chief priests to bind all that call on thy name.

15 But the Lord said unto him, Go thy way: for he is a chosen vessel unto me, to bear my name before the Gentiles, and kings, and the children of Israel:

16 For I will shew him how great things he must suffer for my name's sake.

17 And Ananias went his way, and entered into the house; and putting *his* hands on him said, Brother Saul, the Lord, *even* Jesus, that appeared unto thee in the way as thou camest, hath sent me, that thou mightest receive thy sight, and be filled with the Holy Ghost.

18 And immediately there fell from his eyes as it had been scales: and he received sight

forthwith, and arose, and was baptized.

19 And when he had received meat, he was strengthened. Then was Saul certain days with the disciples which were at Damascus.

20 And straightway he preached Christ in the synagogues, that he is the Son of God.

21 But all that heard *him* were amazed, and said; Is not this he that destroyed them which called on this name in Jerusalem, and came hither for that intent, that he might bring them bound unto the chief priests?

22 But Saul increased the more in strength, and confounded the Jews which dwelt at Damascus, proving that this is very Christ.

23 ❈ And after that many days were fulfilled, the Jews took counsel to kill him:

24 But their laying await was known of Saul. And they watched the gates day and night to kill him.

25 Then the disciples took him by night, and let *him* down by the wall in a basket.

26 And when Saul was come to Jerusalem, he assayed to join himself to the disciples: but they were all afraid of him, and believed not that he was a disciple.

27 But Barnabas took *him*, and brought *him* to the apostles, and declared unto them how he had seen the Lord in the way, and that he had spoken to him, and how he had preached boldly at Damascus in the name of Jesus.

28 And he was with them coming in and going out at Jerusalem.

29 And he spake boldly in the name of the Lord Jesus, and disputed against the Grecians: but they went about to slay him.

30 *Which* when the brethren knew, they brought him down to Caesarea, and sent him forth to Tarsus.

31 Then had the churches rest throughout all Judaea and Galilee and Samaria, and were edified; and walking in the fear of the Lord, and in the comfort of the Holy Ghost, were multiplied.

32 ❈ And it came to pass, as Peter passed throughout all *quarters*, he came down also to the saints which dwelt at Lydda.

33 And there he found a certain man named Aeneas, which had kept his bed eight years, and was sick of the palsy.

34 And Peter said unto him, Aeneas, Jesus Christ maketh thee whole: arise, and make thy bed. And he arose immediately.

35 And all that dwelt at Lydda and Saron saw him, and turned to the Lord.

36 ❈ Now there was at Joppa a certain disciple named Tabitha, which by interpretation is called Dorcas: this woman was full of good works and almsdeeds which she did.

37 And it came to pass in those days, that she was sick, and died: whom when they had washed, they laid *her* in an upper chamber.

38 And forasmuch as Lydda was nigh to Joppa, and the disciples had heard that Peter was there, they sent unto him two men, desiring *him* that he would not delay to come to them.

39 Then Peter arose and went with them. When he was come, they brought him into the upper chamber: and all the widows stood by him weeping, and shewing the coats and garments which Dorcas made, while she was with them.

40 But Peter put them all forth, and kneeled down, and prayed; and turning *him* to the body said, Tabitha, arise. And she opened her eyes: and when she saw Peter, she sat up.

41 And he gave her *his* hand, and lifted her up, and when he had called the saints and widows, presented her alive.

42 And it was known throughout all Joppa; and many believed in the Lord.

43 And it came to pass, that he tarried many days in Joppa with one Simon a tanner.

10

There was a certain man in Caesarea called Cornelius, a centurion of the band called the Italian *band*,

2 A devout *man*, and one that feared God with all his house, which gave much alms to the people, and prayed to God always.

3 He saw in a vision evidently about the ninth hour of the day an angel of God coming in to him, and saying unto him, Cornelius.

4 And when he looked on him, he was afraid, and said, What is it, Lord? And he said unto him, Thy prayers and thine alms are come up for a memorial before God.

5 And now send men to Joppa, and call for *one* Simon, whose surname is Peter:

6 He lodgeth with one Simon a tanner, whose house is by the sea side: he shall tell thee what thou oughtest to do.

7 And when the angel which spake unto Cornelius was departed, he called two of his household servants, and a devout soldier of them that waited on him continually;

8 And when he had declared all *these* things unto them, he sent them to Joppa.

9 ¶ On the morrow, as they went on their journey, and drew nigh unto the city, Peter went up upon the housetop to pray about the sixth hour:

10 And he became very hungry, and would have eaten: but while they made ready, he fell into a trance,

11 And saw heaven opened, and a certain vessel descending unto him, as it had been a great sheet knit at the four corners, and let down to the earth:

12 Wherein were all manner of fourfooted beasts of the earth, and wild beasts, and creeping things, and fowls of the air.

13 And there came a voice to him, Rise, Peter; kill, and eat.

14 But Peter said, Not so, Lord;

for I have never eaten any thing that is common or unclean.

15 And the voice *spake* unto him again the second time, What God hath cleansed, *that* call not thou common.

16 This was done thrice: and the vessel was received up again into heaven.

17 Now while Peter doubted in himself what this vision which he had seen should mean, behold, the men which were sent from Cornelius had made enquiry for Simon's house, and stood before the gate,

18 And called, and asked whether Simon, which was surnamed Peter, were lodged there.

19 ❅ While Peter thought on the vision, the Spirit said unto him, Behold, three men seek thee.

20 Arise therefore, and get thee down, and go with them, doubting nothing: for I have sent them.

21 Then Peter went down to the men which were sent unto him from Cornelius; and said, Behold, I am he whom ye seek: what *is* the cause wherefore ye are come?

22 And they said, Cornelius the centurion, a just man, and one that feareth God, and of good report among all the nation of the Jews, was warned from God by an holy angel to send for thee into his house, and to hear words of thee.

23 ❅ Then called he them in, and lodged *them*. And on the morrow Peter went away with them, and certain brethren from Joppa ac-

companied him.

24 And the morrow after they entered into Caesarea. And Cornelius waited for them, and had called together his kinsmen and near friends.

25 And as Peter was coming in, Cornelius met him, and fell down at his feet, and worshipped *him*.

26 But Peter took him up, saying, Stand up; I myself also am a man.

27 And as he talked with him, he went in, and found many that were come together.

28 And he said unto them, Ye know how that it is an unlawful thing for a man that is a Jew to keep company, or come unto one of another nation; but God hath shewed me that I should not call any man common or unclean.

29 Therefore came I unto you without gainsaying, as soon as I was sent for: I ask therefore for what intent ye have sent for me?

30 And Cornelius said, Four days ago I was fasting until this hour; and at the ninth hour I prayed in my house, and, behold, a man stood before me in bright clothing,

31 And said, Cornelius, thy prayer is heard, and thine alms are had in remembrance in the sight of God.

32 Send therefore to Joppa, and call hither Simon, whose surname is Peter; he is lodged in the house of *one* Simon a tanner by the sea side: who, when he cometh, shall speak unto thee.

33 Immediately therefore I

sent to thee; and thou hast well done that thou art come. Now therefore are we all here present before God, to hear all things that are commanded thee of God.

34 ¶ Then Peter opened *his* mouth, and said, Of a truth I perceive that God is no respecter of persons:

35 But in every nation he that feareth him, and worketh righteousness, is accepted with him.

36 The word which *God* sent unto the children of Israel, preaching peace by Jesus Christ: (he is Lord of all:)

37 That word, *I say*, ye know, which was published throughout all Judaea, and began from Galilee, after the baptism which John preached;

38 How God anointed Jesus of Nazareth with the Holy Ghost and with power: who went about doing good, and healing all that were oppressed of the devil; for God was with him.

39 And we are witnesses of all things which he did both in the land of the Jews, and in Jerusalem; whom they slew and hanged on a tree:

40 Him God raised up the third day, and shewed him openly;

41 Not to all the people, but unto witnesses chosen before of God, *even* to us, who did eat and drink with him after he rose from the dead.

42 And he commanded us to preach unto the people, and to testify that it is he which was ordained of God *to be* the Judge of quick and dead.

43 To him give all the prophets witness, that through his name whosoever believeth in him shall receive remission of sins.

44 ¶ While Peter yet spake these words, the Holy Ghost fell on all them which heard the word.

45 And they of the circumcision which believed were astonished, as many as came with Peter, because that on the Gentiles also was poured out the gift of the Holy Ghost.

46 For they heard them speak with tongues, and magnify God. Then answered Peter,

47 Can any man forbid water, that these should not be baptized, which have received the Holy Ghost as well as we?

48 ¶ And he commanded them to be baptized in the name of the Lord. Then prayed they him to tarry certain days.

11

And the apostles and brethren that were in Judaea heard that the Gentiles had also received the word of God.

2 And when Peter was come up to Jerusalem, they that were of the circumcision contended with him,

3 Saying, Thou wentest in to men uncircumcised, and didst eat with them.

4 But Peter rehearsed *the matter* from the beginning, and expounded *it* by order unto them, saying,

5 I was in the city of Joppa praying: and in a trance I saw a vision, A certain vessel descend,

as it had been a great sheet, let down from heaven by four corners; and it came even unto me:

6 Upon the which when I had fastened mine eyes, I considered, and saw fourfooted beasts of the earth, and wild beasts, and creeping things, and fowls of the air.

7 And I heard a voice saying unto me, Arise, Peter; slay and eat.

8 But I said, Not so, Lord: for nothing common or unclean hath at any time entered into my mouth.

9 But the voice answered me again from heaven, What God hath cleansed, *that* call not thou common.

10 And this was done three times: and all were drawn up again into heaven.

11 And, behold, immediately there were three men already come unto the house where I was, sent from Caesarea unto me.

12 And the Spirit bade me go with them, nothing doubting. Moreover these six brethren accompanied me, and we entered into the man's house:

13 And he shewed us how he had seen an angel in his house, which stood and said unto him, Send men to Joppa, and call for Simon, whose surname is Peter;

14 Who shall tell thee words, whereby thou and all thy house shall be saved.

15 And as I began to speak, the Holy Ghost fell on them, as on us at the beginning.

16 Then remembered I the word of the Lord, how that he said, John indeed baptized with water; but ye shall be baptized with the Holy Ghost.

17 Forasmuch then as God gave them the like gift as *he did* unto us, who believed on the Lord Jesus Christ; what was I, that I could withstand God?

18 When they heard these things, they held their peace, and glorified God, saying, Then hath God also to the Gentiles granted repentance unto life.

19 ¶ Now they which were scattered abroad upon the persecution that arose about Stephen travelled as far as Phenice, and Cyprus, and Antioch, preaching the word to none but unto the Jews only.

20 And some of them were men of Cyprus and Cyrene, which, when they were come to Antioch, spake unto the Grecians, preaching the Lord Jesus.

21 And the hand of the Lord was with them: and a great number believed, and turned unto the Lord.

22 ¶ Then tidings of these things came unto the ears of the church which was in Jerusalem: and they sent forth Barnabas, that he should go as far as Antioch.

23 Who, when he came, and had seen the grace of God, was glad, and exhorted them all, that with purpose of heart they would cleave unto the Lord.

24 For he was a good man, and full of the Holy Ghost and of faith: and much people was added unto the Lord.

25 Then departed Barnabas to Tarsus, for to seek Saul:

26 And when he had found him, he brought him unto Antioch. And it came to pass, that a whole year they assembled themselves with the church, and taught much people. And the disciples were called Christians first in Antioch.

27 ¶ And in these days came prophets from Jerusalem unto Antioch.

28 And there stood up one of them named Agabus, and signified by the Spirit that there should be great dearth throughout all the world: which came to pass in the days of Claudius Caesar.

29 Then the disciples, every man according to his ability, determined to send relief unto the brethren which dwelt in Judea:

30 Which also they did, and sent it to the elders by the hands of Barnabas and Saul.

12 Now about that time Herod the king stretched forth *his* hands to vex certain of the church.

2 And he killed James the brother of John with the sword.

3 ¶ And because he saw it pleased the Jews, he proceeded further to take Peter also. (Then were the days of unleavened bread.)

4 And when he had apprehended him, he put *him* in prison, and delivered *him* to four quaternions of soldiers to keep him; intending after Easter to bring him forth to the people.

5 Peter therefore was kept in prison: but prayer was made without ceasing of the church unto God for him.

6 ¶ And when Herod would have brought him forth, the same night Peter was sleeping between two soldiers, bound with two chains: and the keepers before the door kept the prison.

7 And, behold, the angel of the Lord came upon *him*, and a light shined in the prison: and he smote Peter on the side, and raised him up, saying, Arise up quickly. And his chains fell off from *his* hands.

8 And the angel said unto him, Gird thyself, and bind on thy sandals. And so he did. And he saith unto him, Cast thy garment about thee, and follow me.

9 And he went out, and followed him; and wist not that it was true which was done by the angel; but thought he saw a vision.

10 When they were past the first and the second ward, they came unto the iron gate that leadeth unto the city; which opened to them of his own accord: and they went out, and passed on through one street; and forthwith the angel departed from him.

11 And when Peter was come to himself, he said, Now I know of a surety, that the Lord hath sent his angel, and hath delivered me out of the hand of Herod, and *from* all the expectation of the people of the Jews.

12 And when he had considered *the thing*, he came to the house of Mary the mother of John, whose surname was Mark; where many were gathered together praying.

13 And as Peter knocked at the door of the gate, a damsel came to hearken, named Rhoda.

14 And when she knew Peter's voice, she opened not the gate for gladness, but ran in, and told how Peter stood before the gate.

15 And they said unto her, Thou art mad. But she constantly affirmed that it was even so. Then said they, It is his angel.

16 But Peter continued knocking: and when they had opened *the door,* and saw him, they were astonished.

17 But he, beckoning unto them with the hand to hold their peace, declared unto them how the Lord had brought him out of the prison. And he said, Go shew these things unto James, and to the brethren. And he departed, and went into another place.

18 Now as soon as it was day, there was no small stir among the soldiers, what was become of Peter.

19 And when Herod had sought for him, and found him not, he examined the keepers, and commanded that *they* should be put to death. And he went down from Judaea to Caesarea, and *there* abode.

20 ¶ And Herod was highly displeased with them of Tyre and Sidon: but they came with one accord to him, and, having made Blastus the king's chamberlain their friend, desired peace; because their country was nourished by the king's *country.*

21 And upon a set day Herod, arrayed in royal apparel, sat upon his throne, and made an oration unto them.

22 And the people gave a shout, *saying, It is* the voice of a god, and not of a man.

23 And immediately the angel of the Lord smote him, because he gave not God the glory: and he was eaten of worms, and gave up the ghost.

24 ¶ But the word of God grew and multiplied.

25 And Barnabas and Saul returned from Jerusalem, when they had fulfilled *their* ministry, and took with them John, whose surname was Mark.

13

Now there were in the church that was at Antioch certain prophets and teachers; as Barnabas, and Simeon that was called Niger, and Lucius of Cyrene, and Manaen, which had been brought up with Herod the tetrarch, and Saul.

2 As they ministered to the Lord, and fasted, the Holy Ghost said, Separate me Barnabas and Saul for the work whereunto I have called them.

3 And when they had fasted and prayed, and laid *their* hands on them, they sent *them* away.

4 ¶ So they, being sent forth by the Holy Ghost, departed unto Seleucia; and from thence they sailed to Cyprus.

5 And when they were at Salamis, they preached the word of God in the synagogues of the Jews: and they had also John to *their* minister.

6 And when they had gone

through the isle unto Paphos, they found a certain sorcerer, a false prophet, a Jew, whose name was Bar-jesus:

7 Which was with the deputy of the country, Sergius Paulus, a prudent man; who called for Barnabas and Saul, and desired to hear the word of God.

8 But Elymas the sorcerer (for so is his name by interpretation) withstood them, seeking to turn away the deputy from the faith.

9 Then Saul, (who also is called Paul,) filled with the Holy Ghost, set his eyes on him,

10 And said, O full of all subtilty and all mischief, thou child of the devil, thou enemy of all righteousness, wilt thou not cease to pervert the right ways of the Lord?

11 And now, behold, the hand of the Lord is upon thee, and thou shalt be blind, not seeing the sun for a season. And immediately there fell on him a mist and a darkness; and he went about seeking some to lead him by the hand.

12 Then the deputy, when he saw what was done, believed, being astonished at the doctrine of the Lord.

13 Now when Paul and his company loosed from Paphos, they came to Perga in Pamphylia: and John departing from them returned to Jerusalem.

14 ¶ But when they departed from Perga, they came to Antioch in Pisidia, and went into the synagogue on the sabbath day, and sat down.

15 And after the reading of the law and the prophets, the rulers of the synagogue sent unto them, saying, Ye men and brethren, if ye have any word of exhortation for the people, say on.

16 Then Paul stood up, and beckoning with his hand said, Men of Israel, and ye that fear God, give audience.

17 The God of this people of Israel chose our fathers, and exalted the people when they dwelt as strangers in the land of Egypt, and with an high arm brought he them out of it.

18 And about the time of forty years suffered he their manners in the wilderness.

19 And when he had destroyed seven nations in the land of Chanaan, he divided their land to them by lot.

20 And after that he gave unto them judges about the space of four hundred and fifty years, until Samuel the prophet.

21 And afterward they desired a king: and God gave unto them Saul the son of Cis, a man of the tribe of Benjamin, by the space of forty years.

22 And when he had removed him, he raised up unto them David to be their king; to whom also he gave testimony, and said, I have found David the son of Jesse, a man after mine own heart, which shall fulfil all my will.

23 Of this man's seed hath God according to his promise raised unto Israel a Saviour, Jesus:

24 When John had first preached

before his coming the baptism of repentance to all the people of Israel.

25 And as John fulfilled his course, he said, Whom think ye that I am? I am not *he*. But, behold, there cometh one after me, whose shoes of *his* feet I am not worthy to loose.

26 Men *and* brethren, children of the stock of Abraham, and whosoever among you feareth God, to you is the word of this salvation sent.

27 For they that dwell at Jerusalem, and their rulers, because they knew him not, nor yet the voices of the prophets which are read every sabbath day, they have fulfilled *them* in condemning *him*.

28 And though they found no cause of death *in him*, yet desired they Pilate that he should be slain.

29 And when they had fulfilled all that was written of him, they took *him* down from the tree, and laid *him* in a sepulchre.

30 But God raised him from the dead:

31 And he was seen many days of them which came up with him from Galilee to Jerusalem, who are his witnesses unto the people.

32 And we declare unto you glad tidings, how that the promise which was made unto the fathers,

33 God hath fulfilled the same unto us their children, in that he hath raised up Jesus again; as it is also written in the second psalm,

Thou art my Son, this day have I begotten thee.

34 And as concerning that he raised him up from the dead, *now* no more to return to corruption, he said on this wise, I will give you the sure mercies of David.

35 Wherefore he saith also in another *psalm*, Thou shalt not suffer thine Holy One to see corruption.

36 For David, after he had served his own generation by the will of God, fell on sleep, and was laid unto his fathers, and saw corruption:

37 But he, whom God raised again, saw no corruption.

38 ¶ Be it known unto you therefore, men *and* brethren, that through this man is preached unto you the forgiveness of sins:

39 And by him all that believe are justified from all things, from which ye could not be justified by the law of Moses.

40 Beware therefore, lest that come upon you, which is spoken of in the prophets;

41 Behold, ye despisers, and wonder, and perish: for I work a work in your days, a work which ye shall in no wise believe, though a man declare it unto you.

42 And when the Jews were gone out of the synagogue, the Gentiles besought that these words might be preached to them the next sabbath.

43 Now when the congregation was broken up, many of the Jews and religious proselytes followed

Paul and Barnabas: who, speaking to them, persuaded them to continue in the grace of God.

44 ¶ And the next sabbath day came almost the whole city together to hear the word of God.

45 But when the Jews saw the multitudes, they were filled with envy, and spake against those things which were spoken by Paul, contradicting and blaspheming.

46 Then Paul and Barnabas waxed bold, and said, It was necessary that the word of God should first have been spoken to you: but seeing ye put it from you, and judge yourselves unworthy of everlasting life, lo, we turn to the Gentiles.

47 For so hath the Lord commanded us, *saying*, I have set thee to be a light of the Gentiles, that thou shouldest be for salvation unto the ends of the earth.

48 And when the Gentiles heard this, they were glad, and glorified the word of the Lord: and as many as were ordained to eternal life believed.

49 And the word of the Lord was published throughout all the region.

50 But the Jews stirred up the devout and honourable women, and the chief men of the city, and raised persecution against Paul and Barnabas, and expelled them out of their coasts.

51 But they shook off the dust of their feet against them, and came unto Iconium.

52 And the disciples were filled with joy, and with the Holy Ghost.

14 And it came to pass in Iconium, that they went both together into the synagogue of the Jews, and so spake, that a great multitude both of the Jews and also of the Greeks believed.

2 But the unbelieving Jews stirred up the Gentiles, and made their minds evil affected against the brethren.

3 Long time therefore abode they speaking boldly in the Lord, which gave testimony unto the word of his grace, and granted signs and wonders to be done by their hands.

4 But the multitude of the city was divided: and part held with the Jews, and part with the apostles.

5 And when there was an assault made both of the Gentiles, and also of the Jews with their rulers, to use *them* despitefully, and to stone them,

6 They were ware of *it*, and fled unto Lystra and Derbe, cities of Lycaonia, and unto the region that lieth round about:

7 And there they preached the gospel.

8 ¶ And there sat a certain man at Lystra, impotent in his feet, being a cripple from his mother's womb, who never had walked:

9 The same heard Paul speak: who stedfastly beholding him, and perceiving that he had faith to be healed,

10 Said with a loud voice, Stand upright on thy feet. And he leaped and walked.

11 And when the people saw what Paul had done, they lifted up their voices, saying in the speech of Lycaonia, The gods are come down to us in the likeness of men.

12 And they called Barnabas, Jupiter; and Paul, Mercurius, because he was the chief speaker.

13 Then the priest of Jupiter, which was before their city, brought oxen and garlands unto the gates, and would have done sacrifice with the people.

14 *Which* when the apostles, Barnabas and Paul, heard *of*, they rent their clothes, and ran in among the people, crying out,

15 And saying, Sirs, why do ye these things? We also are men of like passions with you, and preach unto you that ye should turn from these vanities unto the living God, which made heaven, and earth, and the sea, and all things that are therein:

16 Who in times past suffered all nations to walk in their own ways.

17 Nevertheless he left not himself without witness, in that he did good, and gave us rain from heaven, and fruitful seasons, filling our hearts with food and gladness.

18 And with these sayings scarce restrained they the people, that they had not done sacrifice unto them.

19 ¶ And there came thither certain Jews from Antioch and Iconium, who persuaded the people, and having stoned Paul, drew *him* out of the city, supposing he had been dead.

20 Howbeit, as the disciples stood round about him, he rose up, and came into the city: and the next day he departed with Barnabas to Derbe.

21 And when they had preached the gospel to that city, and had taught many, they returned again to Lystra, and *to* Iconium, and Antioch,

22 Confirming the souls of the disciples, *and* exhorting them to continue in the faith, and that we must through much tribulation enter into the kingdom of God.

23 ¶ And when they had ordained them elders in every church, and had prayed with fasting, they commended them to the Lord, on whom they believed.

24 And after they had passed throughout Pisidia, they came to Pamphylia.

25 ¶ And when they had preached the word in Perga, they went down into Attalia:

26 And thence sailed to Antioch, from whence they had been recommended to the grace of God for the work which they fulfilled.

27 And when they were come, and had gathered the church together, they rehearsed all that God had done with them, and how he had opened the door of faith unto the Gentiles.

28 And there they abode long time with the disciples.

15 And certain men which came down from Judaea taught the brethren, *and*

said, Except ye be circumcised after the manner of Moses, ye cannot be saved.

2 When therefore Paul and Barnabas had no small dissension and disputation with them, they determined that Paul and Barnabas, and certain other of them, should go up to Jerusalem unto the apostles and elders about this question.

3 And being brought on their way by the church, they passed through Phenice and Samaria, declaring the conversion of the Gentiles: and they caused great joy unto all the brethren.

4 And when they were come to Jerusalem, they were received of the church, and *of* the apostles and elders, and they declared all things that God had done with them.

5 But there rose up certain of the sect of the Pharisees which believed, saying, That it was needful to circumcise them, and to command *them* to keep the law of Moses.

6 ¶ And the apostles and elders came together for to consider of this matter.

7 And when there had been much disputing, Peter rose up, and said unto them, Men *and* brethren, ye know how that a good while ago God made choice among us, that the Gentiles by my mouth should hear the word of the gospel, and believe.

8 And God, which knoweth the hearts, bare them witness, giving them the Holy Ghost, even as *he did* unto us;

9 And put no difference between us and them, purifying their hearts by faith.

10 Now therefore why tempt ye God, to put a yoke upon the neck of the disciples, which neither our fathers nor we were able to bear?

11 But we believe that through the grace of the Lord Jesus Christ we shall be saved, even as they.

12 ¶ Then all the multitude kept silence, and gave audience to Barnabas and Paul, declaring what miracles and wonders God had wrought among the Gentiles by them.

13 ¶And after they had held their peace, James answered, saying, Men *and* brethren, hearken unto me:

14 Simeon hath declared how God at the first did visit the Gentiles, to take out of them a people for his name.

15 And to this agree the words of the prophets; as it is written,

16 After this I will return, and will build again the tabernacle of David, which is fallen down; and I will build again the ruins thereof, and I will set it up:

17 That the residue of men might seek after the Lord, and all the Gentiles, upon whom my name is called, saith the Lord, who doeth all these things.

18 Known unto God are all his works from the beginning of the world.

19 Wherefore my sentence is, that we trouble not them, which from among the Gentiles are turned to God:

20 But that we write unto them, that they abstain from pollutions of idols, and *from* fornication, and *from* things strangled, and *from* blood.

21 For Moses of old time hath in every city them that preach him, being read in the synagogues every sabbath day.

22 Then pleased it the apostles and elders with the whole church, to send chosen men of their own company to Antioch with Paul and Barnabas; *namely,* Judas surnamed Barsabas, and Silas, chief men among the brethren:

23 And they wrote *letters* by them after this manner; The apostles and elders and brethren *send* greeting unto the brethren which are of the Gentiles in Antioch and Syria and Cilicia.

24 Forasmuch as we have heard, that certain which went out from us have troubled you with words, subverting your souls, saying, *Ye must* be circumcised, and keep the law; to whom we gave no *such* commandment:

25 It seemed good unto us, being assembled with one accord, to send chosen men unto you with our beloved Barnabas and Paul,

26 Men that have hazarded their lives for the name of our Lord Jesus Christ.

27 We have sent therefore Judas and Silas, who shall also tell *you* the same things by mouth.

28 For it seemed good to the Holy Ghost, and to us, to lay upon you no greater burden than these necessary things;

29 That ye abstain from meats offered to idols, and from blood, and from things strangled, and from fornication: from which if ye keep yourselves, ye shall do well. Fare ye well.

30 So when they were dismissed, they came to Antioch: and when they had gathered the multitude together, they delivered the epistle:

31 *Which* when they had read, they rejoiced for the consolation.

32 And Judas and Silas, being prophets also themselves, exhorted the brethren with many words, and confirmed *them*.

33 And after they had tarried *there* a space, they were let go in peace from the brethren unto the apostles.

34 Notwithstanding it pleased Silas to abide there still.

35 Paul also and Barnabas continued in Antioch, teaching and preaching the word of the Lord, with many others also.

36 ¶ And some days after Paul said unto Barnabas, Let us go again and visit our brethren in every city where we have preached the word of the Lord, *and see* how they do.

37 And Barnabas determined to take with them John, whose surname was Mark.

38 But Paul thought not good to take him with them, who departed from them from Pamphylia, and went not with them to the work.

39 And the contention was so sharp between them, that they

213

departed asunder one from the other: and so Barnabas took Mark, and sailed unto Cyprus;

40 And Paul chose Silas, and departed, being recommended by the brethren unto the grace of God.

41 And he went through Syria and Cilicia, confirming the churches.

16 Then came he to Derbe and Lystra: and, behold, a certain disciple was there, named Timotheus, the son of a certain woman, which was a Jewess, and believed; but his father *was* a Greek:

2 Which was well reported of by the brethren that were at Lystra and Iconium.

3 Him would Paul have to go forth with him; and took and circumcised him because of the Jews which were in those quarters: for they knew all that his father was a Greek.

4 ¶ And as they went through the cities, they delivered them the decrees for to keep, that were ordained of the apostles and elders which were at Jerusalem.

5 And so were the churches established in the faith, and increased in number daily.

6 ¶ Now when they had gone throughout Phrygia and the region of Galatia, and were forbidden of the Holy Ghost to preach the word in Asia,

7 After they were come to Mysia, they assayed to go into Bithynia: but the Spirit suffered them not.

8 And they passing by Mysia came down to Troas.

9 And a vision appeared to Paul in the night; There stood a man of Macedonia, and prayed him, saying, Come over into Macedonia, and help us.

10 And after he had seen the vision, immediately we endeavoured to go into Macedonia, assuredly gathering that the Lord had called us for to preach the gospel unto them.

11 Therefore loosing from Troas, we came with a straight course to Samothracia, and the next *day* to Neapolis;

12 And from thence to Philippi, which is the chief city of that part of Macedonia, *and* a colony: and we were in that city abiding certain days.

13 And on the sabbath we went out of the city by a river side, where prayer was wont to be made; and we sat down, and spake unto the women which resorted *thither.*

14 ¶ And a certain woman named Lydia, a seller of purple, of the city of Thyatira, which worshipped God, heard *us:* whose heart the Lord opened, that she attended unto the things which were spoken of Paul.

15 And when she was baptized, and her household, she besought *us,* saying, If ye have judged me to be faithful to the Lord, come into my house, and abide *there.* And she constrained us.

16 ¶ And it came to pass, as we went to prayer, a certain damsel possessed with a spirit of divina-

tion met us, which brought her masters much gain by soothsaying:

17 The same followed Paul and us, and cried, saying, These men are the servants of the most high God, which shew unto us the way of salvation.

18 And this did she many days. But Paul, being grieved, turned and said to the spirit, I command thee in the name of Jesus Christ to come out of her. And he came out the same hour.

19 ¶ And when her masters saw that the hope of their gains was gone, they caught Paul and Silas, and drew *them* into the marketplace unto the rulers,

20 And brought them to the magistrates, saying, These men, being Jews, do exceedingly trouble our city,

21 And teach customs, which are not lawful for us to receive, neither to observe, being Romans.

22 And the multitude rose up together against them: and the magistrates rent off their clothes, and commanded to beat *them*.

23 And when they had laid many stripes upon them, they cast *them* into prison, charging the jailor to keep them safely:

24 Who, having received such a charge, thrust them into the inner prison, and made their feet fast in the stocks.

25 ¶ And at midnight Paul and Silas prayed, and sang praises unto God: and the prisoners heard them.

26 And suddenly there was a great earthquake, so that the foundations of the prison were shaken: and immediately all the doors were opened, and every one's bands were loosed.

27 And the keeper of the prison awaking out of his sleep, and seeing the prison doors open, he drew out his sword, and would have killed himself, supposing that the prisoners had been fled.

28 But Paul cried with a loud voice, saying, Do thyself no harm: for we are all here.

29 Then he called for a light, and sprang in, and came trembling, and fell down before Paul and Silas,

30 And brought them out, and said, Sirs, what must I do to be saved?

31 And they said, Believe on the Lord Jesus Christ, and thou shalt be saved, and thy house.

32 And they spake unto him the word of the Lord, and to all that were in his house.

33 And he took them the same hour of the night, and washed *their* stripes; and was baptized, he and all his, straightway.

34 And when he had brought them into his house, he set meat before them, and rejoiced, believing in God with all his house.

35 ¶ And when it was day, the magistrates sent the serjeants, saying, Let those men go.

36 And the keeper of the prison told this saying to Paul, The magistrates have sent to let you go: now therefore depart, and go

in peace.

37 But Paul said unto them, They have beaten us openly uncondemned, being Romans, and have cast *us* into prison; and now do they thrust us out privily? nay verily; but let them come themselves and fetch us out.

38 And the serjeants told these words unto the magistrates: and they feared, when they heard that they were Romans.

39 And they came and besought them, and brought *them* out, and desired *them* to depart out of the city.

40 And they went out of the prison, and entered into *the house of* Lydia: and when they had seen the brethren, they comforted them, and departed.

17

Now when they had passed through Amphipolis and Apollonia, they came to Thessalonica, where was a synagogue of the Jews:

2 And Paul, as his manner was, went in unto them, and three sabbath days reasoned with them out of the scriptures,

3 Opening and alleging, that Christ must needs have suffered, and risen again from the dead; and that this Jesus, whom I preach unto you, is Christ.

4 And some of them believed, and consorted with Paul and Silas; and of the devout Greeks a great multitude, and of the chief women not a few.

5 ¶ But the Jews which believed not, moved with envy, took unto them certain lewd fellows of the baser sort, and gathered a company, and set all the city on an uproar, and assaulted the house of Jason, and sought to bring them out to the people.

6 And when they found them not, they drew Jason and certain brethren unto the rulers of the city, crying, These that have turned the world upside down are come hither also;

7 Whom Jason hath received: and these all do contrary to the decrees of Caesar, saying that there is another king, *one* Jesus.

8 And they troubled the people and the rulers of the city, when they heard these things.

9 And when they had taken security of Jason, and of the other, they let them go.

10 ¶ And the brethren immediately sent away Paul and Silas by night unto Berea: who coming *thither* went into the synagogue of the Jews.

11 These were more noble than those in Thessalonica, in that they received the word with all readiness of mind, and searched the scriptures daily, whether those things were so.

12 Therefore many of them believed; also of honourable women which were Greeks, and of men, not a few.

13 But when the Jews of Thessalonica had knowledge that the word of God was preached of Paul at Berea, they came thither also, and stirred up the people.

14 And then immediately the brethren sent away Paul to go as it were to the sea: but Silas and Timotheus abode there still.

15 And they that conducted Paul brought him unto Athens: and receiving a commandment unto Silas and Timotheus for to come to him with all speed, they departed.

16 ¶ Now while Paul waited for them at Athens, his spirit was stirred in him, when he saw the city wholly given to idolatry.

17 Therefore disputed he in the synagogue with the Jews, and with the devout persons, and in the market daily with them that met with him.

18 Then certain philosophers of the Epicureans, and of the Stoicks, encountered him. And some said, What will this babbler say? other some, He seemeth to be a setter forth of strange gods: because he preached unto them Jesus, and the resurrection.

19 And they took him, and brought him unto Areopagus, saying, May we know what this new doctrine, whereof thou speakest, *is*?

20 For thou bringest certain strange things to our ears: we would know therefore what these things mean.

21 (For all the Athenians and strangers which were there spent their time in nothing else, but either to tell, or to hear some new thing.)

22 ¶ Then Paul stood in the midst of Mars' hill, and said, Ye men of Athens, I perceive that in all things ye are too superstitious.

23 For as I passed by, and beheld your devotions, I found an altar with this inscription, TO THE UNKNOWN GOD. Whom therefore ye ignorantly worship, him declare I unto you.

24 God that made the world and all things therein, seeing that he is Lord of heaven and earth, dwelleth not in temples made with hands;

25 Neither is worshipped with men's hands, as though he needed any thing, seeing he giveth to all life, and breath, and all things;

26 And hath made of one blood all nations of men for to dwell on all the face of the earth, and hath determined the times before appointed, and the bounds of their habitation;

27 That they should seek the Lord, if haply they might feel after him, and find him, though he be not far from every one of us:

28 For in him we live, and move, and have our being; as certain also of your own poets have said, For we are also his offspring.

29 Forasmuch then as we are the offspring of God, we ought not to think that the Godhead is like unto gold, or silver, or stone, graven by art and man's device.

30 And the times of this ignorance God winked at; but now commandeth all men every where to repent:

31 Because he hath appointed a day, in the which he will judge the world in righteousness by *that* man whom he hath ordained; *whereof* he hath given assurance unto all *men*, in that he hath raised him from the dead.

32 ¶ And when they heard of the resurrection of the dead, some mocked: and others said, We will hear thee again of this *matter.*

33 So Paul departed from among them.

34 Howbeit certain men clave unto him, and believed: among the which *was* Dionysius the Areopagite, and a woman named Damaris, and others with them.

18

After these things Paul departed from Athens, and came to Corinth;

2 And found a certain Jew named Aquila, born in Pontus, lately come from Italy, with his wife Priscilla; (because that Claudius had commanded all Jews to depart from Rome:) and came unto them.

3 And because he was of the same craft, he abode with them, and wrought: for by their occupation they were tentmakers.

4 And he reasoned in the synagogue every sabbath, and persuaded the Jews and the Greeks.

5 And when Silas and Timotheus were come from Macedonia, Paul was pressed in the spirit, and testified to the Jews *that* Jesus *was* Christ.

6 And when they opposed themselves, and blasphemed, he shook *his* raiment, and said unto them, Your blood *be* upon your own heads; I *am* clean; from henceforth I will go unto the Gentiles.

7 And he departed thence, and entered into a certain *man's* house, named Justus, *one* that worshipped God, whose house joined hard to the synagogue.

8 And Crispus, the chief ruler of the synagogue, believed on the Lord with all his house; and many of the Corinthians hearing believed, and were baptized.

9 Then spake the Lord to Paul in the night by a vision, Be not afraid, but speak, and hold not thy peace:

10 For I am with thee, and no man shall set on thee to hurt thee: for I have much people in this city.

11 And he continued *there* a year and six months, teaching the word of God among them.

12 ¶ And when Gallio was the deputy of Achaia, the Jews made insurrection with one accord against Paul, and brought him to the judgment seat,

13 Saying, This *fellow* persuadeth men to worship God contrary to the law.

14 And when Paul was now about to open *his* mouth, Gallio said unto the Jews, If it were a matter of wrong or wicked lewdness, O *ye* Jews, reason would that I should bear with you:

15 But if it be a question of words and names, and *of* your law, look ye *to it;* for I will be no judge of such *matters.*

16 And he drave them from the judgment seat.

17 Then all the Greeks took Sosthenes, the chief ruler of the synagogue, and beat *him* before the judgment seat. And Gallio cared for none of those things.

18 ¶ And Paul *after this* tarried *there* yet a good while, and then took his leave of the brethren, and sailed thence into Syria, and with him Priscilla and Aquila; having shorn *his* head in Cenchrea; for he had a vow.

19 And he came to Ephesus, and left them there: but he himself entered into the synagogue, and reasoned with the Jews.

20 When they desired *him* to tarry longer time with them, he consented not;

21 But bade them farewell, saying, I must by all means keep this feast that cometh in Jerusalem: but I will return again unto you, if God will. And he sailed from Ephesus.

22 And when he had landed at Caesarea, and gone up, and saluted the church, he went down to Antioch.

23 And after he had spent some time *there*, he departed, and went over *all* the country of Galatia and Phrygia in order, strengthening all the disciples.

24 ¶ And a certain Jew named Apollos, born at Alexandria, an eloquent man, and mighty in the scriptures, came to Ephesus.

25 This man was instructed in the way of the Lord; and being fervent in the spirit, he spake and taught diligently the things of the Lord, knowing only the baptism of John.

26 And he began to speak boldly in the synagogue: whom when Aquila and Priscilla had heard, they took him unto *them*, and expounded unto him the way of God more perfectly.

27 And when he was disposed to pass into Achaia, the brethren wrote, exhorting the disciples to receive him: who, when he was come, helped them much which had believed through grace:

28 For he mightily convinced the Jews, *and that* publickly, shewing by the scriptures that Jesus was Christ.

19

And it came to pass, that, while Apollos was at Corinth, Paul having passed through the upper coasts came to Ephesus: and finding certain disciples,

2 He said unto them, Have ye received the Holy Ghost since ye believed? And they said unto him, We have not so much as heard whether there be any Holy Ghost.

3 And he said unto them, Unto what then were ye baptized? And they said, Unto John's baptism.

4 Then said Paul, John verily baptized with the baptism of repentance, saying unto the people, that they should believe on him which should come after him, that is, on Christ Jesus.

5 When they heard *this*, they were baptized in the name of the Lord Jesus.

6 And when Paul had laid *his* hands upon them, the Holy Ghost came on them; and they spake with tongues, and prophesied.

7 And all the men were about twelve.

8 ¶ And he went into the synagogue, and spake boldly for the

space of three months, disputing and persuading the things concerning the kingdom of God.

9 But when divers were hardened, and believed not, but spake evil of that way before the multitude, he departed from them, and separated the disciples, disputing daily in the school of one Tyrannus.

10 And this continued by the space of two years; so that all they which dwelt in Asia heard the word of the Lord Jesus, both Jews and Greeks.

11 And God wrought special miracles by the hands of Paul:

12 So that from his body were brought unto the sick handkerchiefs or aprons, and the diseases departed from them, and the evil spirits went out of them.

13 ¶ Then certain of the vagabond Jews, exorcists, took upon them to call over them which had evil spirits the name of the Lord Jesus, saying, We adjure you by Jesus whom Paul preacheth.

14 And there were seven sons of one Sceva, a Jew, and chief of the priests, which did so.

15 And the evil spirit answered and said, Jesus I know, and Paul I know; but who are ye?

16 And the man in whom the evil spirit was leaped on them, and overcame them, and prevailed against them, so that they fled out of that house naked and wounded.

17 And this was known to all the Jews and Greeks also dwelling at Ephesus; and fear fell on them all, and the name of the Lord Jesus was magnified.

18 And many that believed came, and confessed, and shewed their deeds.

19 Many of them also which used curious arts brought their books together, and burned them before all men: and they counted the price of them, and found it fifty thousand pieces of silver.

20 So mightily grew the word of God and prevailed.

21 ¶ After these things were ended, Paul purposed in the spirit, when he had passed through Macedonia and Achaia, to go to Jerusalem, saying, After I have been there, I must also see Rome.

22 So he sent into Macedonia two of them that ministered unto him, Timotheus and Erastus; but he himself stayed in Asia for a season.

23 And the same time there arose no small stir about that way.

24 For a certain man named Demetrius, a silversmith, which made silver shrines for Diana, brought no small gain unto the craftsmen;

25 Whom he called together with the workmen of like occupation, and said, Sirs, ye know that by this craft we have our wealth.

26 Moreover ye see and hear, that not alone at Ephesus, but almost throughout all Asia, this Paul hath persuaded and turned away much people, saying that they be no gods, which are made with hands:

27 So that not only this our craft is in danger to be set at nought; but also that the temple of the great goddess Diana should be despised, and her magnificence should be destroyed, whom all Asia and the world worshippeth.

28 And when they heard *these sayings*, they were full of wrath, and cried out, saying, Great *is* Diana of the Ephesians.

29 And the whole city was filled with confusion: and having caught Gaius and Aristarchus, men of Macedonia, Paul's companions in travel, they rushed with one accord into the theatre.

30 And when Paul would have entered in unto the people, the disciples suffered him not.

31 And certain of the chief of Asia, which were his friends, sent unto him, desiring *him* that he would not adventure himself into the theatre.

32 Some therefore cried one thing, and some another: for the assembly was confused; and the more part knew not wherefore they were come together.

33 And they drew Alexander out of the multitude, the Jews putting him forward. And Alexander beckoned with the hand, and would have made his defence unto the people.

34 But when they knew that he was a Jew, all with one voice about the space of two hours cried out, Great *is* Diana of the Ephesians.

35 And when the townclerk had appeased the people, he said, Ye men of Ephesus, what man is

there that knoweth not how that the city of the Ephesians is a worshipper of the great goddess Diana, and of the *image* which fell down from Jupiter?

36 Seeing then that these things cannot be spoken against, ye ought to be quiet, and to do nothing rashly.

37 For ye have brought hither these men, which are neither robbers of churches, nor yet blasphemers of your goddess.

38 Wherefore if Demetrius, and the craftsmen which are with him, have a matter against any man, the law is open, and there are deputies: let them implead one another.

39 But if ye enquire any thing concerning other matters, it shall be determined in a lawful assembly.

40 For we are in danger to be called in question for this day's uproar, there being no cause whereby we may give an account of this concourse.

41 And when he had thus spoken, he dismissed the assembly.

20 And after the uproar was ceased, Paul called unto *him* the disciples, and embraced *them*, and departed for to go into Macedonia.

2 And when he had gone over those parts, and had given them much exhortation, he came into Greece,

3 And *there* abode three months. And when the Jews laid wait for him, as he was about to sail into Syria, he purposed to re-

turn through Macedonia.

4 And there accompanied him into Asia Sopater of Berea; and of the Thessalonians, Aristarchus and Secundus; and Gaius of Derbe, and Timotheus; and of Asia, Tychicus and Trophimus.

5 These going before tarried for us at Troas.

6 And we sailed away from Philippi after the days of unleavened bread, and came unto them to Troas in five days; where we abode seven days.

7 (And upon the first *day* of the week, when the disciples came together to break bread, Paul preached unto them, ready to depart on the morrow; and continued his speech until midnight.

8 And there were many lights in the upper chamber, where they were gathered together.

9 And there sat in a window a certain young man named Eutychus, being fallen into a deep sleep: and as Paul was long preaching, he sunk down with sleep, and fell down from the third loft, and was taken up dead.

10 And Paul went down, and fell on him, and embracing *him* said, Trouble not yourselves; for his life is in him.

11 When he therefore was come up again, and had broken bread, and eaten, and talked a long while, even till break of day, so he departed.

12 And they brought the young man alive, and were not a little comforted.

13 (And we went before to ship, and sailed unto Assos, there intending to take in Paul: for so had he appointed, minding himself to go afoot.

14 And when he met with us at Assos, we took him in, and came to Mitylene.

15 And we sailed thence, and came the next *day* over against Chios; and the next *day* we arrived at Samos, and tarried at Trogyllium; and the next *day* we came to Miletus.

16 For Paul had determined to sail by Ephesus, because he would not spend the time in Asia: for he hasted, if it were possible for him, to be at Jerusalem the day of Pentecost.

17 (And from Miletus he sent to Ephesus, and called the elders of the church.

18 And when they were come to him, he said unto them, Ye know, from the first day that I came into Asia, after what manner I have been with you at all seasons,

19 Serving the Lord with all humility of mind, and with many tears, and temptations, which befell me by the lying in wait of the Jews:

20 *And* how I kept back nothing that was profitable *unto you*, but have shewed you, and have taught you publickly, and from house to house,

21 Testifying both to the Jews, and also to the Greeks, repentance toward God, and faith toward our Lord Jesus Christ.

22 And now, behold, I go bound in the spirit unto Jerusalem, not

knowing the things that shall befall me there:

23 Save that the Holy Ghost witnesseth in every city, saying that bonds and afflictions abide me.

24 But none of these things move me, neither count I my life dear unto myself, so that I might finish my course with joy, and the ministry, which I have received of the Lord Jesus, to testify the gospel of the grace of God.

25 And now, behold, I know that ye all, among whom I have gone preaching the kingdom of God, shall see my face no more.

26 Wherefore I take you to record this day, that I am pure from the blood of all men.

27 For I have not shunned to declare unto you all the counsel of God.

28 ❮ Take heed therefore unto yourselves, and to all the flock, over the which the Holy Ghost hath made you overseers, to feed the church of God, which he hath purchased with his own blood.

29 For I know this, that after my departing shall grievous wolves enter in among you, not sparing the flock.

30 Also of your own selves shall men arise, speaking perverse things, to draw away disciples after them.

31 Therefore watch, and remember, that by the space of three years I ceased not to warn every one night and day with tears.

32 And now, brethren, I commend you to God, and to the word of his grace, which is able to build you up, and to give you an inheritance among all them which are sanctified.

33 I have coveted no man's silver, or gold, or apparel.

34 Yea, ye yourselves know, that these hands have ministered unto my necessities, and to them that were with me.

35 I have shewed you all things, how that so labouring ye ought to support the weak, and to remember the words of the Lord Jesus, how he said, It is more blessed to give than to receive.

36 ❮ And when he had thus spoken, he kneeled down, and prayed with them all.

37 And they all wept sore, and fell on Paul's neck, and kissed him,

38 Sorrowing most of all for the words which he spake, that they should see his face no more. And they accompanied him unto the ship.

21 And it came to pass, that after we were gotten from them, and had launched, we came with a straight course unto Coos, and the day following unto Rhodes, and from thence unto Patara:

2 And finding a ship sailing over unto Phenicia, we went aboard, and set forth.

3 Now when we had discovered Cyprus, we left it on the left hand, and sailed into Syria, and landed at Tyre: for there the ship was to unlade her burden.

4 ¶ And finding disciples, we tarried there seven days: who said to Paul through the Spirit, that he should not go up to Jerusalem.

5 And when we had accomplished those days, we departed and went our way; and they all brought us on our way, with wives and children, till *we were* out of the city: and we kneeled down on the shore, and prayed.

6 And when we had taken our leave one of another, we took ship; and they returned home again.

7 And when we had finished *our* course from Tyre, we came to Ptolemais, and saluted the brethren, and abode with them one day.

8 And the next *day* we that were of Paul's company departed, and came into Caesarea: and we entered into the house of Philip the evangelist, which was *one* of the seven; and abode with him.

9 And the same man had four daughters, virgins, which did prophesy.

10 And as we tarried *there* many days, there came down from Judaea a certain prophet, named Agabus.

11 And when he was come unto us, he took Paul's girdle, and bound his own hands and feet, and said, Thus saith the Holy Ghost, So shall the Jews at Jerusalem bind the man that owneth this girdle, and shall deliver *him* into the hands of the Gentiles.

12 And when we heard these things, both we, and they of that place, besought him not to go up to Jerusalem.

13 Then Paul answered, What mean ye to weep and to break mine heart? for I am ready not to be bound only, but also to die at Jerusalem for the name of the Lord Jesus.

14 ¶ And when he would not be persuaded, we ceased, saying, The will of the Lord be done.

15 And after those days we took up our carriages, and went up to Jerusalem.

16 There went with us also *certain* of the disciples of Caesarea, and brought with them one Mnason of Cyprus, an old disciple, with whom we should lodge.

17 And when we were come to Jerusalem, the brethren received us gladly.

18 And the *day* following Paul went in with us unto James; and all the elders were present.

19 And when he had saluted them, he declared particularly what things God had wrought among the Gentiles by his ministry.

20 And when they heard *it*, they glorified the Lord, and said unto him, Thou seest, brother, how many thousands of Jews there are which believe; and they are all zealous of the law:

21 And they are informed of thee, that thou teachest all the Jews which are among the Gentiles to forsake Moses, saying that they ought not to circumcise *their* children, neither to walk after the customs.

22 What is it therefore? the mul-

titude must needs come together: for they will hear that thou art come.

23 Do therefore this that we say to thee: We have four men which have a vow on them;

24 Them take, and purify thyself with them, and be at charges with them, that they may shave *their* heads: and all may know that those things, whereof they were informed concerning thee, are nothing; but *that* thou thyself also walkest orderly, and keepest the law.

25 As touching the Gentiles which believe, we have written *and* concluded that they observe no such thing, save only that they keep themselves from *things* offered to idols, and from blood, and from strangled, and from fornication.

26 Then Paul took the men, and the next day purifying himself with them entered into the temple, to signify the accomplishment of the days of purification, until that an offering should be offered for every one of them.

27 ℂ And when the seven days were almost ended, the Jews which were of Asia, when they saw him in the temple, stirred up all the people, and laid hands on him,

28 Crying out, Men of Israel, help: This is the man, that teacheth all *men* every where against the people, and the law, and this place: and further brought Greeks also into the temple, and hath polluted this holy place.

29 (For they had seen before with him in the city Trophimus an Ephesian, whom they supposed that Paul had brought into the temple.)

30 And all the city was moved, and the people ran together: and they took Paul, and drew him out of the temple: and forthwith the doors were shut.

31 ℂ And as they were about to kill him, tidings came unto the chief captain of the band, that all Jerusalem was in an uproar.

32 Who immediately took soldiers and centurions, and ran down unto them: and when they saw the chief captain and the soldiers, they left beating of Paul.

33 Then the chief captain came near, and took him, and commanded *him* to be bound with two chains; and demanded who he was, and what he had done.

34 And some cried one thing, some another, among the multitude: and when he could not know the certainty for the tumult, he commanded him to be carried into the castle.

35 And when he came upon the stairs, so it was, that he was borne of the soldiers for the violence of the people.

36 For the multitude of the people followed after, crying, Away with him.

37 ℂ And as Paul was to be led into the castle, he said unto the chief captain, May I speak unto thee? Who said, Canst thou speak Greek?

38 Art not thou that Egyptian, which before these days madest

225

an uproar, and leddest out into the wilderness four thousand men that were murderers?

39 But Paul said, I am a man *which am a* Jew of Tarsus, *a city* in Cilicia, a citizen of no mean city: and, I beseech thee, suffer me to speak unto the people.

40 And when he had given him licence, Paul stood on the stairs, and beckoned with the hand unto the people. And when there was made a great silence, he spake unto *them* in the Hebrew tongue, saying,

22

Men, brethren, and fathers, hear ye my defence *which I make* now unto you.

2 (And when they heard that he spake in the Hebrew tongue to them, they kept the more silence: and he saith,)

3 I am verily a man *which am a* Jew, born in Tarsus, *a city* in Cilicia, yet brought up in this city at the feet of Gamaliel, *and* taught according to the perfect manner of the law of the fathers, and was zealous toward God, as ye all are this day.

4 And I persecuted this way unto the death, binding and delivering into prisons both men and women.

5 As also the high priest doth bear me witness, and all the estate of the elders: from whom also I received letters unto the brethren, and went to Damascus, to bring them which were there bound unto Jerusalem, for to be punished.

6 And it came to pass, that, as I made my journey, and was come nigh unto Damascus about noon, suddenly there shone from heaven a great light round about me.

7 And I fell unto the ground, and heard a voice saying unto me, Saul, Saul, why persecutest thou me?

8 And I answered, Who art thou, Lord? And he said unto me, I am Jesus of Nazareth, whom thou persecutest.

9 And they that were with me saw indeed the light, and were afraid; but they heard not the voice of him that spake to me.

10 And I said, What shall I do, Lord? And the Lord said unto me, Arise, and go into Damascus; and there it shall be told thee of all things which are appointed for thee to do.

11 And when I could not see for the glory of that light, being led by the hand of them that were with me, I came into Damascus.

12 And one Ananias, a devout man according to the law, having a good report of all the Jews which dwelt *there*,

13 Came unto me, and stood, and said unto me, Brother Saul, receive thy sight. And the same hour I looked up upon him.

14 And he said, The God of our fathers hath chosen thee, that thou shouldest know his will, and see that Just One, and shouldest hear the voice of his mouth.

15 For thou shalt be his witness unto all men of what thou hast seen and heard.

16 And now why tarriest thou?

arise, and be baptized, and wash away my sins, calling on the name of the Lord.

17 And it came to pass, that, when I was come again to Jerusalem, even while I prayed in the temple, I was in a trance;

18 And saw him saying unto me, Make haste, and get thee quickly out of Jerusalem: for they will not receive thy testimony concerning me.

19 And I said, Lord, they know that I imprisoned and beat in every synagogue them that believed on thee:

20 And when the blood of thy martyr Stephen was shed, I also was standing by, and consenting unto his death, and kept the raiment of them that slew him.

21 And he said unto me, Depart: for I will send thee far hence unto the Gentiles.

22 ¶And they gave him audience unto this word, and *then* lifted up their voices, and said, Away with such a *fellow* from the earth: for it is not fit that he should live.

23 And as they cried out, and cast off *their* clothes, and threw dust into the air,

24 The chief captain commanded him to be brought into the castle, and bade that he should be examined by scourging; that he might know wherefore they cried so against him.

25 ¶And as they bound him with thongs, Paul said unto the centurion that stood by, Is it lawful for you to scourge a man that is a Roman, and uncondemned?

26 When the centurion heard *that*, he went and told the chief captain, saying, Take heed what thou doest: for this man is a Roman.

27 Then the chief captain came, and said unto him, Tell me, art thou a Roman? He said, Yea.

28 And the chief captain answered, With a great sum obtained I this freedom. And Paul said, But I was *free* born.

29 Then straightway they departed from him which should have examined him: and the chief captain also was afraid, after he knew that he was a Roman, and because he had bound him.

30 On the morrow, because he would have known the certainty wherefore he was accused of the Jews, he loosed him from *his* bands, and commanded the chief priests and all their council to appear, and brought Paul down, and set him before them.

23

And Paul, earnestly beholding the council, said, Men *and* brethren, I have lived in all good conscience before God until this day.

2 ¶And the high priest Ananias commanded them that stood by him to smite him on the mouth.

3 Then said Paul unto him, God shall smite thee, *thou* whited wall: for sittest thou to judge me after the law, and commandest me to be smitten contrary to the law?

4 And they that stood by said, Revilest thou God's high priest?

5 Then said Paul, I wist not,

brethren, that he was the high priest: for it is written, Thou shalt not speak evil of the ruler of thy people.

6 ¶ But when Paul perceived that the one part were Sadducees, and the other Pharisees, he cried out in the council, Men *and* brethren, I am a Pharisee, the son of a Pharisee: of the hope and resurrection of the dead I am called in question.

7 And when he had so said, there arose a dissension between the Pharisees and the Sadducees: and the multitude was divided.

8 For the Sadducees say that there is no resurrection, neither angel, nor spirit: but the Pharisees confess both.

9 And there arose a great cry: and the scribes *that were* of the Pharisees' part arose, and strove, saying, We find no evil in this man: but if a spirit or an angel hath spoken to him, let us not fight against God.

10 And when there arose a great dissension, the chief captain, fearing lest Paul should have been pulled in pieces of them, commanded the soldiers to go down, and to take him by force from among them, and to bring *him* into the castle.

11 ¶ And the night following the Lord stood by him, and said, Be of good cheer, Paul: for as thou hast testified of me in Jerusalem, so must thou bear witness also at Rome.

12 ¶ And when it was day, certain of the Jews banded together, and bound themselves under a curse, saying that they would neither eat nor drink till they had killed Paul.

13 And they were more than forty which had made this conspiracy.

14 And they came to the chief priests and elders, and said, We have bound ourselves under a great curse, that we will eat nothing until we have slain Paul.

15 Now therefore ye with the council signify to the chief captain that he bring him down unto you to morrow, as though ye would enquire something more perfectly concerning him: and we, or ever he come near, are ready to kill him.

16 ¶ And when Paul's sister's son heard of their lying in wait, he went and entered into the castle, and told Paul.

17 Then Paul called one of the centurions unto *him*, and said, Bring this young man unto the chief captain: for he hath a certain thing to tell him.

18 So he took him, and brought *him* to the chief captain, and said, Paul the prisoner called me unto *him*, and prayed me to bring this young man unto thee, who hath something to say unto thee.

19 Then the chief captain took him by the hand, and went *with him* aside privately, and asked *him*, What is that thou hast to tell me?

20 And he said, The Jews have agreed to desire thee that thou wouldest bring down Paul to morrow into the council, as though they would enquire some-

what of him more perfectly.

21 But do not thou yield unto them: for there lie in wait for him of them more than forty men, which have bound themselves with an oath, that they will neither eat nor drink till they have killed him: and now are they ready, looking for a promise from thee.

22 So the chief captain *then* let the young man depart, and charged *him, See* thou tell no man that thou hast shewed these things to me.

23 ¶ And he called unto *him* two centurions, saying, Make ready two hundred soldiers to go to Caesarea, and horsemen threescore and ten, and spearmen two hundred, at the third hour of the night;

24 And provide *them* beasts, that they may set Paul on, and bring *him* safe unto Felix the governor.

25 And he wrote a letter after this manner:

26 Claudius Lysias unto the most excellent governor Felix *sendeth* greeting.

27 This man was taken of the Jews, and should have been killed of them: then came I with an army, and rescued him, having understood that he was a Roman.

28 And when I would have known the cause wherefore they accused him, I brought him forth into their council:

29 Whom I perceived to be accused of questions of their law, but to have nothing laid to his charge worthy of death or of bonds.

30 And when it was told me how that the Jews laid wait for the man, I sent straightway to thee, and gave commandment to his accusers also to say before thee what *they had* against him. Farewell.

31 Then the soldiers, as it was commanded them, took Paul, and brought *him* by night to Antipatris.

32 On the morrow they left the horsemen to go with him, and returned to the castle:

33 Who, when they came to Caesarea, and delivered the epistle to the governor, presented Paul also before him.

34 And when the governor had read *the letter,* he asked of what province he was. And when he understood that *he was* of Cilicia;

35 I will hear thee, said he, when thine accusers are also come. And he commanded him to be kept in Herod's judgment hall.

24 And after five days Ananias the high priest descended with the elders, and *with* a certain orator *named* Tertullus, who informed the governor against Paul.

2 And when he was called forth, Tertullus began to accuse *him,* saying, Seeing that by thee we enjoy great quietness, and that very worthy deeds are done unto this nation by thy providence,

3 We accept *it* always, and in all

229

places, most noble Felix, with all thankfulness.

4 Notwithstanding, that I be not further tedious unto thee, I pray thee that thou wouldest hear us of thy clemency a few words.

5 For we have found this man *a pestilent fellow,* and a mover of sedition among all the Jews throughout the world, and a ringleader of the sect of the Nazarenes:

6 Who also hath gone about to profane the temple: whom we took, and would have judged according to our law.

7 But the chief captain Lysias came *upon us,* and with great violence took *him* away out of our hands,

8 Commanding his accusers to come unto thee: by examining of whom thyself mayest take knowledge of all these things, whereof we accuse him.

9 And the Jews also assented, saying that these things were so.

10 ¶ Then Paul, after that the governor had beckoned unto him to speak, answered, Forasmuch as I know that thou hast been of many years a judge unto this nation, I do the more cheerfully answer for myself:

11 Because that thou mayest understand, that there are yet but twelve days since I went up to Jerusalem for to worship.

12 And they neither found me in the temple disputing with any man, neither raising up the people, neither in the synagogues, nor in the city:

13 Neither can they prove the things whereof they now accuse me.

14 But this I confess unto thee, that after the way which they call heresy, so worship I the God of my fathers, believing all things which are written in the law and in the prophets:

15 And have hope toward God, which they themselves also allow, that there shall be a resurrection of the dead, both of the just and unjust.

16 And herein do I exercise myself, to have always a conscience void to offence toward God, and *toward* men.

17 Now after many years I came to bring alms to my nation, and offerings.

18 Whereupon certain Jews from Asia found me purified in the temple, neither with multitude, nor with tumult.

19 Who ought to have been here before thee, and object, if they had ought against me.

20 Or else let these same *here* say, if they have found any evil doing in me, while I stood before the council,

21 Except it be for this one voice, that I cried standing among them, Touching the resurrection of the dead I am called in question by you this day.

22 And when Felix heard these things, having more perfect knowledge of *that* way, he deferred them, and said, When Lysias the chief captain shall come down, I will know the uttermost of your matter.

23 And he commanded a centurion to keep Paul, and to let *him* have liberty, and that he should forbid none of his acquaintance to minister or come unto him.

24 ¶ And after certain days, when Felix came with his wife Drusilla, which was a Jewess, he sent for Paul, and heard him concerning the faith in Christ.

25 And as he reasoned of righteousness, temperance, and judgment to come, Felix trembled, and answered, Go thy way for this time; when I have a convenient season, I will call for thee.

26 He hoped also that money should have been given him of Paul, that he might loose him: wherefore he sent for him the oftener, and communed with him.

27 ¶ But after two years Porcius Festus came into Felix' room: and Felix, willing to shew the Jews a pleasure, left Paul bound.

25 Now when Festus was come into the province, after three days he ascended from Caesarea to Jerusalem.

2 Then the high priest and the chief of the Jews informed him against Paul, and besought him,

3 And desired favour against him, that he would send for him to Jerusalem, laying wait in the way to kill him.

4 But Festus answered, that Paul should be kept at Caesarea, and that he himself would depart shortly *thither*.

5 Let them therefore, said he, which among you are able, go down with *me*, and accuse this man, if there be any wickedness in him.

6 And when he had tarried among them more than ten days, he went down unto Caesarea; and the next day sitting on the judgment seat commanded Paul to be brought.

7 And when he was come, the Jews which came down from Jerusalem stood round about, and laid many and grievous complaints against Paul, which they could not prove.

8 ¶ While he answered for himself, Neither against the law of the Jews, neither against the temple, nor yet against Caesar, have I offended any thing at all.

9 But Festus, willing to do the Jews a pleasure, answered Paul, and said, Wilt thou go up to Jerusalem, and there be judged of these things before me?

10 ¶ Then said Paul, I stand at Caesar's judgment seat, where I ought to be judged: to the Jews have I done no wrong, as thou very well knowest.

11 For if I be an offender, or have committed any thing worthy of death, I refuse not to die: but if there be none of these things whereof these accuse me, no man may deliver me unto them. I appeal unto Caesar.

12 Then Festus, when he had conferred with the council, answered, Hast thou appealed unto Caesar? unto Caesar shalt thou go.

13 And after certain days king Agrippa and Bernice came unto Caesarea to salute Festus.

14 And when they had been there many days, Festus declared Paul's cause unto the king, saying, There is a certain man left in bonds by Felix:

15 About whom, when I was at Jerusalem, the chief priests and the elders of the Jews informed *me*, desiring *to have* judgment against him.

16 To whom I answered, It is not the manner of the Romans to deliver any man to die, before that he which is accused have the accusers face to face, and have licence to answer for himself concerning the crime laid against him.

17 Therefore, when they were come hither, without any delay on the morrow I sat on the judgment seat, and commanded the man to be brought forth.

18 Against whom when the accusers stood up, they brought none accusation of such things as I supposed:

19 But had certain questions against him of their own superstition, and of one Jesus, which was dead, whom Paul affirmed to be alive.

20 And because I doubted of such manner of questions, I asked *him* whether he would go to Jerusalem, and there be judged of these matters.

21 But when Paul had appealed to be reserved unto the hearing of Augustus, I commanded him to be kept till I might send him to Caesar.

22 Then Agrippa said unto Festus, I would also hear the man

myself. To morrow, said he, thou shalt hear him.

23 And on the morrow, when Agrippa was come, and Bernice, with great pomp, and was entered into the place of hearing, with the chief captains, and principal men of the city, at Festus' commandment Paul was brought forth.

24 And Festus said, King Agrippa, and all men which are here present with us, ye see this man, about whom all the multitude of the Jews have dealt with me, both at Jerusalem, and *also* here, crying that he ought not to live any longer.

25 But when I found that he had committed nothing worthy of death, and that he himself hath appealed to Augustus, I have determined to send him.

26 Of whom I have no certain thing to write unto my lord. Wherefore I have brought him forth before you, and specially before thee, O king Agrippa, that, after examination had, I might have somewhat to write.

27 For it seemeth to me unreasonable to send a prisoner, and not withal to signify the crimes *laid* against him.

26

Then Agrippa said unto Paul, Thou art permitted to speak for thyself. Then Paul stretched forth the hand, and answered for himself:

2 I think myself happy, king Agrippa, because I shall answer for myself this day before thee touching all the things whereof I am accused of the Jews:

3 Especially *because I know*

thee to be expert in all customs and questions which are among the Jews: wherefore I beseech thee to hear me patiently.

4 My manner of life from my youth, which was at the first among mine own nation at Jerusalem, know all the Jews;

5 Which knew me from the beginning, if they would testify, that after the most straitest sect of our religion I lived a Pharisee.

6 And now I stand and am judged for the hope of the promise made of God, unto our fathers:

7 Unto which *promise* our twelve tribes, instantly serving God day and night, hope to come. For which hope's sake, king Agrippa, I am accused of the Jews.

8 Why should it be thought a thing incredible with you, that God should raise the dead?

9 I verily thought with myself, that I ought to do many things contrary to the name of Jesus of Nazareth.

10 Which thing I also did in Jerusalem: and many of the saints did I shut up in prison, having received authority from the chief priests; and when they were put to death, I gave my voice against *them*.

11 And I punished them oft in every synagogue, and compelled *them* to blaspheme; and being exceedingly mad against them, I persecuted *them* even unto strange cities.

12 ❦ Whereupon as I went to Damascus with authority and commission from the chief priests,

13 At midday, O king, I saw in the way a light from heaven, above the brightness of the sun, shining round about me and them which journeyed with me.

14 And when we were all fallen to the earth, I heard a voice speaking unto me, and saying in the Hebrew tongue, Saul, Saul, why persecutest thou me? *it is* hard for thee to kick against the pricks.

15 And I said, Who art thou, Lord? And he said, I am Jesus whom thou persecutest.

16 But rise, and stand upon thy feet: for I have appeared unto thee for this purpose, to make thee a minister and a witness both of these things which thou hast seen, and of those things in the which I will appear unto thee;

17 Delivering thee from the people, and *from* the Gentiles, unto whom now I send thee,

18 To open their eyes, *and* to turn *them* from darkness to light, and *from* the power of Satan unto God, that they may receive forgiveness of sins, and inheritance among them which are sanctified by faith that is in me.

19 ❦ Whereupon, O king Agrippa, I was not disobedient unto the heavenly vision:

20 But shewed first unto them of Damascus, and at Jerusalem, and throughout all the coasts of Judaea, and *then* to the Gentiles, that they should repent and turn to God, and do works meet for repentance.

21 For these causes the Jews caught me in the temple, and went about to kill me.

22 Having therefore obtained help of God, I continue unto this day, witnessing both to small and great, saying none other things than those which the prophets and Moses did say should come:

23 That Christ should suffer, and that he should be the first that should rise from the dead, and should shew light unto the people, and to the Gentiles.

24 And as he thus spake for himself, Festus said with a loud voice, Paul, thou art beside thyself; much learning doth make thee mad.

25 But he said, I am not mad, most noble Festus; but speak forth the words of truth and soberness.

26 For the king knoweth of these things, before whom also I speak freely: for I am persuaded that none of these things are hidden from him; for this thing was not done in a corner.

27 King Agrippa, believest thou the prophets? I know that thou believest.

28 Then Agrippa said unto Paul, Almost thou persuadest me to be a Christian.

29 And Paul said, I would to God, that not only thou, but also all that hear me this day, were both almost, and altogether such as I am, except these bonds.

30 And when he had thus spoken, the king rose up, and the governor, and Bernice, and they that sat with them:

31 And when they were gone aside, they talked between themselves, saying, This man doeth nothing worthy of death or of bonds.

32 Then said Agrippa unto Festus, This man might have been set at liberty, if he had not appealed unto Caesar.

27 And when it was determined that we should sail into Italy, they delivered Paul and certain other prisoners unto one named Julius, a centurion of Augustus' band.

2 And entering into a ship of Adramyttium, we launched, meaning to sail by the coasts of Asia; one Aristarchus, a Macedonian of Thessalonica, being with us.

3 And the next day we touched at Sidon. And Julius courteously entreated Paul, and gave him liberty to go unto his friends to refresh himself.

4 And when we had launched from thence, we sailed under Cyprus, because the winds were contrary.

5 And when we had sailed over the sea of Cilicia and Pamphylia, we came to Myra, a city of Lycia.

6 And there the centurion found a ship of Alexandria sailing into Italy; and he put us therein.

7 And when we had sailed slowly many days, and scarce were come over against Cnidus, the wind not suffering us, we sailed under Crete, over against Salmone;

8 And, hardly passing it, came unto a place which is called The fair havens; nigh whereunto was the city *of* Lasea.

9 ¶ Now when much time was spent, and when sailing was now dangerous, because the fast was now already past, Paul admonished *them,*

10 And said unto them, Sirs, I perceive that this voyage will be with hurt and much damage, not only of the lading and ship, but also of our lives.

11 Nevertheless the centurion believed the master and the owner of the ship, more than those things which were spoken by Paul.

12 And because the haven was not commodious to winter in, the more part advised to depart thence also, if by any means they might attain to Phenice, *and there* to winter; *which is* an haven of Crete, and lieth toward the south west and north west.

13 And when the south wind blew softly, supposing that they had obtained *their* purpose, loosing *thence,* they sailed close by Crete.

14 ¶ But not long after there arose against it a tempestuous wind, called Euroclydon.

15 And when the ship was caught, and could not bear up into the wind, we let *her* drive.

16 And running under a certain island which is called Clauda, we had much work to come by the boat:

17 Which when they had taken up, they used helps, undergirding the ship; and, fearing lest they should fall into the quicksands, strake sail, and so were driven.

18 And we being exceedingly tossed with a tempest, the next *day* they lightened the ship;

19 And the third *day* we cast out with our own hands the tackling of the ship.

20 And when neither sun nor stars in many days appeared, and no small tempest lay on *us,* all hope that we should be saved was then taken away.

21 ¶ But after long abstinence Paul stood forth in the midst of them, and said, Sirs, ye should have hearkened unto me, and not have loosed from Crete, and to have gained this harm and loss.

22 And now I exhort you to be of good cheer: for there shall be no loss of *any man's* life among you, but of the ship.

23 For there stood by me this night the angel of God, whose I am, and whom I serve,

24 Saying, Fear not, Paul; thou must be brought before Caesar: and, lo, God hath given thee all them that sail with thee.

25 Wherefore, sirs, be of good cheer: for I believe God, that it shall be even as it was told me.

26 Howbeit we must be cast upon a certain island.

27 But when the fourteenth night was come, as we were driven up and down in Adria, about midnight the shipmen deemed that they drew near to some country;

28 And sounded, and found *it*

twenty fathoms: and when they had gone a little further, they sounded again, and found *it* fifteen fathoms.

29 Then fearing lest we should have fallen upon rocks, they cast four anchors out of the stern, and wished for the day.

30 And as the shipmen were about to flee out of the ship, when they had let down the boat into the sea, under colour as though they would have cast anchors out of the foreship.

31 Paul said to the centurion and to the soldiers, Except these abide in the ship, ye cannot be saved.

32 Then the soldiers cut off the ropes of the boat, and let her fall off.

33 And while the day was coming on, Paul besought *them* all to take meat, saying, This day is the fourteenth day that ye have tarried and continued fasting, having taken nothing.

34 Wherefore I pray you to take *some* meat: for this is for your health: for there shall not an hair fall from the head of any of you.

35 And when he had thus spoken, he took bread, and gave thanks to God in presence of them all: and when he had broken *it*, he began to eat.

36 Then were they all of good cheer, and they also took *some* meat.

37 And we were in all in the ship two hundred threescore and sixteen souls.

38 And when they had eaten enough, they lightened the ship, and cast out the wheat into the sea.

39 And when it was day, they knew not the land: but they discovered a certain creek with a shore, into the which they were minded, if it were possible, to thrust in the ship.

40 And when they had taken up the anchors, they committed *themselves* unto the sea, and loosed the rudder bands, and hoised up the mainsail to the wind, and made toward shore.

41 ¶ And falling into a place where two seas met, they ran the ship aground; and the forepart stuck fast, and remained unmoveable, but the hinder part was broken with the violence of the waves.

42 And the soldiers' counsel was to kill the prisoners, lest any of them should swim out, and escape.

43 But the centurion, willing to save Paul, kept them from *their* purpose; and commanded that they which could swim should cast *themselves* first *into the sea*, and get to land:

44 And the rest, some on boards, and some on *broken pieces* of the ship. And so it came to pass, that they escaped all safe to land.

28

And when they were escaped, then they knew that the island was called Melita.

2 And the barbarous people shewed us no little kindness: for they kindled a fire, and received us every one, because of

the present rain, and because of the cold.

3 ¶ And when Paul had gathered a bundle of sticks, and laid *them* on the fire, there came a viper out of the heat, and fastened on his hand.

4 And when the barbarians saw the *venomous* beast hang on his hand, they said among themselves, No doubt this man is a murderer, whom, though he hath escaped the sea, yet vengeance suffereth not to live.

5 And he shook off the beast into the fire, and felt no harm.

6 Howbeit they looked when he should have swollen, or fallen down dead suddenly: but after they had looked a great while, and saw no harm come to him, they changed their minds, and said that he was a god.

7 In the same quarters were possessions of the chief man of the island, whose name was Publius; who received us, and lodged us three days courteously.

8 ¶ And it came to pass, that the father of Publius lay sick of a fever and of a bloody flux: to whom Paul entered in, and prayed, and laid his hands on him, and healed him.

9 So when this was done, others also, which had diseases in the island, came, and were healed:

10 Who also honoured us with many honours; and when we departed, they laded *us* with such things as were necessary.

11 ¶ And after three months we departed in a ship of Alexandria, which had wintered in the isle, whose sign was Castor and Pollux.

12 And landing at Syracuse, we tarried *there* three days.

13 And from thence we fetched a compass, and came to Rhegium: and after one day the south wind blew, and we came the next day to Puteoli:

14 Where we found brethren, and were desired to tarry with them seven days: and so we went toward Rome.

15 And from thence, when the brethren heard of us, they came to meet us as far as Appii forum, and The three taverns: whom when Paul saw, he thanked God, and took courage.

16 And when we came to Rome, the centurion delivered the prisoners to the captain of the guard: but Paul was suffered to dwell by himself with a soldier that kept him.

17 ¶ And it came to pass, that after three days Paul called the chief of the Jews together: and when they were come together, he said unto them, Men *and* brethren, though I have committed nothing against the people, or customs of our fathers, yet was I delivered prisoner from Jerusalem into the hands of the Romans.

18 Who, when they had examined me, would have let *me* go, because there was no cause of death in me.

19 But when the Jews spake against *it*, I was constrained to appeal unto Caesar; not that I had ought to accuse my nation of.

20 For this cause therefore have

I called for you, to see *you*, and to speak with *you*: because that for the hope of Israel I am bound with this chain.

21 And they said unto him, We neither received letters out of Judaea concerning thee, neither any of the brethren that came shewed or spake any harm of thee.

22 But we desire to hear of thee what thou thinkest: for as concerning this sect, we know that every where it is spoken against.

23 And when they had appointed him a day, there came many to him into *his* lodging; to whom he expounded and testified the kingdom of God, persuading them concerning Jesus, both out of the law of Moses, and *out of* the prophets, from morning till evening.

24 And some believed the things which were spoken, and some believed not.

25 And when they agreed not among themselves, they departed, after that Paul had spoken one word, Well spake the Holy Ghost by Esaias the prophet unto our fathers,

26 Saying, Go unto this people, and say, Hearing ye shall hear, and shall not understand; and seeing ye shall see, and not perceive:

27 For the heart of this people is waxed gross, and their ears are dull of hearing, and their eyes have they closed; lest they should see with *their* eyes, and hear with *their* ears, and understand with *their* heart, and should be converted, and I should heal them.

28 Be it known therefore unto you, that the salvation of God is sent unto the Gentiles, and *that* they will hear it.

29 And when he had said these words, the Jews departed, and had great reasoning · among themselves.

30 And Paul dwelt two whole years in his own hired house, and received all that came in unto him,

31 Preaching the kingdom of God, and teaching those things which concern the Lord Jesus Christ, with all confidence, no man forbiddin him.

THE EPISTLE OF PAUL THE APOSTLE
TO THE

ROMANS

1 Paul, a servant of Jesus Christ, called *to be* an apostle, separated unto the gospel of God,

2 (Which he had promised afore by his prophets in the holy scriptures,)

3 Concerning his Son Jesus Christ our Lord, which was made of the seed of David according to the flesh;

4 And declared *to be* the Son

of God with power, according to the spirit of holiness, by the resurrection from the dead:

5 By whom we have received grace and apostleship, for obedience to the faith among all nations, for his name:

6 Among whom are ye also the called of Jesus Christ:

7 To all that be in Rome, beloved of God, called *to be* saints: Grace to you and peace from God our Father, and the Lord Jesus Christ.

8 First, I thank my God through Jesus Christ for you all, that your faith is spoken of throughout the whole world.

9 For God is my witness, whom I serve with my spirit in the gospel of his Son, that without ceasing I make mention of you always in my prayers;

10 Making request, if by any means now at length I might have a prosperous journey by the will of God to come unto you.

11 For I long to see you, that I may impart unto you some spiritual gift, to the end ye may be established;

12 That is, that I may be comforted together with you by the mutual faith both of you and me.

13 Now I would not have you ignorant, brethren, that oftentimes I purposed to come unto you, (but was let hitherto,) that I might have some fruit among you also, even as among other Gentiles.

14 I am debtor both to the Greeks, and to the Barbarians; both to the wise, and to the unwise.

15 So, as much as in me is, I am ready to preach the gospel to you that are at Rome also.

16 ⦅ For I am not ashamed of the gospel of Christ: for it is the power of God unto salvation to every one that believeth; to the Jew first, and also to the Greek.

17 For therein is the righteousness of God revealed from faith to faith: as it is written, The just shall live by faith.

18 For the wrath of God is revealed from heaven against all ungodliness and unrighteousness of men, who hold the truth in unrighteousness;

19 Because that which may be known of God is manifest in them; for God hath shewed *it* unto them.

20 For the invisible things of him from the creation of the world are clearly seen, being understood by the things that are made, *even* his eternal power and Godhead; so that they are without excuse:

21 ⦅ Because that, when they knew God, they glorified *him* not as God, neither were thankful; but became vain in their imaginations, and their foolish heart was darkened.

22 Professing themselves to be wise, they became fools,

23 And changed the glory of the uncorruptible God into an image made like to corruptible man, and to birds, and fourfooted beasts, and creeping things.

24 Wherefore God also gave

them up to uncleanness through the lusts of their own hearts, to dishonour their own bodies between themselves:

25 Who changed the truth of God into a lie, and worshipped and served the creature more than the Creator, who is blessed for ever. Amen.

26 For this cause God gave them up unto vile affections: for even their women did change the natural use into that which is against nature:

27 And likewise also the men, leaving the natural use of the woman, burned in their lust one toward another; men with men working that which is unseemly, and receiving in themselves that recompence of their error which was meet.

28 And even as they did not like to retain God in *their* knowledge, God gave them over to a reprobate mind, to do those things which are not convenient;

29 Being filled with all unrighteousness, fornication, wickedness, covetousness, maliciousness; full of envy, murder, debate, deceit, malignity; whisperers,

30 Backbiters, haters of God, despiteful, proud, boasters, inventors of evil things, disobedient to parents,

31 Without understanding, covenantbreakers, without natural affection, implacable, unmerciful:

32 Who knowing the judgment of God, that they which commit such things are worthy of death, not only do the same, but have pleasure in them that do them.

2 Therefore thou art inexcusable, O man, whosoever thou art that judgest: for wherein thou judgest another, thou condemnest thyself; for thou that judgest doest the same things.

2 But we are sure that the judgment of God is according to truth against them which commit such things.

3 And thinkest thou this, O man, that judgest them which do such things, and doest the same, that thou shalt escape the judgment of God?

4 Or despisest thou the riches of his goodness and forbearance and longsuffering; not knowing that the goodness of God leadeth thee to repentance?

5 ¶ But after thy hardness and impenitent heart treasurest up unto thyself wrath against the day of wrath and revelation of the righteous judgment of God;

6 Who will render to every man according to his deeds:

7 To them who by patient continuance in well doing seek for glory and honour and immortality, eternal life:

8 But unto them that are contentious, and do not obey the truth, but obey unrighteousness, indignation and wrath,

9 Tribulation and anguish, upon every soul of man that doeth evil, of the Jew first, and also of the Gentile;

10 But glory, honour, and peace, to every man that worketh good, to the Jew first, and also to the

Gentile:

11 For there is no respect of persons with God.

12 For as many as have sinned without law shall also perish without law: and as many as have sinned in the law shall be judged by the law;

13 (For not the hearers of the law *are* just before God, but the doers of the law shall be justified.

14 For when the Gentiles, which have not the law, do by nature the things contained in the law, these, having not the law, are a law unto themselves:

15 Which shew the work of the law written in their hearts, their conscience also bearing witness, and *their* thoughts the mean while accusing or else excusing one another;)

16 In the day when God shall judge the secrets of men by Jesus Christ according to my gospel.

17 Behold, thou art called a Jew, and restest in the law, and makest thy boast of God,

18 And knowest *his* will, and approvest the things that are more excellent, being instructed out of the law;

19 And art confident that thou thyself art a guide of the blind, a light of them which are in darkness,

20 An instructor of the foolish, a teacher of babes, which hast the form of knowledge and of the truth in the law.

21 Thou therefore which teachest another, teachest thou not thyself? thou that preachest a man should not steal, dost thou steal?

22 Thou that sayest a man should not commit adultery, dost thou commit adultery? thou that abhorrest idols, dost thou commit sacrilege?

23 Thou that makest thy boast of the law, through breaking the law dishonourest thou God?

24 For the name of God is blasphemed among the Gentiles through you, as it is written.

25 For circumcision verily profiteth, if thou keep the law: but if thou be a breaker of the law, thy circumcision is made uncircumcision.

26 Therefore if the uncircumcision keep the righteousness of the law, shall not his uncircumcision be counted for circumcision?

27 And shall not uncircumcision which is by nature, if it fulfil the law, judge thee, who by the letter and circumcision dost transgress the law?

28 For he is not a Jew, which is one outwardly; neither *is that* circumcision, which is outward in the flesh:

29 But he *is* a Jew, which is one inwardly; and circumcision *is that* of the heart, in the spirit, *and* not in the letter; whose praise *is* not of men, but of God.

3 What advantage then hath the Jew? or what profit *is there* of circumcision?

2 Much every way: chiefly, because that unto them were committed the oracles of God.

3 For if some did not believe? shall their unbelief make the faith of God without effect?

4 God forbid: yea, let God be true, but every man a liar; as it is written, That thou mightest be justified in thy sayings, and mightest overcome when thou art judged.

5 But if our unrighteousness commend the righteousness of God, what shall we say? Is God unrighteous who taketh vengeance? (I speak as a man)

6 God forbid: for then how shall God judge the world?

7 For if the truth of God hath more abounded through my lie unto his glory; why yet am I also judged as a sinner?

8 And not rather, (as we be slanderously reported, and as some affirm that we say,) Let us do evil, that good may come? whose damnation is just.

9 What then? are we better than they? No, in no wise: for we have before proved both Jews and Gentiles, that they are all under sin;

10 As it is written, There is none righteous, no, not one:

11 There is none that understandeth, there is none that seeketh after God.

12 They are all gone out of the way, they are together become unprofitable; there is none that doeth good, no, not one.

13 Their throat is an open sepulchre; with their tongues they have used deceit; the poison of asps is under their lips:

14 Whose mouth is full of cursing and bitterness:

15 Their feet are swift to shed blood:

16 Destruction and misery are in their ways:

17 And the way of peace have they not known:

18 There is no fear of God before their eyes.

19 Now we know that what things soever the law saith, it saith to them who are under the law: that every mouth may be stopped, and all the world may become guilty before God.

20 ℂ Therefore by the deeds of the law there shall no flesh be justified in his sight: for by the law is the knowledge of sin.

21 But now the righteousness of God without the law is manifested, being witnessed by the law and the prophets;

22 Even the righteousness of God which is by faith of Jesus Christ unto all and upon all them that believe: for there is no difference:

23 For all have sinned, and come short of the glory of God;

24 Being justified freely by his grace through the redemption that is in Christ Jesus:

25 Whom God hath set forth to be a propitiation through faith in his blood, to declare his righteousness for the remission of sins that are past, through the forbearance of God;

26 To declare, I say, at this time his righteousness: that he might be just, and the justifier of him

which believeth in Jesus.

27 Where *is* boasting then? It is excluded. By what law? of works? Nay: but by the law of faith.

28 Therefore we conclude that a man is justified by faith without the deeds of the law.

29 *Is he* the God of the Jews only? *is he* not also of the Gentiles? Yes, of the Gentiles also:

30 Seeing *it is* one God, which shall justify the circumcision by faith, and uncircumcision through faith.

31 Do we then make void the law through faith? God forbid: yea, we establish the law.

4 What shall we say then that Abraham our father, as pertaining to the flesh, hath found?

2 For if Abraham were justified by works, he hath *whereof* to glory; but not before God.

3 For what saith the scripture? Abraham believed God, and it was counted unto him for righteousness.

4 Now to him that worketh is the reward not reckoned of grace, but of debt.

5 But to him that worketh not, but believeth on him that justifieth the ungodly, his faith is counted for righteousness.

6 Even as David also describeth the blessedness of the man, unto whom God imputeth righteousness without works,

7 *Saying,* Blessed *are* they whose iniquities are forgiven, and whose sins are covered.

8 Blessed *is* the man to whom the Lord will not impute sin.

9 *Cometh* this blessedness then upon the circumcision *only,* or upon the uncircumcision also? for we say that faith was reckoned to Abraham for righteousness.

10 How was it then reckoned? when he was in circumcision, or in uncircumcision? Not in circumcision, but in uncircumcision.

11 And he received the sign of circumcision, a seal of the righteousness of the faith which *he had yet* being uncircumcised: that he might be the father of all them that believe, though they be not circumcised; that righteousness might be imputed unto them also:

12 And the father of circumcision to them who are not of the circumcision only, but who also walk in the steps of that faith of our father Abraham, which *he had* being *yet* uncircumcised.

13 ℂ For the promise, that he should be the heir of the world, *was* not to Abraham, or to his seed, through the law, but through the righteousness of faith.

14 For if they which are of the law *be* heirs, faith is made void, and the promise made of none effect:

15 Because the law worketh wrath: for where no law is, *there is* no transgression.

16 Therefore *it is* of faith, that *it might be* by grace; to the end the promise might be sure to all the seed; not to that only which is of

243

the law, but to that also which is of the faith of Abraham; who is the father of us all,

17 (As it is written, I have made thee a father of many nations,) before him whom he believed, *even* God, who quickeneth the dead, and calleth those things which be not as though they were.

18 Who against hope believed in hope, that he might become the father of many nations, according to that which was spoken, So shall thy seed be.

19 And being not weak in faith, he considered not his own body now dead, when he was about an hundred years old, neither yet the deadness of Sarah's womb:

20 He staggered not at the promise of God through unbelief; but was strong in faith, giving glory to God;

21 And being fully persuaded that, what he had promised, he was able also to perform.

22 And therefore it was imputed to him for righteousness.

23 ¶Now it was not written for his sake alone, that it was imputed to him;

24 But for us also, to whom it shall be imputed, if we believe on him that raised up Jesus our Lord from the dead;

25 Who was delivered for our offences, and was raised again for our justification.

5 Therefore being justified by faith, we have peace with God through our Lord Jesus Christ:

2 By whom also we have access by faith into this grace wherein we stand, and rejoice in hope of the glory of God.

3 And not only *so*, but we glory in tribulations also: knowing that tribulation worketh patience;

4 And patience, experience; and experience, hope:

5 And hope maketh not ashamed; because the love of God is shed abroad in our hearts by the Holy Ghost which is given unto us.

6 For when we were yet without strength, in due time Christ died for the ungodly.

7 For scarcely for a righteous man will one die: yet peradventure for a good man some would even dare to die.

8 But God commendeth his love toward us, in that, while we were yet sinners, Christ died for us.

9 Much more then, being now justified by his blood, we shall be saved from wrath through him.

10 For if, when we were enemies, we were reconciled to God by the death of his Son, much more, being reconciled, we shall be saved by his life.

11 And not only *so*, but we also joy in God through our Lord Jesus Christ, by whom we have now received the atonement.

12 Wherefore, as by one man sin entered into the world, and death by sin; and so death passed upon all men, for that all have sinned:

13 (For until the law sin was in the world: but sin is not imputed

244

when there is no law.

14 Nevertheless death reigned from Adam to Moses, even over them that had not sinned after the similitude of Adam's transgression, who is the figure of him that was to come.

15 But not as the offence, so also *is* the free gift. For if through the offence of one many be dead, much more the grace of God, and the gift by grace, *which is* by one man, Jesus Christ, hath abounded unto many.

16 And not as *it was* by one that sinned, *so is* the gift: for the judgment *was* by one to condemnation, but the free gift *is* of many offences unto justification.

17 ¶For if by one man's offence death reigned by one; much more they which receive abundance of grace and of the gift of righteousness shall reign in life by one, Jesus Christ.)

18 Therefore as by the offence of one *judgment came* upon all men to condemnation; even so by the righteousness of one *the free gift came* upon all men unto justification of life.

19 For as by one man's disobedience many were made sinners, so by the obedience of one shall many be made righteous.

20 Moreover the law entered, that the offence might abound. But where sin abounded, grace did much more abound:

21 That as sin hath reigned unto death, even so might grace reign through righteousness unto eternal life by Jesus Christ our Lord.

6 What shall we say then? Shall we continue in sin, that grace may abound?

2 God forbid. How shall we, that are dead to sin, live any longer therein?

3 Know ye not, that so many of us as were baptized into Jesus Christ were baptized into his death?

4 Therefore we are buried with him by baptism into death: that like as Christ was raised up from the dead by the glory of the Father, even so we also should walk in newness of life.

5 For if we have been planted together in the likeness of his death, we shall be also *in the likeness of his* resurrection:

6 Knowing this, that our old man is crucified with *him*, that the body of sin might be destroyed, that henceforth we should not serve sin.

7 For he that is dead is freed from sin.

8 Now if we be dead with Christ, we believe that we shall also live with him:

9 Knowing that Christ being raised from the dead dieth no more; death hath no more dominion over him.

10 For in that he died, he died unto sin once: but in that he liveth, he liveth unto God.

11 Likewise reckon ye also yourselves to be dead indeed unto sin, but alive unto God through Jesus Christ our Lord.

12 ¶Let not sin therefore reign in your mortal body, that ye should

obey it in the lusts thereof.

13 Neither yield ye your members *as* instruments of unrighteousness unto sin: but yield yourselves unto God, as those that are alive from the dead, and your members *as* instruments of righteousness unto God.

14 For sin shall not have dominion over you: for ye are not under the law, but under grace.

15 What then? shall we sin, because we are not under the law, but under grace? God forbid.

16 Know ye not, that to whom ye yield yourselves servants to obey, his servants ye are to whom ye obey; whether of sin unto death, or of obedience unto righteousness?

17 But God be thanked, that ye were the servants of sin, but ye have obeyed from the heart that form of doctrine which was delivered you.

18 Being then made free from sin, ye became the servants of righteousness.

19 I speak after the manner of men because of the infirmity of your flesh: for as ye have yielded your members servants to uncleanness and to iniquity unto iniquity; even so now yield your members servants to righteousness unto holiness.

20 For when ye were the servants of sin, ye were free from righteousness.

21 What fruit had ye then in those things whereof ye are now ashamed? for the end of those things *is* death.

22 But now being made free from sin, and become servants to God, ye have your fruit unto holiness, and the end everlasting life.

23 ¶ For the wages of sin *is* death; but the gift of God *is* eternal life through Jesus Christ our Lord.

7 Know ye not, brethren, (for I speak to them that know the law,) how that the law hath dominion over a man as long as he liveth?

2 For the woman which hath an husband is bound by the law to *her* husband so long as he liveth; but if the husband be dead, she is loosed from the law of *her* husband.

3 So then if, while *her* husband liveth, she be married to another man, she shall be called an adulteress: but if her husband be dead, she is free from that law; so that she is no adulteress, though she be married to another man.

4 Wherefore, my brethren, ye also are become dead to the law by the body of Christ; that ye should be married to another, *even* to him who is raised from the dead, that we should bring forth fruit unto God.

5 For when we were in the flesh, the motions of sins, which were by the law, did work in our members to bring forth fruit unto death.

6 But now we are delivered from the law, that being dead wherein we were held; that we should serve in newness of spirit, and not *in* the oldness of the letter.

7 ¶ What shall we say then? *Is* the law sin? God forbid. Nay, I had not known sin, but by the law: for I had not known lust, except the law had said, Thou shalt not covet.

8 But sin, taking occasion by the commandment, wrought in me all manner of concupiscence. For without the law sin *was* dead.

9 For I was alive without the law once: but when the commandment came, sin revived, and I died.

10 And the commandment, which *was* ordained to life, I found *to be* unto death.

11 For sin, taking occasion by the commandment, deceived me, and by it slew *me*.

12 ¶ Wherefore the law *is* holy, and the commandment holy, and just, and good.

13 Was then that which is good made death unto me? God forbid. But sin, that it might appear sin, working death in me by that which is good; that sin by the commandment might become exceeding sinful.

14 For we know that the law is spiritual: but I am carnal, sold under sin.

15 For that which I do I allow not: for what I would, that do I not; but what I hate, that do I.

16 If then I do that which I would not, I consent unto the law that *it is* good.

17 Now then it is no more I that do it, but sin that dwelleth in me.

18 For I know that in me (that is, in my flesh,) dwelleth no good thing: for to will is present with me; but *how* to perform that which is good I find not.

19 For the good that I would I do not: but the evil which I would not, that I do.

20 Now if I do that I would not, it is no more I that do it, but sin that dwelleth in me.

21 I find then a law, that, when I would do good, evil is present with me.

22 For I delight in the law of God after the inward man:

23 But I see another law in my members, warring against the law of my mind, and bringing me into captivity to the law of sin which is in my members.

24 O wretched man that I am! who shall deliver me from the body of this death?

25 I thank God through Jesus Christ our Lord. So then with the mind I myself serve the law of God; but with the flesh the law of sin.

8

There is therefore now no condemnation to them which are in Christ Jesus, who walk not after the flesh, but after the Spirit.

2 For the law of the Spirit of life in Christ Jesus hath made me free from the law of sin and death.

3 For what the law could not do, in that it was weak through the flesh, God sending his own Son in the likeness of sinful flesh, and for sin, condemned sin in the flesh:

4 That the righteousness of the

law might be fulfilled in us, who walk not after the flesh, but after the Spirit.

5 ℭ For they that are after the flesh do mind the things of the flesh; but they that are after the Spirit the things of the Spirit.

6 For to be carnally minded *is* death; but to be spiritually minded *is* life and peace.

7 Because the carnal mind *is* enmity against God: for it is not subject to the law of God, neither indeed can be.

8 So then they that are in the flesh cannot please God.

9 But ye are not in the flesh, but in the Spirit, if so be that the Spirit of God dwell in you. Now if any man have not the Spirit of Christ, he is none of his.

10 And if Christ *be* in you, the body *is* dead because of sin; but the Spirit *is* life because of righteousness.

11 But if the Spirit of him that raised up Jesus from the dead dwell in you, he that raised up Christ from the dead shall also quicken your mortal bodies by his Spirit that dwelleth in you.

12 Therefore, brethren, we are debtors, not to the flesh, to live after the flesh.

13 For if ye live after the flesh, ye shall die: but if ye through the Spirit do mortify the deeds of the body, ye shall live.

14 ℭ For as many as are led by the Spirit of God, they are the sons of God.

15 For ye have not received the spirit of bondage again to fear;

but ye have received the Spirit of adoption, whereby we cry, Abba, Father.

16 The Spirit itself beareth witness with our spirit, that we are the children of God:

17 And if children, then heirs; heirs of God, and joint-heirs with Christ; if so be that we suffer with **him**, that we may be also glorified together.

18 ℭ For I reckon that the sufferings of this present time are not worthy *to be compared* with the glory which shall be revealed in us.

19 For the earnest expectation of the creature waiteth for the manifestation of the sons of God.

20 For the creature was made subject to vanity, not willingly, but by reason of him who hath subjected *the same* in hope,

21 Because the creature itself also shall be delivered from the bondage of corruption into the glorious liberty of the children of God.

22 For we know that the whole creation groaneth and travaileth in pain together until now.

23 And not only *they,* but ourselves also, which have the firstfruits of the Spirit, even we ourselves groan within ourselves, waiting for the adoption, *to wit,* the redemption of our body.

24 For we are saved by hope: but hope that is seen is not hope: for what a man seeth, why doth he yet hope for?

25 But if we hope for that we

see not, *then* do we with patience wait for *it*.

26 ¶ Likewise the Spirit also helpeth our infirmities: for we know not what we should pray for as we ought: but the Spirit itself maketh intercession for us with groanings which cannot be uttered.

27 And he that searcheth the hearts knoweth what *is* the mind of the Spirit, because he maketh intercession for the saints according to *the will of* God.

28 ¶ And we know that all things work together for good to them that love God, to them who are the called according to *his* purpose.

29 For whom he did foreknow, he also did predestinate *to be* conformed to the image of his Son, that he might be the firstborn among many brethren.

30 Moreover whom he did predestinate, them he also called: and whom he called, them he also justified: and whom he justified, them he also glorified.

31 What shall we then say to these things? If God *be* for us, who *can be* against us?

32 He that spared not his own Son, but delivered him up for us all, how shall he not with him also freely give us all things?

33 Who shall lay any thing to the charge of God's elect? *It is* God that justifieth.

34 Who *is* he that condemneth? *It is* Christ that died, yea rather, that is risen again, who is even at the right hand of God, who also maketh intercession for us.

35 ¶ Who shall separate us from the love of Christ? *shall* tribulation, or distress, or persecution, or famine, or nakedness, or peril, or sword?

36 As it is written, For thy sake we are killed all the day long; we are accounted as sheep for the slaughter.

37 Nay, in all these things we are more than conquerors through him that loved us.

38 For I am persuaded, that neither death, nor life, nor angels, nor principalities, nor powers, nor things present, nor things to come,

39 Nor height, nor depth, nor any other creature, shall be able to separate us from the love of God, which is in Christ Jesus our Lord.

9

I say the truth in Christ, I lie not, my conscience also bearing me witness in the Holy Ghost,

2 That I have great heaviness and continual sorrow in my heart.

3 For I could wish that myself were accursed from Christ for my brethren, my kinsmen according to the flesh:

4 Who are Israelites; to whom *pertaineth* the adoption, and the glory, and the covenants, and the giving of the law, and the service *of God*, and the promises;

5 Whose *are* the fathers, and of whom *as* concerning the flesh Christ *came*, who is over all, God blessed for ever. Amen.

6 ¶ Not as though the word of

249

God hath taken none effect. For they *are* not all Israel, which are of Israel:

7 Neither, because they are the seed of Abraham, *are they* all children: but, In Isaac shall thy seed be called.

8 That is, They which are the children of the flesh, these *are* not the children of God: but the children of the promise are counted for the seed.

9 For this *is* the word of promise, At this time will I come, and Sarah shall have a son.

10 And not only *this*; but when Rebecca also had conceived by one, *even* by our father Isaac;

11 (For *the children* being not yet born, neither having done any good or evil, that the purpose of God according to election might stand, not of works, but of him that calleth;)

12 It was said unto her, The elder shall serve the younger.

13 As it is written, Jacob have I loved, but Esau have I hated.

14 ¶ What shall we say then? *Is there* unrighteousness with God? God forbid.

15 For he saith to Moses, I will have mercy on whom I will have mercy, and I will have compassion on whom I will have compassion.

16 So then *it is* not of him that willeth, nor of him that runneth, but of God that sheweth mercy.

17 For the scripture saith unto Pharaoh, Even for this same purpose have I raised thee up, that I might shew my power in thee,

and that my name might be declared throughout all the earth.

18 Therefore hath he mercy on whom he will *have mercy*, and whom he will he hardeneth.

19 Thou wilt say then unto me, Why doth he yet find fault? For who hath resisted his will?

20 Nay but, O man, who art thou that repliest against God? Shall the thing formed say to him that formed *it*, Why hast thou made me thus?

21 Hath not the potter power over the clay, of the same lump to make one vessel unto honour, and another unto dishonour?

22 *What* if God, willing to shew *his* wrath, and to make his power known, endured with much long-suffering the vessels of wrath fitted to destruction:

23 And that he might make known the riches of his glory on the vessels of mercy, which he had afore prepared unto glory,

24 Even us, whom he hath called, not of the Jews only, but also of the Gentiles?

25 ¶ As he saith also in Osee, I will call them my people, which were not my people; and her beloved, which was not beloved.

26 And it shall come to pass, *that* in the place where it was said unto them, Ye *are* not my people; there shall they be called the children of the living God.

27 Esaias also crieth concerning Israel, Though the number of the children of Israel be as the sand of the sea, a remnant shall be saved:

28 For he will finish the work, and cut *it* short in righteousness: because a short work will the Lord make upon the earth.

29 And as Esaias said before, Except the Lord of Sabaoth had left us a seed, we had been as Sodoma, and been made like unto Gomorrha.

30 What shall we say then? That the Gentiles, which followed not after righteousness, have attained to righteousness, even the righteousness which is of faith.

31 But Israel, which followed after the law of righteousness, hath not attained to the law of righteousness.

32 Wherefore? Because *they sought it* not by faith, but as it were by the works of the law. For they stumbled at that stumblingstone;

33 As it is written, Behold, I lay in Sion a stumblingstone and rock of offence: and whosoever believeth on him shall not be ashamed.

10 Brethren, my heart's desire and prayer to God for Israel is, that they might be saved.

2 For I bear them record that they have a zeal of God, but not according to knowledge.

3 For they being ignorant of God's righteousness, and going about to establish their own righteousness, have not submitted themselves unto the righteousness of God.

4 For Christ *is* the end of the law for righteousness to every one that believeth.

5 For Moses describeth the righteousness which is of the law, That the man which doeth those things shall live by them.

6 But the righteousness which is of faith speaketh on this wise, Say not in thine heart, Who shall ascend into heaven? (that is, to bring Christ down *from above*:)

7 Or, Who shall descend into the deep? (that is, to bring up Christ again from the dead.)

8 But what saith it? The word is nigh thee, *even* in thy mouth, and in thy heart: that is, the word of faith, which we preach;

9 That if thou shalt confess with thy mouth the Lord Jesus, and shalt believe in thine heart that God hath raised him from the dead, thou shalt be saved.

10 For with the heart man believeth unto righteousness; and with the mouth confession is made unto salvation.

11 ¶ For the scripture saith, Whosoever believeth on him shall not be ashamed.

12 For there is no difference between the Jew and the Greek: for the same Lord over all is rich unto all that call upon him.

13 For whosoever shall call upon the name of the Lord shall be saved.

14 How then shall they call on him in whom they have not believed? and how shall they believe in him of whom they have not heard? and how shall they hear without a preacher?

15 And how shall they preach,

except they be sent? as it is written, How beautiful are the feet of them that preach the gospel of peace, and bring glad tidings of good things!

16 But they have not all obeyed the gospel. For Esaias saith, Lord, who hath believed our report?

17 So then faith *cometh* by hearing, and hearing by the word of God.

18 But I say, Have they not heard? Yes verily, their sound went into all the earth, and their words unto the ends of the world.

19 But I say, Did not Israel know? First Moses saith, I will provoke you to jealousy by *them that are* no people, *and* by a foolish nation I will anger you.

20 But Esaias is very bold, and saith, I was found of them that sought me not; I was made manifest unto them that asked not after me.

21 But to Israel he saith, All day long I have stretched forth my hands unto a disobedient and gainsaying people.

11 I say then, Hath God cast away his people? God forbid. For I also am an Israelite, of the seed of Abraham, *of* the tribe of Benjamin.

2 God hath not cast away his people which he foreknew. Wot ye not what the scripture saith of Elias? how he maketh intercession to God against Israel, saying,

3 Lord, they have killed thy prophets, and digged down thine altars; and I am left alone, and they seek my life.

4 But what saith the answer of God unto him? I have reserved to myself seven thousand men, who have not bowed the knee to *the image of* Baal.

5 Even so then at this present time also there is a remnant according to the election of grace.

6 And if by grace, then *is it* no more of works: otherwise grace is no more grace. But if *it be* of works, then is it no more grace: otherwise work is no more work.

7 What then? Israel hath not obtained that which he seeketh for; but the election hath obtained it, and the rest were blinded.

8 (According as it is written, God hath given them the spirit of slumber, eyes that they should not see, and ears that they should not hear,) unto this day.

9 And David saith, Let their table be made a snare, and a trap, and a stumblingblock, and a recompense unto them:

10 Let their eyes be darkened, that they may not see, and bow down their back alway.

11 ¢ I say then, Have they stumbled that they should fall? God forbid: but *rather* through their fall salvation *is* come unto the Gentiles, for to provoke them to jealousy.

12 Now if the fall of them *be* the riches of the world, and the diminishing of them the riches of the Gentiles; how much more their fulness?

13 For I speak to you Gentiles, inasmuch as I am the apostle of the Gentiles, I magnify mine office:

14 If by any means I may provoke to emulation *them which are* my flesh, and might save some of them.

15 For if the casting away of them *be* the reconciling of the world, what *shall* the receiving *of them be*, but life from the dead?

16 ¶ For if the firstfruit *be* holy, the lump *is* also *holy*: and if the root *be* holy, so *are* the branches.

17 And if some of the branches be broken off, and thou, being a wild olive tree, wert graffed in among them, and with them partakest of the root and fatness of the olive tree;

18 Boast not against the branches. But if thou boast, thou bearest not the root, but the root thee.

19 Thou wilt say then, The branches were broken off, that I might be graffed in.

20 Well; because of unbelief they were broken off, and thou standest by faith. Be not highminded, but fear:

21 For if God spared not the natural branches, *take heed* lest he also spare not thee.

22 Behold therefore the goodness and severity of God: on them which fell, severity; but toward thee, goodness, if thou continue in *his* goodness: otherwise thou also shalt be cut off.

23 And they also, if they abide not still in unbelief, shall be graffed in: for God is able to graff them in again.

24 For if thou wert cut out of the olive tree which is wild by nature, and wert graffed contrary to nature into a good olive tree: how much more shall these, which be the natural *branches*, be graffed into their own olive tree?

25 For I would not, brethren, that ye should be ignorant of this mystery, lest ye should be wise in your own conceits; that blindness in part is happened to Israel, until the fulness of the Gentiles be come in.

26 ¶ And so all Israel shall be saved: as it is written, There shall come out of Sion the Deliverer, and shall turn away ungodliness from Jacob:

27 For this *is* my covenant unto them, when I shall take away their sins.

28 As concerning the gospel, *they are* enemies for your sakes: but as touching the election, *they are* beloved for the father's sakes.

29 For the gifts and calling of God *are* without repentance.

30 For as ye in times past have not believed God, yet have now obtained mercy through their unbelief:

31 Even so have these also now not believed, that through your mercy they also may obtain mercy.

32 For God hath concluded them all in unbelief, that he might have mercy upon all.

33 O the depth of the riches both of the wisdom and knowledge of God! how unsearchable *are* his judgments, and his ways past finding out!

34 For who hath known the mind of the Lord? or who hath been his counsellor?

35 Or who hath first given to him, and it shall be recompensed unto him again?

36 For of him, and through him, and to him, *are* all things: to whom *be* glory for ever. Amen.

12 I beseech you therefore, brethren, by the mercies of God, that ye present your bodies a living sacrifice, holy, acceptable unto God, *which is* your reasonable service.

2 And be not conformed to this world: but be ye transformed by the renewing of your mind, that ye may prove what *is* that good, and acceptable, and perfect, will of God.

3 For I say, through the grace given unto me, to every man that is among you, not to think *of himself* more highly than he ought to think; but to think soberly, according as God hath dealt to every man the measure of faith.

4 For as we have many members in one body, and all members have not the same office:

5 So we, *being* many, are one body in Christ, and every one members one of another.

6 Having then gifts differing according to the grace that is given to us, whether prophecy, *let us* *prophesy* according to the proportion of faith;

7 Or ministry, *let us wait* on *our* ministering: or he that teacheth, on teaching;

8 Or he that exhorteth, on exhortation: he that giveth, *let him do it* with simplicity; he that ruleth, with diligence; he that sheweth mercy, with cheerfulness.

9 ¶ *Let* love be without dissimulation. Abhor that which is evil; cleave to that which is good.

10 *Be* kindly affectioned one to another with brotherly love; in honour preferring one another;

11 Not slothful in business; fervent in spirit; serving the Lord;

12 Rejoicing in hope; patient in tribulation; continuing instant in prayer;

13 Distributing to the necessity of saints; given to hospitality.

14 Bless them which persecute you: bless, and curse not.

15 Rejoice with them that do rejoice, and weep with them that weep.

16 *Be* of the same mind one toward another. Mind not high things, but condescend to men of low estate. Be not wise in your own conceits.

17 Recompense to no man evil for evil. Provide things honest in the sight of all men.

18 If it be possible, as much as lieth in you, live peaceably with all men.

19 Dearly beloved, avenge not yourselves, but *rather* give place unto wrath: for it is written, Ven-

geance *is* mine; I will repay, saith the Lord.

20 Therefore if thine enemy hunger, feed him; if he thirst, give him drink: for in so doing thou shalt heap coals of fire on his head.

21 Be not overcome of evil, but overcome evil with good.

13 Let every soul be subject unto the higher powers. For there is no power but of God: the powers that be are ordained of God.

2 Whosoever therefore resisteth the power, resisteth the ordinance of God: and they that resist shall receive to themselves damnation.

3 For rulers are not a terror to good works, but to the evil. Wilt thou then not be afraid of the power? do that which is good, and thou shalt have praise of the same:

4 For he is the minister of God to thee for good. But if thou do that which is evil, be afraid; for he beareth not the sword in vain: for he is the minister of God, a revenger to *execute* wrath upon him that doeth evil.

5 Wherefore ye must needs be subject, not only for wrath, but also for conscience sake.

6 For for this cause pay ye tribute also: for they are God's ministers, attending continually upon this very thing.

7 Render therefore to all their dues: tribute to whom tribute *is due*; custom to whom custom; fear to whom fear; honour to

whom honour.

8 ¶ Owe no man any thing, but to love one another: for he that loveth another hath fulfilled the law.

9 For this, Thou shalt not commit adultery, Thou shalt not kill, Thou shalt not steal, Thou shalt not bear false witness, Thou shalt not covet; and if *there be* any other commandment, it is briefly comprehended in this saying, namely, Thou shalt love thy neighbour as thyself.

10 Love worketh no ill to his neighbour: therefore love *is* the fulfilling of the law.

11 ¶ And that, knowing the time, that now *it is* high time to awake out of sleep: for now *is* our salvation nearer than when we believed.

12 The night is far spent, the day is at hand: let us therefore cast off the works of darkness, and let us put on the armour of light.

13 Let us walk honestly, as in the day; not in rioting and drunkenness, not in chambering and wantonness, not in strife and envying.

14 But put ye on the Lord Jesus Christ, and make not provision for the flesh, to *fulfil* the lusts *thereof*.

14 Him that is weak in the faith receive ye, *but* not to doubtful disputations.

2 For one believeth that he may eat all things: another, who is weak, eateth herbs.

3 ¶ Let not him that eateth de-

spise him that eateth not; and let not him which eateth not judge him that eateth: for God hath received him.

4 Who art thou that judgest another man's servant? to his own master he standeth or falleth. Yea, he shall be holden up: for God is able to make him stand.

5 One man esteemeth one day above another: another esteemeth every day *alike*. Let every man be fully persuaded in his own mind.

6 He that regardeth the day, regardeth *it* unto the Lord; and he that regardeth not the day, to the Lord he doth not regard *it*. He that eateth, eateth to the Lord, for he giveth God thanks; and he that eateth not, to the Lord he eateth not, and giveth God thanks.

7 For none of us liveth to himself, and no man dieth to himself.

8 For whether we live, we live unto the Lord; and whether we die, we die unto the Lord: whether we live therefore, or die, we are the Lord's.

9 For to this end Christ both died, and rose, and revived, that he might be Lord both of the dead and living.

10 But why dost thou judge thy brother? or why dost thou set at nought thy brother? for we shall all stand before the judgment seat of Christ.

11 For it is written, As I live, saith the Lord, every knee shall bow to me, and every tongue shall confess to God.

12 So then every one of us shall give account of himself to God.

13 Let us not therefore judge one another any more: but judge this rather, that no man put a stumblingblock or an occasion to fall in *his* brother's way.

14 I know, and am persuaded by the Lord Jesus, that *there is* nothing unclean of itself: but to him that esteemeth any thing to be unclean, to him *it is* unclean.

15 But if thy brother be grieved with *thy* meat, now walkest thou not charitably. Destroy not him with thy meat, for whom Christ died.

16 Let not then your good be evil spoken of:

17 For the kingdom of God is not meat and drink; but righteousness, and peace, and joy in the Holy Ghost.

18 For he that in these things serveth Christ *is* acceptable to God, and approved of men.

19 Let us therefore follow after the things which make for peace, and things wherewith one may edify another.

20 For meat destroy not the work of God. All things indeed *are* pure; but *it is* evil for that man who eateth with offence.

21 *It is* good neither to eat flesh, nor to drink wine, nor *any thing* whereby thy brother stumbleth, or is offended, or is made weak.

22 Hast thou faith? have *it* to thyself before God. Happy *is* he that condemneth not himself in that thing which he alloweth.

23 And he that doubteth is damned if he eat, because *he eat-*

eth not of faith: for whatsoever *is* not of faith is sin.

15 We then that are strong ought to bear the infirmities of the weak, and not to please ourselves.

2 Let every one of us please *his* neighbour for *his* good to edification.

3 For even Christ pleased not himself; but, as it is written, The reproaches of them that reproached thee fell on me.

4 For whatsoever things were written aforetime were written for our learning, that we through patience and comfort of the scriptures might have hope.

5 Now the God of patience and consolation grant you to be likeminded one toward another according to Christ Jesus:

6 That ye may with one mind *and* one mouth glorify God, even the Father of our Lord Jesus Christ.

7 Wherefore receive ye one another, as Christ also received us to the glory of God.

8 Now I say that Jesus Christ was a minister of the circumcision for the truth of God, to confirm the promises *made* unto the fathers:

9 And that the Gentiles might glorify God for *his* mercy; as it is written, For this cause I will confess to thee among the Gentiles, and sing unto thy name.

10 And again he saith, Rejoice, ye Gentiles, with his people.

11 And again, Praise the Lord, all ye Gentiles; and laud him, all ye people.

12 And again, Esaias saith, There shall be a root of Jesse, and he that shall rise to reign over the Gentiles; in him shall the Gentiles trust.

13 Now the God of hope fill you with all joy and peace in believing, that ye may abound in hope, through the power of the Holy Ghost.

14 And I myself also am persuaded of you, my brethren, that ye also are full of goodness, filled with all knowledge, able also to admonish one another.

15 ¶ Nevertheless, brethren, I have written the more boldly unto you in some sort, as putting you in mind, because of the grace that is given to me of God,

16 That I should be the minister of Jesus Christ to the Gentiles, ministering the gospel of God, that the offering up of the Gentiles might be acceptable, being sanctified by the Holy Ghost.

17 I have therefore whereof I may glory through Jesus Christ in those things which pertain to God.

18 For I will not dare to speak of any of those things which Christ hath not wrought by me, to make the Gentiles obedient, by word and deed,

19 Through mighty signs and wonders, by the power of the Spirit of God; so that from Jerusalem, and round about unto Illyricum, I have fully preached the gospel of Christ.

20 Yea, so have I strived to preach the gospel, not where

Christ was named, lest I should build upon another man's foundation:

21 But as it is written, To whom he was not spoken of, they shall see: and they that have not heard shall understand.

22 For which cause also I have been much hindered from coming to you.

23 But now having no more place in these parts, and having a great desire these many years to come unto you;

24 Whensoever I take my journey into Spain, I will come to you: for I trust to see you in my journey, and to be brought on my way thitherward by you, if first I be somewhat filled with your *company*.

25 But now I go unto Jerusalem to minister unto the saints.

26 For it hath pleased them of Macedonia and Achaia to make a certain contribution for the poor saints which are at Jerusalem.

27 It hath pleased them verily; and their debtors they are. For if the Gentiles have been made partakers of their spiritual things, their duty is also to minister unto them in carnal things.

28 When therefore I have performed this, and have sealed to them this fruit, I will come by you into Spain.

29 And I am sure that, when I come unto you, I shall come in the fulness of the blessing of the gospel of Christ.

30 Now I beseech you, brethren, for the Lord Jesus Christ's sake, and for the love of the Spirit, that ye strive together with me in *your* prayers to God for me;

31 That I may be delivered from them that do not believe in Judaea; and that my service which *I have* for Jerusalem may be accepted of the saints;

32 That I may come unto you with joy by the will of God, and may with you be refreshed.

33 Now the God of peace *be* with you all. Amen.

16 I commend unto you Phebe our sister, which is a servant of the church which is at Cenchrea:

2 That ye receive her in the Lord, as becometh saints, and that ye assist her in whatsoever business she hath need of you: for she hath been a succourer of many, and of myself also.

3 Greet Priscilla and Aquila my helpers in Christ Jesus:

4 Who have for my life laid down their own necks: unto whom not only I give thanks, but also all the churches of the Gentiles.

5 Likewise *greet* the church that is in their house. Salute my well-beloved Epaenetus, who is the firstfruits of Achaia unto Christ.

6 Greet Mary, who bestowed much labour on us.

7 Salute Andronicus and Junia, my kinsmen, and my fellowprisoners, who are of note among the apostles, who also were in Christ before me.

8 Greet Amplias my beloved in the Lord.

9 Salute Urbane, our helper in Christ, and Stachys my beloved.

10 Salute Apelles approved in Christ. Salute them which are of Aristobulus' *household.*

11 Salute Herodion my kinsman. Greet them that be of the *household* of Narcissus, which are in the Lord.

12 Salute Tryphena and Tryphosa, who labour in the Lord. Salute the beloved Persis, which laboured much in the Lord.

13 Salute Rufus chosen in the Lord, and his mother and mine.

14 Salute Asyncritus, Phlegon, Hermas, Patrobas, Hermes, and the brethren which are with them.

15 Salute Philologus, and Julia, Nereus, and his sister, and Olympas, and all the saints which are with them.

16 Salute one another with an holy kiss. The churches of Christ salute you.

17 ¶ Now I beseech you, brethren, mark them which cause divisions and offences contrary to the doctrine which ye have learned; and avoid them.

18 For they that are such serve not our Lord Jesus Christ, but their own belly; and by good words and fair speeches deceive the hearts of the simple.

19 For your obedience is come abroad unto all *men.* I am glad therefore on your behalf: but yet I would have you wise unto that which is good, and simple concerning evil.

20 And the God of peace shall bruise Satan under your feet shortly. The grace of our Lord Jesus Christ *be* with you. Amen.

21 ¶ Timotheus my workfellow, and Lucius, and Jason, and Sosipater, my kinsmen, salute you.

22 I Tertius, who wrote *this* epistle, salute you in the Lord.

23 Gaius mine host, and of the whole church, saluteth you. Erastus the chamberlain of the city saluteth you, and Quartus a brother.

24 The grace of our Lord Jesus Christ *be* with you all. Amen.

25 Now to him that is of power to stablish you according to my gospel, and the preaching of Jesus Christ, according to the revelation of the mystery, which was kept secret since the world began,

26 But now is made manifest, and by the scriptures of the prophets, according to the commandment of the everlasting God, made known to all nations for the obedience of faith:

27 To God only wise, *be* glory through Jesus Christ for ever. Amen.

¶ Written to the Romans from Corinthus, *and sent* by Phebe servant of the church at Cenchrea.

259

THE FIRST EPISTLE OF PAUL THE APOSTLE
TO THE

CORINTHIANS

1 Paul called *to be* an apostle of Jesus Christ through the will of God, and Sosthenes *our* brother,

2 Unto the church of God which is at Corinth, to them that are sanctified in Christ Jesus, called *to be* saints, with all that in every place call upon the name of Jesus Christ our Lord, both theirs and ours:

3 Grace *be* unto you, and peace, from God our Father, and *from* the Lord Jesus Christ.

4 I thank my God always on your behalf, for the grace of God which is given you by Jesus Christ;

5 That in every thing ye are enriched by him, in all utterance, and *in* all knowledge;

6 Even as the testimony of Christ was confirmed in you:

7 So that ye come behind in no gift; waiting for the coming of our Lord Jesus Christ:

8 Who shall also confirm you unto the end, *that ye may be* blameless in the day of our Lord Jesus Christ.

9 God *is* faithful, by whom ye were called unto the fellowship of his Son Jesus Christ our Lord.

10 ¶ Now I beseech you, brethren, by the name of our Lord Jesus Christ, that ye all speak the same thing, and *that* there be no divisions among you; but *that* ye be perfectly joined together in the same mind and in the same judgment.

11 For it hath been declared unto me of you, my brethren, by them *which are of the house* of Chloe, that there are contentions among you.

12 ¶ Now this I say, that every one of you saith, I am of Paul; and I of Apollos; and I of Cephas; and I of Christ.

13 Is Christ divided? was Paul crucified for you? or were ye baptized in the name of Paul?

14 I thank God that I baptized none of you, but Crispus and Gaius;

15 Lest any should say that I had baptized in mine own name.

16 And I baptized also the household of Stephanas: besides, I know not whether I baptized any other.

17 For Christ sent me not to baptize, but to preach the gospel: not with wisdom of words, lest the cross of Christ should be made of none effect.

18 For the preaching of the cross is to them that perish foolishness; but unto us which are saved it is the power of God.

19 For it is written, I will destroy the wisdom of the wise, and will bring to nothing the understanding of the prudent.

20 Where *is* the wise? where *is* the scribe? where *is* the dis-

puter of this world? hath not God made foolish the wisdom of this world?

21 For after that in the wisdom of God the world by wisdom knew not God, it pleased God by the foolishness of preaching to save them that believe.

22 For the Jews require a sign, and the Greeks seek after wisdom:

23 But we preach Christ crucified, unto the Jews a stumblingblock, and unto the Greeks foolishness;

24 But unto them which are called, both Jews and Greeks, Christ the power of God, and the wisdom of God.

25 Because the foolishness of God is wiser than men; and the weakness of God is stronger than men.

26 For ye see your calling, brethren, how that not many wise men after the flesh, not many mighty, not many noble, *are called*;

27 But God hath chosen the foolish things of the world to confound the wise; and God hath chosen the weak things of the world to confound the things which are mighty;

28 And base things of the world, and things which are despised, hath God chosen, *yea*, and things which are not, to bring to nought things that are:

29 That no flesh should glory in his presence.

30 But of him are ye in Christ Jesus, who of God is made unto us wisdom, and righteousness, and sanctification, and redemption:

31 That, according as it is written, He that glorieth, let him glory in the Lord.

2 And I, brethren, when I came to you, came not with excellency of speech or of wisdom, declaring unto you the testimony of God.

2 For I determined not to know any thing among you, save Jesus Christ, and him crucified.

3 And I was with you in weakness, and in fear, and in much trembling.

4 And my speech and my preaching *was* not with enticing words of man's wisdom, but in demonstration of the Spirit and of power:

5 That your faith should not stand in the wisdom of men, but in the power of God.

6 Howbeit we speak wisdom among them that are perfect: yet not the wisdom of this world, nor of the princes of this world, that come to nought:

7 But we speak the wisdom of God in a mystery, *even* the hidden *wisdom*, which God ordained before the world unto our glory:

8 Which none of the princes of this world knew: for had they known *it*, they would not have crucified the Lord of glory.

9 But as it is written, Eye hath not seen, nor ear heard, neither have entered into the heart of man, the things which God hath

prepared for them that love him.

10 But God hath revealed *them* unto us by his Spirit: for the Spirit searcheth all things, yea, the deep things of God.

11 For what man knoweth the things of a man, save the spirit of man which is in him? even so the things of God knoweth no man, but the Spirit of God.

12 Now we have received, not the spirit of the world, but the spirit which is of God; that we might know the things that are freely given to us of God.

13 Which things also we speak, not in the words which man's wisdom teacheth, but which the Holy Ghost teacheth; comparing spiritual things with spiritual.

14 But the natural man receiveth not the things of the Spirit of God: for they are foolishness unto him: neither can he know *them*, because they are spiritually discerned.

15 But he that is spiritual judgeth all things, yet he himself is judged of no man.

16 For who hath known the mind of the Lord, that he may instruct him? But we have the mind of Christ.

3 And I, brethren, could not speak unto you as unto spiritual, but as unto carnal, *even* as unto babes in Christ.

2 I have fed you with milk, and not with meat: for hitherto ye were not able *to bear it*, neither yet now are ye able.

3 ❡ For ye are yet carnal: for whereas *there is* among you en-

vying, and strife, and divisions, are ye not carnal, and walk as men?

4 For while one saith, I am of Paul; and another, I *am* of Apollos; are ye not carnal?

5 Who then is Paul, and who *is* Apollos, but ministers by whom ye believed, even as the Lord gave to every man?

6 I have planted, Apollos watered; but God gave the increase.

7 So then neither is he that planteth any thing, neither he that watereth; but God that giveth the increase.

8 Now he that planteth and he that watereth are one: and every man shall receive his own reward according to his own labour.

9 For we are labourers together with God: ye are God's husbandry, *ye are* God's building.

10 According to the grace of God which is given unto me, as a wise masterbuilder, I have laid the foundation, and another buildeth thereon. But let every man take heed how he buildeth thereupon.

11 ❡ For other foundation can no man lay than that is laid, which is Jesus Christ.

12 Now if any man build upon this foundation gold, silver, precious stones, wood, hay, stubble;

13 Every man's work shall be made manifest: for the day shall declare it; because it shall be revealed by fire; and the fire shall try every man's work of what sort it is.

14 If any man's work abide

which he hath built thereupon, he shall receive a reward.

15 If any man's work shall be burned, he shall suffer loss: but he himself shall be saved; yet so as by fire.

16 ¶Know ye not that ye are the temple of God, and *that* the Spirit of God dwelleth in you?

17 If any man defile the temple of God, him shall God destroy; for the temple of God is holy, which *temple* ye are.

18 Let no man deceive himself. If any man among you seemeth to be wise in this world, let him become a fool, that he may be wise.

19 For the wisdom of this world is foolishness with God. For it is written, He taketh the wise in their own craftiness.

20 And again, The Lord knoweth the thoughts of the wise, that they are vain.

21 Therefore let no man glory in men. For all things are yours;

22 Whether Paul, or Apollos, or Cephas, or the world, or life, or death, or things present, or things to come; all are yours;

23 And ye are Christ's; and Christ *is* God's.

4 Let a man so account of us, as of the ministers of Christ, and stewards of the mysteries of God.

2 Moreover it is required in stewards, that a man be found faithful.

3 But with me it is a very small thing that I should be judged of you, or of man's judgment: yea, I

judge not mine own self.

4 For I know nothing by myself; yet am I not hereby justified: but he that judgeth me is the Lord.

5 Therefore judge nothing before the time, until the Lord come, who both will bring to light the hidden things of darkness, and will make manifest the counsels of the hearts: and then shall every man have praise of God.

6 And these things, brethren, I have in a figure transferred to myself and *to* Apollos for your sakes; that ye might learn in us not to think of *men* above that which is written, that no one of you be puffed up for one against another.

7 For who maketh thee to differ *from another*? and what hast thou that thou didst not receive? now if thou didst receive *it*, why dost thou glory, as if thou hadst not received *it*?

8 Now ye are full, now ye are rich, ye have reigned as kings without us: and I would to God ye did reign, that we also might reign with you.

9 For I think that God hath set forth us the apostles last, as it were appointed to death: for we are made a spectacle unto the world, and to angels, and to men.

10 We *are* fools for Christ's sake, but ye *are* wise in Christ; we *are* weak, but ye *are* strong; ye *are* honourable, but we *are* despised.

11 Even unto this present hour we both hunger, and thirst, and

are naked, and are buffeted, and have no certain dwellingplace;

12 And labour, working with our own hands: being reviled, we bless; being persecuted, we suffer it:

13 Being defamed, we intreat: we are made as the filth of the world, *and are* the offscouring of all things unto this day.

14 I write not these things to shame you, but as my beloved sons I warn *you*.

15 For though ye have ten thousand instructers in Christ, yet *have ye* not many fathers: for in Christ Jesus I have begotten you through the gospel.

16 Wherefore I beseech you, be ye followers of me.

17 For this cause have I sent unto you Timotheus, who is my beloved son, and faithful in the Lord, who shall bring you into remembrance of my ways which be in Christ, as I teach every where in every church.

18 Now some are puffed up, as though I would not come to you.

19 ¶ But I will come to you shortly, if the Lord will, and will know, not the speech of them which are puffed up, but the power.

20 For the kingdom of God *is* not in word, but in power.

21 What will ye? shall I come unto you with a rod, or in love, and *in* the spirit of meekness?

5 It is reported commonly *that there is* fornication among you, and such fornication as is not so much as named among the Gentiles, that one

should have his father's wife.

2 And ye are puffed up, and have not rather mourned, that he that hath done this deed might be taken away from among you.

3 For I verily, as absent in body, but present in spirit, have judged already, as though I were present, *concerning* him that hath so done this deed,

4 In the name of our Lord Jesus Christ, when ye are gathered together, and my spirit, with the power of our Lord Jesus Christ,

5 To deliver such an one unto Satan for the destruction of the flesh, that the spirit may be saved in the day of the Lord Jesus.

6 Your glorying *is* not good. Know ye not that a little leaven leaveneth the whole lump?

7 ¶ Purge out therefore the old leaven, that ye may be a new lump, as ye are unleavened. For even Christ our passover is sacrificed for us:

8 Therefore let us keep the feast, not with old leaven, neither with the leaven of malice and wickedness; but with the unleavened *bread* of sincerity and truth.

9 I wrote unto you in an epistle not to company with fornicators:

10 Yet not altogether with the fornicators of this world, or with the covetous, or extortioners, or with idolaters; for then must ye needs go out of the world.

11 But now I have written unto you not to keep company, if any man that is called a brother be a fornicator, or covetous, or an idolater, or a railer, or a drunk-

ard, or an extortioner; with such an one no not to eat.

12 For what have I to do to judge them also that are without? do not ye judge them that are within?

13 But them that are without God judgeth. Therefore put away from among yourselves that wicked person.

6 Dare any of you, having a matter against another, go to law before the unjust, and not before the saints?

2 Do ye not know that the saints shall judge the world? and if the world shall be judged by you, are ye unworthy to judge the smallest matters?

3 Know ye not that we shall judge angels? how much more things that pertain to this life?

4 If then ye have judgments of things pertaining to this life, set them to judge who are least esteemed in the church.

5 I speak to your shame. Is it so, that there is not a wise man among you? no, not one that shall be able to judge between his brethren?

6 But brother goeth to law with brother, and that before the unbelievers.

7 Now therefore there is utterly a fault among you, because ye go to law one with another. Why do ye not rather take wrong? why do ye not rather *suffer yourselves to* be defrauded?

8 Nay, ye do wrong, and defraud, and that *your* brethren.

9 ¶ Know ye not that the unrigh-

teous shall not inherit the kingdom of God? Be not deceived: neither fornicators, nor idolaters, nor adulterers, nor effeminate, nor abusers of themselves with mankind,

10 Nor thieves, nor covetous, nor drunkards, nor revilers, nor extortioners, shall inherit the kingdom of God.

11 And such were some of you: but ye are washed, but ye are sanctified, but ye are justified in the name of the Lord Jesus, and by the Spirit of our God.

12 All things are lawful unto me, but all things are not expedient: all things are lawful for me, but I will not be brought under the power of any.

13 Meats for the belly, and the belly for meats: but God shall destroy both it and them. Now the body *is* not for fornication, but for the Lord; and the Lord for the body.

14 And God hath both raised up the Lord, and will also raise up us by his own power.

15 ¶ Know ye not that your bodies are the members of Christ? shall I then take the members of Christ, and make *them* the members of an harlot? God forbid.

16 What? know ye not that he which is joined to an harlot is one body? for two, saith he, shall be one flesh.

17 But he that is joined unto the Lord is one spirit.

18 Flee fornication. Every sin that a man doeth is without the body; but he that committeth fornication sinneth against his

own body.

19 What? know ye not that your body is the temple of the Holy Ghost *which is* in you, which ye have of God, and ye are not your own?

20 For ye are bought with a price: therefore glorify God in your body, and in your spirit, which are God's.

7 Now concerning the things whereof ye wrote unto me: *It is* good for a man not to touch a woman.

2 Nevertheless, *to avoid* fornication, let every man have his own wife, and let every woman have her own husband.

3 Let the husband render unto the wife due benevolence: and likewise also the wife unto the husband.

4 The wife hath not power of her own body, but the husband: and likewise also the husband hath not power of his own body, but the wife.

5 Defraud ye not one the other, except *it be* with consent for a time, that ye may give yourselves to fasting and prayer; and come together again, that Satan tempt you not for your incontinency.

6 But I speak this by permission, *and* not of commandment.

7 For I would that all men were even as I myself. But every man hath his proper gift of God, one after this manner, and another after that.

8 I say therefore to the unmarried and widows, It is good for them if they abide even as I.

9 But if they cannot contain, let them marry: for it is better to marry than to burn.

10 ¶ And unto the married I command, *yet* not I, but the Lord, Let not the wife depart from *her* husband:

11 But and if she depart, let her remain unmarried, or be reconciled to *her* husband: and let not the husband put away *his* wife.

12 But to the rest speak I, not the Lord: If any brother hath a wife that believeth not, and she be pleased to dwell with him, let him not put her away.

13 And the woman which hath an husband that believeth not, and if he be pleased to dwell with her, let her not leave him.

14 For the unbelieving husband is sanctified by the wife, and the unbelieving wife is sanctified by the husband: else were your children unclean; but now are they holy.

15 But if the unbelieving depart, let him depart. A brother or a sister is not under bondage in such *cases*: but God hath called us to peace.

16 For what knowest thou, O wife, whether thou shalt save *thy* husband? or how knowest thou, O man, whether thou shalt save *thy* wife?

17 ¶ But as God hath distributed to every man, as the Lord hath called every one, so let him walk. And so ordain I in all churches.

18 Is any man called being circumcised? let him not become uncircumcised. Is any called in uncircumcision? let him not be

circumcised.

19 Circumcision is nothing, and uncircumcision is nothing, but the keeping of the commandments of God.

20 Let every man abide in the same calling wherein he was called.

21 Art thou called *being* a servant? care not for it: but if thou mayest be made free, use *it* rather.

22 For he that is called in the Lord, *being* a servant, is the Lord's freeman: likewise also he that is called, *being* free, is Christ's servant.

23 Ye are bought with a price; be not ye the servants of men.

24 Brethren, let every man, wherein he is called, therein abide with God.

25 ❡ Now concerning virgins I have no commandment of the Lord: yet I give my judgment, as one that hath obtained mercy of the Lord to be faithful.

26 I suppose therefore that this is good for the present distress, *I say*, that *it is* good for a man so to be.

27 Art thou bound unto a wife? seek not to be loosed. Art thou loosed from a wife? seek not a wife.

28 But and if thou marry, thou hast not sinned; and if a virgin marry, she hath not sinned. Nevertheless such shall have trouble in the flesh: but I spare you.

29 But this I say, brethren, the time *is* short: it remaineth, that both they that have wives be as though they had none;

30 And they that weep, as though they wept not; and they that rejoice, as though they rejoiced not; and they that buy, as though they possessed not;

31 And they that use this world, as not abusing *it*: for the fashion of this world passeth away.

32 But I would have you without carefulness. He that is unmarried careth for the things that belong to the Lord, how he may please the Lord:

33 But he that is married careth for the things that are of the world, how he may please *his* wife.

34 There is difference *also* between a wife and a virgin. The unmarried woman careth for the things of the Lord, that she may be holy both in body and in spirit: but she that is married careth for the things of the world, how she may please *her* husband.

35 And this I speak for your own profit; not that I may cast a snare upon you, but for that which is comely, and that ye may attend upon the Lord without distraction.

36 But if any man think that he behaveth himself uncomely toward his virgin, if she pass the flower of *her* age, and need so require, let him do what he will, he sinneth not: let them marry.

37 Nevertheless he that standeth stedfast in his heart, having no necessity, but hath power over his own will, and hath so decreed in his heart that he will keep his virgin, doeth well.

38 So then he that giveth *her* in marriage doeth well; but he that giveth *her* not in marriage doeth better.

39 The wife is bound by the law as long as her husband liveth; but if her husband be dead, she is at liberty to be married to whom she will; only in the Lord.

40 But she is happier if she so abide, after my judgment: and I think also that I have the Spirit of God.

8 Now as touching things offered unto idols, we know that we all have knowledge. Knowledge puffeth up, but charity edifieth.

2 And if any man think that he knoweth any thing, he knoweth nothing yet as he ought to know.

3 But if any man love God, the same is known of him.

4 As concerning therefore the eating of those things that are offered in sacrifice unto idols, we know that an idol *is* nothing in the world, and that *there is* none other God but one.

5 For though there be that are called gods, whether in heaven or in earth, (as there be gods many, and lords many,)

6 But to us *there is but* one God, the Father, of whom *are* all things, and we in him; and one Lord Jesus Christ, by whom *are* all things, and we by him.

7 Howbeit *there is* not in every man that knowledge: for some with conscience of the idol unto this hour eat *it* as a thing offered unto an idol; and their conscience being weak is defiled.

8 ¢ But meat commendeth us not to God: for neither, if we eat, are we the better; neither, if we eat not, are we the worse.

9 But take heed lest by any means this liberty of yours become a stumblingblock to them that are weak.

10 For if any man see thee which hast knowledge sit at meat in the idol's temple, shall not the conscience of him which is weak be emboldened to eat those things which are offered to idols;

11 And through thy knowledge shall the weak brother perish, for whom Christ died?

12 But when ye sin so against the brethren, and wound their weak conscience, ye sin against Christ.

13 Wherefore, if meat make my brother to offend, I will eat no flesh while the world standeth, lest I make my brother to offend.

9 Am I not an apostle? am I not free? have I not seen Jesus Christ our Lord? are not ye my work in the Lord?

2 If I be not an apostle unto others, yet doubtless I am to you: for the seal of mine apostleship are ye in the Lord.

3 Mine answer to them that do examine me is this,

4 Have we not power to eat and to drink?

5 Have we not power to lead about a sister, a wife, as well as other apostles, and *as* the brethren of the Lord, and Cephas?

6 Or I only and Barnabas, have

not we power to forbear working?

7 ¶ Who goeth a warfare any time at his own charges? who planteth a vineyard, and eateth not of the fruit thereof? or who feedeth a flock, and eateth not of the milk of the flock?

8 Say I these things as a man? or saith not the law the same also?

9 For it is written in the law of Moses, Thou shalt not muzzle the mouth of the ox that treadeth out the corn. Doth God take care for oxen?

10 Or saith he *it* altogether for our sakes? For our sakes, no doubt, *this* is written: that he that ploweth should plow in hope; and that he that thresheth in hope should be partaker of his hope.

11 If we have sown unto you spiritual things, *is it* a great thing if we shall reap your carnal things?

12 If others be partakers of *this* power over you, *are* not we rather? Nevertheless we have not used this power; but suffer all things, lest we should hinder the gospel of Christ.

13 Do ye not know that they which minister about holy things live *of the things* of the temple? and they which wait at the altar are partakers with the altar?

14 Even so hath the Lord ordained that they which preach the gospel should live of the gospel.

15 ¶ But I have used none of these things: neither have I written these things, that it should be so done unto me: for *it were* better for me to die, than that any man should make my glorying void.

16 For though I preach the gospel, I have nothing to glory of: for necessity is laid upon me; yea, woe is unto me, if I preach not the gospel!

17 For if I do this thing willingly, I have a reward: but if against my will, a dispensation *of the gospel* is committed unto me.

18 What is my reward then? *Verily* that, when I preach the gospel, I may make the gospel of Christ without charge, that I abuse not my power in the gospel.

19 ¶ For though I be free from all *men*, yet have I made myself servant unto all, that I might gain the more.

20 And unto the Jews I became as a Jew, that I might gain the Jews; to them that are under the law, as under the law, that I might gain them that are under the law;

21 To them that are without law, as without law, (being not without law to God, but under the law to Christ,) that I might gain them that are without law.

22 To the weak became I as weak, that I might gain the weak: I am made all things to all *men*, that I might by all means save some.

23 And this I do for the gospel's sake, that I might be partaker thereof with *you*.

24 Know ye not that they which run in a race run all, but one receiveth the prize? So run, that ye may obtain.

25 And every man that striveth for the mastery is temperate in all things. Now they *do it* to obtain a corruptible crown; but we an incorruptible.

26 I therefore so run, not as uncertainly; so fight I, not as one that beateth the air:

27 But I keep under my body, and bring *it* into subjection: lest that by any means, when I have preached to others, I myself should be a castaway.

10

Moreover, brethren, I would not that ye should be ignorant, how that all our fathers were under the cloud, and all passed through the sea;

2 And were all baptized unto Moses in the cloud and in the sea;

3 And did all eat the same spiritual meat;

4 ℂ And did all drink the same spiritual drink: for they drank of that spiritual Rock that followed them: and that Rock was Christ.

5 But with many of them God was not well pleased: for they were overthrown in the wilderness.

6 Now these things were our examples, to the intent we should not lust after evil things, as they also lusted.

7 ℂ Neither be ye idolaters, as *were* some of them; as it is written, The people sat down to eat and drink, and rose up to play.

8 Neither let us commit fornication, as some of them committed, and fell in one day three and twenty thousand.

9 Neither let us tempt Christ, as some of them also tempted, and were destroyed of serpents.

10 Neither murmur ye, as some of them also murmured, and were destroyed of the destroyer.

11 ℂ Now all these things happened unto them for ensamples: and they are written for our admonition, upon whom the ends of the world are come.

12 Wherefore let him that thinketh he standeth take heed lest he fall.

13 There hath no temptation taken you but such as is common to man: but God *is* faithful, who will not suffer you to be tempted above that ye are able; but will with the temptation also make a way to escape, that ye may be able to bear *it*.

14 Wherefore, my dearly beloved, flee from idolatry.

15 I speak as to wise men; judge ye what I say.

16 ℂ The cup of blessing which we bless, is it not the communion of the blood of Christ? The bread which we break, is it not the communion of the body of Christ?

17 For we *being* many are one bread, *and* one body: for we are all partakers of that one bread.

18 Behold Israel after the flesh: are not they which eat of the sacrifices partakers of the altar?

19 What say I then? that the idol is any thing, or that which is offered in sacrifice to idols is any thing?

20 But *I* say, that the things

which the Gentiles sacrifice, they sacrifice to devils, and not to God: and I would not that ye should have fellowship with devils.

21 Ye cannot drink the cup of the Lord, and the cup of devils: ye cannot be partakers of the Lord's table, and of the table of devils.

22 Do we provoke the Lord to jealousy? are ye stronger than he?

23 ¶ All things are lawful for me, but all things are not expedient: all things are lawful for me, but all things edify not.

24 Let no man seek his own, but every man another's *wealth*.

25 Whatsoever is sold in the shambles, *that* eat, asking no question for conscience sake:

26 For the earth *is* the Lord's, and the fulness thereof.

27 If any of them that believe not bid you *to a feast*, and ye be disposed to go; whatsoever is set before you, eat, asking no question for conscience sake.

28 But if any man say unto you, This is offered in sacrifice unto idols, eat not for his sake that shewed it, and for conscience sake: for the earth *is* the Lord's, and the fulness thereof.

29 Conscience, I say, not thine own, but of the other: for why is my liberty judged of another *man's* conscience?

30 For if I by grace be a partaker, why am I evil spoken of for that for which I give thanks?

31 Whether therefore ye eat, or drink, or whatsoever ye do, do all to the glory of God.

32 Give none offence, neither to the Jews, nor to the Gentiles, nor to the church of God:

33 Even as I please all *men* in all *things*, not seeking mine own profit, but the *profit* of many, that they may be saved.

11 Be ye followers of me, even as I also *am* of Christ.

2 Now I praise you, brethren, that ye remember me in all things, and keep the ordinances, as I delivered *them* to you.

3 But I would have you know, that the head of every man is Christ; and the head of the woman *is* the man; and the head of Christ *is* God.

4 Every man praying or prophesying, having *his* head covered, dishonoureth his head.

5 But every woman that prayeth or prophesieth with *her* head uncovered dishonoureth her head: for that is even all one as if she were shaven.

6 For if the woman be not covered, let her also be shorn: but if it be a shame for a woman to be shorn or shaven, let her be covered.

7 For a man indeed ought not to cover *his* head, forasmuch as he is the image and glory of God: but the woman is the glory of the man.

8 For the man is not of the woman: but the woman of the man.

9 Neither was the man created

for the woman; but the woman for the man.

10 For this cause ought the woman to have power on *her* head because of the angels.

11 Nevertheless neither is the man without the woman, neither the woman without the man, in the Lord.

12 For as the woman *is* of the man, even so *is* the man also by the woman; but all things of God.

13 Judge in yourselves: is it comely that a woman pray unto God uncovered?

14 Doth not even nature itself teach you, that, if a man have long hair, it is a shame unto him?

15 But if a woman have long hair, it is a glory to her: for *her* hair is given her for a covering.

16 But if any man seem to be contentious, we have no such custom, neither the churches of God.

17 ¶ Now in this that I declare *unto you* I praise *you* not, that ye come together not for the better, but for the worse.

18 For first of all, when ye come together in the church, I hear that there be divisions among you; and I partly believe it.

19 For there must be also heresies among you, that they which are approved may be made manifest among you.

20 ¶ When ye come together therefore into one place, *this* is not to eat the Lord's supper.

21 For in eating every one taketh before *other* his own supper: and one is hungry, and another is drunken.

22 What? have ye not houses to eat and to drink in? or despise ye the church of God, and shame them that have not? What shall I say to you? shall I praise you in this? I praise *you* not.

23 ¶ For I have received of the Lord that which also I delivered unto you, That the Lord Jesus the *same* night in which he was betrayed took bread:

24 And when he had given thanks, he brake *it,* and said, Take, eat: this is my body, which is broken for you: this do in remembrance of me.

25 After the same manner also *he took* the cup, when he had supped, saying, This cup is the new testament in my blood: this do ye, as oft as ye drink *it,* in remembrance of me.

26 For as often as ye eat this bread, and drink this cup, ye do shew the Lord's death till he come.

27 Wherefore whosoever shall eat this bread, and drink *this* cup of the Lord, unworthily, shall be guilty of the body and blood of the Lord.

28 But let a man examine himself, and so let him eat of *that* bread, and drink of *that* cup.

29 For he that eateth and drinketh unworthily, eateth and drinketh damnation to himself, not discerning the Lord's body.

30 For this cause many *are* weak and sickly among you, and many sleep.

31 For if we would judge ourselves, we should not be judged.

32 But when we are judged, we are chastened of the Lord, that we should not be condemned with the world.

33 Wherefore, my brethren, when ye come together to eat, tarry one for another.

34 And if any man hunger, let him eat at home; that ye come not together unto condemnation. And the rest will I set in order when I come.

12

Now concerning spiritual *gifts*, brethren, I would not have you ignorant.

2 Ye know that ye were Gentiles, carried away unto these dumb idols, even as ye were led.

3 Wherefore I give you to understand, that no man speaking by the Spirit of God calleth Jesus accursed: and *that* no man can say that Jesus is the Lord, but by the Holy Ghost.

4 Now there are diversities of gifts, but the same Spirit.

5 And there are differences of administrations, but the same Lord.

6 And there are diversities of operations, but it is the same God which worketh all in all.

7 But the manifestation of the Spirit is given to every man to profit withal.

8 For to one is given by the Spirit the word of wisdom; to another the word of knowledge by the same Spirit;

9 To another faith by the same Spirit; to another the gifts of healing by the same Spirit;

10 To another the working of miracles; to another prophecy; to another discerning of spirits; to another *divers* kinds of tongues; to another the interpretation of tongues:

11 But all these worketh that one and the selfsame Spirit, dividing to every man severally as he will.

12 ¶ For as the body is one, and hath many members, and all the members of that one body, being many, are one body: so also *is* Christ.

13 For by one Spirit are we all baptized into one body, whether *we be* Jews or Gentiles, whether *we be* bond or free; and have been all made to drink into one Spirit.

14 For the body is not one member, but many.

15 If the foot shall say, Because I am not the hand, I am not of the body; is it therefore not of the body?

16 And if the ear shall say, Because I am not the eye, I am not of the body; is it therefore not of the body?

17 If the whole body *were* an eye, where *were* the hearing? If the whole *were* hearing, where *were* the smelling?

18 But now hath God set the members every one of them in the body, as it hath pleased him.

19 And if they were all one member, where *were* the body?

20 But now *are they* many members, yet but one body.

21 And the eye cannot say unto the hand, I have no need of thee: nor again the head to the feet, I have no need of you.

22 Nay, much more those members of the body, which seem to be more feeble, are necessary:

23 And those *members* of the body, which we think to be less honourable, upon these we bestow more abundant honour; and our uncomely *parts* have more abundant comeliness.

24 For our comely *parts* have no need: but God hath tempered the body together, having given more abundant honour to that *part* which lacked.

25 That there should be no schism in the body; but *that* the members should have the same care one for another.

26 And whether one member suffer, all the members suffer with it; or one member be honoured, all the members rejoice with it.

27 ℂ Now ye are the body of Christ, and members in particular.

28 And God hath set some in the church, first apostles, secondarily prophets, thirdly teachers, after that miracles, then gifts of healings, helps, governments, diversities of tongues.

29 *Are* all apostles? *are* all prophets? *are* all teachers? *are* all workers of miracles?

30 Have all the gifts of healing? do all speak with tongues? do all interpret?

31 But covet earnestly the best gifts: and yet shew I unto you a more excellent way.

13 Though I speak with the tongues of men and of angels, and have not charity, I am become *as* sounding brass, or a tinkling cymbal.

2 And though I have *the gift of* prophecy, and understand all mysteries, and all knowledge; and though I have all faith, so that I could remove mountains, and have not charity, I am nothing.

3 And though I bestow all my goods to feed *the poor*, and though I give my body to be burned, and have not charity, it profiteth me nothing.

4 Charity suffereth long, *and* is kind; charity envieth not; charity vaunteth not itself, is not puffed up,

5 Doth not behave itself unseemly, seeketh not her own, is not easily provoked, thinketh no evil;

6 Rejoiceth not in iniquity, but rejoiceth in the truth;

7 Beareth all things, believeth all things, hopeth all things, endureth all things.

8 Charity never faileth: but whether *there be* prophecies, they shall fail; whether *there be* tongues, they shall cease; whether *there be* knowledge, it shall vanish away.

9 For we know in part, and we prophesy in part.

10 But when that which is perfect is come, then that which is in part shall be done away.

11 When I was a child, I spake as a child, I understood as a child, I thought as a child: but when I became a man, I put away childish things.

12 For now we see through a glass, darkly; but then face to face: now I know in part; but then shall I know even as also I am known.

13 And now abideth faith, hope, charity, these three; but the greatest of these is charity.

14 Follow after charity, and desire spiritual *gifts*, but rather that ye may prophesy.

2 For he that speaketh in an *unknown* tongue speaketh not unto men, but unto God: for no man understandeth *him*; howbeit in the spirit he speaketh mysteries.

3 But he that prophesieth speaketh unto men *to* edification, and exhortation, and comfort.

4 He that speaketh in an *unknown* tongue edifieth himself; but he that prophesieth edifieth the church.

5 I would that ye all spake with tongues, but rather that ye prophesied: for greater *is* he that prophesieth than he that speaketh with tongues, except he interpret, that the church may receive edifying.

6 Now, brethren, if I come unto you speaking with tongues, what shall I profit you, except I shall speak to you either by revelation, or by knowledge, or by prophesying, or by doctrine?

7 And even things without life

giving sound, whether pipe or harp, except they give a distinction in the sounds, how shall it be known what is piped or harped?

8 For if the trumpet give an uncertain sound, who shall prepare himself to the battle?

9 So likewise ye, except ye utter by the tongue words easy to be understood, how shall it be known what is spoken? for ye shall speak into the air.

10 There are, it may be, so many kinds of voices in the world, and none of them *is* without signification.

11 Therefore if I know not the meaning of the voice, I shall be unto him that speaketh a barbarian, and he that speaketh *shall be* a barbarian unto me.

12 Even so ye, forasmuch as ye are zealous of spiritual *gifts*, seek that ye may excel to the edifying of the church.

13 Wherefore let him that speaketh in an *unknown* tongue pray that he may interpret.

14 For if I pray in an *unknown* tongue, my spirit prayeth, but my understanding is unfruitful.

15 What is it then? I will pray with the spirit, and I will pray with the understanding also: I will sing with the spirit, and I will sing with the understanding also.

16 Else when thou shalt bless with the spirit, how shall he that occupieth the room of the unlearned say Amen at thy giving of thanks, seeing he understandeth not what thou sayest?

17 For thou verily givest thanks

well, but the other is not edified.

18 I thank my God, I speak with tongues more than ye all:

19 Yet in the church I had rather speak five words with my understanding, that *by my voice* I might teach others also, than ten thousand words in an **unknown** tongue.

20 Brethren, be not children in understanding: howbeit in malice be ye children, but in understanding be men.

21 In the law it is written, With *men of* other tongues and other lips will I speak unto this people; and yet for all that will they not hear me, saith the Lord.

22 Wherefore tongues are for a sign, not to them that believe, but to them that believe not: but prophesying **serveth** not for them that believe not, but for them which believe.

23 ¶ If therefore the whole church be come together into one place, and all speak with tongues, and there come in *those that are* unlearned, or unbelievers, will they not say that ye are mad?

24 But if all prophesy, and there come in one that believeth not, or *one* unlearned, he is convinced of all, he is judged of all:

25 And thus are the secrets of his heart made manifest; and so falling down on *his* face he will worship God, and report that God is in you of a truth.

26 How is it then, brethren? when ye come together, every one of you hath a psalm, hath a doctrine, hath a tongue, hath a revelation, hath an interpreta-

tion. Let all things be done unto edifying.

27 If any man speak in an *unknown* tongue, *let it be* by two, or at the most *by* three, and *that* by course; and let one interpret.

28 But if there be no interpreter, let him keep silence in the church; and let him speak to himself, and to God.

29 Let the prophets speak two or three, and let the other judge.

30 If *any thing* be revealed to another that sitteth by, let the first hold his peace.

31 For ye may all prophesy one by one, that all may learn, and all may be comforted.

32 And the spirits of the prophets are subject to the prophets.

33 For God is not *the author* of confusion, but of peace, as in all churches of the saints.

34 Let your women keep silence in the churches: for it is not permitted unto them to speak; but *they are commanded* to be under obedience as also saith the law.

35 And if they will learn any thing, let them ask their husbands at home: for it is a shame for women to speak in the church.

36 What? came the word of God out from you? or came it unto you only?

37 If any man think himself to be a prophet, or spiritual, let him acknowledge that the things that I write unto you are the commandments of the Lord.

38 But if any man be ignorant, let him be ignorant.

39 Wherefore, brethren, covet

to prophesy, and forbid not to speak with tongues.

40 Let all things be done decently and in order.

15 Moreover, brethren, I declare unto you the gospel which I preached unto you, which also ye have received, and wherein ye stand;

2 By which also ye are saved, if ye keep in memory what I preached unto you, unless ye have believed in vain.

3 For I delivered unto you first of all that which I also received, how that Christ died for our sins according to the scriptures;

4 And that he was buried, and that he rose again the third day according to the scriptures:

5 And that he was seen of Cephas, then of the twelve:

6 After that, he was seen of above five hundred brethren at once; of whom the greater part remain unto this present, but some are fallen asleep.

7 After that, he was seen of James; then of all the apostles.

8 And last of all he was seen of me also, as of one born out of due time.

9 For I am the least of the apostles, that am not meet to be called an apostle, because I persecuted the church of God.

10 But by the grace of God I am what I am: and his grace which *was bestowed* upon me was not in vain; but I laboured more abundantly than they all: yet not I, but the grace of God which was with me.

11 Therefore whether *it were* I or they, so we preach, and so ye believed.

12 ¶ Now if Christ be preached that he rose from the dead, how say some among you that there is no resurrection of the dead?

13 But if there be no resurrection of the dead, then is Christ not risen:

14 And if Christ be not risen, then *is* our preaching vain, and your faith *is* also vain.

15 Yea, and we are found false witnesses of God; because we have testified of God that he raised up Christ: whom he raised not up, if so be that the dead rise not.

16 For if the dead rise not, then is not Christ raised:

17 And if Christ be not raised, your faith *is* vain; ye are yet in your sins.

18 Then they also which are fallen asleep in Christ are perished.

19 If in this life only we have hope in Christ, we are of all men most miserable.

20 ¶ But now is Christ risen from the dead, *and* become the firstfruits of them that slept.

21 For since by man *came* death, by man *came* also the resurrection of the dead.

22 For as in Adam all die, even so in Christ shall all be made alive.

23 But every man in his own order: Christ the firstfruits; afterward they that are Christ's at his coming.

24 Then *cometh* the end, when he shall have delivered up the kingdom to God, even the Father; when he shall have put down all rule and all authority and power.

25 For he must reign, till he hath put all enemies under his feet.

26 The last enemy *that* shall be destroyed *is* death.

27 For he hath put all things under his feet. But when he saith, all things are put under *him, it is* manifest that he is excepted, which did put all things under him.

28 And when all things shall be subdued unto him, then shall the Son also himself be subject unto him that put all things under him, that God may be all in all.

29 Else what shall they do which are baptized for the dead, if the dead rise not at all? why are they then baptized for the dead?

30 And why stand we in jeopardy every hour?

31 I protest by your rejoicing which I have in Christ Jesus our Lord, I die daily.

32 If after the manner of men I have fought with beasts at Ephesus, what advantageth it me, if the dead rise not? let us eat and drink; for to morrow we die.

33 Be not deceived: evil communications corrupt good manners.

34 Awake to righteousness, and sin not; for some have not the knowledge of God: I speak *this* to your shame.

35 ¶ But some *man* will say, How are the dead raised up? and with what body do they come?

36 *Thou* fool, that which thou sowest is not quickened, except it die:

37 And that which thou sowest, thou sowest not that body that shall be, but bare grain, it may chance of wheat, or of some other *grain*:

38 But God giveth it a body as it hath pleased him, and to every seed his own body.

39 All flesh *is* not the same flesh: but *there is* one *kind of* flesh of men, another flesh of beasts, another of fishes, *and* another of birds.

40 *There are* also celestial bodies, and bodies terrestrial: but the glory of the celestial *is* one, and the *glory* of the terrestrial *is* another.

41 *There is* one glory of the sun, and another glory of the moon, and another glory of the stars: for *one* star differeth from *another* star in glory.

42 So also *is* the resurrection of the dead. It is sown in corruption; it is raised in incorruption:

43 It is sown in dishonour; it is raised in glory: it is sown in weakness; it is raised in power:

44 It is sown a natural body; it is raised a spiritual body. There is a natural body, and there is a spiritual body.

45 And so it is written, The first man Adam was made a living soul; the last Adam *was made* a quickening spirit.

46 Howbeit that *was* not first

which is spiritual, but that which is natural; and afterward that which is spiritual.

47 The first man *is* of the earth, earthy; the second man *is* the Lord from heaven.

48 As *is* the earthy, such *are* they also that are earthy: and as *is* the heavenly, such *are* they also that are heavenly.

49 And as we have borne the image of the earthy, we shall also bear the image of the heavenly.

50 Now this I say, brethren, that flesh and blood cannot inherit the kingdom of God; neither doth corruption inherit incorruption.

51 ¶ Behold, I shew you a mystery; We shall not all sleep, but we shall all be changed,

52 In a moment, in the twinkling of an eye, at the last trump: for the trumpet shall sound, and the dead shall be raised incorruptible, and we shall be changed.

53 For this corruptible must put on incorruption, and this mortal *must* put on immortality.

54 So when this corruptible shall have put on incorruption, and this mortal shall have put on immortality, then shall be brought to pass the saying that is written, Death is swallowed up in victory.

55 O death, where *is* thy sting? O grave, where *is* thy victory?

56 The sting of death *is* sin; and the strength of sin *is* the law.

57 But thanks *be* to God, which giveth us the victory through our Lord Jesus Christ.

58 Therefore, my beloved brethren, be ye stedfast, unmoveable, always abounding in the work of the Lord, forasmuch as ye know that your labour is not in vain in the Lord.

16

Now concerning the collection for the saints, as I have given order to the churches of Galatia, even so do ye.

2 Upon the first *day* of the week let every one of you lay by him in store, as God hath prospered him, that there be no gatherings when I come.

3 And when I come, whomsoever ye shall approve by *your* letters, them will I send to bring your liberality unto Jerusalem.

4 And if it be meet that I go also, they shall go with me.

5 ¶ Now I will come unto you, when I shall pass through Macedonia: for I do pass through Macedonia.

6 And it may be that I will abide, yea, and winter with you, that ye may bring me on my journey whithersoever I go.

7 For I will not see you now by the way; but I trust to tarry a while with you, if the Lord permit.

8 But I will tarry at Ephesus until Pentecost.

9 For a great door and effectual is opened unto me, and *there are* many adversaries.

10 Now if Timotheus come, see that he may be with you without fear: for he worketh the work of the Lord, as I also *do*.

11 Let no man therefore despise him: but conduct him forth in peace, that he may come unto me: for I look for him with the brethren.

12 As touching *our* brother Apollos, I greatly desired him to come unto you with the brethren: but his will was not at all to come at this time; but he will come when he shall have convenient time.

13 Watch ye, stand fast in the faith, quit you like men, be strong.

14 Let all your things be done with charity.

15 I beseech you, brethren, (ye know the house of Stephanas, that it is the firstfruits of Achaia, and *that* they have addicted themselves to the ministry of the saints,)

16 That ye submit yourselves unto such, and to every one that helpeth with *us*, and laboureth.

17 I am glad of the coming of Stephanas and Fortunatus and Achaicus: for that which was lacking on your part they have supplied.

18 For they have refreshed my spirit and yours: therefore acknowledge ye them that are such.

19 ¶ The churches of Asia salute you. Aquila and Priscilla salute you much in the Lord, with the church that is in their house.

20 All the brethren greet you. Greet ye one another with an holy kiss.

21 The salutation of *me* Paul with mine own hand.

22 If any man love not the Lord Jesus Christ, let him be Anathema Maran-atha.

23 The grace of our Lord Jesus Christ *be* with you.

24 My love *be* with you all in Christ Jesus. Amen.

¶ The first *epistle* to the Corinthians was written from Philippi by Stephanas and Fortunatus, and Achaicus and Timotheus.

THE SECOND EPISTLE OF PAUL THE APOSTLE TO THE

CORINTHIANS

1 Paul, an apostle of Jesus Christ by the will of God, and Timothy *our* brother, unto the church of God which is at Corinth, with all the saints which are in all Achaia:

2 Grace *be* to you and peace from God our Father, and *from* the Lord Jesus Christ.

3 ¶ Blessed *be* God, even the Father of our Lord Jesus Christ, the Father of mercies, and the God of all comfort;

4 Who comforteth us in all our tribulation, that we may be able to comfort them which are in any

trouble, by the comfort wherewith we ourselves are comforted of God.

5 For as the sufferings of Christ abound in us, so our consolation also aboundeth by Christ.

6 And whether we be afflicted, *it is* for your consolation and salvation, which is effectual in the enduring of the same sufferings which we also suffer: or whether we be comforted, *it is* for your consolation and salvation.

7 And our hope of you *is* stedfast, knowing, that as ye are partakers of the sufferings, so *shall ye be* also of the consolation.

8 For we would not, brethren, have you ignorant of our trouble which came to us in Asia, that we were pressed out of measure, above strength, insomuch that we despaired even of life:

9 But we had the sentence of death in ourselves, that we should not trust in ourselves, but in God which raiseth the dead:

10 Who delivered us from so great a death, and doth deliver: in whom we trust that he will yet deliver *us*;

11 Ye also helping together by prayer for us, that for the gift *bestowed* upon us by the means of many persons thanks may be given by many on our behalf.

12 ¶ For our rejoicing is this, the testimony of our conscience, that in simplicity and godly sincerity, not with fleshly wisdom, but by the grace of God, we have had our conversation in the world, and more abundantly to youward.

13 For we write none other things unto you, than what ye read or acknowledge; and I trust ye shall acknowledge even to the end;

14 As also ye have acknowledged us in part, that we are your rejoicing, even as ye also *are* ours in the day of the Lord Jesus.

15 And in this confidence I was minded to come unto you before, that ye might have a second benefit;

16 And to pass by you into Macedonia, and to come again out of Macedonia unto you, and of you to be brought on my way toward Judaea.

17 When I therefore was thus minded, did I use lightness? or the things that I purpose, do I purpose according to the flesh, that with me there should be yea yea, and nay nay?

18 But *as* God *is* true, our word toward you was not yea and nay.

19 For the Son of God, Jesus Christ, who was preached among you by us, *even* by me and Silvanus and Timotheus, was not yea and nay, but in him was yea.

20 For all the promises of God in him *are* yea, and in him Amen, unto the glory of God by us.

21 Now he which stablisheth us with you in Christ, and hath anointed us, *is* God;

22 Who hath also sealed us, and given the earnest of the Spirit in our hearts.

23 Moreover I call God for a record upon my soul, that to spare you I came not as yet unto

281

Corinth.

24 Not for that we have domination over your faith, but are helpers of your joy: for by faith ye stand.

2 But I determined this with myself, that I would not come again to you in heaviness.

2 For if I make you sorry, who is he then that maketh me glad, but the same which is made sorry by me?

3 And I wrote this same unto you, lest, when I came, I should have sorrow from them of whom I ought to rejoice; having confidence in you all, that my joy is *the joy* of you all.

4 For out of much affliction and anguish of heart I wrote unto you with many tears; not that ye should be grieved, but that ye might know the love which I have more abundantly unto you.

5 ❧ But if any have caused grief, he hath not grieved me, but in part: that I may not overcharge you all.

6 Sufficient to such a man is this punishment, which *was inflicted* of many.

7 So that contrariwise ye *ought* rather to forgive *him*, and comfort *him*, lest perhaps such a one should be swallowed up with overmuch sorrow.

8 Wherefore I beseech you that ye would confirm *your* love toward him.

9 For to this end also did I write, that I might know the proof of you, whether ye be obedient in all things.

10 To whom ye forgive any thing, I *forgive* also: for if I forgave any thing, to whom I forgave *it*, for your sakes *forgave I it* in the person of Christ;

11 Lest Satan should get an advantage of us: for we are not ignorant of his devices.

12 Furthermore, when I came to Troas to *preach* Christ's gospel, and a door was opened unto me of the Lord,

13 I had no rest in my spirit, because I found not Titus my brother: but taking my leave of them, I went from thence into Macedonia.

14 ❧ Now thanks *be* unto God, which always causeth us to triumph in Christ, and maketh manifest the savour of his knowledge by us in every place.

15 For we are unto God a sweet savour of Christ, in them that are saved, and in them that perish:

16 To the one *we are* the savour of death unto death; and to the other the savour of life unto life. And who *is* sufficient for these things?

17 For we are not as many, which corrupt the word of God: but as of sincerity, but as of God, in the sight of God speak we in Christ.

3 Do we begin again to commend ourselves? or need we, as some *others*, epistles of commendation to you, or *letters* of commendation from you?

2 Ye are our epistle written in our hearts, known and read of all men:

3 *Forasmuch* as *ye are* manifestly declared to be the epistle of Christ ministered by us, written not with ink, but with the Spirit of the living God; not in tables of stone, but in fleshy tables of the heart.

4 And such trust have we through Christ to God-ward:

5 Not that we are sufficient of ourselves to think any thing as of ourselves; but our sufficiency *is* of God;

6 ᶜWho also hath made us able ministers of the new testament; not of the letter, but of the spirit: for the letter killeth, but the spirit giveth life.

7 But if the ministration of death, written *and* engraven in stones, was glorious, so that the children of Israel could not stedfastly behold the face of Moses for the glory of his countenance; which *glory* was to be done away:

8 How shall not the ministration of the spirit be rather glorious?

9 For if the ministration of condemnation *be* glory, much more doth the ministration of righteousness exceed in glory.

10 For even that which was made glorious had no glory in this respect, by reason of the glory that excelleth.

11 For if that which is done away *was* glorious, much more that which remaineth *is* glorious.

12 Seeing then that we have such hope, we use great plainness of speech:

13 And not as Moses, *which* put a vail over his face, that the children of Israel could not stedfastly look to the end of that which is abolished:

14 But their minds were blinded: for until this day remaineth the same vail untaken away in the reading of the old testament; which *vail* is done away in Christ.

15 But even unto this day, when Moses is read, the vail is upon their heart.

16 Nevertheless when it shall turn to the Lord, the vail shall be taken away.

17 Now the Lord is that Spirit: and where the Spirit of the Lord *is*, there *is* liberty.

18 But we all, with open face beholding as in a glass the glory of the Lord, are changed into the same image from glory to glory, *even* as by the Spirit of the Lord.

4 Therefore seeing we have this ministry, as we have received mercy, we faint not;

2 But have renounced the hidden things of dishonesty, not walking in craftiness, nor handling the word of God deceitfully; but by manifestation of the truth commending ourselves to every man's conscience in the sight of God.

3 But if our gospel be hid, it is hid to them that are lost:

4 In whom the god of this world hath blinded the minds of them which believe not, lest the light of the glorious gospel of Christ, who is the image of God, should shine unto them.

283

5 For we preach not ourselves, but Christ Jesus the Lord; and ourselves your servants for Jesus' sake.

6 For God, who commanded the light to shine out of darkness, hath shined in our hearts, to *give* the light of the knowledge of the glory of God in the face of Jesus Christ.

7 But we have this treasure in earthen vessels, that the excellency of the power may be of God, and not of us.

8 *We are* troubled on every side, yet not distressed; *we are* perplexed, but not in despair;

9 Persecuted, but not forsaken; cast down, but not destroyed;

10 Always bearing about in the body the dying of the Lord Jesus, that the life also of Jesus might be made manifest in our body.

11 For we which live are alway delivered unto death for Jesus' sake, that the life also of Jesus might be made manifest in our mortal flesh.

12 So then death worketh in us, but life in you.

13 We having the same spirit of faith, according as it is written, I believed, and therefore have I spoken; we also believe, and therefore speak;

14 Knowing that he which raised up the Lord Jesus shall raise up us also by Jesus, and shall present *us* with you.

15 For all things *are* for your sakes, that the abundant grace might through the thanksgiving of many redound to the glory of God.

16 For which cause we faint not; but though our outward man perish, yet the inward *man* is renewed day by day.

17 For our light affliction, which is but for a moment, worketh for us a far more exceeding *and* eternal weight of glory;

18 While we look not at the things which are seen, but at the things which are not seen: for the things which are seen *are* temporal; but the things which are not seen *are* eternal.

5 For we know that if our earthly house of *this* tabernacle were dissolved, we have a building of God, an house not made with hands, eternal in the heavens.

2 For in this we groan, earnestly desiring to be clothed upon with our house which is from heaven:

3 If so be that being clothed we shall not be found naked.

4 For we that are in *this* tabernacle do groan, being burdened: not for that we would be unclothed, but clothed upon, that mortality might be swallowed up of life.

5 Now he that hath wrought us for the selfsame thing *is* God, who also hath given unto us the earnest of the Spirit.

6 Therefore *we are* always confident, knowing that, whilst we are at home in the body, we are absent from the Lord:

7 (For we walk by faith, not by sight:)

8 We are confident, *I say*, and

willing rather to be absent from the body, and to be present with the Lord.

9 ❡ Wherefore we labour, that, whether present or absent, we may be accepted of him.

10 For we must all appear before the judgment seat of Christ; that every one may receive the things *done* in *his* body, according to that he hath done, whether *it be* good or bad.

11 Knowing therefore the terror of the Lord, we persuade men; but we are made manifest unto God; and I trust also are made manifest in your consciences.

12 For we commend not ourselves again unto you, but give you occasion to glory on our behalf, that ye may have somewhat to *answer* them which glory in appearance, and not in heart.

13 For whether we be beside ourselves, *it is* to God: or whether we be sober, *it is* for your cause.

14 For the love of Christ constraineth us; because we thus judge, that if one died for all, then were all dead:

15 And *that* he died for all, that they which live should not henceforth live unto themselves, but unto him which died for them, and rose again.

16 Wherefore henceforth know we no man after the flesh: yea, though we have known Christ after the flesh, yet now henceforth know we him no more.

17 Therefore if any man *be* in Christ, *he is* a new creature: old things are passed away; behold,

all things are become new.

18 ❡ And all things *are* of God, who hath reconciled us to himself by Jesus Christ, and hath given to us the ministry of reconciliation;

19 To wit, that God was in Christ, reconciling the world unto himself, not imputing their trespasses unto them; and hath committed unto us the word of reconciliation.

20 Now then we are ambassadors for Christ, as though God did beseech *you* by us: we pray *you* in Christ's stead, be ye reconciled to God.

21 For he hath made him *to be* sin for us, who knew no sin; that we might be made the righteousness of God in him.

6 We then, *as* workers together *with him*, beseech *you* also that ye receive not the grace of God in vain.

2 (For he saith, I have heard thee in a time accepted, and in the day of salvation have I succoured thee: behold, now *is* the accepted time; behold, now *is* the day of salvation.)

3 Giving no offence in any thing, that the ministry be not blamed:

4 But in all *things* approving ourselves as the ministers of God, in much patience, in afflictions, in necessities, in distresses,

5 In stripes, in imprisonments, in tumults, in labours, in watchings, in fastings;

6 By pureness, by knowledge, by longsuffering, by kindness,

285

by the Holy Ghost, by love unfeigned,

7 By the word of truth, by the power of God, by the armour of righteousness on the right hand and on the left,

8 By honour and dishonour, by evil report and good report: as deceivers, and *yet* true;

9 As unknown, and *yet* well known; as dying, and, behold, we live; as chastened, and *not* killed;

10 As sorrowful, yet alway rejoicing; as poor, yet making many rich; as having nothing, and *yet* possessing all things.

11 O *ye* Corinthians, our mouth is open unto you, our heart is enlarged.

12 Ye are not straitened in us, but ye are straitened in your own bowels.

13 Now for a recompence in the same, (I speak as unto *my* children,) be ye also enlarged.

14 Be ye not unequally yoked together with unbelievers: for what fellowship hath righteousness with unrighteousness? and what communion hath light with darkness?

15 ¶ And what concord hath Christ with Belial? or what part hath he that believeth with an infidel?

16 And what agreement hath the temple of God with idols? for ye are the temple of the living God; as God hath said, I will dwell in them, and walk in *them*; and I will be their God, and they shall be my people.

17 Wherefore come out from among them, and be ye separate, saith the Lord, and touch not the unclean *thing*; and I will receive you.

18 And will be a Father unto you, and ye shall be my sons and daughters, saith the Lord Almighty.

7 Having therefore these promises, dearly beloved, let us cleanse ourselves from all filthiness of the flesh and spirit, perfecting holiness in the fear of God.

2 Receive us; we have wronged no man, we have corrupted no man, we have defrauded no man.

3 ¶ I speak not *this* to condemn *you*: for I have said before, that ye are in our hearts to die and live with *you*.

4 Great *is* my boldness of speech toward you, great *is* my glorying of you: I am filled with comfort, I am exceeding joyful in all our tribulation.

5 For, when we were come into Macedonia, our flesh had no rest, but we were troubled on every side; without *were* fightings, within *were* fears.

6 Nevertheless God, that comforteth those that are cast down, comforted us by the coming of Titus;

7 And not by his coming only, but by the consolation wherewith he was comforted in you, when he told us your earnest desire, your mourning, your fervent mind toward me; so that I rejoiced the more.

8 For though I made you sorry with a letter, I do not repent, though I did repent: for I perceive that the same epistle hath made you sorry, though *it were* but for a season.

9 ¶ Now I rejoice, not that ye were made sorry, but that ye sorrowed to repentance: for ye were made sorry after a godly manner, that ye might receive damage by us in nothing.

10 For godly sorrow worketh repentance to salvation not to be repented of: but the sorrow of the world worketh death.

11 For behold this selfsame thing, that ye sorrowed after a godly sort, what carefulness it wrought in you, yea, *what* clearing of yourselves, yea, *what* indignation, yea, *what* fear, yea, *what* vehement desire, yea, *what* zeal, yea, *what* revenge! In all *things* ye have approved yourselves to be clear in this matter.

12 Wherefore, though I wrote unto you, *I did it* not for his cause that had done the wrong, nor for his cause that suffered wrong, but that our care for you in the sight of God might appear unto you.

13 Therefore we were comforted in your comfort: yea, and exceedingly the more joyed we for the joy of Titus, because his spirit was refreshed by you all.

14 For if I have boasted any thing to him of you, I am not ashamed; but as we spake all things to you in truth, even so our boasting, which *I made* before Titus, is found a truth.

15 And his inward affection is more abundant toward you, whilst he remembereth the obedience of you all, how with fear and trembling ye received him.

16 I rejoice therefore that I have confidence in you in all *things.*

8 Moreover, brethren, we do you to wit of the grace of God bestowed on the churches of Macedonia;

2 How that in a great trial of affliction the abundance of their joy and their deep poverty abounded unto the riches of their liberality.

3 For to *their* power, I bear record, yea, and beyond *their* power *they were* willing of themselves;

4 Praying us with much intreaty that we would receive the gift, and *take upon us* the fellowship of the ministering to the saints.

5 And *this they did,* not as we hoped, but first gave their own selves to the Lord, and unto us by the will of God.

6 Insomuch that we desired Titus, that as he had begun, so he would also finish in you the same grace also.

7 Therefore, as ye abound in every *thing, in* faith, and utterance, and knowledge, and *in* all diligence, and *in* your love to us, *see* that ye abound in this grace also.

8 I speak not by commandment, but by occasion of the forwardness of others, and to prove the sincerity of your love.

9 For ye know the grace of our

Lord Jesus Christ, that, though he was rich, yet for your sakes he became poor, that ye through his poverty might be rich.

10 And herein I give *my* advice: for this is expedient for you, who have begun before, not only to do, but also to be forward a year ago.

11 Now therefore perform the doing of *it*; that as *there was* a readiness to will, so *there may be* a performance also out of that which ye have.

12 For if there be first a willing mind, *it is* accepted according to that a man hath, *and* not according to that he hath not.

13 For *I mean* not that other men be eased, and ye burdened:

14 But by an equality, *that* now at this time your abundance *may be a supply* for their want, that their abundance also may be *a supply* for your want: that there may be equality:

15 As it is written, He that *had gathered* much had nothing over; and he that *had gathered* little had no lack.

16 ¶ But thanks *be* to God, which put the same earnest care into the heart of Titus for you.

17 For indeed he accepted the exhortation; but being more forward, of his own accord he went unto you.

18 And we have sent with him the brother, whose praise *is* in the gospel throughout all the churches;

19 And not *that* only, but who was also chosen of the churches to travel with us with this grace, which is administered by us to the glory of the same Lord, and *declaration of* your ready mind:

20 Avoiding this, that no man should blame us in this abundance which is administered by us:

21 Providing for honest things, not only in the sight of the Lord, but also in the sight of men.

22 And we have sent with them our brother, whom we have oftentimes proved diligent in many things, but now much more diligent, upon the great confidence which *I have* in you.

23 Whether *any do enquire* of Titus, *he is* my partner and fellowhelper concerning you: or our brethren *be enquired of*, they are the messengers of the churches, *and* the glory of Christ.

24 Wherefore shew ye to them, and before the churches, the proof of your love, and of our boasting on your behalf.

9

For as touching the ministering to the saints, it is superfluous for me to write to you:

2 For I know the forwardness of your mind, for which I boast of you to them of Macedonia, that Achaia was ready a year ago; and your zeal hath provoked very many.

3 Yet have I sent the brethren, lest our boasting of you should be in vain in this behalf; that, as I said, ye may be ready:

4 Lest haply if they of Macedonia come with me, and find you unprepared, we (that we say not,

ye) should be ashamed in this same confident boasting.

5 Therefore I thought it necessary to exhort the brethren, that they would go before unto you, and make up beforehand your bounty, whereof ye had notice before, that the same might be ready, as *a matter of* bounty, and not as *of* covetousness.

6 But this I *say*, He which soweth sparingly shall reap also sparingly; and he which soweth bountifully shall reap also bountifully.

7 Every man according as he purposeth in his heart, *so let him give*; not grudgingly, or of necessity: for God loveth a cheerful giver.

8 And God *is* able to make all grace abound toward you; that ye, always having all sufficiency in all *things*, may abound to every good work:

9 (As it is written, He hath dispersed abroad; he hath given to the poor: his righteousness remaineth for ever.

10 Now he that ministereth seed to the sower both minister bread for *your* food, and multiply your seed sown, and increase the fruits of your righteousness;)

11 Being enriched in every thing to all bountifulness, which causeth through us thanksgiving to God.

12 For the administration of this service not only supplieth the want of the saints, but is abundant also by many thanksgivings unto God;

13 Whiles by the experiment of this ministration they glorify God for your professed subjection unto the gospel of Christ, and for *your* liberal distribution unto them, and unto all *men*;

14 And by their prayer for you, which long after you for the exceeding grace of God in you.

15 Thanks *be* unto God for his unspeakable gift.

10

Now I Paul myself beseech you by the meekness and gentleness of Christ, who in presence *am* base among you, but being absent am bold toward you:

2 But I beseech *you*, that I may not be bold when I am present with that confidence, wherewith I think to be bold against some, which think of us as if we walked according to the flesh.

3 For though we walk in the flesh, we do not war after the flesh:

4 (For the weapons of our warfare *are* not carnal, but mighty through God to the pulling down of strong holds;)

5 Casting down imaginations, and every high thing that exalteth itself against the knowledge of God, and bringing into captivity every thought to the obedience of Christ;

6 And having in a readiness to revenge all disobedience, when your obedience is fulfilled.

7 Do ye look on things after the outward appearance? If any man trust to himself that he is Christ's, let him of himself think this again, that, as he *is* Christ's,

even so *are* we Christ's.

8 For though I should boast somewhat more of our authority, which the Lord hath given us for edification, and not for your destruction, I should not be ashamed:

9 That I may not seem as if I would terrify you by letters.

10 For *his* letters, say they, *are* weighty and powerful; but *his* bodily presence *is* weak, and *his* speech contemptible.

11 Let such an one think this, that, such as we are in word by letters when we are absent, such *will we be* also in deed when we are present.

12 ¶ For we dare not make ourselves of the number, or compare ourselves with some that commend themselves: but they measuring themselves by themselves, and comparing themselves among themselves, are not wise.

13 But we will not boast of things without *our* measure, but according to the measure of the rule which God hath distributed to us, a measure to reach even unto you.

14 For we stretch not ourselves beyond *our measure*, as though we reached not unto you: for we are come as far as to you also in *preaching* the gospel of Christ:

15 Not boasting of things without *our* measure, *that is*, of other men's labours; but having hope, when your faith is increased, that we shall be enlarged by you according to our rule abundantly,

16 To preach the gospel in the *regions* beyond you, *and* not to boast in another man's line of things made ready to our hand.

17 But he that glorieth, let him glory in the Lord.

18 For not he that commendeth himself is approved, but whom the Lord commendeth.

11 Would to God ye could bear with me a little in *my* folly: and indeed bear with me.

2 For I am jealous over you with godly jealousy: for I have espoused you to one husband, that I may present *you as* a chaste virgin to Christ.

3 But I fear, lest by any means, as the serpent beguiled Eve through his subtilty, so your minds should be corrupted from the simplicity that is in Christ.

4 For if he that cometh preacheth another Jesus, whom we have not preached, or *if* ye receive another spirit, which ye have not received, or another gospel, which ye have not accepted, ye might well bear with *him*.

5 For I suppose I was not a whit behind the very chiefest apostles.

6 But though *I be* rude in speech, yet not in knowledge; but we have been throughly made manifest among you in all things.

7 Have I committed an offence in abasing myself that ye might be exalted, because I have preached to you the gospel of God freely?

8 I robbed other churches, taking wages *of them*, to do you service.

9 And when I was present with you, and wanted, I was chargeable to no man: for that which was lacking to me the brethren which came from Macedonia supplied: and in all *things* I have kept myself from being burdensome unto you, and *so* will I keep *myself*.

10 As the truth of Christ is in me, no man shall stop me of this boasting in the regions of Achaia.

11 Wherefore? because I love you not? God knoweth.

12 But what I do, that I will do, that I may cut off occasion from them which desire occasion; that wherein they glory, they may be found even as we.

13 For such *are* false apostles, deceitful workers, transforming themselves into the apostles of Christ.

14 And no marvel; for Satan himself is transformed into an angel of light.

15 Therefore *it is* no great thing if his ministers also be transformed as the ministers of righteousness; whose end shall be according to their works.

16 ¶ I say again, Let no man think me a fool; if otherwise, yet as a fool receive me, that I may boast myself a little.

17 That which I speak, I speak *it* not after the Lord, but as it were foolishly, in this confidence of boasting.

18 Seeing that many glory after the flesh, I will glory also.

19 For ye suffer fools gladly, seeing ye *yourselves* are wise.

20 For ye suffer, if a man bring you into bondage, if a man devour *you*, if a man take *of you*, if a man exalt himself, if a man smite you on the face.

21 I speak as concerning reproach, as though we had been weak. Howbeit whereinsoever any is bold, (I speak foolishly,) I am bold also.

22 Are they Hebrews? so *am* I. Are they Israelites? so *am* I. Are they the seed of Abraham? so *am* I.

23 ¶ Are they ministers of Christ? (I speak as a fool) I *am* more; in labours more abundant, in stripes above measure, in prisons more frequent, in deaths oft.

24 Of the Jews five times received I forty *stripes* save one.

25 Thrice was I beaten with rods, once was I stoned, thrice I suffered shipwreck, a night and a day I have been in the deep;

26 *In* journeyings often, in perils of waters, *in* perils of robbers, *in* perils by *mine own* countrymen, *in* perils by the heathen, *in* perils in the city, *in* perils in the wilderness, *in* perils in the sea, *in* perils among false brethren;

27 In weariness and painfulness, in watchings often, in hunger and thirst, in fastings often, in cold and nakedness.

28 Beside those things that are without, that which cometh upon me daily, the care of all the

churches.

29 Who is weak, and I am not weak? who is offended, and I burn not?

30 If I must needs glory, I will glory of the things which concern mine infirmities.

31 The God and Father of our Lord Jesus Christ, which is blessed for evermore, knoweth that I lie not.

32 In Damascus the governor under Aretas the king kept the city of the Damascenes with a garrison, desirous to apprehend me:

33 And through a window in a basket was I let down by the wall, and escaped his hands.

12

It is not expedient for me doubtless to glory. I will come to visions and revelations of the Lord.

2 I knew a man in Christ above fourteen years ago, (whether in the body, I cannot tell; or whether out of the body, I cannot tell: God knoweth;) such an one caught up to the third heaven.

3 And I knew such a man, (whether in the body, or out of the body, I cannot tell: God knoweth;)

4 How that he was caught up into paradise, and heard unspeakable words, which it is not lawful for a man to utter.

5 Of such an one will I glory: yet of myself I will not glory, but in mine infirmities.

6 For though I would desire to glory, I shall not be a fool; for I will say the truth: but *now* I forbear, lest any man should think of me above that which he seeth me *to be*, or *that* he heareth of me.

7 And lest I should be exalted above measure through the abundance of the revelations, there was given to me a thorn in the flesh, the messenger of Satan to buffet me, lest I should be exalted above measure.

8 For this thing I besought the Lord thrice, that it might depart from me.

9 (And he said unto me, My grace is sufficient for thee: for my strength is made perfect in weakness. Most gladly therefore will I rather glory in my infirmities, that the power of Christ may rest upon me.

10 Therefore I take pleasure in infirmities, in reproaches, in necessities, in persecutions, in distresses for Christ's sake: for when I am weak, then am I strong.

11 (I am become a fool in glorying; ye have compelled me: for I ought to have been commended of you: for in nothing am I behind the very chiefest apostles, though I be nothing.

12 Truly the signs of an apostle were wrought among you in all patience, in signs, and wonders, and mighty deeds.

13 For what is it wherein ye were inferior to other churches, except *it be* that I myself was not burdensome to you? forgive me this wrong.

14 Behold, the third time I am ready to come to you; and I will

292

not be burdensome to you: for I seek not yours, but you: for the children ought not to lay up for the parents, but the parents for the children.

15 And I will very gladly spend and be spent for you; though the more abundantly I love you, the less I be loved.

16 But be it so, I did not burden you: nevertheless, being crafty, I caught you with guile.

17 Did I make a gain of you by any of them whom I sent unto you?

18 I desired Titus, and with *him* I sent a brother. Did Titus make a gain of you? walked we not in the same spirit? *walked we* not in the same steps?

19 Again, think ye that we excuse ourselves unto you? we speak before God in Christ: but *we do* all things, dearly beloved, for your edifying.

20 For I fear, lest, when I come, I shall not find you such as I would, and *that* I shall be found unto you such as ye would not: lest *there be* debates, envyings, wraths, strifes, backbitings, whisperings, swellings, tumults:

21 *And* lest, when I come again, my God will humble me among you, and *that* I shall bewail many which have sinned already, and have not repented of the uncleanness and fornication and lasciviousness which they have committed.

13 This *is* the third *time* I am coming to you. In the mouth of two or three witnesses shall every word be established.

2 I told you before, and foretell you, as if I were present, the second time; and being absent now I write to them which heretofore have sinned, and to all other, that, if I come again, I will not spare:

3 Since ye seek a proof of Christ speaking in me, which to you-ward is not weak, but is mighty in you.

4 For though he was crucified through weakness, yet he liveth by the power of God. For we also are weak in him, but we shall live with him by the power of God to-ward you.

5 Examine yourselves, whether ye be in the faith; prove your own selves. Know ye not your own selves, how that Jesus Christ is in you, except ye be reprobates?

6 But I trust that ye shall know that we are not reprobates.

7 Now I pray to God that ye do no evil; not that we should appear approved, but that ye should do that which is honest, though we be as reprobates.

8 For we can do nothing against the truth, but for the truth.

9 For we are glad, when we are weak, and ye are strong: and this also we wish, *even* your perfection.

10 Therefore I write these things being absent, lest being present I should use sharpness, according to the power which the Lord hath given me to edification, and not to destruction.

11 ❡ Finally, brethren, farewell.

293

Be perfect, be of good comfort, be of one mind, live in peace; and the God of love and peace shall be with you.

12 Greet one another with a holy kiss.

13 All the saints salute you.

14 The grace of the Lord Jesus Christ, and the love of God, and the communion of the Holy Ghost, *be* with you all. Amen.

❡The second *epistle* to the Corinthians was written from Philippi, *a city of* Macedonia, by Titus and Lucas.

THE EPISTLE OF PAUL THE APOSTLE
TO THE

GALATIANS

1 Paul, an apostle, (not of men, neither by man, but by Jesus Christ, and God the Father, who raised him from the dead;)

2 And all the brethren which are with me, unto the churches of Galatia;

3 Grace *be* to you and peace from God the Father, and *from* our Lord Jesus Christ,

4 Who gave himself for our sins, that he might deliver us from this present evil world, according to the will of God and our Father:

5 To whom *be* glory for ever and ever. Amen.

6 ❡ I marvel that ye are so soon removed from him that called you into the grace of Christ unto another gospel:

7 Which is not another; but there be some that trouble you, and would pervert the gospel of Christ.

8 ❡ But though we, or an angel from heaven, preach any other gospel unto you than that which we have preached unto you, let him be accursed.

9 As we said before, so say I now again, If any *man* preach any other gospel unto you than that ye have received, let him be accursed.

10 For do I now persuade men, or God? or do I seek to please men? for if I yet pleased men, I should not be the servant of Christ.

11 But I certify you, brethren, that the gospel which was preached of me is not after man.

12 For I neither received it of man, neither was I taught *it*, but by the revelation of Jesus Christ.

13 For ye have heard of my conversation in time past in the Jews' religion, how that beyond measure I persecuted the church of God, and wasted it:

14 And profited in the Jews' religion above many my equals in mine own nation, being more exceedingly zealous of the traditions of my fathers.

15 But when it pleased God, who separated me from my mother's womb, and called *me* by his grace,

16 To reveal his Son in me, that I might preach him among the heathen; immediately I conferred not with flesh and blood:

17 Neither went I up to Jerusalem to them which were apostles before me; but I went into Arabia, and returned again unto Damascus.

18 Then after three years I went up to Jerusalem to see Peter, and abode with him fifteen days.

19 But other of the apostles saw I none, save James the Lord's brother.

20 Now the things which I write unto you, behold, before God, I lie not.

21 Afterwards I came into the regions of Syria and Cilicia;

22 And was unknown by face unto the churches of Judaea which were in Christ:

23 But they had heard only, That he which persecuted us in times past now preacheth the faith which once he destroyed.

24 And they glorified God in me.

2 Then fourteen years after I went up again to Jerusalem with Barnabas, and took Titus with *me* also.

2 And I went up by revelation, and communicated unto them that gospel which I preach among the Gentiles, but privately to them which were of reputation, lest by any means I should run, or had run, in vain.

3 But neither Titus, who was with me, being a Greek, was compelled to be circumcised:

4 And that because of false brethren unawares brought in, who came in privily to spy out our liberty which we have in Christ Jesus, that they might bring us into bondage:

5 To whom we gave place by subjection, no, not for an hour; that the truth of the gospel might continue with you.

6 But of these who seemed to be somewhat, (whatsoever they were, it maketh no matter to me: God accepteth no man's person:) for they who seemed *to be somewhat* in conference added nothing to me:

7 But contrariwise, when they saw that the gospel of the uncircumcision was committed unto me, as *the gospel* of the circumcision *was* unto Peter;

8 (For he that wrought effectually in Peter to the apostleship of the circumcision, the same was mighty in me toward the Gentiles:)

9 And when James, Cephas, and John, who seemed to be pillars, perceived the grace that was given unto me, they gave to me and Barnabas the right hands of fellowship; that we *should go* unto the heathen, and they unto the circumcision.

10 Only *they would* that we should remember the poor; the same which I also was forward to do.

11 But when Peter was come

to Antioch, I withstood him to the face, because he was to be blamed.

12 For before that certain came from James, he did eat with the Gentiles: but when they were come, he withdrew and separated himself, fearing them which were of the circumcision.

13 And the other Jews dissembled likewise with him; insomuch that Barnabas also was carried away with their dissimulation.

14 But when I saw that they walked not uprightly according to the truth of the gospel, I said unto Peter before *them* all, If thou, being a Jew, livest after the manner of Gentiles, and not as do the Jews, why compellest thou the Gentiles to live as do the Jews?

15 ¶ We *who are* Jews by nature, and not sinners of the Gentiles,

16 Knowing that a man is not justified by the works of the law, but by the faith of Jesus Christ, even we have believed in Jesus Christ, that we might be justified by the faith of Christ, and not by the works of the law: for by the works of the law shall no flesh be justified.

17 But if, while we seek to be justified by Christ, we ourselves also are found sinners, *is* therefore Christ the minister of sin? God forbid.

18 For if I build again the things which I destroyed, I make myself a transgressor.

19 For I through the law am dead to the law, that I might live

unto God.

20 I am crucified with Christ: nevertheless I live; yet not I, but Christ liveth in me: and the life which I now live in the flesh I live by the faith of the Son of God, who loved me, and gave himself for me.

21 I do not frustrate the grace of God: for if righteousness *come* by the law, then Christ is dead in vain.

3 O foolish Galatians, who hath bewitched you, that ye should not obey the truth, before whose eyes Jesus Christ hath been evidently set forth, crucified among you?

2 This only would I learn of you, Received ye the Spirit by the works of the law, or by the hearing of faith?

3 Are ye so foolish? having begun in the Spirit, are ye now made perfect by the flesh?

4 Have ye suffered so many things in vain? if *it be* yet in vain.

5 He therefore that ministereth to you the Spirit, and worketh miracles among you, *doeth he it* by the works of the law, or by the hearing of faith?

6 Even as Abraham believed God, and it was accounted to him for righteousness.

7 Know ye therefore that they which are of faith, the same are the children of Abraham.

8 And the scripture, foreseeing that God would justify the heathen through faith, preached before the gospel unto Abraham,

saying, In thee shall all nations be blessed.

9 So then they which be of faith are blessed with faithful Abraham.

10 For as many as are of the works of the law are under the curse: for it is written, Cursed *is* every one that continueth not in all things which are written in the book of the law to do them.

11 But that no man is justified by the law in the sight of God, *it is* evident: for, The just shall live by faith.

12 And the law is not of faith: but, The man that doeth them shall live in them.

13 Christ hath redeemed us from the curse of the law, being made a curse for us: for it is written, Cursed *is* every one that hangeth on a tree:

14 That the blessing of Abraham might come on the Gentiles through Jesus Christ; that we might receive the promise of the Spirit through faith.

15 Brethren, I speak after the manner of men; Though *it be* but a man's covenant, yet *if it be* confirmed, no man disannulleth, or addeth thereto.

16 Now to Abraham and his seed were the promises made. He saith not, And to seeds, as of many; but as of one, And to thy seed, which is Christ.

17 And this I say, *that* the covenant, that was confirmed before of God in Christ, the law, which was four hundred and thirty years after, cannot disannul, that it should make the promise of none effect.

18 For if the inheritance *be* of the law, *it is* no more of promise: but God gave *it* to Abraham by promise.

19 Wherefore then **serveth** the law? It was added because of transgressions, till the seed should come to whom the promise was made; *and it was* ordained by angels in the hand of a mediator.

20 Now a mediator is not *a mediator* of one, but God is one.

21 *Is* the law then against the promises of God? God forbid: for if there had been a law given which could have given life, verily righteousness should have been by the law.

22 But the scripture hath concluded all under sin, that the promise by faith of Jesus Christ might be given to them that believe.

23 But before faith came, we were kept under the law, shut up unto the faith which should afterwards be revealed.

24 Wherefore the law was our schoolmaster *to bring us* unto Christ, that we might be justified by faith.

25 But after that faith is come, we are no longer under a schoolmaster.

26 For ye are all the children of God by faith in Christ Jesus.

27 For as many of you as have been baptized into Christ have put on Christ.

28 There is neither Jew nor Greek, there is neither bond nor

297

free, there is neither male nor female: for ye are all one in Christ Jesus.

29 And if ye *be* Christ's, then are ye Abraham's seed, and heirs according to the promise.

4 Now I say, *That* the heir, as long as he is a child, differeth nothing from a servant, though he be lord of all;

2 But is under tutors and governors until the time appointed of the father.

3 Even so we, when we were children, were in bondage under the elements of the world:

4 But when the fulness of the time was come, God sent forth his Son, made of a woman, made under the law,

5 To redeem them that were under the law, that we might receive the adoption of sons.

6 And because ye are sons, God hath sent forth the Spirit of his Son into your hearts, crying, Abba, Father.

7 Wherefore thou art no more a servant, but a son; and if a son, then an heir of God through Christ.

8 Howbeit then, when ye knew not God, ye did service unto them which by nature are no gods.

9 But now, after that ye have known God, or rather are known of God, how turn ye again to the weak and beggarly elements, whereunto ye desire again to be in bondage?

10 Ye observe days, and months, and times, and years.

11 I am afraid of you, lest I have bestowed upon you labour in vain.

12 Brethren, I beseech you, be as I *am*; for I *am* as ye *are*: ye have not injured me at all.

13 Ye know how through infirmity of the flesh I preached the gospel unto you at the first.

14 And my temptation which was in my flesh ye despised not, nor rejected; but received me as an angel of God, *even* as Christ Jesus.

15 Where is then the blessedness ye spake of? for I bear you record, that, if *it had been* possible, ye would have plucked out your own eyes, and have given them to me.

16 Am I therefore become your enemy, because I tell you the truth?

17 They zealously affect you, *but* not well; yea, they would exclude you, that ye might affect them.

18 But *it is* good to be zealously affected always in *a good thing*, and not only when I am present with you.

19 My little children, of whom I travail in birth again until Christ be formed in you,

20 I desire to be present with you now, and to change my voice; for I stand in doubt of you.

21 Tell me, ye that desire to be under the law, do ye not hear the law?

22 ❡ For it is written, that Abraham had two sons, the one by a bondmaid, the other by a freewoman.

23 But he *who was* of the bondwoman was born after the flesh; but he of the freewoman *was* by promise.

24 Which things are an allegory: for these are the two covenants; the one from the mount Sinai, which gendereth to bondage, which is Agar.

25 For this Agar is mount Sinai in Arabia, and answereth to Jerusalem which now is, and is in bondage with her children.

26 But Jerusalem which is above is free, which is the mother of us all.

27 For it is written, Rejoice, *thou* barren; thou bearest not; break forth and cry, thou that travailest not: for the desolate hath many more children than she which hath an husband.

28 Now we, brethren, as Isaac was, are the children of promise.

29 But as then he that was born after the flesh persecuted him *that was born* after the Spirit, even so *it is* now.

30 Nevertheless what saith the scripture? Cast out the bondwoman and her son: for the son of the bondwoman shall not be heir with the son of the freewoman.

31 So then, brethren, we are not children of the bondwoman, but of the free.

5 Stand fast therefore in the liberty wherewith Christ hath made us free, and be not entangled again with the yoke of bondage.

2 Behold, I Paul say unto you, that if ye be circumcised, Christ shall profit you nothing.

3 For I testify again to every man that is circumcised, that he is a debtor to do the whole law.

4 Christ is become of no effect unto you, whosoever of you are justified by the law; ye are fallen from grace.

5 For we through the Spirit wait for the hope of righteousness by faith.

6 For in Jesus Christ neither circumcision availeth any thing, nor uncircumcision; but faith which worketh by love.

7 Ye did run well; who did hinder you that ye should not obey the truth?

8 This persuasion *cometh* not of him that calleth you.

9 A little leaven leaveneth the whole lump.

10 I have confidence in you through the Lord, that ye will be none otherwise minded: but he that troubleth you shall bear his judgment, whosoever he be.

11 And I, brethren, if I yet preach circumcision, why do I yet suffer persecution? then is the offence of the cross ceased.

12 I would they were even cut off which trouble you.

13 For, brethren, ye have been called unto liberty; only *use* not liberty for an occasion to the flesh, but by love serve one another.

14 For all the law is fulfilled in one word, *even* in this; Thou shalt love thy neighbour as thyself.

15 But if ye bite and devour one another, take heed that ye be not consumed one of another.

16 *This* I say then, Walk in the Spirit, and ye shall not fulfil the lust of the flesh.

17 For the flesh lusteth against the Spirit, and the Spirit against the flesh: and these are contrary the one to the other: so that ye cannot do the things that ye would.

18 But if ye be led of the Spirit, ye are not under the law.

19 ¶ Now the works of the flesh are manifest, which are *these*; Adultery, fornication, uncleanness, lasciviousness,

20 Idolatry, witchcraft, hatred, variance, emulations, wrath, strife, seditions, heresies,

21 Envyings, murders, drunkenness, revellings, and such like: of the which I tell you before, as I have also told *you* in time past, that they which do such things shall not inherit the kingdom of God.

22 ¶ But the fruit of the Spirit is love, joy, peace, longsuffering, gentleness, goodness, faith,

23 Meekness, temperance : against such there is no law.

24 And they that are Christ's have crucified the flesh with the affections and lusts.

25 If we live in the Spirit, let us also walk in the Spirit.

26 Let us not be desirous of vain glory, provoking one another, envying one another.

6 Brethren, if a man be overtaken in a fault, ye which

are spiritual, restore such an one in the spirit of meekness; considering thyself, lest thou also be tempted.

2 Bear ye one another's burdens, and so fulfil the law of Christ.

3 For if a man think himself to be something, when he is nothing, he deceiveth himself.

4 But let every man prove his own work, and then shall he have rejoicing in himself alone, and not in another.

5 For every man shall bear his own burden.

6 ¶ Let him that is taught in the word communicate unto him that teacheth in all good things.

7 Be not deceived; God is not mocked: for whatsoever a man soweth, that shall he also reap.

8 For he that soweth to his flesh shall of the flesh reap corruption; but he that soweth to the Spirit shall of the Spirit reap life everlasting.

9 And let us not be weary in well doing: for in due season we shall reap, if we faint not.

10 As we have therefore opportunity, let us do good unto all *men*, especially unto them who are of the household of faith.

11 ¶ Ye see how large a letter I have written unto you with mine own hand.

12 As many as desire to make a fair shew in the flesh, they constrain you to be circumcised; only lest they should suffer persecution for the cross of Christ.

13 For neither they themselves

who are circumcised keep the law; but desire to have you circumcised, that they may glory in your flesh.

14 But God forbid that I should glory, save in the cross of our Lord Jesus Christ, by whom the world is crucified unto me, and I unto the world.

15 For in Christ Jesus neither circumcision availeth any thing, nor uncircumcision, but a new creature.

16 And as many as walk according to this rule, peace *be* on them, and mercy, and upon the Israel of God.

17 From henceforth let no man trouble me: for I bear in my body the marks of the Lord Jesus.

18 Brethren, the grace of our Lord Jesus Christ *be* with your spirit. Amen.

¶ Unto the Galatians written from Rome.

THE EPISTLE OF PAUL THE APOSTLE TO THE

EPHESIANS

1 Paul, an apostle of Jesus Christ by the will of God, to the saints which are at Ephesus, and to the faithful in Christ Jesus:

2 Grace *be* to you, and peace, from God our Father, and *from* the Lord Jesus Christ.

3 Blessed *be* the God and Father of our Lord Jesus Christ, who hath blessed us with all spiritual blessings in heavenly *places* in Christ:

4 According as he hath chosen us in him before the foundation of the world, that we should be holy and without blame before him in love:

5 Having predestinated us unto the adoption of children by Jesus Christ to himself, according to the good pleasure of his will,

6 ¶ To the praise of the glory of his grace, wherein he hath made us accepted in the beloved.

7 In whom we have redemption through his blood, the forgiveness of sins, according to the riches of his grace;

8 Wherein he hath abounded toward us in all wisdom and prudence;

9 Having made known unto us the mystery of his will, according to his good pleasure which he hath purposed in himself:

10 That in the dispensation of the fulness of times he might gather together in one all things in Christ, both which are in heaven, and which are on earth; *even* in him:

11 In whom also we have obtained an inheritance, being predestinated according to the purpose of him who worketh all things after the counsel of his own will:

301

12 That we should be to the praise of his glory, who first trusted in Christ.

13 In whom ye also *trusted*, after that ye heard the word of truth, the gospel of your salvation: in whom also after that ye believed, ye were sealed with that holy Spirit of promise,

14 Which is the earnest of our inheritance until the redemption of the purchased possession, unto the praise of his glory.

15 ¶ Wherefore I also, after I heard of your faith in the Lord Jesus, and love unto all the saints,

16 Cease not to give thanks for you, making mention of you in my prayers;

17 That the God of our Lord Jesus Christ, the Father of glory, may give unto you the spirit of wisdom and revelation in the knowledge of him:

18 The eyes of your understanding being enlightened; that ye may know what is the hope of his calling, and what the riches of the glory of his inheritance in the saints,

19 And what *is* the exceeding greatness of his power to us-ward who believe, according to the working of his mighty power,

20 Which he wrought in Christ, when he raised him from the dead, and set *him* at his own right hand in the heavenly *places*,

21 ¶ Far above all principality, and power, and might, and dominion, and every name that is named, not only in this world, but also in that which is to come:

22 And hath put all *things* under his feet, and gave him *to be* the head over all *things* to the church,

23 Which is his body, the fulness of him that filleth all in all.

2 And you *hath he quickened*, who were dead in trespasses and sins;

2 Wherein in time past ye walked according to the course of this world, according to the prince of the power of the air, the spirit that now worketh in the children of disobedience:

3 Among whom also we all had our conversation in times past in the lusts of our flesh, fulfilling the desires of the flesh and of the mind; and were by nature the children of wrath, even as others.

4 But God, who is rich in mercy, for his great love wherewith he loved us,

5 Even when we were dead in sins, hath quickened us together with Christ, (by grace ye are saved;)

6 And hath raised *us* up together, and made *us* sit together in heavenly *places* in Christ Jesus:

7 That in the ages to come he might shew the exceeding riches of his grace, in *his* kindness toward us through Christ Jesus.

8 For by grace are ye saved through faith; and that not of yourselves: *it is* the gift of God:

9 Not of works, lest any man should boast.

10 For we are his workmanship, created in Christ Jesus unto good

works, which God hath before ordained that we should walk in them.

11 Wherefore remember, that ye *being* in time past Gentiles in the flesh, who are called Uncircumcision by that which is called the Circumcision in the flesh made by hands;

12 That at that time ye were without Christ, being aliens from the commonwealth of Israel, and strangers from the covenants of promise, having no hope, and without God in the world:

13 But now in Christ Jesus ye who sometimes were far off are made nigh by the blood of Christ.

14 For he is our peace, who hath made both one, and hath broken down the middle wall of partition *between us*;

15 Having abolished in his flesh the enmity, *even* the law of commandments *contained* in ordinances; for to make in himself of twain one new man, *so* making peace;

16 And that he might reconcile both unto God in one body by the cross, having slain the enmity thereby:

17 And came and preached peace to you which were afar off, and to them that were nigh.

18 For through him we both have access by one Spirit unto the Father.

19 Now therefore ye are no more strangers and foreigners, but fellowcitizens with the saints, and of the household of God;

20 And are built upon the foundation of the apostles and prophets, Jesus Christ himself being the chief corner *stone*;

21 In whom all the building fitly framed together groweth unto an holy temple in the Lord:

22 In whom ye also are builded together for an habitation of God through the Spirit.

3 For this cause I Paul, the prisoner of Jesus Christ for you Gentiles,

2 If ye have heard of the dispensation of the grace of God which is given me to you-ward:

3 How that by revelation he made known unto me the mystery; (as I wrote afore in few words,

4 Whereby, when ye read, ye may understand my knowledge in the mystery of Christ)

5 Which in other ages was not made known unto the sons of men, as it is now revealed unto his holy apostles and prophets by the Spirit;

6 That the Gentiles should be fellowheirs, and of the same body, and partakers of his promise in Christ by the gospel:

7 Whereof I was made a minister, according to the gift of the grace of God given unto me by the effectual working of his power.

8 Unto me, who am less than the least of all saints, is this grace given, that I should preach among the Gentiles the unsearchable riches of Christ;

9 And to make all *men* see what

is the fellowship of the mystery, which from the beginning of the world hath been hid in God, who created all things by Jesus Christ:

10 To the intent that now unto the principalities and powers in heavenly *places* might be known by the church the manifold wisdom of God,

11 According to the eternal purpose which he purposed in Christ Jesus our Lord:

12 In whom we have boldness and access with confidence by the faith of him.

13 Wherefore I desire that ye faint not at my tribulations for you, which is your glory.

14 For this cause I bow my knees unto the Father of our Lord Jesus Christ,

15 Of whom the whole family in heaven and earth is named,

16 That he would grant you, according to the riches of his glory, to be strengthened with might by his Spirit in the inner man;

17 That Christ may dwell in your hearts by faith; that ye, being rooted and grounded in love,

18 May be able to comprehend with all saints what *is* the breadth, and length, and depth, and height;

19 And to know the love of Christ, which passeth knowledge, that ye might be filled with all the fulness of God.

20 Now unto him that is able to do exceeding abundantly above all that we ask or think, according to the power that worketh in us,

21 Unto him *be* glory in the church by Christ Jesus throughout all ages, world without end. Amen.

4

I therefore, the prisoner of the Lord, beseech you that ye walk worthy of the vocation wherewith ye are called,

2 With all lowliness and meekness, with longsuffering, forbearing one another in love;

3 Endeavouring to keep the unity of the Spirit in the bond of peace.

4 *There is* one body, and one Spirit, even as ye are called in one hope of your calling;

5 One Lord, one faith, one baptism,

6 One God and Father of all, who *is* above all, and through all, and in you all.

7 But unto every one of us is given grace according to the measure of the gift of Christ.

8 Wherefore he saith, When he ascended up on high, he led captivity captive, and gave gifts unto men.

9 (Now that he ascended, what is it but that he also descended first into the lower parts of the earth?

10 He that descended is the same also that ascended up far above all heavens, that he might fill all things.)

11 And he gave some, apostles; and some, prophets; and some, evangelists; and some, pastors and teachers;

12 For the perfecting of the

saints, for the work of the ministry, for the edifying of the body of Christ:

13 Till we all come in the unity of the faith, and of the knowledge of the Son of God, unto a perfect man, unto the measure of the stature of the fulness of Christ:

14 That we *henceforth* be no more children, tossed to and fro, and carried about with every wind of doctrine, by the sleight of men, *and* cunning craftiness, whereby they lie in wait to deceive;

15 But ‚speaking the truth in love, may grow up into him in all things, which is the head, *even* Christ:

16 From whom the whole body fitly joined together and compacted by that which every joint supplieth, according to the effectual working in the measure of every part, maketh increase of the body unto the edifying of itself in love.

17 ¶ This I say therefore, and testify in the Lord, that ye henceforth walk not as other Gentiles walk, in the vanity of their mind,

18 Having the understanding darkened, being alienated from the life of God through the ignorance that is in them, because of the blindness of their heart:

19 Who being past feeling have given themselves over unto lasciviousness, to work all uncleanness with greediness.

20 But ye have not so learned Christ;

21 If so be that ye have heard him, and have been taught by him, as the truth is in Jesus:

22 That ye put off concerning the former conversation the old man, which is corrupt according to the deceitful lusts;

23 And be renewed in the spirit of your mind;

24 And that ye put on the new man, which after God is created in righteousness and true holiness.

25 ¶ Wherefore putting away lying, speak every man truth with his neighbour: for we are members one of another.

26 Be ye angry, and sin not: let not the sun go down upon your wrath:

27 Neither give place to the devil.

28 Let him that stole steal no more: but rather let him labour, working with *his* hands the thing which is good, that he may have to give to him that needeth.

29 Let no corrupt communication proceed out of your mouth, but that which is good to the use of edifying, that it may minister grace unto the hearers.

30 And grieve not the holy Spirit of God, whereby ye are sealed unto the day of redemption.

31 Let all bitterness, and wrath, and anger, and clamour, and evil speaking, be put away from you, with all malice:

32 And be ye kind one to another, tenderhearted, forgiving one another, even as God for Christ's sake hath forgiven you.

5 Be ye therefore followers of God, *as* dear children;

2 And walk in love, as Christ also hath loved us, and hath given himself for us an offering and a sacrifice to God for a sweetsmelling savour.

3 ¶ But fornication, and all uncleanness, or covetousness, let it not be once named among you, as becometh saints;

4 Neither filthiness, nor foolish talking, nor jesting, which are not convenient: but rather giving of thanks.

5 For this ye know, that no whoremonger, nor unclean person, nor covetous man, who is an idolater, hath any inheritance in the kingdom of Christ and of God.

6 Let no man deceive you with vain words: for because of these things cometh the wrath of God upon the children of disobedience.

7 Be not ye therefore partakers with them.

8 For ye were sometimes darkness, but now *are ye* light in the Lord: walk as children of light:

9 (For the fruit of the Spirit *is* in all goodness and righteousness and truth;)

10 Proving what is acceptable unto the Lord.

11 And have no fellowship with the unfruitful works of darkness, but rather reprove *them*.

12 For it is a shame even to speak of those things which are done of them in secret.

13 But all things that are re-proved are made manifest by the light: for whatsoever doth make manifest is light.

14 Wherefore he saith, Awake thou that sleepest, and arise from the dead, and Christ shall give thee light.

15 ¶ See then that ye walk circumspectly, not as fools, but as wise,

16 Redeeming the time, because the days are evil.

17 Wherefore be ye not unwise, but understanding what the will of the Lord *is*.

18 ¶ And be not drunk with wine, wherein is excess; but be filled with the Spirit;

19 Speaking to yourselves in psalms and hymns and spiritual songs, singing and making melody in your heart to the Lord;

20 Giving thanks always for all things unto God and the Father in the name of our Lord Jesus Christ;

21 Submitting yourselves one to another in the fear of God.

22 ¶ Wives, submit yourselves unto your own husbands, as unto the Lord.

23 For the husband is the head of the wife, even as Christ is the head of the church: and he is the saviour of the body.

24 Therefore as the church is subject unto Christ, so *let* the wives *be* to their own husbands in every thing.

25 Husbands, love your wives, even as Christ also loved the church, and gave himself for it;

26 That he might sanctify and

306

cleanse it with the washing of water by the word,

27 That he might present it to himself a glorious church, not having spot, or wrinkle, or any such thing; but that it should be holy and without blemish.

28 So ought men to love their wives as their own bodies. He that loveth his wife loveth himself.

29 For no man ever yet hated his own flesh; but nourisheth and cherisheth it, even as the Lord the church:

30 For we are members of his body, of his flesh, and of his bones.

31 For this cause shall a man leave his father and mother, and shall be joined unto his wife, and they two shall be one flesh.

32 This is a great mystery: but I speak concerning Christ and the church.

33 Nevertheless let every one of you in particular so love his wife even as himself; and the wife see that she reverence her husband.

6 Children, obey your parents in the Lord: for this is right.

2 Honour thy father and mother; which is the first commandment with promise;

3 That it may be well with thee, and thou mayest live long on the earth.

4 And, ye fathers, provoke not your children to wrath: but bring them up in the nurture and admonition of the Lord.

5 ¶Servants, be obedient to them

that are your masters according to the flesh, with fear and trembling, in singleness of your heart, as unto Christ;

6 Not with eyeservice, as menpleasers; but as the servants of Christ, doing the will of God from the heart;

7 With good will doing service, as to the Lord, and not to men:

8 Knowing that whatsoever good thing any man doeth, the same shall he receive of the Lord, whether he be bond or free.

9 And, ye masters, do the same things unto them, forbearing threatening: knowing that your Master also is in heaven; neither is there respect of persons with him.

10 ¶ Finally, my brethren, be strong in the Lord, and in the power of his might.

11 Put on the whole armour of God, that ye may be able to stand against the wiles of the devil.

12 For we wrestle not against flesh and blood, but against principalities, against powers, against the rulers of the darkness of this world, against spiritual wickedness in high places.

13 Wherefore take unto you the whole armour of God, that ye may be able to withstand in the evil day, and having done all, to stand.

14 Stand therefore, having your loins girt about with truth, and having on the breastplate of righteousness;

15 And your feet shod with the preparation of the gospel of

peace:

16 Above all, taking the shield of faith, wherewith ye shall be able to quench all the fiery darts of the wicked.

17 And take the helmet of salvation, and the sword of the Spirit, which is the word of God:

18 Praying always with all prayer and supplication in the Spirit, and watching thereunto with all perseverance and supplication for all saints;

19 And for me, that utterance may be given unto me, that I may open my mouth boldly, to make known the mystery of the gospel,

20 For which I am an ambassador in bonds: that therein I may speak boldly, as I ought to speak.

21 But that ye also may know my affairs, *and* how I do, Tychicus, a beloved brother and faithful minister in the Lord, shall make known to you all things:

22 Whom I have sent unto you for the same purpose, that ye might know our affairs, and *that* he might comfort your hearts.

23 Peace *be* to the brethren, and love with faith, from God the Father and the Lord Jesus Christ.

24 Grace *be* with all them that love our Lord Jesus Christ in sincerity. Amen.

C Written from Rome unto the Ephesians by Tychicus.

THE EPISTLE OF PAUL THE APOSTLE
TO THE

PHILIPPIANS

1 Paul and Timotheus, the servants of Jesus Christ, to all the saints in Christ Jesus which are at Philippi, with the bishops and deacons:

2 Grace *be* unto you, and peace, from God our Father, and *from* the Lord Jesus Christ.

3 C I thank my God upon every remembrance of you,

4 Always in every prayer of mine for you all making request with joy,

5 For your fellowship in the gospel from the first day until now;

6 Being confident of this very thing, that he which hath begun a good work in you will perform *it* until the day of Jesus Christ:

7 Even as it is meet for me to think this of you all, because I have you in my heart; inasmuch as both in my bonds, and in the defence and confirmation of the gospel, ye all are partakers of my grace.

8 For God is my record, how greatly I long after you all in the bowels of Jesus Christ.

9 And this I pray, that your love may abound yet more and more

in knowledge and *in* all judgment;

10 That ye may approve things that are excellent; that ye may be sincere and without offence till the day of Christ.

11 Being filled with the fruits of righteousness, which are by Jesus Christ, unto the glory and praise of God.

12 But I would ye should understand, brethren, that the things *which happened* unto me have fallen out rather unto the furtherance of the gospel;

13 So that my bonds in Christ are manifest in all the palace, and in all other *places*;

14 And many of the brethren in the Lord, waxing confident by my bonds, are much more bold to speak the word without fear.

15 Some indeed preach Christ even of envy and strife; and some also of good will:

16 The one preach Christ of contention, not sincerely, supposing to add affliction to my bonds:

17 But the other of love, knowing that I am set for the defence of the gospel.

18 What then? notwithstanding, every way, whether in pretence, or in truth, Christ is preached; and I therein do rejoice, yea, and will rejoice.

19 For I know that this shall turn to my salvation through your prayer, and the supply of the Spirit of Jesus Christ,

20 According to my earnest expectation and *my* hope, that in

nothing I shall be ashamed, but *that* with all boldness, as always, *so* now also Christ shall be magnified in my body, whether *it be* by life, or by death.

21 ¶For to me to live *is* Christ, and to die *is* gain.

22 But if I live in the flesh, this *is* the fruit of my labour: yet what I shall choose I wot not.

23 For I am in a strait betwixt two, having a desire to depart, and to be with Christ; which is far better:

24 Nevertheless to abide in the flesh *is* more needful for you.

25 And having this confidence, I know that I shall abide and continue with you all for your furtherance and joy of faith;

26 That your rejoicing may be more abundant in Jesus Christ for me by my coming to you again.

27 Only let your conversation be as it becometh the gospel of Christ: that whether I come and see you, or else be absent, I may hear of your affairs, that ye stand fast in one spirit, with one mind striving together for the faith of the gospel;

28 And in nothing terrified by your adversaries: which is to them an evident token of perdition, but to you of salvation, and that of God.

29 For unto you it is given in the behalf of Christ, not only to believe on him, but also to suffer for his sake;

30 Having the same conflict which ye saw in me, and now

hear *to be* in me.

2 If *there be* therefore any consolation in Christ, if any comfort of love, if any fellowship of the Spirit, if any bowels and mercies,

2 Fulfil ye my joy, that ye be likeminded, having the same love, *being* of one accord, of one mind.

3 *Let* nothing *be done* through strife or vainglory; but in lowliness of mind let each esteem other better than themselves.

4 Look not every man on his own things, but every man also on the things of others.

5 Let this mind be in you, which was also in Christ Jesus:

6 Who, being in the form of God, thought it not robbery to be equal with God:

7 But made himself of no reputation, and took upon him the form of a servant, and was made in the likeness of men:

8 And being found in fashion as a man, he humbled himself, and became obedient unto death, even the death of the cross.

9 Wherefore God also hath highly exalted him, and given him a name which is above every name:

10 That at the name of Jesus every knee should bow, of *things* in heaven, and *things* in earth, and *things* under the earth;

11 And *that* every tongue should confess that Jesus Christ *is* Lord, to the glory of God the Father.

12 Wherefore, my beloved, as ye have always obeyed, not as in my presence only, but now much more in my absence, work out your own salvation with fear and trembling.

13 For it is God which worketh in you both to will and to do of *his* good pleasure.

14 Do all things without murmurings and disputings:

15 That ye may be blameless and harmless, the sons of God, without rebuke, in the midst of a crooked and perverse nation, among whom ye shine as lights in the world;

16 Holding forth the word of life; that I may rejoice in the day of Christ, that I have not run in vain, neither laboured in vain.

17 Yea, and if I be offered upon the sacrifice and service of your faith, I joy, and rejoice with you all.

18 For the same cause also do ye joy, and rejoice with me.

19 But I trust in the Lord Jesus to send Timotheus shortly unto you, that I also may be of good comfort, when I know your state.

20 For I have no man likeminded, who will naturally care for your state.

21 For all seek their own, not the things which are Jesus Christ's.

22 But ye know the proof of him, that, as a son with the father, he hath served with me in the gospel.

23 Him therefore I hope to send presently, so soon as I shall see

how it will go with me.

24 But I trust in the Lord that I also myself shall come shortly.

25 Yet I supposed it necessary to send to you Epaphroditus, my brother, and companion in labour, and fellowsoldier, but your messenger, and he that ministered to my wants.

26 For he longed after you all, and was full of heaviness, because that ye had heard that he had been sick.

27 For indeed he was sick nigh unto death: but God had mercy on him; and not on him only, but on me also, lest I should have sorrow upon sorrow.

28 I sent him therefore the more carefully, that, when ye see him again, ye may rejoice, and that I may be the less sorrowful.

29 Receive him therefore in the Lord with all gladness; and hold such in reputation:

30 Because for the work of Christ he was nigh unto death, not regarding his life, to supply your lack of service toward me.

3 Finally, my brethren, rejoice in the Lord. To write the same things to you, to me indeed *is* not grievous, but for you *it is* safe.

2 Beware of dogs, beware of evil workers, beware of the concision.

3 For we are the circumcision, which worship God in the spirit, and rejoice in Christ Jesus, and have no confidence in the flesh.

4 Though I might also have confidence in the flesh. If any other man thinketh that he hath whereof he might trust in the flesh, I more:

5 Circumcised the eighth day, of the stock of Israel, *of* the tribe of Benjamin, an Hebrew of the Hebrews; as touching the law, a Pharisee;

6 Concerning zeal, persecuting the church; touching the righteousness which is in the law, blameless.

7 ¶ But what things were gain to me, those I counted loss for Christ.

8 Yea doubtless, and I count all things *but* loss for the excellency of the knowledge of Christ Jesus my Lord: for whom I have suffered the loss of all things, and do count them *but* dung, that I may win Christ,

9 And be found in him, not having mine own righteousness, which is of the law, but that which is through the faith of Christ, the righteousness which is of God by faith:

10 That I may know him, and the power of his resurrection, and the fellowship of his sufferings, being made conformable unto his death;

11 If by any means I might attain unto the resurrection of the dead.

12 Not as though I had already attained, either were already perfect: but I follow after, if that I may apprehend that for which also I am apprehended of Christ Jesus.

13 Brethren, I count not myself to have apprehended: but *this*

one thing *I do*, forgetting those things which are behind, and reaching forth unto those things which are before,

14 I press toward the mark for the prize of the high calling of God in Christ Jesus.

15 Let us therefore, as many as be perfect, be thus minded: and if in any thing ye be otherwise minded, God shall reveal even this unto you.

16 Nevertheless, whereto we have already attained, let us walk by the same rule, let us mind the same thing.

17 Brethren, be followers together of me, and mark them which walk so as ye have us for an ensample.

18 (For many walk, of whom I have told you often, and now tell you even weeping, *that they are* the enemies of the cross of Christ:

19 Whose end *is* destruction, whose God *is their* belly, and *whose* glory *is* in their shame, who mind earthly things.)

20 For our conversation is in heaven; from whence also we look for the Saviour, the Lord Jesus Christ:

21 Who shall change our vile body, that it may be fashioned like unto his glorious body, according to the working whereby he is able even to subdue all things unto himself.

4 Therefore, my brethren dearly beloved and longed for, my joy and crown, so stand fast in the Lord, *my* dearly be-loved.

2 I beseech Euodias, and beseech Syntyche, that they be of the same mind in the Lord.

3 And I intreat thee also, true yokefellow, help those women which laboured with me in the gospel, with Clement also, and *with* other my fellowlabourers, whose names *are* in the book of life.

4 Rejoice in the Lord alway: *and* again I say, Rejoice.

5 ❪ Let your moderation be known unto all men. The Lord *is* at hand.

6 Be careful for nothing; but in every thing by prayer and supplication with thanksgiving let your requests be made known unto God.

7 And the peace of God, which passeth all understanding, shall keep your hearts and minds through Christ Jesus.

8 ❪ Finally, brethren, whatsoever things are true, whatsoever things *are* honest, whatsoever things *are* just, whatsoever things *are* pure, whatsoever things *are* lovely, whatsoever things *are* of good report; if *there be* any virtue, and if *there be* any praise, think on these things.

9 Those things, which ye have both learned, and received, and heard, and seen in me, do: and the God of peace shall be with you.

10 ❪ But I rejoiced in the Lord greatly, that now at the last your care of me hath flourished again; wherein ye were also careful, but ye lacked opportunity.

11 Not that I speak in respect of want: for I have learned, in whatsoever state I am, *therewith* to be content.

12 I know both how to be abased, and I know how to abound: every where and in all things I am instructed both to be full and to be hungry, both to abound and to suffer need.

13 I can do all things through Christ which strengtheneth me.

14 Notwithstanding ye have well done, that ye did communicate with my affliction.

15 Now ye Philippians know also, that in the beginning of the gospel, when I departed from Macedonia, no church communicated with me as concerning giving and receiving, but ye only.

16 For even in Thessalonica ye sent once and again unto my necessity.

17 Not because I desire a gift: but I desire fruit that may abound to your account.

18 But I have all, and abound: I am full, having received of Epaphroditus the things *which were sent* from you, an odour of a sweet smell, a sacrifice acceptable, wellpleasing to God.

19 But my God shall supply all your need according to his riches in glory by Christ Jesus.

20 Now unto God and our Father *be* glory for ever and ever. Amen.

21 Salute every saint in Christ Jesus. The brethren which are with me greet you.

22 All the saints salute you, chiefly they that are of Caesar's household.

23 The grace of our Lord Jesus Christ *be* with you all. Amen.

¶ It was written to the Philippians from Rome by Epaphroditus.

THE EPISTLE OF PAUL THE APOSTLE
TO THE

COLOSSIANS

1 Paul, an apostle of Jesus Christ by the will of God, and Timotheus *our* brother,

2 To the saints and faithful brethren in Christ which are at Colosse: Grace *be* unto you, and peace, from God our Father and the Lord Jesus Christ.

3 ¶ We give thanks to God and the Father of our Lord Jesus Christ, praying always for you,

4 Since we heard of your faith

in Christ Jesus, and of the love *which ye have* to all the saints,

5 For the hope which is laid up for you in heaven, whereof ye heard before in the word of the truth of the gospel;

6 Which is come unto you, as *it is* in all the world; and bringeth forth fruit, as *it doth* also in you, since the day ye heard *of it*, and knew the grace of God in truth:

7 As ye also learned of Epa-

phras our dear fellowservant, who is for you a faithful minister of Christ;

8 Who also declared unto us your love in the Spirit.

9 ¶ For this cause we also, since the day we heard *it*, do not cease to pray for you, and to desire that ye might be filled with the knowledge of his will in all wisdom and spiritual understanding;

10 That ye might walk worthy of the Lord unto all pleasing, being fruitful in every good work, and increasing in the knowledge of God;

11 Strengthened with all might, according to his glorious power, unto all patience and longsuffering with joyfulness;

12 Giving thanks unto the Father, which hath made us meet to be partakers of the inheritance of the saints in light:

13 Who hath delivered us from the power of darkness, and hath translated *us* into the kingdom of his dear Son:

14 In whom we have redemption through his blood, *even* the forgiveness of sins:

15 Who is the image of the invisible God, the firstborn of every creature:

16 For by him were all things created, that are in heaven, and that are in earth, visible and invisible, whether *they be* thrones, or dominions, or principalities, or powers: all things were created by him, and for him:

17 And he is before all things, and by him all things consist.

18 And he is the head of the body, the church: who is the beginning, the firstborn from the dead; that in all *things* he might have the preeminence.

19 ¶ For it pleased *the Father* that in him should all fulness dwell;

20 And, having made peace through the blood of his cross, by him to reconcile all things unto himself; by him, *I say*, whether *they be* things in earth, or things in heaven.

21. And you, that were sometime alienated and enemies in *your* mind by wicked works, yet now hath he reconciled

22 In the body of his flesh through death, to present you holy and unblameable and unreproveable in his sight:

23 If ye continue in the faith grounded and settled, and *be* not moved away from the hope of the gospel, which ye have heard, *and* which was preached to every creature which is under heaven; whereof I Paul am made a minister;

24 Who now rejoice in my sufferings for you, and fill up that which is behind of the afflictions of Christ in my flesh for his body's sake, which is the church:

25 Whereof I am made a minister, according to the dispensation of God which is given to me for you, to fulfil the word of God;

26 *Even* the mystery which hath been hid from ages and from generations, but now is made manifest to his saints:

27 To whom God would make

known what *is* the riches of the glory of this mystery among the Gentiles; which is Christ in you, the hope of glory:

28 Whom we preach, warning every man, and teaching every man in all wisdom; that we may present every man perfect in Christ Jesus:

29 Whereunto I also labour, striving according to his working, which worketh in me mightily.

2 For I would that ye knew what great conflict I have for you, and *for* them at Laodicea, and *for* as many as have not seen my face in the flesh;

2 That their hearts might be comforted, being knit together in love, and unto all riches of the full assurance of understanding, to the acknowledgement of the mystery of God, and of the Father, and of Christ;

3 In whom are hid all the treasures of wisdom and knowledge.

4 And this I say, lest any man should beguile you with enticing words.

5 For though I be absent in the flesh, yet am I with you in the spirit, joying and beholding your order, and the stedfastness of your faith in Christ.

6 As ye have therefore received Christ Jesus the Lord, *so* walk ye in him:

7 Rooted and built up in him, and stablished in the faith, as ye have been taught, abounding therein with thanksgiving.

8 ¶ Beware lest any man spoil you through philosophy and vain deceit, after the tradition of men, after the rudiments of the world, and not after Christ.

9 For in him dwelleth all the fulness of the Godhead bodily.

10 And ye are complete in him, which is the head of all principality and power:

11 In whom also ye are circumcised with the circumcision made without hands, in putting off the body of the sins of the flesh by the circumcision of Christ:

12 Buried with him in baptism, wherein also ye are risen with *him* through the faith of the operation of God, who hath raised him from the dead.

13 And you, being dead in your sins and the uncircumcision of your flesh, hath he quickened together with him, having forgiven you all trespasses;

14 Blotting out the handwriting of ordinances that was against us, which was contrary to us, and took it out of the way, nailing it to his cross;

15 *And* having spoiled principalities and powers, he made a shew of them openly, triumphing over them in it.

16 Let no man therefore judge you in meat, or in drink, or in respect of an holyday, or of the new moon, or of the sabbath *days*:

17 Which are a shadow of things to come; but the body *is* of Christ.

18 Let no man beguile you of your reward in a voluntary humility and worshipping of an-

gels, intruding into those things which he hath not seen, vainly puffed up by his fleshly mind,

19 And not holding the Head, from which all the body by joints and bands having nourishment ministered, and knit together, increaseth with the increase of God.

20 Wherefore if ye be dead with Christ from the rudiments of the world, why, as though living in the world, are ye subject to ordinances,

21 (Touch not; taste not; handle not;

22 Which all are to perish with the using;) after the commandments and doctrines of men?

23 Which things have indeed a shew of wisdom in will worship, and humility, and neglecting of the body: not in any honour to the satisfying of the flesh.

3 If ye then be risen with Christ, seek those things which are above, where Christ sitteth on the right hand of God.

2 Set your affection on things above, not on things on the earth.

3 For ye are dead, and your life is hid with Christ in God.

4 When Christ, *who is* our life, shall appear, then shall ye also appear with him in glory.

5 Mortify therefore your members which are upon the earth; fornication, uncleanness, inordinate affection, evil concupiscence, and covetousness, which is idolatry:

6 For which things' sake the wrath of God cometh on the children of disobedience:

7 In the which ye also walked some time, when ye lived in them.

8 But now ye also put off all these; anger, wrath, malice, blasphemy, filthy communication out of your mouth.

9 ¶Lie not one to another, seeing that ye have put off the old man with his deeds;

10 And have put on the new *man*, which is renewed in knowledge after the image of him that created him:

11 Where there is neither Greek nor Jew, circumcision nor uncircumcision, Barbarian, Scythian, bond *nor* free: but Christ *is* all, and in all.

12 Put on therefore, as the elect of God, holy and beloved, bowels of mercies, kindness, humbleness of mind, meekness, longsuffering;

13 Forbearing one another, and forgiving one another, if any man have a quarrel against any: even as Christ forgave you, so also *do* ye.

14 And above all these things *put on* charity, which is the bond of perfectness.

15 And let the peace of God rule in your hearts, to the which also ye are called in one body; and be ye thankful.

16 Let the word of Christ dwell in you richly in all wisdom; teaching and admonishing one another in psalms and hymns and spiritual songs, singing with grace in your hearts to the Lord.

17 And whatsoever ye do in word or deed, *do* all in the name of the Lord Jesus, giving thanks to God and the Father by him.

18 Wives, submit yourselves unto your own husbands, as it is fit in the Lord.

19 Husbands, love *your* wives, and be not bitter against them.

20 Children, obey *your* parents in all things: for this is well pleasing unto the Lord.

21 Fathers, provoke not your children *to anger*, lest they be discouraged.

22 Servants, obey in all things *your* masters according to the flesh; not with eyeservice, as menpleasers; but in singleness of heart, fearing God;

23 And whatsoever ye do, do *it* heartily, as to the Lord, and not unto men;

24 Knowing that of the Lord ye shall receive the reward of the inheritance: for ye serve the Lord Christ.

25 But he that doeth wrong shall receive for the wrong which he hath done: and there is no respect of persons.

4 Masters, give unto *your* servants that which is just and equal; knowing that ye also have a Master in heaven.

2 ¶ Continue in prayer, and watch in the same with thanksgiving;

3 Withal praying also for us, that God would open unto us a door of utterance, to speak the mystery of Christ, for which I am also in bonds:

4 That I may make it manifest, as I ought to speak.

5 ¶ Walk in wisdom toward them that are without, redeeming the time.

6 Let your speech *be* alway with grace, seasoned with salt, that ye may know how ye ought to answer every man.

7 All my state shall Tychicus declare unto you, *who is* a beloved brother, and a faithful minister and fellowservant in the Lord:

8 Whom I have sent unto you for the same purpose, that he might know your estate, and comfort your hearts;

9 With Onesimus, a faithful and beloved brother, who is *one* of you. They shall make known unto you all things which *are done* here.

10 ¶ Aristarchus my fellowprisoner saluteth you, and Marcus, sister's son to Barnabas, (touching whom ye received commandments: if he come unto you, receive him;)

11 And Jesus, which is called Justus, who are of the circumcision. These only *are* my fellowworkers unto the kingdom of God, which have been a comfort unto me.

12 Epaphras, who is *one* of you, a servant of Christ, saluteth you, always labouring fervently for you in prayers, that ye may stand perfect and complete in all the will of God.

13 For I bear him record, that he hath a great zeal for you, and them *that are* in Laodicea, and them in Hierapolis.

14 Luke, the beloved physician, and Demas, greet you.

15 Salute the brethren which are in Laodicea, and Nymphas, and the church which is in his house.

16 And when this epistle is read among you, cause that it be read also in the church of the Laodiceans; and that ye likewise read the *epistle* from Laodicea.

17 And say to Archippus, Take heed to the ministry which thou hast received in the Lord, that thou fulfil it.

18 The salutation by the hand of me Paul. Remember my bonds. Grace *be* with you. Amen.

❡ Written from Rome to the Colossians by Tychicus and Onesimus.

THE FIRST EPISTLE OF PAUL THE APOSTLE
TO THE
THESSALONIANS

1 Paul, and Silvanus, and Timotheus, unto the church of the Thessalonians *which is in* God the Father and *in* the Lord Jesus Christ: Grace *be* unto you, and peace, from God our Father, and the Lord Jesus Christ.

2 ❡ We give thanks to God always for you all, making mention of you in our prayers;

3 Remembering without ceasing your work of faith, and labour of love, and patience of hope in our Lord Jesus Christ, in the sight of God and our Father;

4 Knowing, brethren beloved, your election of God.

5 For our gospel came not unto you in word only, but also in power, and in the Holy Ghost, and in much assurance; as ye know what manner of men we were among you for your sake.

6 And ye became followers of us, and of the Lord, having received the word in much affliction, with joy of the Holy Ghost.

7 ❡ So that ye were ensamples to all that believe in Macedonia and Achaia.

8 For from you sounded out the word of the Lord not only in Macedonia and Achaia, but also in every place your faith to God-ward is spread abroad; so that we need not to speak any thing.

9 For they themselves shew of us what manner of entering in we had unto you, and how ye turned to God from idols to serve the living and true God;

10 And to wait for his Son from heaven, whom he raised from the dead, *even* Jesus, which delivered us from the wrath to come.

2 For yourselves, brethren, know our entrance in unto you, that it was not in vain:

2 But even after that we had suffered before, and were shamefully entreated, as ye know, at Philippi, we were bold in our God to speak unto you the gospel of God with much contention.

3 For our exhortation *was* not of deceit, nor of uncleanness, nor in guile:

4 But as we were allowed of God to be put in trust with the gospel, even so we speak; not as pleasing men, but God, which trieth our hearts.

5 For neither at any time used we flattering words, as ye know, nor a cloke of covetousness; God *is* witness:

6 Nor of men sought we glory, neither of you, nor *yet* of others, when we might have been burdensome, as the apostles of Christ.

7 But we were gentle among you, even as a nurse cherisheth her children:

8 So being affectionately desirous of you, we were willing to have imparted unto you, not the gospel of God only, but also our own souls, because ye were dear unto us.

9 For ye remember, brethren, our labour and travail: for labouring night and day, because we would not be chargeable unto any of you, we preached unto you the gospel of God.

10 Ye *are* witnesses, and God *also*, how holily and justly and unblameably we behaved ourselves among you that believe:

11 As ye know how we exhorted and comforted and charged every one of you, as a father *doth* his children,

12 That ye would walk worthy of God, who hath called you unto his kingdom and glory.

13 For this cause also thank we God without ceasing, because, when ye received the word of God which ye heard of us, ye received *it* not *as* the word of men, but as it is in truth, the word of God, which effectually worketh also in you that believe.

14 For ye, brethren, became followers of the churches of God which in Judaea are in Christ Jesus: for ye also have suffered like things of your own countrymen, even as they *have* of the Jews:

15 Who both killed the Lord Jesus, and their own prophets, and have persecuted us; and they please not God, and are contrary to all men:

16 Forbidding us to speak to the Gentiles that they might be saved, to fill up their sins alway: for the wrath is come upon them to the uttermost.

17 But we, brethren, being taken from you for a short time in presence, not in heart, endeavoured the more abundantly to see your face with great desire.

18 Wherefore we would have come unto you, even I Paul, once and again; but Satan hindered us.

19 For what *is* our hope, or joy, or crown of rejoicing? *Are* not even ye in the presence of our Lord Jesus Christ at his coming?

20 For ye are our glory and joy.

3 Wherefore when we could no longer forbear, we thought it good to be left at Athens alone;

2 And sent Timotheus, our

brother, and minister of God, and our fellowlabourer in the gospel of Christ, to establish you, and to comfort you concerning your faith:

3 That no man should be moved by these afflictions: for yourselves know that we are appointed thereunto.

4 For verily, when we were with you, we told you before that we should suffer tribulation; even as it came to pass, and ye know.

5 For this cause, when I could no longer forbear, I sent to know your faith, lest by some means the tempter have tempted you, and our labour be in vain.

6 But now when Timotheus came from you unto us, and brought us good tidings of your faith and charity, and that ye have good remembrance of us always, desiring greatly to see us, as we also *to see* you:

7 Therefore, brethren, we were comforted over you in all our affliction and distress by your faith:

8 For now we live, if ye stand fast in the Lord.

9 ¶ For what thanks can we render to God again for you, for all the joy wherewith we joy for your sakes before our God;

10 Night and day praying exceedingly that we might see your face, and might perfect that which is lacking in your faith?

11 Now God himself and our Father, and our Lord Jesus Christ, direct our way unto you.

12 And the Lord make you to increase and abound in love one toward another, and toward all *men*, even as we *do* toward you:

13 To the end he may stablish your hearts unblameable in holiness before God, even our Father, at the coming of our Lord Jesus Christ with all his saints.

4 Furthermore then we beseech you, brethren, and exhort *you* by the Lord Jesus, that as ye have received of us how ye ought to walk and to please God, *so* ye would abound more and more.

2 For ye know what commandments we gave you by the Lord Jesus.

3 For this is the will of God, *even* your sanctification, that ye should abstain from fornication:

4 That every one of you should know how to possess his vessel in sanctification and honour;

5 Not in the lust of concupiscence, even as the Gentiles which know not God:

6 That no *man* go beyond and defraud his brother in *any* matter: because that the Lord *is* the avenger of all such, as we also have forewarned you and testified.

7 For God hath not called us unto uncleanness, but unto holiness.

8 He therefore that despiseth, despiseth not man, but God, who hath also given unto us his holy Spirit.

9 ¶ But as touching brotherly love ye need not that I write unto you: for ye yourselves are taught of

God to love one another.

10 And indeed ye do it toward all the brethren which are in all Macedonia: but we beseech you, brethren, that ye increase more and more;

11 And that ye study to be quiet, and to do your own business, and to work with your own hands, as we commanded you;

12 That ye may walk honestly toward them that are without, and *that* ye may have lack of nothing.

13 ¶ But I would not have you to be ignorant, brethren, concerning them which are asleep, that ye sorrow not, even as others which have no hope.

14 For if we believe that Jesus died and rose again, even so them also which sleep in Jesus will God bring with him.

15 For this we say unto you by the word of the Lord, that we which are alive *and* remain unto the coming of the Lord shall not prevent them which are asleep.

16 For the Lord himself shall descend from heaven with a shout, with the voice of the archangel, and with the trump of God: and the dead in Christ shall rise first:

17 Then we which are alive *and* remain shall be caught up together with them in the clouds, to meet the Lord in the air: and so shall we ever be with the Lord.

18 Wherefore comfort one another with these words.

5 But of the times and the seasons, brethren, ye have no need that I write unto you.

2 For yourselves know perfectly that the day of the Lord so cometh as a thief in the night.

3 For when they shall say, Peace and safety; then sudden destruction cometh upon them, as travail upon a woman with child; and they shall not escape.

4 But ye, brethren, are not in darkness, that that day should overtake you as a thief.

5 Ye are all the children of light, and the children of the day: we are not of the night, nor of darkness.

6 ¶ Therefore let us not sleep, as *do* others; but let us watch and be sober.

7 For they that sleep sleep in the night; and they that be drunken are drunken in the night.

8 But let us, who are of the day, be sober, putting on the breastplate of faith and love; and for an helmet, the hope of salvation.

9 For God hath not appointed us to wrath, but to obtain salvation by our Lord Jesus Christ,

10 Who died for us, that, whether we wake or sleep, we should live together with him.

11 Wherefore comfort yourselves together, and edify one another, even as also ye do.

12 And we beseech you, brethren, to know them which labour among you, and are over you in the Lord, and admonish you;

13 And to esteem them very highly in love for their work's sake. *And* be at peace among yourselves.

14 Now we exhort you, brethren, warn them that are unruly, comfort the feebleminded, support the weak, be patient toward all *men*.

15 See that none render evil for evil unto any man; but ever follow that which is good, both among yourselves, and to all *men*.

16 Rejoice evermore.

17 Pray without ceasing.

18 In every thing give thanks: for this is the will of God in Christ Jesus concerning you.

19 Quench not the Spirit.

20 Despise not prophesyings.

21 Prove all things; hold fast that which is good.

22 Abstain from all appearance of evil.

23 And the very God of peace sanctify you wholly; and *I pray God* your whole spirit and soul and body be preserved blameless unto the coming of our Lord Jesus Christ.

24 Faithful *is* he that calleth you, who also will do *it*.

25 Brethren, pray for us.

26 Greet all the brethren with an holy kiss.

27 I charge you by the Lord that this epistle be read unto all the holy brethren.

28 The grace of our Lord Jesus Christ *be* with you. Amen.

C The first *epistle* unto the Thessalonians was written from Athens.

THE SECOND EPISTLE OF PAUL THE APOSTLE
TO THE

THESSALONIANS

1 Paul, and Silvanus, and Timotheus, unto the church of the Thessalonians in God our Father and the Lord Jesus Christ:

2 Grace unto you, and peace, from God our Father and the Lord Jesus Christ.

3 C We are bound to thank God always for you, brethren, as it is meet, because that your faith groweth exceedingly, and the charity of every one of you all toward each other aboundeth;

4 C So that we ourselves glory in you in the churches of God for your patience and faith in all your persecutions and tribulations that ye endure:

5 *Which is* a manifest token of the righteous judgment of God, that ye may be counted worthy of the kingdom of God, for which ye also suffer:

6 Seeing *it is* a righteous thing with God to recompense tribulation to them that trouble you;

7 And to you who are troubled rest with us, when the Lord Jesus shall be revealed from heaven with his mighty angels,

8 In flaming fire taking ven-

geance on them that know not God, and that obey not the gospel of our Lord Jesus Christ:

9 Who shall be punished with everlasting destruction from the presence of the Lord, and from the glory of his power;

10 When he shall come to be glorified in his saints, and to be admired in all them that believe (because your testimony among you was believed) in that day.

11 Wherefore also we pray always for you, that our God would count you worthy of *this* calling, and fulfil all the good pleasure of *his* goodness, and the work of faith with power:

12 That the name of our Lord Jesus Christ may be glorified in you, and ye in him, according to the grace of our God and the Lord Jesus Christ.

2 Now we beseech you, brethren, by the coming of our Lord Jesus Christ, and *by* our gathering together unto him,

2 That ye be not soon shaken in mind, or be troubled, neither by spirit, nor by word, nor by letter as from us, as that the day of Christ is at hand.

3 ¶ Let no man deceive you by any means: for *that day shall not come*, except there come a falling away first, and that man of sin be revealed, the son of perdition;

4 Who opposeth and exalteth himself above all that is called God, or that is worshipped; so that as God sitteth in the temple of God, shewing himself that he is God.

5 Remember ye not, that, when I was yet with you, I told you these things?

6 And now ye know what withholdeth that he might be revealed in his time.

7 For the mystery of iniquity doth already work: only he who now letteth *will let*, until he be taken out of the way.

8 ¶ And then shall that Wicked be revealed, whom the Lord shall consume with the spirit of his mouth, and shall destroy with the brightness of his coming:

9 *Even him*, whose coming is after the working of Satan with all power and signs and lying wonders,

10 And with all deceivableness of unrighteousness in them that perish; because they received not the love of the truth, that they might be saved.

11 And for this cause God shall send them strong delusion, that they should believe a lie:

12 That they all might be damned who believed not the truth, but had pleasure in unrighteousness.

13 But we are bound to give thanks alway to God for you, brethren beloved of the Lord, because God hath from the beginning chosen you to salvation through sanctification of the Spirit and belief of the truth:

14 Whereunto he called you by our gospel, to the obtaining of the glory of our Lord Jesus Christ.

15 Therefore, brethren, stand

323

fast, and hold the traditions which ye have been taught, whether by word, or our epistle.

16 ❡ Now our Lord Jesus Christ himself, and God, even our Father, which hath loved us, and hath given *us* everlasting consolation and good hope through grace,

17 Comfort your hearts, and stablish you in every good word and work.

3 Finally, brethren, pray for us, that the word of the Lord may have *free* course, and be glorified, even as *it is* with you:

2 And that we may be delivered from unreasonable and wicked men: for all *men* have not faith.

3 But the Lord is faithful, who shall stablish you, and keep *you* from evil.

4 And we have confidence in the Lord touching you, that ye both do and will do the things which we command you.

5 ❡ And the Lord direct your hearts into the love of God, and into the patient waiting for Christ.

6 Now we command you, brethren, in the name of our Lord Jesus Christ, that ye withdraw yourselves from every brother that walketh disorderly, and not after the tradition which he received of us.

7 For yourselves know how ye ought to follow us: for we behaved not ourselves disorderly among you;

8 Neither did we eat any man's bread for nought; but wrought with labour and travail night and day, that we might not be chargeable to any of you:

9 Not because we have not power, but to make ourselves an ensample unto you to follow us.

10 For even when we were with you, this we commanded you, that if any would not work, neither should he eat.

11 For we hear that there are some which walk among you disorderly, working not at all, but are busybodies.

12 Now them that are such we command and exhort by our Lord Jesus Christ, that with quietness they work, and eat their own bread.

13 But ye, brethren, be not weary in well doing.

14 And if any man obey not our word by this epistle, note that man, and have no company with him, that he may be ashamed.

15 Yet count *him* not as an enemy, but admonish *him* as a brother.

16 ❡ Now the Lord of peace himself give you peace always by all means. The Lord *be* with you all.

17 The salutation of Paul with mine own hand, which is the token in every epistle: so I write.

18 The grace of our Lord Jesus Christ be with you all. Amen.

❡ The second *epistle* to the Thessalonians was written from Athens.

324

THE FIRST EPISTLE OF PAUL THE APOSTLE
TO

TIMOTHY

1 Paul, an apostle of Jesus Christ by the commandment of God our Saviour, and Lord Jesus Christ, *which is* our hope;

2 Unto Timothy, *my* own son in the faith: Grace, mercy, *and* peace, from God our Father and Jesus Christ our Lord.

3 ❡ As I besought thee to abide still at Ephesus, when I went into Macedonia, that thou mightest charge some that they teach no other doctrine,

4 Neither give heed to fables and endless genealogies, which minister questions, rather than godly edifying which is in faith: *so do.*

5 ❡ Now the end of the commandment is charity out of a pure heart, and *of* a good conscience, and *of* faith unfeigned:

6 From which some having swerved have turned aside unto vain jangling;

7 Desiring to be teachers of the law; understanding neither what they say, nor whereof they affirm.

8 But we know that the law *is* good, if a man use it lawfully;

9 Knowing this, that the law is not made for a righteous man, but for the lawless and disobedient, for the ungodly and for sinners, for unholy and profane, for murderers of fathers and murderers of mothers, for manslayers,

10 For whoremongers, for them that defile themselves with mankind, for menstealers, for liars, for perjured persons, and if there be any other thing that is contrary to sound doctrine;

11 ❡ According to the glorious gospel of the blessed God, which was committed to my trust.

12 And I thank Christ Jesus our Lord, who hath enabled me, for that he counted me faithful, putting me into the ministry;

13 Who was before a blasphemer, and a persecutor, and injurious: but I obtained mercy, because I did *it* ignorantly in unbelief.

14 And the grace of our Lord was exceeding abundant with faith and love which is in Christ Jesus.

15 This *is* a faithful saying, and worthy of all acceptation, that Christ Jesus came into the world to save sinners; of whom I am chief.

16 Howbeit for this cause I obtained mercy, that in me first Jesus Christ might shew forth all longsuffering, for a pattern to them which should hereafter believe on him to life everlasting.

17 Now unto the King eternal, immortal, invisible, the only wise God, *be* honour and glory for ever and ever. Amen.

18 This charge I commit unto thee, son Timothy, according to

the prophecies which went before on thee, that thou by them mightest war a good warfare;

19 Holding faith, and a good conscience; which some having put away concerning faith have made shipwreck:

20 Of whom is Hymenaeus and Alexander; whom I have delivered unto Satan, that they may learn not to blaspheme.

2 I exhort therefore, that, first of all, supplications, prayers, intercessions, *and* giving of thanks, be made for all men;

2 For kings, and *for* all that are in authority; that we may lead a quiet and peaceable life in all godliness and honesty.

3 For this *is* good and acceptable in the sight of God our Saviour;

4 Who will have all men to be saved, and to come unto the knowledge of the truth.

5 For *there is* one God, and one mediator between God and men, the man Christ Jesus;

6 Who gave himself a ransom for all, to be testified in due time.

7 Whereunto I am ordained a preacher, and an apostle, (I speak the truth in Christ, *and* lie not;) a teacher of the Gentiles in faith and verity.

8 I will therefore that men pray every where, lifting up holy hands, without wrath and doubting.

9 ¶ In like manner also, that women adorn themselves in modest apparel, with shamefacedness and sobriety; not with broided hair, or gold, or pearls, or costly array;

10 But (which becometh women professing godliness) with good works.

11 Let the woman learn in silence with all subjection.

12 But I suffer not a woman to teach, nor to usurp authority over the man, but to be in silence.

13 For Adam was first formed, then Eve.

14 And Adam was not deceived, but the woman being deceived was in the transgression.

15 ¶ Notwithstanding she shall be saved in childbearing, if they continue in faith and charity and holiness with sobriety.

3 This *is* a true saying, If a man desire the office of a bishop, he desireth a good work.

2 A bishop then must be blameless, the husband of one wife, vigilant, sober, of good behaviour; given to hospitality, apt to teach;

3 Not given to wine, no striker, not greedy of filthy lucre; but patient, not a brawler, not covetous;

4 One that ruleth well his own house, having his children in subjection with all gravity;

5 (For if a man know not how to rule his own house, how shall he take care of the church of God?)

6 Not a novice, lest being lifted up with pride he fall into the condemnation of the devil.

7 Moreover he must have a good report of them which are without; lest he fall into reproach and the snare of the devil.

8 Likewise *must* the deacons *be* grave, not doubletongued, not given to much wine, not greedy of filthy lucre;

9 Holding the mystery of the faith in a pure conscience.

10 And let these also first be proved; then let them use the office of a deacon, being *found* blameless.

11 Even so *must their* wives *be* grave, not slanderers, sober, faithful in all things.

12 Let the deacons be the husbands of one wife, ruling their children and their own houses well.

13 For they that have used the office of a deacon well purchase to themselves a good degree, and great boldness in the faith which is in Christ Jesus.

14 ¶ These things write I unto thee, hoping to come unto thee shortly:

15 But if I tarry long, that thou mayest know how thou oughtest to behave thyself in the house of God, which is the church of the living God, the pillar and ground of the truth.

16 And without controversy great is the mystery of godliness: God was manifest in the flesh, justified in the Spirit, seen of angels, preached unto the Gentiles, believed on in the world, received up into glory.

4 Now the Spirit speaketh expressly, that in the latter times some shall depart from the faith, giving heed to seducing spirits, and doctrines of devils;

2 Speaking lies in hypocrisy; having their conscience seared with a hot iron;

3 Forbidding to marry, *and commanding* to abstain from meats, which God hath created to be received with thanksgiving of them which believe and know the truth.

4 For every creature of God *is* good, and nothing to be refused, if it be received with thanksgiving:

5 For it is sanctified by the word of God and prayer.

6 ¶ If thou put the brethren in remembrance of these things, thou shalt be a good minister of Jesus Christ, nourished up in the words of faith and of good doctrine, whereunto thou hast attained.

7 But refuse profane and old wives' fables, and exercise thyself *rather* unto godliness.

8 For bodily exercise profiteth little: but godliness is profitable unto all things, having promise of the life that now is, and of that which is to come.

9 This *is* a faithful saying, and worthy of all acceptation.

10 For therefore we both labour and suffer reproach, because we trust in the living God, who is the Saviour of all men, specially of those that believe.

11 These things command and teach.

12 Let no man despise thy youth; but be thou an example of the believers, in word, in conversation, in charity, in spirit, in faith, in purity.

13 Till I come, give attendance to reading, to exhortation, to doctrine.

14 Neglect not the gift that is in thee, which was given thee by prophecy, with the laying on of the hands of the presbytery.

15 Meditate upon these things; give thyself wholly to them; that thy profiting may appear to all.

16 Take heed unto thyself, and unto the doctrine; continue in them: for in doing this thou shalt both save thyself, and them that hear thee.

5 Rebuke not an elder, but intreat *him* as a father; *and* the younger men as brethren;

2 The elder women as mothers; the younger as sisters, with all purity.

3 ¶ Honour widows that are widows indeed.

4 But if any widow have children or nephews, let them learn first to shew piety at home, and to requite their parents: for that is good and acceptable before God.

5 Now she that is a widow indeed, and desolate, trusteth in God, and continueth in supplications and prayers night and day.

6 But she that liveth in pleasure is dead while she liveth.

7 And these things give in charge, that they may be blameless.

8 But if any provide not for his own, and specially for those of his own house, he hath denied the faith, and is worse than an infidel.

9 Let not a widow be taken into the number under threescore years old, having been the wife of one man.

10 Well reported of for good works; if she have brought up children, if she have lodged strangers, if she have washed the saints' feet, if she have relieved the afflicted, if she have diligently followed every good work.

11 But the younger widows refuse: for when they have begun to wax wanton against Christ, they will marry;

12 Having damnation, because they have cast off their first faith.

13 And withal they learn *to be* idle, wandering about from house to house; and not only idle, but tattlers also and busybodies, speaking things which they ought not.

14 I will therefore that the younger women marry, bear children, guide the house, give none occasion to the adversary to speak reproachfully.

15 For some are already turned aside after Satan.

16 If any man or woman that believeth have widows, let them relieve them, and let not the church be charged; that it may relieve them that are widows indeed.

17 ¶ Let the elders that rule well be counted worthy of double honour, especially they who la-

bour in the word and doctrine.

18 For the scripture saith, Thou shalt not muzzle the ox that treadeth out the corn. And, The labourer *is* worthy of his reward.

19 Against an elder receive not an accusation, but before two or three witnesses.

20 Them that sin rebuke before all, that others also may fear.

21 ¶ I charge *thee* before God, and the Lord Jesus Christ, and the elect angels, that thou observe these things without preferring one before another, doing nothing by partiality.

22 ¶ Lay hands suddenly on no man, neither be partaker of other men's sins: keep thyself pure.

23 Drink no longer water, but use a little wine for thy stomach's sake and thine often infirmities.

24 Some men's sins are open beforehand, going before to judgment; and some *men* they follow after.

25 Likewise also the good works *of some* are manifest beforehand; and they that are otherwise cannot be hid.

6 Let as many servants as are under the yoke count their own masters worthy of all honour, that the name of God and *his* doctrine be not blasphemed.

2 And they that have believing masters, let them not despise *them*, because they are brethren; but rather do *them* service, because they are faithful and beloved, partakers of the benefit. These things teach and exhort.

3 If any man teach otherwise,

and consent not to wholesome words, *even* the words of our Lord Jesus Christ, and to the doctrine which is according to godliness;

4 He is proud, knowing nothing, but doting about questions and strifes of words, whereof cometh envy, strife, railings, evil surmisings,

5 Perverse disputings of men of corrupt minds, and destitute of the truth, supposing that gain is godliness: from such withdraw thyself.

6 ¶ But godliness with contentment is great gain.

7 For we brought nothing into *this* world, *and it is* certain we can carry nothing out.

8 And having food and raiment let us be therewith content.

9 But they that will be rich fall into temptation and a snare, and *into* many foolish and hurtful lusts, which drown men in destruction and perdition.

10 For the love of money is the root of all evil: which while some coveted after, they have erred from the faith, and pierced themselves through with many sorrows.

11 ¶ But thou, O man of God, flee these things; and follow after righteousness, godliness, faith, love, patience, meekness.

12 Fight the good fight of faith, lay hold on eternal life, whereunto thou art also called, and hast professed a good profession before many witnesses.

13 I give thee charge in the

sight of God, who quickeneth all things, and *before* Christ Jesus, who before Pontius Pilate witnessed a good confession;

14 That thou keep *this* commandment without spot, unrebukeable, until the appearing of our Lord Jesus Christ:

15 Which in his times he shall shew, *who is* the blessed and only Potentate, the King of kings, and Lord of lords;

16 Who only hath immortality, dwelling in the light which no man can approach unto; whom no man hath seen, nor can see: to whom *be* honour and power everlasting. Amen.

17 Charge them that are rich in this world, that they be not highminded, nor trust in uncertain riches, but in the living God,

who giveth us richly all things to enjoy;

18 That they do good, that they be rich in good works, ready to distribute, willing to communicate;

19 Laying up in store for themselves a good foundation against the time to come, that they may lay hold on eternal life.

20 O Timothy, keep that which is committed to thy trust, avoiding profane *and* vain babblings, and oppositions of science falsely so called:

21 With whom some professing have erred concerning the faith. Grace *be* with thee. Amen.

¶ The first to Timothy was written from Laodicea, which is the chiefest city of Phrygia Pacatiana.

THE SECOND EPISTLE OF PAUL THE APOSTLE
TO
TIMOTHY

1 Paul, an apostle of Jesus Christ by the will of God, according to the promise of life which is in Christ Jesus,

2 To Timothy, *my* dearly beloved son: Grace, mercy, *and* peace, from God the Father and Christ Jesus our Lord.

3 I thank God, whom I serve from *my* forefathers with pure conscience, that without ceasing I have remembrance of thee in my prayers night and day;

4 Greatly desiring to see thee, being mindful of thy tears, that I

may be filled with joy;

5 When I call to remembrance the unfeigned faith that is in thee, which dwelt first in thy grandmother Lois, and thy mother Eunice; and I am persuaded that in thee also.

6 ¶ Wherefore I put thee in remembrance that thou stir up the gift of God, which is in thee by the putting on of my hands.

7 For God hath not given us the spirit of fear; but of power, and of love, and of a sound mind.

8 Be not thou therefore ashamed

of the testimony of our Lord, nor of me his prisoner: but be thou partaker of the afflictions of the gospel according to the power of God;

9 Who hath saved us, and called *us* with an holy calling, not according to our works, but according to his own purpose and grace, which was given us in Christ Jesus before the world began;

10 But is now made manifest by the appearing of our Saviour Jesus Christ, who hath abolished death, and hath brought life and immortality to light through the gospel:

11 Whereunto I am appointed a preacher, and an apostle, and a teacher of the Gentiles.

12 For the which cause I also suffer these things: nevertheless I am not ashamed: for I know whom I have believed, and am persuaded that he is able to keep that which I have committed unto him against that day.

13 Hold fast the form of sound words, which thou hast heard of me, in faith and love which is in Christ Jesus.

14 That good thing which was committed unto thee keep by the Holy Ghost which dwelleth in us.

15 This thou knowest, that all they which are in Asia be turned away from me; of whom are Phygellus and Hermogenes.

16 The Lord give mercy unto the house of Onesiphorus; for he oft refreshed me, and was not ashamed of my chain:

17 But, when he was in Rome, he sought me out very diligently, and found *me.*

18 The Lord grant unto him that he may find mercy of the Lord in that day: and in how many things he ministered unto me at Ephesus, thou knowest very well.

2 Thou therefore, my son, be strong in the grace that is in Christ Jesus.

2 And the things that thou hast heard of me among many witnesses, the same commit thou to faithful men, who shall be able to teach others also.

3 Thou therefore endure hardness, as a good soldier of Jesus Christ.

4 No man that warreth entangleth himself with the affairs of *this* life; that he may please him who hath chosen him to be a soldier.

5 And if a man also strive for masteries, *yet* is he not crowned, except he strive lawfully.

6 The husbandman that laboureth must be first partaker of the fruits.

7 Consider what I say; and the Lord give thee understanding in all things.

8 Remember that Jesus Christ of the seed of David was raised from the dead according to my gospel:

9 Wherein I suffer trouble, as an evil doer, *even* unto bonds; but the word of God is not bound.

10 Therefore I endure all things for the elect's sakes, that they may also obtain the salvation which is in Christ Jesus with

331

eternal glory.

11 *It* is a faithful saying: For if we be dead with *him*, we shall also live with *him*:

12 If we suffer, we shall also reign with *him*: if we deny *him*, he also will deny us:

13 If we believe not, *yet* he abideth faithful: he cannot deny himself.

14 Of these things put *them* in remembrance, charging *them* before the Lord that they strive not about words to no profit, *but* to the subverting of the hearers.

15 Study to shew thyself approved unto God, a workman that needeth not to be ashamed, rightly dividing the word of truth.

16 But shun profane *and* vain babblings: for they will increase unto more ungodliness.

17 And their word will eat as doth a canker: of whom is Hymenaeus and Philetus;

18 Who concerning the truth have erred, saying that the resurrection is past already; and overthrow the faith of some.

19 ¶ Nevertheless the foundation of God standeth sure, having this seal, The Lord knoweth them that are his. And, Let every one that nameth the name of Christ depart from iniquity.

20 But in a great house there are not only vessels of gold and of silver, but also of wood and of earth; and some to honour, and some to dishonour.

21 If a man therefore purge himself from these, he shall be a vessel unto honour, sanctified, and meet for the master's use, *and* prepared unto every good work.

22 Flee also youthful lusts: but follow righteousness, faith, charity, peace, with them that call on the Lord out of a pure heart.

23 But foolish and unlearned questions avoid, knowing that they do gender strifes.

24 And the servant of the Lord must not strive; but be gentle unto all *men*, apt to teach, patient,

25 In meekness instructing those that oppose themselves; if God peradventure will give them repentance to the acknowledging of the truth;

26 And *that* they may recover themselves out of the snare of the devil, who are taken captive by him at his will.

3 This know also, that in the last days perilous times shall come.

2 For men shall be lovers of their own selves, covetous, boasters, proud, blasphemers, disobedient to parents, unthankful, unholy,

3 Without natural affection, trucebreakers, false accusers, incontinent, fierce, despisers of those that are good,

4 Traitors, heady, highminded, lovers of pleasures more than lovers of God;

5 Having a form of godliness, but denying the power thereof: from such turn away.

6 ¶ For of this sort are they which

creep into houses, and lead captive silly women laden with sins, led away with divers lusts,

7 Ever learning, and never able to come to the knowledge of the truth.

8 Now as Jannes and Jambres withstood Moses, so do these also resist the truth: men of corrupt minds, reprobate concerning the faith.

9 But they shall proceed no further: for their folly shall be manifest unto all *men*, as theirs also was.

10 But thou hast fully known my doctrine, manner of life, purpose, faith, longsuffering, charity, patience,

11 Persecutions, afflictions, which came unto me at Antioch, at Iconium, at Lystra; what persecutions I endured: but out of *them* all the Lord delivered me.

12 Yea, and all that will live godly in Christ Jesus shall suffer persecution.

13 But evil men and seducers shall wax worse and worse, deceiving, and being deceived.

14 But continue thou in the things which thou hast learned and hast been assured of, knowing of whom thou hast learned *them*;

15 And that from a child thou hast known the holy scriptures, which are able to make thee wise unto salvation through faith which is in Christ Jesus.

16 All scripture *is* given by inspiration of God, and is profitable for doctrine, for reproof, for correction, for instruction in righteousness:

17 That the man of God may be perfect, throughly furnished unto all good works.

4 I charge *thee* therefore before God, and the Lord Jesus Christ, who shall judge the quick and the dead at his appearing and his kingdom;

2 Preach the word; be instant in season, out of season; reprove, rebuke, exhort with all longsuffering and doctrine.

3 For the time will come when they will not endure sound doctrine; but after their own lusts shall they heap to themselves teachers, having itching ears;

4 And they shall turn away *their* ears from the truth, and shall be turned unto fables.

5 But watch thou in all things, endure afflictions, do the work of an evangelist, make full proof of thy ministry.

6 ❡ For I am now ready to be offered, and the time of my departure is at hand.

7 I have fought a good fight, I have finished *my* course, I have kept the faith:

8 Henceforth there is laid up for me a crown of righteousness, which the Lord, the righteous judge, shall give me at that day: and not to me only, but unto all them also that love his appearing.

9 ❡ Do thy diligence to come shortly unto me:

10 For Demas hath forsaken me, having loved this present world,

and is departed unto Thessalonica; Crescens to Galatia, Titus unto Dalmatia.

11 Only Luke is with me. Take Mark, and bring him with thee: for he is profitable to me for the ministry.

12 And Tychicus have I sent to Ephesus.

13 The cloke that I left at Troas with Carpus, when thou comest, bring *with thee*, and the books, *but* especially the parchments.

14 Alexander the coppersmith did me much evil: the Lord reward him according to his works:

15 Of whom be thou ware also; for he hath greatly withstood our words.

16 At my first answer no man stood with me, but all *men* forsook me: *I pray God* that it may not be laid to their charge.

17 Notwithstanding the Lord stood with me, and strengthened me; that by me the preaching might be fully known, and *that* all the Gentiles might hear: and I was delivered out of the mouth of the lion.

18 And the Lord shall deliver me from every evil work, and will preserve *me* unto his heavenly kingdom: to whom *be* glory for ever and ever. Amen.

19 Salute Prisca and Aquila, and the household of Onesiphorus.

20 Erastus abode at Corinth: but Trophimus have I left at Miletum sick.

21 Do thy diligence to come before winter. Eubulus greeteth thee, and Pudens, and Linus, and Claudia, and all the brethren.

22 The Lord Jesus Christ *be* with thy spirit. Grace *be* with you. Amen.

❁The second *epistle* unto Timotheus, ordained the first bishop of the church of the Ephesians, was written from Rome, when Paul was brought before Nero the second time.

THE EPISTLE OF PAUL
TO
TITUS

1 Paul, a servant of God, and an apostle of Jesus Christ, according to the faith of God's elect, and the acknowledging of the truth which is after godliness;

2 In hope of eternal life, which God, that cannot lie, promised before the world began;

3 But hath in due times manifested his word through preaching, which is committed unto me according to the commandment of God our Saviour;

4 To Titus, *mine* own son after the common faith: Grace, mercy, *and* peace, from God the Father and the Lord Jesus Christ our Saviour.

5 ❁For this cause left I thee in

Crete, that thou shouldest set in order the things that are wanting, and ordain elders in every city, as I had appointed thee:

6 If any be blameless, the husband of one wife, having faithful children not accused of riot or unruly.

7 For a bishop must be blameless, as the steward of God; not selfwilled, not soon angry, not given to wine, no striker, not given to filthy lucre;

8 But a lover of hospitality, a lover of good men, sober, just, holy, temperate;

9 Holding fast the faithful word as he hath been taught, that he may be able by sound doctrine both to exhort and to convince the gainsayers.

10 ¶ For there are many unruly and vain talkers and deceivers, specially they of the circumcision:

11 Whose mouths must be stopped, who subvert whole houses, teaching things which they ought not, for filthy lucre's sake.

12 One of themselves, *even* a prophet of their own, said, The Cretians *are* alway liars, evil beasts, slow bellies.

13 This witness is true. Wherefore rebuke them sharply, that they may be sound in the faith;

14 Not giving heed to Jewish fables, and commandments of men, that turn from the truth.

15 Unto the pure all things *are* pure: but unto them that are defiled and unbelieving *is* nothing pure; but even their mind and conscience is defiled.

16 They profess that they know God; but in works they deny *him*, being abominable, and disobedient, and unto every good work reprobate.

2

But speak thou the things which become sound doctrine:

2 That the aged men be sober, grave, temperate, sound in faith, in charity, in patience.

3 The aged women likewise, that *they be* in behaviour as becometh holiness, not false accusers, not given to much wine, teachers of good things;

4 That they may teach the young women to be sober, to love their husbands, to love their children,

5 *To be* discreet, chaste, keepers at home, good, obedient to their own husbands, that the word of God be not blasphemed.

6 Young men likewise exhort to be sober minded.

7 In all things shewing thyself a pattern of good works: in doctrine *shewing* uncorruptness, gravity, sincerity,

8 Sound speech, that cannot be condemned; that he that is of the contrary part may be ashamed, having no evil thing to say of you.

9 *Exhort* servants to be obedient unto their own masters, *and* to please *them* well in all *things*; not answering again;

10 Not purloining, but shewing all good fidelity; that they may adorn the doctrine of God our

335

Saviour in all things.

11 For the grace of God that bringeth salvation hath appeared to all men,

12 Teaching us that, denying ungodliness and worldly lusts, we should live soberly, righteously, and godly, in this present world;

13 Looking for that blessed hope, and the glorious appearing of the great God and our Saviour Jesus Christ;

14 Who gave himself for us, that he might redeem us from all iniquity, and purify unto himself a peculiar people, zealous of good works.

15 These things speak, and exhort, and rebuke with all authority. Let no man despise thee.

3 Put them in mind to be subject to principalities and powers, to obey magistrates, to be ready to every good work,

2 To speak evil of no man, to be no brawlers, *but* gentle, shewing all meekness unto all men.

3 For we ourselves also were sometimes foolish, disobedient, deceived, serving divers lusts and pleasures, living in malice and envy, hateful, *and* hating one another.

4 But after that the kindness and love of God our Saviour toward man appeared,

5 Not by works of righteousness which we have done, but according to his mercy he saved us, by the washing of regeneration, and renewing of the Holy Ghost;

6 Which he shed on us abundantly through Jesus Christ our Saviour;

7 That being justified by his grace, we should be made heirs according to the hope of eternal life.

8 *This is* a faithful saying, and these things I will that thou affirm constantly, that they which have believed in God might be careful to maintain good works. These things are good and profitable unto men.

9 But avoid foolish questions, and genealogies, and contentions, and strivings about the law; for they are unprofitable and vain.

10 A man that is an heretick after the first and second admonition reject;

11 Knowing that he that is such is subverted, and sinneth, being condemned of himself.

12 ❧ When I shall send Artemas unto thee, or Tychicus, be diligent to come unto me to Nicopolis: for I have determined there to winter.

13 Bring Zenas the lawyer and Apollos on their journey diligently, that nothing be wanting unto them.

14 And let ours also learn to maintain good works for necessary uses, that they be not unfruitful.

15 All that are with me salute thee. Greet them that love us in the faith. Grace *be* with you all. Amen.

❧ It was written to Titus, ordained the first bishop of the church of the Cretians, from Nicopolis of Macedonia.

THE EPISTLE OF PAUL
TO

PHILEMON

PAUL, a prisoner of Jesus Christ, and Timothy *our* brother, unto Philemon our dearly beloved, and fellowlabourer,

2 And to *our* beloved Apphia, and Archippus our fellowsoldier, and to the church in thy house:

3 Grace to you, and peace, from God our Father and the Lord Jesus Christ.

4 ¶ I thank my God, making mention of thee always in my prayers,

5 Hearing of thy love and faith, which thou hast toward the Lord Jesus, and toward all saints;

6 That the communication of thy faith may become effectual by the acknowledging of every good thing which is in you in Christ Jesus.

7 For we have great joy and consolation in thy love, because the bowels of the saints are refreshed by thee, brother.

8 Wherefore, though I might be much bold in Christ to enjoin thee that which is convenient,

9 Yet for love's sake I rather beseech *thee*, being such an one as Paul the aged, and now also a prisoner of Jesus Christ.

10 ¶ I beseech thee for my son Onesimus, whom I have begotten in my bonds:

11 Which in time past was to thee unprofitable, but now profitable to thee and to me:

12 Whom I have sent again: thou therefore receive him, that is, mine own bowels:

13 Whom I would have retained with me, that in thy stead he might have ministered unto me in the bonds of the gospel:

14 But without thy mind would I do nothing; that thy benefit should not be as it were of necessity, but willingly.

15 For perhaps he therefore departed for a season, that thou shouldest receive him for ever;

16 Not now as a servant, but above a servant, a brother beloved, specially to me, but how much more unto thee, both in the flesh, and in the Lord?

17 If thou count me therefore a partner, receive him as myself.

18 If he hath wronged thee, or oweth *thee* ought, put that on mine account;

19 I Paul have written *it* with mine own hand, I will repay *it*: albeit I do not say to thee how thou owest unto me even thine own self besides.

20 Yea, brother, let me have joy of thee in the Lord: refresh my bowels in the Lord.

21 Having confidence in thy obedience I wrote unto thee, knowing that thou wilt also do more than I say.

22 ¶ But withal prepare me also a lodging: for I trust that through

your prayers I shall be given unto you.

23 There salute thee Epaphras, my fellowprisoner in Christ Jesus;

24 Marcus, Aristarchus, Demas, Lucas, my fellowlabourers.

25 The grace of our Lord Jesus Christ *be* with your spirit. Amen.

€ Written from Rome to Philemon, by Onesimus a servant.

THE EPISTLE TO THE

HEBREWS

1 God, who at sundry times and in divers manners spake in time past unto the fathers by the prophets,

2 Hath in these last days spoken unto us *by his* Son, whom he hath appointed heir of all things, by whom also he made the worlds;

3 Who being the brightness of *his* glory, and the express image of his person, and upholding all things by the word of his power, when he had by himself purged our sins, sat down on the right hand of the Majesty on high:

4 Being made so much better than the angels, as he hath by inheritance obtained a more excellent name than they.

5 For unto which of the angels said he at any time, Thou *art* my Son, this day have I begotten thee? And again, I will be to him a Father, and he shall be to me a Son?

6 And again, when he bringeth in the firstbegotten into the world, he saith, And let all the angels of God worship him.

7 And of the angels he saith,

Who maketh his angels spirits, and his ministers a flame of fire.

8 But unto the Son *he saith*, Thy throne, O God, *is* for ever and ever: a sceptre of righteousness *is* the sceptre of thy kingdom.

9 Thou hast loved righteousness, and hated iniquity; therefore God, *even* thy God, hath anointed thee with the oil of gladness above thy fellows.

10 And, Thou, Lord, in the beginning hast laid the foundation of the earth; and the heavens are the works of thine hands:

11 They shall perish; but thou remainest; and they all shall wax old as doth a garment;

12 And as a vesture shalt thou fold them up, and they shall be changed: but thou art the same, and thy years shall not fail.

13 But to which of the angels said he at any time, Sit on my right hand, until I make thine enemies thy footstool?

14 Are they not all ministering spirits, sent forth to minister for them who shall be heirs of salvation?

2 Therefore we ought to give the more earnest heed to the things which we have heard, lest at any time we should let *them* slip.

2 For if the word spoken by angels was stedfast, and every transgression and disobedience received a just recompence of reward;

3 How shall we escape, if we neglect so great salvation; which at the first began to be spoken by the Lord, and was confirmed unto us by them that heard *him*;

4 God also bearing *them* witness, both with signs and wonders, and with divers miracles, and gifts of the Holy Ghost, according to his own will?

5 ¶ For unto the angels hath he not put in subjection the world to come, whereof we speak.

6 But one in a certain place testified, saying, What is man, that thou art mindful of him? or the son of man, that thou visitest him?

7 Thou madest him a little lower than the angels; thou crownedst him with glory and honour, and didst set him over the works of thy hands:

8 Thou hast put all things in subjection under his feet. For in that he put all in subjection under him, he left nothing *that is* not put under him. But now we see not yet all things put under him.

9 But we see Jesus, who was made a little lower than the angels for the suffering of death, crowned with glory and honour; that he by the grace of God should taste death for every man.

10 For it became him, for whom *are* all things, and by whom *are* all things, in bringing many sons unto glory, to make the captain of their salvation perfect through sufferings.

11 For both he that sanctifieth and they who are sanctified *are* all of one: for which cause he is not ashamed to call them brethren,

12 Saying, I will declare thy name unto my brethren, in the midst of the church will I sing praise unto thee.

13 And again, I will put my trust in him. And again, Behold I and the children which God hath given me.

14 Forasmuch then as the children are partakers of flesh and blood, he also himself likewise took part of the same; that through death he might destroy him that had the power of death, that is, the devil;

15 And deliver them who through fear of death were all their lifetime subject to bondage.

16 For verily he took not on *him the nature of* angels; but he took on *him* the seed of Abraham.

17 Wherefore in all things it behoved him to be made like unto *his* brethren, that he might be a merciful and faithful high priest in things *pertaining* to God, to make reconciliation for the sins of the people.

18 For in that he himself hath suffered being tempted, he is able to succour them that are tempted.

3 Wherefore, holy brethren, partakers of the heavenly calling, consider the Apostle and High Priest of our profession, Christ Jesus;

2 Who was faithful to him that appointed him, as also Moses *was faithful* in all his house.

3 For this *man* was counted worthy of more glory than Moses, inasmuch as he who hath builded the house hath more honour than the house.

4 For every house is builded by some *man*; but he that built all things *is* God.

5 And Moses verily *was* faithful in all his house, as a servant, for a testimony of those things which were to be spoken after;

6 But Christ as a son over his own house; whose house are we, if we hold fast the confidence and the rejoicing of the hope firm unto the end.

7 ¶ Wherefore (as the Holy Ghost saith, To day if ye will hear his voice,

8 Harden not your hearts, as in the provocation, in the day of temptation in the wilderness:

9 When your fathers tempted me, proved me, and saw my works forty years.

10 Wherefore I was grieved with that generation, and said, They do alway err in *their* heart; and they have not known my ways.

11 So I sware in my wrath, They shall not enter into my rest.)

12 Take heed, brethren, lest there be in any of you an evil heart of unbelief, in departing from the living God.

13 But exhort one another daily, while it is called To day; lest any of you be hardened through the deceitfulness of sin.

14 For we are made partakers of Christ, if we hold the beginning of our confidence stedfast unto the end;

15 While it is said, To day if ye will hear his voice, harden not your hearts, as in the provocation.

16 For some, when they had heard, did provoke: howbeit not all that came out of Egypt by Moses.

17 But with whom was he grieved forty years? *was it* not with them that had sinned, whose carcases fell in the wilderness?

18 And to whom sware he that they should not enter into his rest, but to them that believed not?

19 So we see that they could not enter in because of unbelief.

4 Let us therefore fear, lest a promise being left *us* of entering into his rest, any of you should seem to come short of it.

2 For unto us was the gospel preached, as well as unto them: but the word preached did not profit them, not being mixed with faith in them that heard *it.*

3 For we which have believed do enter into rest, as he said, As I have sworn in my wrath, if they shall enter into my rest: although the works were finished from the foundation of the world.

4 For he spake in a certain place of the seventh *day* on this wise, And God did rest the seventh day from all his works.

5 And in this *place* again, If they shall enter into my rest.

6 Seeing therefore it remaineth that some must enter therein, and they to whom it was first preached entered not in because of unbelief:

7 Again, he limiteth a certain day, saying in David, To day, after so long a time; as it is said, To day if ye will hear his voice, harden not your hearts.

8 For if Jesus had given them rest, then would he not afterward have spoken of another day.

9 There remaineth therefore a rest to the people of God.

10 For he that is entered into his rest, he also hath ceased from his own works, as God *did* from his.

11 Let us labour therefore to enter into that rest, lest any man fall after the same example of unbelief.

12 ¶ For the word of God *is* quick, and powerful, and sharper than any twoedged sword, piercing even to the dividing asunder of soul and spirit, and of the joints and marrow, and *is* a discerner of the thoughts and intents of the heart.

13 Neither is there any creature that is not manifest in his sight: but all things *are* naked and opened unto the eyes of him with whom we have to do.

14 ¶ Seeing then that we have a great high priest, that is passed into the heavens, Jesus the Son of God, let us hold fast *our* profession.

15 For we have not an high priest which cannot be touched with the feeling of our infirmities; but was in all points tempted like as *we are, yet* without sin.

16 Let us therefore come boldly unto the throne of grace, that we may obtain mercy, and find grace to help in time of need.

5 For every high priest taken from among men is ordained for men in things *pertaining* to God, that he may offer both gifts and sacrifices for sins:

2 Who can have compassion on the ignorant, and on them that are out of the way; for that he himself also is compassed with infirmity.

3 And by reason hereof he ought, as for the people, so also for himself, to offer for sins.

4 And no man taketh this honour unto himself, but he that is called of God, as *was* Aaron.

5 ¶ So also Christ glorified not himself to be made an high priest; but he that said unto him, Thou art my Son, to day have I begotten thee.

6 As he saith also in another *place*, Thou *art* a priest for ever after the order of Melchisedec.

7 Who in the days of his flesh, when he had offered up prayers and supplications with strong crying and tears unto him that was able to save him from death, and was heard in that he feared;

8 Though he were a Son, yet

341

learned he obedience by the things which he suffered;

9 And being made perfect, he became the author of eternal salvation unto all them that obey him;

10 Called of God an high priest after the order of Melchisedec.

11 ¶ Of whom we have many things to say, and hard to be uttered, seeing ye are dull of hearing.

12 For when for the time ye ought to be teachers, ye have need that one teach you again which *be* the first principles of the oracles of God; and are become such as have need of milk, and not of strong meat.

13 For every one that useth milk *is* unskilful in the word of righteousness: for he is a babe.

14 But strong meat belongeth to them that are of full age, *even* those who by reason of use have their senses exercised to discern both good and evil.

6 Therefore leaving the principles of the doctrine of Christ, let us go on unto perfection; not laying again the foundation of repentance from dead works, and of faith toward God,

2 Of the doctrine of baptisms, and of laying on of hands, and of resurrection of the dead, and of eternal judgment.

3 And this will we do, if God permit.

4 For *it is* impossible for those who were once enlightened, and have tasted of the heavenly gift, and were made partakers of the Holy Ghost,

5 And have tasted the good word of God, and the powers of the world to come,

6 If they shall fall away, to renew them again unto repentance; seeing they crucify to themselves the Son of God afresh, and put *him* to an open shame.

7 For the earth which drinketh in the rain that cometh oft upon it, and bringeth forth herbs meet for them by whom it is dressed, receiveth blessing from God:

8 But that which beareth thorns and briers *is* rejected, and *is* nigh unto cursing; whose end *is* to be burned.

9 But, beloved, we are persuaded better things of you, and things that accompany salvation, though we thus speak.

10 For God *is* not unrighteous to forget your work and labour of love, which ye have shewed toward his name, in that ye have ministered to the saints, and do minister.

11 And we desire that every one of you do shew the same diligence to the full assurance of hope unto the end:

12 That ye be not slothful, but followers of them who through faith and patience inherit the promises.

13 ¶ For when God made promise to Abraham, because he could swear by no greater, he sware by himself,

14 Saying, Surely blessing I will bless thee, and multiplying I will multiply thee.

342

And so, after he had patiently endured, he obtained the promise.

16 For men verily swear by the greater: and an oath for confirmation *is* to them an end of all strife.

17 Wherein God, willing more abundantly to shew unto the heirs of promise the immutability of his counsel, confirmed *it* by an oath:

18 That by two immutable things, in which *it was* impossible for God to lie, we might have a strong consolation, who have fled for refuge to lay hold upon the hope set before us:

19 Which *hope* we have as an anchor of the soul, both sure and stedfast, and which entereth into that within the veil;

20 Whither the forerunner is for us entered, *even* Jesus, made an high priest for ever after the order of Melchisedec.

7 For this Melchisedec, king of Salem, priest of the most high God, who met Abraham returning from the slaughter of the kings, and blessed him;

2 To whom also Abraham gave a tenth part of all; first being by interpretation King of righteousness, and after that also King of Salem, which is, King of peace;

3 Without father, without mother, without descent, having neither beginning of days, nor end of life; but made like unto the Son of God; abideth a priest continually.

4 Now consider how great this man *was*, unto whom even the patriarch Abraham gave the tenth of the spoils.

5 And verily they that are of the sons of Levi, who receive the office of the priesthood, have a commandment to take tithes of the people according to the law, that is, of their brethren, though they come out of the loins of Abraham:

6 But he whose descent is not counted from them received tithes of Abraham, and blessed him that had the promises.

7 And without all contradiction the less is blessed of the better.

8 And here men that die receive tithes; but there he *receiveth them*, of whom it is witnessed that he liveth.

9 And as I may so say, Levi also, who receiveth tithes, payed tithes in Abraham.

10 For he was yet in the loins of his father, when Melchisedec met him.

11 ¶ If therefore perfection were by the Levitical priesthood, (for under it the people received the law,) what further need *was there* that another priest should rise after the order of Melchisedec, and not be called after the order of Aaron?

12 For the priesthood being changed, there is made of necessity a change also of the law.

13 For he of whom these things are spoken pertaineth to another tribe, of which no man gave attendance at the altar.

14 For *it is* evident that our Lord

343

sprang out of Juda; of which tribe Moses spake nothing concerning priesthood.

15 And it is yet far more evident: for that after the similitude of Melchisedec there ariseth another priest,

16 Who is made, not after the law of a carnal commandment, but after the power of an endless life.

17 For he testifieth, Thou *art* a priest for ever after the order of Melchisedec.

18 For there is verily a disannulling of the commandment going before for the weakness and unprofitableness thereof.

19 For the law made nothing perfect, but the bringing in of a better hope *did*; by the which we draw nigh unto God.

20 And inasmuch as not without an oath *he was made priest*:

21 (For those priests were made without an oath; but this with an oath by him that said unto him, The Lord sware and will not repent, Thou *art* a priest for ever after the order of Melchisedec:)

22 By so much was Jesus made a surety of a better testament.

23 And they truly were many priests, because they were not suffered to continue by reason of death:

24 But this *man*, because he continueth ever, hath an unchangeable priesthood.

25 Wherefore he is able also to save them to the uttermost that come unto God by him, seeing he ever liveth to make intercession for them.

26 For such an high priest became us, *who is* holy, harmless, undefiled, separate from sinners, and made higher than the heavens;

27 Who needeth not daily, as those high priests, to offer up sacrifice, first for his own sins, and then for the people's: for this he did once, when he offered up himself.

28 For the law maketh men high priests which have infirmity; but the word of the oath, which was since the law, *maketh* the Son, who is consecrated for evermore.

8 Now of the things which we have spoken *this is* the sum: We have such an high priest, who is set on the right hand of the throne of the Majesty in the heavens;

2 A minister of the sanctuary, and of the true tabernacle, which the Lord pitched, and not man.

3 For every high priest is ordained to offer gifts and sacrifices: wherefore *it is* of necessity that this man have somewhat also to offer.

4 For if he were on earth, he should not be a priest, seeing that there are priests that offer gifts according to the law:

5 Who serve unto the example and shadow of heavenly things, as Moses was admonished of God when he was about to make the tabernacle: for, See, saith he, *that* thou make all things according to the pattern shewed to thee in the mount.

6 ¶ But now hath he obtained a

more excellent ministry, by how much also he is the mediator of a better covenant, which was established upon better promises.

7 For if that first *covenant* had been faultless, then should no place have been sought for the second.

8 For finding fault with them, he saith, Behold, the days come, saith the Lord, when I will make a new covenant with the house of Israel and with the house of Judah:

9 Not according to the covenant that I made with their fathers in the day when I took them by the hand to lead them out of the land of Egypt; because they continued not in my covenant, and I regarded them not, saith the Lord.

10 For this *is* the covenant that I will make with the house of Israel after those days, saith the Lord; I will put my laws into their mind, and write them in their hearts: and I will be to them a God, and they shall be to me a people:

11 And they shall not teach every man his neighbour, and every man his brother, saying, Know the Lord: for all shall know me, from the least to the greatest.

12 For I will be merciful to their unrighteousness, and their sins and their iniquities will I remember no more.

13 In that he saith, A new *covenant*, he hath made the first old. Now that which decayeth and waxeth old *is* ready to vanish away.

9 Then verily the first *covenant* had also ordinances of divine service, and a worldly sanctuary.

2 For there was a tabernacle made; the first, wherein *was* the candlestick, and the table, and the shewbread; which is called the sanctuary.

3 And after the second veil, the tabernacle which is called the Holiest of all;

4 Which had the golden censer, and the ark of the covenant overlaid round about with gold, wherein *was* the golden pot that had manna, and Aaron's rod that budded, and the tables of the covenant;

5 And over it the cherubims of glory shadowing the mercyseat; of which we cannot now speak particularly.

6 Now when these things were thus ordained, the priests went always into the first tabernacle, accomplishing the service *of God*.

7 But into the second *went* the high priest alone once every year, not without blood, which he offered for himself, and *for* the errors of the people:

8 The Holy Ghost this signifying, that the way into the holiest of all was not yet made manifest, while as the first tabernacle was yet standing:

9 Which *was* a figure for the time then present, in which were offered both gifts and sacrifices, that could not make him that did the service perfect, as pertaining to the conscience;

10 **Which stood** only in meats and drinks, and divers washings, and carnal ordinances, imposed *on them* until the time of reformation.

11 ¢ But Christ being come an high priest of good things to come, by a greater and more perfect tabernacle, not made with hands, that is to say, not of this building;

12 Neither by the blood of goats and calves, but by his own blood he entered in once into the holy place, having obtained eternal redemption *for us.*

13 For if the blood of bulls and of goats, and the ashes of an heifer sprinkling the unclean, sanctifieth to the purifying of the flesh;

14 How much more shall the blood of Christ, who through the eternal Spirit offered himself without spot to God, purge your conscience from dead works to serve the living God?

15 And for this cause he is the mediator of the new testament, that by means of death, for the redemption of the transgressions *that were* under the first testament, they which are called might receive the promise of eternal inheritance.

16 For where a testament *is*, there must also of necessity be the death of the testator.

17 For a testament *is* of force after men are dead: otherwise it is of no strength at all while the testator liveth.

18 Whereupon neither the first *testament* was dedicated without blood.

19 For when Moses had spoken every precept to all the people according to the law, he took the blood of calves and of goats, with water, and scarlet wool, and hyssop, and sprinkled both the book, and all the people,

20 Saying, This *is* the blood of the testament which God hath enjoined unto you.

21 Moreover he sprinkled with blood both the tabernacle, and all the vessels of the ministry.

22 And almost all things are by the law purged with blood; and without shedding of blood is no remission.

23 *It was* therefore necessary that the patterns of things in the heavens should be purified with these; but the heavenly things themselves with better sacrifices than these.

24 For Christ is not entered into the holy places made with hands, *which are* the figures of the true; but into heaven itself, now to appear in the presence of God for us:

25 Nor yet that he should offer himself often, as the high priest entereth into the holy place every year with blood of others;

26 For then must he often have suffered since the foundation of the world: but now once in the end of the world hath he appeared to put away sin by the sacrifice of himself.

27 And as it is appointed unto men once to die, but after this the judgment:

346

28 So Christ was once offered to bear the sins of many; and unto them that look for him shall he appear the second time without sin unto salvation.

10

For the law having a shadow of good things to come, *and* not the very image of the things, can never with those sacrifices which they offered year by year continually make the comers thereunto perfect.

2 For then would they not have ceased to be offered? because that the worshippers once purged should have had no more conscience of sins.

3 But in those *sacrifices there is* a remembrance again *made* of sins every year.

4 For *it is* not possible that the blood of bulls and of goats should take away sins.

5 Wherefore when he cometh into the world, he saith, Sacrifice and offering thou wouldest not, but a body hast thou prepared me:

6 In burnt offerings and *sacrifices* for sin thou hast had no pleasure.

7 Then said I, Lo, I come (in the volume of the book it is written of me,) to do thy will, O God.

8 Above when he said, Sacrifice and offering and burnt offerings and *offering* for sin thou wouldest not, neither hadst pleasure *therein*; which are offered by the law;

9 Then said he, Lo, I come to do thy will, O God. He taketh away

the first, that he may establish the second.

10 ¶ By the which will we are sanctified through the offering of the body of Jesus Christ once *for all.*

11 And every priest standeth daily ministering and offering oftentimes the same sacrifices, which can never take away sins:

12 But this man, after he had offered one sacrifice for sins for ever, sat down on the right hand of God;

13 From henceforth expecting till his enemies be made his footstool.

14 For by one offering he hath perfected for ever them that are sanctified.

15 *Whereof* the Holy Ghost also is a witness to us: for after that he had said before,

16 This *is* the covenant that I will make with them after those days, saith the Lord, I will put my laws into their hearts, and in their minds will I write them;

17 And their sins and iniquities will I remember no more.

18 Now where remission of these *is, there is* no more offering for sin.

19 ¶ Having therefore, brethren, boldness to enter into the holiest by the blood of Jesus,

20 By a new and living way, which he hath consecrated for us, through the veil, that is to say, his flesh;

21 And *having* an high priest over the house of God;

22 Let us draw near with a true

heart in full assurance of faith, having our hearts sprinkled from an evil conscience, and our bodies washed with pure water.

23 Let us hold fast the profession of *our* faith without wavering; (for he *is* faithful that promised;)

24 And let us consider one another to provoke unto love and to good works:

25 Not forsaking the assembling of ourselves together, as the manner of some *is*; but exhorting *one another*: and so much the more, as ye see the day approaching.

26 For if we sin wilfully after that we have received the knowledge of the truth, there remaineth no more sacrifice for sins,

27 But a certain fearful looking for of judgment and fiery indignation, which shall devour the adversaries.

28 He that despised Moses' law died without mercy under two or three witnesses:

29 Of how much sorer punishment, suppose ye, shall he be thought worthy, who hath trodden under foot the Son of God, and hath counted the blood of the covenant, wherewith he was sanctified, an unholy thing, and hath done despite unto the Spirit of grace?

30 For we know him that hath said, Vengeance *belongeth* unto me, I will recompense, saith the Lord. And again, The Lord shall judge his people.

31 *It is* a fearful thing to fall into the hands of the living God.

32 But call to remembrance the former days, in which, after ye were illuminated, ye endured a great fight of afflictions;

33 Partly, whilst ye were made a gazingstock both by reproaches and afflictions; and partly, whilst ye became companions of them that were so used.

34 For ye had compassion of me in my bonds, and took joyfully the spoiling of your goods, knowing in yourselves that ye have in heaven a better and an enduring substance.

35 Cast not away therefore your confidence, which hath great recompence of reward.

36 For ye have need of patience, that, after ye have done the will of God, ye might receive the promise.

37 For yet a little while, and he that shall come will come, and will not tarry.

38 Now the just shall live by faith: but if *any man* draw back, my soul shall have no pleasure in him.

39 But we are not of them who draw back unto perdition; but of them that believe to the saving of the soul.

11 Now faith is the substance of things hoped for, the evidence of things not seen.

2 For by it the elders obtained a good report.

3 Through faith we understand that the worlds were framed by the word of God, so that things which are seen were not made of things which do appear.

4 ❡ By faith Abel offered unto God a more excellent sacrifice than Cain, by which he obtained witness that he was righteous, God testifying of his gifts: and by it he being dead yet speaketh.

5 ❡ By faith Enoch was translated that he should not see death; and was not found, because God had translated him: for before his translation he had this testimony, that he pleased God.

6 But without faith *it is* impossible to please *him*: for he that cometh to God must believe that he is, and *that* he is a rewarder of them that diligently seek him.

7 ❡ By faith Noah, being warned of God of things not seen as yet, moved with fear, prepared an ark to the saving of his house; by the which he condemned the world, and became heir of the righteousness which is by faith.

8 ❡ By faith Abraham, when he was called to go out into a place which he should after receive for an inheritance, obeyed; and he went out, not knowing whither he went.

9 By faith he sojourned in the land of promise, as *in* a strange country, dwelling in tabernacles with Isaac and Jacob, the heirs with him of the same promise:

10 For he looked for a city which hath foundations, whose builder and maker *is* God.

11 Through faith also Sara herself received strength to conceive seed, and was delivered of a child when she was past age, because she judged him faithful who had promised.

12 Therefore sprang there even of one, and him as good as dead, *so many* as the stars of the sky in multitude, and as the sand which is by the sea shore innumerable.

13 These all died in faith, not having received the promises, but having seen them afar off, and were persuaded of *them*, and embraced *them*, and confessed that they were strangers and pilgrims on the earth.

14 For they that say such things declare plainly that they seek a country.

15 And truly, if they had been mindful of that *country* from whence they came out, they might have had opportunity to have returned.

16 But now they desire a better *country*, that is, an heavenly: wherefore God is not ashamed to be called their God: for he hath prepared for them a city.

17 By faith Abraham, when he was tried, offered up Isaac: and he that had received the promises offered up his only begotten *son*,

18 Of whom it was said, That in Isaac shall thy seed be called:

19 Accounting that God *was* able to raise *him* up, even from the dead; from whence also he received him in a figure.

20 ❡ By faith Isaac blessed Jacob and Esau concerning things to come.

21 ❡ By faith Jacob, when he was a dying, blessed both the sons of Joseph; and worshipped, *leaning* upon the top of his staff.

22 ❡ By faith Joseph, when he

died, made mention of the departing of the children of Israel; and gave commandment concerning his bones.

23 ¶ By faith Moses, when he was born, was hid three months of his parents, because they saw *he was* a proper child; and they were not afraid of the king's commandment.

24 ¶ By faith Moses, when he was come to years, refused to be called the son of Pharaoh's daughter;

25 Choosing rather to suffer affliction with the people of God, than to enjoy the pleasures of sin for a season;

26 Esteeming the reproach of Christ greater riches than the treasures in Egypt: for he had respect unto the recompence of the reward.

27 By faith he forsook Egypt, not fearing the wrath of the king: for he endured, as seeing him who is invisible.

28 Through faith he kept the passover, and the sprinkling of blood, lest he that destroyed the firstborn should touch them.

29 By faith they passed through the Red sea as by dry *land*: which the Egyptians assaying to do were drowned.

30 ¶ By faith the walls of Jericho fell down, after they were compassed about seven days.

31 ¶ By faith the harlot Rahab perished not with them that believed not, when she had received the spies with peace.

32 ¶ And what shall I more say?

for the time would fail me to tell of Gedeon, and of Barak, and of Samson, and of Jephthae; of David also, and Samuel, and of the prophets:

33 Who through faith subdued kingdoms, wrought righteousness, obtained promises, stopped the mouths of lions,

34 Quenched the violence of fire, escaped the edge of the sword, out of weakness were made strong, waxed valiant in fight, turned to flight the armies of the aliens.

35 Women received their dead raised to life again: and others were tortured, not accepting deliverance; that they might obtain a better resurrection:

36 And others had trial of *cruel* mockings and scourgings, yea, moreover of bonds and imprisonment:

37 They were stoned, they were sawn asunder, were tempted, were slain with the sword: they wandered about in sheepskins and goatskins; being destitute, afflicted, tormented;

38 (Of whom the world was not worthy:) they wandered in deserts, and *in* mountains, and *in* dens and caves of the earth.

39 And these all, having obtained a good report through faith, received not the promise:

40 God having provided some better thing for us, that they without us should not be made perfect.

12 Wherefore seeing we also are compassed

about with so great a cloud of witnesses, let us lay aside every weight, and the sin which doth so easily beset us, and let us run with patience the race that is set before us,

2 Looking unto Jesus the author and finisher of our faith; who for the joy that was set before him endured the cross, despising the shame, and is set down at the right hand of the throne of God.

3 For consider him that endured such contradiction of sinners against himself, lest ye be wearied and faint in your minds.

4 Ye have not yet resisted unto blood, striving against sin.

5 And ye have forgotten the exhortation which speaketh unto you as unto children, My son, despise not thou the chastening of the Lord, nor faint when thou art rebuked of him:

6 For whom the Lord loveth he chasteneth, and scourgeth every son whom he receiveth.

7 If ye endure chastening, God dealeth with you as with sons; for what son is he whom the father chasteneth not?

8 But if ye be without chastisement, whereof all are partakers, then are ye bastards, and not sons.

9 Furthermore, we have had fathers of our flesh which corrected us, and we gave them reverence: shall we not much rather be in subjection unto the Father of spirits, and live?

10 For they verily for a few days chastened us after their own pleasure; but he for our profit, that we might be partakers of his holiness.

11 Now no chastening for the present seemeth to be joyous, but grievous: nevertheless afterward it yieldeth the peaceable fruit of righteousness unto them which are exercised thereby.

12 Wherefore lift up the hands which hang down, and the feeble knees;

13 And make straight paths for your feet, lest that which is lame be turned out of the way; but let it rather be healed.

14 Follow peace with all men, and holiness, without which no man shall see the Lord:

15 Looking diligently lest any man fail of the grace of God; lest any root of bitterness springing up trouble you, and thereby many be defiled;

16 Lest there be any fornicator, or profane person, as Esau, who for one morsel of meat sold his birthright.

17 For ye know how that afterward, when he would have inherited the blessing, he was rejected: for he found no place of repentance, though he sought it carefully with tears.

18 For ye are not come unto the mount that might be touched, and that burned with fire, nor unto blackness, and darkness, and tempest,

19 And the sound of a trumpet, and the voice of words; which voice they that heard intreated that the word should not be spoken to them any more:

20 (For they could not endure

that which was commanded, And if so much as a beast touch the mountain, it shall be stoned, or thrust through with a dart:

21 And so terrible was the sight, *that* Moses said, I exceedingly fear and quake):

22 But ye are come unto mount Sion, and unto the city of the living God, the heavenly Jerusalem, and to an innumerable company of angels,

23 To the general assembly and church of the firstborn, which are written in heaven, and to God the Judge of all, and to the spirits of just men made perfect,

24 And to Jesus the mediator of the new covenant, and to the blood of sprinkling, that speaketh better things than *that of* Abel.

25 ¶ See that ye refuse not him that speaketh. For if they escaped not who refused him that spake on earth, much more *shall not* we *escape*, if we turn away from him that *speaketh* from heaven:

26 Whose voice then shook the earth: but now he hath promised, saying, Yet once more I shake not the earth only, but also heaven.

27 And this *word*, Yet once more, signifieth the removing of those things that are shaken, as of things that are made, that those things which cannot be shaken may remain.

28 Wherefore we receiving a kingdom which cannot be moved, let us have grace, whereby we may serve God acceptably with reverence and godly fear:

29 For our God *is* a consuming fire.

13

Let brotherly love continue.

2 Be not forgetful to entertain strangers: for thereby some have entertained angels unawares.

3 Remember them that are in bonds, as bound with them; *and* them which suffer adversity, as being yourselves also in the body.

4 ¶ Marriage *is* honourable in all, and the bed undefiled: but whoremongers and adulterers God will judge.

5 ¶ *Let your* conversation *be* without covetousness; *and be* content with such things as ye have: for he hath said, I will never leave thee, nor forsake thee.

6 So that we may boldly say, The Lord *is* my helper, and I will not fear what man shall do unto me.

7 ¶ Remember them which have the rule over you, who have spoken unto you the word of God: whose faith follow, considering the end of *their* conversation.

8 Jesus Christ the same yesterday, and to day, and for ever.

9 ¶ Be not carried about with divers and strange doctrines. For *it is* a good thing that the heart be established with grace; not with meats, which have not profited them that have been occupied therein.

10 ¶ We have an altar, whereof they have no right to eat which serve the tabernacle.

11 For the bodies of those beasts, whose blood is brought into the sanctuary by the high

priest for sin, are burned without the camp.

12 Wherefore Jesus also, that he might sanctify the people with his own blood, suffered without the gate.

13 Let us go forth therefore unto him without the camp, bearing his reproach.

14 For here have we no continuing city, but we seek one to come.

15 By him therefore let us offer the sacrifice of praise to God continually, that is, the fruit of *our* lips giving thanks to his name.

16 ℂ But to do good and to communicate forget not: for with such sacrifices God is well pleased.

17 Obey them that have the rule over you, and submit yourselves: for they watch for your souls, as they that must give account, that they may do it with joy, and not with grief: for that *is* unprofitable for you.

18 ℂ Pray for us: for we trust we have a good conscience, in all things willing to live honestly.

19 But I beseech *you* the rather to do this, that I may be restored to you the sooner.

20 ℂ Now the God of peace, that brought again from the dead our Lord Jesus, that great shepherd of the sheep, through the blood of the everlasting covenant,

21 Make you perfect in every good work to do his will, working in you that which is well pleasing in his sight, through Jesus Christ; to whom *be* glory for ever and ever. Amen.

22 And I beseech you, brethren suffer the word of exhortation: for I have written a letter unto you in few words.

23 Know ye that *our* brother Timothy is set at liberty; with whom, if he come shortly, I will see you.

24 Salute all them that have the rule over you, and all the saints. They of Italy salute you.

25 Grace *be* with you all. Amen.

ℂ Written to the Hebrews from Italy by Timothy.

THE EPISTLE OF

JAMES

1 James, a servant of God and of the Lord Jesus Christ, to the twelve tribes which are scattered abroad, greeting.

2 My brethren, count it all joy when ye fall into divers temptations;

3 Knowing *this*, that the trying of your faith worketh patience.

4 But let patience have *her* perfect work, that ye may be perfect

and entire, wanting nothing.

5 ¶ If any of you lack wisdom, let him ask of God, that giveth to all *men* liberally, and upbraideth not; and it shall be given him.

6 But let him ask in faith, nothing wavering. For he that wavereth is like a wave of the sea driven with the wind and tossed.

7 For let not that man think that he shall receive any thing of the Lord.

8 A double minded man *is* unstable in all his ways.

9 Let the brother of low degree rejoice in that he is exalted:

10 But the rich, in that he is made low: because as the flower of the grass he shall pass away.

11 For the sun is no sooner risen with a burning heat, but it withereth the grass, and the flower thereof falleth, and the grace of the fashion of it perisheth: so also shall the rich man fade away in his ways.

12 Blessed *is* the man that endureth temptation: for when he is tried, he shall receive the crown of life, which the Lord hath promised to them that love him.

13 ¶ Let no man say when he is tempted, I am tempted of God: for God cannot be tempted with evil, neither tempteth he any man:

14 But every man is tempted, when he is drawn away of his own lust, and enticed.

15 Then when lust hath conceived, it bringeth forth sin: and sin, when it is finished, bringeth forth death.

16 Do not err, my beloved brethren.

17 Every good gift and every perfect gift is from above, and cometh down from the Father of lights, with whom is no variableness, neither shadow of turning.

18 Of his own will begat he us with the word of truth, that we should be a kind of firstfruits of his creatures.

19 ¶ Wherefore, my beloved brethren, let every man be swift to hear, slow to speak, slow to wrath:

20 For the wrath of man worketh not the righteousness of God.

21 Wherefore lay apart all filthiness and superfluity of naughtiness, and receive with meekness the engrafted word, which is able to save your souls.

22 But be ye doers of the word, and not hearers only, deceiving your own selves.

23 For if any be a hearer of the word, and not a doer, he is like unto a man beholding his natural face in a glass:

24 For he beholdeth himself, and goeth his way, and straightway forgetteth what manner of man he was.

25 But whoso looketh into the perfect law of liberty, and continueth *therein,* he being not a forgetful hearer, but a doer of the work, this man shall be blessed in his deed.

26 If any man among you seem to be religious, and bridleth not his tongue, but deceiveth his own

heart, this man's religion *is* vain.

27 Pure religion and undefiled before God and the Father is this, To visit the fatherless and widows in their affliction, *and* to keep himself unspotted from the world.

2 My brethren, have not the faith of our Lord Jesus Christ, *the Lord* of glory, with respect of persons.

2 For if there come unto your assembly a man with a gold ring, in goodly apparel, and there come in also a poor man in vile raiment;

3 And ye have respect to him that weareth the gay clothing, and say unto him, Sit thou here in a good place; and say to the poor, Stand thou there, or sit here under my footstool:

4 Are ye not then partial in yourselves, and are become judges of evil thoughts?

5 Hearken, my beloved brethren, Hath not God chosen the poor of this world rich in faith, and heirs of the kingdom which he hath promised to them that love him?

6 But ye have despised the poor. Do not rich men oppress you, and draw you before the judgment seats?

7 Do not they blaspheme that worthy name by the which ye are called?

8 If ye fulfil the royal law according to the scripture, Thou shalt love thy neighbour as thyself, ye do well:

9 But if ye have respect to persons, ye commit sin, and are convinced of the law as transgressors,

10 For whosoever shall keep the whole law, and yet offend in one *point*, he is guilty of all.

11 For he that said, Do not commit adultery, said also, Do not kill. Now if thou commit no adultery, yet if thou kill, thou art become a transgressor of the law.

12 So speak ye, and so do, as they that shall be judged by the law of liberty.

13 For he shall have judgment without mercy, that hath shewed no mercy; and mercy rejoiceth against judgment.

14 ❡ What *doth it* profit, my brethren, though a man say he hath faith, and have not works? can faith save him?

15 If a brother or sister be naked, and destitute of daily food,

16 And one of you say unto them, Depart in peace, be *ye* warmed and filled; notwithstanding ye give them not those things which are needful to the body; what *doth it* profit?

17 Even so faith, if it hath not works, is dead, being alone.

18 Yea, a man may say, Thou hast faith, and I have works: shew me thy faith without thy works, and I will shew thee my faith by my works.

19 Thou believest that there is one God; thou doest well: the devils also believe, and tremble.

20 But wilt thou know, O vain man, that faith without works is

dead?

21 Was not Abraham our father justified by works, when he had offered Isaac his son upon the altar?

22 Seest thou how faith wrought with his works, and by works was faith made perfect?

23 And the scripture was fulfilled which saith, Abraham believed God, and it was imputed unto him for righteousness: and he was called the Friend of God.

24 Ye see then how that by works a man is justified, and not by faith only.

25 Likewise also was not Rahab the harlot justified by works, when she had received the messengers, and had sent *them* out another way?

26 For as the body without the spirit is dead, so faith without works is dead also.

3 My brethren, be not many masters, knowing that we shall receive the greater condemnation.

2 For in many things we offend all. If any man offend not in word, the same *is* a perfect man, *and* able also to bridle the whole body.

3 Behold, we put bits in the horses' mouths, that they may obey us; and we turn about their whole body.

4 Behold also the ships, which though *they be* so great, and *are* driven of fierce winds, yet are they turned about with a very small helm, whithersoever the governor listeth.

5 Even so the tongue is a little member, and boasteth great things. Behold, how great a matter a little fire kindleth!

6 And the tongue *is* a fire, a world of iniquity: so is the tongue among our members, that it defileth the whole body, and setteth on fire the course of nature; and it is set on fire of hell.

7 For every kind of beasts, and of birds, and of serpents, and of things in the sea, is tamed, and hath been tamed of mankind:

8 But the tongue can no man tame; *it is* an unruly evil, full of deadly poison.

9 Therewith bless we God, even the Father; and therewith curse we men, which are made after the similitude of God.

10 Out of the same mouth proceedeth blessing and cursing. My brethren, these things ought not so to be.

11 Doth a fountain send forth at the same place sweet *water* and bitter?

12 Can the fig tree, my brethren, bear olive berries? either a vine, figs? so *can* no fountain both yield salt water and fresh.

13 ¶ Who *is* a wise man and endued with knowledge among you? let him shew out of a good conversation his works with meekness of wisdom.

14 But if ye have bitter envying and strife in your hearts, glory not, and lie not against the truth.

15 This wisdom descendeth not from above, but *is* earthly, sensual, devilish.

16 For where envying and strife *is*, there *is* confusion and every evil work.

17 But the wisdom that is from above is first pure, then peaceable, gentle, *and* easy to be intreated, full of mercy and good fruits, without partiality, and without hypocrisy.

18 And the fruit of righteousness is sown in peace of them that make peace.

4 From whence *come* wars and fightings among you? *come they* not hence, *even* of your lusts that war in your members?

2 Ye lust, and have not: ye kill, and desire to have, and cannot obtain: ye fight and war, yet ye have not, because ye ask not.

3 Ye ask, and receive not, because ye ask amiss, that ye may consume *it* upon your lusts.

4 Ye adulterers and adulteresses, know ye not that the friendship of the world is enmity with God? whosoever therefore will be a friend of the world is the enemy of God.

5 Do ye think that the scripture saith in vain, The spirit that dwelleth in us lusteth to envy?

6 But he giveth more grace. Wherefore he saith, God resisteth the proud, but giveth grace unto the humble.

7 Submit yourselves therefore to God. Resist the devil, and he will flee from you.

8 Draw nigh to God, and he will draw nigh to you. Cleanse *your* hands, *ye* sinners; and purify *your* hearts, *ye* double minded.

9 Be afflicted, and mourn, and weep: let your laughter be turned to mourning, and *your* joy to heaviness.

10 Humble yourselves in the sight of the Lord, and he shall lift you up.

11 Speak not evil one of another, brethren. He that speaketh evil of *his* brother, and judgeth his brother, speaketh evil of the law, and judgeth the law: but if thou judge the law, thou art not a doer of the law, but a judge.

12 There is one lawgiver, who is able to save and to destroy: who art thou that judgest another?

13 Go to now, ye that say, To day or to morrow we will go into such a city, and continue there a year, and buy and sell, and get gain:

14 Whereas ye know not what *shall be* on the morrow. For what *is* your life? It is even a vapour, that appeareth for a little time, and then vanisheth away.

15 For that ye *ought* to say, If the Lord will, we shall live, and do this, or that.

16 But now ye rejoice in your boastings: all such rejoicing is evil.

17 Therefore to him that knoweth to do good, and doeth *it* not, to him it is sin.

5 Go to now, *ye* rich men, weep and howl for your miseries that shall come upon *you*.

2 Your riches are corrupted, and your garments are motheaten.

3 Your gold and silver is cankered; and the rust of them shall be a witness against you, and shall eat your flesh as it were fire. Ye have heaped treasure together for the last days.

4 Behold, the hire of the labourers who have reaped down your fields, which is of you kept back by fraud, crieth: and the cries of them which have reaped are entered into the ears of the Lord of sabaoth.

5 Ye have lived in pleasure on the earth, and been wanton; ye have nourished your hearts, as in a day of slaughter.

6 Ye have condemned *and* killed the just; *and* he doth not resist you.

7 ⟨ Be patient therefore, brethren, unto the coming of the Lord. Behold, the husbandman waiteth for the precious fruit of the earth, and hath long patience for it, until he receive the early and latter rain.

8 Be ye also patient; stablish your hearts: for the coming of the Lord draweth nigh.

9 Grudge not one against another, brethren, lest ye be condemned: behold, the judge standeth before the door.

10 Take, my brethren, the prophets, who have spoken in the name of the Lord, for an example of suffering affliction, and of patience.

11 Behold, we count them happy which endure. Ye have heard of the patience of Job, and have seen the end of the Lord; that the Lord is very pitiful, and of tender mercy.

12 But above all things, my brethren, swear not, neither by heaven, neither by the earth, neither by any other oath: but let your yea be yea; and *your* nay, nay; lest ye fall into condemnation.

13 ⟨ Is any among you afflicted? let him pray. Is any merry? let him sing psalms.

14 Is any sick among you? let him call for the elders of the church; and let them pray over him, anointing him with oil in the name of the Lord:

15 And the prayer of faith shall save the sick, and the Lord shall raise him up; and if he have committed sins, they shall be forgiven him.

16 Confess *your* faults one to another, and pray one for another, that ye may be healed. The effectual fervent prayer of a righteous man availeth much.

17 Elias was a man subject to like passions as we are, and he prayed earnestly that it might not rain: and it rained not on the earth by the space of three years and six months.

18 And he prayed again, and the heaven gave rain, and the earth brought forth her fruit.

19 ⟨ Brethren, if any of you do err from the truth, and one convert him;

20 Let him know, that he which converteth the sinner from the error of his way shall save a soul from death, and shall hide a multitude of sins.

THE FIRST EPISTLE OF

PETER

1 Peter, an apostle of Jesus Christ, to the strangers scattered throughout Pontus, Galatia, Cappadocia, Asia, and Bithynia,

2 Elect according to the foreknowledge of God the Father, through sanctification of the Spirit, unto obedience and sprinkling of the blood of Jesus Christ: Grace unto you, and peace, be multiplied.

3 Blessed *be* the God and Father of our Lord Jesus Christ, which according to his abundant mercy hath begotten us again unto a lively hope by the resurrection of Jesus Christ from the dead,

4 To an inheritance incorruptible, and undefiled, and that fadeth not away, reserved in heaven for you,

5 Who are kept by the power of God through faith unto salvation ready to be revealed in the last time.

6 Wherein ye greatly rejoice, though now for a season, if need be, ye are in heaviness through manifold temptations:

7 That the trial of your faith, being much more precious than of gold that perisheth, though it be tried with fire, might be found unto praise and honour and glory at the appearing of Jesus Christ:

8 Whom having not seen, ye love; in whom, though now ye see *him* not, yet believing, ye rejoice with joy unspeakable and full of glory:

9 Receiving the end of your faith, *even* the salvation of *your* souls.

10 ❪Of which salvation the prophets have enquired and searched diligently, who prophesied of the grace *that should come* unto you:

11 Searching what, or what manner of time the Spirit of Christ which was in them did signify, when it testified beforehand the sufferings of Christ, and the glory that should follow.

12 Unto whom it was revealed, that not unto themselves, but unto us they did minister the things, which are now reported unto you by them that have preached the gospel unto you with the Holy Ghost sent down from heaven; which things the angels desire to look into.

13 ❪Wherefore gird up the loins of your mind, be sober, and hope to the end for the grace that is to be brought unto you at the revelation of Jesus Christ;

14 As obedient children, not fashioning yourselves according to the former lusts in your ignorance:

15 But as he which hath called you is holy, so be ye holy in all manner of conversation;

16 Because it is written, Be ye holy; for I am holy.

17 And if ye call on the Father, who without respect of persons judgeth according to every man's

work, pass the time of your sojourning *here* in fear:

18 Forasmuch as ye know that ye were not redeemed with corruptible things, as silver and gold, from your vain conversation *received* by tradition from your fathers;

19 But with the precious blood of Christ, as of a lamb without blemish and without spot:

20 Who verily was foreordained before the foundation of the world, but was manifest in these last times for you,

21 Who by him do believe in God, that raised him up from the dead, and gave him glory; that your faith and hope might be in God.

22 Seeing ye have purified your souls in obeying the truth through the Spirit unto unfeigned love of the brethren, *see that ye* love one another with a pure heart fervently:

23 Being born again, not of corruptible seed, but of incorruptible, by the word of God, which liveth and abideth for ever.

24 For all flesh *is* as grass, and all the glory of man as the flower of grass. The grass withereth, and the flower thereof falleth away:

25 But the word of the Lord endureth for ever. And this is the word which by the gospel is preached unto you.

2 Wherefore laying aside all malice, and all guile, and hypocrisies, and envies, and all evil speakings,

2 As newborn babes, desire the sincere milk of the word, that ye may grow thereby:

3 If so be ye have tasted that the Lord *is* gracious.

4 ¶ To whom coming, *as unto* a living stone, disallowed indeed of men, but chosen of God, *and* precious,

5 Ye also, as lively stones, are built up a spiritual house, an holy priesthood, to offer up spiritual sacrifices, acceptable to God by Jesus Christ.

6 Wherefore also it is contained in the scripture, Behold, I lay in Sion a chief corner stone, elect, precious: and he that believeth on him shall not be confounded.

7 Unto you therefore which believe *he is* precious: but unto them which be disobedient, the stone which the builders disallowed, the same is made the head of the corner,

8 And a stone of stumbling, and a rock of offense, *even to them* which stumble at the word, being disobedient: whereunto also they were appointed.

9 But ye *are* a chosen generation, a royal priesthood, an holy nation, a peculiar people; that ye should shew forth the praises of him who hath called you out of darkness into his marvellous light;

10 Which in time past *were* not a people, but *are* now the people of God: which had not obtained mercy, but now have obtained mercy.

11 ¶ Dearly beloved, I beseech *you* as strangers and pilgrims, abstain from fleshly lusts, which

war against the soul;

12 Having your conversation honest among the Gentiles: that, whereas they speak against you as evildoers, they may by your good works, which they shall behold, glorify God in the day of visitation.

13 ¶ Submit yourselves to every ordinance of man for the Lord's sake: whether it be to the king, as supreme;

14 Or unto governors, as unto them that are sent by him for the punishment of evildoers, and for the praise of them that do well.

15 For so is the will of God, that with well doing ye may put to silence the ignorance of foolish men:

16 As free, and not using your liberty for a cloke of maliciousness, but as the servants of God.

17 Honour all men. Love the brotherhood. Fear God. Honour the king.

18 ¶ Servants, be subject to your masters with all fear; not only to the good and gentle, but also to the froward.

19 For this is thankworthy, if a man for conscience toward God endure grief, suffering wrongfully.

20 For what glory is it, if, when ye be buffeted for your faults, ye shall take it patiently? but if, when ye do well, and suffer for it, ye take it patiently, this is acceptable with God.

21 For even hereunto were ye called: because Christ also suffered for us, leaving us an example, that ye should follow his steps:

22 Who did no sin, neither was guile found in his mouth:

23 Who, when he was reviled, reviled not again; when he suffered, he threatened not; but committed himself to him that judgeth righteously:

24 Who his own self bare our sins in his own body on the tree, that we, being dead to sins, should live unto righteousness: by whose stripes ye were healed.

25 For ye were as sheep going astray; but are now returned unto the Shepherd and Bishop of your souls.

3 Likewise, ye wives, be in subjection to your own husbands; that, if any obey not the word, they also may without the word be won by the conversation of the wives;

2 While they behold your chaste conversation coupled with fear.

3 Whose adorning let it not be that outward adorning of plaiting the hair, and of wearing of gold, or of putting on of apparel;

4 But let it be the hidden man of the heart, in that which is not corruptible, even the ornament of a meek and quiet spirit, which is in the sight of God of great price.

5 For after this manner in the old time the holy women also, who trusted in God, adorned themselves, being in subjection unto their own husbands:

6 Even as Sara obeyed Abraham, calling him lord: whose daughters ye are, as long as ye do

well, and are not afraid with any amazement.

7 Likewise, ye husbands, dwell with *them* according to knowledge, giving honour unto the wife, as unto the weaker vessel, and as being heirs together of the grace of life; that your prayers be not hindered.

8 ¶ Finally, *be ye* all of one mind, having compassion one of another, love as brethren, *be* pitiful, *be* courteous:

9 Not rendering evil for evil, or railing for railing: but contrariwise blessing; knowing that ye are thereunto called, that ye should inherit a blessing.

10 For he that will love life, and see good days, let him refrain his tongue from evil, and his lips that they speak no guile:

11 Let him eschew evil, and do good; let him seek peace, and ensue it.

12 ¶ For the eyes of the Lord *are* over the righteous, and his ears *are open* unto their prayers: but the face of the Lord *is* against them that do evil.

13 And who *is* he that will harm you, if ye be followers of that which is good?

14 But and if ye suffer for righteousness' sake, happy *are ye*: and be not afraid of their terror, neither be troubled;

15 But sanctify the Lord God in your hearts: and *be* ready always to give an answer to every man that asketh you a reason of the hope that is in you with meekness and fear:

16 Having a good conscience; that, whereas they speak evil of you, as of evildoers, they may be ashamed that falsely accuse your good conversation in Christ.

17 For *it is* better, if the will of God be so, that ye suffer for well doing, than for evil doing.

18 ¶ For Christ also hath once suffered for sins, the just for the unjust, that he might bring us to God, being put to death in the flesh, but quickened by the Spirit:

19 By which also he went and preached unto the spirits in prison;

20 Which sometime were disobedient, when once the longsuffering of God waited in the days of Noah, while the ark was a preparing, wherein few, that is, eight souls were saved by water.

21 The like figure whereunto *even* baptism doth also now save us (not the putting away of the filth of the flesh, but the answer of a good conscience toward God,) by the resurrection of Jesus Christ:

22 Who is gone into heaven, and is on the right hand of God; angels and authorities and powers being made subject unto him.

4 Forasmuch then as Christ hath suffered for us in the flesh, arm yourselves likewise with the same mind: for he that hath suffered in the flesh hath ceased from sin;

2 That he no longer should live the rest of *his* time in the flesh to the lusts of men, but to the will of God.

3 For the time past of *our* life may suffice us to have wrought the will of the Gentiles, when we walked in lasciviousness, lusts, excess of wine, revellings, banquetings, and abominable idolatries:

4 Wherein they think it strange that ye run not with *them* to the same excess of riot, speaking evil of *you*:

5 Who shall give account to him that is ready to judge the quick and the dead.

6 For for this cause was the gospel preached also to them that are dead, that they might be judged according to men in the flesh, but live according to God in the spirit.

7 But the end of all things is at hand: be ye therefore sober, and watch unto prayer.

8 And above all things have fervent charity among yourselves: for charity shall cover the multitude of sins.

9 Use hospitality one to another without grudging.

10 As every man hath received the gift, *even so* minister the same one to another, as good stewards of the manifold grace of God.

11 If any man speak, *let him speak* as the oracles of God; if any man minister, *let him do it* as of the ability which God giveth: that God in all things may be glorified through Jesus Christ, to whom be praise and dominion for ever and ever. Amen.

12 Beloved, think it not strange concerning the fiery trial which is to try you, as though some strange thing happened unto you:

13 But rejoice, inasmuch as ye are partakers of Christ's sufferings; that, when his glory shall be revealed, ye may be glad also with exceeding joy.

14 If ye be reproached for the name of Christ, happy *are ye*; for the spirit of glory and of God resteth upon you: on their part he is evil spoken of, but on your part he is glorified.

15 But let none of you suffer as a murderer, or *as* a thief, or *as* an evildoer, or as a busybody in other men's matters.

16 Yet if *any man suffer* as a Christian, let him not be ashamed; but let him glorify God on this behalf.

17 For the time *is come* that judgment must begin at the house of God: and if *it* first *begin* at us, what shall the end *be* of them that obey not the gospel of God?

18 And if the righteous scarcely be saved, where shall the ungodly and the sinner appear?

19 Wherefore let them that suffer according to the will of God commit the keeping of their souls *to him* in well doing, as unto a faithful Creator.

5 The elders which are among you I exhort, who am also an elder, and a witness of the sufferings of Christ, and also a partaker of the glory that shall be revealed:

2 Feed the flock of God which is among you, taking the over-

sight *thereof*, not by constraint, but willingly; not for filthy lucre, but of a ready mind;

3 Neither as being lords over *God's* heritage, but being ensamples to the flock.

4 And when the chief Shepherd shall appear, ye shall receive a crown of glory that fadeth not away.

5 Likewise, ye younger, submit yourselves unto the elder. Yea, all *of you* be subject one to another, and be clothed with humility: for God resisteth the proud, and giveth grace to the humble.

6 Humble yourselves therefore under the mighty hand of God, that he may exalt you in due time:

7 Casting all your care upon him; for he careth for you.

8 Be sober, be vigilant; because your adversary the devil, as a roaring lion, walketh about, seeking whom he may devour:

9 Whom resist stedfast in the faith, knowing that the same afflictions are accomplished in your brethren that are in the world.

10 But the God of all grace, who hath called us unto his eternal glory by Christ Jesus, after that ye have suffered a while, make you perfect, stablish, strengthen, settle *you*.

11 To him *be* glory and dominion for ever and ever. Amen.

12 By Silvanus, a faithful brother unto you, as I suppose, I have written briefly, exhorting, and testifying that this is the true grace of God wherein ye stand.

13 The *church that is* at Babylon, elected together with *you*, saluteth you; and *so doth* Marcus my son.

14 Greet ye one another with a kiss of charity. Peace *be* with you all that are in Christ Jesus. Amen.

THE SECOND EPISTLE OF

PETER

1 Simon Peter, a servant and an apostle of Jesus Christ, to them that have obtained like precious faith with us through the righteousness of God and our Saviour Jesus Christ:

2 Grace and peace be multiplied unto you through the knowledge of God, and of Jesus our Lord,

3 According as his divine power hath given unto us all things

that *pertain* unto life and godliness, through the knowledge of him that hath called us to glory and virtue:

4 Whereby are given unto us exceeding great and precious promises: that by these ye might be partakers of the divine nature, having escaped the corruption that is in the world through lust.

5 ¶ And beside this, giving all dil-

igence, add to your faith virtue; and to virtue knowledge;

6 And to knowledge temperance; and to temperance patience; and to patience godliness;

7 And to godliness brotherly kindness; and to brotherly kindness charity.

8 For if these things be in you, and abound, they make *you that ye shall* neither *be* barren nor unfruitful in the knowledge of our Lord Jesus Christ.

9 But he that lacketh these things is blind, and cannot see afar off, and hath forgotten that he was purged from his old sins.

10 Wherefore the rather, brethren, give diligence to make your calling and election sure: for if ye do these things, ye shall never fall:

11 For so an entrance shall be ministered unto you abundantly into the everlasting kingdom of our Lord and Saviour Jesus Christ.

12 ¶ Wherefore I will not be negligent to put you always in remembrance of these things, though ye know *them*, and be established in the present truth.

13 Yea, I think it meet, as long as I am in this tabernacle, to stir you up by putting *you* in remembrance;

14 Knowing that shortly I must put off *this* my tabernacle, even as our Lord Jesus Christ hath shewed me.

15 Moreover I will endeavour that ye may be able after my decease to have these things always in remembrance.

16 For we have not followed cunningly devised fables, when we made known unto you the power and coming of our Lord Jesus Christ, but were eyewitnesses of his majesty.

17 For he received from God the Father honour and glory, when there came such a voice to him from the excellent glory, This is my beloved Son, in whom I am well pleased.

18 And this voice which came from heaven we heard, when we were with him in the holy mount.

19 We have also a more sure word of prophecy; whereunto ye do well that ye take heed, as unto a light that shineth in a dark place, until the day dawn, and the day star arise in your hearts:

20 Knowing this first, that no prophecy of the scripture is of any private interpretation.

21 For the prophecy came not in old time by the will of man: but holy men of God spake *as they were* moved by the Holy Ghost.

2 But there were false prophets also among the people, even as there shall be false teachers among you, who privily shall bring in damnable heresies, even denying the Lord that bought them, and bring upon themselves swift destruction.

2 And many shall follow their pernicious ways; by reason of whom the way of truth shall be evil spoken of.

3 And through covetousness

shall they with feigned words make merchandise of you: whose judgment now of a long time lingereth not, and their damnation slumbereth not.

4 For if God spared not the angels that sinned, but cast *them* down to hell, and delivered *them* into chains of darkness, to be reserved unto judgment;

5 And spared not the old world, but saved Noah the eighth *person*, a preacher of righteousness, bringing in the flood upon the world of the ungodly;

6 And turning the cities of Sodom and Gomorrha into ashes condemned *them* with an overthrow, making *them* an ensample unto those that after should live ungodly;

7 And delivered just Lot, vexed with the filthy conversation of the wicked:

8 (For that righteous man dwelling among them, in seeing and hearing, vexed *his* righteous soul from day to day with *their* unlawful deeds;)

9 The Lord knoweth how to deliver the godly out of temptations, and to reserve the unjust unto the day of judgment to be punished:

10 But chiefly them that walk after the flesh in the lust of uncleanness, and despise government. Presumptuous *are they*, selfwilled, they are not afraid to speak evil of dignities.

11 Whereas angels, which are greater in power and might, bring not railing accusation against them before the Lord.

12 But these, as natural brute beasts, made to be taken and destroyed, speak evil of the things that they understand not; and shall utterly perish in their own corruption;

13 And shall receive the reward of unrighteousness, *as* they that count it pleasure to riot in the day time. Spots *they are* and blemishes, sporting themselves with their own deceivings while they feast with you;

14 Having eyes full of adultery, and that cannot cease from sin; beguiling unstable souls: an heart they have exercised with covetous practices; cursed children:

15 Which have forsaken the right way, and are gone astray, following the way of Balaam *the son* of Bosor, who loved the wages of unrighteousness;

16 But was rebuked for his iniquity: the dumb ass speaking with man's voice forbad the madness of the prophet.

17 These are wells without water, clouds that are carried with a tempest; to whom the mist of darkness is reserved for ever.

18 For when they speak great swelling *words* of vanity, they allure through the lusts of the flesh, *through much* wantonness, those that were clean escaped from them who live in error.

19 While they promise them liberty, they themselves are the servants of corruption: for of whom a man is overcome, of the same is he brought in bondage.

20 For if after they have es-

caped the pollutions of the world through the knowledge of the Lord and Saviour Jesus Christ, they are again entangled therein, and overcome, the latter end is worse with them than the beginning.

21 For it had been better for them not to have known the way of righteousness, than, after they have known *it*, to turn from the holy commandment delivered unto them.

22 But it is happened unto them according to the true proverb, The dog *is* turned to his own vomit again; and the sow that was washed to her wallowing in the mire.

3 This second epistle, beloved, I now write unto you; in *both* which I stir up your pure minds by way of remembrance:

2 That ye may be mindful of the words which were spoken before by the holy prophets, and of the commandment of us the apostles of the Lord and Saviour:

3 Knowing this first, that there shall come in the last days scoffers, walking after their own lusts,

4 And saying, Where is the promise of his coming? for since the fathers fell asleep, all things continue as *they were* from the beginning of the creation.

5 For this they willingly are ignorant of, that by the word of God the heavens were of old, and the earth standing out of the water and in the water:

6 Whereby the world that then was, being overflowed with water, perished:

7 But the heavens and the earth, which are now, by the same word are kept in store, reserved unto fire against the day of judgment and perdition of ungodly men.

8 ¶ But, beloved, be not ignorant of this one thing, that one day *is* with the Lord as a thousand years, and a thousand years as one day.

9 The Lord is not slack concerning his promise, as some men count slackness; but is longsuffering to us-ward, not willing that any should perish, but that all should come to repentance.

10 But the day of the Lord will come as a thief in the night; in the which the heavens shall pass away with a great noise, and the elements shall melt with fervent heat, the earth also and the works that are therein shall be burned up.

11 *Seeing* then *that* all these things shall be dissolved, what manner *of persons* ought ye to be in *all* holy conversation and godliness,

12 Looking for and hasting unto the coming of the day of God, wherein the heavens being on fire shall be dissolved, and the elements shall melt with fervent heat?

13 Nevertheless we, according to his promise, look for new heavens and a new earth, wherein dwelleth righteousness.

14 Wherefore, beloved, seeing that ye look for such things, be

diligent that ye may be found of him in peace, without spot, and blameless.

15 ¶ And account *that* the long-suffering of our Lord *is* salvation; even as our beloved brother Paul also according to the wisdom given unto him hath written unto you;

16 As also in all *his* epistles, speaking in them of these things; in which are some things hard to be understood, which they that are unlearned and unstable wrest, as *they do* also the other scriptures, unto their own destruction.

17 Ye therefore, beloved, seeing ye know *these things* before, beware lest ye also, being led away with the error of the wicked, fall from your own stedfastness.

18 But grow in grace, and *in* the knowledge of our Lord and Saviour Jesus Christ. To him *be* glory both now and for ever. Amen.

THE FIRST EPISTLE OF

JOHN

1 That which was from the beginning, which we have heard, which we have seen with our eyes, which we have looked upon, and our hands have handled, of the Word of life;

2 (For the life was manifested, and we have seen *it*, and bear witness, and shew unto you that eternal life, which was with the Father, and was manifested unto us;)

3 That which we have seen and heard declare we unto you, that ye also may have fellowship with us: and truly our fellowship *is* with the Father, and with his Son Jesus Christ.

4 And these things write we unto you, that your joy may be full.

5 This then is the message which we have heard of him, and declare unto you, that God is light, and in him is no darkness at all.

6 If we say that we have fellowship with him, and walk in darkness, we lie, and do not the truth:

7 But if we walk in the light, as he is in the light, we have fellowship one with another, and the blood of Jesus Christ his Son cleanseth us from all sin.

8 If we say that we have no sin, we deceive ourselves, and the truth is not in us.

9 If we confess our sins, he is faithful and just to forgive us *our* sins, and to cleanse us from all unrighteousness.

10 If we say that we have not sinned, we make him a liar, and his word is not in us.

2 MY little children, these things write I unto you, that

ye sin not. And if any man sin, we have an advocate with the Father, Jesus Christ the righteous:

2 And he is the propitiation for our sins: and not for ours only, but also for *the sins of* the whole world.

3 ¶And hereby we do know that we know him, if we keep his commandments.

4 He that saith, I know him, and keepeth not his commandments, is a liar, and the truth is not in him.

5 But whoso keepeth his word, in him verily is the love of God perfected: hereby know we that we are in him.

6 He that saith he abideth in him ought himself also so to walk, even as he walked.

7 Brethren, I write no new commandment unto you, but an old commandment which ye had from the beginning. The old commandment is the word which ye have heard from the beginning.

8 Again, a new commandment I write unto you, which thing is true in him and in you: because the darkness is past, and the true light now shineth.

9 He that saith he is in the light, and hateth his brother, is in darkness even until now.

10 He that loveth his brother abideth in the light, and there is none occasion of stumbling in him.

11 But he that hateth his brother is in darkness, and walketh in darkness, and knoweth not whither he goeth, because that darkness hath blinded his eyes.

12 I write unto you, little children, because your sins are forgiven you for his name's sake.

13 I write unto you, fathers, because ye have known him *that is* from the beginning. I write unto you, young men, because ye have overcome the wicked one. I write unto you, little children, because ye have known the Father.

14 I have written unto you, fathers, because ye have known him *that is* from the beginning. I have written unto you, young men, because ye are strong, and the word of God abideth in you, and ye have overcome the wicked one.

15 ¶ Love not the world, neither the things that *are* in the world. If any man love the world, the love of the Father is not in him.

16 For all that *is* in the world, the lust of the flesh, and the lust of the eyes, and the pride of life, is not of the Father, but is of the world.

17 And the world passeth away, and the lust thereof: but he that doeth the will of God abideth for ever.

18 ¶ Little children, it is the last time: and as ye have heard that antichrist shall come, even now are there many antichrists; whereby we know that it is the last time.

19 They went out from us, but they were not of us; for if they had been of us, they would *no doubt* have continued with us: but *they went out*, that they might be made manifest that they

were not all of us.

20 But ye have an unction from the Holy One, and ye know all things.

21 I have not written unto you because ye know not the truth, but because ye know it, and that no lie is of the truth.

22 Who is a liar but he that denieth that Jesus is the Christ? He is antichrist, that denieth the Father and the Son.

23 Whosoever denieth the Son, the same hath not the Father: *[but] he that acknowledgeth the Son hath the Father also.*

24 Let that therefore abide in you, which ye have heard from the beginning. If that which ye have heard from the beginning shall remain in you, ye also shall continue in the Son, and in the Father.

25 And this is the promise that he hath promised us, *even* eternal life.

26 These *things* have I written unto you concerning them that seduce you.

27 But the anointing which ye have received of him abideth in you, and ye need not that any man teach you: but as the same anointing teacheth you of all things, and is truth, and is no lie, and even as it hath taught you, ye shall abide in him.

28 And now, little children, abide in him; that, when he shall appear, we may have confidence, and not be ashamed before him at his coming.

29 If ye know that he is righ-

teous, ye know that every one that doeth righteousness is born of him.

3 Behold, what manner of love the Father hath bestowed upon us, that we should be called the sons of God: therefore the world knoweth us not, because it knew him not.

2 Beloved, now are we the sons of God, and it doth not yet appear what we shall be: but we know that, when he shall appear, we shall be like him; for we shall see him as he is.

3 And every man that hath this hope in him purifieth himself, even as he is pure.

4 Whosoever committeth sin transgresseth also the law: for sin is the transgression of the law.

5 And ye know that he was manifested to take away our sins; and in him is no sin.

6 Whosoever abideth in him sinneth not: whosoever sinneth hath not seen him, neither known him.

7 Little children, let no man deceive you: he that doeth righteousness is righteous, even as he is righteous.

8 He that committeth sin is of the devil; for the devil sinneth from the beginning. For this purpose the Son of God was manifested, that he might destroy the works of the devil.

9 Whosoever is born of God doth not commit sin; for his seed remaineth in him: and he cannot sin, because he is born of God.

10 In this the children of God

are manifest, and the children of the devil: whosoever doeth not righteousness is not of God, neither he that loveth not his brother.

11 ¶ For this is the message that ye heard from the beginning, that we should love one another.

12 Not as Cain, *who* was of that wicked one, and slew his brother. And wherefore slew he him? Because his own works were evil, and his brother's righteous.

13 Marvel not, my brethren, if the world hate you.

14 We know that we have passed from death unto life, because we love the brethren. He that loveth not *his* brother abideth in death.

15 Whosoever hateth his brother is a murderer: and ye know that no murderer hath eternal life abiding in him.

16 Hereby perceive we the love *of God*, because he laid down his life for us: and we ought to lay down *our* lives for the brethren.

17 But whoso hath this world's good, and seeth his brother have need, and shutteth up his bowels *of compassion* from him, how dwelleth the love of God in him?

18 My little children, let us not love in word, neither in tongue; but in deed and in truth.

19 And hereby we know that we are of the truth, and shall assure our hearts before him.

20 For if our heart condemn us, God is greater than our heart, and knoweth all things.

21 Beloved, if our heart con-

demn us not, *then* have we confidence toward God.

22 And whatsoever we ask, we receive of him, because we keep his commandments, and do those things that are pleasing in his sight.

23 And this is his commandment, That we should believe on the name of his Son Jesus Christ, and love one another, as he gave us commandment.

24 And he that keepeth his commandments dwelleth in him, and he in him. And hereby we know that he abideth in us, by the Spirit which he hath given us.

4 Beloved, believe not every spirit, but try the spirits whether they are of God: because many false prophets are gone out into the world.

2 Hereby know ye the Spirit of God: Every spirit that confesseth that Jesus Christ is come in the flesh is of God:

3 And every spirit that confesseth not that Jesus Christ is come in the flesh is not of God: and this is that *spirit* of antichrist, whereof ye have heard that it should come; and even now already is it in the world.

4 Ye are of God, little children, and have overcome them: because greater is he that is in you, than he that is in the world.

5 They are of the world: therefore speak they of the world, and the world heareth them.

6 We are of God: he that knoweth God heareth us; he that is not of God heareth not us.

Hereby know we the spirit of truth, and the spirit of error.

7 ¶ Beloved, let us love one another: for love is of God; and every one that loveth is born of God, and knoweth God.

8 He that loveth not knoweth not God; for God is love.

9 In this was manifested the love of God toward us, because that God sent his only begotten Son into the world, that we might live through him.

10 Herein is love, not that we loved God, but that he loved us, and sent his Son to be the propitiation for our sins.

11 Beloved, if God so loved us, we ought also to love one another.

12 No man hath seen God at any time. If we love one another, God dwelleth in us, and his love is perfected in us.

13 Hereby know we that we dwell in him, and he in us, because he hath given us of his Spirit.

14 And we have seen and do testify that the Father sent the Son to be the Saviour of the world.

15 Whosoever shall confess that Jesus is the Son of God, God dwelleth in him, and he in God.

16 And we have known and believed the love that God hath to us. God is love; and he that dwelleth in love dwelleth in God, and God in him.

17 Herein is our love made perfect, that we may have boldness in the day of judgment: because as he is, so are we in this world.

18 There is no fear in love; but perfect love casteth out fear: because fear hath torment. He that feareth is not made perfect in love.

19 We love him, because he first loved us.

20 ¶ If a man say, I love God, and hateth his brother, he is a liar: for he that loveth not his brother whom he hath seen, how can he love God whom he hath not seen?

21 And this commandment have we from him, That he who loveth God love his brother also.

5 Whosoever believeth that Jesus is the Christ is born of God: and every one that loveth him that begat loveth him also that is begotten of him.

2 By this we know that we love the children of God, when we love God, and keep his commandments.

3 For this is the love of God, that we keep his commandments: and his commandments are not grievous.

4 For whatsoever is born of God overcometh the world: and this is the victory that overcometh the world, even our faith.

5 Who is he that overcometh the world, but he that believeth that Jesus is the Son of God?

6 ¶ This is he that came by water and blood, even Jesus Christ; not by water only, but by water and blood. And it is the Spirit that beareth witness, because the Spirit is truth.

7 For there are three that bear record in heaven, the Father, the Word, and the Holy Ghost: and these three are one.

8 And there are three that bear witness in earth, the Spirit, and the water, and the blood: and these three agree in one.

9 If we receive the witness of men, the witness of God is greater: for this is the witness of God which he hath testified of his Son.

10 He that believeth on the Son of God hath the witness in himself: he that believeth not God hath made him a liar; because he believeth not the record that God gave of his Son.

11 And this is the record, that God hath given to us eternal life, and this life is in his Son.

12 He that hath the Son hath life; *and* he that hath not the Son of God hath not life.

13 These things have I written unto you that believe on the name of the Son of God; that ye may know that ye have eternal life, and that ye may believe on the name of the Son of God.

14 And this is the confidence that we have in him, that, if we ask any thing according to his will, he heareth us:

15 And if we know that he hear us, whatsoever we ask, we know that we have the petitions that we desired of him.

16 If any man see his brother sin a sin *which is* not unto death, he shall ask, and he shall give him life for them that sin not unto death. There is a sin unto death: I do not say that he shall pray for it.

17 All unrighteousness is sin: and there is a sin not unto death.

18 We know that whosoever is born of God sinneth not; but he that is begotten of God keepeth himself, and that wicked one toucheth him not.

19 *And* we know that we are of God, and the whole world lieth in wickedness.

20 And we know that the Son of God is come, and hath given us an understanding, that we may know him that is true, and we are in him that is true, *even* in his Son Jesus Christ. This is the true God, and eternal life.

21 Little children, keep yourselves from idols. Amen.

THE SECOND EPISTLE OF

JOHN

THE elder unto the elect lady and her children, whom I love in the truth; and not I only, but also all they that have known the truth;

2 For the truth's sake, which dwelleth in us, and shall be with us for ever.

3 Grace be with you, mercy,

and peace, from God the Father, and from the Lord Jesus Christ, the Son of the Father, in truth and love.

4 I rejoiced greatly that I found of thy children walking in truth, as we have received a commandment from the Father.

5 And now I beseech thee, lady, not as though I wrote a new commandment unto thee, but that which we had from the beginning, that we love one another.

6 And this is love, that we walk after his commandments. This is the commandment, That, as ye have heard from the beginning, ye should walk in it.

7 ¶ For many deceivers are entered into the world, who confess not that Jesus Christ is come in the flesh. This is a deceiver and an antichrist.

8 Look to yourselves, that we lose not those things which we have wrought, but that we receive a full reward.

9 Whosoever transgresseth, and abideth not in the doctrine of Christ, hath not God. He that abideth in the doctrine of Christ, he hath both the Father and the Son.

10 If there come any unto you, and bring not this doctrine, receive him not into *your* house, neither bid him God speed:

11 For he that biddeth him God speed is partaker of his evil deeds.

12 ¶ Having many things to write unto you, I would not *write* with paper and ink: but I trust to come unto you, and speak face to face, that our joy may be full.

13 The children of thy elect sister greet thee. Amen.

THE THIRD EPISTLE OF

JOHN

THE elder unto the wellbeloved Gaius, whom I love in the truth.

2 Beloved, I wish above all things that thou mayest prosper and be in health, even as thy soul prospereth.

3 For I rejoiced greatly, when the brethren came and testified of the truth that is in thee, even as thou walkest in the truth.

4 I have no greater joy than to hear that my children walk in truth.

5 Beloved, thou doest faithfully whatsoever thou doest to the brethren, and to strangers;

6 Which have borne witness of thy charity before the church: whom if thou bring forward on their journey after a godly sort, thou shalt do well:

7 Because that for his name's sake they went forth, taking

nothing of the Gentiles.

8 We therefore ought to receive such, that we might be fellowhelpers to the truth.

9 ¶ I wrote unto the church: but Diotrephes, who loveth to have the preeminence among them, receiveth us not.

10 Wherefore, if I come, I will remember his deeds which he doeth, prating against us with malicious words: and not content therewith, neither doth he himself receive the brethren, and forbiddeth them that would, and casteth *them* out of the church.

11 Beloved, follow not that which is evil, but that which is good. He that doeth good is of God: but he that doeth evil hath not seen God.

12 ¶ Demetrius hath good report of all *men*, and of the truth itself: yea, and we *also* bear record; and ye know that our record is true.

13 I had many things to write, but I will not with ink and pen write unto thee:

14 But I trust I shall shortly see thee, and we shall speak face to face. Peace *be* to thee. *Our* friends salute thee. Greet the friends by name.

THE EPISTLE OF

JUDE

J UDE, the servant of Jesus Christ, and brother of James, to them that are sanctified by God the Father, and preserved in Jesus Christ, *and* called:

2 Mercy unto you, and peace, and love, be multiplied.

3 Beloved, when I gave all diligence to write unto you of the common salvation, it was needful for me to write unto you, and exhort *you* that ye should earnestly contend for the faith which was once delivered unto the saints.

4 ¶ For there are certain men crept in unawares, who were before of old ordained to this condemnation, ungodly men, turning the grace of our God into lasciviousness, and denying the only Lord God, and our Lord Jesus Christ.

5 I will therefore put you in remembrance, though ye once knew this, how that the Lord, having saved the people out of the land of Egypt, afterward destroyed them that believed not.

6 And the angels which kept not their first estate, but left their own habitation, he hath reserved in everlasting chains under darkness unto the judgment of the great day.

7 Even as Sodom and Gomorrha, and the cities about them in like manner, giving themselves over to fornication, and going

after strange flesh, are set forth for an example, suffering the vengeance of eternal fire.

8 Likewise also these *filthy* dreamers defile the flesh, despise dominion, and speak evil of dignities.

9 Yet Michael the archangel, when contending with the devil he disputed about the body of Moses, durst not bring against him a railing accusation, but said, The Lord rebuke thee.

10 But these speak evil of those things which they know not: but what they know naturally, as brute beasts, in those things they corrupt themselves.

11 Woe unto them! for they have gone in the way of Cain, and ran greedily after the error of Balaam for reward, and perished in the gainsaying of Core.

12 These are spots in your feasts of charity, when they feast with you, feeding themselves without fear: clouds *they are* without water, carried about of winds; trees whose fruit withereth, without fruit, twice dead, plucked up by the roots;

13 Raging waves of the sea, foaming out their own shame; wandering stars, to whom is reserved the blackness of darkness for ever.

14 And Enoch also, the seventh from Adam, prophesied of these, saying, Behold, the Lord cometh with ten thousands of his saints,

15 To execute judgment upon all, and to convince all that are ungodly among them of all their ungodly deeds which they

have ungodly committed, and of all their hard *speeches* which ungodly sinners have spoken against him.

16 These are murmurers, complainers, walking after their own lusts; and their mouth speaketh great swelling *words*, having men's persons in admiration because of advantage.

17 But, beloved, remember ye the words which were spoken before of the apostles of our Lord Jesus Christ;

18 How that they told you there should be mockers in the last time, who should walk after their own ungodly lusts.

19 These be they who separate themselves, sensual, having not the Spirit.

20 ⦅But ye, beloved, building up yourselves on your most holy faith, praying in the Holy Ghost,

21 Keep yourselves in the love of God, looking for the mercy of our Lord Jesus Christ unto eternal life.

22 And of some have compassion, making a difference:

23 And others save with fear, pulling *them* out of the fire; hating even the garment spotted by the flesh.

24 Now unto him that is able to keep you from falling, and to present *you* faultless before the presence of his glory with exceeding joy,

25 To the only wise God our Saviour, *be* glory and majesty, dominion and power, both now and ever. Amen.

THE BOOK OF
REVELATION

1 The Revelation of Jesus Christ, which God gave unto him, to shew unto his servants things which must shortly come to pass; and he sent and signified *it* by his angel unto his servant John:

2 Who bare record of the word of God, and of the testimony of Jesus Christ, and of all things that he saw.

3 Blessed *is* he that readeth, and they that hear the words of this prophecy, and keep those things which are written therein: for the time *is* at hand.

4 ¶ John to the seven churches which are in Asia: Grace *be* unto you, and peace, from him which is, and which was, and which is to come; and from the seven Spirits which are before his throne;

5 And from Jesus Christ, *who is* the faithful witness, *and* the first begotten of the dead, and the prince of the kings of the earth. Unto him that loved us, and washed us from our sins in his own blood,

6 And hath made us kings and priests unto God and his Father; to him *be* glory and dominion for ever and ever. Amen.

7 ¶ Behold, he cometh with clouds; and every eye shall see him, and they *also* which pierced him: and all kindreds of the earth shall wail because of him. Even so, Amen.

8 ¶ I am Alpha and Omega, the beginning and the ending, saith the Lord, which is, and which was, and which is to come, the Almighty.

9 ¶ I John, who also am your brother, and companion in tribulation, and in the kingdom and patience of Jesus Christ, was in the isle that is called Patmos, for the word of God, and for the testimony of Jesus Christ.

10 I was in the Spirit on the Lord's day, and heard behind me a great voice, as of a trumpet,

11 Saying, I am Alpha and Omega, the first and the last: and, What thou seest, write in a book, and send *it* unto the seven churches which are in Asia; unto Ephesus, and unto Smyrna, and unto Pergamos, and unto Thyatira, and unto Sardis, and unto Philadelphia, and unto Laodicea.

12 And I turned to see the voice that spake with me. And being turned, I saw seven golden candlesticks;

13 And in the midst of the seven candlesticks *one* like unto the Son of man, clothed with a garment down to the foot, and girt about the paps with a golden girdle.

14 His head and *his* hairs *were* white like wool, as white as snow; and his eyes *were* as a flame of fire;

15 And his feet like unto fine brass, as if they burned in a fur-

nace; and his voice as the sound of many waters.

16 And he had in his right hand seven stars: and out of his mouth went a sharp twoedged sword: and his countenance *was* as the sun shineth in his strength.

17 And when I saw him, I fell at his feet as dead. And he laid his right hand upon me, saying unto me, Fear not; I am the first and the last:

18 I *am* he that liveth, and was dead; and, behold, I am alive for evermore, Amen; and have the keys of hell and of death.

19 Write the things which thou hast seen, and the things which are, and the things which shall be hereafter;

20 The mystery of the seven stars which thou sawest in my right hand, and the seven golden candlesticks. The seven stars are the angels of the seven churches: and the seven candlesticks which thou sawest are the seven churches.

2 Unto the angel of the church of Ephesus write; These things saith he that holdeth the seven stars in his right hand, who walketh in the midst of the seven golden candlesticks;

2 I know thy works, and thy labour, and thy patience, and how thou canst not bear them which are evil: and thou hast tried them which say they are apostles, and are not, and hast found them liars:

3 And hast borne, and hast patience, and for my name's sake hast laboured, and hast not fainted.

4 Nevertheless I have *somewhat* against thee, because thou hast left thy first love.

5 Remember therefore from whence thou art fallen, and repent, and do the first works; or else I will come unto thee quickly, and will remove thy candlestick out of his place, except thou repent.

6 But this thou hast, that thou hatest the deeds of the Nicolaitanes, which I also hate.

7 He that hath an ear, let him hear what the Spirit saith unto the churches; To him that overcometh will I give to eat of the tree of life, which is in the midst of the paradise of God.

8 (And unto the angel of the church in Smyrna write; These things saith the first and the last, which was dead, and is alive;

9 I know thy works, and tribulation, and poverty, (but thou art rich) and I *know* the blasphemy of them which say they are Jews, and are not, but *are* the synagogue of Satan.

10 Fear none of those things which thou shalt suffer: behold, the devil shall cast *some* of you into prison, that ye may be tried: and ye shall have tribulation ten days. Be thou faithful unto death, and I will give thee the crown of life.

11 He that hath an ear, let him hear what the Spirit saith unto the churches; He that overcometh shall not be hurt of the second death.

12 (And to the angel of the

church in Pergamos write; These things saith he which hath the sharp sword with two edges;

13 I know thy works, and where thou dwellest, *even* where Satan's seat *is*: and thou holdest fast my name, and hast not denied my faith, even in those days wherein Antipas *was* my faithful martyr, who was slain among you, where Satan dwelleth.

14 But I have a few things against thee, because thou hast there them that hold the doctrine of Balaam, who taught Balac to cast a stumblingblock before the children of Israel, to eat things sacrificed unto idols, and to commit fornication.

15 So hast thou also them that hold the doctrine of the Nicolaitanes, which thing I hate.

16 Repent; or else I will come unto thee quickly, and will fight against them with the sword of my mouth.

17 He that hath an ear, let him hear what the Spirit saith unto the churches; To him that overcometh will I give to eat of the hidden manna, and will give him a white stone, and in the stone a new name written, which no man knoweth saving he that receiveth *it*.

18 ¶ And unto the angel of the church in Thyatira write; These things saith the Son of God, who hath his eyes like unto a flame of fire, and his feet *are* like fine brass;

19 I know thy works, and charity, and service, and faith, and thy patience, and thy works; and the last *to be* more than the first.

20 Notwithstanding I have a few things against thee, because thou sufferest that woman Jezebel, which calleth herself a prophetess, to teach and to seduce my servants to commit fornication, and to eat things sacrificed unto idols.

21 And I gave her space to repent of her fornication; and she repented not.

22 Behold, I will cast her into a bed, and them that commit adultery with her into great tribulation, except they repent of their deeds.

23 And I will kill her children with death; and all the churches shall know that I am he which searcheth the reins and hearts: and I will give unto every one of you according to your works.

24 But unto you I say, and unto the rest in Thyatira, as many as have not this doctrine, and which have not known the depths of Satan, as they speak; I will put upon you none other burden.

25 But that which ye have *already* hold fast till I come.

26 And he that overcometh, and keepeth my works unto the end, to him will I give power over the nations:

27 And he shall rule them with a rod of iron; as the vessels of a potter shall they be broken to shivers: even as I received of my Father.

28 And I will give him the morning star.

29 He that hath an ear, let him

379

hear what the Spirit saith unto the churches.

3 And unto the angel of the church in Sardis write; These things saith he that hath the seven Spirits of God, and the seven stars; I know thy works, that thou hast a name that thou livest, and art dead.

2 Be watchful, and strengthen the things which remain, that are ready to die: for I have not found thy works perfect before God.

3 Remember therefore how thou hast received and heard, and hold fast, and repent. If therefore thou shalt not watch, I will come on thee as a thief, and thou shalt not know what hour I will come upon thee.

4 Thou hast a few names even in Sardis which have not defiled their garments; and they shall walk with me in white: for they are worthy.

5 He that overcometh, the same shall be clothed in white raiment; and I will not blot out his name out of the book of life, but I will confess his name before my Father, and before his angels.

6 He that hath an ear, let him hear what the Spirit saith unto the churches.

7 ⁌And to the angel of the church in Philadelphia write; These things saith he that is holy, he that is true, he that hath the key of David, he that openeth, and no man shutteth; and shutteth, and no man openeth;

8 I know thy works: behold, I have set before thee an open door, and no man can shut it: for thou hast a little strength, and hast kept my word, and hast not denied my name.

9 Behold, I will make them of the synagogue of Satan, which say they are Jews, and are not, but do lie; behold, I will make them to come and worship before thy feet, and to know that I have loved thee.

10 Because thou hast kept the word of my patience, I also will keep thee from the hour of temptation, which shall come upon all the world, to try them that dwell upon the earth.

11 Behold, I come quickly: hold that fast which thou hast, that no man take thy crown.

12 Him that overcometh will I make a pillar in the temple of my God, and he shall go no more out: and I will write upon him the name of my God, and the name of the city of my God, *which is* new Jerusalem, which cometh down out of heaven from my God: and *I will write upon him* my new name.

13 He that hath an ear, let him hear what the Spirit saith unto the churches.

14 ⁌And unto the angel of the church of the Laodiceans write; These things saith the Amen, the faithful and true witness, the beginning of the creation of God;

15 I know thy works, that thou art neither cold nor hot: I would thou wert cold or hot.

16 So then because thou art lukewarm, and neither cold nor hot, I will spue thee out of my

mouth.

17 Because thou sayest, I am rich, and increased with goods, and have need of nothing: and knowest not that thou art wretched, and miserable, and poor, and blind, and naked:

18 I counsel thee to buy of me gold tried in the fire, that thou mayest be rich; and white raiment, that thou mayest be clothed, and *that* the shame of thy nakedness do not appear; and anoint thine eyes with eyesalve, that thou mayest see.

19 As many as I love, I rebuke and chasten: be zealous therefore, and repent.

20 (Behold, I stand at the door, and knock: if any man hear my voice, and open the door, I will come in to him, and will sup with him, and he with me.

21 To him that overcometh will I grant to sit with me in my throne, even as I also overcame, and am set down with my Father in his throne.

22 He that hath an ear, let him hear what the Spirit saith unto the churches.

4 After this I looked, and, behold, a door *was* opened in heaven: and the first voice which I heard *was* as it were of a trumpet talking with me; which said, Come up hither, and I will shew thee things which must be hereafter.

2 And immediately I was in the spirit: and, behold, a throne was set in heaven, and *one* sat on the throne.

3 And he that sat was to look upon like a jasper and a sardine stone: and *there was* a rainbow round about the throne, in sight like unto an emerald.

4 (And round about the throne *were* four and twenty seats: and upon the seats I saw four and twenty elders sitting, clothed in white raiment; and they had on their heads crowns of gold.

5 And out of the throne proceeded lightnings and thunderings and voices: and *there were* seven lamps of fire burning before the throne, which are the seven Spirits of God.

6 (And before the throne *there was* a sea of glass like unto crystal: and in the midst of the throne, and round about the throne, *were* four beasts full of eyes before and behind.

7 And the first beast *was* like a lion, and the second beast like a calf, and the third beast had a face as a man, and the fourth beast *was* like a flying eagle.

8 And the four beasts had each of them six wings about *him*; and *they were* full of eyes within: and they rest not day and night, saying, Holy, holy, holy, Lord God Almighty, which was, and is, and is to come.

9 (And when those beasts give glory and honour and thanks to him that sat on the throne, who liveth for ever and ever,

10 The four and twenty elders fall down before him that sat on the throne, and worship him that liveth for ever and ever, and cast their crowns before the throne,

381

saying,

11 Thou art worthy, O Lord, to receive glory and honour and power: for thou hast created all things, and for thy pleasure they are and were created.

5 And I saw in the right hand of him that sat on the throne a book written within and on the backside, sealed with seven seals.

2 And I saw a strong angel proclaiming with a loud voice, Who is worthy to open the book, and to loose the seals thereof?

3 And no man in heaven, nor in earth, neither under the earth, was able to open the book, neither to look thereon.

4 And I wept much, because no man was found worthy to open and to read the book, neither to look thereon.

5 And one of the elders saith unto me, Weep not: behold, the Lion of the tribe of Juda, the Root of David, hath prevailed to open the book, and to loose the seven seals thereof.

6 And I beheld, and, lo, in the midst of the throne and of the four beasts, and in the midst of the elders, stood a Lamb as it had been slain, having seven horns and seven eyes, which are the seven Spirits of God sent forth into all the earth.

7 And he came and took the book out of the right hand of him that sat upon the throne.

8 And when he had taken the book, the four beasts and four *and* twenty elders fell down before the Lamb, having every one of them harps, and golden vials full of odours, which are the prayers of saints.

9 ¶And they sung a new song, saying, Thou art worthy to take the book, and to open the seals thereof: for thou wast slain, and hast redeemed us to God by thy blood out of every kindred, and tongue, and people, and nation;

10 And hast made us unto our God kings and priests: and we shall reign on the earth.

11 And I beheld, and I heard the voice of many angels round about the throne and the beasts and the elders: and the number of them was ten thousand times ten thousand, and thousands of thousands;

12 Saying with a loud voice, Worthy is the Lamb that was slain to receive power, and riches, and wisdom, and strength, and honour, and glory, and blessing.

13 And every creature which is in heaven, and on the earth, and under the earth, and such as are in the sea, and all that are in them, heard I saying, Blessing, and honour, and glory, and power, *be* unto him that sitteth upon the throne, and unto the Lamb for ever and ever.

14 And the four beasts said, Amen. And the four *and* twenty elders fell down and worshipped him that liveth for ever and ever.

6 And I saw when the Lamb opened one of the seals, and I heard, as it were the noise of thunder, one of the four beasts saying, Come and see.

2 And I saw, and behold a white horse: and he that sat on him had a bow; and a crown was given unto him: and he went forth conquering, and to conquer.

3 ¶ And when he had opened the second seal, I heard the second beast say, Come and see.

4 And there went out another horse *that was* red: and *power* was given to him that sat thereon to take peace from the earth, and that they should kill one another: and there was given unto him a great sword.

5 ¶ And when he had opened the third seal, I heard the third beast say, Come and see. And I beheld, and lo a black horse; and he that sat on him had a pair of balances in his hand.

6 And I heard a voice in the midst of the four beasts say, A measure of wheat for a penny, and three measures of barley for a penny; and *see* thou hurt not the oil and the wine.

7 ¶ And when he had opened the fourth seal, I heard the voice of the fourth beast say, Come and see.

8 And I looked, and behold a pale horse: and his name that sat on him was Death, and Hell followed with him. And power was given unto them over the fourth part of the earth, to kill with sword, and with hunger, and with death, and with the beasts of the earth.

9 ¶ And when he had opened the fifth seal, I saw under the altar the souls of them that were slain for the word of God, and for the testimony which they held:

10 And they cried with a loud voice, saying, How long, O Lord, holy and true, dost thou not judge and avenge our blood on them that dwell on the earth?

11 And white robes were given unto every one of them; and it was said unto them, that they should rest yet for a little season, until their fellowservants also and their brethren, that should be killed as they *were*, should be fulfilled.

12 ¶ And I beheld when he had opened the sixth seal, and, lo, there was a great earthquake; and the sun became black as sackcloth of hair, and the moon became as blood;

13 And the stars of heaven fell unto the earth, even as a fig tree casteth her untimely figs, when she is shaken of a mighty wind.

14 And the heaven departed as a scroll when it is rolled together; and every mountain and island were moved out of their places.

15 And the kings of the earth, and the great men, and the rich men, and the chief captains, and the mighty men, and every bondman, and every free man, hid themselves in the dens and in the rocks of the mountains;

16 And said to the mountains and rocks, Fall on us, and hide us from the face of him that sitteth on the throne, and from the wrath of the Lamb:

17 For the great day of his wrath is come; and who shall be able to stand?

7 And after these things I saw four angels standing on the four corners of the earth, holding the four winds of the earth, that the wind should not blow on the earth, nor on the sea, nor on any tree.

2 And I saw another angel ascending from the east, having the seal of the living God: and he cried with a loud voice to the four angels, to whom it was given to hurt the earth and the sea,

3 Saying, Hurt not the earth, neither the sea, nor the trees, till we have sealed the servants of our God in their foreheads.

4 € And I heard the number of them which were sealed: *and there were* sealed an hundred *and* forty *and* four thousand of all the tribes of the children of Israel.

5 Of the tribe of Juda *were* sealed twelve thousand. Of the tribe of Reuben *were* sealed twelve thousand. Of the tribe of Gad *were* sealed twelve thousand.

6 Of the tribe of Aser *were* sealed twelve thousand. Of the tribe of Nephthalim *were* sealed twelve thousand. Of the tribe of Manasses *were* sealed twelve thousand.

7 Of the tribe of Simeon *were* sealed twelve thousand. Of the tribe of Levi *were* sealed twelve thousand. Of the tribe of Issachar *were* sealed twelve thousand.

8 Of the tribe of Zabulon *were* sealed twelve thousand. Of the tribe of Joseph *were* sealed twelve thousand. Of the tribe of Benjamin *were* sealed twelve thousand.

9 € After this I beheld, and, lo, a great multitude, which no man could number, of all nations, and kindreds, and people, and tongues, stood before the throne, and before the Lamb, clothed with white robes, and palms in their hands;

10 And cried with a loud voice, saying, Salvation to our God which sitteth upon the throne, and unto the Lamb.

11 And all the angels stood round about the throne, and *about* the elders and the four beasts, and fell before the throne on their faces, and worshipped God,

12 Saying, Amen: Blessing, and glory, and wisdom, and thanksgiving, and honour, and power, and might, *be* unto our God for ever and ever. Amen.

13 And one of the elders answered, saying unto me, What are these which are arrayed in white robes? and whence came they?

14 And I said unto him, Sir, thou knowest. And he said to me, These are they which came out of great tribulation, and have washed their robes, and made them white in the blood of the Lamb.

15 Therefore are they before the throne of God, and serve him day and night in his temple: and he that sitteth on the throne shall dwell among them.

16 They shall hunger no more, neither thirst any more; neither

shall the sun light on them, nor any heat.

17 For the Lamb which is in the midst of the throne shall feed them, and shall lead them unto living fountains of waters: and God shall wipe away all tears from their eyes.

8 And when he had opened the seventh seal, there was silence in heaven about the space of half an hour.

2 And I saw the seven angels which stood before God; and to them were given seven trumpets.

3 And another angel came and stood at the altar, having a golden censer; and there was given unto him much incense, that he should offer *it* with the prayers of all saints upon the golden altar which was before the throne.

4 And the smoke of the incense, *which came* with the prayers of the saints, ascended up before God out of the angel's hand.

5 And the angel took the censer, and filled it with fire of the altar, and cast *it* into the earth: and there were voices, and thunderings, and lightnings, and an earthquake.

6 ¶ And the seven angels which had the seven trumpets prepared themselves to sound.

7 The first angel sounded, and there followed hail and fire mingled with blood, and they were cast upon the earth: and the third part of trees was burnt up, and all green grass was burnt up.

8 And the second angel sounded, and as it were a great mountain burning with fire was cast into the sea: and the third part of the sea became blood;

9 And the third part of the creatures which were in the sea, and had life, died; and the third part of the ships were destroyed.

10 And the third angel sounded, and there fell a great star from heaven, burning as it were a lamp, and it fell upon the third part of the rivers, and upon the fountains of waters;

11 And the name of the star is called Wormwood: and the third part of the waters became wormwood; and many men died of the waters, because they were made bitter.

12 And the fourth angel sounded, and the third part of the sun was smitten, and the third part of the moon, and the third part of the stars; so as the third part of them was darkened, and the day shone not for a third part of it, and the night likewise.

13 And I beheld, and heard an angel flying through the midst of heaven, saying with a loud voice, Woe, woe, woe, to the inhabiters of the earth by reason of the other voices of the trumpet of the three angels, which are yet to sound!

9 And the fifth angel sounded, and I saw a star fall from heaven unto the earth: and to him was given the key of the bottomless pit.

2 And he opened the bottomless pit; and there arose a smoke out of the pit, as the smoke of a great furnace; and the sun and the air were darkened by reason of the

smoke of the pit.

3 And there came out of the smoke locusts upon the earth: and unto them was given power, as the scorpions of the earth have power.

4 And it was commanded them that they should not hurt the grass of the earth, neither any green thing, neither any tree; but only those men which have not the seal of God in their foreheads.

5 And to them it was given that they should not kill them, but that they should be tormented five months: and their torment *was* as the torment of a scorpion, when he striketh a man.

6 And in those days shall men seek death, and shall not find it; and shall desire to die, and death shall flee from them.

7 And the shapes of the locusts *were* like unto horses prepared unto battle; and on their heads *were* as it were crowns like gold, and their faces *were* as the faces of men.

8 And they had hair as the hair of women, and their teeth were as *the teeth* of lions.

9 And they had breastplates, as it were breastplates of iron; and the sound of their wings *was* as the sound of chariots of many horses running to battle.

10 And they had tails like unto scorpions, and there were stings in their tails: and their power *was* to hurt men five months.

11 And they had a king over them, *which is* the angel of the bottomless pit, whose name in the Hebrew tongue *is* Abaddon,

but in the Greek tongue hath *his* name Apollyon.

12 ❡ One woe is past; *and,* behold, there come two woes more hereafter.

13 And the sixth angel sounded, and I heard a voice from the four horns of the golden altar which is before God,

14 Saying to the sixth angel which had the trumpet, Loose the four angels which are bound in the great river Euphrates.

15 And the four angels were loosed, which were prepared for an hour, and a day, and a month, and a year, for to slay the third part of men.

16 And the number of the army of the horsemen *were* two hundred thousand thousand: and I heard the number of them.

17 And thus I saw the horses in the vision, and them that sat on them, having breastplates of fire, and of jacinth, and brimstone: and the heads of the horses *were* as the heads of lions; and out of their mouths issued fire and smoke and brimstone.

18 By these three was the third part of men killed, by the fire, and by the smoke, and by the brimstone, which issued out of their mouths.

19 For their power is in their mouth, and in their tails: for their tails *were* like unto serpents, and had heads, and with them they do hurt.

20 And the rest of the men which were not killed by these plagues yet repented not of the works of their hands, that they

should not worship devils, and idols of gold, and silver, and brass, and stone, and of wood: which neither can see, nor hear, nor walk:

21 Neither repented they of their murders, nor of their sorceries, nor of their fornication, nor of their thefts.

10 And I saw another mighty angel come down from heaven, clothed with a cloud: and a rainbow *was* upon his head, and his face *was* as it were the sun, and his feet as pillars of fire:

2 And he had in his hand a little book open: and he set his right foot upon the sea, and *his* left *foot* on the earth,

3 And cried with a loud voice, as *when* a lion roareth: and when he had cried, seven thunders uttered their voices.

4 And when the seven thunders had uttered their voices, I was about to write: and I heard a voice from heaven saying unto me, Seal up those things which the seven thunders uttered, and write them not.

5 ⸿ And the angel which I saw stand upon the sea and upon the earth lifted up his hand to heaven,

6 And sware by him that liveth for ever and ever, who created heaven, and the things that therein are, and the earth, and the things that therein are, and the sea, and the things which are therein, that there should be time no longer:

7 But in the days of the voice of the seventh angel, when he shall begin to sound, the mystery of God should be finished, as he hath declared to his servants the prophets.

8 ⸿ And the voice which I heard from heaven spake unto me again, and said, Go *and* take the little book which is open in the hand of the angel which standeth upon the sea and upon the earth.

9 And I went unto the angel, and said unto him, Give me the little book. And he said unto me, Take *it*, and eat it up; and it shall make thy belly bitter, but it shall be in thy mouth sweet as honey.

10 And I took the little book out of the angel's hand, and ate it up; and it was in my mouth sweet as honey: and as soon as I had eaten it, my belly was bitter.

11 And he said unto me, Thou must prophesy again before many peoples, and nations, and tongues, and kings.

11 And there was given me a reed like unto a rod: and the angel stood, saying, Rise, and measure the temple of God, and the altar, and them that worship therein.

2 But the court which is without the temple leave out, and measure it not; for it is given unto the Gentiles: and the holy city shall they tread under foot forty *and* two months.

3 ⸿ And I will give *power* unto my two witnesses, and they shall prophesy a thousand two hundred *and* threescore days, clothed in sackcloth.

4 These are the two olive trees,

and the two candlesticks standing before the God of the earth.

5 And if any man will hurt them, fire proceedeth out of their mouth, and devoureth their enemies: and if any man will hurt them, he must in this manner be killed.

6 These have power to shut heaven, that it rain not in the days of their prophecy; and have power over waters to turn them to blood, and to smite the earth with all plagues, as often as they will.

7 And when they shall have finished their testimony, the beast that ascendeth out of the bottomless pit shall make war against them, and shall overcome them, and kill them.

8 And their dead bodies **shall lie** in the street of the great city, which spiritually is called Sodom and Egypt, where also our Lord was crucified.

9 And they of the people and kindreds and tongues and nations shall see their dead bodies three days and an half, and shall not suffer their dead bodies to be put in graves.

10 And they that dwell upon the earth shall rejoice over them, and make merry, and shall send gifts one to another; because these two prophets tormented them that dwelt on the earth.

11 And after three days and an half the spirit of life from God entered into them, and they stood upon their feet; and great fear fell upon them which saw them.

12 And they heard a great voice from heaven saying unto them, Come up hither. And they ascended up to heaven in a cloud; and their enemies beheld them.

13 (And the same hour was there a great earthquake, and the tenth part of the city fell, and in the earthquake were slain of men seven thousand: and the remnant were affrighted, and gave glory to the God of heaven.

14 The second woe is past; *and*, behold, the third woe cometh quickly.

15 (And the seventh angel sounded; and there were great voices in heaven, saying, The kingdoms of this world are become *the kingdoms* of our Lord, and of his Christ; and he shall reign for ever and ever.

16 And the four and twenty elders, which sat before God on their seats, fell upon their faces, and worshipped God,

17 Saying, We give thee thanks, O Lord God Almighty, which art, and wast, and art to come; because thou hast taken to thee thy great power, and hast reigned.

18 And the nations were angry, and thy wrath is come, and the time of the dead, that they should be judged, and that thou shouldest give reward unto thy servants the prophets, and to the saints, and them that fear thy name, small and great; and shouldest destroy them which destroy the earth.

19 And the temple of God was opened in heaven, and there was seen in his temple the ark of his testament: and there were

lightnings, and voices, and thunderings, and an earthquake, and great hail.

12 And there appeared a great wonder in heaven; a woman clothed with the sun, and the moon under her feet, and upon her head a crown of twelve stars:

2 And she being with child cried, travailing in birth, and pained to be delivered.

3 ¶ And there appeared another wonder in heaven; and behold a great red dragon, having seven heads and ten horns, and seven crowns upon his heads.

4 And his tail drew the third part of the stars of heaven, and did cast them to the earth: and the dragon stood before the woman which was ready to be delivered, for to devour her child as soon as it was born.

5 ¶ And she brought forth a man child, who was to rule all nations with a rod of iron: and her child was caught up unto God, and *to* his throne.

6 And the woman fled into the wilderness, where she hath a place prepared of God, that they should feed her there a thousand two hundred *and* threescore days.

7 And there was war in heaven: Michael and his angels fought against the dragon; and the dragon fought and his angels,

8 And prevailed not; neither was their place found any more in heaven.

9 ¶ And the great dragon was cast out, that old serpent, called the Devil, and Satan, which deceiveth the whole world: he was cast out into the earth, and his angels were cast out with him.

10 And I heard a loud voice saying in heaven, Now is come salvation, and strength, and the kingdom of our God, and the power of his Christ: for the accuser of our brethren is cast down, which accused them before our God day and night.

11 And they overcame him by the blood of the Lamb, and by the word of their testimony; and they loved not their lives unto the death.

12 Therefore rejoice, *ye* heavens, and *ye* that dwell in them. Woe to the inhabiters of the earth and of the sea! for the devil is come down unto you, having great wrath, because he knoweth that he hath but a short time.

13 ¶ And when the dragon saw that he was cast unto the earth, he persecuted the woman which brought forth the man *child*.

14 And to the woman were given two wings of a great eagle, that she might fly into the wilderness, into her place, where she is nourished for a time, and times, and half a time, from the face of the serpent.

15 And the serpent cast out of his mouth water as a flood after the woman, that he might cause her to be carried away of the flood.

16 And the earth helped the woman, and the earth opened her mouth, and swallowed up the

389

flood which the dragon cast out of his mouth.

17 And the dragon was wroth with the woman, and went to make war with the remnant of her seed, which keep the commandments of God, and have the testimony of Jesus Christ.

13

And I stood upon the sand of the sea, and saw a beast rise up out of the sea, having seven heads and ten horns, and upon his horns ten crowns, and upon his heads the name of blasphemy.

2 And the beast which I saw was like unto a leopard, and his feet were as *the feet* of a bear, and his mouth as the mouth of a lion: and the dragon gave him his power, and his seat, and great authority.

3 And I saw one of his heads as it were wounded to death; and his deadly wound was healed: and all the world wondered after the beast.

4 And they worshipped the dragon which gave power unto the beast: and they worshipped the beast, saying, Who *is* like unto the beast? who is able to make war with him?

5 And there was given unto him a mouth speaking great things and blasphemies; and power was given unto him to continue forty *and* two months.

6 And he opened his mouth in blasphemy against God, to blaspheme his name, and his tabernacle, and them that dwell in heaven.

7 And it was given unto him to make war with the saints, and to overcome them: and power was given him over all kindreds, and tongues, and nations.

8 And all that dwell upon the earth shall worship him, whose names are not written in the book of life of the Lamb slain from the foundation of the world.

9 If any man have an ear, let him hear.

10 He that leadeth into captivity shall go into captivity: he that killeth with the sword must be killed with the sword. Here is the patience and the faith of the saints.

11 ℭ And I beheld another beast coming up out of the earth; and he had two horns like a lamb, and he spake as a dragon.

12 And he exerciseth all the power of the first beast before him, and causeth the earth and them which dwell therein to worship the first beast, whose deadly wound was healed.

13 And he doeth great wonders, so that he maketh fire come down from heaven on the earth in the sight of men,

14 And deceiveth them that dwell on the earth by *the means of* those miracles which he had power to do in the sight of the beast; saying to them that dwell on the earth, that they should make an image to the beast, which had the wound by a sword, and did live.

15 And he had power to give life unto the image of the beast, that the image of the beast should

390

both speak, and cause that as many as would not worship the image of the beast should be killed.

16 And he causeth all, both small and great, rich and poor, free and bond, to receive a mark in their right hand, or in their foreheads:

17 And that no man might buy or sell, save he that had the mark, or the name of the beast, or the number of his name.

18 ❡ Here is wisdom. Let him that hath understanding count the number of the beast: for it is the number of a man; and his number *is* Six hundred threescore *and* six.

14

And I looked, and, lo, a Lamb stood on the mount Sion, and with him an hundred forty *and* four thousand, having his Father's name written in their foreheads.

2 And I heard a voice from heaven, as the voice of many waters, and as the voice of a great thunder: and I heard the voice of harpers harping with their harps:

3 And they sung as it were a new song before the throne, and before the four beasts, and the elders: and no man could learn that song but the hundred *and* forty *and* four thousand, which were redeemed from the earth.

4 These are they which were not defiled with women; for they are virgins. These are they which follow the Lamb whithersoever he goeth. These were redeemed from among men, *being* the firstfruits unto God and to the Lamb.

5 And in their mouth was found no guile: for they are without fault before the throne of God.

6 ❡ And I saw another angel fly in the midst of heaven, having the everlasting gospel to preach unto them that dwell on the earth, and to every nation, and kindred, and tongue, and people,

7 Saying with a loud voice, Fear God, and give glory to him; for the hour of his judgment is come: and worship him that made heaven, and earth, and the sea, and the fountains of waters.

8 ❡ And there followed another angel, saying, Babylon is fallen, is fallen, that great city, because she made all nations drink of the wine of the wrath of her fornication.

9 ❡ And the third angel followed them, saying with a loud voice, If any man worship the beast and his image, and receive *his* mark in his forehead, or in his hand,

10 The same shall drink of the wine of the wrath of God, which is poured out without mixture into the cup of his indignation; and he shall be tormented with fire and brimstone in the presence of the holy angels, and in the presence of the Lamb:

11 And the smoke of their torment ascendeth up for ever and ever: and they have no rest day nor night, who worship the beast and his image, and whosoever receiveth the mark of his name.

12 Here is the patience of the saints: here *are* they that keep the commandments of God, and the faith of Jesus.

13 ¶ And I heard a voice from heaven saying unto me, Write, Blessed *are* the dead which die in the Lord from henceforth: Yea, saith the Spirit, that they may rest from their labours; and their works do follow them.

14 And I looked, and behold a white cloud, and upon the cloud *one* sat like unto the Son of man, having on his head a golden crown, and in his hand a sharp sickle.

15 ¶ And another angel came out of the temple, crying with a loud voice to him that sat on the cloud, Thrust in thy sickle, and reap: for the time is come for thee to reap; for the harvest of the earth is ripe.

16 And he that sat on the cloud thrust in his sickle on the earth; and the earth was reaped.

17 And another angel came out of the temple which is in heaven, he also having a sharp sickle.

18 And another angel came out from the altar, which had power over fire; and cried with a loud cry to him that had the sharp sickle, saying, Thrust in thy sharp sickle, and gather the clusters of the vine of the earth; for her grapes are fully ripe.

19 And the angel thrust in his sickle into the earth, and gathered the vine of the earth, and cast *it* into the great winepress of the wrath of God.

20 And the winepress was trodden without the city, and blood came out of the winepress, even unto the horse bridles, by the space of a thousand *and* six hundred furlongs.

15 And I saw another sign in heaven, great and marvellous, seven angels having the seven last plagues; for in them is filled up the wrath of God.

2 And I saw as it were a sea of glass mingled with fire: and them that had gotten the victory over the beast, and over his image, and over his mark, *and* over the number of his name, stand on the sea of glass, having the harps of God.

3 ¶ And they sing the song of Moses the servant of God, and the song of the Lamb, saying, Great and marvellous *are* thy works, Lord God Almighty; just and true *are* thy ways, thou King of saints.

4 Who shall not fear thee, O Lord, and glorify thy name? for *thou* only *art* holy: for all nations shall come and worship before thee; for thy judgments are made manifest.

5 ¶ And after that I looked, and, behold, the temple of the tabernacle of the testimony in heaven was opened:

6 And the seven angels came out of the temple, having the seven plagues, clothed in pure and white linen, and having their breasts girded with golden girdles.

7 And one of the four beasts gave unto the seven angels seven golden vials full of the wrath of God, who liveth for ever and ever.

8 And the temple was filled

with smoke from the glory of God, and from his power; and no man was able to enter into the temple, till the seven plagues of the seven angels were fulfilled.

16

And I heard a great voice out of the temple saying to the seven angels, Go your ways, and pour out the vials of the wrath of God upon the earth.

2 And the first went, and poured out his vial upon the earth; and there fell a noisome and grievous sore upon the men which had the mark of the beast, and *upon* them which worshipped his image.

3 And the second angel poured out his vial upon the sea; and it became as the blood of a dead *man:* and every living soul died in the sea.

4 And the third angel poured out his vial upon the rivers and fountains of waters; and they became blood.

5 And I heard the angel of the waters say, Thou art righteous, O Lord, which art, and wast, and shalt be, because thou hast judged thus.

6 For they have shed the blood of saints and prophets, and thou hast given them blood to drink; for they are worthy.

7 And I heard another out of the altar say, Even so, Lord God Almighty, true and righteous *are* thy judgments.

8 And the fourth angel poured out his vial upon the sun; and power was given unto him to scorch men with fire.

9 And men were scorched with great heat, and blasphemed the name of God, which hath power over these plagues: and they repented not to give him glory.

10 And the fifth angel poured out his vial upon the seat of the beast; and his kingdom was full of darkness; and they gnawed their tongues for pain,

11 And blasphemed the God of heaven because of their pains and their sores, and repented not of their deeds.

12 And the sixth angel poured out his vial upon the great river Euphrates; and the water thereof was dried up, that the way of the kings of the east might be prepared.

13 (And I saw three unclean spirits like frogs *come* out of the mouth of the dragon, and out of the mouth of the beast, and out of the mouth of the false prophet.

14 For they are the spirits of devils, working miracles, *which* go forth unto the kings of the earth and of the whole world, to gather them to the battle of that great day of God Almighty.

15 (Behold, I come as a thief. Blessed *is* he that watcheth, and keepeth his garments, lest he walk naked, and they see his shame.

16 And he gathered them together into a place called in the Hebrew tongue Armageddon.

17 (And the seventh angel poured out his vial into the air; and there came a great voice out of the temple of heaven, from the throne, saying, It is done.

18 And there were voices, and thunders, and lightnings; and there was a great earthquake, such as was not since men were upon the earth, so mighty an earthquake, *and* so great.

19 And the great city was divided into three parts, and the cities of the nations fell: and great Babylon came in remembrance before God, to give unto her the cup of the wine of the fierceness of his wrath.

20 And every island fled away, and the mountains were not found.

21 And there fell upon men a great hail out of heaven, *every stone* about the weight of a talent: and men blasphemed God because of the plague of the hail; for the plague thereof was exceeding great.

17

And there came one of the seven angels which had the seven vials, and talked with me, saying unto me, Come hither; I will shew unto thee the judgment of the great whore that sitteth upon many waters:

2 With whom the kings of the earth have committed fornication, and the inhabitants of the earth have been made drunk with the wine of her fornication.

3 So he carried me away in the spirit into the wilderness: and I saw a woman sit upon a scarlet coloured beast, full of names of blasphemy, having seven heads and ten horns.

4 And the woman was arrayed in purple and scarlet colour, and decked with gold and precious stones and pearls, having a golden cup in her hand full of abominations and filthiness of her fornication:

5 And upon her forehead *was* a name written, MYSTERY, BABYLON THE GREAT, THE MOTHER OF HARLOTS AND ABOMINATIONS OF THE EARTH.

6 And I saw the woman drunken with the blood of the saints, and with the blood of the martyrs of Jesus: and when I saw her, I wondered with great admiration.

7 And the angel said unto me, Wherefore didst thou marvel? I will tell thee the mystery of the woman, and of the beast that carrieth her, which hath the seven heads and ten horns.

8 ¶ The beast that thou sawest was, and is not; and shall ascend out of the bottomless pit, and go into perdition: and they that dwell on the earth shall wonder, whose names were not written in the book of life from the foundation of the world, when they behold the beast that was, and is not, and yet is.

9 And here *is* the mind which hath wisdom. The seven heads are seven mountains, on which the woman sitteth.

10 And there are seven kings: five are fallen, and one is, *and* the other is not yet come; and when he cometh, he must continue a short space.

11 And the beast that was, and is not, even he is the eighth, and is of the seven, and goeth into perdition.

12 And the ten horns which thou sawest are ten kings, which have received no kingdom as yet; but receive power as kings one hour with the beast.

13 These have one mind, and shall give their power and strength unto the beast.

14 These shall make war with the Lamb, and the Lamb shall overcome them: for he is Lord of lords, and King of kings: and they that are with him *are* called, and chosen, and faithful.

15 And he saith unto me, The waters which thou sawest, where the whore sitteth, are peoples, and multitudes, and nations, and tongues.

16 And the ten horns which thou sawest upon the beast, these shall hate the whore, and shall make her desolate and naked, and shall eat her flesh, and burn her with fire.

17 For God hath put in their hearts to fulfill his will, and to agree, and give their kingdom unto the beast, until the words of God shall be fulfilled.

18 And the woman which thou sawest is that great city, which reigneth over the kings of the earth.

18 And after these things I saw another angel come down from heaven, having great power; and the earth was lightened with his glory.

2 And he cried mightily with a strong voice, saying, Babylon the great is fallen, is fallen, and is become the habitation of devils,

and the hold of every foul spirit, and a cage of every unclean and hateful bird.

3 For all nations have drunk of the wine of the wrath of her fornication, and the kings of the earth have committed fornication with her, and the merchants of the earth are waxed rich through the abundance of her delicacies.

4 And I heard another voice from heaven, saying, Come out of her, my people, that ye be not partakers of her sins, and that ye receive not of her plagues.

5 For her sins have reached unto heaven, and God hath remembered her iniquities.

6 Reward her even as she rewarded you, and double unto her double according to her works: in the cup which she hath filled fill to her double.

7 How much she hath glorified herself, and lived deliciously, so much torment and sorrow give her: for she saith in her heart, I sit a queen, and am no widow, and shall see no sorrow.

8 Therefore shall her plagues come in one day, death, and mourning, and famine; and she shall be utterly burned with fire: for strong *is* the Lord God who judgeth her.

9 ¶ And the kings of the earth, who have committed fornication and lived deliciously with her, shall bewail her, and lament for her, when they shall see the smoke of her burning,

10 Standing afar off for the fear of her torment, saying, Alas, alas that great city Babylon, that

395

mighty city! for in one hour is thy judgment come.

11 And the merchants of the earth shall weep and mourn over her; for no man buyeth their merchandise any more:

12 The merchandise of gold, and silver, and precious stones, and of pearls, and fine linen, and purple, and silk, and scarlet, and all thyine wood, and all manner vessels of ivory, and all manner vessels of most precious wood, and of brass, and iron, and marble,

13 And cinnamon, and odours, and ointments, and frankincense, and wine, and oil, and fine flour, and wheat, and beasts, and sheep, and horses, and chariots, and slaves, and souls of men.

14 And the fruits that thy soul lusted after are departed from thee, and all things which were dainty and goodly are departed from thee, and thou shalt find them no more at all.

15 The merchants of these things, which were made rich by her, shall stand afar off for the fear of her torment, weeping and wailing,

16 And saying, Alas, alas that great city, that was clothed in fine linen, and purple, and scarlet, and decked with gold, and precious stones, and pearls!

17 For in one hour so great riches is come to nought. And every shipmaster, and all the company in ships, and sailors, and as many as trade by sea, stood afar off,

18 And cried when they saw the smoke of her burning, saying, What city is like unto this great city!

19 And they cast dust on their heads, and cried, weeping and wailing, saying, Alas, alas that great city, wherein were made rich all that had ships in the sea by reason of her costliness! for in one hour is she made desolate.

20 ¶ Rejoice over her, thou heaven, and ye holy apostles and prophets; for God hath avenged you on her.

21 And a mighty angel took up a stone like a great millstone, and cast it into the sea, saying, Thus with violence shall that great city Babylon be thrown down, and shall be found no more at all.

22 And the voice of harpers, and musicians, and of pipers, and trumpeters, shall be heard no more at all in thee; and no craftsman, of whatsoever craft he be, shall be found any more in thee; and the sound of a millstone shall be heard no more at all in thee;

23 And the light of a candle shall shine no more at all in thee; and the voice of the bridegroom and of the bride shall be heard no more at all in thee: for thy merchants were the great men of the earth; for by thy sorceries were all nations deceived.

24 And in her was found the blood of prophets, and of saints, and of all that were slain upon the earth.

19

And after these things I heard a great voice of much people in heaven, saying, Alleluia; Salvation, and glory, and honour, and power, unto the Lord our God:

2 For true and righteous *are* his judgments: for he hath judged the great whore, which did corrupt the earth with her fornication, and hath avenged the blood of his servants at her hand.

3 And again they said, Alleluia. And her smoke rose up for ever and ever.

4 And the four and twenty elders and the four beasts fell down and worshipped God that sat on the throne, saying, Amen; Alleluia.

5 And a voice came out of the throne, saying, Praise our God, all ye his servants, and ye that fear him, both small and great.

6 And I heard as it were the voice of a great multitude, and as the voice of many waters, and as the voice of mighty thunderings, saying, Alleluia: for the Lord God omnipotent reigneth.

7 ¶ Let us be glad and rejoice, and give honour to him: for the marriage of the Lamb is come, and his wife hath made herself ready.

8 And to her was granted that she should be arrayed in fine linen, clean and white: for the fine linen is the righteousness of saints.

9 And he saith unto me, Write, Blessed *are* they which are called unto the marriage supper of the Lamb. And he saith unto me, These are the true sayings of God.

10 And I fell at his feet to worship him. And he said unto me, See *thou do it* not: I am thy fellowservant, and of thy brethren that have the testimony of Jesus: worship God: for the testimony of Jesus is the spirit of prophecy.

11 And I saw heaven opened, and behold a white horse; and he that sat upon him *was* called Faithful and True, and in righteousness he doth judge and make war.

12 His eyes *were* as a flame of fire, and on his head *were* many crowns; and he had a name written, that no man knew, but he himself.

13 And he *was* clothed with a vesture dipped in blood: and his name is called The Word of God.

14 And the armies *which were* in heaven followed him upon white horses, clothed in fine linen, white and clean.

15 And out of his mouth goeth a sharp sword, that with it he should smite the nations: and he shall rule them with a rod of iron: and he treadeth the winepress of the fierceness and wrath of Almighty God.

16 And he hath on *his* vesture and on his thigh a name written, KING OF KINGS, AND LORD OF LORDS.

17 And I saw an angel standing in the sun; and he cried with a loud voice, saying to all the fowls that fly in the midst of heaven, Come and gather yourselves together unto the supper of the great God;

18 That ye may eat the flesh of kings, and the flesh of captains, and the flesh of mighty men, and

the flesh of horses, and of them that sit on them, and the flesh of all *men*, *both* free and bond, both small and great.

19 ¶ And I saw the beast, and the kings of the earth, and their armies, gathered together to make war against him that sat on the horse, and against his army.

20 And the beast was taken, and with him the false prophet that wrought miracles before him, with which he deceived them that had received the mark of the beast, and them that worshipped his image. These both were cast alive into a lake of fire burning with brimstone.

21 And the remnant were slain with the sword of him that sat upon the horse, which *sword* proceeded out of his mouth: and all the fowls were filled with their flesh.

20 And I saw an angel come down from heaven, having the key of the bottomless pit and a great chain in his hand.

2 And he laid hold on the dragon, that old serpent, which is the Devil, and Satan, and bound him a thousand years,

3 And cast him into the bottomless pit, and shut him up, and set a seal upon him, that he should deceive the nations no more, till the thousand years should be fulfilled: and after that he must be loosed a little season.

4 ¶ And I saw thrones, and they sat upon them, and judgment was given unto them: and I *saw* the souls of them that were beheaded for the witness of Jesus, and for the word of God, and which had not worshipped the beast, neither his image, neither had received *his* mark upon their foreheads, or in their hands; and they lived and reigned with Christ a thousand years.

5 But the rest of the dead lived not again until the thousand years were finished. This *is* the first resurrection.

6 Blessed and holy *is* he that hath part in the first resurrection: on such the second death hath no power, but they shall be priests of God and of Christ, and shall reign with him a thousand years.

7 ¶ And when the thousand years are expired, Satan shall be loosed out of his prison,

8 And shall go out to deceive the nations which are in the four quarters of the earth, Gog, and Magog, to gather them together to battle: the number of whom *is* as the sand of the sea.

9 And they went up on the breadth of the earth, and compassed the camp of the saints about, and the beloved city: and fire came down from God out of heaven, and devoured them.

10 And the devil that deceived them was cast into the lake of fire and brimstone, where the beast and the false prophet *are*, and shall be tormented day and night for ever and ever.

11 And I saw a great white throne, and him that sat on it, from whose face the earth and the heaven fled away; and there was found no place for them.

12 ¶ And I saw the dead, small and great, stand before God; and the books were opened: and another book was opened, which is *the book* of life: and the dead were judged out of those things which were written in the books, according to their works.

13 And the sea gave up the dead which were in it; and death and hell delivered up the dead which were in them: and they were judged every man according to their works.

14 And death and hell were cast into the lake of fire. This is the second death.

15 And whosoever was not found written in the book of life was cast into the lake of fire.

21 And I saw a new heaven and a new earth: for the first heaven and the first earth were passed away; and there was no more sea.

2 And I John saw the holy city, new Jerusalem, coming down from God out of heaven, prepared as a bride adorned for her husband.

3 And I heard a great voice out of heaven saying, Behold, the tabernacle of God *is* with men, and he will dwell with them, and they shall be his people, and God himself shall be with them, *and be* their God.

4 And God shall wipe away all tears from their eyes; and there shall be no more death, neither sorrow, nor crying, neither shall there be any more pain: for the former things are passed away.

5 And he that sat upon the throne said, Behold, I make all things new. And he said unto me, Write: for these words are true and faithful.

6 And he said unto me, It is done. I am Alpha and Omega, the beginning and the end. I will give unto him that is athirst of the fountain of the water of life freely.

7 He that overcometh shall inherit all things; and I will be his God, and he shall be my son.

8 But the fearful, and unbelieving, and the abominable, and murderers, and whoremongers, and sorcerers, and idolaters, and all liars, shall have their part in the lake which burneth with fire and brimstone: which is the second death.

9 ¶ And there came unto me one of the seven angels which had the seven vials full of the seven last plagues, and talked with me, saying, Come hither, I will shew thee the bride, the Lamb's wife.

10 And he carried me away in the spirit to a great and high mountain, and shewed me that great city, the holy Jerusalem, descending out of heaven from God,

11 Having the glory of God: and her light *was* like unto a stone most precious, even like a jasper stone, clear as crystal;

12 And had a wall great and high, *and* had twelve gates, and at the gates twelve angels, and names written thereon, which are *the names* of the twelve tribes of the children of Israel:

13 On the east three gates;

on the north three gates; on the south three gates; and on the west three gates.

14 And the wall of the city had twelve foundations, and in them the names of the twelve apostles of the Lamb.

15 And he that talked with me had a golden reed to measure the city, and the gates thereof, and the wall thereof.

16 And the city lieth foursquare, and the length is as large as the breadth: and he measured the city with the reed, twelve thousand furlongs. The length and the breadth and the height of it are equal.

17 And he measured the wall thereof, an hundred *and* forty *and* four cubits, *according to* the measure of a man, that is, of the angel.

18 And the building of the wall of it was *of* jasper: and the city *was* pure gold, like unto clear glass.

19 And the foundations of the wall of the city *were* garnished with all manner of precious stones. The first foundation *was* jasper; the second, sapphire; the third, a chalcedony; the fourth, an emerald;

20 The fifth, sardonyx; the sixth, sardius; the seventh, chrysolyte; the eighth, beryl; the ninth, a topaz; the tenth, a chrysoprasus; the eleventh, a jacinth; the twelfth, an amethyst.

21 And the twelve gates *were* twelve pearls: every several gate was of one pearl: and the street of the city *was* pure gold, as it were transparent glass.

22 And I saw no temple therein: for the Lord God Almighty and the Lamb are the temple of it.

23 And the city had no need of the sun, neither of the moon, to shine in it: for the glory of God did lighten it, and the Lamb *is* the light thereof.

24 And the nations of them which are saved shall walk in the light of it: and the kings of the earth do bring their glory and honour into it.

25 And the gates of it shall not be shut at all by day: for there shall be no night there.

26 And they shall bring the glory and honour of the nations into it.

27 And there shall in no wise enter into it any thing that defileth, neither *whatsoever* worketh abomination, or *maketh* a lie: but they which are written in the Lamb's book of life.

22 And he shewed me a pure river of water of life, clear as crystal, proceeding out of the throne of God and of the Lamb.

2 ¶ In the midst of the street of it, and on either side of the river, *was there* the tree of life, which bare twelve *manner of* fruits, *and* yielded her fruit every month: and the leaves of the tree *were* for the healing of the nations.

3 And there shall be no more curse: but the throne of God and of the Lamb shall be in it; and his servants shall serve him:

4 And they shall see his face; and his name *shall be* in their foreheads.

5 And there shall be no night there; and they need no candle, neither light of the sun; for the Lord God giveth them light: and they shall reign for ever and ever.

6 And he said unto me, These sayings *are* faithful and true: and the Lord God of the holy prophets sent his angel to shew unto his servants the things which must shortly be done.

7 Behold, I come quickly: blessed *is* he that keepeth the sayings of the prophecy of this book.

8 And I John saw these things, and heard *them.* And when I had heard and seen, I fell down to worship before the feet of the angel which shewed me these things.

9 Then saith he unto me, See *thou do it* not: for I am thy fellowservant, and of thy brethren the prophets, and of them which keep the sayings of this book: worship God.

10 And he saith unto me, Seal not the sayings of the prophecy of this book: for the time is at hand.

11 He that is unjust, let him be unjust still: and he which is filthy, let him be filthy still: and he that is righteous, let him be righteous still: and he that is holy, let him be holy still.

12 And, behold, I come quickly; and my reward *is* with me, to give every man according as his work shall be.

13 I am Alpha and Omega, the beginning and the end, the first and the last.

14 Blessed *are* they that do his commandments, that they may have right to the tree of life, and may enter in through the gates into the city.

15 For without *are* dogs, and sorcerers, and whoremongers, and murderers, and idolaters, and whosoever loveth and maketh a lie.

16 I Jesus have sent mine angel to testify unto you these things in the churches. I am the root and the offspring of David, *and* the bright and morning star.

17 And the Spirit and the bride say, Come. And let him that heareth say, Come. And let him that is athirst come. And whosoever will, let him take the water of life freely.

18 For I testify unto every man that heareth the words of the prophecy of this book, If any man shall add unto these things, God shall add unto him the plagues that are written in this book:

19 And if any man shall take away from the words of the book of this prophecy, God shall take away his part out of the book of life, and out of the holy city, and *from* the things which are written in this book.

20 He which testifieth these things saith, Surely I come quickly. Amen. Even so, come, Lord Jesus.

21 The grace of our Lord Jesus Christ *be* with you all. Amen.

The End

ISBN : 9780999804919

Published by One Million Words LLC

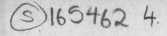

D0702213

Praise for Gail Godwin

"Gail Godwin is one of the best writers we have today."
—*Atlanta Journal-Constitution*

"Godwin's plots are compelling; her atmospheres and imagery are bewitching."
—*The Christian Science Monitor*

"Godwin moves us, not by high-voltage language, but by a generous-spirited chronicling of the aches and illusions that flesh is heir to."
—*Chicago Sun-Times Book Week*

"Gail Godwin is a wonderful writer."
—*The Boston Globe*

Mr. Bedford
and the Muses

Also by Gail Godwin

NOVELS

The Perfectionists, 1970

Glass People, 1972

The Odd Woman, 1974

Violet Clay, 1978

A Mother and Two Daughters, 1982

The Finishing School, 1984

A Southern Family, 1987

Father Melancholy's Daughter, 1991

The Good Husband, 1994

SHORT STORIES

Dream Children, 1976

Mr. Bedford and the Muses, 1983

Mr. Bedford
and the Muses

by
Gail Godwin

Ballantine Books • New York

Copyright © 1976, 1978, 1979, 1983 by Gail Godwin

All rights reserved under International and Pan-American Copyright Conventions. Published in the United States by Ballantine Books, a division of Random House, Inc., New York, and distributed in Canada by Random House of Canada Limited, Toronto.

http://www.randomhouse.com

This edition published by arrangement with Viking Penguin, a division of Penguin Books USA, Inc.

"A Cultural Exchange" appeared originally in Atlantic Monthly; *"Mr. Bedford" was published originally in condensed form under the title "The Unlikely Family" in* Redbook; *"A Father's Pleasures" and "Amanuensis" appeared originally in* Cosmopolitan, *and "The Angry-Year" in* McCall's. *"Amanuensis" was subsequently included in the* 1980 Prize Stories/O. Henry Awards Collection.

Grateful acknowledgment is made to Warner Bros. Music, Inc., for permission to reprint a selection from "Carolina in the Morning," lyrics by Gus Kahn, music by Walter Donaldson. Copyright © 1922 (renewed) Warner Bros. Inc. All rights reserved.

Library of Congress Catalog Card Number: 96-96064

ISBN: 0-345-39021-0

Cover design by Dreu Pennington-McNeil
Cover art © Prudence See 1995

Manufactured in the United States of America
First Ballantine Books Edition: August 1996
10 9 8 7 6 5 4 3 2 1

to Gingie

Contents

Mr. Bedford

I began keeping a journal when I was thirteen. Sometimes, now, I look with incredulity at the bulk of volumes widening along my shelf and I am reminded of the old lady who confesses to a stranger that she has always had a weakness for pancakes. "There's nothing wrong with having a weakness for pancakes," the stranger says. "Really?" she cries, relieved, and takes him up to her attic to show him her hundreds and hundreds of pancakes stacked neatly in tiers.

People say, "Oh, they must be so useful to your writing. All that material." But in fact the majority of the agonies, furies, passions, and dreads, penned in various inks in a handwriting that has changed from a stiff baroque upright to a looser, loopy slant, are as cold as those pancakes in the attic. Yet I go on with my vice. I look forward to it at the end of the day as some people do to a drink. Occasionally I indulge in a retrospective read and come away wishing that girl and then that woman had paid more attention to what was going on around her rather than heaping up more cold pancakes. But once in a while I come across something still warm. It connects me to my living past and starts my imagination glowing, as in the case of Mr. Bedford's story, written down carefully one spring afternoon in the London of 1963, within an hour after that strange and memorable couple, the Eastons, had told it to me.

My life with the Eastons began when I arrived in London in the spring of 1962. I lived with them, except for one winter's defection, until the autumn of 1964. Even today, when I try to describe the Eastons to people, I end up talking for thirty or forty minutes, growing more agitated, and finally demanding of my listeners: "Who *were* the Eastons, anyway?" And, as most people are perfectly willing to pass judgment on people they've never met, the answers are as peremptory as they are varied. "Con artists," says one person. "Victims!" insists another. "Their kind is a dying breed," remarks a third. But the minute I reread Mr. Bedford's story in my old journal, I knew that the Eastons, whatever they were, are very alive in me.

Easton is not their real name, of course. For obvious reasons, I'll change all the names, including my own. Also, made-up names make it easier to invent when you come to memory gaps. And this sometimes leads to bonuses. In the middle of "inventing," you discover you are remembering. Or, even better, you discover the real truth that lay buried beneath the literal happenings.

Only Mr. Bedford's name I won't change. It was his story that reconnected me to that chunk of raw past that now quivers to be shaped into meaning. We take our Muses where we find them, and you, Mr. Bedford, are the Muse of this story. As you once carried your candle into dark rooms for the Eastons, lead me now, in your diligent, slow-footed way, through the precarious realm of fiction-in-progress. You may keep your real name; your relatives won't sue.

The ad in the *Evening Standard* offered a bed-sitter in South Kensington, two meals included, seven guineas a week, "Student or young prof. person preferred." I had to ask someone what a guinea was, and was told that it was a fancy way to ask for more money (seven guineas being seven pounds, seven shillings). But I could still afford it, and I was a "young prof. person." So I called, or "rang up," as I would learn to say, and the woman who answered the telephone had an American voice with an Eastern Seaboard drawl. Her tone was warm and cultivated. She seemed pleased I was American, too, and even more pleased when I told her I'd be working for our Embassy. "Aren't you *lucky!*" she said. She told me to get off the 74 bus at

Old Brompton Road across from the Boltons and walk around the grassy circle to Tregunter Road. "It's the big gray house. It has a brass knocker shaped like a lion's head." She laughed. "You can move in right away if you like the room," she said. "But by all means stay and have supper with us." I was impressed by her spontaneous generosity. I had been in London less than a week and was still not certain what to make of the so-called British reserve.

I really congratulated myself on my luck when I saw the Boltons. It was just the sort of London I had imagined myself living in, knowing even as I conjured it up that I could not afford it on a GS-2 salary: a sweep of grand houses banked by well-kept lawns; old trees that, even though still bare, were tall and plentiful enough to form a cordon between the Brompton Road traffic and this austere preserve. Tregunter Road was shabbier, but the big gray house with the brass knocker still retained the ghost of former grandeur, even though its portico paint was peeling badly.

Mrs. Easton also retained the ghost of her better years. She carried herself extremely well in her baggy sweater and too-long tweed skirt, and her thoroughbred outlines were still apparent. She had a classic face, though wrinkled, and wore her faded blond hair pulled back behind her ears and fastened with a tortoiseshell barrette. "I'm *so* glad you rang when you did, Carrie," she said, "because immediately afterward a lovely young man telephoned from Leeds—he's joining Reuters (you know, the news service) and they had seen our ad and teletyped it up to him—but I told him I was pretty sure we'd already rented it. I see you've brought your bag—wasn't it heavy? Let's leave it just inside the door for now. I want you to meet Mr. Easton first and then he'll show you the room." She had a way of talking and smiling through her teeth at the same time that I found both unnerving and classy. We went past a large common room where a balding young man in a three-piece suit sat on a sofa reading a newspaper and another male of indeterminate age, also wearing a suit, was playing a Bach prelude rather badly on an old upright piano painted red.

"Do you have other tenants?" I asked, following her long, neatly shod feet down a gloomy corridor filled with promising supper smells. Somehow, from the way she had talked on the phone, I had assumed it would just be the three of us.

"Oh yes," she replied in her sunny, closed-mouth way, "we can accommodate seven. One is away at the moment, however, for the Easter holidays."

We passed a purple velvet curtain behind which someone was playing a Charles Aznavour record, then turned right into another corridor. Mrs. Easton knocked softly on a tall door with carved moldings. "Whit, dear, it's us," she called in a slightly placatory tone, then allowed a moment or two to pass before she opened it. A tall man stood erectly, with his back to us, in front of a fireplace that had a gas heater in the grate instead of a real fire. He wore well-pressed cavalry twills and a Harris tweed jacket with suede patches at the elbows. Then, with rather theatrical timing, he did an about-face. His cheeks were flushed and his light-blue eyes were a little watery and his hair was mostly gone, but he, too, still carried the outlines of a former beauty. He wore a maroon-and-gray tie that looked regimental, and also some tiny decoration in his buttonhole.

"Whit, this is Carrie Ames," said Mrs. Easton. "Carrie, this is my husband, Whitmore Easton." There was pride in her voice as she drawled out those last four words. I assumed he must be someone important, and/or she was still in love with him.

Mr. Easton shook my hand and looked me over. "So you'll be working for David Bruce, huh? Well, he's a capable chap. Gives wonderful parties, so I'm told. I was fond of Winant myself. He was ambassador here during the war. Amiable fellow. Took his own life, you know. I knew him when he was governor of New Hampshire. His second term."

"Are you two from New Hampshire?" I asked.

"No, I'm from New York and Lee, here, is from Connecticut. Say, Carrie, can I get you a drink? Darling"—he turned to his wife—"how about a drink?"

"Thank you, dear. I'll have a glass of sherry."

I said, "That sounds fine."

"Wonderful." He went to a sideboard. The room was filled with lots of large, dark-stained furniture. There was the smell of a nice perfume in the overheated air. Mrs. Easton displaced a Siamese cat from the sofa, explaining to him that he must defer to their guest. "This is Enrico," she said, fondling the cat in her arms. She wore a large pear-shaped diamond with two emerald baguettes on her wedding finger. The cat wriggled and sprang out of her arms with an ill-humored meow and stalked off to a hassock.

"Poor Rico," said Mrs. Easton, "he misses Elba. He had more freedom there. And he still hasn't forgiven us for the animal quarantine. We only recently got him back."

"You lived on Elba?" I sat down in Enrico's place. The sofa was a hideous old brown horsehair, but someone had draped a beautiful sea-green mohair shawl all along the back.

Mr. Easton joined us with the drinks. "I'm having something a wee bit stronger," he said, winking at me. He had poured himself half a tumblerful of gin with a dollop of tonic water. "Here's to Carrie," he said, raising the tumbler. We all drank to me. Mrs. Easton, with the air of a confidante, told me how for seven years she and Mr. Easton had run a little *pensione* in Portoferraio. "We met so many lovely people, mostly English, and we began to get homesick for some real civilization. And then this young man, Martin Eglantine, who owns this house and the one behind, across the garden, where your room is—listen to that, Whit!"—and she laughed, screwing up her eyes—"I'm already thinking of it as Carrie's room."

"Eglantine's a real entrepreneur," said Mr. Easton. "He owns dozens of houses like this, all over London. Buys 'em up quick as I can snap my fingers." He snapped his fingers, looked surprised to see that his glass was empty, and got up to refill it. I caught a shadow of annoyance on Mrs. Easton's face.

"Anyway," she went on brightly, smiling through her teeth, "Martin was very impressed with our *pensione*, and when we said we were ready to make a change, he offered us the use of these houses."

"But how long has it been since you've been *home?*"

"Oh, about eight years," said Mr. Easton jovially from the sideboard.

"No, Whit, it'll be ten years the thirtieth of this month," Mrs. Easton corrected him.

There was a silence in the room. The gas heater sighed. A clock ticked. Mr. Easton sloshed gin into the tumbler.

"But don't you miss the United States?" I asked, more to break the silence than anything else, and earned a look from Mrs. Easton that I would come to know and dread. I called it, in my journals, "the scrunch," because her whole face bunched up into a mask of wrinkles. The eyes became little slits of light— and malevolent light, at that—and the lips disappeared altogether. And you knew you had done something unforgivably *gauche*.

But this first time the apparition was mercifully brief, and the next moment she was drawling through her teeth, "Of course we miss it, but . . . well, honestly, Carrie, England has so much to offer, and, frankly, Mr. Easton and I are more English in our *values* than we are American."

"Carrie, if you look out those French windows you'll see a big white mansion to your left," said Mr. Easton. "That's Douglas Fairbanks Junior's house. I knew him in Cairo. We met at a houseboat party on the Nile. Interesting fellow, but I always thought he had terrible taste in women."

I don't think it once occurred to me that I could choose not to take "my room." Even before I saw its unprepossessing layout—though it was no worse than the average room perpetrated on "students and young professional persons" all over the civilized world—I knew I was going to live here. I knew it even as I followed Mr. Easton's military pace down the narrow garden path that connected the big gray house with the less impressive row house behind, and he knew it, too, because he had brought along my suitcase. In less than an hour, the Eastons had wound me fast into their net. It was a net composed of obligation, fascination, and intrigue. I liked them, didn't quite trust them, de-sired their approval, and knew, with the instinct of one who likes to stir life up, that wherever they were would never be dull.

"Well, no movie star's mansion on this side," said Mr. Eas-ton, as we looked out "my window" upon a solid block of coun-cil flats, "but you get the morning sun. It'll be easier to get up for work. We furnish linen service. Three towels a week, one change of sheets. What? Oh, a bookcase. Sure, sure. Ask Lee, I'm pretty sure there's one in the attic over at the other house. What we do is, you see, we give you the basics and then you fill in the rest according to your individual taste. Jean-Louis—that's our French textile salesman—has his room all filled with velvets and brocades. Alexander—he's a turf accountant (we call it bookie back home)—he lives in that passage with the purple curtain, we passed it on the way out. He can't afford the full rent, but he's an interesting chap, so we let him fix up that pas-sage and have his meals for a little less than you guys pay— which reminds me, rent is payable a week in advance and on Thursday, if possible. Keeps things uniform. Get Alexander to show you his passage. He's fixed it up like a Victorian brothel. Here's your gas fire. First you put in your shilling—I'll put the first one in for good luck—and then you light it." He did a deep knee bend, amazingly limber for his age, and demonstrated. Then rose again, tilting toward me as if he'd lost his balance momentarily. "Well, I expect you'll want to wash up before supper." His face was crimson as he backed out of the room. I couldn't be sure whether he had actually patted my bottom or just brushed against it with his hand in the act of getting to his feet.

Just before supper, Mrs. Easton, wearing a handsome black bib apron with thin white stripes over her clothes, emerged from the kitchen and introduced me to my fellow boarders. She reiterated that one was away for Easter. Of the present number, I was the only girl. Mrs. Easton explained that she and her husband took their meal separately, in their own quarters. "We feel you young people are less inhibited that way." Then she went back to the kitchen and served the plates, which Mr. Easton carried out two at a time. The couple took their own plates on a tray and disappeared.

"Did you know Colonel and Mrs. Easton back in America?" asked Alexander, the turf accountant who lived in the passage.

I said no, I'd met them only this afternoon.

"Pity. We were hoping you could give us the gen on them."

"Sorry. I didn't even know he was a colonel."

"He has a DSO," said a baby-faced young man with dark eyes and beautiful long lashes. "The British gave it to him for blowing up an enemy train in World War Two. He drinks too much, but she's terribly nice. And such a terrific cook. Mmm." He parodied someone licking his chops, then took a delicate forkful of lasagne.

"Even if her servings are the size of a postage stamp," said Alexander. "That's fine for Carlos here, he can sit in his room all day eating pâté and reading novels. Carlos's father is the finance minister of Mexico."

"Alexander," said Carlos, blushing deeply, "you embarrass me."

An arrogant-appearing young man in a turtleneck sweater who was reading something in his lap while he ate gave a snort of laughter. He was the best-looking of the bunch.

"I don't see why, Carlos. I'm just saving Carrie a bit of time. She's curious about us, we're curious about her. And being such a bloody international group, we don't have access to all the shortcuts one has with one's own countrymen. That's why I was hoping she could give us the gen on the Eastons. We're all keen on placing people, Carlos."

"That's not true," protested Carlos, blinking rapidly. "It's what a person is in himself that counts."

"Rubbish," said Alexander. "What am I 'in myself'? A bloody cipher. One more human being. Whereas if you can place my accent—Yorkshire, working class—and then if you can tell I'm wearing a thirty-guinea, made-to-measure suit, and if you go in my passage and if you know anything about antiques and can recognize what I've managed to accumulate on my sodding salary, *then* you're on the road to finding out who I am. And intend to become."

"A crook?" inquired a balding young man genially, without looking up from his food. He was the one in the three-piece suit I had seen reading a newspaper earlier.

"That's Colin," Alexander told me. "He's a clerk at Barclays Bank. He earns ten pounds a week. But *his* suit is off the peg."

"Oh, really, Alexander," said Colin, continuing to eat.

The arrogant man in the turtleneck gave another snort of laughter. I had retained his name from Mrs. Easton's introductions, though his had not been one she had lingered over indulgently, as in the case of Alexander and Jean-Louis the textile salesman, or with relish, as in the case of Carlos Paredes y Broncas. The antisocial man's name was Nigel Farthingale. He ate a piece of endive with his little finger sticking out and turned the page of the book on his lap.

"Oh Colin," I said, "I wonder if you could advise me. I was in the Canary Islands just before coming here and this British lady told me I would get a better rate of exchange if I cashed my American Express dollars into pounds down there. So now I'm carrying around all these loose pound notes. Would I lose a lot if I were to turn them back into traveler's checks?"

"You might lose more if you don't," said Colin.

"Nevair carry more cash than you can afford to lose," said the French textile salesman with real feeling, looking up from his meal for the first time. There was genuine alarm on his handsome, plump face. He wore his paisley silk foulard tied so high on his neck that he appeared to have no chin.

"Oh, Carrie probably comes from a very rich family," said Alexander. "All Americans are rich."

"Rubbish," I said. But in such a way that they might think he'd hit on the truth. "You must get a lot of good tips," I said, "being a turf accountant, Alexander."

"Yes, but I don't gamble. Investment is more my nature." Alexander was the thinnest grown-person I'd ever seen. His cheeks were so hollow he looked as if he were constantly sucking a sweet.

"Then why work in such a place?"

"It's as good as any, till my ship comes in. Besides, I rather enjoy watching how people of all classes can make equally bloody asses of themselves."

The Eastons reappeared. Mr. Easton cleared the table while Mrs. Easton poured coffee and served around a platter of cookies in the common room. She had taken off her apron and dabbed on a little of the nice perfume, and now, with the air of a grand lady entertaining a group of young people in her own home, she proceeded to devote herself to each of us in turn. I came first because I was new, and she explained to the group that I would be working at the Embassy on Grosvenor Square and then asked me what my duties would be, exactly, and turned things over to me with the smoothness of a talk-show hostess. I said I wasn't sure as to the exact scope of my duties, the job didn't start till Monday, but that I would be with a new program that was supposed to encourage British people to take their holidays in the United States.

"I'd adore taking a holiday in America," said Alexander. "Why not get your department to send me over as a publicity stunt? I'll go everywhere and send back good reports."

Appreciative laughter. Except for arrogant Nigel, who sat with the air of one restrained, his demitasse cup balanced upon his closed book.

Then Mrs. Easton looked fondly at Carlos and inquired whether he had *studied* any today. "Carlos is cramming for Cambridge," she explained to me.

There followed another set-to between Alexander and Carlos, in which Alexander said Carlos would be a bloody expert on the novels of Mary Renault when he got to Cambridge, and Carlos, blinking and blushing, protested that he had studied all morning and read *The Bull from the Sea* only in the afternoon. "And besides, Mrs. Easton"—he appealed to her like a favorite child—"it *is* history."

"Of course it is, Carlos, but you mustn't neglect your other subjects." Then, squaring her shoulders a little, she turned to Nigel Farthingale. "Any luck with your auditions?" she drawled, forcing her smile wider.

With a scornful glance at her, as if to say, Must we play this ridiculous farce?, he offered her his book. "I'm reading for the part of Jack next Tuesday. It won't be a very grand production, but then"—with a curl of his lip—"beggars can't be choosers, can they?"

I thought she flinched at this, but when she saw the book she cried, "Oh! *The Importance of Being Earnest.* Nigel, you're not going to believe this, but *I* once played Jack when we did this at our boarding school." She folded her hands on the book, closed her eyes for a minute, and then leaped up like a girl from her chair. She began pacing around our little circle and we watched, fascinated, as her stride grew more masculine. Then she held out the book in front of her, as if it had suddenly become much larger and taken on weight. "Is *this* the handbag, Miss Prism?" she asked, in a husky male voice. "Examine it carefully before you speak. The happiness of more than one person depends on your answer."

We were all charmed with her as she stood before us, in the tweed skirt whose length had been right about ten years before, holding out the library book as if it really were a bag large enough to hold a manuscript . . . or a baby . . . but then Nigel cruelly revoked the spell by saying, "It's 'the happiness of more than one *life*,' actually," and Mrs. Easton visibly recalled herself. You saw the years pile up again—for a moment she had been a girl, or a boy, with youth's whole life before her—and then she spoke once more through her teeth as she said, "You're right, I'm sure, Nigel. After all, it was such a long time ago." She handed him back his book. And resumed her place at the coffeepot.

Some desultory conversation ensued. Jean-Louis described

his success on a selling trip in Bristol, from which he had returned only that day, and had complimentary things to say about the sherry of that city; Alexander described a lamp he had seen in a shop in the King's Road that would be just bloody perfect for his passage, only it cost eighteen quid. Mr. Easton joined us. He sat down at the red piano and ran his fingers over the keys, then embarked on the first few bars of the "Moonlight Sonata." "Hey, Carrie," he called over his shoulder, "ever hear of a place called Rhinebeck, New York?"

It was at this moment that Nigel Farthingale chose to acknowledge my existence for the first time. "Come, Carrie," he said, rising abruptly, "it's time someone showed you the inside of an English pub."

I was in a quandary, one that would become a staple of my association with the Eastons: that of choosing between the call of freedom and the demands of "civilization"—one of Mrs. Easton's pet words. I had been eyeing the arrogant Nigel all through dinner, fantasizing just such an invitation as this, but why did it have to come at such an inopportune time? Mrs. Easton was just now beaming her scrunched look at Nigel with a formidable intensity. But, fearsome as the scrunch was, I dreaded any encroachment on my free choice more. This was a boardinghouse, after all, not a convent.

"Well, okay," I told Nigel. I slung my purse over my arm and followed him out of the room. Just as we reached the door, Mr. Easton hurried up behind us and took Nigel aside. "Can I count on it *this* Thursday?" I heard him ask.

"They're a frightful couple, frightful. When he started on *his* act, I felt it my duty to spare you. You'll get it yet, all the new ones do. The beautiful lady at the piano in the manor house in Rhinebeck, New York, playing the 'Moonlight Sonata,' only she turns out to have a tail. They're mean, dishonest, petty people. I think they've done something awful, that's why she can't even go home to see her grandchild. And they play favorites. They blow hot and cold on you, and they're terrible snobs. They court you as long as you're useful and do things their way, but they gossip behind your back and he tells the most awful lies. It's nothing but plot and counterplot from morning till night in that house."

"But what do you think they've done—that they can't go home?"

"Oh, who knows. Embezzled money, maybe. Perhaps they were spies. One day I was alone with her—I was in their good graces then, she thought me frightfully charming—and she showed me all these photographs of a child. 'He's almost nine years old and I've never laid eyes on him,' she said, and began to sniffle. I asked why, was it a question of money, and she laid her hand on my arm in that confidential way she has and said, 'Oh, Nigel, it's much more complicated than that.' She turned nasty on me after that, probably regretted confiding even that much. I'm getting out of there as soon as possible. I'm a bit strapped at the moment, but as soon as I get something . . . I'm seeing a chap at the BBC tomorrow. . . ."

I regretted coming out with him. The beer was warm and tasted bitter, and all exhilaration of freedom had long since fled. On and on ranted Nigel, always about the Eastons, his voice rising to a whine as he catalogued their faults. He was probably angry because Mr. Easton was closing in on him about the rent; I was a mere sounding board. I said I was tired and offered to pay for our beers, since he was strapped. He gallantly refused and said he'd go along with me tomorrow and show me where the American Express office was, as it was quite near where he had his appointment.

The next morning, as soon as breakfast was over and the dining room had cleared out, I prepared to reinstate myself with the Eastons. Mr. Easton, wearing a soft blue wool shirt with his tweed jacket today (and the little decoration on his lapel), was moving briskly around the common room, humming to himself as he emptied ashtrays and gathered up stray newspapers. I went over to him with my purse and explained that I was on my way to American Express to get all my pounds changed into traveler's checks, so could I just give him my seven guineas in advance now, though it was only Wednesday.

"Sit down, sit down," he said. He himself sat down and patted a place beside him on the couch. "A man should never take money from a woman while standing up," he said jovially. I counted out seven pounds from my envelope and then added seven shillings from my change purse. "Much appreciated," he said. "And how did the inside of an English pub look to you?" I made a sour face and shrugged. "I think it's a matter of who shows it to you. I'm going to try again." There, that should make things clear and win me back into their good graces. "Poor Nigel," he said to me, slipping my rent in his wallet, "he came to London hoping to make it big as an actor and, well, he just hasn't got what it takes. He's turning bitter and blaming it on everybody else. We've been very patient with him. Lee even baked him a cake for his thirtieth birthday and he never even thanked her." "It must be terrible to turn thirty and not be what you had hoped to be," I said, truly shocked that Nigel should be that old. "He's riding with me to the American Express office to show me where it is, but only because he has to go that way, anyway." "Sure, why not?" said Mr. Easton.

Mrs. Easton came out of the kitchen, drying her hands on a dish towel.

"Carrie wasn't too impressed with the inside of an English pub," said Mr. Easton. "Seems the company left something to be desired."

"Well, I'm not surprised," said Mrs. Easton. Her manner brightened toward me. "Carrie, come into the kitchen, if you have a moment, and I'll show you something simply splendid."

An impressive-sized fish had been laid out on the chopping board. "Isn't he wonderful?" crooned Mrs. Easton. "Daphne Heathcock brought him back with her on the train. In a wooden box packed with ice. The Heathcocks have been so lovely to us. He's an M.P. Daphne is a lovely girl, I want you two to be friends. She slept in this morning, she was tired from the trip."

"What kind of fish is it?"

"Why, it's a salmon. He's one of the first of the spring run. Honestly, I admire this fish. Do you realize he's been at least twice to sea? Look, you can tell from the scales. This fellow has gone through unbelievable hardships just to get back to his hometown river and start a family."

"How do you know it's a he?"

"Why, because of the hooked jaw. The hens have a rounded jaw; also, their sides are fatter. My father was a great salmon fisherman. He fished the Restigouche, up in Canada. Have you ever heard of the Restigouche Salmon Club?" It seemed to disappoint her that I hadn't. "Well, boy," she said to the salmon, "I'll do my best for you. I'm going to poach you and serve you with a Flemish sauce. I do hope you'll be here for dinner, Carrie. I wouldn't want you to miss this treat."

Nigel Farthingale obligingly pointed out the sights to me as we rode to Piccadilly on the top deck of the bus. He did not mention the Eastons. It was as if he knew I had gone over to the enemy and he needed to preserve his strength for his own battles. His face looked gray and worried as he walked me down the Haymarket in London's muted spring sunshine, and as he talked about his appointment—he was trying to get into television commercials—his breath was not good. I pitied him as I wished him luck at the entrance to American Express, but I was relieved he planned to leave the Eastons soon. This morning he was a walking portent of all I did not want to happen to me.

I went into the brightly lit office, found the banking window, and opened my purse. The envelope was still there, but the sheaf of pounds that had been inside was gone.

"Wait a minute, sit down and start over. Lee's just gone out for some nutmeg, she won't be long. Now let's try and reconstruct what you did with your purse from the time you paid me your rent till the time you opened your purse at American Express."

I had found Mr. Easton in their room, making up the horse-hair sofa, which apparently converted to a bed at night. A pair of Mrs. Easton's stockings hung over the back of a chair, and I think he had been drinking when I knocked. The gas fire was not lit in the grate and it was cold in the room.

"Well, I think I left my purse on the sofa in the common room when Mrs. Easton called me to look at the salmon. And when I came back, you and Nigel were standing there talking."

"Wait a minute," said Mr. Easton, snapping his fingers. "I was out of the room for a few seconds. I went to the dustbin. When I came back, Nigel was there, waiting for you. I hate to say this, but it sure looks like Nigel. He owes two weeks' back rent. How much did you have in the envelope, Carrie?"

To this day I can't say why I lied. It still embarrasses me to think of that lie, and I wouldn't admit it now except that it is inextricable from this story. But that will come later.

"A hundred and fifty pounds," I told Mr. Easton, when the sum had been not quite fifty.

Mrs. Easton returned. "Who let Rico out into the hall?" (She had the Siamese cat in her arms.) "Oh, Carrie. I thought you'd gone to town."

"Sorry, darling," said Mr. Easton, "he must have slipped out. . . . Carrie's had all her money stolen."

"Oh *no!*" cried Mrs. Easton. She put down the cat. Then she removed her stockings from the back of the chair and put them away in a drawer. "When did this happen? And where?"

"We've been reconstructing," Mr. Easton said. "Apparently, our out-of-work actor was in the common room with Carrie's purse. I had just stepped out to empty the—"

"But where was Carrie without her purse?" said Mrs. Easton, looking from one to the other of us.

"In the kitchen with you," he said.

"Oh dear," said Mrs. Easton vexedly.

"I'm terribly sorry this had to happen today," I said, "I mean the day of your salmon dinner."

"It's not *your* fault," she said, but looking at me as if she really thought it was. "Well, Whit, what do you think we ought to do?"

"Call Scotland Yard," he said.

"You're joking," she said.

"No I'm not. With a hundred and fifty pounds involved, we have no choice."

"A hundred and fifty pounds? You were carrying around that much in cash, Carrie?"

I nodded miserably, my misery largely a result of the lie. Had I wanted to impress upon them my distress by tripling the amount? Or to build my fake image as a rich girl? Or was I just an awful liar, as Nigel had accused Mr. Easton of being?

"But won't they come and go through everyone's *room?*" Mrs. Easton asked Mr. Easton, getting the beginnings of her scrunch. "If you two think it's Nigel—and I join you in thinking so—why not just wait until he comes back and confront him?"

"What if he never comes back?" said Mr. Easton. "He may just take the money and scram."

"And leave his things behind?"

"Tell you what," said Mr. Easton. "It's up to Carrie, of course. We'll wait and see if Nigel does come back, and if he does, *then* I'll call the Yard."

"I hate the thought of them going through the rooms," she said. "I mean, what will Carlos think? What will *Daphne* think?"

"They'll think that if it ever happens to them we'll be just as thorough. And they'll probably find it exciting," said Mr. Easton. "If it comes to that. And, frankly, I don't think it will."

Around four o'clock, Mr. Easton came and rapped on my door like a conspirator and told me that Nigel had returned and that Inspector Roper of the CID would be along shortly. I was to come and wait in the Eastons' room, where we would go over the facts with Roper, and then Mr. Easton would summon Nigel and "confront him out of the blue" with the law. He seemed animated by all the excitement, and I noticed he had changed into a clean shirt and put the regimental-looking tie back on.

When Inspector Roper arrived, he found us grouped in a cozy tableau of domestic distress. The gas fire hissing merrily in the grate. The beautiful sea-green mohair shawl draped once more over the back of the old horsehair sofa bed. Mr. Easton standing at attention; Mrs. Easton, with her good posture, sitting beside me on the sofa, making a gesture with her hands halfway between warming them and wringing them. The American *jeune fille*, eyes open abnormally wide with horror at the possibility of being discovered by Scotland Yard in an "exaggeration"—a look that passes as shock at having been robbed by the English before she's been a week on their shores. And Enrico the cat crouched elegantly on his hassock.

Poor Nigel did not have a chance. By the time he was summoned to the room, the Eastons and Roper were old friends. Roper had heard about the blown-up armament train that had got Colonel Easton his DSO, and the CID inspector had identified Mrs. Easton's perfume as Je Reviens and told us how, briefly, before the war, he had sold beauty products for Worth in the provinces. He asked me where in America I lived and said, "I've always wanted to go there and drink a mint julep in the proper surroundings."

Nigel was incensed when he found out what he was suspected of, and the more defensive he got the more hoity-toity his accent became, which did not help his case with Roper, whose vowels were more in the Alexander category. Nigel denied stealing my money and, with the condescension of an Oxford undergraduate inviting a common policeman to his room for sherry, invited Roper to "come upstairs and conduct a search."

Roper returned alone, looking sheepish, and said that of course he had found nothing. "The bloke's had ample opportunity to dispose of it," he said, "but I'm fairly certain I've put the wind up him. Of course, that doesn't help your case, Miss Ames, but quite honestly, just between us, you oughtn't to be carrying round large amounts of cash like that . . . it's just asking for it, you know. What I'm most concerned with, if you want to know, is that you don't judge England by this one bloke. We're not all of us like that, you can be sure."

"Of *course* not," said Mrs. Easton. "England is the most civilized nation on earth."

"Thank you, ma'am, which is exactly the reason why I

can't escort that insolent young liar to his just deserts: in this country a man is innocent until he's proven guilty. And I've got nothing to convict him on, you see."

"I understand," I said. Though I was a little disappointed with Scotland Yard.

"But will you be all right?" asked Roper.

"Oh, we'll take good care of her," said Mr. Easton, putting his arm around my shoulders. "And she's got a nice job at the American Embassy, starting Monday."

"Well, then," said Roper, "you're all right, then, aren't you? Mind you, this all goes down in the books. We may get him yet. But if by chance we don't, Miss Ames, try to look back on this as a learning experience. But don't judge the English by it!"

Just before the great salmon dinner, when some of us were gathered in the common room, Jean-Louis playing his bad Bach on the red upright, Alexander leafing through an old *Queen* from the magazine rack, Mr. Easton came in and took me aside.

"Flash bulletin," he said. "Farthingale's done a flit. I went up to his room after Roper left. I was going to have a man-to-man talk with him, see if I couldn't shame him into giving your money back. Not a trace. He'd cleared out. And owing two weeks' rent."

"Oh God," I said, feeling totally responsible for everything.

"I called the Yard, but Roper wasn't back yet. I left word. Listen, Carrie, do us a favor, will you? Don't mention the robbery to the others. Mrs. Easton is worried that it'll give the house a bad name. I'll just tell them he left. Okay? And I'll keep you posted on developments from the Yard."

"Okay," I agreed, feeling I'd been let off lightly.

The salmon was a success. It was the first time I'd ever eaten it fresh, and it remains to this day my favorite delicacy. Daphne, its purveyor, was much thanked, and the merits of the fish extolled by French, English, Mexican, and American consumers alike. "Jolly good," Daphne would reply, or, "I'm *so* glad." She would have been recognized as an English girl any-where in the world by her tissue-paper-thin skin (which was al-ready beginning to crinkle around the eyes, though she was only nineteen), and her expressionless features, and her inward-turning teeth. But I found her aloofness fascinating and read into her half-a-dozen stock phrases (which consisted of the two already quoted, plus variations around the adjectives "boring" and "super," and "One hopes so," and "I shouldn't be at all sur-prised") infinite nuances and levels of meaning. Like many English people of her class that I would meet, *she* seemed to find her frugal vocabulary adequate to meet the situations of a day; it was up to me to supply the shades of difference. Mrs. Easton had told me Daphne was studying shorthand and typing at a little establishment off Bond Street, and I asked Daphne if she planned to be a secretary.

"One hopes so," she replied, transporting a modest bite of salmon, her fork prongs-down, to her small mouth.

"Among Daphne's crowd, 'shorthand/typing' is shorthand for husband-hunting," put in Alexander.

"Don't be boring," said Daphne, though she blushed scar-let.

"*C'est parfait,*" murmured Jean-Louis, not looking up from his plate. "And the sauce is exquisite, as well."

"Did you get your notes changed into something safer?" inquired Colin good-naturedly.

"Mmm," I said vaguely, pretending to have a mouthful of salmon.

"I say," said Alexander. "Do you think you can get a carton of Pall Malls for me at your PX? I can advance you the money now, if you like."

"Did you hear Nigel left?" said Carlos. "Mrs. Easton said he moved out this afternoon without even giving a day's notice."

"Well, I shan't miss him," said Alexander.

"Always had his nose in the air ... or in a book," said Colin.

"And he treated Mrs. Easton badly last evening," said

Carlos. "There was no need for him to correct that one little word."

"I think he was not very—how do you put it?—solvent," said Jean-Louis.

"He was boring," said Daphne.

"Well, at least he had the decency to leave before the meal," said Alexander. "Our portions are that much larger. But you fancied him, didn't you, Carrie?"

"Not I," I said.

Thus the waters closed over Nigel Farthingale. No more was heard of him, not even via Scotland Yard, and my money was never found. (However, fifteen years would pass, and one night, back in the States, while irritably switching TV channels, I would come upon Nigel in the act of denying yet another crime. This time he was being accused of making off with his mother-in-law's bedtime novel so he could read it himself. It was not a very good program—its U.S. appearance was undoubtedly due to our current rage for "anything English"—but I stayed with it for a while in order to watch Nigel. He had aged, of course, but then who hadn't, and his hair was different and he wore a sad, droopy mustache in keeping with his farcical role. He was clad in a nightshirt that showed his potbelly, and he *had* stolen his mother-in-law's novel, and his wife, who was on Mummy's side, clobbered him with it when he was discovered red-handed with it, in his own bed. The whole thing depressed me very much and I switched it off. As Nigel's silly, puffy face shrank to a pinpoint of light, I said uselessly, "I think I owe you an apology.")

After dinner, we all adjourned to the common room and Mrs. Easton emerged without her apron, accepted our profuse compliments on the salmon, and poured coffee. She asked Daphne if she had enjoyed her Easter vacation.

"It was super, thank you very much."

Mr. Easton joined us after he had put the dishes to soak.

"So old Nigel's cleared off, has he?" said Alexander.

"Yep. Got an urgent call from Hollywood. Had to rush right off," said Mr. Easton, sitting down at the piano.

Everybody laughed.

He played a few bars of the "Moonlight Sonata" and then told us about the time he had gone "on a matter of business" from New York City to the house of a very wealthy man in Rhinebeck, New York. "While the butler went off to announce me, I wandered about the room, looking at the paintings and so on, and then I heard this same music coming from somewhere . . . only the person was playing it much better than I do, with real talent and feeling. And I found myself going in search of it. I went through one magnificent room after another until finally I reached the most beautiful room of them all. It overlooked the Hudson and at that moment the sun was just setting. A beautiful woman sat at a grand piano; she was in three-quarter profile, so I could see her but she didn't see me. Well, I stood there admiring this vision of loveliness. I was a young man, life was just beginning for me, as it is for all of you now, and that woman in those surroundings seemed the epitome of all I hoped to win for myself: love, accomplishment, beauty, elegance, wealth. I stood on the threshold of that room, watching her like a man in a dream, and then, when it came time for her to turn the page of her music, I saw a long tail whip up from under her dress, do the job for her, and then disappear under her dress again. She went right on playing, without a break. Shortly after that, the man I'd come to see on business joined me and she heard us and stopped playing and came over to be introduced. She was his daughter. Later, after he and I had done our business, he asked me to stay and dine with them. He said his daughter didn't often have the pleasure of interesting company her own age. I thanked him and explained I had to get back to New York on urgent business. I rode all the way back to the city having one martini after another in the club car."

"And what sort of a tail was it, exactly?" asked Carlos in the tones of one who knows the story well enough to move on to its subtler embellishments.

"Oh, slender, graceful, efficient," said Mr. Easton. "Everything you'd want in a tail, really."

I was practically on the floor with hilarity.

"That is, if one wanted a tail," said Alexander.

At this point, cool Daphne almost fell off her chair laughing.

"And did it," I gasped, "did it have hair on it?"

This brought a communal shriek. Now everyone was rolling and pitching and snorting. Mrs. Easton was laughing so hard she held her stomach as if in pain, Colin had his round face buried in his hands, and Jean-Louis, cackling like a madman, took out a gorgeous square of silk and mopped the tears from his eyes.

"Did it have hair?" repeated Mr. Easton, swinging around on his piano stool to face me. Like a good performer, he had kept control of himself and only a slight twitch of his mouth betrayed his mirth. "Well, Carrie, as I recollect, it had a thin layer of hair. Not that you could see bare skin or anything. Just, you know"—his right hand stroked a sensuous curve in the air—"the right amount of hair for a ladylike tail."

The London evening closed around our happy circle, and presently, still flushed from laughing, Mrs. Easton got up to turn on a lamp. Anyone happening to pass our window then would have seen such a picture as might make his heart quicken with longing . . . or nostalgia . . . or eagerness to get home: depending on his own domestic circumstances.

In the following weeks, my energies and attentions were directed more upon Grosvenor Square than upon the goings-on at "Tregunter," as all the inmates called it, even though half of us had rooms in the shabbier house, behind, on Cathcart Road. We three "travel consultants," in our temporary quarters on the fourth floor of the Embassy, were all in our early twenties: one from California, one from Missouri, one from North Carolina. We were expected to look personable and be enthusiastic and pleasant as we doled out scenic brochures and city maps and worked out timetables, if required, for the potential British visitors to the U.S. who had seen our ads and braved their way past the Marine guards to inquire further. To those who had stayed at home in Lancs or Hants or Weston super Mare or Berwick upon Tweed and penned inquiries beginning with "I am extremely sorry to bother you" from houses with picturesque names like Tidmarsh Cottage or Eel Grange, we were expected, when not busy with "live" customers, to write warm, helpful replies, enclosing the appropriate brochures. When it was discovered that the girl from Missouri had been signing all her letters "Love, Betty Ann McRae," our supervisor, an ex–airline stewardess and the bane of my workday existence, took to screening all our letters and returning them for revision if "the tone was off" or, as once or twice in my case, "they showed too much imagination."

Colleen Drury (or "Dreary," as we called her behind her back) was an earnest woman in her forties. During slow hours, she told us stories of her grim childhood in a dead Midwestern town she had been determined to escape. Her mother had told her she was ugly, and, often, when Colleen was sleeping, would come into Colleen's bedroom and snatch her pillow from under her head. When our boss, Mr. Miles, discovered Colleen, she had been "retired" from the skies by her airline and was working as a tour planner in its London office. She was not a bad-looking woman. She liked to tell us how she was once aboard a flight with JFK when he was still a senator, and he called her over and told her, "You look a lot like my wife." There was a resemblance, in the facial structure and the hair, and Colleen frankly played it up in her choice of clothes and shoes and the little pillbox hats she always wore to Embassy receptions. She even spoke in a whispery, girlish voice that sounded exactly like the parody of Jackie on a record about the Kennedys in the White House that was all the rage that year. But poor Colleen had a witch's chin and suffered from chronic conjunctivitis and from a variety of back problems that would bring her ramrod-straight to the office one day and stooping the next. She was a spinster but, as she confided to us, she had been on the verge of marriage several times, once even having left her suitcase, as required, in the rectory of a certain village to establish residence during the period of the banns. But at the last minute, she told us, she always lost her nerve and couldn't go through with it. She was a stickler for etiquette and protocol and adored poring over manuals that told you how to address nobility and who sits where and leaves when. One morning, our post brought a letter from an earl inquiring about the ninety-nine-dollars-for-ninety-nine-days bus ticket offered by Greyhound, and Colleen spent the better part of that day rushing up and down on the elevator, from and to the USIS library, consulting *Debrett's* and *Burke's* and R. W. Chapman's *Names, Designations & Appellations*. She humbly submitted her final draft to Mr. Miles, our good-humored, unflappable director, who seemed always on his way out for an appointment. He skimmed it, standing on the threshold of the exit, and said, "Seems fine to me, Colleen. Be sure and save his seal, my nephew is making a collection."

I spent a great deal of time fretting about Colleen. She could just walk through the room and make me feel guilty. Every time I talked to her, I came away feeling I had either betrayed or incriminated myself. I discussed it with the other two, who admitted they felt the same, only not as violently as I did. "It's because she's earned this job and we haven't," said the girl from California, who was secretly engaged but wanted her year of independence before she settled down. She and I had had political entrées to our Stateside interviews with Mr. Miles. "It's because this job is the center of her life, while we have other things we care about more," said the loving Betty Ann from Missouri, who was newly wed to a handsome, strapping Texan doing a year at the London School of Economics. "I guess you're right," said I, who still drifted becalmed, uncertain, upon my ocean of possibilities. I looked upon this job as a sort of glamorous lifeboat (the glamour being the London part) that would keep me financially afloat till the winds of love and accomplishment bestirred themselves and set me on my course.

/ / /

The Eastons' name does not make its initial appearance in my journal until almost a month has elapsed from the day I entered their house. Or, rather, Martin Eglantine's house. The entire Nigel-robbery episode is summed up in the scrawled rubric "Just trying to survive!," followed by a long column of pounds, shillings, and pence in which emergency expenses are worked out till the first payday. (Mr. Miles, always good about these things, advanced a loan.) "The Eastons hang their clothes over the backs of chairs when they go to bed at night" is sandwiched inauspiciously between the conclusion of a diatribe against Colleen Drury (ending with the resolution "Do not converse with her except when absolutely necessary!") and an exchange among the "inmates" that I must have found recordable:

> ALEXANDER (*throwing down the Sunday color supplement*): Just look at the Queen! Why can't she dress properly?
> COLIN: I'm afraid that's not her fault, old boy.
> ALEXANDER: You can be dowdy and elegant at the same time.
> JEAN-LOUIS: Tell me, Carrie, what is considered a gude salarie in America?

One night, very late, the door to my room had swung shut while I was in the bathroom. I ran shivering across the connecting garden to the main house to borrow the Eastons' spare key. It took several knocks to wake them. "Carrie! What's wrong?" asked Mr. Easton, in striped flannel pajamas, when he finally opened the door. He seemed relieved when he learned I only wanted the key. From the doorway, I could see Mrs. Easton under the bedclothes in their pulled-out horsehair sofa bed. "All right now, dear?" she drawled sleepily at me. I also saw his twills, the Harris tweed, and the maroon-and-gray tie laid out neatly on a chair, and her too-long skirt and the baggy sweater draped on another chair, and their shoes beneath their respective chairs. I found the sight both touching and sinister. As though they might have to get dressed in a hurry, I thought, recalling Nigel's hints at their dark past.

All the inmates of the "youth brothel," as Mr. Easton sometimes called it, were intrigued by the Eastons' friends. There were not many, but among them numbered several whose correspondence could have added to Mr. Miles's nephew's seal collection. There was an old lady with pinkish hair and a slightly soiled lavender suit that looked like an old Chanel who arrived most Saturdays to take tea with Mrs. Easton. She drove up in a wobbly, ancient Morris Minor, tooted the horn twice (which was the signal for Mr. Easton to remove Enrico to the kitchen), and first coaxed and then dragged an angry, rheumy-eyed pug from the front seat of the Morris. The pug's name was Donna Elvira; the Eastons addressed the old lady as "Principessa." The Principessa and Donna Elvira would go off to the Eastons' room to have tea with Mrs. Easton, and Mr. Easton would chop vegetables or cube meat for a curry and keep Enrico company in the kitchen. When tea was over, the Principessa would come to the kitchen (leaving Mrs. Easton outside in the hall in charge of Donna Elvira) and say in her hoarse, heavily accented English, "Dear Whit, I have come to say good-bye." Then they would chat for a minute, during which time the old lady would always remark, "That looks delicious, is that beef or pork?" or, "Oh, what a pretty cheese," and Mr. Easton would insist on wrapping some up for her. Once she went so far as to admire Enrico's stock of tins, which were kept on a shelf over the sink, and Mr. Easton persuaded her to take one for Donna Elvira, whose palate had gone off her usual brand, the Principessa said.

"She lost everything during the war and had to flee Italy," Mrs. Easton told us. "Now she's just a raggle-taggle gypsy like us, even though the blood of the Medicis flows in her veins."

"She can't afford even a full square meal a day, but she has a Goya painting hanging in her bed-sitting room," said Mr. Easton.

"Well, she'll always have a decent tea and some scraps for her Sunday lunch as long as the blood flows in *our* veins, be it ever so sluggish," said Mrs. Easton. "But it's just a drawing, darling, not a painting." Mrs. Easton almost always corrected her husband's exaggerations, even though it pained her, you could tell. "This Chelsea pensioner came up to us on the street and wanted twenty-five shillings for a postcard," he would say. "No, darling. Four shillings," she would amend.

Then there were Lord and Lady Monleigh. He was the Eastons' age, in his early sixties; she was a handsome, languid woman about twenty years younger—his second wife. She wrote novels under her maiden name, but her book-jacket photos always showed her posed inside or outside "Houndsdene Hall, the country seat of the Marquess and Marchioness of Monleigh." Once a fortnight, the Eastons left us a cold supper and took the bus to Belgrave Square to dine at the Monleighs' town house, and about that often Lord and Lady Monleigh came to Tregunter and dined off trays in the Eastons' room and then joined us for coffee. Lord Monleigh was fascinated by our ménage (he had no children) and loved to draw us out. He was a stout little man with pointed ears like a gnome's and extremely intelligent eyes that fastened on people and things, avid to extract their essences. He asked Alexander if he might visit the famous antique-filled passage he had heard so much about, and when they returned, Alexander was saying, "You're quite welcome, sir, it's a distinct improvement to show it to someone who knows what he's seeing." He wanted to know Jean-Louis's travel routes when he went selling his silks around the provinces, and insisted upon giving him names of acquaintances who might be of help. "What delights you most about the English?" he demanded of me. "And what about us disappoints you most?" "I love their subtlety," I said. "But sometimes they ... well ... lack *vigor*." (That popular Camelot word.) "Mmm," he mused, pulling at a gnomish ear. "P'raps you'll find we make up for it with durability." Mrs. Easton nodded at Lord Monleigh as if she were a schoolgirl listening to her favorite teacher.

He asked Carlos what he'd been cramming for. "Ah yes, grammar. My nephew found a good one on his entrance examination to Sandhurst. 'What is wrong with this sentence: Our Christmas turkey did not come, so we had to eat one of our friends.' "

It sometimes occurred to me to wonder why Lady Monleigh, the novelist of the two, who slouched elegantly in her chair, smoking her Russian cigarettes and cocooned in some private reverie, was not asking these questions. I studied her discreetly, for I planned to write novels, too, once everything was sorted out in my lifeboat. Well, maybe she was absorbing it silently, all this valuable human data her husband so obligingly ferreted out for her. But I took out her latest novel from the lending library and found little evidence of it.

One Sunday the Eastons invited me to their room to take tea with two young men who had boarded with them in Portoferraio, where the Eastons seemed to have acquired all their present friends. I went expecting to meet contemporaries and was disappointed to find two middle-aged men, one with graying hair and the other gone completely silver. But the tea was comforting from other aspects. The Eastons approved of me that day, and glowed every time my portion of the discourse proved lively or intelligent. They behaved like kinsmen taking credit for an American cousin they had decided to present to their select circle. One reason I was able to shine as I did was that, as soon as I entered their room and saw the other guests, I was able to relax: Eros was not among them. The other was that Mr. Easton served sherry as well as tea.

One of the topics we discussed was that of taste. Christopher, the silver-haired one, was redecorating his part of the Chelsea house he shared with Mark, the graying-haired one. Christopher owned the house, or rather had one of those ninety-nine-year leases that pass for ownership in England; and Mark, a barrister, rented the downstairs floor. Mr. Easton, who'd had a head start on the afternoon's spirits, proclaimed that if you hadn't grown up among good things, your taste was always going to be a little off. There would always be some garish lapse to trip you up and give the whole show away.

"Oh, I disagree, Whit, darling," said Mrs. Easton animatedly, looking very happy to be having just this sort of conversation in just this sort of civilized circumstance, at tea. "I think it comes down to whether a person has an innate feel for *proportion* in all the activities of life, whether it's selecting a chair to go in a room or"—she cast about in her head for a minute—"or washing the dishes."

"I'm fascinated," said Christopher, leaning forward and recrossing his ankles. (Both visitors wore identical shoes: mudbrown suede lace-ups.) "Do tell us, Mrs. Easton, how one washes the dishes in good taste."

"All right, I will! Whit does. My husband does." She beamed at Mr. Easton, who had raised his eyebrows quizzically and, under the umbrella of her compliment, took this opportunity to top everyone's glass with more sherry. "The way our little household works, here at Tregunter, is that after the main meal we all take coffee together in the big room. I attach great importance to this; I think it fosters a sense of family life; often when young people are starting out on their own, living in digs, they tend to forget ... well ... that there's anything but themselves. Their isolation leads them into a kind of brooding selfishness that's neither healthy nor productive." Her forehead clouded, she began to get her scrunch. (Of whom was she thinking?)

"I know exactly what you mean," put in Mark, whose round, boyish face somewhat offset the graying temples. "When I first came up to town, I took a sort of masochistic pleasure in dragging myself home each night to my dreadful North London digs and contemplating how, once again, the world had failed to recognize my genius that day. Now if I'd had *you* to pour me a reassuring cup of coffee and ... have I said something amusing, Carrie?"

"Just your description. I love it, it's perfect." I started to add, That's just how *I* feel, but thought better of it. I was learning.

"But the dishes, the dishes!" cried Christopher, who could be somewhat shrill.

"Yes . . . Well, *after* we've all had our coffee hour, Whit insists on doing them. You see, he wants me to save my hands," Mrs. Easton went on, casting a rather critical look down at her hands and the diamond ring with the emerald baguettes. "But I always keep him company. And I must say he goes about it in such a *manly* way, sort of making it into an organized, workmanlike thing . . . like carpentry, or something. It becomes tasteful because he makes it into a perfectly appropriate task for a man like himself to be doing." The blood rose to her face, as it always did when she became emotional.

Mr. Easton put down his sherry glass and crossed the room and kissed his wife on the forehead. "A tasteful kiss," he explained to us.

I couldn't have been more surprised when, a few days later, Mark telephoned me at the office and asked me if I would like to go for a drive in his new Fiat the following Sunday. He had given no indication during tea of finding me anything more than part of the Easton "family." I stopped by the Eastons' room to report this development, and also to ask tactfully, for the third time, if it would be possible for me to have that bookcase Mr. Easton had promised.

"Oh, I'm so glad," said Mrs. Easton. "Mark is just the nicest boy. Frankly, Carrie, it's the sort of thing we were hoping for. It's so important to go out with the right kind of men, especially in England."

"With an Englishman," said Mr. Easton, "you don't even have to flirt. They're immovable for weeks and then all of a sudden they fall flat on their faces."

"But it hasn't even been a week," I said.

"Well, then, dear, he must have thought you were very special," said Mrs. Easton.

I thought this would be a good time to mention the book-case.

"Yes, of course you need one," said Mrs. Easton. "And we're going to see that you get one even if we have to buy it."

"But isn't there a lot of furniture up in the attic?" I asked. "Mr. Easton said . . ."

"Whit, shall we tell her?" said Mrs. Easton portentously.

"Might as well. Just don't say anything to the others. We were going to announce it at the coffee hour tonight," he said.

They told me Martin Eglantine had decided to put both the house on Tregunter and the house on Cathcart on the market.

"He wants us out in a month," said Mr. Easton.

"Isn't that awful?" cried Mrs. Easton. "After he practically begged us to come here!"

The prospect of eviction had a bonding effect on our household. After Mr. Easton's grim announcement at the evening coffee hour, nobody wanted to leave the common room. We all sat around decrying Mr. Eglantine's mercenary inclinations and wondering what we were going to do. Carlos and Alexander took up a collection and brought back three large bottles of cider from the corner pub. We began congregating in one another's rooms. Usually it was Carlos's room because he kept two heaters going and had such pretty pillows and decorations. Also a steady supply of delectable snacks.

"Do you know the Eastons didn't even have a bloody *lease?*" said Alexander. "How naive can you be?"

"They assumed he was a gentleman and therefore there was no need," said Carlos.

"They are a charming couple," said Jean-Louis, "but I think they are not practical people always."

"The point is," continued Alexander, "we're out on our ears in less than a month."

"But maybe they'll find something by then," I said. "They go out looking every day. Maybe they'll find an even nicer house than Tregunter. And, frankly, the rooms over in Cathcart are nothing to write home about."

"But they're rooms," said Alexander. "I can't even afford a proper room. And what if the new house they do find doesn't have a passage?"

"Don't be silly, Alexander. They'll always make a place for you," said Carlos. "You amuse them. I feel perfectly confident they will find something."

"One hopes so," sighed Daphne, who had been standing with her back to us, looking out at the delicate green that had begun to assert itself in gardens and on trees, despite the still-raw air. "There they go off now, as a matter of fact."

We all gathered at Carlos's window in time to see the Eastons sally forth on another day of house-hunting. She wore the tweed jacket that matched her old skirt and, as it was windy, had borrowed back the sea-green mohair shawl from the sofa. He was in his regimental best and carried a rolled-up newspaper section as if it were a swagger stick. He tapped it against his thigh in rhythm to their step, and, as always, she leaned on his arm. There was a poignancy in the way they assaulted the pavement with their long-legged strides; something in their attitude reminded me of a painting I had seen of Adam and Eve being ejected from the Garden, the urgency of their situation sweetened by the sharing of it. We watched them possessively out of sight. It had not occurred to any of us to go off alone and look for a place.

"It's a Procrustean bed, whichever way you make it," Mr. Easton told us one evening, as he poured coffee. Mrs. Easton was so exhausted, she had not emerged from their room after supper. "Up in Notting Hill or over in Bayswater there are lots of big houses available for groups like us. The owners figure, I guess, we can't bring the neighborhood down much lower than it already is. But who wants to live in the middle of Wogville? Whereas, we've seen several nice houses in Knightsbridge or

South Kensington or over in Chelsea that would be fine for *us*—they don't even mind Rico—but they put their foot down when it comes to boarders. Zoning regulations, you see."

"Why tell them?" asked Alexander.

Mr. Easton seemed to have considered this already. "You guys aren't exactly invisible, you know. You all go out the front door every morning and come back every evening."

"I meant why tell them we're boarders?"

"Oh? What would you be, then? My bastard children?" Mr. Easton surveyed our circle, as if testing out the visible credibility of this. Daphne, who'd had her silky reddish hair cut that day, sat placidly knitting an argyle sock; Carlos was looking particularly cherubic in a new white cashmere turtleneck from his latest buying spree in the Burlington Arcade; Jean-Louis had taken out a small notebook and was calculating figures in it while he munched an oatmeal cookie; I was still in my office clothes because I had detoured over to Better Books in Charing Cross Road in order to buy two new American novels—Richard Yates's *Revolutionary Road* and Reynolds Price's *A Long and Happy Life*—which I planned to read over the weekend; Colin, though no older than the rest of us, gave an impression of middle-aged stodginess, possibly because of his balding head and his three-piece bank-clerk suit; then we had a new boarder, Ian, who had taken Nigel's room and who *was* slightly older. His hair was already gray and his face wore a constant look of strain. He sold office furniture. And then, of course, there was Alexander, looking like a skeletal and sinister ecclesiastic these days, since he had taken to wearing a black polo shirt with his dark suit.

Alexander took out a PX cigarette from a flat silver case and lit it with an expensive-looking lighter. His sharp cheeks, slightly scarred from acne, sucked hungrily at the flame. "Why not?" he said. "Why not say we're your family?"

Several weeks passed. Martin Eglantine had granted the Eastons an extra month's grace, but Mr. Easton was obliged to conduct prospective buyers through the two houses, and movers came and took away the sofa, the rug, and the upright piano in our common room. Mrs. Easton's cooking suffered and her eyes were often red. Carlos cut his finger badly, opening a tin of pâté, and had to go to the emergency room of St. Stephen's Hospital. The girls in the office persuaded me to look for something on my own, and I went as far as telephoning several places. But I knew I wouldn't follow through. Staying in this drama was somehow more important. More important, even, than getting settled so I could write my own novel in the evenings, a task that was beginning to assume more urgency than before, since I had subtracted Reynolds Price's birth date from the date of publication of his first novel. (Ian, the new boarder, had actually seen me doing this arithmetic in the flyleaf of the book, as a few of us hung dispiritedly about the common room one gray Saturday; he surprised me by saying, "I used to do that, too." "Don't you anymore?" I asked. "Not once they all started being younger," he said. He himself was reading Trollope. He had taken a first in history at Oxford some years before, "but things just didn't work out," and now he sold metal desks and typing chairs. He ate no midday meal and walked to work in order to afford his room at Tregunter. "I like the spirit of the Eastons," he said. "And I do so hate eating alone." He had beautiful, white, manicured hands, which he clasped and unclasped as he talked.)

And then, just before supper one evening, Mr. Easton, already three sheets to the wind, told us with flushed face that there would be an important announcement after the meal.

"I have good news and bad news," began Mr. Easton, as we all clustered around on the few remaining chairs and on some hassocks and pillows Mrs. Easton had brought down from the attic during these last weeks of depletion. "The good news is, we've taken a lease on a house. It's on Old Church Street, in Chelsea, about half a block from the river . . . wait a minute . . . wait a minute"—he held up his hand in warning against our cheers and sighs of relief. "The bad news is, it's a small house.

Smaller than we'd hoped for, but, well, Mrs. Easton and I are in a little more of a bind than you people, when you come to think of it. I mean, you're young, most of you make a salary, it's not the end of the world if you have to pack your bags and start all over. To put it frankly, Mrs. Easton and I are kind of tired, and that's why we decided to go on and take this little dollhouse in Chelsea. It's one of those row houses, thin as a pencil from the outside, the rooms going one behind the other toward the back. There are four floors. There's the basement floor, which has a storage room and a small bathroom. Then there are two rooms on the ground floor, one facing the street, the other facing the back garden, which is just a walled-in patio. Then you go up the steps and on the first landing there's the kitchen. It also looks out on the garden, or patio. Then you go up a few more steps and you get to the first floor (we'd call it the second, back in the States) and that's the drawing room / dining room. Just one room running the length of the house, from back to front. You guys with me, so far?"

We were. But the light had gone out of our faces. One more floor to go and only two possible bedrooms, so far. Carlos pulled at the loose bandage on his finger. Ian's beautiful white hands were shaking, even though they were clasped on his Trollope.

"Okay. Go up some more steps, you come to the second landing. Here there's a little room that the owner's wife uses as a sewing room. Very small room, but it gets lots of light. It's the room directly above the kitchen and it also looks out over the back garden. And then we come to the top floor, where we have a large bathroom, and the master bedroom, and another small bedroom behind. The master bedroom looks toward the street and the small one toward the garden. And that's it, gang." He spread his hands in a gesture of having no more to offer. He had remained standing the whole time. Mrs. Easton sat on a pillow on the floor with her legs tucked girlishly under her skirt. She had all the coffee things spread around her. "Would anyone like more coffee or another cookie?" she asked, smiling through her teeth. Nobody did.

"Is there a passage?" inquired Alexander.

"No, Alexander," Mr. Easton said with great meaning. "There is no passage."

"Bloody hell," said Alexander. But I noticed he seemed less upset than one would have expected. Carlos looked much more upset on Alexander's behalf.

"We figure," Mr. Easton went on, "that we've got six possible bedrooms to work with."

"I count only five," said Colin, who had listened with rigid attention to the description. "Two on the ground, one on the second landing, two on the top."

"Right you are," said Mr. Easton. "But Lee and I plan to convert the basement storage room for our use. Of course, we'll have to live in one of those ground-floor rooms until we make the basement habitable, but without the rent from those rooms we couldn't hack it. It just wouldn't pay, with anything under five paying guests. As it is, we're going to be forced to raise the rent to ten guineas."

Colin's face worked strangely. Then, abruptly, the young bank clerk got up and left the room.

"I can't stand it, Whit," said Mrs. Easton, looking up beseechingly at her husband. "It's like breaking up a family. I think *I'm* going to cry."

Ian got to his feet. "This is, of course, a great disappointment for me," he said. "But why make it difficult for you, as well? I have enjoyed being in this 'family' immensely, even though it has only been for a short time. Naturally I can't scrape together the ten, but I'm warning you"—and here he took Mrs. Easton's rather yellowish freckled hand in his own two beautiful white ones—"I shall visit you whenever I'm in need of a bit of spirit . . . if that's agreeable to you."

"Oh, it certainly *is!*" she cried, emotion and relief filling her voice. She looked up at him gratefully. "You *will* come and take tea with us sometimes? *Promise* us, Ian?"

He promised, and shook Mr. Easton's hand and, in his rather effeminate way, went away to his room with his novel.

"That's what I call a real gentleman," exclaimed Mrs. Easton passionately.

"Yep," agreed Mr. Easton, "that's the genuine article. But as my commanding officer used to say after a battle, let's pause for a minute, out of respect for our fallen comrades, and then count heads for the coming fray. Daphne, you think you'd like to come to Chelsea with us?"

The girl, who had kept her eyes lowered and had continued her knitting during the entire episode, looked up and said, in an almost chastened tone, "I should like that very much. If you'll have me. My school finishes in August. But if I might stay for the summer?"

"That would please us very much," said Mrs. Easton.

"Carrie? I take it you'll join us?" asked Mr. Easton.

"Actually," said Mrs. Easton, "the room we *tentatively* have in mind for you has two built-in bookshelves, one on either side of the fireplace. And the cutest little alcoves where Mrs. Henning keeps two *very nice* porcelain figurines. Though I'm certain she'll remove those."

"Then Carrie will have a place for her Rodin and her Giacometti," said Mr. Easton, with a wink at me.

"You know you can count me in," I said. A fireplace! In the bedroom!

"In fact, Daphne, we thought you two girls could share the top floor. And then whoever was in the sewing room on the landing—we thought maybe Carlos, because he needs the light for his studying all day—would have to share the big bathroom. But I'm sure the three of you could work out a civilized arrangement."

"Just don't all try to climb in the tub at the same time," said Mr. Easton jovially. "It's not big enough."

"I'll be above the kitchen, then," said Carlos. "Shall I be able to contain myself with all those good cooking odors?"

"Not to worry, Carlos. You'll have your pâté to console you."

Everyone looked nervously toward Alexander as he spoke.

How was he "taking" it: the fact that there was no passage for him and his turf accountant's salary.

"Alexander," burst out Carlos, "you could share with me. You're out in the daytime, so I could study, and then if you don't snore, or anything, at night, we could *muddle through*, as the English say." He sank back on his floor cushion, aglow with magnanimity.

"Thank you, Carlos, but I have no intention of muddling through."

"Actually," Mrs. Easton broke in, "there's a tiny stone *shed* in the little garden area. Whit and I thought Alexander might not mind that during the summer months for a little less rent. We mentioned it to him earlier so that he wouldn't get upset when Whit made the announcement to the group, but we didn't want to say anything to Colin, because he might have thought we were playing favorites." Then she beamed at Carlos. "You see, Carlos, we feel just as you do. Life would not be the same without Alexander."

"As a matter of fact, it was Alexander who gave us the idea that—" began Mr. Easton, but Mrs. Easton interrupted him.

"And we thought Jean-Louis could take his choice of one of the ground-floor rooms. And we'll live in the other till we get the storage room fixed up. And then, of course, we'll have to get another boarder *pronto*, or Whit and I will be in debtors' prison."

So Colin and Ian were dispensable, I was thinking, while Alexander was not. And how deftly the Eastons had managed everything: in less than a half hour, the two dispensables had been eased out and the rest of us had been assigned our spaces. And yet there was a certain comfort in being stage-managed like this. I was pretty sure I had got the master bedroom, and this indicated my stock was very high indeed with the Eastons.

Then Mrs. Easton got a very mischievous look on her face and said, "Shall I tell our little anecdote, Whit, or shall you?"

"You tell it. I knew you were dying to when you stopped me a minute ago."

"No, darling, I just thought we ought to finish up where everybody would be. You tell stories much better than I do."

"Nope. You tell it or nobody does." They were playing to us now.

"Please, Mrs. Easton," we cried.

"Go on, darling," said Mr. Easton. "You tell them while I just step into the kitchen and wash the dishes 'in good taste.' " And he tiptoed ostentatiously away, relieved, I think, that his own part of the performance had gone so well.

"Well," began Mrs. Easton, "as you know, we haven't had an easy time finding a house. The ones that were easily available were exactly the ones we didn't want; and the owners of the ones we found suitable simply put their foot down when it came to paying guests. We were getting *extremely* discouraged, and I guess it showed on our faces because Lord Monleigh noticed it when we dined at Belgrave Square last Tuesday. That was how the Hennings' house happened to come up. Mrs. Henning's father and Lord Monleigh keep their horses at the same stable near Hyde Park, and one day, while the two men were waiting for their mounts, they got into conversation. It turns out *Mr.* Henning is in the foreign service and has to go to the Far East for three years. And Mrs. Henning is just sick about going—they had just bought this adorable house in Chelsea and furnished it exactly as they liked, with antiques—but Mr. Henning is a young career officer and has to go where he's told if he's to advance. They're terribly worried about letting their house to the wrong people, which is why Mrs. Henning's father was asking Lord Monleigh if he didn't have some friend who needed a pied-à-terre in London and would take care of all their nice things. Lord Monleigh said he couldn't think of anyone off hand, but he'd keep it in mind. 'I never thought to suggest you two,' he told Whit and me, 'because I knew you were looking for something larger for your charming *family.*' And then Whit told him what Alexander had said the other evening, about telling potential landlords you all were his bastard children. Lord and Lady Monleigh thought that so amusing. And then we four got into a fascinating discussion—honestly, we always have such good talk when we go to them—about what a family is. It's so many things, really. In many cultures, it includes whoever lives in a household, including the servants. The Latin word simply *means* the servants. And Lord Monleigh was telling us that in Holinshed's *Chronicles*—which mentions his own family, by the way—the term 'family' is used when describing the retinue of any nobleman. Really, when you consider all the historical and etymological possibilities, what *we* think of as 'family'—the nuclear or conjugal family—is only a very, very small corner of the pie.

"Anyway, to make a long story short, Whit and I decided to go and look at the Henning house. We telephoned them and said we'd been at Lord Monleigh's and he'd mentioned it to us. They were *very* warm to us, and she was practically in tears when Whit sat down at the little rosewood piano and played a Chopin mazurka. 'Now I know it will be taken care of,' she said. 'I've been having these awful nightmares about little boys smearing jam between the keys and carving their initials in my Duncan Phyfe table.' 'Well,' Whit told her, 'we haven't got a single little boy. On this side of the Atlantic. We have a grandchild, of course. But even he's beyond the jam-smearing stage.' And then *I* said, 'What Mr. Easton and I are looking for is a tasteful, compact house, so that I can care for it myself, but an ample enough house so that we can have various members of our family stay with us when necessary.' 'Of course,' she said, and then we all had a very nice tea in their drawing room, which is a little overcrowded with all her knickknacks, but they can be removed. We discussed terms and Whit and I asked if we could let them know today . . . and we had to plan things, you see, because the budget is going to be *very* tight. Also, we didn't want to seem too eager. Well, anyway"—and she clasped her hands together and smiled, taking us in rather closely to judge our reactions—"late this afternoon, Whit called and said we'd take it. The lease will be drawn up tomorrow by their solicitor and they will leave England on the fifteenth of next month. Mrs. Henning got on the phone to me after the men were finished and you know what she said? She said, 'I have good feelings about this, Mrs. Easton.

I can feel you love our house and that at the end of three years we shall find it even better than we left it.' And I want to tell you something . . ." Here Mrs. Easton screwed up her face in a special way she had, a sort of cousin to her scrunch, to convey she meant business. "She *shall* find it better than she left it. And that is the main thing, isn't it?" She allowed her words to sink in. Then she asked brightly, "Are there any questions?"

"When can we see the house?" asked Carlos.

"Well, you can see the *house* any time you want. It's number twenty-one Old Church Street. I see no harm in any of you walking over to see it. Just please don't go all at once and stand outside and gape like orphans. As soon as we've signed the lease and they've gone down to the country—they're spending their last fortnight with his mother—Whit and I will take you over, one or two at a time, to have a look. It's really *very* charming. I think we are all going to be happy in this house, if we pull together. I think . . . well, they will understand that Lord Monleigh did them a great favor in finding us, when they return at the end of three years."

"Have you told Lord Monleigh, then?" asked Alexander, offering Mrs. Easton a look a complicity.

She did not return it. "As a matter of fact, I'm off to write them a note this very minute. To thank them. I'm sure he'll be so pleased. He finds you all so interesting. And he'll be happy for *us*. After all," she concluded, rising a little stiffly from her floor cushion, "we are his friends. He hardly knows that Mrs. Henning's father from the stables."

And off she went in her narrow Italian walking shoes to the kitchen. "How are you doing, darling?" we heard her ask. We were supposed to hear. Meanwhile, we could imagine the triumphant unspoken relief that charged the kitchen when their eyes communicated. "Fine, fine," came his answer. "I'm off to write a *thank-you letter to the Monleighs*," she said, very audibly. "Oh! Good idea. Good idea," came the reply.

"Anyone for the pub?" asked Alexander. "Daphne?"

"No, thank you. I must go and practice my typing exercise."

"Jean-Louis?"

"Eh . . . *non*. I must make my monthly report to Monsieur Duval." Duval was his boss in Marseilles.

Alexander, Carlos, and I went out into an evening that was, at long last, beginning to feel like spring.

"Well, that was a masterful bloody performance if ever there was one," said Alexander.

"Do you think she *will* write to Lord Monleigh?" asked Carlos.

"Oh yes. It will be a masterful letter. He'll find the whole thing amusing. Lord and Lady Monleigh like to be amused. It's their last resource. And it's just the sort of thing they'd like their rum American friends to do."

"I thought Daphne's reaction was interesting," I said.

"Daphne has no reactions," said Alexander.

"Exactly!" I cried, loving everything about this evening. "But what was she thinking underneath?"

"Possibly what 'the Monleighs' will think: that it's jolly good fun and no skin off her own nose. On the contrary, Daphne's comforts will improve."

"That's not the way to the pub, Alexander," said Carlos.

"Who's going to the pub? I'm going to go and gape like an orphan at our new house. Though I don't suppose my shed will be visible from the street."

Before I lived at 21 Old Church Street, I had a vague mental concept labeled "the ideal room," composed of parts of rooms I had seen, or read about in novels. It should be ample, but not too ample to be cozy; it should be a room with a personality and history of its own, but allow space for *my* personality and history to develop. The window would offer either a view or a stimulating vista. Its prime function would be to provide a fertile site for the growth of an intricate and active imagination.

When the Eastons took me, one quiet Sunday, down the narrow little Chelsea street to show me the house (which I had already seen at night), and Mrs. Easton led me, with some ceremony, up the softly red-carpeted stairs to the top floor and into the master bedroom, I recognized it as an incarnation of my concept. It was not large, though it was the biggest bedroom in the house, corresponding to the dimensions of the drawing room directly below, but its aspect was generous. I had been prepared for the fireplace, but not for the gray-blue velvet-cushioned window seats, or the double bed with its canopy. The wallpaper depicted bygone English rural life: shepherdesses, haymaking, the occasional cavalier in plumed hat galloping by. The creamy white bookcases awaited my books; a small table desk with a leather top, my notebooks; a three-way mirror on a kidney-shaped dressing table, my self-scrutinies and vanities; and the marvelous canopied bed, my dreams and daydreams. I threw my arms around Mrs. Easton. "I'm afraid I'll die before I get to live here!" I said rapturously.

"We thought you'd appreciate it the most," she said, beaming.

Our first days in the new house were idyllic. Mrs. Easton went around smiling constantly; she planted geraniums in the window boxes; she clearly belonged in a house like this. Mr. Easton went about efficiently with his toolbox, repairing window sashes, fixing a back entrance / exit flap for Enrico's trips to and from the garden. We all went out the door in the morning (all except Carlos, who remained in his bright "sewing room" cramming for Cambridge) looking forward to our return journeys from our jobs (or, in Daphne's case, from school), when we would alight from the 19 bus or the 22 on the King's Road and come back through the bright yellow door, knowing we had four good hours of daylight and a good supper ahead of us. Mrs. Easton was extremely pleased with her new kitchen, with its quantities of afternoon and evening light and its accurate oven and American-sized refrigerator with freezer. Her culinary imagination stretched itself, and we never knew what we might be trying for the first time in our lives: I had never had cold trout in aspic; Daphne and Alexander and Jean-Louis had never tasted fried okra and tomatoes; none of us had ever had chilled grape soup—including Mrs. Easton, who scrunched her face afterward and pronounced it a "mistake." In the new house, Mrs. Easton served our plates through a little window between the dining room and the landing outside the kitchen, and she and Mr. Easton took their meals in the kitchen. When Lord and Lady Monleigh dined at Old Church Street (Alexander had been right, they seemed to think the whole thing very amusing) they now sat with us at Mrs. Henning's Duncan Phyfe table, which Mrs. Easton kept polished to such a high gloss that, as several times happened, when one of us spilled a drop of water it simply huddled docilely upon the wax till it could be wiped away with a napkin.

When Alexander had finished decorating his garden shed, he invited us all to have a look, two at a time, as it would only hold three people comfortably, and for the occasion he had a bottle of PX champagne. This event occurred on an evening in early June when Lord and Lady Monleigh were dining for the first time with us in the new house. The Marquess and Marchioness were of course the first to go in, and when they emerged from the little stone hut into the small garden, where we were all gathered, waiting our turn, Lord Monleigh said, "That boy most certainly has an eye!" and even Lady Monleigh was more aroused than usual from her habitual torpor. "Do you know," she told her husband, "it rather reminds me of Lord Salton's Chinese Room ... on a smaller scale, of course. In an odd way, I somehow like it better." She giggled and took out a black cigarette with a gold tip, and Alexander whipped out his lighter and lit it with the expertise of a maître d'.

"But what will you do in winter, my boy?" asked Monleigh.

"Oh, I shall be quite comfortable," replied Alexander. "That wall is almost thirty centimeters thick. I shall plug in my heater in the new electrical outlet I installed and be warm as toast. The hangings provide insulation, too, you know."

"Quite so, quite so. What a pity you can't see our tapestries down in Warwickshire. I think you'd enjoy them."

"I should like very much to see them."

"Well! Well . . . er . . . if you are ever down our way, you must be sure to let us know. If we're not at home, our house-keeper will be glad to show them. And if we are, all the more delightful."

"Thank you, my lord. I shall remember your kind offer."

And Alexander was to do just that. In his own ripe time.

The Eastons had been doing some speedy decorating of their basement headquarters. For, any day, a Spanish secretary from Shell Oil in Madrid would be moving into the ground-floor room they had been using. They had found her through one of their connections, and Shell Oil had obligingly sent a month's rent in advance to hold the room. One evening toward the end of June, we were all invited down to drink a glass of sherry and inspect the Eastons' new bedroom, which they had christened "Le Cave Rouge." They had painted the walls of the Hennings' basement storage room a deep red (possibly to encourage an illusion of heat, because the room never lost its slight dankness) and hung some nice Piranesi etchings and a map of Elba; some of the small pieces of furniture that had crowded the rest of the house had been brought down here; Mr. Easton had installed a thin bamboo curtain over the long slit of a window high in the wall, so that what light there was could come in but passers-by could not look down and see in. Mrs. Easton, who liked to make the best of things, told us how it comforted her, late at night, to lie in bed and hear the footsteps of the two policemen walking down Old Church Street on their night beat. "You can even see their legs and feet silhouetted by the street-lamp." Enrico the cat lay curled on the pillows of the bed, where some of us sat.

"Oh," said Carlos. "Who is reading Proust?"

"I am," said Mrs. Easton. "I can't tell you, I was so thrilled when I saw the Hennings had a complete set in that big book-case in the drawing room. I think they must have picked them up at some auction, because the nameplates inside aren't theirs. In fact, I doubt if they bought most of their books for reading.

Except for their *Debrett's* and *Burke's Peerage*—I'm sure they read *them*. It's so nice for me to be reading Proust again; it's going to be my summer entertainment. My last husband burned my Proust, along with all my other books, when I left him to marry Whit. He telephoned me and said, 'You might as well come and get your'—well, I won't use the adjective he used—'your *books*,' and when I got to our old house, he had dumped my entire library on the front lawn and set fire to it."

"Oh no!" we cried. "How horrible of him!"

"Yes, it was," she said. "He was not usually horrible, but jealousy makes people do vile things. Oh, well"—and she reached over and touched Mr. Easton's arm. He jumped slightly; he had been gazing down at his polished shoe, in a sort of stupor. Was he drinking more since I had begun bringing their booze from the PX, where a quart of gin cost exactly one fifth of what they'd been paying at the off-license? "What, dear?" he asked. "I was just about to say," explained Mrs. Easton with a smile that stopped short of her eyes when she saw how far gone he was, "that in spite of all our setbacks, I've got what I want." "What is that? Oh. Oh!" When it dawned on him that she meant *him*, he covered the hand she had laid on his sleeve with his own hand and patted it as though he meant to protect her from something.

On the very first morning in my ideal room, I was awakened by a sound I had never heard before in my life, a ceremonial clatter in the street below that grew louder until the house rocked. I fought my way out of the canopied bed's luxurious embrace and ran to the window and saw row after row of horsemen trotting their black steeds up the narrow street. The rising sun glinted orange on the silver helmets with their tall, waving plumes. What a sight! The room had certainly lived up to its promise of a vista. It was, I would find out from the Eastons, the Queen's Household Guards: this was their ordinary exercise route, along the Embankment and up Old Church Street. On that first morning, the sight acted as a heraldic stimulus. I dressed and went out and walked by the Thames. So much to be done. And the long English summer day to get it done in. When I returned to the house, Mrs. Easton was just starting our breakfasts and I went up to my room to write down some resolutions. There was a large square of morning sun on the leather desktop. Everything about the room's aspect invited me to sit down at that desk and begin the creative task. If only I did not have to go to the office on Grosvenor Square and deal with Colleen and the British tourists. I wrote my resolutions in a round, upright script and, in doing so, had the imitative sensation of beginning a novel—which had been one of the resolutions. Then I went downstairs and sat in my customary place at the Duncan Phyfe table and Mrs. Easton passed me my poached egg and toast through the little window.

In July I received a cablegram from Arden Speer, a friend from college. It said: ARRIVING LONDON EARLY AUGUST. HOW ABOUT A ROOMMATE? The reply was prepaid. This unexpected missive put me in a quandary. Arden and I had met, our senior year, in an editorial-writing class for journalism majors. When Arden's father had died, he had left her and her mother a small empire of newspapers and radio stations in our home state, and Arden was expected to take them over eventually. She was a strikingly lovely girl, with very white skin, lively green eyes, and thick black hair with red lights in it. She smiled often, and with apparent candor, which I considered fairly heroic, given her awful luck. Two years before, she and her mother had been driving back from an ASNE convention at night when their rear tire blew out. Arden, being that rarity, a Southern belle who knows how to change a tire, got out and began jacking up the wheel while her mother stood holding a flashlight for her. Then a drunken driver had careened out of the darkness, sideswiped the kneeling girl, and dragged her a hundred and fifty yards down the highway. Her right leg was broken in three places and the left one had to be amputated just below the knee. When she came out of the anesthetic and the doctor told her this, she replied, "Well, thank you for saving my life." That was the kind of girl she was. During our last year of college, we had gotten in the habit of having lunch together after our journalism class. We would go slowly down the steps (besides her prosthesis she used a cane, as the right leg, which had not healed straight, was in a brace) to her Ford convertible, which she was permitted to park just outside the building, and we would drive out of town to a hamburger joint we liked, and sit in her car, drinking chocolate malts and eating the hamburgers and talking. She never mentioned her accident, or the fact she was crippled; I had heard the details from her aunt, my old school nurse, who had cared for her after the accident. Our conversations had a quaintly uplifting tone to them: we spoke about our goals; we talked about books we liked, or "writing"; we never gossiped or complained. I always felt on my best behavior with Arden, as if I must live up to her image of me (she had assured me that I had it in me to "do great things").

Which was one of the three reasons for my quandary: it was one thing to have twice-weekly lunches based on shared ideals and mutual respect, but I was not quite sure I could keep up the self I had presented to Arden on an around-the-clock basis.

Reason number two was that Arden knew something about me that I didn't want known here: namely, that I had been married and divorced. I had sent Arden a wedding invitation and she had mailed back a very nice silver serving dish; by the time I got around to thanking her for the dish, I was already separated, but I was too cowardly to tell her. I waited till I was out of the country and then wrote her, saying it had been a terrible mistake, but now, at least, I had embarked on my vocation. From all our talks about Thomas Wolfe and Hemingway and Henry James, she would understand it was necessary for me to go to Europe to begin. But if she came, she would want to see what I'd written, and, though she was very discreet and could be depended on to keep a secret, she would not understand why I was posing as a girl who had never been married; she might think there was something morally murky about this. Why not just be myself, who had made a mistake?

Reason number three made me the most uneasy. In my letters home I had represented myself as the brave young adventuress, living alone as I forged my craft in a strange land. Even my mother, who knew I lived in some kind of boardinghouse, did not know the full extent of the coddling I got at Old Church Street. Why, Mrs. Easton even changed our beds. I was afraid my expatriate image would be diminished when Arden saw our cozy little fellowship. And seeing it through her eyes, I felt I had shortchanged myself for not taking the plunge and living the true solitary life.

It is evidence of how bound up I was with the Eastons that I went right down to Le Cave Rouge within minutes of receiving the cablegram, scarcely having had time to think the thoughts above. And here, my motives did become murky. Mrs. Easton and I had recently had a confrontation and I wanted to get back in her good graces by offering her something. Arden— Arden's tragic story, Arden's old-fashioned manners, and Arden's income—would, I knew, catch the imagination of the Eastons. And Daphne's shorthand/typing course finished in August, when she would be vacating the room next to mine. In spite of my quandary, it would be comforting to have Arden around. Maybe with her in the next room I would be driven, out of pure shame, to produce some pages for her to read.

Mrs. Easton's and my confrontation had been over Mark, the graying barrister whom I had met in their room at Tregunter. I had seen him often since that spring day when he had taken me driving in his new Fiat. Though he was sixteen years older than I, he seemed younger, after I got to know him, mainly because of his vision of himself as a boy who still had to prove and defend himself in the arena of his peers. He had been called "Pudding Face" by his classmates at Haileybury, and he had a wry, charming way of describing his long struggle to overcome the nickname, first in the army and then at Oxford, and his triumph at reaching the pinnacle of English legal dignity, when he put on his barrister's wig for the first time—only to find he looked more pudding-faced in it than ever. Our fondness for each other was based more on camaraderie than on Eros. We drove around London taking turns deprecating ourselves, and reinforced each other's egos afterward in fashionable little restaurants such as 49 Mossup Place. He had just joined a "water-skiing club," where we went on weekends. It was about an hour's drive out of London, situated on a quarry that had been filled with water, and just large enough to accommodate two outboard motorboats going around at the same time. The American in me found this a laughable hole, considering the membership fee, but the members themselves, mostly professional people in their thirties and forties, found it a lark. Down they came, in their little Renaults and Fiats and the occasional Jaguar or Mercedes sports model, and unloaded their picnic hampers groaning with French bread and Genoa salami and ripe Brie and Fortnum's tinned pâté with truffles and the Algerian wine that was popular just then, and sat around the quarry on tartan blankets (unless it was raining, in which case they crowded into a lean-to) and waited their turn on the list for a boat. One rare warm Sunday (the sun was actually shining) a brownish-gray Bentley came bumping down the road, and everybody got funny looks on their faces and sat up straighter or rearranged their picnic items on their blankets, and a sharp-tongued member named Giles said, "Oh bloody hell, here come the Effing-Joneses."

"Who are the Effing-Joneses?" I asked.

"Shh," said Mark. "Giles means the *Joneses*. The f---ing part is because they monopolize the boats."

"Well, why should they? Make them wait their turn like everybody else."

"That's hardly possible, darling," said Mark.

A small, pale man with a limp got out on the driver's side of the Bentley and went around to open the door for a stocky, brown-haired woman wearing a cotton dress and what looked like white nursing shoes. Then the man unloaded a great deal of equipment from the back seat of the Bentley and the two of them went down the path to a little shack where the more modest members changed. The man and the woman were both frowning and looked as though they had been having a fight. Pretty soon they returned, wearing matching rubber suits that covered them to the wrists and ankles. They took turns monopolizing the best boat. He was a crack slalom skier in spite of the fact that one of his legs was shorter and thinner than the other. She kept falling into the water. At one point a carful of photographers arrived. One of them asked Mark and Giles, our two best skiers, to ski on either side of the woman, all three of them holding on to a long wooden pole; in this way she was able to stay up long enough for the photographers in the boat to snap a picture. The photograph, cropped, appeared on the front page of the next day's *Daily Mail*. She was smiling and looked as if she'd been skiing all her life. PRINCESS MEG SKIS, read the caption.

The Eastons loved this story and told it at once to the Monleighs, and to every new guest at Old Church Street.

It was not my going to the water-skiing club with Mark that raised Mrs. Easton's hackles. As I was leaving for work one morning, she called, "Can you come in the kitchen for a minute, Carrie?"

"Sure. What's up?"

"Carrie, when I went to make your bed yesterday morning, it hadn't been slept in."

"Well, no, I hadn't slept in it. I got home just before breakfast."

"But where were you *all night?*"

"I stayed over at Mark's. We got back late from the club."

Mrs. Easton's face began to assemble itself into the lineaments of a most formidable scrunch. "Well, I'm shocked. That's all."

"But why? I often stay over on the weekends."

"But we didn't *know* you did," she said.

My face felt hot. "Look, Mrs. Easton," I said, assuming an offensive defense, "it's nineteen sixty-*two*."

"I know what year it is, I'm the same age as this century. And even if it were nineteen *seventy*-two I'd still be shocked.

And the fact that you left your door open, so Daphne and Carlos could see right in and know the bed hadn't been *touched*."

"Ah," I said, "you're worried about appearances. I should have known." This was the first time I had ever criticized her to her face.

"That's not it," she flared. "I think it's immoral! And Mr. Easton and I will have to ask you not to do it again as long as you live in this house."

"Very well, I'll move out tomorrow," I said, and stormed down the soft-carpeted stairs and out of the house.

When I returned at the end of the day, beaten down by my boring job, having acknowledged my reluctance to give up my cushy room and Mrs. Easton's gourmet suppers, I found *Swann's Way* on my little leather-topped writing table with a note:

> It's just that we love you and feel responsible for you. After all, you're *one of us*. We think you're a lovely girl with lots of potential and we want you to set more stock on yourself. And speaking of potential, I think it's time you got to know Proust. He is, to my mind, *indispensable* to a young writer and he expresses so many of my own thoughts on the civilized life.
>
> Love,
> Lee Easton

The entry in my journal for the next day reads: "Went to PX. Was invited alone to Le Cave Rouge tonight for brandy and good talk. I was damn lucky to find the Eastons." And then there follows an extensive quote from Proust that ends with the phrase "our social personality is created by the thoughts of other people."

When I went rushing downstairs to Le Cave Rouge the afternoon I received Arden's cablegram, I found Mrs. Easton relaxing on the bed with her shoes off; Enrico was asleep on her stomach and *Within a Budding Grove* was propped on his curved back. Mr. Easton sat forward in a wing chair, his army kit of polishes and brushes open on the floor beside him: he was doing all their shoes. Their door was open, but I knocked on the molding.

"Oh, hello, Carrie," said Mrs. Easton testily, looking up at me over the tops of her reading glasses.

"Come in, come in," said Mr. Easton, too heartily. There was that in the faces and voices of both, or so I imagined, that testified to hours of their discussing me with the maledictive energy peculiar to married couples who have learned to deflect their resentments and boredoms away from each other and onto the nearest victim.

"I've just had a cablegram—" I began.

"Oh dear," said Mrs. Easton. "Not bad news, I hope."

"No, actually, it's good." I told them about Arden, emphasizing the points that would arouse their interest most. "Of course, she thinks I just have a flat somewhere and wants to share it with me," I concluded.

"She sounds like a lovely girl. But such a horrible thing to happen to someone so young, on the brink of life. It's fortunate, though, that she has the means to . . . well, make her life as comfortable as possible," said Mrs. Easton.

"Is she able to climb stairs?" asked Mr. Easton. "If not, Lee, why don't we give her the Spanish girl's room? It's on the ground floor, at least."

"No, darling, I think it's more important for her to be on the same floor with a bathroom. And the Spanish girl's room isn't one of the nicer rooms, though I'm sure it will be nice enough for her if she ever gets here. Daphne's room is the ideal choice. That way she can be near a bathroom and"—she relented and smiled at me for the first time—"near her friend."

"Didja ever hear anything like that Spanish girl?" Mr. Easton asked me. "Supposed to be here six weeks ago, but her husband doesn't want her to come, so he keeps getting sick on her."

"No, darling, only three weeks ago," Mrs. Easton characteristically corrected her exaggerating spouse. "But it *is* annoying. I rang up that man at Shell Oil again today and told him we'd have to have a deposit to hold that room any longer. I really can't understand that girl's husband. Doesn't he know what it will mean to their income—the fact that her boss is sending her here to perfect her English so she'll be more valuable to the office in Madrid?"

And I could feel the red cave of a room, always a little damp, warm toward me, as the three of us disparaged the lot of the poor Spanish girl, whose policeman husband was doing everything in his power to keep her from partaking of the debauched English life.

"Isn't that cablegram prepaid-reply?" asked Mr. Easton at last. "Arden's probably sitting down there in Carolina wondering if you want her." (Already she was "Arden.")

"If you're really sure she'd like it here, we could just word the reply right here . . . oops, sorry, Rico. . . ." Mrs. Easton got up to fetch a pencil, and within minutes a glowing description of our domicile stretched the limits of the allotted words.

"Gosh," I said when Mrs. Easton put the pencil down, "*you* should be a writer."

"It's too late to be anything but what I am, Carrie," she replied with a thin smile, "and even that is a full-time job. Whit will take this to the post office for you, he's going out presently. From what you say, I think Arden will fit in very well."

Before I reached the top of the stairs, I heard their voices begin: that muted, conspiratorial buzz which was constantly at work, authoring and ordering and interpreting our household—their creation, the kingdom over which they ruled.

Mark drove me out to Heathrow to meet Arden. It was a chilly, drizzling August night. The plane was late. Mark and I stood outside the barrier and watched the passengers go through customs. At last, Arden swung through a door, followed by a porter who looked quite happy to be carrying her two blue suitcases.

"That's her," I told Mark. She had given up her cane since I last saw her, and the brace had been removed from her leg. She propelled herself independently with a little lurching limp.

"What an attractive girl," said Mark. Arden had spotted me and was waving and smiling. "But I should have thought your American technology could devise a better leg than that one."

"No, no. The crooked one is her own, it didn't heal right. It's the straight, realistic-looking one that's artificial."

The Eastons had been watching for us, and no sooner had Mark's Fiat pulled to the curb than the door to 21 Old Church Street was flung open and, for a moment, the handsome older couple stood framed against the softly lit interior and the red-carpeted stairs. Then Mr. Easton marched out into the drizzle and took charge of Arden's luggage. Mrs. Easton hugged Arden on the threshold of the door. "Welcome to our house," she said feelingly, smiling broadly through her teeth. "We're so glad you're here at last." Then she turned to Mark and said, "It was so good of you to bring them. Won't you come in for a moment? It's very late, but . . ."

Mark the gentleman took the hint. "I'm sure Arden must be very tired. May I come another time?"

The glazed chintz bedspread had been turned back in Arden's room, and there was a little silver pitcher full of late-summer flowers on her dresser. Arden and I sat on the bed talking, after the Eastons had given us tea and biscuits in front of the drawing room fire and then excused themselves for bed.

"What an interesting couple," said Arden. "Very . . . picturesque. The whole thing is picturesque. The way she's furnished the house."

"No, this foreign-service couple owns the house. The Eastons just rented it furnished. In fact, I'm not quite sure the owners realized so many of us were going to live here." I thought I'd better go easy on Arden's high ideals the first night.

"How interesting. I wonder why they've chosen to live

over here. They're obviously well-bred people. He went to Exeter."

"How do you know?"

"He was wearing an Exeter tie. I once had a boyfriend who went to Exeter. He wrote me the fattest letters you ever did see. Now I realize it was probably because he was bored to death. Once he invited me to go up there to a dance. I didn't go, I've forgotten why."

There was a lull in our dialogue. From Alexander's shed below, in the garden, drifted snatches of Charles Aznavour. I wondered if Arden now regretted not going to the dance; I wondered what conclusions she would draw when she saw that Mr. Easton wore that tie almost exclusively. Arden would meet the others tomorrow. Now I gave her amusing, quick sketches of Alexander, Carlos, Jean-Louis, and Daphne (who had left only yesterday, reluctant to go at all because at the last minute she had begun going out with the heir to the biscuit company whose products we'd just been eating downstairs). The Spanish girl had at last arrived, over her husband's angry protests, and was settling into English ways, now that she had some more words and Mrs. Easton had explained to her why it was not agreeable to come to the table wearing rollers in her hair. And I described Lord and Lady Monleigh, and the old Principessa who had lost everything under Mussolini except her Goya. She had been too ill lately to come to us on her genteel scavenges, so now Mrs. Easton took a care package to her on Saturday afternoons.

"You are the smartest thing, Carrie."

"Me? Why?"

"You have an instinct for locating the action. Are you writing about these people?"

"Not yet. I still have quite a backlog before I even *get* to England. Honestly, Arden, it gets me down when I think of all I haven't written about. And there's more piling up every day."

"Well," she said, in her upbeat drawl, "you have to start somewhere."

"I *have* started. Several places. The trouble is, I'll be working on one thing and then it flags and I think of another thing I want to write, and it seems much more interesting. So I start on it, and then it bogs down, and I look at the rough drafts of both things and feel depressed because neither of them amounts to anything yet. Then I think of ten more things I want to write about and I panic and can't put one word in front of the other."

"Hmm," said Arden. She cocked her head to one side, looking at me. Arden always looked at people the whole time they were talking, and often after they'd stopped, as if she could read a kind of subtext in their faces. "Maybe the best thing for you would be to finish something. Maybe you can help *me* out some. I plan to send home a series of five-minute tapes on aspects of England, for Mother to run on our stations. I know the radio audience of Ruffin County isn't exactly what you had in mind, but there is something to be said for having a deadline . . . and *some* audience. I was going to ask you to do this, anyway. You must know all kinds of special things about London, having lived here six months."

"I don't know. When you're living in a place, you always feel there's plenty of time to see it, so you keep putting it off."

"Well," said Arden brightly, "my project will help you get started. We can go out and explore and then come home and write up our impressions and dictate them into my machine."

"So this is to be a working visit for you, then?"

"Oh," said Arden, getting a foxy look on her face, "I have several reasons for coming to England." Then, adroitly, she switched subjects and I found myself telling more than I'd meant to reveal about my short, ill-fated marriage. I stopped short of the sexual details, however, because there was something about Arden that discouraged prurience, just as there was something about Arden that discouraged too much complaining. She said, "Of course, I understand," when I told her I'd just as soon people here didn't know I was divorced, and the ease of her reply relieved me greatly.

/ / /

Arden "fitted right in" at 21 Old Church Street, as Mrs. Easton remarked about twenty times a day. Arden delighted in the household, and the household delighted in Arden. Her enthusiasm stepped up the tempo of life, especially during the first few weeks. On Arden's first "official" evening, the day after she arrived, Mrs. Easton outdid herself with a steak-and-kidney pie, Mr. Easton did his number at the piano about the lovely Rhinebeck lady with the tail, Alexander and Carlos staged one of their conversational tussles, and even I was pressed into service. ("Carrie," said Mr. Easton, "tell Arden about those friends of yours, the Effing-Joneses, you met down at the ski club.") Three nights after Arden's arrival, my journal notes, we played charades in the drawing room. Mrs. Easton, wearing a paper wig, was Justice Walk, the quaint alleyway across the street. Arden took Isabel, otherwise known as "the Spanish girl," to Madame Tussaud's with her in a taxi, and Isabel, enslaved by this kindness (it was the first time anybody had actually invited her out), began crocheting Arden a shawl. "Alexander, have you seen that new play, *The Premise?*" Arden asked one Saturday lunchtime. "Can't afford the theater on my pittance, I'm afraid," said Alexander. "Well, will you be my guest tonight?" said Arden. "I reckon I'm old-fashioned, but I like to have an escort, and also it's fun to have someone to discuss it with afterward." "I'd be honored," said Alexander. "Is this jersey all right, or shall I wear a tie?" "A tie, I think," said Arden.

When the Marquess and Marchioness of Monleigh came to dine with us, Arden amused them extremely by interviewing them on her little battery-powered tape machine ("Could you tell our listeners in Ruffin County something about your novels, Lady Monleigh? . . . Lord Monleigh, I wonder if you would explain to us exactly what a marquess *is*") and showing them the little red celluloid discs, on which their words were recorded, which would fit flat into an ordinary envelope and be mailed home to Mother the following day.

"What a game gel," exclaimed Lord Monleigh, when Arden had clumped back upstairs to put away her machine.

"Yes, we think she is just . . . well"—Mrs. Easton screwed up her face in the intensity of searching for the right superlative—"first-*rate*. She uses every minute of her day in a way you seldom see among young people. And her energy! When you consider it's twice the effort for *her* to get from one room to another . . ."

"Quite," said Lady Monleigh, sinking back languidly onto the sofa pillows and lighting up one of her gold-tipped, black, Russian cigarettes.

I excused myself and went upstairs to do some writing. Mrs. Easton's remark about using every minute of one's day had not fallen on deaf ears. Whether I imagined it or not, I was beginning to detect a coldness in their attitude toward me that seemed to increase in direct proportion to their growing warmth toward Arden. It was as though they could not have two favorite American girls at once and had chosen Arden as the superior version. And, though I had stopped staying over at Mark's (our affair, never at white heat, had begun to cool), Arden reported to me that Mr. Easton had told her, "Carrie's a great girl, but she doesn't come home at night." I explained to Arden that Mr. Easton had a bad habit of exaggerating things, and she seemed to accept the explanation. But things turned really sinister a few days later. Coming out of my room one afternoon, I heard the Eastons chatting with Arden in the kitchen below. "Say, listen, Arden," Mr. Easton was saying, "don't carry around too much cash. Carrie had a hundred and fifty pounds stolen her first day in England." "No, darling, actually it was only a hundred and fifty dollars," came Mrs. Easton's habitual correction of her husband's exaggeration.

I tiptoed back into my room, closed the door softly, and lay down on the canopied bed, where I spent more and more of my free time now. So. The evidence was in. The Eastons had stolen my money, Mrs. Easton luring me into the kitchen at Tregunter to look at the salmon while Mr. Easton rifled the envelope from which he had seen me extract bills. Mrs. Easton was right: the actual sum had been fifty pounds, or somewhere between a hundred and forty and a hundred and fifty dollars in those days. I felt queasy at the thought of those two coolly robbing me, but I felt even queasier that, all along, the two of them had known I had lied when I told them it was a hundred and fifty pounds.

"The Eastons are very charming," Arden said, when we were curled up on my bed one evening, working up a tape on Chelsea Old Church, at the foot of our street, where, Arden had found out, Henry James's funeral service had been held, "even though he drinks a little too much."

"Oh yes, they can be very charming, but all the same . . ." And I heard myself go into a tirade that carried a sense of déjà vu. How the Eastons were snobs and played favorites and blew hot and cold. How they wooed you as long as you did things their way, but how they sat down there in Le Cave Rouge and plotted and gossiped about you. I told Arden my theory about the stolen money and about how the Eastons had misrepresented themselves to get this house. Though Arden kept nodding and letting me go on, her face froze into a polite little mask. I could see that she did not want to believe anything too bad about the Eastons. Well, neither had I, that time in the pub when Nigel Farthingale was heaping accusations on them. I hadn't cared, as long as I could bask in the security of their establishment and be entertained by their strange and interesting ways. But somehow I thought Arden was being overly defensive about them; I could see it written on her face: a sort of horror that I might say more than she wanted to hear. Why?

"And I think they've done something awful because she can't go back to the States to see her daughter's little boy," I went on, unable to stop.

"Did she say she couldn't go back?"

"She's said lots of times she would *adore* to go back, only it just isn't possible. And she gets this meaningful look on her face, as if she'd like to say more but can't. And you know yourself how she whips out those photos of little Steve whenever she gets an opportunity."

"I got the impression," said Arden, after a moment's silence, "that they just don't have the money. Which would also account for their having to take in boarders, even though they represented themselves as a couple alone to the owners. There's no question in my mind that they've come down a long way from where they started ... but ... Carrie! Stealing your money! That's a serious allegation. Are you really sure?"

"Look. I left my purse beside him when she called me into the kitchen. He had only to reach in and take that wad of pounds. I even made it easier for him, because I had fastened them together with a rubber band. Of course, they tried to blame it on this out-of-work actor who got scared by the whole thing and sneaked away the same day without paying his rent."

I could see Arden doubted my theory. But I couldn't give her the real piece of evidence because it would have meant telling her about my lie and that would have undermined her belief in everything I told her after that.

So, when she frowned and said, "I guess I'm just not able to believe that about the Eastons," I said, "Oh, what does it matter now," and in a few minutes Arden's bright, upbeat voice was reading into the tape machine what we had written about the many devastations and rebuildings of Chelsea Old Church for the subsequent enlightenment of the listeners of Ruffin County.

Things got worse between me and the Eastons. Grudges compounded. One week I just did not feel like taking the long trek out to the PX in order to buy Alexander's cigarettes and Mr. Easton's gin. "Hey, Carrie," said Mr. Easton the next day, "haven't you forgotten something?" I told him I was sorry but there had been too much work at my office for me to go to the PX. "No, no," he said, a one-upping glint in his watery eyes, "I meant your rent." He'd got me. For the first time since I'd been with them, I was late with my weekly check. "More coffee, Carrie?" said Mrs. Easton one morning, screwing up her face at me as she offered the pot through the little window between the dining room and the kitchen landing. Her smile had always been through clenched teeth—on the day we met she had smiled at me like that—but now I saw it as a malevolent grimace, beamed at me.

One night, about nine, she came up to my room. The house was very quiet. Arden, Alexander, and Isabel had gone to a movie (*Viridiana*) in a taxi; Carlos was spending the evening with his mother, who had arrived in London to console him (he had not gotten into Cambridge) and was staying at the Connaught; Jean-Louis had gone back to France for a periodic report to his boss. I know all this because I had written it in my journal. "Is it my fault that tonight I feel there is absolutely no one in the world who gives a damn about me?" I had just written, in fact, when Mrs. Easton tapped softly on my door.

"Hello, Carrie. Oh, I'm disturbing you."

"No, you're not. I was just feeling sorry for myself in my journal." (Now why had I said that?)

"But you have no cause to feel sorry for yourself," she drawled. "May I?" And she dipped her graying blond head down and crawled under the canopy into bed with me. "Oh my! No wonder you spend so much time in here. It's like . . . a womb. Oh my! Don't let me fall asleep here. I might never wake up." She laid her head back on the spare pillow and smoothed her old tweed skirt over her trim legs. With her eyes closed and that smile on her face, she looked like the Cheshire Cat. "No, Carrie," she said with her eyes closed, "*you* haven't any cause to feel sorry for yourself. As I was saying to Whit only the other night, you are a very fortunate girl. You have a fabulous job, you have a nice man to take you out, and you're young and attractive. Whit thinks you're very attractive. He said you have such an infectious laugh and that you carry yourself well."

"Did he say that?" I wondered what else they had said, down there in Le Cave Rouge.

"He certainly did. Whit thinks the world of you. As I do. Why, you're practically like a daughter."

"How is your daughter, by the way?"

"Thank you, Penny is fine. I just had a letter." She sat up

and hugged her knees. I had a sudden image of us as two girls in boarding school, having a heart-to-heart on the bed. "It's hard to believe, but Penny just celebrated her fortieth birthday."

"Don't you wish you could have been there!" I said, hoping to bait her.

"Well, of course I wish it, Carrie, but there's no point brooding about the impossible." She peered approvingly over the tips of her knees at her handsome new Belgian shoes. She had ordered them from an ad in *The New Yorker*, to which her daughter had given her a five-year subscription. The Eastons devoured their *New Yorker*s. "Well, we're still okay," Mr. Easton would say, after looking at the cartoons every week. He said that if a day came when they couldn't understand any of the jokes in *The New Yorker*, they would know they had become hopeless expatriates. The whole household had been consulted about those shoes; the ad had been passed around at after-dinner coffee in the drawing room. "Seventy-five dollars, isn't that awful?" cried Mrs. Easton. "But of course they're handmade, they'll last for years." She stuck out one of her slim, long feet for us to examine. "*These* are almost ten years old. They were the first pair of shoes I bought when we got to Elba." "Buy them, buy them," encouraged Mr. Easton. "Can't skimp on shoes. My mother always used to say, 'You can tell a lady by her shoes.'" "Come on, Mrs. Easton, have them," said Alexander, in a rare moment of tenderness. "We'll all be jolly glad to eat tripe and onions for an entire month if you'll have those shoes." "Well . . . I'll have to think about it," she said. But she had ordered them. And we hadn't had tripe and onions once.

Now, looking at their sleek brown surfaces, I wondered if my stolen pounds had helped pay for them. "But why do you say it's impossible?" I went on mercilessly. "Why should it be impossible for you to go back home, once in a while, to see your daughter? And your grandson."

"Oh, Carrie . . ." And Mrs. Easton heaved such a tragic sigh that I felt ashamed of myself. "It's all so complicated."

"Complicated how?" At that moment, I felt sure I was going to find out their "secret." The atmosphere of the quiet house, the schoolgirlish coziness under my canopy, encouraged intimacy. But then (did she sense some untrustworthiness in me, some impurity of motive?) the moment passed, and she said, "Money complications. Money, or the lack of it, always makes things extremely complicated."

"But," I persisted, a bit callously (to have been so close!), "couldn't she send you the fare? I mean, you've often said how well her husband is doing in his law practice. . . ."

But she had shut down on me. "No, Carrie, life is for the young. They need their money for their own life. I've had mine, and it's been a full one. In a way, I feel sorry for the young people growing up now. I truly believe the generation to which Whit and I belong had the best years of our country. So much energy . . . and high ideals . . . and a lovely formality to things . . . and *romance*. No, I have nothing to complain about. I grew up having the best, and I had it most of my life, and now I've got my memories and . . . I've got the man I love."

"That's the most important thing," I said, picturing Mr. Easton's red face and the way he *wove*, rather than walked, into the room each evening for after-dinner coffee.

"I agree. Which reminds me, I've had a letter from Daphne. Her biscuit suitor is being *very* attentive. He writes her every day and sends flowers several times a week. Things look extremely promising."

"That's nice." I had nothing against Daphne, but I could not get too excited about her impending romantic fortunes. I frankly couldn't imagine her being passionately in love, even for the sake of all those biscuits.

"*We* think so. The thing is, Daphne would like to come back to us. In fact, she'd like to come as soon as possible. Of course, Arden has taken her old room and is likely to be in it for . . . an indefinite time . . . and the Spanish girl is due to stay through November. But I thought, when Carlos goes, Daphne might not mind his room. It's very light and cheery, even though it's rather tiny. But"—she laughed—"if things progress as they seem to be doing, Daphne won't be *in* this house for very long."

"Well, here's wishing her luck," I said, "but I thought Carlos was keeping his room till he got back from Paris. Isn't his mother taking him to Paris?"

"That's right. Carlos will need his room for his things, for six more weeks. Señora Paredes y Broncas plans to have some clothes made, and you know fittings take a while. And frankly, Carrie, here is where you can help us out, if you will."

"Help out? Me?"

"Yes, dear. Whit and I were wondering if you would be willing to share your room with Daphne. It would only be till Carlos vacates his room. And it would mean everything to Daphne. You see, she feels she has a *base* here. And . . . well . . . it's so important for a girl when she's trying . . . when the man is at the peak of his interest but hasn't declared himself yet . . . it's important for her to have the proper backdrop. Of course, the ideal backdrop at such a time is a loving family—so the man sees that she is cherished and then he doesn't try to take advantage—but Daphne's family is way up there, practically in Scotland. And so, Carrie"—she laid her left hand with the diamond-and-emerald ring persuasively on top of my hands, which were folded on top of my closed journal—"*we'll* be her family . . . till he's in the bag!"

This last caused me to snort with laughter, despite the fact that I was stunned by her proposal: *share my room?* Had I come all the way across the ocean to crawl into bed every night with an English girl? "Listen, Mrs. Easton," I said, trying to let her down without evoking the terrible scrunch, "I'd love to help, but I really need the privacy for my writing."

"We know how you feel about your writing," she said, her face compressing into the first signs of the dreaded look, "but I honestly don't see how Daphne will cramp your style. I mean, she'll be home in the daytime, while you're at work, and she'll be going out most evenings with her young man."

"What about weekends? I usually like to do something up here when I'm home on weekends."

"Well, I'm sure we can work out some sort of schedule. I hadn't noticed you were home *that much* on weekends, myself."

There was an awful stretch of silence. Both of us lay side by side on the bed looking straight ahead. My face felt numb. What I wanted most in the world was for her to go. I heard myself saying, "I know I don't please you, Mrs. Easton. I wish I could."

"Well, of course you please me, Carrie. And you'd please me more if you felt happier about yourself. You've got so much going for you, if you'd have a little courage. You have to believe in yourself. Jane Austen believed in *her*self. And she wrote her books on the dining-room table, between all her social and domestic obligations. You know, I've always believed it does people good to have limits. Limits on their time, limits on their space. It forces them to make something of themselves."

"You think so?" I was just stalling for time now. I knew she had won. At least I could give the appearance of grace in defeat.

"I really do, Carrie."

Within a few minutes, we had embraced, and she had gone over to the window and looked out, asking, "Do the guardsmen still thrill you when they come by in the morning? They do me—even though I only see their horses' hooves." And then she noticed that the velvet window-seat covers were a bit spotty, and unzipped them from the pillows and took them away with her.

I opened my journal and continued writing: "I have promised to share my room with Daphne for six weeks. Maybe it will work out. She'll get a husband and I will be *forced* into making better use of my time and finishing something."

I heard the front door slam. I went to the window and peered covertly from behind the curtain. Arm in arm, the Eastons were heading down Justice Walk to their favorite pub, where they went on select occasions when they had something to celebrate.

"She conned you!" cried the girl from California, when I told my colleagues at work the next day.

"But won't you mind sleeping in the same bed?" asked

the happily married Betty Ann, who had signed her letters "love."

"But at least," put in Colleen, who was hovering over our desks, preparing to distribute the morning letters among us, "you'll be able to *save* a little. She probably gave you a reduction, since you'll be sharing."

"She didn't actually say anything about a reduction." Just like Colleen, to put her finger unerringly on where I had been stupid.

"Then insist on one," said the girl from California. "Do it first thing, when you get back tonight. Boy, do those two know how to work their tenants. I'll bet the Mexican boy is paying full price just to keep his things in his room. They'll be *making* money on this deal."

On returning to Old Church Street, I went straight to Mrs. Easton, who was peeling potatoes in the kitchen. She greeted me with unusual warmth. To keep myself from weakening, I went gracelessly to the point. "Everything was decided so quickly last night," I said, "that I didn't get a chance to ask what kind of reduction you and Mr. Easton will give me for those six weeks when I'll be sharing my room. I mean," I went on more aggressively, "you all will be making money on this thing, specially with Carlos not even eating here for most of the time."

"Making money we will not be, Carrie. If you knew all the little expenses: that stopped-up toilet last week cost us almost ten pounds because it was on a weekend and the plumber had to come from Croydon."

"Well, that's not my fault. You told me yourself the Spanish girl was the one who flushed the sanitary napkin."

"It's not a question of whose *fault*, Carrie. This is a household. We all work together to make life as pleasant as possible. And there are other expenses that . . . well . . . Mr. Easton and I haven't liked to harp on. I mean"—and she narrowed her eyes—"we're Americans and we understand that Americans like more heat; but, between you and Arden, those upstairs heaters are going constantly on the weekend and, as Arden is home all day as well, our electric bill is becoming astronomical."

"I still think I should get some kind of discount," I said. "I didn't stop up the toilet and I don't stay home all day and run up your heating bill. And I *am* going to be inconvenienced by having to share my room."

"Very well," she said coldly. "I'll speak to Mr. Easton and we'll let you know what we can do."

They agreed to a two-pound weekly reduction, to begin the following Thursday, when Daphne would be arriving. But it was a Pyrrhic victory. In the next few days, their disapproval of me became positively hostile. They froze me out during after-dinner coffee conversations. Mrs. Easton asked me whether I would mind using a pencil when I wrote in bed, as it was hard on her hands to have to scrub the ink out of my sheets before sending them to the laundry. Every time I came out of my bedroom, it seemed they were discussing me sotto voce in the kitchen below, just loud enough for me to hear. (I was probably meant to hear.)

"I can't get over it. I mean, it's just so terribly petty when she makes thirty pounds a week." (Mrs. Easton.)

"Some people are like that. Can't bear to part with a nickel if they can avoid it." (Mr. Easton.)

One night, late, I went down to the dark kitchen to get some ice water. As luck would have it, I left the freezer door open while I emptied the cubes out of the ice tray and Mr. Easton chose that moment to materialize in his striped flannel pajamas. "Keep this thing shut, will you?" he slurred, slamming the door. From the fumes that emanated out of him, I judged he must be more gin than human and I decided to say nothing, get my ice, and leave the kitchen. I concentrated on transferring the cubes into the glass. I filled the glass with water. I refilled the ice tray. I stiffened my shoulders and got past him and replaced the tray in the freezer. "Whassa matter, cat got your tongue?" His breath came suddenly close to my ear. His hand gripped my buttock, quite intentionally, through my nightgown, gripped it so hard that the next morning when I examined myself over my shoulder in the triple mirror there were bruise marks where his fingers had been.

"You have no choice!" cried the girls at the Travel Service.

"It's time you got out of that hostel setup anyway," said the girl from California, who had spoken with an air of detached superiority ever since she had announced she would be leaving us after Christmas—first to go skiing in Zermatt, then to go home and get married.

Colleen suggested we telephone the man at Embassy housing and see what he had on the books. "I agree with the others," she said gravely, "it's time you weaned yourself from the Eastons."

By lunchtime, I was being shown through a series of ground-floor rooms in a gaunt brick row house on Green Street, a three-minute walk from the Embassy. The only trouble was, the Travel Service had recently moved to its own new office (opened with a gala party, Alistair Cooke and the Duke of Bedford in attendance) in Piccadilly. But I would still be able to walk to work from here.

"This is the situation," said the man from Embassy housing. "The old girl who owns this house wants to sell it, but she can't till next May because the two fags who live upstairs have a watertight lease till then. So she figures she may as well get what she can from these downstairs rooms."

"They certainly are partitioned off in a weird way," I said.

"Yes, well, you've got to remember this was built as a one-family dwelling. It was a nice house in its day. James Mason, the actor, owns the one like it, to the right; he's kept his in one piece."

"It's a little *dark*. . . ."

"England is dark. If you don't want it, I have a new gal with HEW who'll probably take it. . . ."

"I'll take it," I said, feeling that my honor was at stake.

/ / /

"Can we talk later?" I murmured to Arden, who sat next to me on the glazed chintz couch in the drawing room. Mrs. Easton, in her customary chair, poured after-dinner coffee into demitasse cups, adding a spoonful of sugar crystals shaped like small colored rocks for most of us. She handed me my cup with her pained smile.

"Of course we can," said Arden, "only it had better be now, because I've promised to give Isabel an English lesson this evening."

As we went upstairs, I realized the mood was wrong for what I was going to propose. Arden was happy in this house, she was becoming entrenched in its communal rituals. I had even heard the small sigh that escaped her as she put down her demitasse cup and limped ahead of me from the lamplit, people-filled room. Everyone was discussing the railway strike slated for the following day, and Alexander was trying to persuade Jean-Louis to go halves with him in renting a car so they could drive around London picking up pretty girls.

"Well," said Arden brightly, closing the door of her room rather slowly against their laughter. "What's up?"

"I've rented an apartment—a whole floor, in Mayfair—and I was wondering if you might like to share it. We could each have a bedroom, and then there's this august drawing room in the front of the house, the old lady's even left some Victorian chairs and a sofa and what they call a tallboy—"

"Carrie, I have something to tell you," she interrupted. "Of course, I was going to tell you in a few days when all the arrangements were definite. . . . We've never talked about my accident, have we?"

And she proceeded to relate a terse, objective version, almost like a combined police-and-medical report, of the story I had heard, in more human and dramatic detail, from her aunt. Her voice was the same spritely, interested voice she used when recording her "Aspects of England" reports for the listeners of

Ruffin County. It was as if the violence, although regrettable, had happened to someone else. There was, of course, no mention of the brave reply to the doctor's news.

"But as you can see, the right leg hasn't healed as it should, and after a great deal of reading up on the matter, I decided to consult the man who is considered the best in the field, Sir Rupert Wentworth-Stokes. Last week we went over the X rays and he says there's a pretty good chance of a successful operation. He'll take part of my hipbone and reshape the tibia. But we won't know for certain for two months. Half of that time, I have to stay in bed. I haven't even told Mother, and I'm not going to until I know the results. I've told the Eastons, of course, because they will have to care for me, and she has been just splendid about it. I know they have their faults, Carrie, and I'm aware that you all are on the outs. I really think you're wise to leave, things being as they are."

"What have they said to you?"

"I don't think anything can be gained by going into that," she said rather primly. Then, with more warmth, she appealed to me to keep my fingers crossed and pray for her, "and please come visit me in the hospital."

"I guess I'd better. They won't let me visit you here, once I leave."

"Oh, Carrie, they don't hate you *that* much!" she exclaimed. Then hastily revised her tactlessness: "A cooling-off period will put things in perspective on both sides."

On my first night in Green Street I imagined them discussing me over coffee in the Chelsea drawing room.

"I wonder how Carrie's getting on in her new flat." (Alexander—more to "set things up" than out of any genuine concern.)

"I'll bet she's going to miss your cooking, Mrs. Easton." (Carlos.)

"Of course we were sorry to see her go, but it's what she wanted." (Mrs. Easton.)

"The real reason was, though we don't want to shock any of you guys, Carrie felt her nightlife was too constricted here." (Mr. Easton.)

"I'm not quite sure what you mean, Mr. Easton." (Arden, who could be depended upon to be loyal.)

"Oh, nothing. Nothing." (Mr. Easton, with ominous significance.) "We were hurt, of course. She's been with us two years and then bang! Less than a week's notice."

"Six months, darling." (Mrs. Easton.) "Though in some ways it did seem like two years." (Exchanging a wry look with Alexander.)

"It cannot be cheap, having a flat in Mayfair." (Jean-Louis.)

"Oh, Carrie's got more money than she knows what to do with." (Mr. Easton.)

"Really?" (Arden, who knew better, tightrope-walking between defending her friend and placating one of the two people in England who had agreed to take care of her when she was flat on her back.)

"Personally, I'll be so glad to see Daphne again!" (Mrs. Easton.)

"Hey, Isabel. Now that your English is better, how would you like to hear a strange story? Ever heard of a place called Rhinebeck, New York?"

And Mr. Easton, breathing a little heavily from gin, would sit down at the Hennings' elegant rosewood piano and ripple his large fingers over the keys. He had a surprisingly light and accurate touch. Anyone happening to be walking along Old Church Street in the autumn dusk would look up at the lighted window, the geraniums glowing in the window boxes, and hear the opening bars of the "Moonlight Sonata," or, subsequently, the shouts of laughter, and think to himself, or herself: Ah, the family! Nothing can ever replace it!

I thought about the Chelsea house a lot, my first few weeks on Green Street. If Old Church Street had embodied domestic coziness to the point of stultifying my young soul, then Green Street certainly embodied its opposite. The Central Line ran directly beneath my bed. As I figured it—and I had plenty of long evenings to lie there and figure it—my flat was exactly the midpoint between Marble Arch and Bond Street, because, beneath me, the trains seemed to achieve their highest speed. Above me, every evening without fail, the two men upstairs took a long bath together, overflowing the drain. In the daytime, I would look down at what had once been a little courtyard but was now a swamp filled with stagnant green muck from the improper drainage. The men laughed as they bathed, and, from the cadence of their alternating voices, seemed to be telling each other about their day. And then there was the odd arrangement of the flat itself. The front room I never used, because it was on the other side of the partition and just inside the entrance to the house. Behind the partition, which is where my life began, was a hallway with first a tiny kitchen and then a tiny bathroom to the right. Edwards, the man who came to wash the windows, told me that the kitchen and bathroom had been added when the old lady had decided to turn the house into flats. My narrow little bedroom at the rear of the house, which I liked best of the rooms because of all its built-in wardrobes and cupboards and shelves, had been, he said, the butler's pantry. And the larger room next to it (which I kept locked at night, because it led—via a dark, winding passageway—to the basement, which couldn't be locked) had been the butler's bed-sitting room. Edwards told me that the little courtyard filled with stagnant drainwater had formerly been a beautiful garden where the family sat on Sundays.

Arden had to wait till mid-November for her operation, Sir Rupert's schedule was so full; she progressed so well that she was able to come to my Christmas party, which I held in the butler's bed-sitting room. She arrived looking radiant, in a long, high-necked white dress and the new shawl Isabel had crocheted for her. Her hair was piled, Gibson Girl–style, on her head, and five healthy pink toes stuck out from the cast on her right leg. In Arden's retinue were Alexander, Isabel, Jean-Louis, and the

Easton's newest boarder, a rather frail-looking young man with a large hawk nose and red cheeks, whom Arden introduced simply as "Peter, who has taken Carlos's room." Peter stuck close to Arden, anticipating her desires for a fresh drink or another sandwich. "He was awfully helpful last month," Arden told me, during one of Peter's brief absences, "he spelled the Eastons in taking care of me. He's cramming for Oxford and has been reading to me about the Hapsburgs, whom I find fascinating." When anyone asked Arden how she'd broken her leg, Peter would answer, "Had a bit of a fall on her skis," and, as soon as the person turned away, he and Arden would nudge each other and giggle.

"Well, how are things going with Daphne and her cookie heir?" I asked Alexander, who looked sleek and prosperous in his new dinner clothes. He seemed to have filled out a bit, too. Encouraged by Arden, he had a lucrative evening sideline: he had signed up with an escort service.

"Oh, Daphne's still very keen. The trouble is, *he* doesn't seem quite keen enough. The Eastons think he's starting to bolt."

"Too bad. And how are the Eastons, not that I care."

"Cunning as always. They shall ask me all about your flat, not that they care. What would you take for that horrid bamboo firescreen?"

"If it's horrid, why do you ask?"

"I know a horrid rich chap who might fancy it."

"Well, I'm sorry, but it belongs to the old lady who owns this house. All the furniture does."

"Pity. We could divide the spoils. She'd never miss half of it."

"Alexander, you're getting worse."

"That's where you're wrong. I'm getting better. One of these days I shall have perfected myself."

"For what?"

"For what I'm for." He laughed and offered me a cigarette from his case. "Still don't smoke? Good girl. I must say, I miss your PX cigarettes awfully."

"How old is that Peter, who seems to adore Arden?"

"Nineteen. The Eastons are worried."

"Why? Nineteen's old enough to take care of yourself."

"Mmm. Depends on one's circumstances, I suppose."

"Isabel's English has certainly improved," I said. (She stood not far from us, surrounded by a little circle of men. "I like the way Anglo-Saxon meng stay free like boys," she was saying. "In es-Spain, the mang, he come out from his mother and go under his wife.") "So, what *are* Peter's circumstances, then?"

"Well, Peter was entrusted to the Eastons, you might say, by their perennially useful friends, Lord and Lady Monleigh. Lady Monleigh was at school with Peter's mother. Also"—Alexander paused, relishing his role as informant—"Peter's father died last year. Which makes Peter the sixteenth Duke of Harleigh."

"Well, good for him. But the Eastons needn't worry. Arden's much too old for him, he's just good company while her leg's healing. She more or less told me so herself."

"Did she? I shall pass it on to the Eastons. It will make things less uncomfortable for Arden."

"You mean they're making her uncomfortable?"

"Cooling off, you might say."

"Those two! They'd turn on God Himself if He lived with them three months."

"They would ... unless He knew how to handle them."

"And you do?"

"Oh"—he sucked thoughtfully on his cigarette, affecting a sort of James Bond insouciance—"we rub along."

It was London's coldest winter in eighty-two years. Thirty-two people died in a fog. Out of sheer lassitude I made an omelet almost every night in my tiny kitchen. The girl from California had resigned and was skiing in Switzerland before going home to plan her wedding. The happily married Betty Ann and I sat side by side behind our counter in the new office. Behind us was a giant wooden sculpture, in orange, of the United States. The wind shrieked around the corners of the plate-glass windows of our reception room, which we called "the Fishbowl" because anybody walking along Sackville or Vigo Street could look in on us as we sat there. Anybody could *come* in—that's why we were there—and a motley assortment did, though not always to ask questions about travel in the United States of America. We had our favorites. There was the policeman we saved stamps for, who would stop by to get them and always tell us one or two stories about his profession. He gave us advice for handling lunatics: "Act interested in a disinterested way. Agree with them while walking them to the door." Then there was the nice old goldsmith who quoted Greek and Roman poets in the original and took me to see the swearing-in of the new Lord Mayor. The servants' chef at Buckingham Palace dropped in on us whenever he came from his tailor. It was he who gave me the omelet recipe: "You want to leave the middle just a wee bit runny before you fold it over." He promised—and later kept his promise—to get us inside the palace gate for the Trooping of the Colour and show us the servants' apartments afterward. Then I had befriended a hobo who had been raised in London but had traveled by boxcar to more places in the United States than I had. He brought me gifts—a plump grapefruit from Soho, an excellent penknife that I still carry—and I would type the latest pages of his memoirs while he walked up and down outside so that Mr. Miles would not worry that we had a loiterer in the reception room. The hobo wrote, he explained in a confidential voice that never rose above a hoarse whisper, standing up in the Central Post Office every night; he used the backs of telegraph forms and a pencil chained to the wall.

Colleen was out with her back a lot. It had not been a good winter for her, she was turning into an old woman overnight, she lamented to us. Her hair was going gray and two of her teeth had died.

When we had no customers, and if I had caught up with the hobo's memoirs for the day, I might get out my own manuscript and work on it. The hobo had been an inspiration as well as a reproach. I figured if he could stand up every night in the post office and write, I ought to be able to produce something sitting down in a Mies van der Rohe chair in front of a new IBM. Mr. Miles was very obliging about what we did with our spare time, as long as we answered all the letters first and stopped doing whatever we were doing when a live customer came in. I was writing about my marriage. If it came out the way I wanted, the novel would be a sort of American *Madame Bovary*. Betty Ann was reading a magazine article, one gloomy afternoon, that proved that if a divorced woman had not remarried within four years, her chances decreased sharply. I thought of poor Colleen. I thought of myself. Betty Ann confided to me that she was pregnant and her husband wanted her to quit so they could have a holiday in Greece before she was too far along.

After work I would walk home to Green Street, crack some eggs, and eat my omelet while reading and listening to the BBC. Then I would wash the dish and the fork and the pan and retreat for the night with my book and transistor to the butler's pantry, where I would feel the fast trains rumble under me and hear the men upstairs talking and splashing. I would read and write in my journal until the Home Service played "God Save the Queen" and went off the air, and sometimes after that.

Arden's cast came off and she was the possessor of a lovely straight leg. She took me to dinner to celebrate and told me she was going to splurge and order a new prosthesis as well: there was a place in New York that fashioned them so you could wear high heels. "Mother is urging me to come home, but I thought I'd stay and see the English spring," she said. Peter had promised to drive her to Oxford. "Peter has been just wonderful. Despite the difference in our ages, he's one of the most rewarding friends I've ever had. I never get tired of talking to him and it's nice just being in the same room with him." She told me how Peter could sit in a straight chair, with plugs in his ears, and read for a solid hour without once looking up. "He'll often sit in my room and read for an entire afternoon."

"And how are the Eastons taking it?"

"Taking what, Carrie?" She looked annoyed.

"I mean, his being in your room so much. Mrs. Easton can be funny about how things look."

"Well, she's welcome to come in at any time. There'll be nothing to look at. You were right about the Eastons, they do blow hot and cold on you. It's smile one minute and whisper the next, and you wonder what you've done. But *my* conscience is clear, and they'll just have to put up with me till I get ready to leave. I'm not going to let them spoil my last months in England."

"If you ever need my butler's sitting room, you're welcome to it. That awful sofa pulls out into a bed."

"Thank you, but I don't think I'll be needing it." She tilted her chin defiantly and, for some reason, blushed. "They may think what they like, but they wouldn't *dare* say it to my face. Oh no, they're too resourceful for that." She gave an uncharacteristically cynical little laugh. "*Much* too resourceful!"

The following Saturday, about four-thirty in the afternoon, my doorbell shrilled. I peeked out cautiously, keeping the chain latched, in case it was one of the local panhandlers, a seven-foot grizzled Negro, who announced himself as Yahweh. (I always gave him a half crown, but never allowed him inside the front door.) It was Arden, with a face like a death mask. She carried the smaller of her blue suitcases. "Just tell me if I'm inconveniencing you, Carrie. If I am, I can go on to a hotel, I've kept my taxi."

"Not at all! You look terrible. Here, let me run down and pay him for you."

"No, thank you, I can manage, if you'll just take the bag." She descended the few steps proudly on her straight legs and paid the driver, calling out a "Thank you" in her Southern accent as he pulled away.

She held on till we were in the inner sanctuary of my flat, behind the partition, and then she began to cry standing up, still holding her purse. I propelled her to my bed in the butler's pantry and then did what the English do on such occasions: made her a cup of tea.

This is what had happened. For the past few weeks, the Eastons had been acting "chilly." Whenever Mr. Easton, in his tipsy states, came upon Arden alone, he would say, "Hiya, Duchess," and wink at her. Arden said she hadn't wanted to tell me this during our talk the week before because we were celebrating her successful operation and also she just didn't want to say it aloud, hoping if she ignored it he might stop saying it. "And it wasn't as if it were malevolent, it was just . . . presumptuous. But this afternoon was another matter."

She then broke down again, collected herself, and, in a dead, even voice, with none of her usual upbeat cadences, told how she and Peter had been reading and talking, this rainy Saturday afternoon, in her room. "Since the Eastons have been acting so funny, I always make it a point to keep my door ajar, so if they want to creep up and look in, they are perfectly welcome, only they never do." Arden had to go to the bathroom and excused herself to Peter and, when she got halfway down the thickly carpeted hallway, heard Mrs. Easton talking on the telephone, which was in the hallway on the floor below. "She was talking in that way people talk when they're really absorbed in doing somebody in. To be perfectly honest, I probably would have stopped to listen even if I hadn't heard my name. But, once I heard it, I went back to the banister, where you can hear every word. Every word comes floating up. Every horrible, fully shaped word. She wasn't talking loudly, but she was talking under the assumption my door upstairs was closed and I was behind it." Arden paused and put down her teacup. She sat very straight on the edge of my bed. With her hard, white face and her lipsticked gash of a mouth, she looked ten years older. And in her long-sleeved white blouse with its ruffled collar, she did look like a duchess, though a very aggrieved one.

"But who was she talking to? What did she say, Arden?"

"She was talking to Lady Monleigh. They were discussing Peter's 'unfortunate attachment' to me. And then Mrs. Easton summed me up in a phrase."

"Which was . . . ?"

"I don't think I can repeat it. I'm not trying to be mysterious or make you think it was something worse than it was . . . though it was pretty bad. I can't repeat it because"—she faltered—"I don't want it to pass my lips. If it did . . . if it did, you see, it would bring me a step nearer thinking of myself like that. And if I thought of myself like that, it would make me a different person from what I am now . . . and what I am trying to be."

"Okay," I said, "I understand." Having already begun to imagine the sort of phrase that would be unspeakable for her.

"What I can't get over"—and here she began to shed tears—"is, that woman nursed me. She took complete care of me for three weeks. She had to bring me a bedpan for three whole weeks, and she did it . . . she did all of it with such grace and such kindness. There will always be gratitude in my heart for that woman who reduced me to such an unkind description. It's like being torn into two pieces. But I'll never set foot in that house again."

"But Arden, what about all your things? I mean, you're welcome to stay here, I'd love it, but won't you have to tell her something?"

"Oh, Alexander can always bring me my things. That's no problem." She laughed that harsh, cynical laugh I had heard for the first time a week before. "He'll do anything for a price. As for her, I think she already knows. After I heard . . . what I heard . . . I went back to my room and told Peter I was going to stay with you for a few days. I packed a few things and went downstairs and called a taxi. She was in the kitchen. She asked me, 'Arden, you'll be back for dinner, won't you?' And I looked her straight in the eye and said I didn't know when I would be back. I think that's when it registered. Because she looked almost stricken . . . I even felt sorry for her, Carrie. And then she said very quietly, 'Well, you will let us know you're all right, won't you?' 'Oh, yes, Mrs. Easton, we'll be in touch,' I said. I guess I sounded threatening because she flinched. She was probably thinking about how she was going to repay all that money."

"Oh God, Arden, what money?"

"The Eastons have borrowed over a hundred pounds from me."

"Oh, Arden. You'll never get it back."

"I will insist on having every penny of it back before I leave England."

"And what about Peter? He'll be sorry to see you leave the house. Of course, he can come and visit you here. I'm away at work all day, you can just pretend this is your own flat."

"Thank you, Carrie. Peter will want to come and visit me, no doubt, especially since I shall be going back to the States sooner than I'd planned. But I'd rather he came when you're home. That boy has such a simple, trusting nature. He could be so easily compromised in his position. And our friendship has been too special for me to want to do that. It's very clear to me now that the Eastons aren't even capable of understanding the kind of thing Peter and I have. It's not in their spiritual vocabulary. Because *nothing can be gained by it.* Excuse me, I just remembered I never did get to the bathroom. When I heard her talking down there—"

And Arden got up hurriedly and went to my bathroom, where I could hear her being sick.

One cold and glittery-bright March day, I was standing near the windows of our ground-floor office, "the Fishbowl," looking out. The new girl and I had already answered all the mail. She sat behind the counter, reading one of the Bollingen Foundation volumes of C. G. Jung. She was a serious, introverted person, and no one liked her very much because Mr. Miles had been about to hire a laughing, sociable girl when a telegram came from Washington telling him to hire this one because her father was a friend of the Speaker of the House. She was so cool to the customers that Colleen and I (yes, we had become friends, of a sort) played a trick on her: we wrote a letter to the Travel Service from a "customer" who felt he had been insulted by "that dark girl who's always reading the psychology books." But she turned the tables on us. She opened the letter and marched right upstairs and presented it to Mr. Miles, who, on calling Colleen and me to his office, said he recognized my style. "You can do better than this, girls," he said, dismissing us with a wave of his hand.

I was standing near the windows thinking that it would soon be exactly one year to the day since I had arrived in London. In that year, I seemed to have drifted in circles on the sea of my destiny. Neither the winds of love nor those of accomplishment had seen fit to bestir themselves and set me on my course. I had not seen Mark since Boxing Day, when, English gentleman to the end, he had stopped by with a gift, a Scotch tam-o'-shanter. The other man in my life, an ex-student of F. R. Leavis who now worked for the *Yorkshire Post*, had found me too frivolous and sent me a farewell letter that concluded with: "Your main concern should be how you're going to fill in the time between now and your funeral." As for the accomplishment department, well, the American *Madame Bovary* was bogged down at chapter nine of a projected twenty chapters. And all around me, as if to mock my unaccomplished desires, everybody else seemed to be skimming past, the wind filling their sails.

Arden had stayed three weeks with me. Peter and Alexander together had packed up her things and brought them to Green Street. Peter had come to supper a couple of times, and the two of them had had long talks in the butler's bed-sitting room, which I had turned over to her. From the looks of it, there was a sort of courtly love attachment between them. There was no doubt that he worshiped her, but they probably went no further than a few sad kisses at the end, if that. On second and third acquaintance, Peter seemed more noble to me, a bit more finely marked than the average nineteen-year-old. This was probably because I knew he was a duke. Arden also may have been influenced by this, but mainly, I believe, she liked him for himself—and because he appreciated her. She cried much of the night before she flew back to the States, but two weeks later wrote me a letter saying how invigorating it was to be home again, and how different "everything" looked from there. She mentioned twice a "very personable" man named Bruce ("just got his M.A. in communications from our old Alma Mater"), whom her mother had hired to manage their new TV station.

And Colleen and I had received a joint postcard from Betty Ann saying that she and her husband were having an "ecstatic" time in Greece. Signed "love," of course.

And my hobo had finished Book One of his memoirs. To my surprise, several chapters had been printed in *The News of the World*. He'd had a tentative offer to appear on a TV program. He was busy at work on Book Two, even though he had not yet found a publisher for the first volume.

And here was I, age twenty-five, with only two more years to go, according to Betty Ann's magazine article, before my matrimonial chances plummeted; here was I, playing office pranks with my old-maid supervisor and typing Book Two of a hobo's manuscript.

When down the sidewalk of Vigo Street sailed a familiar figure, her faded blond head bowed against the wind, the sea-green mohair shawl trailing majestically in her wake. Her toes, I noticed for the first time, turned in just a little as she took the pavement with long-legged strides. She was wearing the Belgian loafers. There was something portentous about her gait, as if nothing could detain her from her mission. Could it be that she was going to glide right by our offices? Maybe she thought I still worked in the Embassy building on Grosvenor Square, and was hurrying somewhere else.

I knocked urgently on the plate-glass window. She looked up, looked in, and lifted her hand in incidental greeting as she turned into our doorway without ever slowing. She *had* been on her way to see me, even if I had not seen her first.

"Mrs. Easton!"

"Carrie, dear!"

We embraced. I thought of Arden watching this and felt like Benedict Arnold.

"I had an errand on Bond Street," she said, "and I just couldn't resist stopping in to see how you were." The winter had roughened her complexion a bit more, but she was the same old Mrs. Easton, smiling—genuinely, it seemed—through her teeth. "Gosh, but it's good to see you!" she exclaimed girlishly.

"It's good to see you, too. Listen, come next door to the Thistle and have a beer. Or we could have an early lunch. They have delicious Cornish pasties and Scotch eggs and such things."

"I'd love a beer and a Cornish pasty!"

"Sydney," I called to the dark girl behind the counter, who had not even looked up from her book, "hold the fort. I'm going to lunch."

"My, but she's a dour one," murmured Mrs. Easton, pronouncing it the Scotch way as we headed next door to the pub.

"You got her immediately!" I cried, laughing a bit hysterically and hooking my arm through hers.

The Thistle was patronized mostly by Regent Street haberdashers. It was a jolly, dark place full of the smells of beer hops, pipe smoke, and its excellent hot buffet items. At first, the girls from the Travel Service had been endured as a necessary evil under the same roof. But now our lunchtime presence in a back booth had become acceptable: we ate well, drank like men, and also one strapping haberdasher who was always teasing us by flexing his muscles and announcing, "Made in England, girls," had developed a little crush on Colleen, who couldn't stand him. She thought he was vulgar. "Where's your friend?" he shouted now as Mrs. Easton and I picked our ladylike way through layers of robust pinstriped and pomade-smelling men. I called back to him that Colleen was at the dentist's.

After Mrs. Easton and I had gained our little enclave and got through the busy-ness of ordering what we wanted, an awkwardness came on both of us. Here we were, face-to-face, each of us remembering certain things that had been said and certain things that couldn't be said. What *would* we say now? That was the question. I almost ruined the whole lunch by looking down at her hands on the table and exclaiming, even in the same second I knew I could probably answer my own tactless question, "But where is your lovely *ring?*"

"Yes, it was lovely," she said, after her face had gone through an interesting series of shifts and suppressions, "but

I've had to stop wearing it. My arthritis flared up this winter. As you know, we did what we could with Le Cave Rouge, but it's never quite lost its basement dampness." She held out her hands to me for examination.

"They don't *look* too bad," I said, "but of course it's how they *feel*, probably." (I was pretty sure a ring like that could fetch a hundred pounds without much trouble.)

"Exactly," she said, massaging the fingers gingerly. Then, thank God, our beer and pasties came.

"Well, cheers," said I, raising my glass.

"Cheers, Carrie." She touched hers to mine. "Here's to . . . spring. I can't tell you how good it was to see your face when you saw me. You are one of those people whose faces show what they're feeling, and you seemed really glad to see me." She ducked her head modestly and took a big sip of beer when I assured her this was so. "It's been kind of an awful winter," I added.

"It has not been an easy winter," she said. And then she told me that the old Principessa had died at the end of January. "But, mercifully, in hospital, with all the care she needed. One of us got over to see her every day, and Whit was with her when she died. She didn't know it, of course. She was in an oxygen tent . . . pneumonia." She took a handkerchief and dabbed at the corner of each eye. "*Anyway* . . . 'The old order changeth, yielding place to new . . .' and God knows it's changing. It's going, going, *gone*, if you ask me. I just thank our lucky stars that Whit and I live here in this humane, civilized country, where if one or both of us become ill we can get decent medical care without being millionaires. We had a nice note from Arden, by the way, thanking us for taking care of her. A bit short and cool, when you consider how we waited on her hand-and-foot and how much grief she caused us. I don't know what she told you and I don't want to know. The two of you are old friends and, believe me, old friends get dearer and rarer as you get on in life. But we lost Peter over her, and Lord and Lady Monleigh haven't been the same toward us since he moved out. Arden managed to poison him against us before she went back to America, though I don't suppose I'll ever know what she said. But Lady Monleigh thinks the Dowager Duchess blames *her* for recommending us, and she in turn blames me. Though she hasn't said so in so many words. The English never do, you know." Her eyes narrowed—the beginnings of the scrunch.

"Who have you got staying with you now?" I wanted to change the subject before the great chain of blame, inevitably, reached me.

"Well, Alexander and Jean-Louis are still with us. And we have a darling new French girl, the daughter of Jean-Louis's boss in Marseilles. Monsieur Duval *delivered* her to our house, isn't that wonderfully old-fashioned? *I* think"—and she leaned forward confidentially—"that old Frenchman has it all planned. He wants his daughter and Jean-Louis, whom he'll probably make a partner in his business, to fall in love. He wants them to be close enough to get to know each other, but not *too* close, if you see what I mean. I've given her Peter's old room . . . and Carlos's . . . dear Carlos . . . we had a sweet letter, they're going to take him to the States and try to get him into Dartmouth. From now on, I'm keeping those top three rooms for girls only. They'll use the upstairs bathroom and the boys will use the lower bathroom. There'll be no excuse for all this running up and down and practically living in someone else's room. I do wish Jean-Louis would notice Anne-Marie more . . . he's always so involved in his business. So far it's Alexander who's noticing her, and though we think the world of Alexander he just wouldn't be suitable for a girl like Anne-Marie." She took a forkful of pasty and chewed it meditatively. "Young people could save themselves so much trouble if they understood who was suitable to marry and who wasn't. But who am I to preach? I shunned the fellow my parents had their hearts set on. I married a young painter who was wasting away, though at least he wasn't penniless."

"The one who burned all your Proust?"

"Heavens no!" She laughed gaily. "Gus, burn Proust? He'd

rather have set himself on fire. Poor Gus had TB—we found out shortly after our marriage. We went to a place in Switzerland: Davos. The Germans had a horrible joke, '*Letzte Grüsse aus Davos,*' they'd say. Last greetings from Davos. Unfortunately, it proved true for poor Gus—people still died from TB then, you know. But the strangest thing, Carrie: there was another American couple at Davos, only she was the sick one. But she got better and divorced that husband and remarried and, later, moved to the very next town in Connecticut to where I was living with the man I'd married after losing Gus ... *now* we're talking about the one who burned Proust. Well, this woman—Louise—and I would meet for lunch or play tennis, but years went by and I never met her husband because he was at work—he was in her father's bank in New York. Her father was an extremely wealthy, influential man—he had once run for the presidency, in the early twenties.

"Anyway! One year I told my husband, 'This has gone far enough, we're going to invite Louise and her mystery husband to our New Year's party.' And we did, and they accepted, and in walks Louise with the man I'd been looking for all my life. I knew it the minute he looked at me. That man was Whit."

"Oh, Mrs. Easton. How romantic."

"Yes, isn't it odd the way your fate comes to claim you in these roundabout little connections? Though, Lord knows, Whit and I tried to be honorable and not hurt anyone. I had my little daughter and Whit worked for his father-in-law. And then World War Two came and Whit was commissioned a colonel and sent right to the European Theater and I was sure every letter I got from him would be the last. I had to rent a post-office box in another town in order to get his letters. And it was so awful when Louise would want to have lunch and read me *her* letters from Whit. And then he came home with the DSO and they dragged on together a little longer. She was completely dependent on him—childless women often are that way. But finally Whit and I decided everyone had had their piece of us and now we wanted to have a little of each other before it was too late. I saw my daughter marry and left for Nevada the next week. Whit's divorce took longer because she fought it tooth and nail and her father more or less controlled their purse strings. But I had a little money from a cottage my father had left me, and so we made it. We burned every one of our bridges and were married by a justice of the peace in New York one morning and sailed for Elba that same afternoon on a Greek ship. We had waited for each other fifteen years. He walked into my living room on December 31, 1937."

"The year I was born."

"Was it? What a coincidence. You know, Carrie, since we seem to be having such a cozy time here and I've been spilling secrets, I must tell you what Whit said about you the other night. We were talking about the various young people who've lived with us, first at Tregunter and now at Twenty-one, and he said, 'Well, Daphne's given us the least trouble, and Arden's given us the most, but the one that had the most life in her was old Carrie.' He said to be sure and invite you for supper because he wants to hear what you've been up to. I was wondering if you'd be free this coming Saturday—I thought I'd try a real bouillabaisse in honor of Anne-Marie. Would you come?"

"Well, thank you. I think that would be nice." The old lech, I thought, did he say that or is she just making it up? I'll go, because I am free and she's the best cook in town and it will be fun to reassess the old gang from the perspective of my winter's worth of independence. "Has Daphne left you, then?"

"Oh no, poor Daphne's still with us. She's still in your old room. Her nice boy got away, I'm afraid. The timing was off somehow. It was unfortunate, because she really did care for him. She's being very subdued these days. She sits around pasting on her false fingernails and she has a part-time job typing up inventories for some Levantine who has a gift shop in Chelsea."

"And who has taken Arden's old room?"

"No one, as yet. Isabel moved in for a while, while the leak in her room was being fixed. I'm sure it was caused by Arden—she'd take hour-long baths and fill the tub so full that the water just *poured* out the drainpipe into the street. But Isabel's left us now, and, frankly, Carrie, I'm in no hurry to put just anyone in that room. It's spring now and we can afford to be choosy because the heating bills won't be so high. Do you know, Arden kept two heaters going in her room the whole time she was with us? And, as you know, she was in her room all day. I felt we would have been perfectly within our rights to raise her rent, but Whit wouldn't hear of it. Dear Whit's as scrupulous as an Eagle Scout."

The pub lunch with Mrs. Easton dominated my thoughts for the rest of that week. So often, especially when we are younger, we see other people only in relation to what they are to us; we freeze them into what they are *now*. But her story had broken the ice, or at least made a crack in it (for I am still far from "figuring out" the Eastons, which is why, I suppose, they have remained so tantalizing to my imagination), and, after the lunch, I could glimpse them as fluid creatures still moving in the auras of their colorful pasts. When she lifted her eyes from the Hennings' copy of Proust and looked across the red basement room, whose dampness had provided a perfect alibi for the missing ring (and which husband had given her the big pear-shaped diamond with the emerald baguettes, or had it been a family heirloom, or had she splurged while she waited for "Whit" to disentangle himself from the purse strings, knowing he couldn't buy her a ring and being glad she had the little legacy from her father so she could finance the burning of their bridges?)— when the Mrs. Easton I knew looked across the basement room at the alcoholic trying to fill an hour by polishing all their shoes, she saw, if not the substance, then the shadow of "the man she had been looking for all her life," the man who had written her clandestine letters, each one perhaps "the last," from the heart of all the action, and who had come home a hero. When my ex-landlady looked at my ex-landlord, who had pinched me in the kitchen and almost certainly made off with my money, she saw the man she had wanted and plotted and schemed for, as long as I had been on the earth.

But though I could now pity them their present lives, I did, a little, envy them their pasts. I could now piece together a sort of broken mosaic of the world she had pronounced "going, going, *gone*," a world of privilege in which girls at boarding school took all the men's parts in *The Importance of Being Earnest* and boys at prep school were provided with neckties that would always grant them a certain cachet, even if their lives later went downhill. It was a world in which one's father fished at the Restigouche Salmon Club (Colleen, a Canadian, had been able to enlighten me on that one) and young artist husbands who were "not penniless" wasted away in Swiss sanatoriums. The wars were grand and revenges were grand: a husband, discovering he had been cheated of his rightful time, made a bonfire of his wife's *Remembrance of Things Past* on the lawn. You even burned your bridges in the grand style: you sailed straight for the island where Napoleon himself lay low for a while until he could rally his resources for a second assault on fortune.

It was very possibly because I was under the spell of Mrs. Easton's romance that, on the Friday before the Saturday I was to partake of her bouillabaisse, I went to a party given by some girls who lived in a mews off Green Street and convinced myself I had met the man I had been looking for all my life. Hastings Pickering was twenty-nine, "with intelligent eyes, inner calm, and manliness," as I was to write in my journal after he had left my flat. He worked as a research engineer for a spark plug company in Croydon and told me he had lost his best friend to matrimony the week before. "Now there's nothing for it but for me to find a woman and get married, too," he said, puffing at his pipe as he made me a cup of coffee in my own kitchen because I had drunk too much at the party. He was losing his hair but that was all right because he had a strong, pure, well-sculpted face and a sweet mouth. Eros quivered between us as we lay chastely together on my bed, because there were no comfortable chairs, and listened to the men taking a bath upstairs. Hastings told me his favorite pastimes were sailing and camping, and that he owned a little cottage in Rugby that he rented out. "I mean, one can't say to one's prospective father-in-law, 'Sir, I'm a good chap, I own thirty-six sweaters,' can one?" He told me that in his opinion a man should not try to sleep with a girl till after they were married.

I was in such a state of well-being on Saturday that I took an early bus to Chelsea so I could ride the extra stops and get off by the river and take my old ritual walk along the Embankment. The stretch between the Battersea and Chelsea bridges was where I came closest, I felt, to achieving a true relationship to time. During my first English summer on Old Church Street, I had often walked there to regain perspective when office gripes or Easton intrigues had got me down, and almost always I came back from the walk with a larger sense of life. Following the historic curve of the Thames from the Pleasure Gardens over on the Battersea side to the Chelsea Pensioners' Hospital on my side, I would have regathered my calm to the point of being able to see before and beyond my own existence by the time I passed the Hovis clock. Human beings had walked this bend of river before me and thought about the mutability of their individual lives, and they would still be walking and thinking after I was gone. Thus humbled, I would experience a peculiar elation, and, feeling almost weightless, as if my body had already dispersed into particles and were no longer visible, I would turn and retrace the route, wondering what all the fuss had been about. Somewhere along the way, I would take a deep breath, shuddering as the "I" and the "Now" refilled me. I would become visible again and resume the plotting of my life.

On this particular spring evening, by the time I had performed the ritual and arrived at the yellow door at 21 Old Church Street, it seemed highly possible that by the end of the summer I should have finished the American *Madame Bovary* and might even be married.

Mr. Easton, in his familiar regalia, answered the door and seemed less high than usual for almost six o'clock and heartily glad to see me.

"Carrie! You're looking wonderful. Come in, come in."

"A few contributions to the Cave Rouge cocktail hour," I

said, handing him a brown paper bag from the PX. (Mrs. Easton had invited me to come early, "so the three of us can go downstairs and have a drink and talk.")

"You shouldn't have done that, but we thank you. C'mon up to the kitchen and say hello to Lee—she's just finishing off a poor lobster. Go ahead, go ahead."

I went up the stairs in front of him, highly conscious of our previous encounter in the dark kitchen. Now the warm yellow of lengthening twilight streamed through its windows, and Mrs. Easton, wearing her handsome black bib apron with thin white stripes, turned from where she was cutting up something, put down her knife, and gave me a "cook's kiss," offering me her face but holding her wet hands aloft.

"I'm so tickled you could come, Carrie. I really think this is going to be fun. I managed to get every single ingredient except the *rascasse*, which, of course, you can't get here, as it swims only in the Mediterranean around Marseilles. But I'm sure Anne-Marie will forgive us; she's providing the wine for the evening, isn't that sweet?"

"And Carrie's providing the cocktail hour," said Mr. Easton, peering into the brown bag.

"Oh, *isn't* that nice. Sweetie, why don't you go on down and prepare our drinks while I finish with this lobster? What will you have, Carrie? We've got some medium-dry sherry and gin. And whatever you brought, of course."

"I'd love a sherry."

"Yes, so would I. Do feel free to go upstairs and use your old bathroom, if you'd like to wash up. Why don't you run upstairs anyway and say hello to your old room. Daphne's not home yet. Oh! And do me a big favor and see if you like what I've done to Arden's old room next door. I thought it needed a new personality, after being a sickroom for so long."

And so I went up, you might say, to my fate. I did not linger long at my old room, I did not even cross its threshold; Daphne's imprint was upon it, and its associations for me now were those of its latter period, when I spent more and more time in the canopied bed and no longer got up to look out the window on the mornings the Queen's Guards rode by. In the bluish evening light (for its sun was gone for the day) *it* looked rather like an opulent sickroom.

I went next door to Arden's former room. It was at its best, this time of day. The same warm yellow light that had filled the kitchen below played flatteringly upon the polished surfaces of furniture. The room's aspect had been completely changed since Arden and I lay across her bed, taping "Aspects of England" for the listeners of Ruffin County. The bed had been moved from the center of the room and pushed flush against one wall. There was a desk, by the window, which had not been here before. This room came equipped with a small washbasin, and, to the right of the basin, next to a roomy chiffonier, a narrow, old-fashioned bookcase, with brass handles on its glass doors, had been fitted in. The room now had the feeling of a study where one might also rest, rather than a boudoir where one might also write. Ah, cunning, cunning Mrs. Easton: to break up the monotonous length of mouse-gray carpeting, she had put down a small Oriental rug, with faded lions and hunters, that I had often admired in the old days when it lay, lost among too many other patterns, in the drawing room downstairs. I knew who was going to live next in this room, and the Eastons knew it, too.

I went to the window, where the desk had been placed, to try the new view. There was the tin roof of Alexander's shed, and, beyond, the greening squares of neighboring gardens, the interesting views of other people's homes, the perky London chimney pots with their crooked hats. I put my palms down upon the desk. It was still warm from the afternoon sun. Here in this alert, chaste little room (and since Hastings had expressed his views on sex before marriage, chastity was clearly going to be the order of the summer) I could begin in earnest to write. Here I could (and did) finish the American *Madame Bovary*. (I would send my only manuscript copy to an agency on Baker Street that had placed an ad in the *Evening Standard:* "Wanted: unpublished novels in which women's problems and love interests are predominant. Agreeable terms." Months would pass and I would finally ring up Directory Enquiries and discover that the agency was not listed. I went around to the address. It was an empty flat. If you ever come across a novel about an unhappy young wife named Bentley who lives on a Florida island called Gull Key—no, they might have changed the names; if you ever come across a novel that ends, "If I could do it once, I can do it again; so rises the indestructible pyramid," that's mine.) Here, at this desk, I would sit on weekend afternoons and some weekend evenings, gazing out at the gardens and houses and wondering about my future. The house of the man I would marry next was visible from this window: a dark brick building in which I would repent at leisure for the second time. But time would still, miraculously, be on my side. No crucial bridges would have been burned as yet, and I would eventually return to my own country and have an opportunity to start afresh.

And here, at this desk, in less than a month, I would sit down one warm English afternoon, after sharing drinks and spilling secrets with the Eastons at their favorite pub to celebrate my return, and write down in my journal the story they had told me, probably in exchange for my telling them all the gloomy and dramatic and salacious details of my first marriage.

Mr. Bedford

On the day Mrs. Easton sold her late father's cottage in Bedford, New York, she and Mr. Easton went walking in the fields behind and found a turtle. They named him Mr. Bedford and took him back to their rooftop flat on East Sixty-sixth Street, which a friend was lending them till Mr. Easton's divorce came through. Mr. Bedford slept in the garden in the daytime, and at night would come clunking down the stairs—a kind of combined crawl-fall—and sleep under their bed. It took him hours to follow them from room to room, and sometimes by the time he had gotten to one room, they had already left it for another. One day

Mr. E. found Mr. Bedford half buried in the hot tar on the roof. It took three hours with a bottle of turpentine, fingers, and a spoon to make him comfortable again. When they had parties, sometimes Mr. Easton would fix a lighted candle to the top of Mr. Bedford's shell and he would come marching into the dark dining room all aglow and make the ladies scream. He ate flies, lettuce leaves, and meat. When the Eastons married and left quickly for Elba, because Mr. E. could never pay the kind of alimony he had agreed to pay in order to get the divorce, they took Mr. Bedford along with them on the ship in a hatbox. The bartender on board tried to interest him in whiskey, but Mr. Bedford was not the drinking sort. The family flourished in Elba until one day Mr. Bedford fell from a second-story window during one of his prowls and cracked his shell. Mr. E. again to the rescue with iodine and adhesive tape. The shell grew back, but Mr. Bedford's legs remained slightly paralyzed despite the Eastons' faithful massages. One day some friends came to take the Eastons' picture for the front of a Christmas card. The Eastons and Mr. Bedford were all three posed looking out of a window. Afterward Mr. Bedford was left in his favorite spot on the patio to have a nap in the sun. But when he didn't come in by nighttime, Mrs. Easton got worried and went to look. But he was nowhere to be found, though they both searched for hours. It was thought that a dog had probably carried him away (as had happened before) but this time dropped him somewhere too far from home for his semiparalyzed legs to return him. Mrs. Easton cried for days because Mr. Bedford, she said, besides being an unusually faithful, intelligent character, also had been their last connection with another time and another place, neither of which could ever be returned to.

"How about it, Carrie?" asked Mr. Easton. "D'ya think you can stand it one more time?"

We were gathered together, rosy from wine and the extraordinary bouillabaisse, in the Hennings' well-appointed drawing room, with its glazed chintz sofa and armchairs, its lamps and little tea tables, its good faded Oriental rugs (one now missing), its impressive array of gilt-and-leather bindings (of which the red-and-gold *Debrett's* was placed to gleam most prominently) on the shelves. We were also rosy from laughing, for the Eastons, taking it by turns, had just retold, for my benefit, the priceless story about how, last November, Mrs. Henning had suddenly rung up to announce she was in the country for a quick visit to her ailing mother-in-law and would it be *too* silly of her to want to pop up to London and say hello to her beloved little house? "Well, thank *God* Arden was still in the hospital," said Mrs. Easton. "I could get to work de-inhabiting her room right away." And at this point Mr. Easton had taken up the story, relating in rapid, comic fashion punctuated with exaggerations how he had called an emergency meeting of the inmates. "I gave them to understand they had to have every item of personal clothing, every single sign of their existence, out of their rooms. Everyone packed themselves up in suitcases and we stored everything under a bunch of blankets down in Le Cave Rouge. And then they were under strict orders to be out of the house from two o'clock till seven o'clock on Saturday, when Mrs. Henning was coming to tea. She only stayed from four to five, but you can't be too careful." "And did she suspect?" I asked. "Well," drawled Mrs. Easton philosophically, "I think she suspected some of it, but not *all* of it. I mean, we couldn't un-paint and un-decorate Le Cave Rouge, so we told her we'd made it into a spare guest room when we had extra friends from America. And what we decided to do about Alexander's shed was tell her the truth: 'We've let a very nice boy fix up your garden shed and live there till he gets on his feet in life.' She was simply enchanted by Alexander's shed. She said it would make a perfect little guest house or study for her husband one day. All in all, she was *quite* satisfied with the state of the house." "But boy, were we glad to phone that taxi and send her back to Victoria Station!" Mr. Easton had concluded.

And then he had asked me if, for the sake of Anne-Marie, I could stand to hear the Rhinebeck story one more time.

"I hope to hear it many more times," I said, significantly. Mrs. Easton beamed at me. An unspoken agreement had already been reached between us over cocktails in Le Cave Rouge.

"Anne-Marie's English isn't so good yet, but you'll do a consecutive translation for her, won't you, Jean-Louis?"

"Eh ... certainly." Jean-Louis looked up from his little notebook, in which he had been making a few quick calculations in the interim. He turned politely toward his boss's daughter, who sat beside Alexander on the sofa, her pretty knees close together, a beautiful girl both sultry and unawakened, as yet. (Jean-Louis would marry her, but Alexander, who brooded slyly upon her ripeness as he sucked deeply on his cigarette, would have her first.)

"Daphne? I won't be killing you with boredom, either?"

"I should quite like to hear it, actually," said poor Daphne, the only one who had not made a pig of herself over the bouilla-baisse. She still mourned the loss of the biscuit heir, or perhaps felt the personal failure it implied. But she sat there bravely, examining a false fingernail that had begun to chip. (Years later I would meet Daphne at the glove counter in Bonwit's. She would be married to an American, a veterinarian specializing in Thoroughbred horses, whose profession required the couple to make frequent trips to England. "I suppose you've heard about Alexander's success," she would say, as we ran through the old guest list; no, she was ashamed to say, she was quite out of touch with the Eastons—"We had a bit of a run-in over this chap I was seeing for a while"—but she supposed they were still in London. "But they *can't* still be running a boardinghouse," I said. "They're getting near their eighties." One hoped not, she said, but had I heard of Alexander's in Berkeley Square? "It's so posh there's a waiting list for membership. He's got it furnished with all his antiques. They say the Marchioness of Monleigh set him up, after her husband died. Richard and I dined there with some friends who are members; we could never afford it. Alexander is quite changed. He's put on weight and looks really like somebody. He's the 'new' England, one might say." And she would go on to lament the other changes in the London we knew. "Remember the Boltons? Well, it's *filled* with estate-agent signs—in Arabic!")

"Well, then!" And Mr. Easton sat himself down at the rosewood piano and ran his fingers lightly over the keys. "A bit out of tune, Lee...."

"I know, darling. As soon as we get caught up, we'll have the tuner. He's so expensive," she confided to me, bending her faded blond head toward where I sat, on a silk cushion, beside her well-shod feet. (Our tenancy in that house was more limited than we knew. At the end of the summer, the Eastons would receive a terribly apologetic letter from Mrs. Henning. "... though we'd adore to have you stay on, prices have gone up so that Father feels we really must increase the rent (as allowed for in clause 14) to cover taxes and insurance rises...." That, as Mrs. Easton would say philosophically, is the way the English do things.)

Mr. Easton played the opening passages of the "Moonlight Sonata" and then told us about the time he had gone "on a matter of business" from New York City to the house of a very wealthy man in Rhinebeck, New York. But this time around, I squinted at his profile until I imagined I could see, as through a scrim, that young man winding his way innocently up the Hudson aboard the train of his convoluted destiny. There would be wives (or was he, at this time, already working for the first one's father, the one that controlled the purse strings?), a war; why, even before the day was over, he would meet a beautiful girl with a tail. Or was that—it occurs to me now—just a metaphor for something he was trying to tell us about our own futures: the contest between what we were determined to wrest from fate and what fate, in her sinuous, sporting movements, as playful and sinister as an unexpected tail, would end up wresting from us?

"... I was a young man, life was just beginning for me, as it is for all of you now, and that woman in those surroundings seemed the epitome of all I hoped to win for myself ..."

And, in a moment, Jean-Louis's translated litany of these things: ". . . *amour* . . . *accomplissement* . . . eh . . ." (Look at Anne-Marie, you fool!) ". . . *beauté* . . . *élégance* . . . *prospérité* . . ."

Now I live near Rhinebeck, New York, myself, on the other side of the bridge. I seldom drive over that bridge without scanning the rooftops of those grand riverfront houses, hidden from full view even in winter by careful forestry, and wondering if in one of them lives an old lady who by now may be reconciled to her tail. Thoughts of her inevitably lead to thoughts of the Eastons. To what have they had to reconcile themselves, since I last saw them?

I stayed with them at 21 Old Church Street till the fall and moved with them and five others to a less elegant house in Oakley Gardens, where we coexisted until the following fall, when I again left in a huff, this time (ostensibly) over a cat. They had given me the ground-floor garden room on the condition I let Enrico go in and out of my window, as this house had no back door. Enrico and I had never really got on—perhaps he smelled my ambivalence toward his owners—but when we began sharing a room the animosities bloomed on both sides. I would make him wait till I had finished doing whatever I was doing, when he yowled and scratched on the closed window; conversely, on warm mornings, when it was open, he would pounce on me while I was still asleep and wave his tail, smelling heavily of musk, in my face before demanding to be let out of the bedroom. But the real reason I was leaving was that I was just turned twenty-seven and had broken my engagement to a rugby player and felt that if I were to be an old maid like Colleen Drury I'd rather be one in the privacy of my own flat.

But fate responded with a series of capricious tail-flicks, and I had no sooner settled into my own flat on Beaufort Street than I was moving out again, across the street, to the flat of my husband. ("Colleen married that fellow you all called 'Made in England,'" Mr. Miles, who liked to keep up with his "old girls," would write to me in 1969.) As a wife, I saw Mrs. Easton occasionally, when we shopped at the same fish market on the King's Road. Sometimes she would smile and seem genuinely glad to see me; sometimes she would look in, see me buying my fish, and hurry on past, doing her other errands first.

The last time I saw Mr. Easton was on a damp night when I had been walking alone beside the Embankment and knew suddenly that I was going to leave my husband and go back to America. I decided to go and see the Eastons and tell them. I felt they, of all people, would understand. I hurried up Oakley Street and turned into Oakley Gardens, hoping they'd offer me something to drink (the husband on Beaufort Street did not believe in alcohol); but when I reached their house, the windows of the drawing room were already dark. I went up on the porch, anyway, and peered in, perhaps hoping I could make her materialize (for it was Mrs. Easton I really wanted to see), and that's when I saw him, holding on to the banister post, doing knee-bends in his striped flannel pajamas. Up and down he went, exceedingly limber for a man of his age; he was facing the front door, no doubt seeing his reflection in its glass panes, when, suddenly (I must have stepped forward, or his vision shifted), he looked perfectly horrified, as if he'd seen a ghost, and turned and bolted down the hall and away into the shadows.

Perhaps Arden knows what has become of them. She and I have been in and out of touch over the years (mostly out, I am ashamed to say), but she is the kind of person who won't let too long go by before she checks up on anyone in her life who has meant something to her. While I was writing this, I was tempted to track her down through good old 555-1212, thinking, It is entirely possible that she is not only in correspondence with them but may even be sending them money. For I've heard, through the grapevine, that Arden is now a very rich woman. (And, the last time we met, a very happy one, with her Bruce and their twin daughters. Happy people are quick to forgive: an oblation to fate?) But then I said, No, not until you finish your story.

Once I was writing a story whose whole thrust depended upon the fulcrum of a lucky cousin's idyllic marriage. Feeling closer to this cousin as I imagined her life on paper, I made the mistake of writing to her before I'd finished. Back came a torrent of anguished pages filled with lucklessness and divorce. Now her luck has changed again and things are on the upswing once more. But I never could finish that story.

One of the fascinating aspects of life is that, as long as people are in it, their stories go on, often in the most amazing ways. But another aspect of life is that, sooner or later, it kills people off.

One of the fascinating aspects of fiction is that, inside its boundaries, you can keep people alive for as long as you like. That's why I don't want to hear anything bad or sad about the Eastons, even if it exists, "out there" in life. Not until I've come to the end of my last page and have safely preserved *my* Eastons as they were to me.

In here, in the confines of my fiction, we are all still alive. Some of us are still young, plotting our favorite versions of the love, accomplishment, beauty, elegance, and wealth we hope to win for ourselves. And even for those whose main chances are now a thing of the past, nobody is friendless or destitute or *too* old or in great physical pain; nobody is even in the hospital.

The elegant drawing room is warm from the coal fire Mr. Easton has made in the grate, and Mrs. Henning's lamps play favorably on our faces, flushed from wine and good food and from laughing at the old, old story. But it was new to Anne-Marie, who laughed so hard at Jean-Louis's translation that she has the hiccups. There goes Mrs. Easton, agile as a girl in her Belgian strollers, and willing to serve her lovely young paying guest, to fetch a glass of water. Anyone happening to be walking along Old Church Street in the spring night may look up at our glowing window and sigh and think: Ah, the pleasures of a cozy, well-appointed home! Or may take an invigorating breath and declare: "Fascinating, to look unseen into a little tableau of other people's lives . . . and then move on."

A Father's Pleasures

*R*udolf Geber loved his son with the love we reserve for those to whom we have given our best selves. Sometimes it even seemed to him that he had brought the boy into the world singlehandedly. It had been Rudolf who overcame his wife's resistance to having a baby. She was one of those people who appear to have been born sad and fearful and who go through life this way, for some inner reason nobody else can fathom. Rudolf, a man of charm, to whom life came easily, had been drawn to her because he believed he of all people could make her relaxed and happy. The pregnancy was difficult and she became more sad and fearful than ever. In her seventh month she stopped growing, and Rudolf canceled an important concert tour and stayed by her side. He rushed her to the hospital when it was learned she was toxic. He signed the papers for a cesarean and the infant was transferred straight from the womb to the incubator.

"We have a son," he told her when she came out of the anesthetic. "Only six pounds, but you should see the black fuzz all over his head, the little monkey."

She turned her face to the wall and wept softly. She knew he was lying, she knew the child had been born dead.

Rudolf never told her of the crisis that came a day later. The tiny boy, whom Rudolf already thought of as Paul, named after his own father, had developed a horrifying twitch. Rudolf stood over the incubator, watching helplessly as the little limbs jerked in spasms, as if being pulled on an invisible rack. The pediatrician was called. "Mr. Geber," she said, "this is either a simple calcium deficiency or something much more serious. At this point I cannot tell which. I shall treat him for the calcium deficiency first, as the treatment for the other thing, which involves draining spinal fluid, is dangerous in itself. And we shall pray."

She stayed with the child all night. Rudolf paced in a waiting room whose curtains he never forgot. He prayed to the deities of both his parents. With the remote, hard-nosed God of his mother, who had survived her concentration camp and now lived in Tel Aviv, he bargained Old Testament–style: "If You let the boy live, I will stop hoping for a happy marriage." Then he remembered his father as he had looked the last time Rudolf ever saw him, waving good-bye as the train pulled out of Berlin. It was the summer of 1939. Rudolf, a *Wunderkind* of twelve, was off to England to play a series of concerts. While in Leeds, Rudolf received a letter from his father, with ten English pounds enclosed, giving him the name of a family who would take him in. He stayed with this family for five years, after which he volunteered for the British forces and was sent to Africa. After the war, he visited his mother in what was then called Palestine. She was angry and bitter that what had happened in the world had been allowed to happen. She and Rudolf fell out when he said he preferred to join the forces of Art and Beauty. "You are just a dreamer, like your father," she said. Rudolf thanked her; soon afterward, he went to America. Rudolf's father had died of a heart attack at Theresienstadt, one of the "model" camps the Nazis kept for public-relations purposes. He had been carrying rocks for a rock garden to beautify the camp to which he had volunteered to accompany his wife.

Now, in the waiting room of a New York hospital, Rudolf also prayed to his father's God, the Father of Jesus. But it was his own father's face, with the high forehead and the reddish-brown mustache, he addressed: "If little Paul lives, help me to be as good a father as you were."

/ / /

When Paul was three, his father bought him a recorder. At the end of the morning's scales and arpeggios, Rudolf waited for the small voice to call through the door of his practice room: "Daddy, can we make our music now?" Their "music" consisted of little Paul's blowing boldly on his recorder and Rudolf's improvising around whatever sound the boy made. Rudolf loved this hour. He kept stealing glances at the serious child blowing for all he was worth, his dark eyes widening, his tiny nostrils flaring with the effort. Paul's face was already shaped as it would be as an adult. The funny black fuzz that had covered his head at birth had fallen out soon afterward and his hair was now the same curly russet as his father's. But Paul had inherited his mother's somber temperament.

During Paul's childhood, the mother seemed quite content to hover efficiently in the background of the love between father and son. She made their meals, worried about their health and all the possible catastrophes that might befall them. She acted as secretary for Rudolf's busy professional life. There was a satisfaction in her voice when she could tell someone, "He cannot come to the phone now, he is practicing." Or, "I am sorry, he's away on tour." She read voraciously and had grown more peaceful since Rudolf had taken the pressure off her to become a happy woman.

The summer Paul was six, the family was to have a free trip to Scandinavia. Rudolf was one of the guest artists on a cruise ship. At the last minute, the mother sprained her back. Paul was so disappointed that they decided to hire a nurse for her at home so that Rudolf could take the boy along as planned.

"Don't let him cramp your style," teased Rudolf's wife, who had grown almost jolly now that she couldn't go on the long-awaited free vacation. She came nearest to happiness during setbacks, Rudolf had learned.

"The boy is my style," he replied. He himself did not know exactly what his words meant, they simply sprang to his tongue.

The plush liner was hardly out of sight of land before Rudolf and Paul had captured the imagination of all on board. Each passenger wove his own story around the charming virtuoso and the solemn little fellow who pattered after him like a shadow. Watching the big man and the little one standing side by side at the rail, their look-alike hair blowing, engaged in intense conversation, people would make adjustments to their own memories: "Ah, my father was like that . . . or would have been, had he lived. . . ." "Yes, I, too, was a good father when my children were small. I wonder if they remember all our outings and conversations. . . ." The women on board fantasized worse fates than a sprained back for the absent mother; each imagined in her own way how she would go about making that serious little boy smile and how the attractive father would reward her with his gratitude and affection.

Both Rudolf and Paul were secretly glad to be off on their own. If his mother were here, Paul knew, she would be worrying herself sick about his falling overboard or drowning in the swimming pool or eating rotten food or staying up late to hear his father's music. As for Rudolf, he had determined this voyage should have lasting significance for his son. He himself had never got his fill of his own father. There were gaps of knowledge he would give anything to be able to fill.

"My father never carried a package," he told Paul.

"Why, was he very weak?"

"No, in that society a gentleman didn't. He didn't shave himself, either. He left the house at half-past eight and stopped at his barber's before he went on to his factory. They called him *der elegante Geber*, my father. Did you know that our name means 'the giver' in German?"

"Am I German or American?" Paul wanted to know.

"American. Third generation on your mother's side, first on mine. I am a naturalized citizen."

"Am I Jewish or just part-Jewish?"

"According to Jewish law, you're Jewish because your mother is. It's the same with me."

"What about other laws? What about American law?"

"Well, according to them, you're a mixture of your mother and father and their mothers and fathers and so on. According to American law you're also unique, you're yourself, Paul, with all the rights and privileges a free country grants an individual."

"Are there some parts of me, then, that don't come from anybody and don't belong to anybody?"

Rudolf thought for a minute, impressed by the gravity of the small boy's question. "Of course!" he answered.

One of the other entertainers on the cruise was a voluptuous, rather rowdy flamenco singer who called herself Carmen Cordero. She drank like a fish and her laugh carried clear across the ship. She had her twelve-year-old daughter with her, a quiet, slim girl who deferred to Carmen in everything yet appeared to live her real life in some remote mental kingdom. She reminded Rudolf of a medieval princess. Her name was Liane. Carmen was vague about Liane's father. Liane became attached to little Paul; she mothered him in a sweet, childish way and was teaching him how to swim. The four of them took their meals together and soon formed a makeshift family, the two sociable, talkative parents and the two quiet, withdrawn children. The available women on board thought the elegant pianist utterly wasted on the coarse Cordero.

But Carmen could not have suited Rudolf better. He liked her rowdy frankness, she was the kind of woman you could say anything to; her good humor was as endless as her capacity for Scotch. Also, she kept the other women away. Rudolf was at this time still intent upon honoring his marriage to the letter of the law. So after their respective performances were tucked away, Rudolf and Carmen sat in the bar and drank Glenfiddich—gratis for them, as was everything else on the ship—and talked music or exchanged professional anecdotes. By tacit agreement, Carmen did not bring up Rudolf's marriage and Rudolf asked no questions about the father of Liane.

"Once I was on tour with this Russian accompanist, a huge woman named Nadia Lissenko," Carmen told Rudolf. "In Medicine Hat, Alberta . . . have you ever been there? . . . we had to share a room with only one bed. In the middle of the night I dreamed I was smothering to death. I woke up and there was Nadia on top of me, naked, grinding her massive, soft body against mine. That was when I resolved to learn to accompany myself on guitar."

"It's much better with guitar, your voice is so resonant," said Rudolf. "Certainly I've been to Medicine Hat. It was there . . . no, sorry, it was Moose Jaw, where I had a small fiasco. I was playing from memory a piece by a local composer when suddenly I blanked. So I improvised. A little Scriabin, a little of my own schlock I sometimes use to warm up with. The composer was livid, but he got the best reviews of his life."

Carmen snorted so loudly with laughter that a refined couple on their honeymoon turned to stare. She put her hand on Rudolf's arm. "Your bravura playing, my dear. By the way, it went over big tonight when you dedicated your encore to little Paul. The audience ate it up."

"Yes, Paul loves the 'Kinderscenen,' " said Rudolf.

"It's funny," said Carmen. "A man alone with his little boy is like an aphrodisiac to women, but a woman alone with her little girl scares the hell out of men."

"What's the difference? Lovers come and go, but my son is always my son and your daughter is always your daughter," said Rudolf. "That's what really matters."

"I think I'll have a refill," said Carmen, with a melancholy look at Rudolf.

Little Paul flourished on the cruise. His body turned a healthy pink-brown from his swimming lessons with the patient Liane. Both of them were extremely fair-skinned and Liane saw to it that they constantly rubbed sun cream on themselves and on each other's shoulders. Liane was still perfectly flat-chested and seldom wore a top. She crooned something to Paul as she pulled him through the water and he shouted with laughter. Rudolf, watching them from the side of the pool, felt a little stab of envy.

The boy never let himself go like that, even with him. If only I could give him a sister, thought Rudolf. But the doctor had said it was inadvisable for his wife to have more children, even if Rudolf could talk her into it a second time.

Paul cried when the cruise came to an end and he hugged Liane good-bye. (But a few weeks later he started first grade and became absorbed in the interesting new world of his peers.)

"*Bonne chance!*" cried Carmen affectionately, throwing herself for the first and last time into Rudolf's arms. She gave him a wet kiss, her eyes also wet. "Maybe we'll run into each other in Medicine Hat one of these days!"

"Maybe!" echoed Rudolf pleasantly. He found a taxi for them at the pier and helped Carmen and Liane stow their suitcases on the rack above.

For many years, Rudolf kept in his wallet a snapshot of Paul as he had been on that cruise. In it Paul was wearing his little yellow swimsuit with the green fish leaping up one hip. Paul gazed up at the camera with an impatient but tolerant expression. He was eager to be off to the pool with Liane. But his father wanted to document their trip together and so here he stood, tensed on his legs, trying to oblige. The sun had dusted his aloofly arched little nose with a saddle of freckles. The unsmiling, prim little mouth tugged at Rudolf's heart.

"Dad, please. Couldn't you find something a little more up-to-date?" complained Paul when the creased snapshot, its colors slightly faded, fell out of Rudolf's wallet one day when he was lending his son his Mobil card. Paul now drove; Paul also smoked pot, Rudolf knew, and was probably trying other things that Rudolf chose not to know about. He was in his last year of high school and had been accepted by the college of his choice. The college was on the opposite side of the country. As fathers and sons went, Rudolf and Paul had what people now called a "good relationship." Paul took a genuine interest in his father's professional life, never missed a New York performance, and—though he had long ago discouraged Rudolf's attempts to turn him toward a musical career—had worked up a wicked little imitation of his father at the piano; in the opening bars of Liszt's Third Hungarian Rhapsody the son had managed to capture not only the father's romantic musical mannerisms but also some of his pet rhythmic shifts that audiences had come to identify with the Geber style.

Father and son dined out on the nights the mother went to her Yoga classes. Rudolf treasured these nights and did his best to keep them free. Each kept the other up-to-date on what he was thinking and reading and (most of) what he was doing. During one of these dinners, Paul had confided to Rudolf that he had "had sex" with a girl.

"Just before I left Berlin," said Rudolf, "my father took me for a walk and told me the facts of life. 'Whenever you feel the urge,' he said, 'take a cold shower.' Of course I was only twelve. You'll soon be eighteen. The only fatherly advice I give is, never lose the mystery and the wonder of the female."

"That's your romanticism," Paul said, but not unkindly. "Kids see things differently now."

One evening, after their bachelor meal, Rudolf and Paul stopped in at the nearest Sam Goody's. Rudolf checked from time to time to see whether all of his records were in stock. This evening he was just about to get depressed because he found only the one Chopin Nocturnes album—and that marked down for sale—when a soft woman's voice called to him, "Aren't you Rudolf Geber?"

Rudolf looked up to see an attractive, slim girl striding toward him. She wore a denim jacket embroidered with flowers and a fringed suede skirt that enhanced her long, shapely legs.

"I am," he said, rather flattered that his face should be recognizable to a member of the Rock Generation.

"It's Liane. You know, Carmen's daughter. From the ship." The girl thrust her hand into his. She was smiling at him in a dazed, happy way. "Gosh, I can't believe it. I saw you come in and I said, 'No, it can't be!' "

"But why not? We've always lived here," said Rudolf. "And here is Paul, your old shipboard playmate. Paul, you remember Liane."

"Oh yes," said Paul politely. Exactly the way he responded when his father ran into some professional colleague on the street and introduced him.

"You've grown a bit," Liane told him, with an attempt at humor. She gave him a friendly once-over. Paul was still more of an adolescent than a man; he was slightly overweight and pimply and wore his hair in the slack, unwashed ponytail that was de rigueur among his friends. "It's so *great* to see you again," Liane exclaimed, looking back at the debonair father with his rippling reddish-gray hair and his air of benevolent insouciance.

"How is Carmen?" Rudolf asked.

"Mother's dead. She killed herself in Chicago last year," said Liane in a level voice. Something in the way her body stiffened and her chin lifted brought back to Rudolf how when she was twelve he had likened her to a medieval princess, always with the option of her remote kingdom.

"How terrible! Carmen? But she was always so robust and cheerful!"

"She felt she was getting old and losing her looks. And her voice. She wasn't getting many engagements anymore. I came home from work and found her in the bathtub the night she did it." The girl's face lit suddenly with an almost malevolent brilliance as she related this. It seemed to Rudolf that she might burst into hysterical laughter any minute.

"Look," he said, laying a steadying hand on her arm, "come and have a drink with us. Or perhaps you haven't eaten? We have, but we could keep you company."

"Thank you but I can't. I just came on the floor. I work here."

"Then you live in the city now? I suppose you go to school in the daytime?"

"Oh, I finished with school a long time ago," said Liane, cocking her head at Rudolf in a familiar, rather mocking way. "I've worked since I was sixteen. After Mother died, I thought I might as well work somewhere else. She always wanted to live in this city, but we never got here."

"So you're fulfilling her dream," mused Rudolf, touched. "Poor Carmen. Do you have a phone? We'll call you. Maybe you'd like to join us for dinner some evening when you're not working."

"I'm listed under 'Marmalade,'" said Liane. "It's my cat's name."

Rudolf took her hand again. "We'll certainly call. Very soon! And meanwhile, if you should need us for anything, we're listed under my wife's maiden name, Susannah Weiss."

"Oh, yes. Because you're so famous," said the girl.

"Nonsense," said Rudolf. He kissed her hand.

As he and Paul walked home, Rudolf said, "I think you might have been a little more enthusiastic to see Liane. You once adored her. Poor kid! To find her own mother ... well, we'll keep tabs on her. I'd like her to feel she isn't completely alone in the world."

"She's got Marmalade," said Paul.

That night Rudolf dreamed he was beside a lovely lake. On the far side of the lake rose mountains with snow on their peaks. He recognized the place, it was in Switzerland; his parents had taken him there one summer when he was a very small boy, even before he had begun his precocious career, which made it practically another life. Some children were playing in the shallow water. He wanted to join them, to laugh and splash with them, but for some reason could not. Feeling very sad, he looked closer and saw that little Paul was among them, and so was Liane, a very young Liane, even younger than the one who had played with Paul on the ship. In the dream, her hair was the same russet color as Paul's. Then it came to Rudolf that all the children playing there, at least a half-dozen children, were his and that was why he couldn't play: he was already a grown-up man, a father. This seemed unutterably sad. He turned to his wife, to say so. Perhaps if he told her his sorrow, they could reach a new understanding. But in place of his wife stood Liane, the woman Liane, looking at him in the same familiar, rather mocking way as in the record store. And he realized he was married to Liane, the woman Liane, who understood him all too well, and that all these children were theirs.

Rudolf woke in the soft spring darkness of his practice room, which had doubled these past few years as his bedroom. His wife was getting her master's in clinical psychology and liked to stay up till all hours studying in the bedroom they formerly shared. Rudolf's window was open and a slight breeze ruffled the hanging plants; voices rose from the pavement two floors below, energetic, argumentative, then faded, along with the noise of a pair of footsteps.

Rudolf recalled the weird excitement in Liane's face when she described how she had found her mother. *She felt she was getting old and losing her looks. And her voice. She wasn't getting many engagements anymore.* Poor old Carmen. What would she have been now, about fifty? She was only a few years older than himself. Rudolf would soon be forty-eight. Now it seemed to him that he had been unkind to Carmen by not making love to her on that cruise; she had wanted him and he had not been unattracted to her. No one would have been hurt; everyone had assumed they were sleeping together as it was. But at the time he had been more in love with the image of himself as the faithful, long-suffering husband. A few years later, however, the dam had broken, first with the handsome soprano Francesca Stolfi, whom he had accompanied in Boston. He was at a low point at the time: the "new music" was all the rage, and as Rudolf flatly refused to play Schumann with the evenness of a computer, or clank chains across the inside of a piano and groan and howl as part of his performance, he had fewer engagements as a soloist and more as a classical accompanist. Francesca had been dazzling in the *Frauenliebe und -Leben;* it had seemed only fitting to continue their splendid synchronization offstage. After Boston, he had become an accomplished adulterer, dividing his life mercilessly in half. One half conducted the sensual, cold-blooded liaisons in which Rudolf always made it clear from the beginning that he had no intention of leaving his wife; the other half sat lovingly across the table from his growing boy and did not even blink when Paul asked: "Well, Dad, did you have any fun at all on your tour, or was it all work?"

But the dream had changed Rudolf. He woke from it a different man. His carefully separated halves merged and his whole being seemed to be dissolving into a sea of desires and regrets. I suppose this must be middle age, he thought, letting the sweet, dark thoughts wash over him like a warm bath. If so, it's not too awful.

If Liane had been twelve when Paul was six, then she must now be . . . twenty-four?

Several months later, Rudolf stood in the door of his wife's bedroom. "Do you have a minute?"

She gave a curt nod, without looking up. The bed was covered with books and papers. Rudolf moved a large text on abnormal psychology and a Doris Lessing paperback and sat down. His wife's hair was pulled back and tied girlishly with a ribbon. Her face was shiny and intense from intellectual concentration. She looked over the tops of her reading glasses at Rudolf. For a second it seemed she was trying to remember who he was.

"Have you finished all your exams?" Rudolf asked gently.

"Oh yes. I was just making a few notes while the adrenaline is still high. And you, what's new?"

"Well, I think I'd like a divorce."

"I see. What about Paul?"

"He knows nothing. I thought we'd wait till he is safely across the country in his college. Then I could write to him."

"Very thoughtful of you. As usual. Is it anyone I know?"

"She was on that cruise years ago, the one you couldn't go on. She was just a child at the time. She and Paul played together while her mother and I drank together. I was, of course, faithful to you."

"Of course. I knew exactly when you stopped."

"You did?" Rudolf exclaimed. "How?"

"You became even kinder."

"Susannah . . ." Rudolf reached for his wife's hand. He felt like weeping.

She was regarding him calmly, as though he were one of her psychological specimens. "What is she like?"

"She's had a rough life. Always on tour with her mother. Never did learn who her father was. Now her mother is dead—slit her wrists and allowed her daughter to find her in the tub, can you imagine? And do you know, she has never lived in a real house?"

"Poor girl!" cried Susannah with so much feeling that Rudolf was astounded by her objectivity.

"You really understand, don't you?" he asked softly.

"I understand more than you think," she replied.

Dear Paul,

By now you are settled in at your college. Your mother and I were happy to hear you like your roommate. The only roommates I ever had were in the army, that was my college, but I can't tell you how much pleasure it gives me that I who never completed high school can send you to college in style! Savor *everything*, and when you have time, write me your impressions.

Paul, there is something I have to tell you. Your mother and I are getting divorced. For years now we have been just good friends, and we shall of course go on being good friends. This should not affect your happiness or security in any way. You will still have your home to come to, and your mother will be in it. She has a new job, with a testing service, and is enjoying her work. She plans to write you her own letter.

As for me, I shall not be far away. I have bought a small place in the country, within two hours' drive of the city. (You should have seen the poor Steinway being hoisted down, how it trembled, two floors above the pavement—I couldn't watch! But after a good tuning it will be recovered from its trauma and when you come—perhaps for a few days at Christmas?—it will be ready for your inimitable "Geber Impersonation.")

Paul, I hope this won't be too big a shock. Liane and I love each other and will soon marry. She is living in the house already and seems very happy, though Marmalade has not yet adjusted completely. I know this must all seem very strange to you, but always remember one thing: the love a man has for his son is like no other love in the world. It cannot be diminished or replaced by any other love.

Your Father,
Rudolf

Dear Dad,

I have suspected about you and Mom for some time. I have her letter too and you are right, she sounds fine.

The other news was a bit of a surprise but Liane was very nice to me when I was small. I hope you both will be happy together. Do you think I should write her a letter? Or not?

I probably won't get back east for Christmas. Tom has invited me to go to his parents' place in Acapulco and if it's okay with you I'd really like to go.

I dropped the Logic course and had to sign up for two hours of something to replace it, so am taking Introduction to Computers. Things are pretty hectic, will write again soon.

Love,
Paul

Rudolf found it as easy to make Liane happy as he had found it impossible to make his first wife happy. Liane had uncomplicated wants, expressed them in her quiet, cool way, and rewarded him with smiles and caresses when he fulfilled them. She wanted to live in a house with a fence around it, so Rudolf himself built the fence, even though the house sat all by itself in a little clearing in the woods. She wanted to feel she need not go anywhere for months on end, except to the village to shop, so

Rudolf cut down on his touring, except what was necessary to survive. (They didn't need much: Liane was not extravagant, Paul's college had long ago been saved for, and Susannah had accepted the house in New York in lieu of alimony payments.) Occasionally, Liane would consent to fly somewhere with Rudolf for a concert, but she tired easily and always worried about Marmalade, alone at home. Poor kid's been dragged around the world enough, thought Rudolf, and did not press her to go with him when she preferred to remain behind in their little house in the country. She was a real stay-at-home, his Liane: she liked them to dress up for dinner and light candles and sit like some elegant storybook couple at opposite ends of the dining-room table. She liked Rudolf to play Bach for her after dinner (she was not the voracious evening reader that Susannah had been) and she would recline on the sofa and close her eyes and rhythmically stroke the orange cat on her lap; she did not like Rudolf to play any of his emotional pieces or to use too much pedal, because it upset the cat, who would get up and leave the room. She had wanted an old-fashioned high bed with a canopy, and Rudolf had finally tracked one down and had it rebuilt and covered in a material Liane chose. She maintained rather touching standards of formality concerning their night dress and connubial approaches that whetted Rudolf's already romantic temperament. He marveled at his good fortune: to have this slim, affectionate, regal girl with her simple demands, and yet to be embroiled anew each night in her woman's mystery.

Meanwhile Paul, on the far side of the country, was doing well in college, though Rudolf was nonplussed when his son announced he was majoring in computer science.

"But I wouldn't know a computer if I were standing in front of one! Wait, is that it? He wants to go somewhere Dad can't follow. That's only natural. But aren't the computers enough? I don't see why he has to spend all his free time, all his vacations, going on these wilderness treks with that 'Explorer Club.' Testing his manhood, I guess. Of course, when I was his age we had the war. But when I was his age, I spent all my free time running after women. He doesn't even have a girlfriend."

"Not that he writes home about, anyway," said Liane, with a certain look, both amused and protective, she frequently gave her husband.

In the spring of the year Paul was to graduate, Rudolf was invited to go to Japan as part of a cultural exchange program. He would play a series of concerts and consult with Japanese musicians. He was elated by the prospect, and even when Liane begged off, his excitement was not really diminished. Six weeks in Japan, a mysterious country that always had fascinated him! And the timing was splendid. He could fly west to Paul's graduation, spend a few days with the boy, and then proceed to Tokyo. He read up on Japanese art and culture and commuted three times a week to New York to take a businessman's "crash course" in Japanese. "I learned a new language at twelve," he told Liane. "Wouldn't it be something if I could learn another one at fifty-one? The ideographs aren't so difficult, either; and so precise and beautiful. Did you know Japanese sacred music has a male mode, *ryo*, and a female mode, *ritsu*, in its pentatonic scale? I think I am going to love these people. Are you sure you won't change your mind and come?" But he knew she wouldn't. He had lived with her long enough to know what to stop wanting from Liane: she would not travel with him and she would not have children with him. Poor kid! Hadn't had enough of being a child herself. "Never mind, princess, you and Marmalade stay home and water the tomatoes and keep each other company!" He would miss her, but he needed this new adventure. It was just not in his nature to sit for too long inside a fence.

Liane was disoriented for several days after Rudolf left. She stayed close to the house, as she always did when Rudolf went away for a few days or a week. But this time he would be gone for six weeks. He telephoned every night from the Coast. "You should see Paul. What a metamorphosis. Hard as a rock and with a beard like Eric the Red. And everyone wants him: companies in the West, companies in the East, Alaska, Puerto Rico. He speaks the powerful, secret language of FORTRAN and COBOL. How are you? How is Marmalade? How are the tomatoes? Listen, I have a small announcement to make: I love you."

Finally Marmalade ran out of cat food and Liane made herself walk to the village. Rudolf had taken the car to the airport and left it in long-term parking, as Liane still hadn't learned to drive. She walked stiffly, leaning slightly to one side, a result of walking so often with Rudolf's arm around her; she kept close to the edge of the road and did not look up when cars passed. Even in her scuffed sneakers and long-legged jeans, she seemed not really part of the scene. By the time she reached the village and purchased the cat food, she felt victorious. She took the unprecedented step of having a Coke by herself in an open-air café. As she walked uphill, toward home again, huffing and puffing, a woman runner passed her, friendly loose breasts jogging under her T-shirt. I could do that, thought Liane, with sudden daring. It occurred to her, as though she were waking from a dream, that in two years she would be thirty years old.

Several weeks later, Liane, in shorts and a kerchief tied around her hair, came sprinting up their private road and saw a large, shiny car parked outside the house. A sunburned man with a full reddish-gold beard was sitting on one of the porch chaises, Marmalade on his lap. As Liane carefully unlatched the gate, he roared with laughter. "Who do you expect that fence to keep out? The squirrels?"

Liane looked more closely at the man. Gradually she was able to pick out Paul's finely arched nose, the soft dark eyes, the rather prim little rosebud mouth of the boy she had whispered to and taught how to float like a jellyfish.

"But . . . Rudolf's not here" was all she could think to say. "He's in Japan."

"I know. He told me to look in on you if I decided to come east for some interviews. I decided to come east for some interviews. This is a great little hideaway. I was just kidding about the fence."

"No, you weren't," said Liane.

The two of them stared at each other silently.

"Dad didn't tell me you ran," Paul at last said pleasantly. "From the way he talked, I expected to find you up in a tower, combing your hair."

"My hair does need combing," said Liane, suddenly conscious of how she must look—and smell. "Excuse me a second." She hurried through the cool house, which seemed unusually dim, and took a fast shower and put on a dress and brushed her hair. Her skin felt tingly from the running and her heart was beating rapidly.

She returned to the porch. Paul, his eyes closed, was stretched out full-length on the chaise. Marmalade was draped over his shoulder, her face against his neck, purring loudly.

"You've stolen my cat's affections," said Liane, taking in the sun-drenched scene with the orange cat and the orange man.

"Cats are fickle creatures, it didn't take much doing." Paul opened his eyes to slits and gave her a lazy smile.

"I hope you'll stay for supper. Rudolf left the freezer full of nice steaks and things," said Liane. "Also, of course, you're welcome to stay the night. The guest room has been waiting for you for four years. Or there's a daybed in your father's practice room that's quite comfortable. You might feel more at home among his things."

"Thank you," said Paul. "I always carry my sleeping bag with me. But I'll borrow a couple of square feet of your land, if it's okay. And I'll take you out to dinner. Dad says you don't go out enough."

Paul drove them through a night filled with stars. Liane sat hugging her window, like a girl on her first date. "Your car is huge. It's like a living room."

"It's a rental. One of the companies that's interviewing me is paying for it."

"It must be wonderful to be so special at something that everybody wants you," said Liane.

"Everybody is going a bit far."

"No, that's what Rudolf said on the phone. Everybody wants you and your secret language."

"That sounds exactly like my father," Paul said, laughing. "He has a way of turning everything into a romance."

As they drove home after dinner, Paul asked, "Do you remember, Liane, the night our ship started up the fjord to dock in Oslo? You came to my stateroom and woke me because you said it was a sight I would always remember. Well, I always have remembered it. Do you remember that night?"

"I . . . think so. Yes." It all came back to her: The gentle rocking of the ship. The sudden miraculous appearance of the lights against the strange greenish sky that never really went dark. Her mother in that red costume with the black trim. Carmen, of whom she always felt a little ashamed, and the elegant, sociable father of the little Paul. She remembered holding the little figure in his pajamas against her as they looked out the porthole. His neck smelled of sleep and of the sun cream they rubbed on each other all day. It seemed to her that she had, on that long-ago night, put her face against that little neck, parted her lips, and taken the soft flesh gently between her teeth for a minute. Did he remember that, too? She looked out the window of the speeding car. The stars seemed to have moved closer.

That night, for the first time, Liane found the canopied bed suffocating. She wanted air and space. She turned off the air conditioner, pulled up the shade, opened the window. There, real night air. That was better. But still she couldn't sleep. She padded barefoot through the dark house and got herself a glass of milk. From the kitchen window, she could make out the shadow of Paul, swaddled in the sleeping bag, under the big Scotch pine. On top of the shadow that was Paul's was another shadow: the fickle Marmalade, asleep on Paul's shoulder.

Liane went back to her room, pulled the silk comforter to

the floor, and made herself a cocoon by the open window, through which she could see a handful of stars.

Paul's interview was not for two more days. The next day he went running with Liane. He gave her a driving lesson in the big car. They cooked hamburgers and ate a pint of ice cream between them.

"Rudolf worries that you don't have girlfriends," Liane startled herself by saying. She added quickly, "I told him that, well, sons don't tell their fathers everything."

"Especially fathers like Rudolf. He has to be protected, my father and his ideals."

"Ah, you know that, too," said Liane.

When it came time to say goodnight, they hugged each other in a self-conscious attempt at their old shipboard camaraderie. But Paul no longer smelled like a little boy, and Liane no longer felt like a little girl.

Liane woke to a loud, urgent ringing. At first she thought that she was aboard a ship and it was going down. Then she realized she was in her makeshift silk sleeping bag on the floor of the bedroom and the phone was ringing. The luminous hands of the clock said four a.m.

"I am committing an extravagance"—Rudolf's energetic voice came clearly over the wire—"but who can blame me. You sound sleepy. What time is it? . . . Oh, sorry! I counted in the wrong direction. What an extraordinary connection this is, I can hear you breathing! . . . Yes, a marvelous time. I've got to come back here, for longer. I am going to force you to come and see for yourself. We'll hire a sitter for Marmalade if necessary. Or if Paul takes a job in New York, he might . . . What? He is? Oh, good. I told him he should look in on you. Let me speak to him. . . . What? Oh, typical! Well, go wake the outdoorsman. Tell him a man in Japan wants a word with him."

Liane stumbled through the house and out to the Scotch pine. "Paul! Wake up, Paul!" What a deep sleeper he was. She knelt and shook him gently by the shoulders. "Paul, dear, wake up!"

Paul woke up and took her in his arms.

"Paul, your father is on the phone! Rudolf's on the phone."

"He would be!" Paul said. He kissed her long and deeply.

After the call had been completed, Paul led Liane back to the Scotch pine. "Do you know the last thing he said to me? 'You two enjoy each other!' "

"He's so innocent!" cried Liane, a bittersweet joy rising in her veins.

"This will kill him," moaned Paul, covering the trembling Liane with his body under the canopy of stars.

But of course it did not. Rudolf was one of those people born to survive, even cheerfully, their own worst sorrows and to build new lives upon the ruins of their old ones. It took him time to get over it, but get over it he did. When enough time had passed for him to think of it philosophically, he even decided the whole thing had been orchestrated by him, in some subterranean depth of his psyche, so that he might, after all, attain perfect fatherhood. What more perfect gift to a son than being given the chance to depose the father?

Rudolf rose to the occasion and did all the necessary things. Somebody had to do them. He sold the house in the country, got the divorce, arranged for the Steinway to go into storage. Poor Liane could not stop bawling and Paul would not see him at all. Both of them were quite incapacitated by their love and left everything to him.

Not too long after their marriage, Rudolf returned to Japan and embarked on a long love affair with that country of so much beauty and strangeness. He married a Japanese woman of considerable intellect and loveliness and fathered two more children, a girl and a boy. The boy was a prodigy on the violin by the time he was seven, and Rudolf, on tour, was often asked, "Are you any relation to Izumi Geber?"

But Rudolf would always love Paul the best.

Rudolf Geber played an all-Liszt program to a packed house in New Zealand on the eve of the year 2000. Liszt was "in" again; for almost two decades the world had been in the throes of a flagrant Romantic Revival. Rudolf reversed Liszt's innovation of showing one's profile to the audience: he played the "Dante Sonata" and the "Mephisto Waltz" with his back to the audience, so they could see his fingerwork.

"When a man reaches my age, people aren't interested in his face," he joked afterward, under the midnight skies of high summer in that hemisphere, at the supper of iced champagne and trout held in his honor.

During that last quiet interlude of the "Mephisto" before the storm breaks in a torrent of keys, Rudolf had experienced a moment of ecstasy. There it all is . . . the major and the minor . . . the eternal duality of life . . . the secret places . . . the grandeur of the all-imposing pattern, he thought, not entirely sure whether the words came from his brain or his fingers, or exactly what they meant.

Paul and Liane remained married and lived healthy, ordinary lives. They had no children.

Amanuensis

*J*oylessness. Deadness.
Aridity. Everything
coming to a slow, dry stop.

And on another day, after looking out of the window for an hour, she wrote: *The pond is beginning to freeze around the edges. I am beginning to freeze around the edges.*

And on still another (for she forced herself to honor her work schedule of twenty years): *Nothing.*

Then, as though keeping up the show for an invisible audience who gathered outside her study door each morning to listen for the sound of her electric typewriter, she began copying slyly from books. A passage from *Death in Venice.* The first page of an Isak Dinesen tale. Several pages from Bishop Paget's classic study on the sin of acedia. She typed quickly, in a parody of her old inspired rhythm. Then she would pull the sheet of purloined eloquence from the typewriter and squint at it, willing it to give up its secret of confidence, trying to graft onto herself the feeling of entitlement the other writer had felt when composing this page: the priceless feeling of having the *right* to say . . . precisely what one had said.

Then she gave up that pretense, too, and simply shut the door to her study every morning at nine and sat down in front of the cold machine—a stubborn priestess guarding her altar, even though its flame had gone out.

Outside, in the real world, it was deep winter. Six snowfalls lay, one on top of the other. The trees, sheathed in ice, glittered in the cold sun. The leaves of the rhododendrons she had planted were furled tight as little green cigars. And the pond, the real pond as well as the image she had appropriated to describe the condition of her imagination, was frozen hard and thick.

Her name was Constance LeFevre. Through a combination of violent ambition and single-minded dedication to her talent, she had succeeded in imposing that name on the reading world. When still an undergraduate, she had taken her youth and offered it, without a second thought, to the Great God Art. He had accepted it. Then she began to accrue words that led to pages of what she determined would be a memorable first impression: a saga, based vaguely on her own family, Huguenots who had settled in an upstate New York village in the seventeenth century. From the beginning Constance had the knack of keeping one eye on her own soul and the other on the world's soul, and what resulted was a hefty novel of six hundred pages in which the reader was allowed intimate and detailed knowledge of how a family rose to financial and social and moral power, then fell again. A story the world never tires of. The world was pleased. And Constance had also managed to please herself: she had used this book, as she was to use most of her books, to further or balance her inner life. When she was twenty, her most pressing need was to discover who she was; but whereas the ordinary twenty-year-old would have focused unhesitatingly on the navel, Constance hesitated ... for she wanted to be extraordinary ... and then chose to use a panoply of "historical" characters to play out the drama going on in herself, where deep religious impulse warred with an attraction to frivolity, arrogance with self-doubt, a desire to be famous—notoriously famous—with the opposite desire for a private peace. Constance knew very little about her real ancestors, except for the village where they had settled. She went to that village and haunted the local Historical Society, presided over by little old ladies with old names (one of them was also a LeFevre, but from a "better" branch); Constance didn't need much, all she needed was some convincing underpinning for the saga she would build from her imagination's needs. The most memorable characters came not out of the Historical Society's files but out of Constance's head. She labored over it, this first work of hers; she wrote and rewrote; she was a stickler for details. When the "ancestor" who had made the "family fortune" began to build his fine house, Constance sought out a young architect in the village and asked him to go through the crumbling but haughtily proportioned ruin built by one Augustin DePuy in the 1760s and tell her exactly how such a house was constructed, nail by nail, plank by plank, stone by stone. The architect fell in love with Constance's masculine mind and feminine charm. Her saga came out when she was twenty-three and enjoyed exceptional success for a first novel. Movie rights were purchased, enabling Constance to buy the old DePuy ruin and adjoining acreage; and when she returned, frustrated, from Hollywood a year later, after writing the screenplay that would never be needed, she married her architect, who had created out of the old ruin the exact house built by her character in her book.

Her second book was pure fantasy. It was the kind of story her working-class parents (the "fallen" LeFevres) had neither the invention nor the time to tell her when she was a child; it was the kind of story she planned to read to her own child, as soon as it got out of the womb and became old enough to appreciate it.

Her third novel was a disillusioned account of a failed marriage and all its miscarried hopes (metaphor for Constance's lost child). It was a bit downbeat, but it restored her public's faith. They had found the "fantasy" rather cloying and self-congratulatory. This new novel spoke of the dull kind of suffering they themselves underwent daily; it did well, well enough for Constance to cash her royalties in time to purchase a round-the-world-cruise ticket for her thirtieth birthday.

The ship visited twenty-two ports. Constance talked to many passengers and crew and slept with some of them. She kept exhaustive notes. What interested her at this point in her life was the otherness of other people. She wanted to get out of herself—it was too uncomfortable being in oneself—and be able to slip into the bodies and thoughts of others, speak as they spoke, want what they wanted. She wanted to put as much distance between her writing self (which, through all, had functioned splendidly) and the self that cringed with guilt and sorrow.

Her *Ports of Folly* was proclaimed a tour de force: twenty-two people told their stories and confessed their guilts in twenty-two chapters, each labeled with the name of an exotic port. "A modern *Decameron* in which the plague is the twentieth century," wrote one reviewer.

The next few years of Constance's life sped by in a blur of twenty-pound bond sheets with carbon copies. Her love affairs, her night fears, her social life, even her writing life, she fed back into the jaws of Art, often before the experiences registered fully on her own emotions. When at thirty-five she found a dead-white patch lurking beneath the glossy dark hair on the right side of her head, she covered it over hurriedly and sat down at her typewriter and began to compose *Second Thoughts*, a novel about a playwright who wakes up one day and realizes he has fed the entire first half of his life into his art and is completely drained of all memory and feeling. She produced four hundred pages of this novel and then, suddenly sickened by it, put it away in a drawer.

One of the little old ladies in the village's upper-crust Historical Society passed away. Constance was asked to take her place. Her family's ignominious descent into poverty and ordinariness had been redeemed by her own reputation, and newcomers to the village were told by the little old ladies that Constance lived in the imposing stone house of her *other* ancestor, the grand merchant-statesman Augustin DePuy. Constance accepted the invitation to join the Historical Society. Her new duties gave her a deep satisfaction. The very boredom of having to donate one whole afternoon of her life every week to dressing nicely and sitting behind a table with fresh flowers and asking people to be sure to sign the visitors' book appealed to her. It was healthy, traditional, this once-a-week, unselfish foray into community life. But eventually she got restless, especially when a whole afternoon would creak by without a single visitor, and she began to rifle the old records and files, where she pounced one afternoon on the material for a sensational short novel that, if she drove herself, would coincide with the bicentennial. *Kull's Kill* was written in a six-week burst of energy. It related in a cool raconteur's voice the depraved, incestuous story of an eighteenth-century Dutch immigrant and his daughter and was brought out in the spring of the bicentennial. Reporters drove up the Thruway to the little village (which was not so little anymore since the state university had opened a large branch there) and trudged through still-frozen fields to photograph the little *kill*, or stream, where poor "Kitty Kull" in sadistic mirth had induced her father-lover to bash her head in; then they went down to the Historical Society and photographed the author in pre-Revolutionary costume and frilly white cap sitting demurely behind the desk and extending the visitors' book. Afterward they went through the files—which were, after all, open to the public—and Xeroxed the old document that revealed the *true* name of "Johannes Kull." When *Kull's Kill* became a best-seller (Constance's first), a magazine did a feature on the historical-novel boom: across from a close-up of Constance was a little inset of Jonas Kip's hair-raising confession, preserved in the photostated diary of the judge who had sentenced him to be hanged. The little old lady who was a direct descendant of the unfortunate Kip bore up stoically; she did not, as several other Society members did, cut Constance dead in the supermarket. Constance resigned from the Society, pleading pressing engagements, before they could ask her to quit. She felt a bit queasy about the whole thing, as if she had soiled her own nest. If only she hadn't been so desperate to get another novel out, before her public forgot her! Now her public loved her more than ever, whereas she despised it a little, for having granted to her most vulgar work the popularity she had so long craved. Could it be that, for almost twenty years, she had been courting with all the wiles of her sensitivity a lover with a heavy, insensitive soul?

As soon as the Old Guard dropped Constance, the new local branch of the state university picked her up. She had snubbed its English Department when, several years before, it had approached her about teaching a Creative Writing Seminar. (Was she, Constance LeFevre, expected to appear in a catalogue that listed such "courses" as "Human Relations" and "Oral Communications" as fully accredited academic subjects?!) But now her pride was assuaged when she was invited to give the annual Rose Verplanck Memorial Lecture to the Humanities Department. She worked hard on her lecture and even drove down to New York and bought a new dress for the occasion.

A by-product of Constance's lecture was her brief affair with an associate professor in the English Department named Alan Insel. Almost as soon as she was fully into it, she realized her error in judgment. But then it took her several months to get out of it again because he had made himself so indispensable to her comforts and her vanity. Insel was an affable sort of failure who had managed to erect a civilized edifice around his shortcomings. He courted Constance with formal deference. He let her know that he *knew* her financial and professional successes were far, far above *his*. He had tried and tried to get his novels published, he told her, in an amused tone of voice, as though laughing at himself, but he just hadn't been as lucky in his subject matter as she, and also, he didn't have her *technique*. But still, he let her know, there were a few points of good living he might be able to share with her, a few serendipitous delicacies she might, in her single-minded pursuit of her craft, have overlooked. He drove her, as if she were a princess, across the bridge in his renovated old brown Jaguar and bought her violets from a greenhouse in January; he always had tickets for interesting productions of rare Ibsen or Pirandello; he belonged to a local vineyard cooperative, and his wine bottles bore his own signature in gold on their pretty labels; he told her she was burning the wrong woods in her massive stone fireplace and arranged with his "man" to deliver two cords of the proper ones in early spring, "so the logs will have the whole summer to season." He liked words like *season* and *subtle* and *sensual*. When they went to bed together, he made it a point of honor never to be obvious or predictable. She never knew quite what he was going to do, but the result was ... inevitably ... satisfactory in a languid, *soothing* way. She could let herself go with him precisely because he didn't matter, but also there was something rather demonic and awful about the way his pale and oddly heavy limbs engulfed her and serviced her while his thin, satiric face gleamed at her in a curious, cold complicity.

And then, abruptly, she woke up beside him in her own bed one early spring morning and knew she loathed him and couldn't wait to get him out of the house. She felt guilty, but guilty in the way one feels guilty when about to discommode some clinging slug that has managed to attach itself to one's arm or leg. She allowed him to make their breakfast—he was an eggs Benedict and Bloody Mary man—and, cringing from him more by the minute, she sat across from him in Augustin DePuy's rustic-beamed old kitchen, whose tiny windows her architect/ex-husband had enlarged to let the morning sun in, and she allowed Insel to go on, one last time, in his snug "lecturing" voice, about how she, Constance, had been "lucky in her subject matter" and had mastered her "technique." "Now, if I had your *technique,*" he said, licking a tiny drop of egg yolk from where it had fallen on his finger, "I'd be able to fly us both to Aruba ... did you see that marvelous color ad in the last *New Yorker*, the one with the Updike story ... now, *his* technique ..." And Constance, steeling herself for the strike, told him she had already been to Aruba—it was, if he recalled, the first port of call in her *Ports of Folly*. "But I must correct you, Alan, on one point," she went on, her voice dropping to a dangerous earnestness. "When you talk about technique, I think you are confusing it with talent. The two are not the same."

Several days later he sent her, inside an envelope, a postcard of Gustav Klimt's *The Kiss*. "All relationships need their breathing spells," he had typed neatly on the back. "Perhaps you ought to call me when you feel ready to see me again." At least he was tactful. He had let her off the hook and preserved his own pride in the bargain. Once or twice in the next few weeks she was tempted to call him, when she felt like sharing the leisurely courses of a gourmet meal ... or when she felt in need of oblivion, combined with caresses and flattery. I am too isolated, she told herself, I need to get out more; I would never have stooped to this "relationship"—how I loathe that word— had I not been too long alone all those months I was trying to write that wretched novel about the playwright who offered his youth to Art. And then, on top of that, when the old ladies snubbed me, that hurt, too; being loved and accepted by individual, discerning people in my everyday orbit is important to me; some dumb, anonymous mass that manifests itself in numbers of copies sold is not enough. No, I was at a particularly vulnerable juncture in my life when I took up with Associate Professor Insel, with his talk of "technique." Of course, I wasn't writing. A nonwriting Constance LeFevre is a damned Constance Le-Fevre, and Alan Insel was my Satan Incarnate.

And then, providentially, the State Department invited Constance to go to South America for the entire month of May. They made up a killing itinerary for her—she was to speak on "Current Fiction in the United States" in fourteen cities—and she accepted with alacrity. The trip proved exhausting, not only physically but in a curious spiritual way as well, and Constance returned feeling old and rather knocked out by life, to her Dutch-and-Huguenot-settled village in early June. Sifting through the big cardboard box of mail the post office had saved for her, she plucked out a brief, urbane note from Insel, saying that he had tried to phone her to say good-bye before he left to spend the summer in Greece.

Good riddance! thought Constance, and now I must really get back to what matters. It had been over a year since *Kull's Kill* had been published and, except for a few desultory short stories, the kind she could write with the upper half of her mind, she had not been able to get into anything that lodged at the center of her inner necessities.

She completely forgot Alan Insel.

She withdrew into herself all through that summer and into the autumn and early winter; she saw no one except for a harmless old college friend who came to visit but spent most of her time commuting to New York City for trysts with a married man. After some false starts, Constance got out all her South American notes and the State Department itineraries and began a novel about a successful American businesswoman destined to have a breakdown in Brazil. At first it went splendidly; she clocked herself at ten-page intervals and scribbled calculations: if she kept up this momentum she would be done with the book by spring! The more she thought about it, the more the idea of this novel pleased her: it was exactly right for where she was, both professionally and psychologically; it would be big and realistic and modern, to counterbalance the dark little romance of *Kull's Kill* in her public's eye; and it would be a way of averting her own "midlife crisis" (hateful term!) by foisting it more profitably on an interesting, high-powered woman character. Much more satisfactory than dealing at one remove from her sex with that tiresome male playwright character. The business angle of her new novel fascinated her. She had not done so much research since her Huguenot saga ... could that really have been twenty years ago? She read up on multinationals, subscribed to three financial magazines, and sat down happily on the floor every Sunday and clipped articles from the *Times* Business Section, which formerly she had dropped, along with Sports, in the wire trash bin outside the village drugstore, to keep from weighing her bicycle down.

And then, mysteriously, without any warning, her novel died on her. She knew the signs: the sickening reluctance to begin in the mornings; the dull, heavy joylessness that spread like a greasy film over the world; the feeling that some connection had been severed between herself and the book. It was irrevocable, she knew. She had not been so sad since she had miscarried ... could that have been fifteen years ago?

She mourned the book. She sat in her study and gazed blankly out at a world growing more still and frozen by the day and wondered, without much interest or emotion, what would happen to her next. A few days would go by and then she would be granted a flicker of false hope: where was her courage? She must just start something new—perhaps a story, something quickly finished, to give her back her confidence. Just type a sentence into the machine, see where it led, make a story from it (after all, she was Constance LeFevre, who had made her name from storytelling). "Once there was a spy," she typed, "who did not think of himself as a spy, but simply as a boy who had lost his parents and was good with languages. . . ."

And that was the end of that. Then came the short, despairing, journal-type ejaculations. And then the copying from the works of others. And then a silent Constance tending her cold altar of a typewriter, whose mechanical carriage had gone sluggish after not being turned on in weeks. Constance, barred from her Art; which returns us to the deep-winter morning on which this tale began.

Someone was knocking at the front door. The only people who used Constance's front door were the Jehovah's Witness lady with her little retarded girl and the United Parcel man bringing another bound galley of another first novel with the respectful editor's note clipped to the cover: "Just a few words from you would be of inestimable . . ."

Nonetheless, at the sound of that knock Constance sprang from her typing chair with shameful relief.

It was a young girl, slim and pretty in a piquant sort of way, with a pert face that looked like an acorn under the brown knitted cap pulled down over her ears. She wore a ratty full-length fox fur that must have been some woman's pride and joy in the 1930s, and heavy, round-toed boots like a man's.

"Yes?" said Constance. She saw a dilapidated old car parked in her circular drive.

"I was wondering if I could speak with you for a minute," said the girl, giving Constance a sudden, disarming smile. "I'm not selling anything, I promise. I'm . . . well . . . I'm offering something for free."

"Would you like to come in?" Constance could tell from the smile that the girl thought highly of herself, that she was more often asked into places than not, and that even if Constance had turned her away she would have gone on thinking highly of herself.

"Thank you," the girl said, bestowing another smile on Constance. She had small, sturdy white teeth with little spaces between them. She thrust her cold, firm hand into Constance's as she gave her big boots one last stomp on the doormat. "My name is Jesse Newbold."

"How do you do," said Constance, already impressed by the girl's precise, confident manner. She closed the door on the cold. "Mine is Constance LeFevre."

"Oh, I know who *you* are," said Jesse solemnly. "That's why I finally got up my courage to come over here. Wow, is that some fireplace!"

"The house is over two hundred years old. It's all been done over, of course. It was a ruin when we . . . I . . . Won't you sit down?" Constance sat down first on the roomy sofa and patted a place beside her. How nice this room is, she thought. Her glance passed with fresh appreciation over the massive dark-stained beams, the walls of creamy yellow, the framed drawings and old maps, the ceiling-high shelves crammed with books. It had been weeks since she had sat in this room. The impatiens plant, she noticed, had a whole sheaf of new pink buds. "Now, do tell me what it is you're offering me."

"Well," said Jesse, sitting erectly on the edge of the sofa and shrugging halfway out of the shabby fox coat, "I'm offering myself."

Under the coat she wore a long blue cotton dress sprigged with white flowers. She raised her eyes, which were the same blue as the dress, to meet Constance's puzzled look. Then, as if taking the lid off her proffered gift package, she snatched away her knitted cap. Two short brown-gold clumps of young hair fell neatly to either side of her innocent yet artful face. For a third time, Constance received the charming smile.

"But . . . I don't understand," said Constance. "You mean as a cleaning girl, or what?" She had tried several girls from the college in this capacity, but they had never worked out.

"Cleaning, if you want. Cooking, typing, fending off fans, answering letters—whatever you need. I have come to offer myself as your amanuensis," said Jesse, putting a musical lilt into the old-fashioned word. "And I wouldn't charge a penny!"

"But why?" asked Constance, who was a firm believer in the adage *nobody gets something for nothing*. "I mean, what would you get out of it?"

"Everything!" the girl exclaimed passionately, and Constance was reminded poignantly of her own younger self and how fiercely that self had wanted things. "I'll get to see how you work, how you live. . . . I'll have the satisfaction of knowing I'm freeing you from having to deal with . . . the stuff you've earned the right, through your talent, not to *have* to deal with!"

This part was probably rehearsed, thought Constance.

"Do you . . . um . . . write, yourself?" she asked, feeling depressed at the possibility that this persuasive, charming creature might write terrible prose.

"Oh, I know, I know what you're thinking," said Jesse, massaging the wool cap in her hands. "But you needn't worry, Miss LeFevre. If you'll just give me a chance, I promise you'll never be burdened by *my* paltry efforts. I've come here to relieve your burdens, not add to them."

"But . . . I don't know, Jesse . . . and please call me Constance . . . I really don't know if there's enough for you to do. Since I lost my last maid, I just run a dustcloth over things once a week, when I water the plants. . . . I've never been obsessive about housekeeping . . . how many hours a week did you have in mind?"

"As many or as few as you need," explained the smiling girl. "Let me explain. You see, I'm only taking one course this semester, Earth Science. I have to have one science course before I can transfer . . . I want to transfer to another college. . . . I've got all I can get from these people here. And . . . well . . . I hate wasting time, and since I think you're a great writer and that's what I want to be eventually, how could I spend my time any better than being around you, seeing how you do it? I don't mean I'd be snooping over your shoulder or anything, but I could sort of observe your rhythms, maybe pick up some of your discipline by osmosis."

"I couldn't possibly let you work for nothing," Constance said, "I'd feel so guilty about exploiting you, *I* couldn't work." As soon as she pronounced this lie about her own "work," the impotence of her predicament hit her anew with the force of a physical blow. She found herself dreading the moment her bright visitor would get up to go. "I would insist on paying you," she added severely. As an incentive, she added, "In cash, of course. So there wouldn't be any income tax problem."

"I'll accept whatever you say," replied Jesse. "You can make all the rules. That's the point, too, you know. I can see what rules you *will* make and be educated by that, too. I will get to observe at close hand the mental processes of a successful woman."

Constance waved this last effusion aside. "Shall we say three-fifty an hour, starting tomorrow? Come about this time? I like to have the first hours of the morning for my—" She made a gesture with her hand, rather than pronounce the lie again.

Engagingly, the girl caught Constance's hand and pressed it warmly in both of hers. "I'm thrilled!" she cried.

They smiled at each other with the joy of mutual discovery.

"By the way," said Constance, "how old are you?"

"Almost twenty," said Jesse.

"Ah, twenty was when it all began for me," said Constance with a sigh.

Constance spent the rest of that day walking around her house, seeing her life as the girl—Jesse—must see it. From the girl's view, it must look enviable. She turned over certain of Jesse's phrases with the relish she remembered from certain of her rave reviews.

That evening, Constance rearranged her study. On one table she put all her unanswered mail: the many magazines and journals still in their brown wrappers, the piles of bound galley proofs of other people's novels, with the respectful editors' notes clipped to the covers . . . yes, anyone could see from that table that Constance LeFevre was in demand. Yet, over the last frozen months, it had been all she could do to weed out the bills from the mass of correspondence and make sure they were paid on time.

She took a fresh manila file folder and wrote in large Magic Marker letters on the front: WORK IN PROGRESS, though she had never done such a thing before in her life. She put the folder, with a dozen or so sheets of yellow paper inside, to the left of her typewriter.

Then she turned on the machine and sat in front of it for a while, listening to its hum, smiling bemusedly at her lamplit reflection on the dark glass of the windowpane.

The girl was, as ladies are fond of saying about their good servants, "a gem." Not that Jesse was a mere "servant." Rather, she made you go back and reexamine the nobler uses of the verb *to serve*. Jesse served Constance. Not only that, she had the tact of one's own shadow. She fitted her movements to Constance's; Constance had been often annoyed by cleaning girls and women for no other reason than that they impinged on her space. Jesse had arrived promptly at ten-thirty on her first day. Constance heard the old car drive up, but it had been agreed the day before that Jesse would let herself in. With an uplifted mood, Constance, in her study, heard the girl take off the heavy boots and begin padding softly about the downstairs rooms. The spraying of furniture polish. The thud-*thump*, thud-*thump* of the sponge mop. Constance, in a burst of greeting, had let loose a barrage of sentences on her spy story, which she had resumed in order to pretend she was writing something. Thus the morning passed . . . thud-*thump* from downstairs . . . an answering *rackety-rackety-rack* from upstairs: like a dialogue between them.

At a little past noon, delicious lunch odors wafted upstairs.

"How did you know I adore mushroom soup?" Constance called, coming downstairs. "Mmm! Is that grilled cheese?"

"The soup was in your cabinet," said Jesse, turning to smile at Constance from her station at the stove. Today she wore a long dress of a modest squirrel-gray, with tiny pearl buttons all the way down the front, and one of Constance's old aprons tied tightly around her small waist. "And I always treat myself to a grilled-cheese sandwich when I'm in the midst of exams."

The table was laid with an indigo cloth Constance had forgotten she had. In a bud vase, Jesse had placed a cutting of the blooming impatiens. The vivid splash of fuchsia against the deep blue cloth gave Constance pleasure. "But the table's only set for one, Jesse, aren't you having anything?"

"Oh, I can get something for myself later. I thought you might like to be alone with your thoughts."

"I'd much rather eat with you," said Constance.

"In that case," replied Jesse, her pert face coloring slightly with embarrassment or delight (Constance wasn't sure which), "I'd love to."

"Are your parents alive?" Constance asked delicately, when they were having their soup. She was dying to find out more about her amanuensis.

"Yes, but they've been divorced ever since I can remember. I've always lived with my mother. She works for a dental surgeon in Queens. She's not a very happy person. My father conducts these archaeological digs. For amateurs. You've probably heard of them. Not that *he's* an amateur. He just likes to be out in the field any way he can." Jesse volunteered all this smoothly, rather glibly, as though she'd come to terms with her parents ages ago.

"And do you see much of your father?"

"Not too much," said Jesse, spooning her soup thoughtfully. "Once in a while. But we get along. He lives with someone not much older than me. She and I get along okay. Would you like more mushroom soup?"

Constance watched the girl's lithe gray-clad figure at the stove. I am old enough to be her mother, she thought. What would it have been like, to have had her all these years? Would I be what I am? Would she be as she is? Would she say, when discussing me with others, "She's not a very happy person"?

The two women soon settled into a routine. Jesse came, for five hours, on Mondays, Wednesdays, and Fridays. (Tuesdays and Thursdays were Earth Science days.) She cleaned a bit and prepared lunch. The lunches were always simple but comforting, the sort of food children might fix if the meals were left to them—sardines on toast; canned soups; bacon, lettuce, and tomato sandwiches—but Constance had not enjoyed her food so much in months. After lunch, they went to Constance's study and tackled the correspondence. Constance had been an antisocial "author" in the past, throwing in the wastebasket anything that did not directly further her career. Now, for Jesse's benefit, she found herself filling in the ballots for PEN elections, answering the questionnaires the Author's Guild was always sending about contracts, reprint rights, and so on; she dictated a brief but individual reply to every fan letter, every request to speak or teach at a college. When the correspondence table began to look threateningly bare, Constance resorted to the stacks of bound galleys of other people's novels. The publication dates had already come and gone for many of them. Of the ones still to come, Constance made two piles: the "trashy at a glance" and the "possible." For the "trashy at a glance," she dictated caustic or amusing notes designed either to instruct Jesse that one couldn't be too careful about one's integrity or simply to make the girl snort with laughter. She decided to test her protégée's budding literary acumen on the "possible" ones.

"I just don't have time to read these," she told Jesse. "Why not take one or two of these *deserving*-looking ones home with you. No big deal. Skim through them if you feel like it, scribble something if they strike a chord."

The poor girl turned pale when Constance suggested this. But then she squared her shoulders and said she'd try. Off went the galleys, under the arm of her ratty fox coat, at the end of the day; they were returned in two days' time with neatly typed notes stapled to their covers. A bit labored, thought Constance. Of course she was trying to impress me. To please Jesse, she selected the least pretentious of the girl's critiques, changed a few adjectives, and told Jesse to send it off to the publisher over the

signature of Constance LeFevre. The girl seemed mildly surprised, though not as flattered as Constance would have hoped.
My pretty little acorn is not an easy nut to crack, thought Constance, her curiosity piqued more each day by Jesse Newbold.

In mid-February, Constance came down with the flu. As soon as
she complained of sore throat and feverishness, Jesse made her
take her temperature. 102°. "Why don't I sleep over for a few
days," suggested Jesse. "You go to bed and pamper yourself."

"Dear child, you can't devote your life to me," protested
Constance weakly, though the idea appealed to her.

"Who said anything about life? I'll just go and pick up a
few things from my place. It'll be fun for me to sleep in a two-
hundred-year-old house."

Thus Constance abandoned herself to the process of her illness. She lay under her satin comforter and felt helpless and
cherished. Jesse made tea and soup, lowered the shades, raised
them again, ran up and down the stairs bringing Constance
books she asked for. Then off the girl would go, to her Earth Science lab, to the supermarket for more cans of soup, to the drugstore for more throat lozenges and Kleenex, and Constance
would lie watching the light change outside the window. Already the darkness was that of very early spring, not winter
darkness anymore. In one of the panes of glass was a tiny crack
that winked like a diamond. Constance lay with a book propped
open on her knees, not reading but listening to the silence, waiting for the rattling sound of the old car churning its way back up
the icy drive. Her thoughts—perhaps colored by her fever—
turned to her old age and eventual death. Was there any sort of
afterlife of the consciousness, or did you live on only through
the minds of others? What others? Would any of her books out-
live her? Which ones? She imagined herself leaving this house to
Jesse in her will. She envisioned an elegant little memoir, published some years after her death, in which Jesse, by then an old
lady herself, would tell what it had been like to live with Constance LeFevre on a day-to-day basis. She only hoped Jesse

could write well enough to do justice to the material. So far, except for the "book reports," Constance had seen none of Jesse's writing. But then, the girl had vowed not to burden her with any "paltry efforts."

"You'd make a great nurse, Jesse," said Constance, who by this time was merely luxuriating in sniffles. "That is, if you didn't want to be a writer. Speaking of which . . . don't you think it's time you showed me something? You must let me help you if I can. Turnabout's fair play." For Jesse had refused, absolutely, to accept one penny for nursing Constance.

"I . . . I don't really have anything ready at the moment," stammered the girl.

"Well," pursued Constance, "show me something that's not. Maybe something you're having problems with."

"I'll see what I can come up with," said Jesse, after going very quiet for several minutes.

That night Constance dreamed Jesse was in her room, down at the other end of the hall, writing a story for her. The girl's pen scratched louder and louder, and Constance's sleep grew troubled. So abrasive! What was Jesse writing on? It sounded like a sharp instrument scratching on stone.

Constance woke up. She could still hear the repetitive scratching . . . only, it was coming from outside. She got out of bed and went to the window and pulled back the shade. A full moon gave the snowy landscape an eerie daylight quality. The amanuensis was skating on the frozen pond. Round and round, shoulders hunched forward, hands clasped behind her back. Constance could not make out her face under the knitted cap, but there was an intensity to her skating, as if she were working out her thoughts in the rhythm of it. I'd give anything to know what she is thinking, Constance thought. For one degrading moment, she was tempted to whisk down the hall to Jesse's room and go through her things. Maybe she kept a journal. Constance's heart pounded guiltily as a culprit's. No, that's not fair, she decided, perhaps she'll let me in on her life through the story she's promised to bring me. Constance went back to bed and sat in the dark, her hands laced tightly together, listening to the girl's skates cut and recut into the frozen pond.

Alas, the story Jesse brought was a disappointment. Although competently written, even with skill in places, it was weary and flat. It was about an older man, alone in some tropical climate, self-importantly reviewing his past. Also it seemed he had lost a woman, though Constance wasn't sure whether she had left him or died. Oh, poor girl, thought Constance. But I asked for it and now I must be encouraging and also very, very careful. The man is undoubtedly Jesse's attempt to "get into" her father, the distant archaeologist; she's dispensed with the father's girlfriend, I see. Besides . . . Jesse is only twenty . . . I don't want to nip any later-blooming talent in the bud. Just because I was such a ruthless, early-blooming little go-getter . . . and yet, never once in my young nights did I skate on a frozen pond in the moonlight.

"Jesse, I think it's terribly brave of you to write a story from the point of view of a man . . . and a person of an older generation, as well."

"You do?"

"Yes. And the prose is tight. Well, usually. You probably worked hard on this."

The girl blushed.

"It's an arduous business we've chosen, Jesse. I once spent four hundred pages trying to raise a character from the dead, and failed. What I'm trying to say, my dear, is—" Constance stopped. The girl's face was working in a woeful, rubbery attempt to keep back tears.

"Please," whispered Jesse, "don't call me 'dear.' "

"I'm sorry. But I didn't mean it as an affectation. You are dear to me." Now it was Constance's turn to blush.

"I'm nothing," said Jesse between her teeth, her eyes brimming. "I'm a piece of shit."

"But, Jesse, the story isn't that bad. My God, you're just

beginning. And it has a certain"—she groped for a word and found only the hated evasion Insel had used—"it has a certain tech*nique.* . . ."

"Oh, I don't give a damn about the story!" shrieked Jesse. She dashed out of Constance's study, sobbing. Constance listened to her running down the hall to her room. The door slammed. Constance realized with a strange lift of heart that if Jesse were her own daughter they might be having a scene just like this. I don't give a damn about the story, either, thought Constance. I give a damn about *her.*

At the beginning of March, Jesse insisted on moving back to her own place. "I'll miss having you in the house," Constance told her, trying to be brave, "but of course you must have your own life. I'll be all the more glad to see you on Monday, Wednesday, and Friday. And who knows, maybe next year ... I've been thinking ... if I knew I had someone responsible to stay in the house, I might travel a bit. I've decided I don't really get out enough."

"My plans are so uncertain," murmured the girl.

"Yes, I know. You said you might transfer. But if your new college is in easy distance, you might like to come here for weekends, or for the long vacations. You don't have to decide now. I just want you to know it's an option."

"You're great," said Jesse, but rather dispiritedly, Constance thought.

Since the day of the outburst, neither of them had mentioned the story again. Jesse arrived at the house promptly on her three working days, worked as well as, or even better than, before. Her demeanor had become more subdued and the little acorn face did not smile so readily, but she treated Constance in a new and tender way, with even more attentiveness than when she had had the flu: she asked Constance's advice about her clothes, about books she ought to read; she bought Constance a red carnation and put it in a vase in her study. One afternoon

Constance had to go to the dentist in a sleet storm; when she arrived home, she found a blazing fire in a big stone fireplace and Jesse had stayed late to prepare an "English tea" for them both. It was as if, thought Constance in bed one night, the tears springing to her eyes, the girl were making amends through these extra attentions for her lack of talent.

It was the end of March. The snow still lay on the ground, but there were hopeful patches of raw earth. Constance, up in her study, was feeling good. She could hear the drip, drip of melting snow from the gutters outside, and from downstairs were beginning to emanate the signs of one of Jesse's comforting lunches. How nice *just being* is, thought Constance, listening to the girl clattering about in the kitchen. She responded via her typewriter with some clatter of her own, to keep up the dialogue. For, although the "spy story" was by this time quite long, Constance knew it was not a real story: it was to convince Jesse that she was upstairs plying her Art; it was to give Jesse her reason for being *downstairs*.

A door slammed. A car started up. What had the girl forgotten this time? The child might not be the world's next Jane Austen, but she was a perfectionist when it came to her luncheon productions. Once before, she had rushed out at the last minute to purchase capers.

Constance decided to sneak down and see what was cooking. The table was covered with a clean cloth. In a small porcelain vase was the year's first crocus. On Constance's plate—she had already noticed with alarm that the table was set for one—was an envelope.

Constance picked up the knife beside her plate and slit open the envelope.

"Dear Constance," it said (it was the first time she had seen the girl's handwriting, wobbly and uneven like a much younger person's), "Clam chowder on LOW. Bologna sandwich in fridge. I can't keep this up anymore. You are a really good lady and I can't take any more advantage of you. Please don't try to find me, you have better things to do with your time, and besides, you won't. There is no 'Jesse Newbold.' "

She had first tried to sign herself "Your Amanuensis," but after several spelling mistakes settled for "Your Friend."

Nevertheless, Constance did try to find her. She went to all three instructors of the six sections of Earth Science at the college and described Jesse's appearance and her clothes. "You don't know her name?" they asked, wondering what this harassed woman was up to. "If you'd let me see your class lists, perhaps I could recognize it." Constance pored over girls' names on computer printouts, pouncing on the smallest clue. "How about this Jane Newburg?" she said excitedly. "No, Janie's a special student. She comes in a wheelchair."

Constance made a nuisance of herself at the registrar's office: more lists of names; Constance finally confiding in the registrar. "You might try the police," said the woman, "but otherwise . . . well, frankly, you have so little to go on. Do you know how many students drop in and out of school these days like a country club? Your young secretary may be in California by now."

Constance phoned her researcher, a young man in New York who sometimes looked up things in the library for her; she asked him to call the offices of all the dental surgeons in Queens and find out if any woman who worked for them had a daughter of about twenty enrolled in this branch of the state university. But after a few days, he phoned back and said a lot of the women were suspicious and wouldn't answer until they knew why he was calling. "They're perfectly right," said Constance, suddenly seeing it from their side, and she told the young man to drop the research and how much did she owe him.

Please don't try to find me, you have better things to do with your time, and besides, you won't.

"Okay, Jesse, you win," said Constance aloud, pacing the rooms of the big old house, finding something in every room that reminded her of her vanished amanuensis. "You came out of nowhere and now you've gone back into it again." She stood looking at the bed, which Jesse herself had stripped down to the mattress, then covered neatly with a spread, when she had vacated the room. "You were a gift, and one has no right to report a vanished gift to the police."

The house began to seem like a mausoleum to her. She saw the years stretch out before her; she squinted at herself in the mirror and saw how she would be ten years from now, twenty, thirty. She saw herself as an old woman, dying alone in this house.

She telephoned her architect ex-husband, who had remarried and was living in the next village over. When they split up, she promised him she would let him know before she ever put this house on the market.

He came by that afternoon, bringing with him his small son, who was a little afraid of Constance. He had aged well, her former husband: a slim, wiry man with shaggy gray hair and, behind his steel-rimmed spectacles, a look of earnest absorption, as though he were making a constant effort to work out a floor plan of the world. Now that he belonged safely to another woman, Constance found him attractive again.

"You really mean to sell?" he asked. "Somehow I pictured you hanging on here to the very end."

"Thank you." Constance laughed dryly. "I've just pictured it myself and it's that fate I want to avoid."

"But where will you go? Donny, please don't play with those fire tongs."

"I have decided," announced Constance with significance, "to go *out*."

"Out," he echoed testily, as he had done frequently during their marriage, playing back to Constance the last words of her more ambiguous statements.

"I mean out into the world. Just to live in it. With no ulterior motive. Let things and people come and go on their own terms, without my interference, and see where they'll go *to*. I've decided to give myself a sabbatical from achievement."

"But won't you need a home to come back to when your 'sabbatical' is over?" he asked with genial concern.

"This has stopped being my home. It's more like an imposing shell that has begun to cut off my sensations and my oxygen. If you don't want to buy it, I guess I'll put it on the market."

"I always did love this house. You know that. Some of my best ideas went into this house."

"And your wife? Would she live here?"

"Would she! It's been the one bone of contention between us. How I was too soft and didn't fight you for it."

"Your softness is becoming to you," said Constance. "In fact, I think I'm going to develop *my* softness."

"Oh, Con." He laughed, with his old husband's-knowledge of her. "You say that with such *ambition*."

Constance invested most of the house-money in securities she had learned about during her research for the aborted business-woman-novel. She banked the rest, and bought a yellow Land-Rover, some camping supplies, and traveler's checks, and she set off, with the tremulousness of a young girl, to see what was happening when she didn't interfere. She wanted to catch the outside world off-guard before it froze into her own willed conception of it. She had many adventures, some disappointments, and a few scares. Through it all, she desisted grimly from taking a single note. The active, nomadic life toughened her body and detached her mind—for a while. Then she felt she had proved her point. She felt restless to make up her own world again. Her year had made her more sensitive to the great ebbs and flows of existence: she resolved to take similar excursions in future, whenever she began to feel frozen or stale; but now, she couldn't wait to put all her fresh impressions into a huge new fiction.

She settled down, this time in a city whose energies kept pace with her own, and began to write again. The juices flowed; crosscurrents sizzled on connection; her vitality had regenerated itself. Could that have been she, poor dried-up husk rattling around in that big old house, cringing prematurely at the prospect of her own death?

It was perfectly clear now: Jesse Newbold, whatever her real name or real purpose, had been Constance's angel of release.

And Constance persisted in believing this, even after the mystery was cleared up. One day she received the bound galleys of a small novel. "Mr. Alan Insel has asked us to send you what we consider a striking first novel," wrote the editor of a second-rate publishing house. "Any comment you would care to give would be of inestimable . . ."

The novel was called *The Amanuensis.*

Constance read the novel. She recognized many things. She recognized the contents of her former medicine cabinet and wastebasket. She recognized the menus. She recognized certain conversations in which her remarks were exaggerated to seem calculating or high-flown. Certain habits and gestures of hers were spotlit in a morbid, obsessive glare. She recognized in the omniscient narrator's weary, self-satisfied voice the same voice in the bad story she had once believed Jesse to have written. She did not recognize the Lesbian encounter in which the lonely and grasping woman writer, in bed with the flu, seduces the reluctant young girl—who has taken this job, secretly, only as an "independent study" with an English professor who was cruelly spurned by the woman after he had been given cause to hope. The professor has decided to teach the woman a lesson in unrequited love.

After the girl mysteriously disappears, the woman is distraught and finally kills herself.

Ah, it was a "striking" novel, all right—but not in the sense of "technique."

When Constance had finished the book, she sat for a long time with her hands folded on her lap. He should have left himself out, she thought; it would have been a much better story if he had left himself and *his* motives out altogether. The story is the girl and the woman: all the necessary reflections and reverberations are contained within *them*. All this clutter about his broken heart and his "revenge" and about how the girl is practically illiterate but needs the one English credit to pass out of two years of college to become an airline stewardess ... that lowers the story to ... just an embarrassing personal reality. If an artist had shaped and refined this material—ah, what he might have made of it. Pity I didn't do it myself. Well, maybe I will someday. Life is long.

And also the woman shouldn't have killed herself: it's much harder to make people live.

She amused herself composing witty and malicious "blurbs" to send to Mr. Insel's editor. She even, for a minute, saw herself suing Insel, but of course that might be exactly what he was hoping for: the advance publicity. So, through herself and through Jesse, he had finally hit on a "lucky subject" and managed to get published.

In the end she opted for silence. Let his impoverished production have its short life, the poor little *clef* (so diligently compiled by Jesse) without its *roman*. Constance had her own work-in-progress and was so religiously grateful it was going well that she could pass up the triumph of having the last word. Why, in a way, she owed Insel thanks. He had, after all, provided her with her angel of release.

Had Jesse gotten the credit, the English credit she had needed for her "independent study"? The ambitious side of Constance wanted her to have got it: she had certainly earned it. But the spiritually concerned side of Constance prayed that the girl had told her shabby professor good-bye and go to hell on the same day she had scrawled her contrite farewell to Constance.

Nevertheless, when Constance flew around the country, or between countries, plying her trade, or sometimes just taking a vacation from achievement, she always looked carefully—and rather wistfully—into the faces of the stewardesses when she entered the planes.

St. John

*S*till stunned from the success of his book, Charles bought a woodland cottage in an upstate community with an artistic reputation and retreated to write his second novel.

The silence of the country surprised him almost as much as his unexpected success. Then, through the silence, especially at night, he began to hear too much: strange exploratory scufflings in last fall's leaves outside the bedroom window; the terrified cry of some animal fleeing from its assailant; a sudden single beep from the burglar alarm in the house of the absent rock singer on the other side of the woods; and, once or twice, a sibilant, rueful sigh that he did not *think* came from him.

Weekdays he worked on the book, learned for the first time the primitive masculine pleasure of chopping wood that would provide his own future warmth, and explored the small village, which combined the bohemian aura of the arts colony it had been in the 1920s and '30s with the hippie style it had picked up in the '60s. On weekends he was visited faithfully by a woman he had lived with for a while in the city. They would cook and go for hikes and, when he put her on the bus Sunday nights, he always felt sad that he wouldn't miss her more.

One morning, when he was temporarily stuck on the book and had taken time off to answer the latest packet of mail forwarded from his publisher, the phone rang. The handful of city people who had his unlisted number knew better than to call before noon.

Curious, Charles went to answer.

"Sin gin here," said a brisk, throaty female voice. At least that's what Charles thought she said.

"Hello?" repeated Charles.

"Look, I've just had a call for you," the voice went on, in a hearty English accent, distinctly upperclass. "I told him I wasn't the sin gin he wanted, but could possibly contact you, and then it would be up to you whether you wanted to ring him back."

It dawned on Charles that he and the voice on the phone had the same last name, St. John, only she pronounced hers in that funny English way. At the same time, a mystery was cleared up: a village acquaintance had recently congratulated him on his stirring letter to the local paper, and Charles hadn't the least idea what he had meant.

There were two St. Johns in town; and this other one was getting his calls.

"I'm really sorry about this," he apologized to the woman, "I know I hate to be disturbed by wrong numbers."

"Don't mind in the least, darling. Now look: got a pencil handy? Just jot down this number . . ."

As he wrote down the number, another mystery presented itself. "But how did you get my number?"

"Darling, I really *can't* say. But they were only trying to be helpful, you know, and I can assure you it is safe with me. I am always glad to be of help to an artist."

"Well, thank you," he said, more warmly. "But I'm still sorry my call interrupted your morning."

"No trouble, I assure you. But do try to call him back within the hour; he's expecting you. A nice man, he sounded. They want you to come and speak at their university."

After she hung up, Charles looked up his surname in the phone book. There she was: "S. St. John." He wondered what the *S* was for: Susanna? Serena? Sophie? Or something more English, like Samantha. Or Sybil.

Though he had no intention of flying off to speak at universities—he wanted to get on with the new work, not be admired for the one he'd finished several years ago—he did phone the man back at once. He didn't want "S. St. John" to be bothered twice in one morning. Also, he was afraid she might call back and chide him, "Look, darling, that nice man just rang again. . . ."

He dreamed more in his country life. Dense, involved dreams that left him exhausted and haunted by their rich quality of seeming fully as real as his daytime life. They caught him up in the momentum and intensity of their demands.

If his writing life were as prolific as his dream life, his book would be finished in six weeks.

Every day he plodded on, keeping faith with his idea, reminding himself of the doubts and second thoughts that had accompanied his creation of the book that was now a success. Sometimes it seemed to him he was competing with that book, and he almost resented its big, calm, assured presence out there in the world.

He chopped more wood and kept abreast of his mail: he had been brought up to answer his letters promptly. He drove each finished chapter to his typist, and jogged to the village bookstore and back for daily exercise. He had guessed that it was the bookstore couple who had given S. St. John his number (he had given it to them so they could call when books he ordered came in), but he saw no point in saying anything now that it was done.

She phoned again. "Sin gin here. Look, you just had a call from Alaska. They want you for a Midnight Sun Writers' Conference. I told them I couldn't promise I'd reach you immediately, but I was sure you'd ring them as soon as possible. Don't forget the time difference!"

On weekends, the friend from the city inveterately descended from the Trailways bus, and they drank wine in front of the fireplace, where it was chilly enough now to justify using his wood. In bed, surrounded by the mysterious night noises, he was glad of her company, even if it was no great romance on either side.

/   /   /

His typist was a conversational man in his sixties. He lived in a tiny cabin atop a steep hill in the woods. He had built the cabin himself and arranged it in such a way that he could stand in the center of its one room and tend the woodstove, reach for a dictionary or thesaurus from the shelf above his bed, cook on his two-burner hotplate, or put the kettle on for tea. He told Charles he had learned the pleasures of constricted space during World War II, when he served as an officer on a destroyer. The cabin had no running water, but the typist took what he needed from a nearby stream. Once a week he bathed in a child's plastic bathtub, heating the water in shifts in the kettle. He had been many things in his life, he told Charles: an actor, a banker, a clown, a radio singer, a journalist, and an English professor. He spoke of his different professions as his "incarnations."

The typist had one peculiarity, which Charles had grown used to: he wore women's clothes while at home in his cabin. The first occasion Charles had trudged up the hill with a chapter, the typist had met him at the door in a denim skirt and a woman's red blouse. Charles shook hands with him as if he had been wearing a three-piece suit; Charles had been brought up that way. The second time, when Charles came to pick up his chapter, the typist, wearing a yellow dress and pearls, offered him tea. As the typist dipped the teabag in first one cup, then the other, he chatted in an appreciative way about Charles's chapter: he had not read Charles's first book because it was never in the library, he told Charles, who was happy that it could not yet come between the typist and this new book.

One day, S. St. John phoned with three messages. "It's that time of year," she told him in a more intimate, conspiratorial voice. "They're all making up the schedules"—she pronounced it "*shed*-ules"—"for their visiting lecturers, so we'll just have to grin and bear it, won't we?" Like an old and trusted secretary, she relayed his messages. Against his better judgment, jut as she was "ringing off," Charles asked her what the *S* stood for.

"Absolutely nothing, darling. The phone company insists one put in a first initial, that's all. *S* was just the first initial that came to mind."

"But ..." Charles waded in further. "I mean ... what should I call you?"

"Bless you, darling. I am known simply as Sin gin."

He restrained himself from asking further about a Christian name. So far, she had been brief in their conversations, in no sense encouraging loquaciousness. He said more formally: "Well, once again, thank you. I really wish this wouldn't happen, but I don't know what I can do about it."

"Not to worry," she assured him. "Actually, I don't always see fit to disturb you. Why, only the other evening a young woman from Santa Fe rang me, wanting you. She had read your book and found out from some magazine piece that you lived here now, and she wanted to talk. I explained that you weren't communicating with anyone except your Muse at the moment, but I would convey her message. She adored your book, said it gave her hope. Poor child, we talked for about an hour. The *contretemps* of some people's lives never cease to amaze me. Well, darling, I didn't mean to make a nuisance of myself. I'll ring off now."

"Do you happen to know a woman in town named St. John?" Charles asked his typist, who, despite his hermit's life, seemed to know a great deal about the village. "She pronounces it 'Sin gin.' "

"Oh, that's Magnus St. John's widow," said the typist. Today he wore the denim skirt and a sweater set, for it was cold. The outfit reminded Charles of a pair of nuns who used to visit his mother sometimes; they had just dispensed with their habits, and wore clothes much like these, and didn't know what to do with their handbags. "The one that writes letters to the paper," the typist said. "I'll bet I know why you ask: you've been getting blamed for the letters." The typist gave a low chuckle. From the neck up, with his hollow cheeks, and erudite gray eyes behind the slipping glasses, and balding gray head, he looked like a kindly professor. Well, he had been a professor in one of his previous incarnations. Charles liked him and looked forward to these visits; perhaps even wrote his chapters faster so there would be more opportunities for these sociable occasions.

The typist dipped the teabag back and forth between the steaming cups. "She's quite mad in her harmless way," he said good-humoredly.

"Who was Magnus St. John?"

"You haven't heard of him? No, I guess not. He was a fairly well-known artist in the thirties. But he had the misfortune to fall between two fashions. He came too late with his Matissean aesthetic, and the abstract expressionists considered him a fuddy-duddy. He died about five years ago. Nobody mentions him much anymore, though he exhibited right up until his death at eighty."

"Eighty! Then she's . . . she must be very old, too." Charles was shocked. The voice had sounded much younger on the phone.

"She was quite a bit younger," mused the typist. "But she's certainly no spring chicken anymore." His voice, with its bass resonances, could have been any man's in a bar, discussing a woman past her prime. Charles had been a baby when his father died, and something about the typist brought out his filial response. He tended to forget, for whole chunks of time, that the man sitting opposite him wore a skirt, blouse, and—yes—perfume (a good one, too). A round mirror hung over the china washbasin on the typist's chest of drawers. Did the typist primp before this mirror when he was alone? Solitude brought out all kinds of things in people. Charles wondered what special predilection waited to suprise *him*, some solitary evening.

"You've been getting blamed for the letter about the sewage proposal, I'll bet," said the typist, crossing a hairy leg. He wore ordinary tennis shoes and white socks.

Charles smiled obliquely. He wasn't sure why he didn't tell about St. John's telephone calls: it made an interesting anecdote. "In what way is she mad?"

"Charles, if you weren't a writer, you would make a first-rate district attorney," the typist teased him. "Though the two occupations go together, don't they? You wouldn't like it if I betrayed one client's confidences to another. I mean, what if another customer came to me and said, 'What is Charles St. John's new book about?' Would you expect me to rattle off the plot?"

"Ah, you type for her, too," said Charles, to whom it had suddenly occurred that St. John—or "Sin gin," as he thought of her—could have got his number from the typist. But hadn't the typist just been telling him how discreet he was? Charles decided to let it go.

"Occasionally," said the typist, looking at Charles over the tops of his glasses. "But now that you've gone and got me to admit it, I shall have to revise myself and say, who *doesn't* exhibit an occasional mad streak in these hills? It's part of the elixir of the place. I mean"—and with a gesture he indicated his outfit—"I frightened a lady clear down the hill the other day. She had phoned and asked if I would type up a list of raffle items for her club, and I said, 'Come right on up, I can do it while you wait.' Well!" He laughed delightedly. "The moment I saw her *hat* crest the hill I knew there would be trouble. I was in the yellow outfit . . . she took one look at me through the screen and gave a little yelp and was off in a cloud of dust."

That was the nearest they ever came to discussing the typist's predilection.

About the time the leaves fell, Charles struck a bad patch. His book reached an impasse. His dreams were wearying and confused. In one dream, his mother—dead now—was accusing him of stealing from her. He awoke in tears from that dream. He had been his mother's favorite child, born late in her life, raised by her after his brother and sister had already married and had families of their own. He switched on the bedside lamp and sat up and tried to understand why his sleeping side would punish him so. Was it because of his success? The successful book? That book, set in another era, the era of his mother's youth, could not have been written without all the stories she had told him over the years. The two of them would be walking down a street in the town and his mother would say: "Do you see that man? When he was in high school, he ran away with the band teacher. His father tracked them down and horsewhipped the man and brought his son home and he's been an exemplary citizen ever since." Then she would laugh in her special way, trying to keep her lips closed because she was sensitive about her slightly protruding teeth. And Charles would look at the red-faced old man duck-footing ahead of them in his wrinkled seersucker suit and try to imagine a boy running off with the band teacher, a man. What would it be like to have a passion for a man? Charles would try to imagine himself into the red-faced man's self—then into the man's younger self. *"Tout comprendre, c'est tout pardonner"* had been one of his mother's favorite maxims. She had come to this town years ago as the schoolteacher; that was when all eight grades were in one room, taught by one teacher. His mother had planned to save her salary for several years and go to France; then she had met his father.

After sitting awake for several hours, Charles realized that his mother would wish him only well, wherever she was; he attributed the dream to some short circuit between his uneasiness about the successful book ("his mother's book") and his difficulties with the new book, in which he was trying to "steal back" some of the flame that had propelled him—not without *its* difficulties—through the first.

Then, one Thursday, his dependable woman friend called from the city and announced she wouldn't be arriving on the Friday-evening bus. After playing it cagey for a moment, she admitted she was getting married.

"But you were here only last weekend," said Charles, baffled more than he was heartbroken.

"Yes, I know." She laughed. "I wanted to be sure."

Whatever that meant. After they had said their good-byes and Charles had wished her all the best, he went out into the crisp night and gathered some firewood and, until the crackling logs had diminished to a heap of embers, sat gazing at he scarcely knew what.

His typist finally phoned *him*. "I've been out several times this week. Buying teabags and that sort of thing. I was wondering if I'd missed your call. You're usually a chapter-every-three-weeks guy."

"I'll have something ready soon," Charles said. "I've reached a spot where there are technical problems. I know what I want, but I have to figure out how to get there. It's like . . . well, I have the *impulse*, but I don't yet know how to materialize it. Can *materialize* be used as a transitive verb?"

The typist chuckled in his fatherly manner. "No, but I know what you mean."

One evening in November, Charles was coming out of the bookstore, which opened at eleven in the morning and stayed open until eight in the evening to fit in with the artistic habits of the village. There was a slight fog, which caused the streetlamps to wear fuzzy amber auras. Charles was walking slowly along the main street, enjoying the melancholy feel of the dampness against his face, when he happened to think of "Sin gin." She had not phoned in weeks. Well, what did he expect? The fact that she hadn't phoned simply meant that nobody was phoning him. Simple: after the brief flare-up of his success, the world had taken him at his word that he wanted to be left alone, and gone on to pursue newer successes.

Coming toward him on the same side of the road was the lanky silhouette of a girl, with loose, bouncy hair, pushing her bike. She was wearing jeans, of the old flare-leg variety, out of style now, and she trudged forward with a brisk, determined, quick-march step. As she passed him, he craned forward, out of simple curiosity, to see what she looked like. She was passing under the streetlamp, sheathed in its orange aura, and he saw, with some regret, that she was not a girl, but a woman no longer young, with a rather determined, lipsticked mouth. She started slightly, returned his gaze, then went on by. After they had each gone on for half-a-dozen steps more, he heard her murmur distinctly, "Hello, Charles."

He whirled around. Her silhouette receded into the fog until she became the girl with long, bouncy hair again.

He knew the voice. It was the first time she had ever used his first name. She pronounced it "Chahles."

"Have you seen your latest contribution to civic life?" Smiling, the typist handed Charles the tabloid-size local paper, folded to the letter page. Charles's stomach jolted slightly when he saw the familiar surname. He read the letter, a spirited diatribe against the new breed of town managers who were fattening their pockets by ruining the town. Though the words seemed out of proportion to what the town managers were trying to do (allow a motel to be built), they were magnificent words with a real Shakespearean bite to them: "infamous hooligans . . ." "obloquy . . . base impertinence . . ." "this rank compound of malefactors, rogues, and termagants . . ." "halcyon . . ." "dunghill . . . canker."

Charles handed the paper back to the typist. "I'd hate to get on her bad side," he quipped. But inwardly he envied the sheer energy of her passion. Over a *motel.*

The typist stood up and began making the tea preparations. The tiny woodstove was going and the cabin glowed with warmth. Today's costume consisted of a pleated skirt, which came just above the typist's pale, knobby knees; a white angora sweater; and several gold chains and ornaments. Charles tried to picture the typist, wearing the workpants and jacket that hung in the corner curtained off as a closet, going through some store's racks of skirts, fingering the fluffy sweaters: how, for instance, could he be sure things would fit when he got them home? Did he tell the saleslady he was buying them for his sister, daughter, ladyfriend, or did he just hand over his purchases with his Mastercard and professorial smile?

"Well, Charles," said the typist, with his back to him as he waited for the kettle to boil, "I finally got my turn at your book in the library. I liked it quite a lot. Of course, in the new book, you're taking more chances."

"How . . . do you mean?" inquired Charles, struggling to keep his voice nonchalant.

"Well. Of course, I'm not a fiction writer. One of the incarnations I haven't tried." The typist chuckled, lifting the kettle at the exact second it began to sing. "But it seems to me that in this new book you are trying seriously to represent the psyche of a *modern* man, and that's no easy thing."

Charles sat quite still, trying to imprint the words on his memory to replay at leisure when he got home.

"Not that I'm slighting your old book," the typist went on, performing his frugal ritual of the shared, dunked teabag. "It was a joy. You could just escape right into that earlier, safer time, when characters wore their outlines more firmly . . . like"—he turned, smiling, holding the two flowered china cups in their saucers—"well, like a good set of tailored clothes. The modern character isn't fitted so easily, and I admire you for taking the risk."

"Thank you," murmured Charles, bowing his head low over the steaming tea. He did not want the other man to see how much he had needed this encouragement. After a moment, he took a large swallow of tea and asked: "Do you happen to know if St. John rides a bike?"

"That's her mode of transportation. Keeps her slim as a sylph. Her hands are a sight, though: she refuses to wear gloves in the bitterest cold. Once I offered her a pair of mine when she was here—well, you've guessed by now who types those remarkable letters—but she turned me down. Said I was trying to undermine her toughness."

"How old did you say she was?"

"Ah, I didn't say ... nobody knows how old St. John is. Must be pushing sixty now."

"Oh, I don't think so!" Charles protested. "I mean ... I've only seen her once, in the fog, but she walked like a girl. Of course I could see from her face that she was a woman ... maybe in her thirties ... maybe even forties ... but surely not sixty!"

"What made you so sure it was St. John?"

"The bookstore people had pointed her out to me," Charles lied. Inexplicably. Why wouldn't he confide in the only friend he had in town? But confide exactly what?

"Well, I can see that she has caught your imagination," said the typist, crossing one workboot with heavy woolen red sock over his knee. His predilection did not, apparently, take in shoes. "I'll tell you what I know about her, without betraying anything. Her legend is common knowledge around here. Another customer of mine told it to me. She came here in the late thirties as Magnus St. John's housekeeper. He was English, too, you know, his father and elder brother were peers of the realm. The story was that she—our St. John—was the daughter of an old family servant. Anyway, the story goes that she wanted to come to America and seek her fortune, and Magnus St. John paid her passage on the condition she work it off by cooking and keeping house for him. The rest is fairly commonplace: she was young and must have been very lovely—and penniless; he was a dominating old egotist used to having his way. He married her and kept her here ... and here she sticks, living in that godforsaken shack that was part of the original arts colony compound, up on Bear Cliff Mountain. All those buildings belong to the village Craftsmen's Guild now, but Magnus St. John got it written down somewhere before he died that she could live on there. If you can call it living. Talk about primitive! The roof leaks ... she's got pans and buckets covering half the floor to catch the drips ... but now I am being indiscreet. I've slipped from public hearsay into personal reportage. Let's find another topic. Only I will say that the cavalier in me was wounded when she wouldn't accept my offer of gloves or my considerable carpenter's skill. I

could have repaired that roof, but she said it was the Craftsmen's Guild's duty and she was going to make them do it." He
laughed quietly. "St. John is a real stickler when it comes to
principles."

Charles stopped by the village Copy Center on his way home
from the typist's. He always duplicated his fresh chapter and
sent it off at once to his editor: it gave him a feeling of progress
being made. He liked the atmosphere of the little shop, with its
T-shirt corner, always with several teenagers hunched over the
counter watching the man iron on the slogans and epithets they
had chosen for their shirts; and in another corner was a large
woman in flowing robes and a turban who had set herself up
with a sign in Gothic letters: VILLAGE SCRIBE. She could nota-
rize documents for you, or—Charles had watched her doing it
—write letters for people in the kind of language that got them fur-
thest with banks, insurance companies, and collection agencies.

Charles stood slouched comfortably over the big machine,
feeding in his pages and watching their doubles slide into the
metal tray. At three other machines, other writers fed in their
masterworks. Perhaps they had not enjoyed the fortunate noto-
riety that Charles had, this past year, but in this funky room,
intense with its air of self-promotion and -presentation, he was
just another struggling soul, anonymous in his jeans and goose-
down parka, cloning his latest visions. For many of these people,
the big Xerox and Pitney-Bowes machines would be their ulti-
mate printing presses; but at this moment, while flattening each
page for the flashy passing eye of the camera, they all had hopes.

Sometimes Charles was sorry he had let his editor see these
early chapters. Diplomatically, the man had let Charles know he
was perplexed: why should Charles choose not to build on his
early success with a second "bright," "humane" comedy that
showed "a wisdom far beyond a young man's years"? Why had
he chosen to venture into these dark, uncertain waters with
who-knew-what at the bottom?

Nevertheless, Charles's spirits always lifted when he

popped a new chapter in the mail—he could just make the five o'clock collection if he hurried—and sent it on its way to the first person outside in the real world, beyond this village with its "elixir" of eccentricity.

He was counting backward through the pages of the duplicated chapter when he became aware of someone close behind him. He could hear the rapid, rather ragged breath, and—after losing count—turned, a bit irritably, to inform his successor that he could have the machine just as soon as he would kindly allow Charles to finish counting his pages in peace.

He turned and there she was, thin and frostbitten in her flare jeans and old boots and frayed pea jacket. She clutched a Guatemalan cloth bag full of papers to her chest as though they contained a matter of life and death. She was looking at him as though she had been watching him for some time and waiting for him to notice her.

"Oh, hello, St. John. It is you, isn't it?" He peered forward, an empty gesture, as he could see perfectly well that it was the woman from the foggy evening. Only, oh God, the typist was right, she was old: the dry, wispy hair that flipped up from her shoulders was a too-bright, unnatural gold under the Copy Center's fluorescent lights; the face had seen many winters, despite its structured gauntness; and the hands made him want to weep, with their red, raw joints and skin like shriveled parchment. Why in the world didn't the foolish woman wear gloves?

She surprised Charles by dropping her head shyly and mumbling something in her low British voice about being *so* glad she had run into him. Fumbling hastily in her Guatemalan bag, she brought forth an untidy sheaf of papers, which she pressed into his arms. She told him to hold those, please, while she made copies of some others.

He stood there holding her papers while she went feverishly at the Xerox machine. Then a glance at the clock impressed on him the absurdity of this scene. "Look, St. John, I have to go now," he said almost curtly. "I'll miss the five o'clock mail."

On she went, feeding the machine, her hair flying wildly as

she swooped to collect each new page fresh from the tray. "Just one more second, darling," she said, and what could he do—what could a cavalier do? as the typist would put it—but stand there holding her stuff?

He made it to the post office. He even made it with enough time left over to satisfy her other request. She had entreated him to sign his name to the copy of a letter she had written (typed by you-know-who) and buy a stamped envelope and address it to their representative in Albany.

The letter was a protest against the inhumane trapping of raccoons.

It seemed strange to Charles, who had time to mull it over while he ate supper, that, as soon as St. John had nailed him with her current cause, she was quite willing to let him go: almost eager to see him sprint out of the Copy Center for the post office. It seemed strange that neither of them had mentioned the half-dozen or more times they had spoken on the phone. She was more sure of herself on the phone, more hearty. He had been taken aback, that first time she had called him "darling" on the telephone. But that must be her style of speech; he had heard her call the Village Scribe the same thing as he had rushed from the shop. "We just have to keep trying, dah-ling," St. John had said in her breathy English voice to the large woman in flowing robes. Charles wondered if she had picked up her tony accent from the dominating old Magnus. If so, what had her own speech been like when she was young and lovely, come to seek her fortune in the New World?

And now here she was, rushing around like one possessed for the protection of raccoons, squandering words the Bard himself had used—but on sewage projects and motels.

He could weep for those hands.

By early December, Charles had finished what he estimated to be a third of his book. He felt it would be a good idea to go away. Get clear away. Though the book was at last tightening with a sense of inevitability, he himself was becoming unstrung. The village "elixir" was getting to him. How afraid he had been, a year ago, that success would ruin him, make him boasting and self-centered and trivial, as he had seen it do to others. And so he had, in a sense, exiled himself to this rural place to "keep himself honest." Oh, he was still honest, all right, more so than ever, perhaps, but the virtue was seeking new depths. When he came here, he had thought the village quaint, been tenderly amused by its artistic pretensions. So many "artists"! Everybody he met had been writing a novel or painting a canvas or transcribing the music of a different drummer. He had modestly suppressed his condescension. How, after all, was he better than they were, except in his talent and maybe discipline and luck?

But as the months of silence wrapped around him and the winter wore him down, and his social life dwindled to the book-store and his typist, he began to exist in an almost medieval anonymity. Weren't they all, in a sense, interchangeable, inter-working parts of the same divine machine that drove them on, kept them all furiously typing or sloshing paint or genuflecting in front of the Xerox machine to gather their harvests of dupli-cated pages?

Or scribbling impassioned diatribes against the mounting trash heap of brutality and greed. ("Sweep on, you fat and greasy citizens," she had written, in her most recent letter to the paper. Charles had smiled when he saw it: the Bard again.)

She had phoned him once more. This time it was about a girl he had known in high school. She had read about Charles's success in a back issue of a magazine while waiting to see her gynecologist. "But she hasn't read your book," St. John told him. "She asked me if I thought you'd mind, and I told her I really couldn't say. Anyhow, here's the number. I'm sure it would make her very happy if you called."

"I probably won't," Charles had said, "but thanks anyway, St. John. How is your raccoon campaign coming?"

But she must have picked up the slightest edge of irony in his tone, because she said defensively, "Oh, these things go slowly, but nevertheless one feels one has to take *some* action." She did not call him darling and rang off after a brisk goodnight.

Yes, he really had to go somewhere, take a breather away from his reclusive life in this village. It had aroused the part of his nature that was strange, lonely, and mad. While it had been good for the book, he worried what it was doing to his social self. If he didn't watch it, the first thing he knew, he would be drafting petitions to be kind to mice (he had, actually, become fond of their companionable little gnawing sounds in his garbage pail beneath the sink) or dressing up in women's clothes.

He called an old acquaintance in the city, a gregarious fellow who kept up with the "hot" vacation spots. The man was flattered to hear from Charles and said he would fix the whole thing up with his own travel agent. "You mean it's not too late?" asked Charles. "If this island is so popular, won't everything be booked?" "They always save a block of rooms for people like you," the man said, laughing. "People like me?" "Sure. Bachelors who get the heebie-jeebies right before the big holidays. This is the kind of island that can always use a personable guy like you. You'll make some chick's holiday, and then she'll tell her friends. Christmas falls on a Thursday this year. When you wanna leave?" "Better make it the Saturday before," said Charles. "Man, you got cabin fever!" crowed the gregarious man triumphantly.

Charles marked time through mid-December. He covered his typewriter, as he did not want to begin pecking out another chapter, and took a box of bakery cookies to his typist, who, he had discovered, had a sweet tooth. Then he got out his summer clothes and ironed them, even though they would just get wrinkled again in the suitcase. He tried to read books he had been saving for months, but couldn't keep his mind on any of them. He went to bed early, fell immediately into a deep sleep, and awoke remembering the most disturbing dreams. After haunting him all fall, his mother had faded out of his night life, to be replaced by crowds of strangers, or peripheral people from his past. If these dream figures had anything in common, it was that they were all discovering, and taking pains to let him know, that he was a fraud, an impostor, or—as in one dream—an importer of stolen animal pelts.

A week before Christmas, he was coming out of the A&P at dusk, and a figure pedaled by on a bicycle, shrieked her brakes to a halt, and walked the bicycle backward till she reached Charles. "God bless you, darling, and Merry Christmas," she said. She was wearing a red woolen muffler that made her look like a pretty girl with a red nose in this kind half-light.

"St. John, I've missed you," he heard himself say.

"God bless you," she repeated. Then, clearly moved, she hooked him around the neck with a freezing hand, and pulled him to her and kissed him fervently on the cheek.

The day before Charles's plane left for the island, it began to snow. Charles called the airline. The airline called Charles back. The flight had been rescheduled for the following day. The following day, it snowed as if it would never quit. Charles had at least a dozen conversations with the airline. The thing he could not stand in life was not knowing something. Once he knew, he could adapt. Finally, a reservations clerk told him, "Sir, you are not the only one who wants to get home for Christmas. There are hundreds of families waiting in this very airport to get home."

"I am at home," said Charles. He canceled his flight.

He went to the kitchen, where the mice were having a loud supper in the garbage pail under the sink, and poured himself a large Scotch. He felt elated that he was not going on his trip. Presently, he had a second Scotch, and sat smiling and shaking his head as he drank: he felt absolutely liberated from the tyranny of his "bright," "wise," social self. He went to the window and watched the snow pile itself implacably upon the village, isolating it from the rest of the world. "The art of our necessities is strange," he murmured aloud, quoting the Bard, giving himself courage as he leafed quickly through the phone book to the page of his name.

His tires, radial though they were, would not make it up the last stretch of Bear Cliff Mountain Road. He pulled over to the side, turned the wheels inward, lifted the handbrake, and stepped out into the snowy night. All around him was the sound of clattering snowflakes. Whoever said that snow fell silently? They didn't know, didn't know firsthand. Pulling his collar closer around his neck, he climbed the hill toward the old arts colony. There were only a few lights. Not many people were willing to live here anymore.

I know we are barely acquainted, but I find myself in love with you.

Who had spoken such incredible words? They were words out of an old book, written when the world was young and innocent and the motives of characters fit closer to their skins. They were words addressed by a cavalier to a maiden, after several mutually gratifying glimpses—perhaps some hastily exchanged words—in a strict society. In this fateful snow, the old magic returned, and within the hour, Charles would clasp the woman of his imagination to his heart and speak these honorable words.

Some years later, Charles had lunch with the typist. They ate in a place the typist loved to visit whenever he came to New York. It was a replica of an English pub, only you could have your beer cold, if you wanted. Charles lived in the city now, and the typist (who had shed that incarnation) was an investment consultant for a philanthropic foundation that operated out of Philadelphia. The typist had to take the train to New York once or twice a month to take care of things to do with the foundation, or with his own affairs, and sometimes he delighted Charles by phoning him to ask if he was free.

"I love this pub," said the typist. "Did I ever tell you about the year I spent at school in England?"

"No, you never did," said Charles. The typist always seemed to have one more story to draw out of his kit bag of incarnations. Sometimes Charles would close his eyes and open them quickly and try to remember how this elderly man in the discreet, well-fitting suit had looked in the old days in the yellow outfit and pearls. Had that all been a dream? The typist's father had played him a dirty trick, as the typist put it, by dying at the age of ninety-eight and leaving him, the only surviving family member, a fortune. ("He waited until I had arthritis in my knee joints and emphysema," the typist had told Charles, "and then he knew he could drive me out of those woods and make me come back to town and play ball.")

"Well," said the typist, sipping his beer and looking kindly at Charles over the tops of his glasses, which at least had not changed, "that was just the best year of my boyhood. I loved that school. I was made their first American prefect at the end of my first year—or what I thought was to be my first year. Apparently, I had committed the crime of enjoying myself too much, because when my father met me at the dock and I told him what a dream of a year it had been, he frowned and said: 'Well, remember it, because that's the end of that.'"

"You mean, he wouldn't let you go back to England because you'd enjoyed it?"

"Something like that," said the typist. "Father had his own ideas about what my life should be like." He smiled quietly into his beer. "I had other ideas. And, I'm happy to say, I acted on them. Now I suppose I must pay my debt to the old man before I kick off myself. I'm ready any time; I've had my fun. Those years in the village, where we met, were just tops. I learned many things."

"Me, too," said Charles.

"She died, you know," said the typist.

"I know," said Charles. "It seems crazy, but I still subscribe to that mad little village paper."

"So do I," said the typist. "That's how I knew. Lungs.

Same thing that's going to get me. It was all those years in that damp cabin up there for her, first serving the needs of the great artist—who, as it turned out, wasn't so great—and then flying around town in the cold, fighting the world, without any gloves."

"I gave her a pair of gloves," said Charles, making circles with his forefinger on the table. "They were cashmere. I wanted to get kidskin, lined with rabbit fur, but I knew she wouldn't wear animal pelts. She wouldn't wear the cashmere, either. Nevertheless, I did what I could, that winter, to keep her hands warm."

That was the nearest they ever came to discussing it.

"You know, your second book remains my favorite," said the typist, after a moment. "Though I may be partial, since I got to see it come into being. It had a certain . . . elixir." He smiled.

"A definite touch of madness," Charles recalled wistfully.

He and the typist parted outside the pub, the typist taxiing downtown to the train station, and Charles walking slowly up the avenue toward the bright accoutrements of a successful novelist's, husband's, and father's life.

The Angry-Year

*I*t was 1957, when the Big Bopper and Albert Camus still walked the earth and the Russians sent a dog into space. It was the year I was angry. The whole of my junior year, I went around angry. I had transferred at last from the modest junior college in my hometown to the big, prestigious university with the good program in English. My family was poor, they couldn't afford to send me, so I'd got there with a scholarship based on my freshman and sophomore grades. Yet, once I'd arrived where I'd slaved to get, I seethed from morning till night with a hot, unspecific anger. Everything infuriated me. I went through registration glaring at the coveys of girls with summer tans who welcomed one another back with shrill, delighted cries. I hated their skittish convertibles with the faded tops, bolting the orange traffic lights. I loathed the conformity of their Weejun loafers (though I wore them myself) and the little jeweled pins swinging saucily from their breasts. There was an enemy here who might destroy me unless I routed him out and destroyed him first, but I could not discover his identity.

I did a strange thing, under a sort of compulsion. I went out for sorority rush, although I knew perfectly well I could not afford to join one, even if asked. I dressed myself up and attended the Pan-Hellenic tea and signed the register as a rushee. I went to the first round of parties, hurrying from house to house under the autumn stars. My attitude was a queer blend of arrogance and obsequiousness. At the Chi Omega house I gulped my paper cup of cider and heard myself tell the most astonishing lies. At the Tri Delt house I ate too many cookies and insulted one of the sisters. I was calmer at the other four houses and managed to participate in the established ritual of chitchat without further incidents. Walking back to my dorm afterward, I concluded that I had done no worse than others, though—with the possible exception of the first two houses—I had not made myself memorable. I went over the evening and decided that most of the girls were shallow fools. I made out a budget in my journal to see if I could squeeze sorority dues out of the scholarship, even though there was a clause in the scholarship saying the holder could not join a fraternity or a sorority. I envisioned all six houses bidding for me, and my polite rejection of them. I would remain inscrutably independent. My roommate was a cheerful, sensible girl, a Christian Scientist. She was lying hunched on the floor of our room that evening, "working on" an injury she'd received at basketball tryouts. She said her parents had given her the choice of a sorority or a Volkswagen and she'd taken the VW, of course.

Before rush began, I had met the president of the Dekes, the big fraternity on campus, at a Get Acquainted Dance at the Armory. I was offhand and rather rude to him, and he kept asking me out. I had told him I might go through rush "just for the experience." He seemed pleased, but then Graham seemed pleased by most things. He was a slow, courtly boy from Danville, Virginia. His family owned a textile mill. I never saw him get excited about anything.

The second day of rush, he waited for me beneath a shedding oak while I ran into the Union to check my rushee mailbox. The first day, everyone got six white invitations. The second day, the serious weeding-out began. I came out of the Union enraged, my hands full of tiny bits of white paper. With Graham as my witness, I flung these into the wire trash basket beside the walk. They floated down, like languid snow, upon crumpled newsprint, paper cups, and apple cores.

"I've dropped out of rush," I said. "I've torn up all my silly invitations. There was this poor girl in there. She made me see what a cruel, stupid farce it is. There wasn't a single invitation in her box. She opened it and it was empty and there was this terrible look on her face. Sort of . . . stunned, like those newspaper pictures of people who have just been told their whole family has been wiped out. I refuse to be part of such a thing. You're looking at an Independent, Graham."

Agreeably, he hurried along the leaf-strewn path beside me. It was a splendid, crisp fall day, full of colors, the kind you breathe in exultantly if you're not preoccupied by anger. "Even though I'm a fraternity man myself," he said, "I admire you for taking a stand. Of course you must, feeling the way you do about that girl in there." He never knew how utterly alone his praise made me feel. For Graham really believed that girl existed. His world contained no necessity for inventing such lies, or for raiding a trash basket upstairs in order to have six invitations to tear up and throw away. He continued to take me out. His peaceful personality seemed to bask in the flames of my rebellion. I continued to be amazed that the president of the Dekes would want me as his girl. I never asked myself did I want him.

My second foray into the extracurricular was a visit to the student newspaper, which was published daily. I was curt and defiant. I said there were a lot of hypocrisies in the system I would love to expose. I asked for a personal column. The editor was a wild-eyed, brilliant Jewish boy from New York. He later became a well-known writer. "A mean Mary McCarthy type, that's what we need," he said. He agreed to give me a trial run: three eight-hundred-word columns a week. "And we'll run a half-column shot of you, with your hair flying, like it is now."

I worked very hard on the first three columns. They were titled, in order of appearance: "Worst of Bugs, Extracurricular-alysis" (exhorting harassed freshmen not to load themselves down with band and basketball and chorus and student politics until they'd found their true and central interests); "Spit on Me or I on Thee" (a sermon, lifted in liberal chunks from Camus, in which I cautioned fellow students to judge not that they be not judged); and "The Mythical Booked-Up Maiden" (which put forth the proposition to campus males, who outnumbered the females ten to one, that dozens of beautiful coeds sat home on Saturday evenings because the boys assumed they were dated up for months in advance).

The first two columns were ignored. The third drew an amazing barrage of fan mail from the men's dorms. They offered various, sometimes unprintable, kinds of services to these stay-at-home maidens. The editor was pleased by the response and said I could keep my column. From then on I had my weapon: the powerful Fourth Estate. I titled my column "Without Restrictions," and set about avenging my private frustrations in vitriolic prose, beneath the photo of my flying hair.

Weekends I sat on the comfortable sofa at the Deke house and studied the enemy at close hand. I drank their Scotch and smiled my Mary McCarthy smile. I was surprised to discover that all the Dekes were a little scared of me. The house read "Without Restrictions" faithfully. Graham had told them about my stand that memorable fall day. To him, I was the girl who couldn't stop for fripperies when the world was smothering under a blanket of hypocrisy. The girls who came to the Deke house were another matter. Although they were friendly and polite to me, I couldn't decipher their true feelings. Most of them came from the three top sororities out of the five that hadn't asked me back. They sat draped over the arms of their boyfriends' chairs, or, with their Weejuns tucked chastely beneath their skirts, on the rug. Their faces were composed, above their jeweled pins, shutting out all disquiet. What was their secret? I asked myself. Had their wealth bought them their unshakable serenity, as it had bought their cashmere sweaters and their perfect even teeth? Was it that simple? Or was their poise due to some secret inner powers, such as the Rosicrucians advertised, powers denied me forever because of my innately angry heart? I watched these girls, fascinated; I looked forward to the weekends not because of Graham but because of them. I sat in the circle of Graham's arm and said witty, icy things, while my eyes darted back and forth, observing their languid, seamless gestures, the way they made a special art out of lighting a cigarette, their glossy, lacquered nails cupping the flame, the charms on their bracelets faintly jingling. Were they silently, en masse, smiling at me while condemning me as a fraud?

I was never sure, and my unsureness whetted my vituperation.

"Without Restrictions" dealt with second-semester rush under the subhead *John Paul Jones Had Better Be Your Friend*. The column ran a "tape recording" of a typical rush dialogue.

> SISTER: And what is *youah* name?
> RUSHEE: Mary Kathleen Jones.
> SISTER: Jones! Are you by any chance related to John Paul?
> RUSHEE: I don't believe so. There are lots of Joneses where I come from.
> SISTER: And where is that?
> RUSHEE: Bent Twig.
> SISTER: Bent Twig! Why didn't you say so! Then you must be good friends with the Twigs who own the bank and the funeral parlor and the newspaper and the fish market.
> RUSHEE: Well, I don't know them personally, but of course everybody's heard of the Twigs.
> SISTER: Uh-huh. Well, Mary Catherine—oh, excuse me, Kath*leen*—it's been just grand talking to you. I'd like you to meet Attalee Hunt, our sister from Savannah. Attie, I think Mary Catherine might like a fresh glass of ice water. She seems to have eaten all her ice.

Not long after this, I received the following letter among my fan mail:

> Dear Miss Lewis,
> Your farce is ridiculous and futile. Why this endless stream of poison from a girl who professes to keep late-night company with Kierkegaard and Camus? Why waste

your eye for the delicate and obscure detail on such passing, boring trivia during your short-term lease among the stars? Where is the discrepancy? Your ambivalence haunts me. Do you know who you are? If you did, I think you would be less angry.

Jack Krazowski
211 Kerr Dorm

The letter upset me briefly. I put it out of my mind. I sipped rum punch after the basketball game, in front of a roaring fire at the Deke house. Suzanne Pinkerton, the Chi O who, it was rumored, once loved Graham, studied me curiously over the rim of her steaming mug and asked softly, "Janie, why do you hate us so?" Graham squeezed my shoulder proudly. "Better watch out for this one," he said. He was always saying about me, "Look out, now," or, "Better watch out for this one." That night, his lack of originality annoyed me.

At midterm, I got my first C. The sight of the letter-grade gave me a shock. I remembered my former industrious scholarship, the feeling I'd had for years that A's were my birthright. Now my mental sharpness was blurred by this constant association with people who demanded little of my mind. All my energy went into planning my next printed tirade against some small or imagined slight. Graham took me to the Interfraternity Ball. Before the dance, we were inconvenienced by a new state liquor law that made it necessary for us to drive twenty miles into the next county in order to purchase our bottles of J&B. Several days later, "Without Restrictions" presented a scathing diatribe against red-neck Baptist legislators who could not hold their liquor and therefore assumed we students at the university could not be trusted, either.

A second letter came from Kerr Dorm.

Dear Miss Lewis,

Have you ever read Ben Franklin's story of the tin whistle? You probably have—you seem to have read everything—so I won't bore you by retelling it. But your latest column put me in mind of little Ben racing about the house in manic despair, blowing stubbornly on the useless whistle for which he had given all his money.

Yours truly,
Jack Krazowski

I went to the library that evening for the first time in weeks. It was a balmy evening, almost spring, and I looked forward to browsing among shelves of books once more. In a *Benjamin Franklin Reader*, I tracked down the story of the tin whistle, how when Ben as a child had been given a gift of money and sent off to a toy store he had been "charmed" by the sound of another boy's whistle and given all his money for it at once.

I then came home and went whistling all over the house, much pleased by my whistle, but disturbing all the family. My brothers and sisters and cousins, understanding the bargain I had made, told me I had given four times as much for it as it was worth; put me in mind what good things I might have bought with the rest of my money; and laughed at me so much for my folly, that I cried with vexation; and the reflection gave me more chagrin than the whistle gave me pleasure.

I left the library and walked slowly back to my dorm. I passed students, some in groups, others solitary, whom I did not know. I wondered who they were and whether their private thoughts were poems or diatribes. Perhaps the one I had just passed would become very famous someday, and someone would say to me, "Oh did you know —— at your university? You were there at the same time." "No, I hung out mainly with the Dekes," I would answer.

I walked past Kerr Dorm nervously. It was the oldest men's dormitory, built of limestone and covered with ivy. It cost less to live there because there was no air conditioning. Which room on the second floor was 211? A pair of feet in white socks hung out of one of the lighted windows. From another came the sound of Brahms's Violin Concerto. I stood beneath the window, listening to the poignant solo of the violin. The stars were out and I was pleased I could recognize so many constellations. Then I heard footsteps and people coming along the walk laughing and I hurried away, not wanting to be discovered mooning outside Jack Krazowski's dorm.

WITHOUT RESTRICTIONS
"Night Sounds"

Last night, about nine, I walked home from the library. The air had that peculiar spring quality which clarifies a drowsy mind and conducts important sounds. As I passed my fellow students I seemed to hear the rhythms of their thoughts: some quick and angry, others slow and meditative. I heard voices out of the future speak to me and I heard my own voice, also in a future time, trying to explain, to justify, the way in which I'd used my short-term lease among the stars . . .

Dear Miss Janie Lewis,

Stick to your tirades, hon. "Night Sounds" are just not you at your best.

Your beer-drinking, frat-hating, establishment-stomping, ever-lovin' buddies from

Bingham Quad

It was Graham's twenty-first birthday. I gave up on men's stores. He had as many cuff links, sweaters, and pocket flasks as they stocked. Also, I had a limited amount to spend, and did not want to risk choosing the wrong brand, an inferior label. I went to the bookstore because here I knew I could trust my taste. Usually, for people I liked, I simply chose a book I wanted myself. Would Graham like a Kierkegaard anthology? The complete poetry of John Donne? I couldn't be sure. I went on to the hobby shelves and examined a glossy volume entitled *A Compleat Guide to the World's Firearms.*

"Looking for new ammunition for your column, Miss

Lewis?" asked an ironic male voice behind me. Somehow I knew who it was. I turned at last to see what Jack Krazowski looked like. He was tall, but otherwise a disappointment. Pale, hawklike face. Horn-rims, faded Levi's, and muddy combat boots. He was holding the Modern Library edition of *Thus Spake Zarasthustra.* His hands were surprisingly graceful and clean.

"I'm looking for a birthday present," I said. "A person I know is being given a surprise birthday party tonight."

"What sort of person?" he asked familiarly. His eyes were such a light blue, he looked as though he were perpetually squinting into the sun.

"One of those persons who have everything already." My sarcastic tone surprised me.

"Oh," he said, not very interested. He was looking at me, rather pleased about something. "You're a lot prettier than that bitchy picture of you they run," he said at last.

"I don't expect you to like my picture any better than you like my column."

"It's getting better. The one about the night sounds showed promise."

"I'm glad you think I have literary promise."

"Oh, that's never been in question. I wasn't referring to that kind of promise when I said you were getting better. Would you like a cup of coffee?"

"I can't. I have to go home and wash my hair for this party. And I haven't even bought a present."

"Let me help you. The purely impersonal shopper's guide. What is your friend like?"

"He's soft-spoken," I said, noting the flicker of disappointment at the masculine pronoun. "Well dressed," I added, looking down at his caked boots. I was being terrible, I couldn't help myself.

"Buy him this." He held up an ornate copy of the *Inferno,* with Doré engravings, on sale for $4.50. "It's a good book, if he wants to read it. And the pictures are nice if he doesn't. He'll be flattered to think that you think he'll read it, anyway."

I caught the implicit snub, but it did seem, somehow, the

perfect choice. And the price was certainly right. I bought the book.

"If he likes it, you have to go to dinner with me sometime," said Jack, who then walked me back to the dorm. He had a loping long-distance walk; I had to run along awkwardly to keep up.

"Were you in the army?" I said. "You walk like you're on a long march."

"Nope. Marines."

"For how long?"

"Four years."

"Good grief, you must be ancient."

"A decrepit twenty-seven in June. I had to get somebody to pay for law school. My old man's a miner. I have nine brothers and sisters."

"Well, I'm an only child. But my father has this problem with his temper and keeps losing jobs. I had these war bonds, luckily, my aunt and uncle used to send me every Christmas, and I cashed them in so I could go to this measly little college in my hometown as a day student. The only reason I'm here is because I made straight A's for two years and did nothing but grind, grind, grind. Now I intend to have some fun." I was shocked at myself. I had not even told my Christian Scientist roommate the whole truth.

We were standing, by this time, at the entrance to my dorm. Jack suddenly gave me a paternal pat on top of my head. "That explains a lot," he said. "Yes. Well, after all my fan mail, I guess you know where I live now. Call me when you're ready to go out to dinner. Any night except Tuesday. That's my night to collect dorm laundry."

I hurried upstairs to wash my hair. I was annoyed at Jack for telling me to call him. Where were his manners? I was sorry I had talked to him about my family, but it had poured out before I could stop it. Under the shower I closed my eyes and luxuriated in thoughts of the evening to come. I felt in control of my life here at last. And Jack had said I was pretty. Maybe we could be friends. We could go off occasionally by ourselves and have quiet conversations. He was not exactly a showpiece, but I had my showpiece already. These were those pre-"Liberation" years, before girls felt guilty about treating men like objects because turnabout is fair play.

Graham liked his present. He said, "This is one classic I have always wanted to read. This is the kind of book you can keep for a lifetime." (And I am sure Graham still has the book.)

In the days that followed I became unusually depressed. All the anger had suddenly gone out of me. I read in the newspaper about a student from Texas who had jumped from the tower due to "pressures from overwork," and every time I thought of this I cried. In fact, I tried to think about it so I could cry. I wrote a column entitled "The Pressures That Bear Us Away," a disconnected, overwrought piece that, when it was published, prompted a call to the newspaper from the Director of Student Health, who pronounced it an irresponsible romanticizing of suicide. The editor called me into his office and more or less issued an ultimatum: Get funny again, or get out. I quickly redeemed myself by "crashing" the sororities' Spring Fashion Show. My next "Without Restrictions" was called "A Visitor from Mars Reports on Pan-Hellenic Couture," and put this shallow annual event in its cosmic place. Graham telephoned, sounding uncharacteristically sad. "I know these things don't seem important to you, Janie, but Suzanne Pinkerton devoted hours of work organizing that show, and she felt your column was unfair." He was as courteous and soft-spoken as ever, but I felt the censure in his words, and imagined his alliance with Suzanne against my clumsy fury.

That afternoon, I called Kerr Dorm, second floor. The phone rang for a long time. At last a boy answered. There was a great commotion in the background, shouts echoing and shower water running. "Who is it you want?" he kept repeating. "You'll have to speak up louder."

"I want Jack Krazowski!" I shouted.

"She wants Jack Krazowski!" he shouted. There was a lot

of male laughter. I was getting ready to hang up in embarrassment.

"Hello," he said. "Don't mind them."

"This is Janie Lewis, from the bookstore," I said.

"I know that. When are we going to dinner? How about tonight?"

"That would be fine. Actually, I've been . . . it will be nice to talk to you."

"I'll be over in about an hour," he said. "I'll shave and put on a suit so you won't be ashamed of me."

"I look forward to it," I said, feeling better.

"I'm glad you finally got around to calling," he said. Was he laughing? I couldn't tell.

When I looked for him in the dorm parlor, I skipped right over him at first. I looked at the boys lounging self-consciously against armchairs and walls, huddling together in groups. One of these boys I recognized as a new Deke, who'd pledged in January. Jack, in a dark suit, turned from the window where he'd been standing. He'd been there all the time, but I had been looking for a boy, not a man.

"I didn't recognize you, all dressed up," I said, hurrying along beside his long-march strides into the early-spring evening. The new Deke looked after us. I supposed it would get back to Graham but I didn't care.

"It's only my charisma," said Jack. "You'll get used to it."

He took me to a steak house on the highway. None of the Greeks ever went there. Everything seemed strangely and pleasantly adult. Jack had borrowed a car, a pedestrian black Plymouth with the radio missing from the dashboard.

"What did you want to talk about?" he said.

"Oh nothing. Everything. I just feel I can be myself around you."

"Can't you be with your other friends? Your friend that had the birthday, for instance?"

"Oh God!" I laughed wildly. Then I amended, "It's just

that ... with a lot of people, I seem to be able to present only certain sides of myself. But with you, I can just let go."

"Knowing what I think I know," he said, "I'm not sure that's a compliment from you."

"What do you mean?"

"Oh, let's pass on that one. If you don't know, it's because you don't want to know yet. Besides, I'm glad you called." He reached over and tapped the back of my neck lightly with his finger, and a queer thing happened to my stomach.

The atmosphere of the steak house had a liberating effect on me. It seemed we were decades away from the college campus. Sitting across from each other in the dark little restaurant, eating our charcoaled steaks and drinking our beers, we might have been two highway travelers going anywhere. "I haven't felt so relaxed all year," I said. "If you only knew how much time I spend talking about nothing with people I don't even like."

"Why do you do it?" Jack asked, watching me closely. The way he had tapped my neck in the car: I hoped he would touch me again.

I said, "When I was growing up, all my friends belonged to a country club. Or, rather, their parents did. This club had the only swimming pool in town. There was another place, a sort of walled-in lake, but a girl had been molested there—a bunch of local hoodlums stood in a circle around her and made her let them feel under her bathing suit—and my mother wouldn't let me go. I was allowed into the country club pool, as a guest, twice a month. Once, a friend tried to sneak me in a third time and the lifeguard caught us and made me leave. My friend decided to stay on. I remember she gave me this sort of pitying look through the fence and said, very cool and sweet, 'We'll have better luck next time, Janie.' I walked back home, over the golf course, and I felt so ashamed."

"It was your so-called friend who should have felt ashamed," said Jack. "Did that ever cross your mind?"

"No, I guess it didn't. Not until now. How funny that it shouldn't have, until now."

"That's because you're in a rut," said Jack. "Do you want to be accepted by people just because they remind you of those rich kids in your hometown? Shouldn't you ask yourself, first of all, whether you accept *them?*"

"I don't know," I said. "It's not that simple. These people do have something. This kind of unshakable quality. I'm so . . . shakable. There's a mystery about these people I need to decipher."

"Mystery!" scoffed Jack. He drummed his long fingers on the checkered tablecloth.

"You have wonderful hands," I said, wanting an excuse to touch him. "Have you ever taken piano?"

"Coal miners' sons aren't in the habit of taking piano lessons," he replied, and I hated the smugness in his voice.

"Why do you play up your proletarian role?" I said.

"I don't know. Do I play it up? Perhaps it's my Budapest defense. Do you know chess? No? I'll have to teach you. It will develop your unshakable powers." He picked up my hand.

"What is a Budapest defense?" I said rapturously.

"A gambit. A sort of counterattack. Get them before they have a chance to get you. You of all people ought to understand."

"I wish you would teach me," I said. "Chess, I mean. No, I don't. I wish you could teach me everything." I did not have to ask myself whether I accepted Jack. There were other ways of knowing.

"Janie," he said. "Too bad we didn't meet earlier."

"But we've got now," I said recklessly. "We've got two more months." I pushed it too quickly, promising more than I was sure I could give.

"We have, if you want it," he said, looking at me carefully.

As soon as we got back to the car, in the dark parking lot behind the steak house, we began kissing. Now and then, a car or a truck would hurtle down the highway, beaming its headlights momentarily on the tall yellow grasses growing wild. Then there was darkness and the stars scattered liberally across a black sky. Suddenly the world was so much bigger. Jack and I existed alone under that sky. We were members of the universe, and anything smaller was a bore.

But when we drove back again, into the lights of the town, and saw students coming out of the movies in pairs, and convertibles skimming around corners, my old paltry fear returned. Jack asked whether I would like to stop off at Harry's, a popular campus hangout, for a cup of coffee, but I said no. I was afraid for his charisma, under the fluorescent lights. It might dissolve, and I would be stuck in Harry's with a coal miner's son and his Budapest defense, and I was not ready yet. He seemed to understand, and drove me to the dorm.

At the front door, he took me by the shoulders and looked searchingly into my face. "Janie, there isn't unlimited time for all there is to do," he said. "Don't waste it. Don't be afraid of doing what you want."

"I enjoyed the dinner," I said, in a turmoil.

He sighed. "Well, you call me when you want another one," he said. "Only it probably won't be steak next time. I'm a poor man, remember."

The spring went quickly, like a 33 record somebody had turned up to 78. Graham became hyperattentive. He'd obviously been told of my stepping out by the new Deke trying to score a few Brownie points. Graham didn't pry. That was not his way. He asked me to accept his pin. I had hoped for this for a long time; it had seemed the answer to so many things. With a dry mouth, feeling a stranger to myself, I accepted the pin in an impressive candlelight ceremony. The brothers stood in a circle around us. Even Suzanne Pinkerton came up to me afterward and took my hand and said, as though she meant it, "I'm so happy for you, Janie."

I saw Jack only once more, at the bookstore. I had gone there to browse, hoping I might meet him.

"That's an elegant pin you've got on," he said, looking straight at my eyes and not at the pin. "Does it mean you're engaged?"

"Not exactly. Kind of engaged to be engaged."

"Hmm. What are those, rubies?"

"They're not tin," I said, without thinking, and could have bitten off my tongue.

"No, I can see that," he said quietly. A remote look came into his face. I remembered how we had kissed under the stars. It would be unthinkable, never to do it again. And yet his remoteness clearly proclaimed we wouldn't.

"Oh well," I said, "things happen. But they also unhappen. Will you be back in the fall?"

"I'm finishing up in June," he said. "I get my law degree in June. Then back to West Virginia, to study for the bar."

"Oh." There was nothing else I could think of to say, yet there was so much going on between us.

He broke the silence. "Well, take care, Janie." Then he went out of the bookstore, bouncing up and down on the balls of his feet, in his long-march style. I had an impulse to run after him. But what would I say when I caught up with him?

After finals, Graham gave a houseparty at his parents' summer cottage at the beach. There was much beer-drinking and water-skiing and necking, and I was so integral a part of the group that I found I could dispense altogether with my Mary McCarthy smile. I shared a bedroom with Suzanne Pinkerton and was able to penetrate her mystique at last. She worried terribly about her small breasts and had sent off secretly for a chest developer, which she used morning and night. She slept with a yellow rabbit, whose fur had come off in patches, which she'd been given as a child. She confided that she was not really in love with the boy who was her date for this houseparty. "There's someone . . . he's in Maine . . . in some ways he reminds me of you, Janie."

"Oh? In what ways?"

"Well, he's real smart, like you . . . and at first he seems, you know, kind of critical. But after you get to know him, he's a wonderful person."

We were lying on the beach one morning, doing our nails

from the same bottle of polish. She said to me, "Marietta Porter is transferring to William and Mary in the fall. There'll be a vacancy at the Chi O house. I could speak to the others if you're interested, Janie."

I was lying on my stomach, listening to the dull, even plash of the sea at low tide, watching Suzanne's polish harden to a fine porcelain sheen on my fingernails. I pretended Jack Krazowski was within listening distance, hearing me utter the finale to that wasted year. But no one was listening as I thanked Suzanne and explained about that clause in my scholarship. No one at all, not even the Spirit of the Times, who had turned her back on us to scan the horizon. There were new things on the way for people to join or to be angry about. The sixties were coming.

Suzanne said, well, she hoped I'd come around to the house and have dinner sometime, she hoped we could get to know each other better. Then she started on her second coat of polish. I lay there beside her, staring at my own nails, getting angrier by the minute because I couldn't love them, even now that I'd made them love me.

Then the boys came back, carrying their surfboards, waving at us while they were still some distance away. Without my glasses I was not sure which of them, in their look-alike plaid bathing trunks, was Graham. The closer they came, the angrier I got, not with the deflected anger that went into the columns of "Without Restrictions," but with a deep, abiding, central anger at the real culprit, the crass conformist who'd been harboring inside the rebel all along. I dug my nails into the sand, ruining the careful polish job. What was the proper procedure for returning a fraternity pin without hurting anyone's feelings?

I don't remember the actual returning of Graham's pin. He must have been hurt, or baffled at the very least. What happened to him later I don't know.

The fall of my senior year I spent ministering to the almost constant anger of a new man, a young psychiatrist in the blackest depths of his training analysis. We spent most of our time together confusing me with his mother. In the spring I rallied and helped to found a new literary magazine on campus. It was called *Shock!!!* and had one triumphant issue before being quashed by the local postmaster. Then I graduated, with no *laudes*, and went out into the world, where I found new people to love and plenty of new things to be angry about.

But ever since the Angry-Year, I have reserved my most energetic fury for the Culprit. Though her powers have diminished as I've grown more sure of mine, she still keeps quarters for herself in some unreachable part of my psyche. She bores from inside at the braver scaffoldings erected by my imagination, and her favorite trick is posing as other people whom I hate until I realize I'm hating myself. She is forever trying to constrain me to the well-trodden paths of expression, even as I write this story. For every mental mile I succeed in traveling without her restrictions, she leadens my heart with her ceaseless plaint: *What are the others thinking? What will others think?*

A Cultural
Exchange

*O*nce I was twenty-one and terrified I would not get the most out of life. I wanted to marry, to travel, to be a writer. Not in that order; not in any order. Perhaps I could bring everything about simultaneously, without having to make any bridge-burning choices. The truth was, I was a person who had spacious ideals, but who was rather timid when it came to facing unknown space.

I went to Copenhagen on a freighter. It was October, the worst month for storms, and I stayed flat on my back in my cabin for most of the trip. The stewardess brought me oranges, and, in my good moments, I sat up and continued work on the long letter I was writing to the man I intended to marry one of these days.

After a week in Copenhagen, I decided to stay for the winter. I wrote to Barney, my intended, that I had "fallen in love with the Danes." Let him worry a little about the ambiguous plural. The real reason, though I couldn't have told you then, was that traveling wearied and depressed me. I found it hard to concentrate on the pure experience of another culture, when I was feeling self-conscious about eating alone, or trying to dissolve little grains of Woolite in a hotel basin that leaked, or constantly being surprised by one more expense I hadn't counted on.

I went to the American Embassy, and the cultural attaché gave me the name of a widower in Klampenborg who took out a lot of books on American culture from the USIS library. "He's not running a boardinghouse or anything, mind you, but he did once say that his family has shrunk and he has too much space and he had been entertaining the thought of taking into the house a well-behaved young person, someone who could help improve his son's English."

And so, on Sunday afternoon, I found myself aboard the electric train, shuttling outward from the city. A rush of cold air came in at each stop: Nordhavn, Svanemøllen, Hellerup, Charlottenlund, Ordrup ... The names of these suburbs vibrated with the secrets of the country I was now going to discover. Secure that I was being met at the end of the line, I could concentrate on the essences along the way.

I saw him before he saw me. He was clearly a gentleman in the old tradition, the way he stood on the station platform, proud and rather aloof, in his chesterfield, his gray-gloved hands on his walking stick. A real patriarch. Then I shrank back as he scanned the windows of my car. But not before I caught the naked wistfulness that played across his features. "We shall look each other over," he had said on the phone, in precise Oxford English. But I had seen, in that eager, lonely look, a predisposition to welcome whatever stepped off the train.

I did just that, pulling up the collar of my polo coat to have something to do with my hands. There was no point in pretending to look up and down the platform, for he was the only person waiting. "Mr. Engelgard? I'm Amanda Sloane. How nice of you to meet me at the station." ("... *a well-behaved young person* ...")

"Rolf Engelgard. It is my pleasure." I could see he was as pleased with my appearance as I had been with his. "I live only there, but first we shall walk a little." He pointed to some white apartment buildings on the slope of a hill. Beyond their flat roofs stretched the glassy gray smoothness of the sea, its horizon topped by a small, misty slice of Sweden. "Are you hungry?" he asked. "Maybe you would like to eat first."

"Oh, I had a late breakfast."

"In that case, we shall wait a little. Would you like a ride into Dryehavn, the King's deer park and hunting lodge? It is lovely just now, before the frost comes. We will lunch after. How would you like that?"

"I'd love it, but I hadn't meant to take up your entire Sunday afternoon."

"Time is something of which I have plenty," he said, taking my arm. "So! First a ride into the park, then lunch at Ryttergarten, then I show you my big old flat. Have you learned any Danish yet?"

"Just *tak*. And *tak for sidst*, and *tusind tak*, and *mange tak*. The people here all speak such good English that it makes me shy. Nevertheless, I'd like to try to learn enough to make myself understood. . . ."

He stopped suddenly. We were mounting a rather steep cement upgrade, away from the Klampenborg station into a leaf-strewn park. His handsome old face went very pale. "I am sorry," he said, breathing very fast. "Last winter I had a little bronchial ailment and still find myself short of breath. It is such a nuisance." He spoke lightly, with an ironic lilt, but his blue eyes were hard with fury. He stood for several minutes, leaning heavily on his stick, glaring at the clean October sky, as if cursing some Viking deity up there.

"We're not in any hurry," I said tactfully. "That's why I like it here. Everyone takes his time."

"The Danes are downright lazy." He started to walk again. "I am a Norwegian. My parents came here when I was a boy."

"What are Norwegians like, then?" I wanted to win his approval.

"Fierce, proud, hardworking. The Danes have a sense of humor, but the Norwegians work harder. My elder son, for example, is Norwegian to the core. My younger, who lives with me, is typical Danish. Almost thirty and still a student."

"And what does your older son do?"

"A lawyer in Copenhagen. We don't speak of him, please."

"Of course," I agreed, embarrassed by the unexpected rebuff. "Where is your car parked?"

"I have no car. They are very dear in this country. I always ride a bicycle until this drat illness."

"Oh, I thought you said something about a ride in the deer park." Eccentric, I was thinking; a bit senile. . . ?

"Ah!"—he now smiled broadly for the first time—"we are in the deer park. Look." He pointed with his stick toward a hill crowned by a small castle, behind which the early-winter sun was already setting at half past one. "We *shall* ride to the King's hunting lodge." He looked down at me, quite pleased with himself. "You wait here, please." He crossed the road and spoke in Danish to a hack driver who stood beside his horses, drinking a bottle of beer.

Soon we were sitting side by side in the open carriage, our legs wrapped in blankets. The driver trotted his pair of bays along the curving path of the woods, where deer grazed close enough for us to see their eyes blink. Engelgard was watching my face avidly for every reaction. "I am so interested to know what you think, all your impressions, Amanda. May I call you Amanda? This will be a new experience for me, too. I have never taken in a lodger. Ever since my wife died, Lars—that is the son who lives with me—has been urging me to let one of our unused rooms. It is such a big flat. It contained twenty-one years of our busy married life, the growing of two boys. I told Lars, 'Whoever comes to live here, *if* I shall find such a person, shall be treated like family.' I could not have it any other way. I wanted a young person. They are more adaptable and straight-forward. You come from the southern part of the United States. Wait, let me guess where. One of the Carolinas."

"North Carolina," I said, amazed, "but how could you tell?"

He smiled radiantly. I suddenly saw how good-looking he must have been as a young man. "I was not manager of Thomas Cook and Sons for thirty years without knowing some Americans. Also I have made a study of American dialects. Languages are my hobby. I speak twelve. Would you like to bet: before you leave us, I shall be able to speak like a—what would you call a native of North Carolina?"

"Well, a lot of people say Tarheel."

"Tarheel! How delightful! And what is the origin of the term?"

"I'm ashamed to say I don't know."

"Never mind, we shall find out. We have plenty of time during these long winter months. I must teach you about North Carolina; you shall show me the Danes." He rubbed his gloved hands together and chuckled. "It will be so good to have interesting conversations with someone young and vital. Poor Lars is at the university all day."

The horses had slowed at the top of a hill. The driver turned to Engelgard and said something in Danish. He replied. When speaking the Scandinavian tongue, his deep voice went up a pitch; he glided softly over the diphthongs, as if he were afraid of mashing them with his strength. *Wait a minute, wait a minute*, the Voice of Experience was warning me, though I hardly ever listened in those days. *Having a fatherly, interpretative landlord your first uncertain winter abroad is one thing; getting involved in the needs of a lonely, authoritative old widower whose moods go up and down like a seesaw is something else.*

"Look there, Tarheel. Have you ever seen so many deer in one place?"

I was already phrasing its beauty in a letter to Barney: the tough, bare lines of the royal hunting lodge; the vast and peaceful sward where hundreds of deer grazed within touching-distance of the Sunday strollers; the whole thing bathed in the russet glow of this uncanny early sunset. I was so excited about being somewhere foreign, at last, and how I would write about it, that I grabbed Mr. Engelgard and committed myself in a rush of exuberant gratitude.

"You certainly do know how to give things a lovely beginning," I said.

He looked studiously at the crowds of deer and people. A tear detached itself from his eye and rolled down his bony cheek.

"How many deer are there in all, I wonder," I went on, pretending I hadn't seen.

"The guidebooks say two thousand," replied the ironic, lilting voice, "but I should think many more than that, myself."

I moved into the enormous, rather dark old flat on Wednesday. Its one advantage was its view of the sea. My room had been Mrs. Engelgard's studio, where she did illustrations for women's magazines. Framed originals of these hung three and four deep on every wall. They showed people wearing slightly out-of-style clothes kissing under leafy trees, little children sitting alone in corners, a girl in an evening dress running away from a gloomy old house, her evening cloak streaming behind her.

Mr. Engelgard had spent all of Monday and Tuesday going through the big oak wardrobe, transferring her things into cardboard boxes. The project was still unfinished when I arrived in the taxi.

The old man had taken the train to town, to do some shopping. It was Lars, the perennial-student son, who helped me settle in.

"All these clotheses shall go away," he said, removing from the floor of the wardrobe several pairs of small walking shoes with mud still caked to the heels. He dropped them gently into the cardboard box. "Poor Father. He worked all day and didn't get nowhere. He spend all the time looking at the things. He loved her so much."

Lars was not a bit like his father. He was short and round, like a troll, and had bright red cheeks and a scruffy beard. His English was as rapid as it was incorrect, for he never paused to search for a word, simply filled in the nearest thing handy. He had switched majors several times and was now in zoology at the University of Copenhagen. "I should have finished my *eksamen* last year, but father went poor and I stay back and take care of him."

"He said he'd been sick." I began hanging my miracle-fiber outfits in Mrs. Engelgard's wardrobe. I decided to keep Lars's physical description vague in my letter to Barney.

"At night, you hear him. He searches for breath. It break

your heart. I sleep in the bed with him. He is unwilling to sleep alone since she die. We hope you shall join us for our supper to-night. Gudrun will cook yellow bean soup. It is gorgeously good, I can tell you. Gudrun is our housekeeper. She is a jolly tart. In the evening she works under the bar at the hotel across the street."

"You mean behind the bar, I hope."

"Behind the bar. You will help my English. It is killing Father. Only, if I wait till I have the right word I never get my thing said. Is better to crash on, don't you think? He who hesitates is last."

"Lost," I corrected, laughing. He would be the brother I never had.

"Lost. Oh, you will be wonderful to have around. And look you—" He walked briskly across the cluttered room to the French doors and pointed proudly to a slab of frozen earth outside. Several twiglike plants, quite dead, stood stiffly erect. "Our garden. In spring, you shall have vegetables and flowers rising out there."

"But I'll be gone by then. I'll go to Paris in the spring."

"Ah, Paris. Yes. But now we enjoy the long Danish winter."

Mr. Engelgard came home long after dark, his arms full of parcels and books checked out of the USIS library. He breathed as though he might collapse any minute. Lars and I were sitting on the sofa in the living room, looking at their family album. "Welcome to our house, Amanda," he said. Then, when he caught his breath, "What did the governor of North Carolina say to the governor of South Carolina?"

"At least I know that one. 'It's a long time between drinks.'"

"Right you are. But watch out: in future they shall not be so easy. I have been to your Embassy and wiped out the Carolina shelf." He dropped a package as he was trying to show me a book, and cursed in Danish. "Lars, do you think you might help me?" he said petulantly to his son.

Lars jumped up at once and took all the parcels. The cork of a wine bottle poked out of one. "Lucky *that* did not drop," he said roguishly, and disappeared into the kitchen.

"Well, now," said Engelgard, slumping heavily into an armchair, "has Lars shown you where to find things? I see he has lost no time in dragging out the family album. Actually I planned to show you it myself, a bit later on, after dinner some night, when you know us better and the pictures mean something. Poor Lars lacks a sense of occasion, but he means well. Do you like your room? It was my wife's studio."

"I love it. All those paintings. The sea outside. All I need now is a typewriter."

"Yes, you are going to begin your writing career. I shall call a man I know about renting you a machine. My wife worked long hours in that room. Late into the night sometimes. Of course, you must feel free to change things around, though personally I think everything looks so appropriate as it is."

"Oh, I wouldn't dream of changing anything," I heard myself declare. All afternoon I had been looking for corners and drawers where I could stash the cactus plants and odd knick-knacks whose value must lie in personal meanings for some family member.

"No, I thought you wouldn't," he said, rewarding me with his smile. "Ah, Lars, my boy, here you are. I thought of a perfect nickname for you today, since we will be speaking more English in this house now."

"What is the name, Father?" Lars asked cheerfully, entering with a tray of drinks. There were two whiskies and some strange, yellowish, oily mixture in a wineglass, on whose bottom bounced a disconsolate black olive. "I have made Amanda a martini, just like in America, so she feels at home."

" 'Frowsy' is the name I have chosen," said Engelgard. He turned his head at such an angle that his son could not see his broad wink to me.

"Hmm. It sounds all right. What do it mean?"

"What *does* it mean. Well, the nearest translation would be—" He was shaking with barely suppressed mirth. "Let's see,

Amanda, wouldn't you say the nearest translation of 'Frowsy' would be 'an American nobleman'?" The old blue eyes coaxed me to be an accomplice.

"Well, yes. I guess that's as good as any," I said. I took a sip of my "martini." Lars had made it with sweet vermouth.

"Frowsy," repeated Lars, rather pleased. "I am Frowsy. How is your martini, the way you like it?"

"Let us drink a toast to the newest member of our family," said Engelgard, raising his own glass, sparing me the necessity of speaking a second untruth.

The next morning, Mr. Engelgard picked up the telephone and spoke familiarly in his musical Danish, and within a few hours a blue portable typewriter was delivered to the flat. We set it up on a large table in the center of my room, and drank a toast to it from Engelgard's schnapps bottle. "When you are a famous writer and they are giving you a cocktail party in a New York skyscraper, go to the window and look out and remember the day we launched your career with a rented typewriter," said the old man. "And remember me a little." Then out he tiptoed ceremoniously, making way for the Muse, and I rolled two sheets and a carbon into the machine and began typing rapidly, knowing he would be listening in the next room.

"Your move, my dear," said Engelgard. It was Saturday night.

Apathetically I moved my queen into the diagonal line of fire from his bishop. My head hurt. *Jeg har en dundrende hovedpine*, according to my Danish phrase book, which was the last thing I needed with eloquent Mr. Engelgard. I have a splitting headache. Outside, the ocean crashed. Frowsy had telephoned from town to say he had run into his brother, Palle, in the bookstore and they would dine together. Englegard had been in the bathroom having a coughing fit when the call came, and I had to relay the message. He glared at the telephone, then smiled dotingly and asked would I like a game of chess. I had thought of going into Copenhagen on the train, sitting for an hour or so in a place where students hung out. But somehow I had slipped into this role of the dutiful daughter, so of course I couldn't go. He'd feel so abandoned, with Frowsy gone as well, to eat with the son of whom we didn't speak.

"Amanda, you aren't keeping your mind on the game. Is something the matter? I never saw you give up your queen without a bloodbath."

"Sorry. I think I'm coming down with something. Do you hear a sort of echo in the room? When I woke up today, my throat was kind of scratchy."

"Why did you not say something?" He came around and felt my forehead. He cursed in Danish. "But, my child, you have a fever! We shall have to move quickly if we are to rout this Danish cold. He hangs on and on and sucks your vitality. That is how my illness began. You must go to bed this minute. That is orders." He looked almost pleased.

"But we haven't finished our game," I said, torn between wanting the eventfulness of a sickbed bustle and feeling trapped, here in this overcrowded flat, with a lonely, autocratic old nurse whose dead wife's apron still hung on the hook behind the kitchen door.

"I would have demolished you in three more moves. See? I take your queen and that leaves your castle defenseless. He cannot budge because he is blocked by your pawn. I take your castle and what stands between me and your king?"

True to his diagnosis, I had contracted the genuine Danish cold. For three days I perspired under the eiderdown, feverishly imagining what kinds of stories had gone with the framed illustrations on my walls, sneezing into Mr. Engelgard's best silk handkerchiefs, which he then boiled, along with the ones he coughed into, in a cooking pot on the back burner of the stove. I ate the oysters he ordered from the hotel across the street. I drank his toddies of whiskey, sugar, and hot water. I slept and dreamed of North Carolina and woke to hear the Danish wind howling and the waves lashing against the strand. Mr. Engelgard pulled up a chair, propped his feet on the foot of my bed, and told stories about the German occupation of Denmark: how, just here, on Strandvej, the Underground had smuggled the Jewish population in fishing boats over to Sweden; how every Danish wife practiced passive resistance by staring at the crotch of every German soldier she passed. And he told me how he and his wife had ridden their bicycles to Rungsted to have tea with Baroness Blixen.

"You had tea with Isak Dinesen!"

"Certainly. My wife illustrated some of her work. If you are a good girl, Amanda, and write very hard, I shall take you to visit her in the spring."

In those days, I kept carbons of all the letters I wrote. I found I could express things in the unselfconscious flow of a letter that simply evaporated when I sat down, consciously, to write a story. But as I reread these carbons now, in my study in upstate New York, I find that I was then so busy creating experiences that I missed the reality.

Dear Barney [Barney's sons in North Carolina must be teenagers by now],

Outside: the howling northern wind. Four hours of daylight. But how I love it, here among the lovable Danes, fantastic schizophrenic race of Peter Pans, telling macabre jokes one minute and shooting themselves the next. [Who on earth was I referring to?] For twenty-five dollars a month [I'm sure it must have been more] I have a perfect setup, a beautiful room overlooking the sea [well, their living room did], very near to Isak Dinesen's house. My landlord is a very close friend of hers and we will dine there next week. Engelgard is a real aristocrat, but he hates being old. His son Lars is a very attractive Dane (don't worry, my American heart belongs to you—eventually). Lars, who is studying zoology at the University of Copenhagen, was showing me the Engelgard family album and there was this picture, browning at the edges, of Mr. Engelgard as a young skier, framed against a Norwegian slope. He was incredibly handsome, a Viking Romeo, cheekbones like brackets (they still are) and a wonderful rakish grin.

After supper the first night I came here, my proud silver-haired host arises from the table (we had yellow bean soup, fried octopus, and Liebfraumilch in my honor) and goes over to the old upright piano with his dead wife's picture on top and proceeds to play and sing in a deep, rich baritone, pausing, however, for shortness of breath, "Nothing could be finer than to be in Carolina in the mor-or-or-ning ..." I almost cried. And did you know (I didn't) that the reason we are called Tarheels is that General Lee said of the N.C. Regiment, "Oh, they'll stick. They've got tar on their heels."

"I think I'll get dressed and take a walk down Strandvej," I said on the second day I had been out of bed. We were having the lunch he'd made: black broth, sardines on toast, and Carlsberg Elephant beer.

"You'll do nothing of the kind," snapped Engelgard.

I burst into tears. It was partly out of frustration over being cooped up so long. But also I knew that my own fear of his displeasure was creating a formidable barrier to my freedom.

"Amanda! Dear me!" He came to me quickly, laid his trembling hand against my face. "Oh, I am sorry. I did not think. Maybe I am so afraid of losing things that I hold on too fiercely. You are of course free to walk at any time you wish. I know what, we will go together. I, too, could use some fresh air. This musty old flat. I could show you the fishing boats, then we will have a little something at the hotel. But you must bundle up snugly. Wear those long black stockings I teased you about."

It was a release to be outside, chaperoned or not. How much I'd missed the sense of just going someplace. The sea was calm and Sweden was clear today. We walked slowly because of his shortness of breath. Gulls dipped, squeaking, up and down in the sky.

"Are things okay between us, Tarheel?" He looked very fit, wearing his chesterfield and a dark-blue woolen scarf knotted high on his neck. His cheeks were pink. Since I had been ill, he seemed to have gained in strength.

"Of course." Tomorrow I would get up early, take the train into Copenhagen, spend the day on my own. It seemed a point of honor to do this, even if, when tomorrow came, I wanted to snuggle in bed. If I didn't get out and go somewhere, I would have nothing to write about.

Sitting in our usual corner in the hotel bar, we drank hot rum. Outside the picture window, the early-afternoon sun was setting. "So you don't think I am a mean old man," said Engelgard.

I said don't be silly.

"Palle, my older boy, the lawyer, you know"—he began suddenly, wiping his lips with the napkin—"after my wife died, I became very morbid. Possibly a bit irritable and demanding. I felt Palle neglected me. He would arrive only to change into clean clothes, then back into town. Sometimes he stayed out all night! One day, we had a showdown. I don't wish to hold a postmortem, but I said, 'As long as you live in my home you behave like a proper son and show some consideration.' He said, 'Very well, Father, I will not live anymore in your home.' And he was gone. He packed his things and moved out the very same night! It shows a certain strength of character, don't you agree? But also a hardness of heart. I haven't seen him since. I keep thinking for a while that perhaps he would ring me up on the telephone. He did not ring. I send Frowsy to find out if he was all right. They have dinner in town now and then. Frowsy will not say if he speaks of me. Sometimes, I confess it, I feel downright sorry for myself and get a bit crotchety. You do forgive me, won't you, for today? You are free to come and go as you please."

"There's nothing to forgive. You were concerned about me. I appreciate having you in my life."

"Honestly?" he asked eagerly.

"Honestly. I'm sure he'll come around. You'll make up."

His face went hard. "You mistake me. It is too late. He will be sorry one day, possibly, but it is over for me."

I took the ten o'clock train to Copenhagen next day. Mr. Engelgard said, "I think I might straighten out your bookshelf while you are in town. You can't want all those dusty foreign books. I shall leave you some space to put in your own, as you buy them."

I nodded agreeably, rather than say I had no intention of accumulating a lot of heavy books to cart around Europe when I went on the road again.

As I crossed the big square in the center of Copenhagen, in bright winter sunshine, I felt like a racehorse being given his head after weeks inside a stable. I strolled down Stroget and looked in the shops. I bought some stretch ski pants for myself, a package of Viennese coffee (his favorite) for Mr. Engelgard, and a new science-fiction anthology for Frowsy. Then I wandered down to Nyhavn, to the port area, and watched the fishwives scream their wares. At a fruit stand I bought a red apple, which I ate ceremoniously while exploring the narrow streets and feeling super-conscious of being in Copenhagen. I played a favorite game with myself, in which I imagined my every action being observed by some person at home. Today it was Barney who watched me munching the apple and trailing my fingers along old walls.

In the late afternoon, I came across a restaurant on the corner of two streets. It was crammed with young people. I went in and ordered a beer and looked helplessly around for somewhere to sit. A handsome young Dane with gold hair and the proverbial sucked-in cheeks waved at me, as though I'd been expected. I sat down with him and his friend, a black man in a dapper tweed suit. Their names were Niels and Jean. Niels was a painter; Jean was a journalist from Marseilles. Their English was rudimentary, but they shared what they had with me; every now and then, some enthusiasm would get the better of them and away they would go, into a fluid, gesticulating French. Niels said he had met lots of American girls seeing the world. "Why you all the time climbing for something?" he asked. "Why is American women so"—he erupted into French, gesticulating to Jean, who supplied him with the word he wanted— "ambitious? You are never in the place where you are, always looking into distance of where you aren't."

"I'm not like that," I said, remembering my pure present-time joy of walking in Nyhavn with my apple.

"May we buy you another beer?" asked Jean, in heavily accented English.

After several more beers, it became easier to communicate. We gestured and laughed a lot and language seemed a silly barrier. We were all young, that was the point. Then we were in another restaurant and I was insisting on buying them both supper, for Niels had explained they could not afford to have more than soup. I told them they could take me to see Christiansborg Castle in return; I was afraid to go by myself in the dark. Then, magically, we were there, a sliver of moon tipped over our heads, our giggling ringing out over the silent battlements and turrets. A palace guard appeared out of the shadows and told us we had to leave. We went to another place and drank more beer and I missed the last train to Klampenborg. I thought this was funny, but Niels and Jean exchanged a look of irritation. "Well, I guess you stay at my place and go first thing tomorrow," said Niels. Our camaraderie was strangely muted as we went through the cobbled streets to Niels's place. Jean and Niels slept on the floor of the living room, giving the bedroom over to me. The sheets were not clean. I heard them giggling together during the early hours of the morning. I slept badly, dreaming that Mr. Englegard came with the police and dragged me into the public square where two fishwives dressed like Nazis flayed me with wet flounders.

When I returned to the flat in Klampenborg, I found it ominously silent. The door to the bedroom Mr. Engelgard shared with his son was closed. As was the door to the living room, where I had spent so much time with the two of them. I went into my room and dropped the packages on the bed. The bookcase had been straightened and some Penguin paperbacks put in. On the table, next to the blue typewriter, was a note from Frowsy.

> Dear Little Sister
>
> If you look you out of the window you shall see a little some thing that look like *oil* on the sea, around the edge. That is ICE!!! Father is not himself today and if I was in your shoe I would leave him be. He is an old man and his moods are his privaledge. He worried for you all the night and though I say dont wait up he must. I come and explain this evening.
>
> > "Frowsy" (American Nobleman)

I did not see Mr. Engelgard for one week. He stayed out of my way and I stayed out of his. Frowsy would come to my room after supper (I was no longer invited to share their meal with them) and we would read our separate books (he was studying for his exams) and talk, after his father had gone to bed early.

"But he said I was free to come and go as I pleased," I protested. "It's unfair! I am an adult, not a child." I told Frowsy the truth, how I had missed the train. For some reason, I felt it necessary to clear my virtue. "Those two weren't even interested in me!" I said.

"Then they was fools," said Frowsy humorously. "I understand perfectly, but Father is the older generation and also Norwegian. That make a difference. We just have to wait till he get over his fury."

I gave him the Viennese coffee to give to his father. Later I saw it, still sealed, placed on my new kitchen "shelf." For now, by decree relayed by a reluctant Frowsy, I was no longer welcome in the living room—that was for "family." One night, when brewing coffee for myself in the kitchen, I discovered I'd run out of sugar. Furtively, I reached for their sugar on the next shelf. Old Engelgard had foreseen this. Their package had a homemade label Scotch-taped to it: ENGELGARD. DO NOT USE! How small-minded could you get, I thought, outraged. I do not have to be a paying prisoner here.

I went into town to American Express and signed up for a bus tour leaving for Spain the week after Christmas. Meanwhile I would sweat out my exile. My rent was paid for the rest of November, and I couldn't leave Denmark till Christmas, because my mother was sending a Christmas box and she'd be hurt if there was no place to send it.

I took long walks in the deer park during the day, to avoid bumping into Mr. Engelgard in the hallway. But the deer were gone. Then I'd come back, furtively make myself a sandwich, and slip off to my room, where, behind the closed door, I would type madly: letters to my mother, to Barney, to old school friends, sometimes just tirades against "the old tyrant," which I would later tear up. Let him think I was writing a great novel. I knew he could hear me. I could hear him, coughing in the next room.

A week before Christmas, he was listening to some carols on the radio. I was in my room, waiting for his next cough. It came. Suddenly, I coughed, too, after he'd finished. I heard him turn down the volume of the carols. He coughed again. I coughed back. Then he called out tentatively, "Amanda?" I combed my hair and went at once to knock on the living-room door.

"Come in."

I opened the door. He was sitting in his chair by the fire, his Norwegian blanket wrapped about his legs. He was holding out his arms to me. I went to him and knelt down beside him and bowed my head in his lap. I cried loudly and he raked my hair with his fingers.

"Oh, no, it is not easy, loving people," he said. "Look, Tarheel, can you forgive a selfish old creature?"

"Me, me," I sobbed. "I'm the one. I should have telephoned. But then it was so late. Oh, it was so sordid. I had to spend the night with awful people."

"Yes," he crooned, some of the old authoritativeness creeping back into his voice. "You *should* have called. I was worried sick. If you are going to be a great writer, little Amanda, you must learn to imagine the feelings of others."

Dearest Barney,

This will be the last communication from Denmark. Friday I take the *solbusen* (means "sun bus") bound for Barcelona via Hamburg, Strasbourg, Colmar, Besançon, Valence, Provence, and the Pyrenees. . . . Christmas among the Danes was the best ever. We stuffed ourselves and lay about in alcoholic goodwill. Father Engelgard had placed the almond in my dish of rice porridge, and so I got the *mandelgave* (almond gift): an aquamarine pendant, set in antique gold. It belonged to his wife. I have not had the heart to tell him I'm leaving yet, but I must do it tonight. It will make him sad and that will make me sad.

"What clever clotheses you Americans have." Frowsy was helping me pack. "In and out of suitcases, yet they never bend."

"Wrinkle," I corrected, pinching him playfully.

"Wrinkle. You have been a good thing for me and my English. But why did you wait so long to tell us you were going?"

"I thought it would be easier."

"Easier for you, maybe. For me, I don't mind. But older people need time to make their brains say yes. It is exactly the way Palle left. Good-bye. Crash. You should have said sooner."

"Oh dear. I've done the wrong thing again." I was angry at Engelgard for refusing to come out of his room and making me feel guilty. "I hate myself," I added, wanting to be told I shouldn't.

"Oh, you are young. You live a little more and change."

Later that morning, the morning I was to leave, a man with a mop bucket and rags and brushes arrived at the flat. He wore white overalls and went straight to work, cleaning.

"Who on earth is that funny little man in the kitchen?" I asked Frowsy.

"Oh, it's Jacobsen. Father asked me to call him for this morning. He comes sometimes when Father wants to spring-clean."

"But it's not spring."

There was an hour to go before my taxi came. Engelgard's bedroom door was shut. When Jacobsen had finished with the bathroom, I went in and took a long bath, soaking and steaming, wanting to be gone. There was still the painful good-bye to have out with old Engelgard.

I had dressed in the pants and sweater I would wear for traveling, and was crouching before Mrs. Engelgard's too-low mirror, combing my hair, when Mr. Engelgard knocked once on the door and called my name. This was it. We would probably both bawl. I opened the door, smiling sadly.

He was dressed in the suit he'd worn the day we met. I had my mouth open to compliment him on his sense of occasion. How nice he looked, with the dark ascot tucked inside his woolen shirt.

"I will appreciate it," he said in his Oxford English, pointing across the hall, "if you will return to my bathroom and wash away the ring you left in my bathtub. I do not feel I should have to do that for you. Especially when the place has just been cleaned by Jacobsen. I want every trace gone, please."

Then he turned and walked back to his room and slammed the door. I never saw him again.

For several Christmases, Frowsy and I exchanged cards. The Christmas after I left, he became engaged to a fellow student, named Birgit. The next Christmas, Birgit had found another. And the following Christmas he wrote, "Father did not make it this year."

Barney also found another, and, I must say, reading over those old carbons, I don't blame him. I also found somebody, and lost him, and found another. Fifteen years passed and my husband and I were staying in the finest hotel in Copenhagen. I am sure the basin did not leak when one tried to dissolve Woolite; I was not there long enough to find out. I looked in the phone book and there was the name, ENGELGARD, and the same address my mother and Barney had written to, during that other winter.

When I said, "Lars?" he didn't know who I was, but when I said, "Frowsy," he cursed in Danish and said, "Amanda, you come out here at once! This minute, do you hear me?" My husband and I took the train through the autumn suburbs and I found my way from Klampenborg station to the flat as if I'd been gone but a few hours.

The man who opened the door was neither short nor round. He no longer looked like a troll. He had shaved the scruffy beard and his hair was golder than I remembered. How could he have grown taller? He was almost thirty when we met. Then I realized it was because he no longer stood next to his father. At first he was terribly nervous. When he handed us our coffee cups, his hands shook. For the first half hour, he addressed all his remarks to my husband. But then he saw me looking around and he said, "You like the way I have decorated. After Father died, I got rid of the old things." He had a slim brown cat who arched her back as he stroked her. "Father would never let us have animals," he said. "One of these days, I may get myself a wife, too, who knows?" Then he laughed like the old Frowsy.

The three of us drove in his new car to Rungsted, along the road that runs by the sea. "So," he said to me, obviously enjoying himself behind the wheel of this sleek machine, "you have become a writer, Amanda, and I have become a zoologist." To my husband he said, "Do you know, if it had not been for your wife, I would have failed those exams. My father was ill and I could not study in bed beside him, and she let me use the table in her room and made coffee when I became sleepy. She rehearsed with me all the bones in the body of a dog, sometimes till three or four in the morning."

"How funny!" I said. "I had forgotten completely about all that. I have been telling Jim what an awful spoiled thing I was."

"Amanda is frequently too hard on herself," said Jim.

We walked through the woods to visit Isak Dinesen's grave. The long, rectangular stone was set flat, under a very old and noble tree. Some beechnuts had fallen on it, near where her name was carved—KAREN BLIXEN—and I put them in my pocket as talismans to make my own writing nobler.

"I tell you something funny," said the attractive Dane, who had at last come to look like my false descriptions of him in letters to Barney. "I don't mean it is funny, but it is typical of Father. The only time he ever mentioned you again was when she died. When he saw it in the newspaper, he got very pink—you know how he went, Amanda, when he began to be furious—and he said, 'Good, good, that will show her. It will be in their newspapers, too, and she will read it and regret she was a poor Tarheel who could not stick and will never meet the greatest writer in Denmark. She will be good and sorry.' I hope you don't mind this little anecdote."

"How could I mind," I said, "when it is so like him?" And with love's delayed reaction, I wished with all my heart that the old man could hear me say it: "I am sorry."

"It is the quirks we come to miss most in our dead," mused our host philosophically, as we walked through the sun-touched woods, back to the car. "I wonder why this is?"

I wondered if I should tell him how much better his English was.

Author's Note

In the old days, storytellers began by invoking the help of their Muses. "Begin it, goddess, at whatever point you will," Homer modestly bids his Muse at the start of *The Odyssey*. In the same spirit—because I wanted guidance—I invoked Mr. Bedford to lead me through the short novel that would bear his name. Now that I am putting his story together with some companions, all of whom had their respective Muses, I feel compelled to acknowledge this welcome band of inspirers who have appeared to me over the years in the most unpredictable disguises.

Mr. Bedford's was the most striking epiphany; so much so that I have since claimed him as my mascot. I collect his images and place them at strategic points around my study, to remind me of the valuable lessons I learned while writing his story, and to warn me against the precipitance that his serene nature deplores.

A few seasons ago, I was in the throes of that occupational malady popularly known as "Writer's Block." Now, Writer's Block has many forms, possibly as many as its antidote: Inspiration. Writer's Block does not mean necessarily that you sit down wordlessly in front of your "cold altar of a typewriter," as Constance LeFevre does at her lowest point in "Amanuensis." Perfect wordlessness may be one of the malady's most honest forms. There is a spiritual purity about that, like the Dark Night of the Soul. No, I was being driven, at the time, by one of the insidious forms of Writer's Block to which my industrious, ambitious nature is prone: Emptiness disguised as Wordiness. And

I had perpetrated over a hundred pages of "a novel" before I understood that my characters had no reason to be in the same book with one another.

I entombed them in a file folder, which I hid from my sight. That evening I watched an English play on television. Later the same night, I had a short dream. I was rushing to catch a flight from England to the United States, but I needed someone to take care of my cat (who, for some reason, had to stay behind in England). And then there suddenly appeared a woman I had known years ago, while working in London, and this woman said she would keep my cat for me if I invited her to come and visit me in the United States.

All the next day, I was absorbed by this dream. It had set me to thinking about that English period of my life, which was in so many ways synonymous with Youthful Expectations—and Dreads. I got out my old journals and browsed for a while in the early 1960s, and that's when I came across the story of Mr. Bedford, as told to me by the very woman who had appeared in my dream.

The next day, I began to write. Because I wanted to write in order to recapture and understand, not because I felt I ought to be writing. I wanted to live in that English time again—but with the perspective that time and distance *and imagination* can bestow. There were memory gaps, but I would fill them in with fiction, which, as every writer knows, is often the best way to get at the important truths that lie buried beneath "what really happened."

Chastened by the recent shame of my hundred empty pages, I resolutely set my pace to one of which Mr. Bedford would approve. I wanted to *find* my story in all that past material, rather than snatch and grab from the material and *impose* a story. That was when I bought my first Mr. Bedford icon and placed it on my desk between the rock from D. H. Lawrence's grave and the beechnut from Isak Dinesen's tree. Go slowly, I told myself: this is a quest, not a race or a contest. And, though the little novel was completed in three months, I will always remember it for the leisurely mood and the sense of discovery that accompanied its progress throughout.

The final proof of its integrity, it seemed to me, was its unpopular length: too long to be a story; too short to be published by itself as a novel. However, just as in the old fable about the race between the tortoise and the hare, "Mr. Bedford" gets there in the end.

Some of the other Muses who inspired stories in this collection have histories too personal for me to elaborate on. It would be fun to tell you how an object left behind in a closet by a houseguest led to my writing "A Father's Pleasures," but I really oughtn't. Nevertheless, I am indebted to that interesting object and its owner.

Likewise, "Amanuensis" would not have come into being had not a certain person suggested herself as a candidate for mine, leading me to imagine all the comforts and drawbacks of having such a person in the house. And Charles St. John, in "St. John," was not the first writer to discover he had a double in town.

Anonymous Muses, you know who you are.

The Muse of "A Cultural Exchange" was Revision, frequently passed over at acknowledgment time because of his low-key and undramatic nature. Most writers have stories that they cut their teeth on, and this was one of mine. Denmark was the first foreign country I lived in, and, full of my adventure, I began writing this story while I was still living it. (It was quite a different story from the one in this volume.) Then, many drafts and some years later, I revisited Denmark and saw the larger landscape and some of the eventualities that had surrounded young Amanda during her sojourn with the Engelgards in Klampenborg, and when I returned home, I got out the old folder, unclipped the yellowing rejection letter from Roger Angell at *The*

New Yorker (which began "I am sorry to disappoint you again . . ." and ended with ". . . but you get better and better"), and fussed around with the story until Revision showed me what I had been trying to say.

I think it will be okay if I tell about the housepainter and his little girl, the Muses of the final version of "The Angry-Year." That, too, was a story that had languished in the limbo of its file folder with a yellowing rejection (from another magazine) clipped to the top. The story was lively and well written, said this rejection, but . . . well . . . it was 1968 and sororities were anachronistic. If only I could *take out* the sorority parts . . . but then, of course, there wouldn't be a story. So sorry. Try us again.

Then we decided to have some downstairs rooms painted.

The first day the painter came, I suspected he was not very impressed with the way the woman of the house spent her time. She was supposed to be a writer; why, then, did she wander around the house so much? When he painted, you could hear the steady *slush-swish* of his brush; but where was the steady sound to prove that I was working?

The second day, he showed up with his three-year-old daughter. "Her mother has some important errands," he explained, smiling in anticipation of the nice surprise he had for this restless, childless woman. "And I thought *you* might enjoy playing with her for a while."

I know what I probably should have done. But the child looked so delighted at the prospect of our playing that I didn't want to be the one to spoil adults for her. So we spent the morning on the floor with crayons.

The next morning, however, I was already fast at work, typing loudly and steadily, when he came. "The Angry-Year" needed a new perspective—I was old enough now to look back with a motherly glance on Janie's social agony and see both the humor and the cause of it—but, except for the silent pauses necessary to find the right words for this new material, the rest of the story had held up pretty well and could be fed into my machine more or less intact. Thus I was provided with two full working days of fuel for my typewriter, whose noise convinced the man downstairs I was a genuine writer and not someone on the lookout for a baby-sitting job.

(There was a bonus, too. It was no longer 1968; sororities were part of the scene again; and magazines were interested in printing stories about them.)

Though Muses do not walk into my dreams every night and announce, "Look here, I'll take care of your living creature if you'll put my story into your next novel," as the "Mr. Bedford" lady did, I am delighted to be able to report that these things do happen. And, even when they aren't happening, which is most of the time, I believe the air around us is thick with what Henry James called "the virus of suggestion." Sometimes it's enough just to keep your eyes and ears open, and answer the door; other times, you might have to exert more energy and go digging into closets. But, "Try to be one of those people on whom nothing is lost!" James advises, and, just as I've taken Mr. Bedford as my official Writing Mascot, I've made those words my motto.

Jerry Bauer

About the Author

GAIL GODWIN was born in Alabama, grew up in Asheville, North Carolina, and received her doctorate in English from the University of Iowa. She has taught at Vassar College and Columbia University and has received a Guggenheim Fellowship and the 1981 Award in Literature from the National Academy and Institute of Arts and Letters. Her short stories, essays, and articles have appeared in numerous magazines and newspapers and her highly praised books include *The Good Husband* and *Violet Clay*. She currently lives in Woodstock, New York.

"That's becoming a habit."

Confusion showed on Jason's face.

"You insisted on doing the same thing last night after the wedding," Gin explained. "You carried me over the threshold."

"I don't remember that."

He shoved his hands in his pockets. "You should rest."

"That's why you brought me up here. To rest."

He nodded, but he refused to look at her.

"I told you I'm not tired."

"No. It's obvious you're wired. You should sleep it off."

"We both know that's unlikely."

She tugged his shirt from his jeans and ran her fingertips along his warm skin. "We both could use a shower."

She shrugged out of her jacket and let it fall to the floor. "Come on, Jason." Why wouldn't he make a move? "Come have some fun with your wife."

DEBRA WEBB

USA TODAY Bestselling Author

READY, AIM...
I DO!

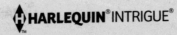

HARLEQUIN® INTRIGUE®

Recycling programs
for this product may
not exist in your area.

ISBN-13: 978-0-373-74770-2

READY, AIM...I DO!

Printed in U.S.A.

www.Harlequin.com

ABOUT THE AUTHOR

Debra Webb wrote her first story at age nine and her first romance at thirteen. It wasn't until she spent three years working for the military behind the Iron Curtain and within the confining political walls of Berlin, Germany, that she realized her true calling. A five-year stint with NASA on the space-shuttle program reinforced her love of the endless possibilities within her grasp as a storyteller. A collision course between suspense and romance was set. Debra has been writing romance, suspense and action-packed romance thrillers since. Visit her at www.debrawebb.com or write to her at P.O. Box 4889, Huntsville, AL 35815.

Books by Debra Webb

HARLEQUIN INTRIGUE

CAST OF CHARACTERS

Jason Grant—A Specialist and former military sniper. Holt has sent Grant out to assist an agent who has been compromised, but he finds himself the primary suspect when a sniper starts attacking civilians in the area.

Ginger Olin—A spy on the trail of a deadly new virus, she needs to identify the buyer, but she picks up an added assignment as authorities try to determine Grant's guilt or innocence.

Emmett Holt—Deputy Director of Mission Recovery. Holt took Lucas Camp's place when he retired. Some believe he will do anything to move to the top.

Thomas Casey—Director of Mission Recovery. Thomas is the consummate Specialist. He handpicks his people and is determined to protect his team.

Lucas Camp—Thomas's closest friend. He will do whatever is necessary to protect his friend and the interests of Mission Recovery.

Victoria Colby-Camp—The semiretired head of the Colby Agency. She and Lucas can't seem to stay out of the business of investigations.

Chapter One

You're next.

Jason Grant couldn't stop thinking about the note he'd received last month. So far he'd come up empty trying to determine the source. He wanted to write it off as a prank, but it wasn't the kind of humor any of his friends or associates indulged in. Although he knew he was considered the next in line for the deputy director post at Mission Recovery, it wasn't how his bosses would announce a promotion.

If this current assignment was any indication, the reality appeared to be that he was next up to either get fired or die of boredom. The sport coat he wore suddenly felt too warm; the tie he'd already loosened still felt too confining.

He looked around the hotel bar. Too early for a big crowd, but there were plenty of people com-

ing and going and gambling. His deep well of
training-induced patience was running dry. Not a
smart thing in his line of work as a Specialist, but
true all the same. Although impatience wasn't
the ideal, he knew the value of being aware of
his strengths and weaknesses throughout a fluc-
tuating operation.

He signaled the bartender for another beer and
thought about what he might have done to de-
serve such a low-level assignment.

Specialists were sent in to recover the impossible situations—not to sit back and watch for potential signs of trouble. Last month he'd been told
to observe, and he had done so. Right up until the
point when Director Casey needed hands-on assistance. This time it felt much the same, except
he had no idea who might be in trouble. In fact,
he had no idea what the hell was going on here.

All he'd been told was that the operative in
place might need backup. He was supposed to
hang out in and around Caesar's Palace, observe
and make himself available to get her out if necessary. They didn't even tell him which *her* he
was looking for.

It didn't feel right. A lot of things in Mission
Recovery weren't feeling right these days.

Still, gut feelings aside, this was the job and
here he was in Sin City. He'd found a cover story
with a nearby convention on security systems

and emerging technologies and booked an upgraded room in the Caesar tower, though he didn't expect to see it much.

He tipped back the dark bottle of beer but didn't risk drinking any more than the half bottle he'd already sipped away. Instead, his eyes scanned the constantly shifting crowd for any female who looked like a covert operative. Evening hours—really any hour in Vegas from what he'd seen so far—meant women were decked out like there was a Bond girl audition nearby. It made for colorful and entertaining scenery, but Jason was ready for action.

This gig of sitting around watching was getting staler than the beer he pretended to drink.

He pulled out his phone and, per his habit, checked the police scanner app for any crime news. For the past two days, aside from a seven-car pileup on Interstate 15 the state troopers suspected had been started by a blown-out front tire of a limousine, it had been mostly routine stuff. Muggings, prostitution, disputes over money or lovers. Nothing that pointed to a spy in trouble. Certainly no high-speed shoot-outs involving high-end automobiles.

He turned his attention to the hockey game televised on the set above the bar. The odds were running like a stock exchange ticker across the bottom of the picture. If something didn't break soon, he might have to resort to the preferred entertainment and place a bet on something.

"Pardon me," the bartender said. "Is your name Grant?"

He nodded. The bartender slid him a shot of tequila with a salt shaker and lime. "Courtesy of the blonde across the way." He jerked his thumb over his shoulder to the other end of the bar.

Grant took a long look and smiled when the woman raised her own shot in salute. The hair was different, probably a wig, and from this distance in the subdued light he couldn't be sure about the eyes. But the dress. He recognized the vibrant emerald dress that skimmed her sensual curves. A certain bold redhead had worn it when she'd crashed a wedding reception in Colorado last month.

At the time he'd considered her the prime suspect behind the cryptic *You're next* note he'd received. But the brief investigation and limited evidence disproved that theory. No one remembered a redhead or even a woman anywhere near the note. In the weeks since, he'd been looking over his shoulder and jumping at shadows, though he'd never admit any such thing. As much as he hated the wide-open, let-it-ride atmosphere in the gambling capital, the constant motion of Vegas was at least curing him of the jumpiness.

What the hell, he thought, and tossed back

the shot. If Olin was the agent in need, the alcohol might dull the edginess he felt whenever he thought about the stunning redhead. Of course, tequila was better known for boosting the potential for trouble than preventing it.

Either way, this being Vegas, he might as well enjoy the ride.

GINGER OLIN SLID a fifty-dollar chip onto number twenty-five and considered herself lucky even before the croupier set the roulette wheel spinning.

Why couldn't all her targets have the good taste to conduct business in Las Vegas? The themes were over the top, but that was the beauty of it. Vegas catered to the bold and overwhelmed the inhibitions of the shy. It made for a delightfully level playing field.

As she strolled through the gaming rooms of Caesar's Palace amid the glamorous theme and thorough details, she noticed the atmosphere exuded luxury with an undercurrent of excited energy. One couldn't help joining in the fun. That energy drew like a magnet, made her feel alive in a way that only this kind of decadence could.

The ball dropped in, and she listened to it zip around the wheel as she scanned the nearby tables for any sign of the man carrying the deadly virus she'd been tracking all over the globe. Hearing the bounce and clatter as the ball landed, she timed her squeal of glee perfectly as the dealer called out the winning number.

"Twenty-five!"

Smiling, she accepted the congratulations and admiring glances along with the slightly taller stack of chips and stepped back from the table. Her target, a slick crime boss out of Europe, was on the move, but who was he here to meet? That was the million-dollar question, and she sought the answer.

She strolled along, just one woman among thousands dressed to the nines and looking for the next place to burn through her money. Waitresses cruised through knots of gamblers and hangers-on in an intricate ballet, trays held high, smiles wide and full of temptation. She supposed some people might find the glitter and glam overdone, but Gin enjoyed it. Here a spy could find the right background to blend with, no matter the circumstances. The perfect playing board for dangerous games.

She spotted her target, an older man with thick gray hair and wire-rimmed glasses, moving toward the craps tables and Gin shadowed him, wondering if he was enjoying the setting as much as she was. The virus wasn't with him, though. Her tracking tag showed it was stationary, probably in his room. Joining the growing crowd cheering on a lucky run at a craps table, she used the raucous, shifting party as cover while she tried to spot the buyer.

Her pulse stuttered when she met the hard, icy gaze of Bernard Isely. He was looking too closely, and not at her well-displayed cleavage. He preferred his women cheap, his vodka expensive, and those who betrayed him dead. He didn't know it yet, but she would soon fall squarely into the last category.

She felt an unprecedented surge of insecurity. Would her wig and contacts be enough to protect her? Her intent was not to dress the same way twice during her stay here. Her well-calculated costuming would, she hoped, be enough to keep her alive throughout and after this assignment.

She dragged her thoughts away from the edge of panic and focused instead on her extensive training and reliable intel. A few weeks ago while she was following a different lead, she'd been told this low life had entered the States, but he should never have been *here*. Not in person. He usually sent someone else to do the face-to-face work.

But there was nothing *usual* about this particular business. His appearance shouldn't have been a shock. She told herself it *wasn't* a shock. Everyone who should know believed his father had commissioned the deadly virus up for sale this weekend. It might not fit his profile, but then this particular exchange wasn't standard fare for the Isely crime family. The son might want to watch his father's greatest coup go out into the criminal world at last. Maybe that was reason enough to take such a high risk.

Regardless, she understood it was his abrupt appearance right across from her that could rattle her. Rattled spies didn't last long. Experience kept her reactions in tune with the excited crowd and her gaze averted from her enemy. Her heart might be in her throat, but there wouldn't be any outward sign of her distress. She had too much practice to give him that advantage.

Immediately she considered her options. This was one of the most wanted and most evasive men of the criminal underworld. They'd almost caught him last month by accident, but somehow he'd slithered out of custody before the right authorities arrived.

The player rolled again and won again, and in the subsequent roar of celebration, Gin slipped back and away, putting the other revelers between her and Isely.

She tagged along on the fringe of a group of women cruising out toward the slot machines. If he was on to her, it would be obvious right away. Unfortunately, her worst-case scenario was confirmed when she spared a glance over her shoulder. It was too late to make a preemptive bold move, but it was still too soon to panic.

There was always a way out.

Well, almost always.

She needed the right crowd or the right loner, she thought, turning toward the low lights of the nearest bar. And she needed one or the other right now.

The crowd was light and most of the patrons were paired up or in small groups. Gin sought the solo acts. There was another blonde woman in a deep emerald dress, only a shade or so darker than Gin's, who might do in a pinch. Gin had the long-lost school chum routine down to a science.

But her first choice would be a man. Men were typically less suspicious and far less likely to admit they couldn't remember a hot chick from a prior rendezvous. She spotted a man in the corner sipping a cup of coffee and squinting into a book that was most likely a tutorial on blackjack. Too serious and sporting a wedding ring, she crossed him off her mental list.

Then she noticed the ideal candidate at the other end of the bar. She strolled right up to the only familiar face she could potentially define as a friend in this town and pressed a light kiss to Specialist Grant's cheek. "Oh, the whims of fate," she said in a flat Midwestern accent.

"More like the whims of my boss," he replied, signaling the bartender.

"Have you been waiting long?"

"A couple of days. What'll you have?"

"White wine," she told the bartender. Taking the barstool next to Jason, she swiveled so her knees brushed against his thigh.

He glanced down and then gave her an interested half-grin. "You don't have to bait me."

"I beg your pardon?"

He leaned closer. "I'm a sure thing, remember?"

She tipped her head back and laughed, playing along. "That's good to know." Studying him, she wondered how much he'd had to drink. Any alcohol beyond a few sips to set his profile meant he was here for pleasure rather than business. Grant, she suspected, wasn't the sort to bend the rules on a mission. His brown eyes were a little unfocused, his pupils dilated. So maybe he wasn't here on business. Still, even in the midst of tying one on, he was her best bet to get out of here.

Using the mirror behind the bar, she checked for Isely. He'd stepped just inside the doorway and was checking out the milling crowd. He didn't come closer, but she could feel his gaze land on her back. If he didn't know for sure, he'd suspected she was trouble. Well, Jason Grant could help her prove otherwise.

The bartender delivered her wine and she sipped, rubbing her palm across Jason's knee. Isely had to believe she was involved with him, that they were simply a couple here to enjoy a long weekend.

"Need a hand?"

"Why, Mr. Grant, that sounds like a wonderful start. I think you're just the lucky charm that would be helpful to me at the craps tables."

He shook his head. "I—ah, don't gamble," he mumbled with a laugh that sounded almost drunken.

Alarms sounded in her head. A man who didn't gamble didn't do Vegas for pleasure. Something was wrong here. "Sweetheart, are you feeling well?"

"Fine." He picked up her hand and stroked her palm with his thumb. "Your hand is…is so soft."

And his was quite strong, but something was clearly wrong. Careful not to break cover, she scanned the room for whoever had drugged him. She needed to get him out of here before he was too loopy to walk.

He started to slump to the side, and she signaled for the bartender to settle the tab. Jason managed a signature and she caught the room number he'd listed along with the drink tally. Two beers wouldn't have put him in this state.

"Why don't we take a walk?" she suggested.

"I'd like that."

"Good." She looped his arm over her shoulder and with hers at his waist she steadied him as they maneuvered through the bar.

The gun she felt in the waistband at the small of his back implied he was on the clock and only solidified her theory that someone had decided he was a target for something. As they exited no one seemed to care, not even Isely, but she couldn't be sure because it took all her concentration to keep Jason upright. His height of just over six feet and lean but muscular build were far more appealing when he was supporting both on his own power.

His hand slid down to cup her bottom and she jumped a little, surprised by his touch. She covered her reaction with a laugh. Maybe he was faking the drunk part. Was he taking advantage and hamming it up, or was there a real problem? It helped the cover, so she wouldn't complain. She guided him toward the main entrance, hoping the fresh air and surroundings would help revive him if this wasn't for show.

"What did you have to drink, sweetheart?" she asked. The crowded streets and traffic noise meant no one could eavesdrop and she wanted as much information as she could get.

"A beer. Not even. Oh!" He jerked a bit. "And you sent me a shot of tequila."

"Ah." As they walked, she checked his pockets. He had his wallet and his room key. She must have interrupted before whoever started this had finished the job. Well, luck was certainly a lady for Jason tonight. She would ask him later why he thought the person who sent him a shot was her.

"You aren't really blonde." He reached over and brushed at the blonde bangs of her wig.

"That's just for fun tonight, remember?"

"*Mmm-hmm.* Where're we going?"

Back to his room if she could manage it. She risked another glance over her shoulder. Damned if Isely wasn't still on her. What would it take to get rid of him?

She'd worn a disguise, stopped shadowing his seller and left the casino where the transaction was slated to occur. "Give a girl a break," she muttered, pausing to catch her breath. Her chosen method of distraction was turning into a serious problem.

Next time, she was going with the old school chum routine. No hormonal interference with that diversion. Running into Jason had looked like a fun, sexy ticket out of trouble, but now he felt like a block of cement dragging her down. She leaned him against a palm tree and kept him there with a hand on his hard chest.

She could leave him and call a cop to help him

back to his room. Practical, but wrong. "Kiss me," she said.

"What?" His eyelids were droopy and his grin was that of a sweet drunk, and still it made butterflies circle in her belly.

"Kiss me," she ordered.

"In a minute." His hands were warm on her waist. "You hafta say 'I do' first."

She followed his gaze. They were standing under the bright neon lights of an Elvis-themed wedding chapel. To her left, Isely was only a few yards away. To her right, one of the brutal men she recognized from his personal security team was even closer and reaching into his jacket.

Damn.

Why couldn't these guys just believe the only thing she was into was her man?

Catching a glimpse of the shoulder holster, she made up her mind. Isely and his crew were known to act first and rationalize later. Drugged, Jason wasn't in any shape to help her. Maybe it was time to play the game their way.

"Well," she said to Jason, marching the fingers of one hand up his shirt while she reached for his gun with the other. She wasn't a great shot left-handed, but she only had to create a diversion if they tried to take her. Flipping off the safety, she kept Jason distracted with her body pressed against his.

Isely's thug had his weapon out now and his attention was locked on her. She didn't know who or what had tipped off Isely, but his intended method of problem solving was clear. As the thug raised his weapon, she fired through Jason's sport coat, aiming for the thug's knee and praying she wouldn't hit anyone else.

People on the street reacted predictably—a sudden flurry of motion set to the soundtrack of panicked screaming. Isely's thug was hopping around in pain—she must have clipped his foot—and people caught sight of his gun. He was swarmed by determined citizens yelling for police assistance.

Jason jumped, a delayed reaction to the sound of the shot. He almost fell, dragging her with him. "Steady, sweetheart. That's just a car back firing," she lied smoothly.

"It's loud out here." He traced the shell of her ear with his fingertip. "Let's get married so I can kiss you," he said.

She tucked the gun back into the holster at his back. "If you insist, honey."

"I do." He sputtered with laughter when he realized what he said. "C'mon." He pushed away from the tree and wobbled toward the chapel entrance with the careful determination of a drunk.

She wasn't sure he'd appreciate her current opinion of Specialist Jason Grant as sweet edging toward adorable, but there wasn't a better way to define him in his diminished state.

Less than an hour later, to the tune of Viva Las Vegas, they were newlyweds with the gold bands, a champagne toast and a "Just Married" limo ride up and down the Strip to prove it.

She wondered how happy her groom would be when he woke up tomorrow morning?

Chapter Two

Emmett Holt steepled his fingers as he reviewed the detailed reports his assistant had sent to his computer. Apparently a sniper was on a killing spree in Las Vegas. Times, targets—hell, even the type of bullets—pointed to Jason Grant, the Specialist who would one day take over this very office. Director Casey had handpicked Grant for the deputy director's chair when Holt eventually moved up to Casey's post, but this development could change everything.

There was never a good time for an agent to go off the deep end, but in light of the recent scandal of false allegations and rumors against the director himself, this was the last thing Mission Recovery needed.

Specialists recruited to their covert agency were above reproach, but it looked for all the world like Grant was about to become the exception. That possibility didn't sit well with Holt. There was only one conclusion in light of this damning data: Grant, or someone who wanted them to believe it was Grant, was waging some sort of vendetta in Las Vegas.

If it was Grant, Holt wondered how he had secured the rifle. To date, their normal contacts in the area denied seeing Grant. Holt knew *someone* was lying, but that in and of itself didn't put Grant in the clear. All Specialists were well-trained in where and how to connect with a helpful associate when they were in the field. He may have purposely gone outside their usual suppliers.

But why? Had he lost it? Or had someone on the other side made him an offer he couldn't refuse?

In the past forty-eight hours the sniper—whoever the hell he was—had picked off a couple of irrelevant targets, caused one serious traffic accident and winged a major player in the drug trade. All of which had been kept out of the media. Considering the damper that kind of publicity could put on tourism, the local authorities had been only too happy to cooperate. The shootings looked perfectly random, but anyone with access to his personnel jacket would put Grant at the top of the suspect list.

The grim accomplishment was more impressive considering the Specialist hadn't missed a single status check-in call since his arrival. Holt suppressed his instincts on the matter. What he believed on a personal level was irrelevant. He had a job to do and no one could ever accuse him of failing to get the job done. He liked Grant as well as he did any of the others but that, too, was irrelevant at the moment.

"Shall I add this to the agenda for the next briefing, sir?" His assistant, Nadine, sat on the opposite side of the desk. Beneath the conservative suit she wore, her posture was particularly rigid as she asked the question. No one wanted to believe the worst. Not even the young assistant he had hired who willingly worked twelve- and fourteen-hour days in an attempt to keep him happy. He vaguely wondered if that was why she kept her hair in a sleek ponytail all the time. He didn't give her time to patronize salons.

He also wondered if she hated him as much as most who had the displeasure of working for him did.

He blinked away the concept. "No. I'll handle it privately." The less anyone knew about this situation the better. If he put it on the agenda for team discussion, Grant might hear about it. And if he knew they were on to him, he'd bolt before they could get a net around him. And if this was Grant, Holt needed to get a net around him as soon as possible.

"Any word from the agent Grant was sent to Las Vegas to support?"

"No, sir."

No surprise there. Everyone knew Vegas remained one of the easiest cities to disappear in. "Maybe the agent managed to get out without Grant's help." Holt said what his assistant expected to hear while his mind worked through the latest developments and numerous other scenarios.

"I'll keep monitoring the news out there," Nadine suggested.

Holt nodded. They both understood the harsh reality and the constricting time frame. He wasn't going to be able to keep the sniper issue quiet much longer. If and when the local police force connected the incidents to a single shooter, they would be obligated to call in federal assistance and warn the public about the threat.

Which meant Holt would be obligated to tell someone in another government agency there was an operative in the area with sharp-shooter expertise, and that would break Grant's cover.

If Jason Grant remained in Las Vegas, with his stellar career as a sniper, he would become a person of interest within the next twenty-four hours. By hour forty-eight, if he couldn't offer a valid alibi for the shootings, he'd be in custody or a wanted suspect. A pawn effectively removed from the dangerous game Holt was playing. No one, particularly his superiors, would be happy with his methods. But that had never stopped him before. It wouldn't now. And that was precisely why they had hired him. He would get the job done, one way or another.

The stakes were high and the risk-to-reward ratio bordered on irrational. But it had to be done, and he was the only one in Mission Recovery who could manage it. On days like this, the baggage of responsibility weighed heavy on his shoulders.

His assistant stood. "Shall I attempt to contact Grant?"

Holt leaned back from his desk and turned a pencil end over end on the arm of his chair. "No need. Until we know more, Specialist Grant's orders don't change. Get me the director as soon as it's morning wherever he is."

"But, sir, he's on his honeymoon."

That was right. The director of Mission Recovery had gotten married last month, but work had prevented an immediate honeymoon. "The world doesn't stop spinning because he fell in love, Nadine," he grumbled. "As much as Thomas Casey would like to think so."

"Of course, sir."

His assistant left the office to carry his reports and orders to the Specialists currently on assignment and those preparing for assignments. Alone, he stared at the pencil in his hand.

He silently assured himself things were going according to the plan and it would all be over soon. Eager as he was to be done with it, he knew rushing the process now would bring the whole damn mess crashing down. On him.

He was the only one who could do this. Likewise, he was the one who would pay in spades if anything went wrong.

"Won't let that happen," he muttered. He'd come too far to bail out now.

Setting the pencil aside, he turned toward his computer and drafted the email his counterpart was expecting. He read it through twice more and then, taking a deep breath, he finally hit *Send*.

Chapter Three

Jason rolled to his back and squinted against the bright sunlight flooding into the room. His head felt stuffed with cotton, which, in any logical universe, should have dulled the incessant ringing in his ears.

"That's your phone, sweetheart. You should answer."

He knew that voice. What the hell was Ginger Olin doing in his hotel room? And why would she be aiming any endearments his way? He flung a hand out in the general direction of the ringing only to have the move stopped short by a warm, soft touch. He dared to open his eyes a crack.

"Careful. I've left you a glass of water." Ginger smiled down at him with a bit too much sympathy as he curled his fingers around the cell phone. "Take the call. I'll be in the shower."

Through slitted eyelids, he watched her saunter away, her body swathed in a hotel robe. He propped himself up on an elbow, struggling to clear the fog from his brain. What was going on here? What the hell was wrong with him?

The phone started ringing again, and he saw the number and stern face of Deputy Director Holt on his screen. Damn. This was one call he couldn't ignore. "Yeah." He cleared the rough edge from his throat, wondering how Ginger had managed to get him so drunk he couldn't remember squat. He never drank on duty. "Grant here."

"Where were you last night? You missed the scheduled check-in."

He opened his mouth to answer and snapped it closed again. He didn't know. Based on his nudity, the state of the bed and the woman in the shower, it wasn't a big leap to figure out what had happened. That still didn't explain this nasty hangover.

"I tried to contact you all night, but your phone was off. I learned this morning that you missed the recovery. If you have any sense of self-preservation, get your ass on the next available flight out of there or consider yourself relieved of duty."

"Sir?" How could he have missed the recovery? Agent Olin was safe, right here in the room with him. She'd been in trouble and he'd gotten her out of it. At least he thought that's how it had gone down. "Sir, I made the recovery," he insisted.

"You've dropped the ball somewhere, Grant, because the package is missing and Agent Conklin never encountered you or your support."

"Give me a second chance. I can meet with security and—"

"I can't. It's too late. Be on the next flight. We will debrief when you arrive."

The line went dead and for a long moment, Jason stared at the screen, utterly dumbfounded. If Olin wasn't the recovery, how had she known the code phrase?

She *had* given him the code phrase, hadn't she? She must have. He wouldn't have taken action unless he'd been sure. Although right now, he couldn't recall exactly what they'd done before coming to the room. It was pretty damn clear what they'd done after they got here.

He rolled to his feet, lost his balance when his vision wavered and landed back on the edge of the bed. He clutched at the mattress until the room stopped spinning. He'd been hung over a few times. Enough to know this wasn't the same thing at all. He'd been drugged. But why? And who would do that?

Carefully he looked around, taking in the view

of his hotel room. Or at least a room that was identical. He spotted his luggage and wished like hell they hadn't upgraded him to a suite. The suitcase across the room might as well have been on the other side of the world.

Desperate, he entertained the idea of crawling over for fresh clothes when he heard the water stop running. He would not let her find him weak as a kitten on his hands and knees in addition to the troubling disorientation plaguing him.

Slowly he turned his head from side to side, then up and down until his dizziness eased off.

The shirt and slacks he'd worn last night were scattered across the floor along with a lace-topped stocking and garter. He half expected to see a bra draped over a lampshade. A memory teased him and he twisted toward the door. Yup. There was the blond wig he'd tugged from her head, eager to get his hands in her glossy red mane.

Something had gone down in this room, or at least she'd made it look that way. He wasn't sure which explanation he wanted to hear most: that it happened, or that he only thought it happened.

He reached for the glass of water on the night-stand and stopped dead. The wide gold band on the ring finger of his left hand glinted in the sunlight. He rubbed at his eyes, but it didn't go away. He was married?

His head and stomach protested as he took in the strewn clothing along with this new information. It certainly looked as if they'd started married life with a bang.

No. Impossible. No way in hell he'd forget his own wedding or the inevitable events leading up to it. No way in hell he'd marry a stranger—and Ginger Olin, CIA operative, fit that description. This had to be some ruse she invented to preserve her cover. Except Holt just said he should have rescued an agent named Conklin.

"Damn it all." He couldn't make sense of the vague scenes flitting through his mind. She owed him some answers. This time when he pushed to his feet, he kept moving forward despite the sudden tilt of the room. He was grateful when the wall kept him from hitting the floor. He pounded a fist on the bathroom door. "Get out here."

She opened the door and a steamy cloud of spicy vanilla scent washed over him. It was so her: lush and tempting. He fought the urge to lean in and inhale deeply.

"Oh, dear," she said with a sly smile as her gaze slid over his body like a touch. He reacted as any man might when faced with the beauty of a gorgeous woman fresh from a shower. Whether his memory ever correctly filled in the details of last night, his body seemed convinced about what they'd done and there was no hiding the part of him demanding an encore performance.

Damn. In his determination to stay on his feet he'd forgotten to cover himself.

One long fingertip trailed across his jaw. "You're looking rough." She opened the door wider. "Come on in. A shower will fix you right up."

Was that a bit of Irish in her voice this morning? If so, was it real? He'd done a little investigating after their last meeting and knew she had a talent for accents. "What did you give me?" He looked past her, ashamed that he wanted to ask for her support to get him across the expanse of the luxurious bathroom.

"The time of your life. Or so you said."

Looking at the woman who'd starred in his fantasies since their one brief conversation last month, it probably had been the time of his life. How unfair that he didn't have full recall. "Not what I meant."

She tucked herself under his arm, keeping him steady as she walked him past the long vanity. "This way, big guy."

Something about the gesture felt familiar. "Did you do this last night?"

"We can talk about last night when your head's clear." She eased back but didn't quite let go. "Steady?"

Barely. "Yes."

"Cold or hot?"

"Pardon?"

"The shower," she clarified, her eyes quickly darting down to his groin and back up again.

"Cold."

"All righty." She reached past him and he saw the glint of gold on her left hand. What did it mean that she apparently had all her faculties and still wore a wedding band as new and shiny as his? Nothing good, he decided when she gave him a little encouraging nudge into the shower.

The cold spray against his scalp and rushing down and over his skin was a brutal shock, but it cleared his head faster than a pot of coffee and restored some measure of control over his lusty hormones.

When he decided he'd tortured himself long enough, he climbed out and reached for a towel on the warmer. The bathroom was empty. Her courtesy and thoughtfulness surprised him—and actually had him a little worried. What the hell was going on? For now he was grateful to find his shaving kit still near the sink closest to the shower. The other sink, which had gone unused since he'd checked in, was surrounded by feminine details, including a flowered bag, a pink toothbrush and a contact lens case pushed to the back of the counter.

Huh? When had that stuff gotten there? Was it his imagination, or was she planning to stay awhile?

Knowing it was risky, he decided to live dangerously and shave anyway. Surviving the experience with only a couple of small nicks, he evaluated his reflection and thought he looked almost normal.

He opened the door to go find some clothes and nearly got rapped on the nose as her hand was raised to knock.

"Whoops," she said, her vivid green gaze direct and clear. "Looks like I'm late." She held out a stack of clothing from his suitcase.

"That was fast."

A small frown drew her brows together. "What do you mean?"

"Married less than twenty-four hours and my wife's already picking out my clothing."

She gave a little huff and shoved the clothing at him, but he saw the blush turning her cheeks a rosy pink. A small victory, but he liked knowing he had some effect on her. Being the one doing all the reacting was no fun.

"Get dressed. Room service should be here soon. Then we can discuss last night in a civilized manner."

"Yes, dear," he said irreverently, closing the door on her frown.

GIN PACED THE room while he dressed. Damn the man for being too handsome for his own good. Or hers. They were in the middle of a serious crisis. Attraction would have to wait. It had proved a serious challenge to ignore his impressive body and the instinctive way he responded to her, both last night and again this morning.

For a hefty tip, the limousine driver had extended the tour when Jason dozed off, then he'd been kind enough to find a drive-through for coffee. The caffeine perked up Jason enough that she could get him into his room. She hadn't counted on it being enough of a stimulant to have him put the moves on her.

The poor man had been so abused by the drug, and still he'd kissed her like it had mattered at the altar, but more specifically when they'd arrived right here. She brought her hands to her lips, remembering. She'd never expected his response to wedded bliss to be so enthusiastic, even if it had been his idea—albeit while under the influence of whatever drug someone had obviously slipped him. He was a test to her self-control, but she'd gotten him safely to the bed before he passed out again.

Once she was sure he would stay unconscious she'd dashed back to her own room and gathered what she needed to set the stage here in his suite. Then she'd returned to his room and searched it, looking for any clue as to why he'd been in Vegas, particularly in the same hotel where a deadly virus was about to change hands. She'd found nothing to point to his purpose or even a possible cover story. The easy explanation was this was just a quick getaway for him, but she didn't believe in coincidence.

Now, while he showered off the last effects of the drug, she cleaned up the mess she'd deliberately made and indulged in what was surely the most girlish moment of her life. She buried her nose in his shirt, remembering his hands in her hair and cruising over her body. The woman who married him for real would be one lucky, well-loved woman.

She shivered, squashing the reaction when the door opened and Jason joined her. His step was steady now, his gaze clear despite the dark circles under his eyes. His thick, sable hair glistened, and even from across the room, she caught the fresh scent of him under the zippy mint of the hotel-brand body wash.

After sleeping next to him all night, making sure he didn't suffer nightmares or worse from the drug, she'd probably be able to pick him out of a lineup with only her nose. Good grief, what was wrong with her?

She twisted the gold band on her finger and searched for the right place to begin. "Could we, umm, talk out there?" *Away from the tangled sheets of the bed.* "I've brewed a pot of coffee, and breakfast will be here any minute."

He agreed with a subtle dip of his chin, and she knew he was evaluating her every move for a motive or a clue.

"Where's my gun?"

"In the closet safe. The code is your birthday."

His eyebrows lifted at that revelation. "Did we, ahh—" He finished with a tilt of his head toward the bed.

"You really don't remember?"

He looked away. "Just bits and pieces."

"Hmm. I should probably be offended," she teased. In reality, she was relieved. His lack of knowledge could work to her advantage. "It was a night *I'll* never forget."

When they were out of the danger zone most people called a bedroom, she poured him a cup of coffee, then slid onto the counter stool. She didn't want to do anything as intimate as sit across from him at the table as if they really were newlyweds. The thought made her chuckle. It didn't get much more intimate than tucking a naked, amorous husband into bed.

When he'd tossed her wig to the floor and pulled the pins from her hair so he could run his hands through it, it had been all she could do not to cave to the temptation he presented. He was handsome and quite striking when dressed. Nude? Well, artists would kill to paint him if they knew what treasures his clothing hid. His body, strong and sculpted, showed the results of his dedication to fitness and preparation. She had relished taking in every single detail.

"You okay?"

"Yes." She sat up straighter. "Thank you. Maybe this would go faster if you just ask whatever is on your mind."

"Are we married?"

"Yes." She handed him the documentation from the Viva Las Vegas wedding chapel. The paperwork was real and almost complete. The marriage license wasn't official, but he didn't seem to notice that. There was the added complication that the marriage wouldn't be considered valid if Jason Grant wasn't his real name. Her sources said it was, but mistakes happened. She still wasn't sure why she'd used *her* real name rather than the alias she'd prepared for this mission.

He tossed the certificate and marriage license to the table and the scowl on his face was enough to have her second-guessing going along with his convenient, drug-induced idea.

He crossed his arms and stared at her. "Why?"

The flippant remark on the tip of her tongue just wouldn't fall. Neither would the truth. Fortunately, she got a momentary reprieve with the arrival of breakfast.

He stalked over to the door, gave a belated glance through the security peephole and yanked the door open. The waiter was all smiles, going on about the pitcher of mimosas and sharing the congratulations for the "happy couple" from the staff. To her shock Jason took it all with a smile worthy of any happy groom, even tipping the man on his way out, but as soon as they were alone, the scowl returned.

"It won't be that bad," she said as he lifted the cover from each plate. She'd placed the order last night when they'd returned to the hotel, but she hadn't expected the elaborate presentation or the mouth-watering aromas. Las Vegas might just become her favorite city, and she'd been all over the world—a few times.

A massive omelet, a plate of bacon and sausage, a stack of pancakes, two flavors of syrup, fresh berries and cream, along with all the other condiments and accompaniments, made for a remarkable display.

"Wow. This smells divine."

He replaced the cover over the omelet she was staring at. "Tell me why you did it and I'll let you eat."

"You don't want to go that route with me," she warned. "I'm hungry." Violence wasn't the way she preferred to have her hands on him, but she'd put up a fight if it was the only way to earn his respect. "You have reach and strength on me, but I have guile, training and a clear head."

"Fair point." He held out a plate. "Start there."

"Where?" She sliced off a portion of the omelet, added a strip of crisp bacon to her plate and returned to the counter and her coffee. As much as she wanted a mimosa, she knew the clear head was a necessity.

"Start with your 'clear head' advantage. Why did you drug me?"

"*I* didn't." She'd merely stepped in and likely saved his life and possibly her own by capitalizing on the moment. "You don't have to believe me, but it's the truth."

His gaze locked with hers, then with an arch of eyebrows, he turned his focus to drizzling syrup over a pancake.

"Is your stomach bothering you?"

"I'm fine."

"Of course you are." And inexplicably she felt obligated to keep him that way.

Although she didn't believe he was the trouble in question, she didn't think it was coincidence that her morning email alert included a caution about a sniper in Las Vegas. From the little she'd been able to dig up on him, Jason had the background and qualifications, but even when he'd been drugged, his sense of right and wrong remained intact.

She'd searched his luggage and found nothing that indicated he had a weapon other than his handgun.

She knew he doubted her about the drugs, and she didn't hold it against him. People didn't join covert agencies for the transparency factor. They chose it for a myriad of other reasons usually starting with some noble concept of honor and duty. Suddenly she wanted to know his motive for joining, wanted to know how it might have morphed or changed since getting into the field, but this wasn't the time.

"What's the last thing you remember?" she asked instead.

"A shot of tequila." He closed his eyes. "I barely remember biting the lime. If you don't want to talk about that, tell me why you did this to us," he said, wiggling his ring finger.

"We'll get there. I promise." She swiped her finger in an X over her heart.

"Not funny."

She laughed. "Wasn't trying to be."

He grunted.

"Come on, Jason. What's the last thing you remember?"

"The wig. You were wearing a wig and I made you take it off when we got here."

She nearly choked on her coffee. "I meant the last thing you remember before we, ah, hooked up."

"You mean before we got married."

"I do, yes." She hadn't heard the poor choice of words until one of his eyebrows lifted. She stifled a laugh, knowing he wouldn't remember enough to understand the joke. "You know what I mean."

"The bar. I was hanging out in the bar waiting for the contact. I didn't expect *you*."

"Same goes," she muttered from behind her coffee cup. "How long had you been there?"

"A couple of hours. I was nursing a beer, keeping an eye on the odds for the hockey game."

"Did you win? I'm up about five hundred dollars since I hit town."

"I don't gamble."

"You're kidding?" Her surprise brought forth another scowl. It amused her. "Well, maybe you don't gamble with money, but clearly you enjoy some level of risk or you wouldn't be the golden boy at Mission Recovery."

"How do you know that?"

"Not because you broke protocol and shared anything. I have my own sources." She rolled her hand, signaling him to continue. "You're at the bar, watching the scores and odds and then what?"

She had to wait while he filled his plate with a slice of the omelet and two sausage links. Then he surprised her, bringing over the coffee carafe and refilling her cup.

"The tequila shot, like I said. The bartender brought it over and said it was from you."

"He used my name?"

"No." He returned to the table. "He pointed to you at the other end of the bar."

"Describe the woman you saw. Please," she added when he shook his head.

"Blonde. Emerald dress that matches a certain eye color."

"You said she was at the other end of the bar. When did she get close enough that you could see her eyes?"

He frowned at his plate. "Your eyes are green. The dress matched your eyes."

She shouldn't be flattered that he knew that, but she was. "I was wearing contacts last night."

"I noticed. And a blond wig."

"Yes." She was starting to really worry they'd both been set up by someone with too much information.

"The dress was just like the one you wore in Colorado last month."

"You're sure?" First of all, she would never wear the same outfit in an op she'd worn at a previous engagement. Men could get away with that kind of thing, but not a woman.

He looked up at her, his expression troubled. "That's the last thing I remember clearly. I was wondering what you were doing here and wearing *that* dress. After that the images are like snippets from a dream. I can't quite hang on to enough to put the pieces together. You walked up and gave me the code phrase for extraction and—"

"Oh, bloody hell."

"What?"

"We've been compromised." Alone but for her reluctant almost-husband, she gave in to the fidgets and started pacing the length of the room. "Something is dreadfully wrong. Yes, I joined you at the bar, but I didn't send you the shot. Drugs and sedatives aren't my style."

"Then whose style is it?"

"I don't know. No one I've been watching would have a reason to drug you." She pushed her hands through her hair, tugged just a little. "I saw lots of people, including a blonde wearing an emerald dress, who I followed to the bar. But once I got there I was focused on you." Because that's all she'd needed to see. She'd let Isely's unexpected appearance rattle her more than she'd thought. A rattled agent fails and she sure had done so here. She swore, turned on her heel and came up hard against Jason's chest. He'd walked up right behind her.

He caught her elbows and held her in place when she might have bounced off of him. "You'll wear a rut in the carpet."

"I don't care. And, for the record, that green dress wasn't the one I was wearing the last time you saw me." There were similarities she had to admit now that she really considered it. It was comparable enough to have a guy thinking it was the same.

"Who's your contact? What's the signal if you need to be pulled out of your mission?" he demanded, dragging her attention back to him.

"I don't have a code phrase or a contact." She pulled herself free of his touch. It was too distracting. "I've never needed help."

"And yet they sent me to backup and offer an exit strategy for an agent in trouble."

"Then they sent you for someone else."

Jason frowned. "That's what my boss said." This he murmured more to himself than to her. "They sure didn't send me to get married. Of all the options to get us out of trouble, why did you do this?" He pointed to the ring on his finger.

"What's the big deal? Got a girl back home?" She wanted him to take the bait and bypass the bigger problem while she figured out a way to salvage her potentially compromised operation.

Instead, she watched the storm brewing in his deep brown eyes.

"It doesn't matter." He turned away. "I wouldn't believe you anyway. But don't count on wearing the pants in this happy union, Mrs. Grant."

"Call me Gin."

He sank back into the chair where she'd draped his sport coat last night. "Now that you have a husband, Mrs. Grant, and I'm him, care to share your next move?"

Now he was just being stubborn. It seemed a shame to have so much handsome man at her fingertips and not be able to do anything fun with him.

"I'm here tracking a product and hopefully I'll get to oversee the sale," she admitted. "Sexy blondes in Las Vegas are everywhere. I thought it would be a foolproof disguise."

"The red *is* memorable," he agreed, eyeing her hair. "Too bad I forgot everything after that."

His eyes raked her from head to toe and she felt as if he saw right through her pale blue cashmere sweater.

If he ignored her barbs, she could ignore his. "It would be nice to get a look at the security footage from the bar. Maybe we can identify the woman who drugged you." Whether that would help with her mission or not was yet to be seen, but perhaps it would convince him that it hadn't been her who'd drugged him.

"Why? You just said sexy blondes are everywhere." He sipped his coffee and took another look at the marriage certificate. "Married by an Elvis impersonator. That is just not me." He shook his head.

"It was your idea last night."

"My brain on drugs." He shrugged, sipped more coffee. "Great. When you're finished with your mission are we going to do a drive-through divorce? I always thought those were an efficient concept."

"Give divorce a lot of thought, do you?"

"Enough."

She recognized a personal trigger point. She wanted to push for the real answers but, married or not, they weren't actually on personal terms yet. "Does the drive-through thing even exist anymore?"

He glared at her. "Guess we'll find out."

"We should be done here in plenty of time to qualify for an annulment.

"Same result."

"Does that mean you'll cooperate?"

"Sure. Marriage is all about compromise. Or so I've heard."

She didn't like the way he said that, and for the first time since bolting into the wedding chapel with an oblivious fiancé on her arm she questioned the wisdom of her rash decision. Well, the second time. Sharing a room with him had pushed her resolve to the brink.

"Getting married was your idea." Had she really needed a kiss from him that badly? She touched her lips again. If she were completely honest with herself she would admit that the kiss had been worth it. "I swear it was your idea."

"You knew I was compromised."

"True, and leaving you in a public place seemed like a really bad idea." She folded her arms over her chest.

"Let me get this straight. You didn't drug me, didn't see who did, but you thought it was okay to haul me into an Elvis-themed chapel and marry me?"

"Not exactly. My first suggestion involved you giving me some cover at the craps tables."

"I don't gamble."

"So you said."

"What else?"

"We went for a walk and I asked you to kiss me." She hurried on when he raised an eyebrow. "But you said we had to be married first. It was all rather gallant." If she didn't think about Isely and his thug flanking them. That was one part she could not afford to mention. Her mission was far too important to compromise for anyone, even the man she'd pretended to marry.

"Gallant?"

"I assumed it was a personality quirk. It fits your whole ex-military persona." She went to the table and pulled out a chair, sitting on her hands so she wouldn't fidget with the breakfast dishes. "But now that we're stuck together it could be an advantage. Just give me forty-eight hours to track this product and sale and then I'll pay the fees to grant you a speedy divorce."

It wouldn't be necessary because the receptionist knew he was intoxicated at the time of the marriage and because they hadn't filed the marriage license, but Gin could tell him the whole story later. No sense burning bridges and tossing away an ally right now. This might be her only chance to experience a marriage. Not to mention she'd been having fantasies about this guy for weeks now.

As a CIA agent, she wasn't the sort of woman a man brought home to his family. She didn't even resemble the sort of woman a man wanted to build a family with. No, she'd learned that hard lesson early in her life.

She was the sort of woman men fantasized about, the woman men liked to show off, but never the woman they kept around. They gave different reasons and it took her longer than she cared to admit to learn those reasons were a re-flection of the men who gave them, not the real-ity of who she was as a person.

When he still hadn't given her an answer, she went for broke. "Please. I really need your help." There, she'd said it. Gin Olin rarely asked for help, but she was no fool and it was clear she couldn't finish this alone.

"Fine. I'll help. Holt gave me an ultimatum. Either I fly back to the office or consider myself fired. The suite is booked through the weekend. If I'm fired I may as well have a little fun with the last perk my job bought me."

"You're willing to risk your job to help me?" Was he serious? Would Mission Recovery really fire him? Emotions she didn't want to try and untangle were suddenly twisting inside her.

He startled her, tugging one of her hands free to hold it. "What are you doing?" she demanded.

"Do we need ground rules?" He raised her hand to his lips and feathered small kisses over her fingers. "Or do you trust me to be the best doting husband ever?"

She yanked her hand away. "Doting?"

"We might even enjoy ourselves."

That was her second biggest fear. Her first was losing the trail of that bio-weapon. "We need ground rules." That was a given. There was just something about this guy that got to her.

As badly as she needed him, she also needed to keep her head on straight.

He sat back. "I'm listening."

"Whatever happens outside of this room stays outside of this room."

"Isn't that just the opposite of how it should be for wedded bliss?"

She ignored him. "I mean it. The 'doting' is for public consumption. Up here, we're just you and me—two covert agents sacrificing for the mission."

His brow furrowed. "Ah, sharing a bed, giving completely of ourselves." He made a tsking sound. "The sacrifices we make."

She rolled her eyes. Snagging another piece of bacon, she nibbled it while she resumed her pacing. What she was about to do was risky, but having a second set of eyes and a capable agent at her back in the casino was her best chance of spotting the buyer.

"Let me fill you in on why I'm here."

He leaned back, laced his fingers behind his head. "I'm all ears." He sniffed. "Wait. What is that smell?"

"Bacon?" She held it up.

"Not unless it's extra crispy." He looked at the dishes and then swiveled around in the chair. "Something smells scorched."

She sighed. "Probably your coat."

"Huh?" He pulled it off the chair and turned it until he found the hole. "Why is there a bullet hole in my sport coat?" He stuck his finger through it, but his eyes were on her. "An explanation, Mrs. Grant?"

"Technically that happened before we exchanged vows."

"Were they shooting at you or me?"

"Me. But I fired first." She paused, thinking it through again. "I was followed into the bar. I thought the disguise and chatting you up would be enough to dissuade him, but you were going loopy on me. So we left, but I was followed again." As much as she'd reviewed it, she couldn't come up with any reason Isely would be onto Jason. Isely shouldn't know her either, but she'd been following the virus for several weeks, and someone might have run a facial recognition that tipped him off. "They were definitely shooting at me," she said confidently.

"All right. Is there a police report?"

"Not that connects us because we ducked into the wedding chapel when people panicked. I fired the gun through your coat. Sorry, that's obvious, I guess." Why did this man make her so nervous? Maybe it was all those waking fantasies about him she'd relished.

He stared at her for a moment. "Did it work? Our marriage ploy?"

"You really don't remember?"

"Could you please stop saying that?"

"Sure. It worked well enough." She came closer and took the coat out of his hands, folding it so the bullet hole was hidden, then she draped it across the top of a different chair. "It made a great diversion."

"Good?"

"Sort of." She hesitated, balanced on the precipice of evading the truth or spilling it all in a messy rush of too much information. Unfortunately she was running out of time before the virus landed in the wrong hands. "Five years ago a European crime family named Isely acquired a lethal strain of influenza. A major sale was interrupted and the virus was confiscated by none other than Thomas Casey. Or so we thought. Testing proved the vials he brought back were fakes. The general consensus, if you assume Thomas Casey isn't a traitor—"

"Which he isn't," he cut in.

"Agreed and proven. But that means someone in the Isely food chain still has the virus. It's come back on the market recently and I've been following the tracking tags on the vials. One is here. I know the seller, but it would be great bonus points if I can identify the buyer."

"That was your assignment in Colorado."

"Among other things. Focus, Grant."

"Oh, I'm dialed in."

She met his intense gaze and nearly shivered in response. The man had an effect on her she could not deny. "Good." She cleared her throat. "I need you to help me identify who's who in this little drama. Two sets of eyes and gadding about in wedded bliss should be enough to get this done. I can watch the tracker tag and you can keep an eye on Isely."

"He's here? Isely?"

She nodded. "He surprised me. I guess he wants to oversee the transaction."

"Are these people I'm supposed to spot wearing name tags or carrying around steel cases with 'live virus' stamped on the side?"

She glared at him. "Lucas Camp gave me the impression you were a competent agent."

"I am."

"He also implied there was more to you than the few lines on your public résumé." She wanted to do a victory dance when she saw how that little barb dug into his ample pride.

"I think we both know résumés are always adjusted to suit the purpose."

Her confidence almost faltered, but she knew she wasn't looking at a hack or wannabe. Jason Grant was a Specialist, and how he got there didn't matter. He was plenty qualified to help her on this. He'd agreed and she should let it go, but she had the sinking feeling there was more to it than a fear of reprimand back at the office.

"Well then." He rolled to his feet and gathered the breakfast dishes, putting them back on the cart. "Let's go downstairs, play the happy couple and see what we see."

"Hang on."

One dark eyebrow lifted in response.

"You haven't explained why you're here."

"Right." He dragged out the word while he bobbed his head. "I don't know. What I gave you is all I have."

"You really expect me to believe that?"

"It's true. My orders were vague. I wasn't told anything other than the code phrase."

"What good is that?"

"Not much." He pushed the cart closer to the door then turned to face her again. "I'd think that would make you happy. I don't have anything to distract me from what you need to accomplish. Now, shall we?"

"Just let me check the status on the package I'm tracking." She pulled out her phone and entered the information. What should have been a simple, quick process felt like an eternity with Jason staring at her. Finally, the feedback came through, confirming the virus vial hadn't moved from the hotel room where the seller was keeping it.

She smiled at him as she tucked her phone away. "It's all good."

Chapter Four

Jason knew she was well-trained and talented—not just because Lucas Camp endorsed her, but because there was so little actual intel on her fieldwork. Last month his friend O'Marron at Interpol had given him the name to go with her stunning face, but beyond that there wasn't much to go on. Her passport records could have fit any number of cover identities, and they probably did.

But her sudden transformation into his blushing bride the very moment they crossed the threshold into the hallway unnerved him. Her hands were everywhere. Not groping, just the small, quick touches of new lovers who feel the slightest distance as an unbearable ache.

And which poet wrote that sappy line so it would get stuck in his head at the worst moment?

Alone in the elevator, she didn't back off. She grinned up at him as she pressed close and kissed him, nipping his lip ever so gently. It was for the cameras, he realized, struggling to keep up with her game and to keep his body in line. Mentally he understood her actions were about their cover, the mission, but physically his body struggled with the concept.

He wanted to blame the drug, but he knew it was out of his system. Lust was the source of his current haze. As much as his body might wish to play along with the marriage game, they had a job to do. And he had to keep things in line.

Still, he'd promised her a doting husband and that's what she would get. As the elevator doors parted, he tugged her toward the shops rather than the casino floor.

"What are you doing? I thought we were going to play some blackjack."

"In a minute." He wanted to put off the gambling as long as possible. "I haven't given you anything yet today." He draped his arm over her shoulders and pressed a kiss to the top of her head. "A doting husband always takes care of his wife first and foremost."

"That's silly," she said with a winning smile. "What could I need more than you?"

Oh, she was good. In a perfect world it would be exactly how he wanted his wife to feel. Contrary to any interpretation of his professional résumé, he'd spent enough time alone to know how he would treat the woman he chose to spend the rest of his life with.

In his line of work he didn't expect to find that forever sort of woman. In truth he didn't expect more than brief, superficial relationships. Not at this stage of the covert ops game anyway. Being a rather sad outlook didn't make it less true. Deep down, under the career accomplishments, he knew he wanted the stability his parents hadn't given him. He'd never so much as whispered it aloud, but he wanted the warm embrace his buddies had walked into after long deployments.

He wanted what his director, Thomas Casey, now had.

This marriage might not be destined to win longest running, but that didn't mean he couldn't enjoy himself for the time they had. Maybe that made him a glutton for punishment because this game would come to an end sooner rather than later, but he refused to allow that to deter him.

As they strolled down a wide corridor that felt more like an indoor mall, he silently commended the casino designers for putting everything within reach so no one had to leave. The clear blue of the fake sky painted on the ceiling made him a little claustrophobic, but it was evidently a system that worked.

"Here." He paused at the window display of a jewelry store. "We'll start here today."

Her hand clutched his in a strong grip. "No." She tugged him along to the next window. "If you want to buy me a present, why not something I need? I forgot my swimsuit."

He wiggled his eyebrows at her. "Fair enough." Not so surprising that she'd be practical, although he had no way of knowing if she really had or hadn't packed a swimsuit. He should have made time to search her luggage.

In the elegant boutique, he teased her, holding up bikini after bikini, each with less material than the one before. She didn't blush or protest— she just played along, dismissing some on color and accepting others. When she had a decent selection, she headed for the dressing room.

She spun around as he followed her. "You can't come in."

He didn't see why not. They were married and he'd certainly given her an eyeful this morning. Based on her ground rules, outside the room was his only chance to see her body. There should be some perks to the setup—besides those drummed up by his too vivid imagination.

"I'll be quick," she said. Though the words were light and the kiss sweet, he heard the steel underneath. She wanted to get out there and find the buyer.

He understood her dedication, appreciated it even. But she'd already gone so far as to marry him, so they could hardly waste the inconvenience and effort by not embracing the part fully. He sat back in the plush chair and checked the police scanner app on his phone for anything strange.

Currently things were calm in the area, so he skimmed the news sites for anything about the shooting last night. Scowling, he read the official report that stated a tourist from Germany had been shot in the foot with his own gun. Interesting way to spin it.

Being relegated to haunt this one casino hadn't been his idea of a great mission, but Gin was certainly perking things up, he thought as she shed her jeans and her bare lower legs appeared below the privacy curtain.

Knowing he couldn't stop the reaction, he went along with it, imagining what she looked like in all the places he couldn't see. If her toes ignited this slow burn of desire...well, it was no wonder he was trying so hard to remember last night.

There was a distinctive grace to her movements as she stepped in and out of several different styles of swimsuit bottoms. Her toes pointed, her calves flexed. She must have been a dancer somewhere in her past.

He almost groaned in protest when she pulled on jeans and slipped back into her heels.

She whipped back the curtain, and a catlike smile spread across her face.

Caught, he grinned at her. "You made a decision?"

A tiny scrap of bikini dangled from her fingertip. "This one should leave you breathless."

He snatched it from her. "Can't wait, sweetheart." He went back to the sales floor, grabbed the first pair of board shorts in his size for himself and was headed for the checkout when she slowed him down. "We just need a couple of other things."

"Like what?"

She shook her head and exchanged a knowing look with the clerk. "My man isn't big on shopping."

"Few of them are," the clerk replied with a kind smile.

Jason regained his patience as Gin found a sheer cover-up, sunscreen and a pair of flip-flops for each of them. They were playing a game here, and just because he found her legs tantalizing didn't mean he'd ever get a look at the whole package. He had to maintain his perspective. This was a vast improvement over milling about waiting for something to happen.

When Gin decided they were set, Jason asked

the clerk to add the charges to their account and deliver the purchases to the room.

"Of course." She tapped a few keys and as he was signing the receipt, the clerk congratulated them both. "Congratulations! You do know you're entered in our wedding sweepstakes this month, right?"

Jason and Gin exchanged a look. "What does that mean?" he asked.

"Each month we give away a destination honeymoon, gift certificates to major retailers and cash. Each night's stay and every purchase you make in the hotel is an added entry."

"That sounds amazing," Gin gushed.

"Doesn't it, though?" the clerk agreed. "Did you have a honeymoon planned?"

"We're just taking the next couple of days here," he replied. "The plan is to do something bigger for our first anniversary."

"Well, Barbados or France would definitely be bigger. Good luck to you."

Gin clung to his arm as they exited the store. When he suggested more window shopping, she cut him off flat. "The seller just walked by. We have to tail him."

"Anything for you, love."

"Stop."

He assumed she wanted him to stop with the endearments, but she'd paused in front of the jewelry store display. Following her lead, he nodded and smiled as she pointed out various pieces.

"He's getting a coffee."

"Okay." That didn't help him much. Three of the five people closest to the serving counter were men. He gave her waist a quick squeeze. "Has the vial moved?"

She drew her phone from her pocket and swiped the screen. "No." She said it with a smile, but he felt the tension humming through her body. "Let's get into the casino. He's a craps and roulette man."

"Not the biologist then."

"How do you know that?"

"I don't. Just seems like a smart man would favor a game with better odds."

"He's representing Isely," she murmured. "How smart can he be?"

Good point. They left the shopping area and passed groups of slot machines and the entrance to the twenty-four-hour buffet on their way to the gambling floor. Delving into the role she'd asked him to play, he matched her slower pace and pretended to look for just the right table to join.

"You've got to give me something better to go on if you want my help."

"Hmm." She drummed her fingertips against his forearm. "Let's try roulette."

"Sucker game," he said for her ears only as

they walked closer. None of the coffee bar customers were nearby, but as Jason scanned the room, he spied a familiar face that filled him with dread. He didn't want to believe it. He couldn't imagine any benign scenario that would put the two of them in the same city.

Gabriel Frost had earned his forbidding reputation by doing the long-range dirty work for the side with the most money. In Europe the man was a cross between a ghost and an urban legend. Kill shots of all complexities were attributed to him. Jason only knew his face because he'd seen it once through a scope during the course of an investigation. It was the reason Interpol had brought him on board—to unravel the shooter's methods. Jason's efforts had brought them closer than they'd ever been, but still they'd been unable to make an arrest.

"Two chances and then I'd like to try some cards," he said, watching Frost head toward the blackjack tables.

She quirked an eyebrow in a silent question but didn't argue. She lost her first bet and lost again on her second. Smiling, she gazed up at him. "Love's better than money any day."

Her sentiment earned them a chorus of *awws* as they left for the card room.

"A kiss for luck?" he asked as they looked around at the various tables.

"Always."

When her lips brushed his, he held her a moment longer. "You're sure this vial originated in Europe?"

"Yes."

"That should do it," he said in a normal voice. He found a seat at the table that gave her the best view of the rest of the floor and him the best view of Frost.

He was up two hundred dollars when Gin whispered in his ear. Although it might have looked like sweet nothings to an outsider, she was telling him her target was on the move again. He had to assume so anyway because he had yet to single out the person she was shadowing.

Jason's newly acquired target sat in front of a growing stack of chips and appeared to be in for a few more hours of play. This wasn't the right place to share his concerns that Isely had brought a shooter to the party, and staying too close might jeopardize the advantage of surprise he knew he had right now. It was best to move.

Jason let her guide him with a deft touch on his arm or at his waist as they moved between tables. They lost a few more chips on a craps game before she declared she wanted to go for a swim. If it meant he got to see her in the bikini, he was all for it.

When they were back in the room, he stowed

the chips in the safe with the gun. "When are you going to tell me who you're shadowing?"

"When you need to know." She was at the table admiring their purchases. "A girl could get used to this kind of service." She tossed the shorts his way. "I'm not sure what to think about Isely's absence." She pulled a tablet out of her suitcase. "Maybe they arrested him last night."

"More likely he's just lying low." And letting Frost do his thing. If she wasn't sharing her secrets with him, he wasn't about to mention the anomaly he'd noticed. He might need the information for leverage later.

"If they picked him up, they're not publicizing it." She sighed and set the tablet aside to pick up the swimsuit. "I'll change in the bedroom."

He pulled the price tags off of the shorts and waited until she was out of sight to strip off his khakis. There wasn't much point in modesty after this morning, but he meant to honor the ground rules. Besides, keeping his distance was the only way to regain his sanity where she was concerned.

"Where did you learn to count cards? Any chance you're undercover with the Gaming Commission?" She laughed and he knew he enjoyed the merry sound too much.

His first instinct was denial, but he heard himself telling her the truth. "My assignments often involve long stretches of boredom. It was something to do."

"I'd think with a skill like that you'd gamble more often."

"I discovered a preference for other calculated risks."

She appeared in the doorway, and he whistled—couldn't stop himself. Her full breasts filled out the revealing cups of the bikini top. Tiny emerald-colored stones glittered on the matching silk. The sheer scarf knotted low on her hips left her midriff bare and did a poor job of covering her lovely legs. She was—in a word—gorgeous.

What were the ground rules again?

Maybe if he knocked his head against the wall, he'd shake loose the memory of those legs twined with his. Of all the things he'd seen in his life, why did his mind block the one memory he knew would keep him warm for the rest of his days?

She spun in a quick circle, hands linked at her back, and stopped with a wink. Playing along, he clutched his heart and pretended to faint onto the love seat.

"You'll cause more than a few heart attacks out there," he promised.

"I hadn't thought of that." She traced the stylized dragon tattoo on his biceps with her fingertip. "You'll leave more than a few hearts stuttering in your wake, too, I think."

"Nah."

She pulled him to his feet and into the bedroom and he had the inevitable hope that she was through with ground rules, too. "Look at us," she said, turning them toward the mirror, her arm linked in his. "We look good together. Like the perfect, newly married couple."

He agreed. Her rich red hair brushed his shoulder and her smooth, alabaster skin was a creamy highlight against his skin tanned from training outside.

"Let's go soak up some sunshine."

"So who are you shadowing, Gin?"

Her face clouded over as she stepped away from him. "Probably just a flunky since I bumped into Isely himself last night. I'd hoped he sent the virus here with someone he trusted, someone who could get us deeper into his operation. My gut says he's up to something."

Jason thought about the sniper. "Criminals usually are."

"I mean something bigger." She pulled a face. "It's not like him to micromanage a standard exchange. He blames that kind of behavior for getting his father killed. I'm just traipsing along behind the tracking tags on the vials." She held up her phone and showed him the status. "This one hasn't moved in two days. Our intel says the sale goes down sometime this weekend."

"Where?"

"Vegas."

"That's too broad a window for one agent to cover."

"Tell me about it. I've been following these little radar blips for weeks."

"How many are there?"

"Three tags that I know of."

"How'd you get the data for tracking?"

She winked at him. "That's classified."

He rolled his eyes. Considering her recent travels, it was a logical assumption that she'd managed that op on her own, too. "Why is it so important to expand your part of the mission?"

"It normally wouldn't matter, but this virus is worse than nasty. It's capable of wiping out a village in less than a week." She started pacing, her hips making the fabric of that scarf sway. "Biological warfare only hurts the innocent. I want to know why it's on American soil."

"Got it," he said, though he suspected there was a bigger reason lurking under the surface. "Any chance your flunky might like the pool?"

"Who knows? But I can watch the blip down there as easily as I can up here."

"Then grab the sunscreen." If they left the room, he could get his hands on her. If they were just killing time, he wanted to enjoy it.

Chapter Five

Gin's pulse fluttered all the way from his suite to the pool. She couldn't get over the reflection of the two of them in the mirror. Something had clicked for her in that moment. Something she couldn't afford to notice and would never consider acting on.

There was an ongoing mission here. Innocent people would die if she failed to follow that signal to the scheduled exchange.

The sobering thought was enough to keep her grounded through the nearly worshipful effort Jason gave to applying the sunscreen to her back. *Doting indeed.* Would he really spoil a wife this way? Would he take such care, or was he just going above and beyond to get under her skin?

Or her sarong.

She pushed her sunglasses up into her hair and squinted at him as he settled on the lounge chair next to hers. "What are you doing?"

"I'm just soaking up the sunshine with my

gorgeous wife. As ordered." He skimmed a finger down her leg, leaving a searing trail along her nerves. "Would you rather we did something else?"

"Of course not." She replaced her sunglasses to cover her reaction to his touch. "This is fabulous." She even managed a contented sigh.

"Good." He was doing something with his phone.

"Problem?"

"Nope, just checking up on a friend."

She hoped that was all he was doing. In his position, she would be trying to figure how who had sent the doped drink and how to get out of an unexpected marriage. The thought was almost as sobering as the idea of a modern-day plague. She scolded herself for the errant thought and flipped over, the better to watch for the people critical to her assignment.

"Do you want to swim?"

"No, thank you." She patted his leg and enjoyed the view as he stripped off his T-shirt. "You go on ahead." His brow furrowed and she knew he thought she wanted to get rid of him. She would have made the same assumption if their roles were reversed. "I promise I'll stay right here. There's no reason to move."

He stood and dropped his sunglasses on the towel before diving into the deep end of the pool with enough grace to make her mouth water. Acting a part or not, she had to admit there was a mutual attraction here. A serious attraction she wanted to explore—time permitting. With every move he made in public, she forgot a little bit about why the ground rules for being alone were so important.

Although it had been fun teasing him that they'd shared something intimate last night, with every passing touch she wanted to see where those kisses might have led if he hadn't been indisposed.

And just where was the woman who had drugged him? It might have been a random con, but she just didn't believe it. Las Vegas and the general anonymity of the hotel scene, worked in the favor of people who wanted to skirt the rules. Gin was excellent with faces, but she had to admit that the constantly shifting landscape presented a challenge. Jason was right—they could talk to the bartender, but most likely they would have to reveal themselves to hotel security. The video record of the bar last night was the only hope they had of getting a lead on the woman who'd sent him the bad drink.

Because the blond wig and emerald dress had been so similar to her own disguise last night, she was more than a little concerned the woman who'd targeted Jason was also somehow related to her case. From behind her oversized dark sunglasses, she watched the other guests at the pool. It wasn't particularly crowded, but they were hardly alone. The staff moved here and there, ever present but never interfering.

No one seemed to care much about Jason swimming a few laps at an easy pace around the people relaxing and playing in the water. Well, no one but a few women with skimpier swimsuits than the one Gin wore. One of them—a blonde—caught at his ankle, and he pulled up short to talk with her.

Not the same woman from the bar last night. Gin could tell from here that the cheek structure was wrong. Plus, she didn't think anyone would risk swimming with a wig on.

The easy smile Jason gave the stranger sent a tide of jealousy surging through Gin. Her toes squeezed the slats of the chair, and she thought going for a swim might be the right choice after all. Every second had that jealousy swirling stronger and stronger around her. It took all of her tremendous self-control to smother the urge to shout at him to show the woman the ring on his finger.

Except that's just what he was doing. The sunlight flashed off the gold band, and the smile he sent Gin's way was full of devotion.

And there went her heart again, doing a little

tap dance of happiness. Keeping her head tilted as if she was reading, she turned the page of the magazine in her lap and mentally reviewed the projections of deaths that one vial of the virus could cause. She was in Las Vegas for a reason. She wasn't here to fall in love with an unattainable man like him.

She'd reached the secondary infection stage numbers when Jason's phone screamed out a Rolling Stones riff. Leaning over, she reached to mute it. If she happened to see the caller identity display *O'Marron*, that wasn't snooping—just an innocent accident.

Seemed like the right rationalization for a wife to make. At least it sounded good in her head.

But she must have leaned too far because her chair suddenly popped and shifted beneath her. Someone screamed and Jason shouted her name. She glanced over her shoulder at him and barely registered the horror on his face when another scream split the air and drew her attention in the other direction.

A lifeguard was on the deck, clutching at her leg, blood running freely between her fingers.

Following instinct, Gin scrambled to help. She was closest, but Jason suddenly was hovering over her, his body so close he dripped pool water over her.

"Go." He gave a nod indicating the nearest cabana.

"But she's hurt." Gin gestured toward the life-guard.

"Your chair."

She twisted around and immediately understood his urgency. One of the slats of the chaise had a clean hole that hadn't been there when she'd taken her seat. A bullet hole. Someone had taken a shot at her.

"Go!"

There was no arguing with that tone even if she had been inclined to do so.

She raced to the cabana, Jason at her side, praying the whole way the shooter wouldn't tag either of them.

Knowing the trip was only a few yards didn't make it any less harrowing. She tried to catch her breath, but Jason spun her in a circle, his big hands brushing lightly over her skin as if he were searching for something.

"What?"

"I can't believe you weren't hit."

She wanted to peek out and check on the life-guard, but Jason blocked her view. "Is she okay?"

"Looked messy but not life threatening. Lower leg. Probably hit by a ricochet of the first bullet."

"First?"

"Yes." He peered through a narrow break in the curtains framing the cabana.

"Can you see the shooter?"

He shook his head and turned back toward her. "Didn't you hear the second shot?"

"I think I missed the first shot. Your phone rang and I—"

"Shh." He pulled her into a quick hug. "We need to get out of here before the cops arrive."

She bobbed her chin in agreement. If they decided they had any helpful information, they could share it through official channels later. Sticking around now might just as easily get either one of them killed or worse—injure another bystander.

She let Jason carve a path as they slipped out of the other side of the cabana and joined the crowd getting pressed back from the scene as paramedics arrived.

He held her hand as they grabbed their things and then made their way back to their room, and she didn't think it was all about acting the part this time. His grip was too strong, just shy of painful, but she didn't pull away. She'd never admit it, but his touch was an anchor she needed after such a close call.

Someone had taken a shot at her.

Gin was well-versed in the physiological responses to adrenaline and fear. She'd trained hard to minimize those effects. Her increased heart rate and rapid breathing were normal, nothing to be embarrassed about. Those effects would settle and probably give way to shaking as soon as they were safely in the room.

But the shaking started in the elevator, and Jason wrapped his arms around her, pulling her close, into the warm security of his solid chest. His heart beat strong and steady in her ear and she let herself cling, enormously grateful for the comfort he offered.

Tears stung her eyes, but she refused to let them fall. She couldn't recall the last time she'd wept, and she'd never done so on a mission.

The elevator car chimed when they reached their floor. By unspoken agreement, they walked in silence down the hallway to their room. She used the brief time to sort out what she'd heard and seen so they could effectively analyze the incident and potential reasons for such a bold strike.

But the truth was she hadn't heard anything... she'd been too distracted.

That was the most dangerous part of all.

Chapter Six

"Mr. Camp on line one, sir."

Holt scowled at the phone. The last thing he needed was Lucas Camp sniffing around and poking his nose into this situation. Holt had planned for every contingency.

Except Camp. Holt had been appointed to this post when Camp had returned to the private sector. A smart man would stay there.

After a quick mental rundown of current operations, he picked up the phone. "This is Holt."

"It's Lucas Camp. Thank you for taking my call."

Holt bit back a curt reply. He didn't have time to waste on distractions. "What do you need, Lucas?"

"I picked up word on a couple of shooting incidents in Las Vegas."

Holt rubbed at his brow. "Going slumming, Lucas, or are you planning your next vacation with the missus?"

"The details were vague, but I wondered if you had anyone in the area."

"No." Holt had to amend the outright lie. "No one I'm willing to discuss with you."

"I understand."

"I don't." Holt leaned forward and went on the offensive. "When Casey went missing last month, I understood your concern. But that's as far as my understanding goes. You're retired, Lucas, and I don't appreciate your interference."

"You were very cooperative in Colorado and I appreciated it," Lucas interjected.

Holt snorted. "Rest assured Thomas has made all his check-ins since he left for his honeymoon." There was nothing else about Colorado they needed to talk about.

"I'm glad to hear it."

Holt gritted his teeth. Thomas Casey and Lucas Camp went way back. After the trouble in Colorado, Casey had probably been checking in with Camp these past weeks, too. He told himself to ease up. This was just another wrinkle in the ever-shifting sands of his plan. But he couldn't shake the gut feeling that Camp knew more than he should about the problems inside Mission Recovery.

"What do you want, Lucas?"

"I want to know if you have someone looking into this thing in Las Vegas."

"Is retirement too boring?" When was this old man going to let it go? "The actions of this office are no longer your concern. Go find a hobby."

The other end of the line was so quiet Holt thought Camp had ended the call. He was about to replace the receiver when Camp finally replied.

"That's a good idea, Holt. I think I'll try gambling."

This time, he heard the click and knew the call was finished. He also understood that Camp's final words had been a warning he would be smart not to ignore. Holt replaced the receiver and sat back, tapping a pencil against the desk blotter. He checked his watch and pulled up a travel website to get an idea of flight availability.

Assuming Camp was in Houston there was any number of flight options that could put him in Vegas in time for dinner. Holt closed the search. It didn't matter.

Even if Camp got to Vegas, he couldn't possibly know where to look or who to look for—other than Grant. Considering the struggle his own people were having keeping Grant contained, he didn't think Camp had better odds.

Who was he kidding?

He broke the pencil he'd been toying with and tossed both pieces into the trash. What was the worst that could happen if Camp managed to interfere? Would one compromised link bring the whole thing tumbling down?

Holt pulled out his cell phone and made a call. A carefully phrased warning was all he could offer, but it would have to suffice.

Houston, 1:20 p.m.

LUCAS CAMP STARED at the telephone. This was wrong.

"I take it that didn't go very well," Victoria Colby-Camp said from the counter where she was preparing lunch.

Lucas had a bad, bad feeling about what Emmett Holt was up to. He placed the phone back into its cradle and joined his wife at the kitchen island. "Holt is up to something. I can feel it. I think I should call Thomas."

Victoria gave him that look, the one that suggested he should rethink that strategy. "Are you certain you want to disturb his honeymoon? Thomas waited a very long time to take a wife. He deserves a proper honeymoon without interruption."

Lucas couldn't deny the validity of her point. "You're right, of course." He kissed his wife's cheek. "I waited quite a while to take a wife, too."

Victoria stopped preparing the salad and smiled at him. "Yes, you did."

He had been in love with Victoria since the first time he laid eyes on her when she was only twenty, but she had belonged to another—his best friend, the late James Colby. But Lucas had waited and now she was his.

"All right." Lucas relented. "I won't call Thomas. I'll just have to go to Vegas and check on this situation personally."

Victoria wiped her hands on a towel. "I think that's an excellent idea," she said to his surprise. "As long as you wait until Jim arrives tomorrow afternoon to pick up the children. He can give us a lift. I'm certain he won't mind flying back to Chicago via Las Vegas."

The Colby Agency jet would certainly make traveling considerably easier. "Very well, my dear. Holt gets a twenty-four-hour reprieve."

"One of these days we're going to have to actually retire," Victoria suggested.

Lucas grinned. "I'll remind you of that the next time an intriguing case comes across the desk of the Colby Agency or to you directly."

"Touché," Victoria confessed. Since they'd announced their retirement they'd been involved in as many cases as ever. The new Colby Agency Houston office had ensured they were never too far from the action.

As if they both needed a reprieve to remind them of what was really important in life, little Luke, their grandson, raced through the living room screaming at the top of his lungs. Eight-year-old Jamie was right on his heels. "Give me my purse!" she wailed.

Jamie had discovered accessories. Before they knew it there would be boyfriends and proms. Time had a way of flying entirely too fast.

Victoria laughed. "How could you possibly consider leaving me at a time like this?"

"What was I thinking?" He joined his wife in laughter as the two children argued over who did what.

Eventually Lucas played the part of negotiator while Victoria finished lunch.

His wife was right. *This* was the most important part of their lives right now.

The rest could wait.

Chapter Seven

Caesar's Palace, Las Vegas,
1:42 p.m.

At the door Gin let Jason swipe the keycard through the lock. He got a red light. He tried a second time and failed again. They exchanged a look, both of them listening for any sounds inside the room. Stepping forward, she tried her keycard, but it failed, too.

With a finger to his lips, he held up a second keycard.

She could only watch and wonder where he'd picked it up as he swiped it through the lock and the light turned green.

As she silently stepped into the room, nothing was out of place. Everything she could see looked precisely as they'd left it, even the shopping bag on the table and Jason's damaged sport coat on the chair. Still, something was off.

She sensed the attack, but didn't have time to brace for it as the room door slammed into her.

Gin let the impact carry her into the wall and then stumbled back into Jason when the intruder kept pushing. She lurched forward, ready and able to handle this, but Jason caught her and pushed her back into the hallway. She bristled, but they would deal with the implied insult later.

Jason drove through the door with his shoulder, pinning whoever was on the other side behind it. She watched the door shift as they struggled, then Jason pulled the door closer and quickly shoved it back against the intruder. As Jason reached around and pulled out a man dressed in a hotel uniform she gaped.

Hands and elbows became a blur in the tight space, but Jason worked him deeper into the suite. She blocked the door, understanding he wanted to prevent an escape. They needed answers.

"You?" The intruder swore and gawked at her and Jason took advantage, landing a solid uppercut, but the intruder recovered. Jason warded off the next hurried advance with swift blocks and a knee strike. The intruder stumbled over the coffee table and it broke with a loud crash, but he rolled away from Jason's next advance.

Gin could see they were evenly matched. Though Jason had muscle mass over the guy, the other man was absorbing the blows and dealing plenty of his own.

Suddenly Jason reared back and she swore when sunlight glinted off the blade of a knife. The intruder feinted toward Jason, who dropped and swung out his leg to trip the other man. The intruder went down and Gin tried to scoot by and get to the weapons in the bedroom safe.

But the intruder jumped up faster than she expected and he caught her. She went still as he jerked her back against him, the cold, sharp edge of his knife pressed against her throat.

Instantly, her training kicked in. Her emotions drew deep inside with the blast of adrenaline, leaving her feeling as cold and hard as the blade of the knife.

Jason took a step and the intruder warned him off.

"Don't even think it," he warned.

"Let her go."

"Not just yet."

"What do you want?" Jason demanded. "Money?"

"Just the woman."

Gin silently commended Jason on the rambling effort and the big worried eyes, but everyone in the room knew this was no simple robbery attempt. Using her eyes, she tried to warn Jason of her intent as the intruder dragged her back toward the door.

"Wait," Jason shouted. "Let me open the safe. We have cash."

He sounded so desperate she almost believed he was worried.

Timing it, she drove her elbow into the intruder's side and twisted her hips, pinning him to the counter. The coffeepot crashed as he waved, tried to regain his balance. With the element of surprise she got her hand up and disarmed him. The knife clattered away and Gin thought it made the odds fair again, but that wasn't giving Jason enough credit.

Jason tackled the intruder and the men fumbled backward, the intruder caught between Jason's advance and the flat-panel television. He pushed Jason off him and they tumbled to the floor, scrapping and rolling for the advantage. This time she made it to the bedroom and, with shaking hands, she punched in the combination to open the small safe. She heard the two trading punches and crashing into things in the other room as she grabbed her revolver.

"Find something to tie him up," Jason called.

With the gun in one hand, she grabbed the roll of duct tape from her suitcase and rushed back out of the bedroom to see the intruder in a heap amid the mess of the broken coffee table and with Jason's knee in his back.

"Nice work," she said, handing him the roll of tape.

"Same goes for you. Where'd you find this?" he asked, accepting her preferred method of bondage.

"I never travel without it."

He shot her a look. "You can be a little scary." He bound the intruder's wrists and feet. "You'll have to show me that move you pulled."

"Anytime."

Jason flipped over the intruder and checked his pockets. "He's not carrying anything but the employee keycard."

"No ID?" She studied the face, the wiry build, but nothing was familiar to her.

"Only the bogus name tag. But I know this guy. His name is Rick Wallace, he works with Gabriel Frost, an assassin I had the misfortune of running into in Europe. He's an independent contractor. He's good and he takes work from the highest bidder. I'd say based on the angle of the shot at the pool, they accessed a room in this tower to take that shot at you." He made a sound that was part grunt, part hum. "I wonder how they managed the uniform and master key."

"Maybe the same way you did?"

His unrepentant grin flashed and she had to admit to herself at least, she found it charming.

"I lifted mine off the housekeeping cart down the hall," he confessed.

"Good hands."

"All the girls say so," he teased with a wicked wink. "This guy probably got his in a kit that accompanied the orders and the down payment. Go ahead and call security."

"Are you sure?"

"I'm not taking the blame for all this damage. Besides, what else are we going to do with him?"

She had a few ideas, none of them legal. "Fine," she said picking up the hotel phone and pressing the key for security. Letting her voice shake, she asked for assistance. "They're on the way," she said when she hung up the phone.

"He looked pretty surprised to see you," Jason said. "You must have been the intended target if he was willing to try to take you at knife point."

"I'd have to agree." She ran her fingertips over the scrape at her throat as she stared out of the window. "But he broke into the room registered in your name." She spun on her heel and glared at the unconscious man. "Wake him up so we can talk to him."

"Not a good idea," he said. "He already knows too much. Let security handle it."

"They won't ask the right questions."

"That might be for the best under the circumstances."

Jason's voice was calm and quiet. He stood beside her but was evidently wise enough not to touch her. His stable presence should have soothed her, but her stomach knotted more. She felt twitchy all over, as if she'd been rolling around in poison ivy instead of lounging poolside. But then again, the poolside fun had ended when someone took that shot at her, so maybe the poison ivy would have been better.

She had to be logical here. Someone had managed to identify them both, even though they hadn't been connected at all before last night. Gin pulled him away from the suite door. "Why are you in town?"

He frowned at her. "I told you—to recover an agent."

"An unnamed agent who has yet to show up." She ran her hands through her hair. "This makes me edgy." She didn't do edgy. "Something else is going on. What was he—" she gestured to the guy on the floor "—doing in here?"

"You got me. Is anything missing?"

"Nothing obvious, but I haven't taken a good look."

"Let's do that."

Swiftly, they searched the room and realized everything was accounted for. Both laptops, her tablet and the small stack of poker chips she'd left on the dresser in the bedroom. She returned her gun to the safe and was checking the status of the virus tracking signal when Jason swore.

"What did you find?"

He lifted the mattress and pointed to a small plastic envelope of ammunition.

"That wasn't here last night," she said.

"Glad we both know that," he said with more than a little irritation. "What are the odds this was left by the previous occupant?"

"Zero." She sighed. "Setting you up for the incident at the pool?"

"It's the wrong ammunition for that shot, but yeah, that's my gut reaction."

She crossed her arms and rubbed at the chill on her skin. "You said you ran into the man, Frost, when you were in Europe. What was your mission?"

"I'll explain while we pack." He snatched the ammunition and zipped it into a concealed compartment in his suitcase. "We have to get out of here."

"Security is on the way," she hissed. "And my op is *here*."

"I understand that," he replied from the closet safe. He pulled weapons, chips and a jewelry box out of the safe and dumped everything into his suitcase.

"We can change rooms," she said, gathering their belongings from the bathroom and tossing his toiletry kit on top of his clothes. "But it's too late to get out of the hotel unnoticed."

"We stand out more if we stay." He pulled on a gray T-shirt that did little to tone down his bright board shorts. With the flip-flops he looked like a surfer in need of a good wave. If only the hair were longer.

"I disagree." She shook her head. "We should go ahead with the report and convince the security team to help us out with surveillance."

"Right, because people in the hospitality industry love hosting sniper bait."

"We have to report the break-in." She stood her ground. This was where she needed to be.

"No," he argued. "Let them find the mess in the course of their investigation. I'm more concerned about who ordered a hit on you and getting you out of range."

"Spoken like a doting husband."

"When in Rome," he muttered.

She laughed, more than a little surprised that she could under the circumstances. This had to be the work of Isely. He was on to her. She should have admitted that when he followed her to the bar last night. Her cover was blown. No two ways about it.

"Seriously," she persisted, "we have to file the

report. This room is booked under your name. As victims of attempted robbery we'll have their sympathy."

"They'll know I'm here for a security conference," he finished for her. "Even my cover story has a military history. The police and security will see the path of the bullet and put us at the scene quickly enough. If they haven't already."

"The hotel video record will clear you."

"Maybe. It depends on the angle. Brown hair, average height—anyone could be me in that pool."

"Running away definitely won't help your case."

He took a deep breath and pushed a hand through his wet hair. "You were booked here under an alias?"

"Of course."

He frowned. "You put Ginger Olin on the marriage license."

She nodded, ignoring the little shiver that skated down her spine as he spoke her name. So he knew her real name. Big deal. She should be pleased that her efforts in Colorado irritated him enough to dig deeper. Why did she keep underestimating him?

"And too many staff know our faces thanks to your little newlywed game."

"That's not so bad. We change rooms, of

course, but we stay and use the temporary fame to our advantage."

"Fine," he said with a heavy sigh, looking around at the mess. "Are you going to claim anything was stolen?"

"No," she gave a nod to his zipped suitcase. "You?"

He shook his head. "Who wants you dead?"

"Any number of people, I suppose, considering my rate of mission success. My intel says none of them are in town." Except Isely.

"But any of them could hire a sniper to deal with you."

She ignored that. "What do we say about this guy?" She nudged the unconscious intruder with her foot.

"Do we have to say anything? We walked in and subdued him. The less we share about him the better our odds if we stay."

"If? Are you going back to the change hotels idea?"

"No. Do you still have the keycard for the room you booked with your alias?"

"Yes. Why?"

"We should go see if anything's wrong there."

"Agreed. But there's nothing to find. I moved all of my things here last night."

Further discussion had to wait as the security team arrived with the hotel manager and a

Las Vegas police officer. When they took in the scene, the hotel security team radioed for help to remove the intruder and refrained from detailed questions until he was out of the way.

She and Jason went through the standard background questions and gave the contact information that matched up with their cover stories. They both applied the right amount of bewildered distress mixed with the temper and shock of the pool shooting and room invasion.

No, none of their valuables were missing. Yes, they'd combined business with pleasure on this trip. No, they didn't have any idea who would want to harm them. Yes, they'd gotten married last night. No, they didn't have any connection to the intruder. And the duct tape was something they'd gotten for their honeymoon. That was the last question on that subject.

"Why did you leave the pool area?" the police officer asked.

Gin opened her mouth, but once more Jason leaped in to answer first.

"That was my fault. I know we should have stayed and given a statement. My wife tried to assist the lifeguard," he said, rubbing her hand where it rested on his thigh. "But I wasn't in the mood to be widowed on our honeymoon. I just wanted her out of there."

"Completely understandable," the hotel manager said with a smile, preempting whatever the officer would have said. "We are so terribly sorry and we'd like to do everything possible to salvage the situation."

Good luck, Gin thought. "Is the lifeguard okay? There seemed to be a lot of blood." She let Jason pull her closer, offering comfort. If this mission fell apart, she would always remember how well he played his role.

After his act here, a real husband might be a bit of a letdown. She pushed the errant thought out of her head. This wasn't the right time to lose focus.

"The lifeguard was stable when the paramedics transported her." The head of security answered that one. "I'm sure she'll make a full recovery."

"That's good news," Gin replied.

"I'll see that your statement is added to the official report about the shooting," the police officer assured. "There may be some follow-up required if it turns out the incident at the pool is related to other recent crimes in the area."

"Other crimes? Plural?" Gin had only heard about one possible strike, and a quick glance at Jason proved he hadn't heard anything before he'd been drugged last night. "What do you mean? What's been going on?"

"I'm not able to elaborate at this time," he explained. "But there is an ongoing investigation related to other shootings."

"Sorry." Gin smiled. "Force of habit."

"She started her career as a police beat reporter. That's how we met," Jason explained. "I was a security consultant for a business that had been targeted by a drug ring."

She watched that sink in to all four faces and gave Jason bonus points for improvisation. She kept her mouth shut, but she would be digging into the details at the earliest opportunity. The ammunition in the bed had her wondering if any of the other shootings were better suited to the particular caliber Wallace had planted.

"Maybe we should just fly home early," Jason suggested.

"No cause for alarm," the manager intervened. "Here at the Palace we've doubled our security presence and coordinated with the Las Vegas police until this is resolved. You'll be safer here than anywhere else on the strip."

"I don't know," she hedged.

"As I said, follow-up may be necessary." The police officer got to his feet. "I think it's best if you stay in town at least through the weekend."

"So let us pamper you." The manager was all smiles. "I've got a penthouse with your name on it and a team of massage therapists standing by."

"Seriously?" Gin squeezed Jason's hand. "That's tempting."

"That's Vegas," the hotel manager added.

"What do you think, honey?"

"I suppose if we have to stay in town anyway..." He hitched his shoulders. "We may as well take them up on the offer."

"It's settled then." The hotel manager reached for his radio, calling in help to move them to the penthouse.

Jason let Gin handle the final exchange of information. Their luggage was whisked away ahead of them, and they were escorted by the manager himself all the way to their new door.

The elevator doors parted on a luxurious vestibule that was nearly as spacious as her original hotel room.

More than the guards standing at the fire exit and elevator, Jason noticed the penthouse was locked with a key.

"I've disabled the electronic lock for your room. Only the key will open it, and you and I have the only two keys." He handed the brass key to Jason. "I hope that goes some distance to restoring your confidence in us."

"Absolutely," Gin said.

Jason nodded, simultaneously impressed and concerned by the extra precautions.

"When your room needs service, just call housekeeping and they will send someone right up to clean it at your convenience."

He supposed that made sense, especially because the intruder had been dressed in a hotel uniform. Their original reservation would show them leaving in less that forty-eight hours.

"We'd rather not create any more trouble or drama for you and your staff," Gin said.

"Please, this is not your fault," the manager said, pushing open the door to the penthouse. "Crime is a part of the Vegas landscape, but I prefer to keep it out of my hotel. Please enjoy the rest of your stay."

Gin gasped and Jason could hardly blame her. His suite a few floors down had been luxurious enough, but he'd only seen a room of this caliber in movies. There were multiple sofas, a kitchen, a dining area, a wet bar and two massage therapists standing like statues near the window.

"We can have dinner delivered at your convenience."

Jason studied the manager instead of the room. "Why do I get the feeling you'd like us to stay tucked away up here for the rest of our stay?"

"Oh no, sir. That's not it at all. Whatever suits you is what we will provide. I was just about to mention your credit line at the casino."

"House money? Talk about above and beyond," Jason said. He drew the heavier curtains together over the sheers, blocking out the late afternoon view of the city. It was stunning as the sun faded and the lights took over, but standing in front of an open window wasn't his idea of a smart move, not even at this altitude.

"What my husband means is thank you." Gin guided the manager toward the door. "We're just a little overwhelmed by your generosity, but we appreciate it very much."

Jason let her smooth over his deliberate cynicism while he explored the rest of the penthouse. He couldn't imagine what this was costing the hotel. Two people could get lost in this place that was better suited to a celebrity traveling with an entourage than to a bride and groom.

Despite the ample space, the lavish décor and the hotel's commitment to anticipate their every need, he couldn't shake the feeling that they'd been neatly trapped. It was a luxurious cell, but it felt like a prison all the same. Being celebrity victims would only make it more of a challenge to do what they'd come here to do.

Well, what he'd come to do since his original recovery mission seemed to be a bust. He kicked that thought out of his head. There would be hell to pay when he got back to the office. Holt was pissed.

Jason decided he might as well make the most

of the rest of the weekend. He wanted to enjoy the lush atmosphere, knew he'd probably never see another room like this on his own dime, yet he couldn't. Not when what had begun as a simple recovery was spiraling out of control. Gin might not be the agent he'd been sent to assist, but she didn't stand a chance with Gabriel Frost hunting her.

The irony of the situation was not lost on him.

Walking through the rooms, he didn't see the beauty or design; he saw the hiding places and firing solutions, the potential injuries that every vase, table or chair could inflict. He knew the adrenaline letdown after the pool attack and the following fight in the room a few floors down was driving him closer to paranoia. But bullets were flying faster than chips lately.

Gin joined him as he closed the curtains in the second bedroom. "What is wrong with you?"

"We're boxed in," he whispered, matching her quiet tone. "There are more eyes on us now. It will be impossible to get anything done."

"Just what do you want to do?" She stepped in close and wrapped her arms around his waist.

He had to remind himself it was an act for Sven and his twin masseuse waiting for them out in the main room. "You know what I mean. This is…" He shook his head. "Over the top."

"So let's adjust our priorities in light of the

new circumstances. A massage is the perfect way to detox after what we've been through."

"I was thinking ice packs and a beer." He glared down at her but knew he couldn't hold out long against the mischievous sparkle in her emerald eyes.

"You want a massage." She caught his hands, laced her fingers with his. "You know you do."

"Not really." The last thing he wanted was to close his eyes. It seemed like every time he blinked he saw that terrible image of the bullet hole in the chair...the bullet that might just as easily have put a hole through her heart.

He pushed her hair back from her neck and examined the red scrape where Wallace had held the knife to her tender skin. Her life had been measured in millimeters today. It was a wonder she didn't need a sedative. "Are you sure you're okay?"

"I'm okay." Her smile looked genuine enough. "But I'd be better with a massage."

"You go ahead. I'll keep watch."

"But you need one, too." She brought her hands to his shoulders and made little circles with her fingertips. "You're all tense."

"Can you blame me?"

"It's complimentary," she sing-songed. "That doesn't happen every day. It's the smart move."

"Unless Sven and his twin are on the enemy's

payroll," he whispered in her ear. "They could snap our necks and call it a day."

"Don't worry. I'll protect you." She tugged his head close and kissed his nose. "Just do your doting husband thing and we'll figure the rest of it out when they're gone."

"Gin," he pleaded. He didn't think it was possible for him to relax in the presence of strangers. "Reschedule for tomorrow."

"Jason," she mimicked his tone. "Our honeymoon's been interrupted by a terrible fright and a burglary." She touched her hand to her heart. "Come on, honey. This is the perfect way to reclaim our time. You know I'm right."

He rolled his eyes but kept his hand in hers as he followed her out to the main room.

Sven and his brother were actually named Paul and Terry and not related at all. For the next ninety minutes, Jason experienced more relaxation than he thought possible with another man's hands on him.

Gin kept up a light commentary for his benefit, and he decided to make it up to her later, assuming she would have preferred to simply sink into the experience rather than chatter for his comfort.

The massage therapists left them with advice to drink plenty of water, skip the alcohol and eat lightly tonight.

When they were finally alone, each of them slumped on the couch, he took a long pull on the bottle of water. "Eat lightly. That explains why the manager comped dinner. They're planning on serving us twigs and leaves."

Gin snorted. "Give it up, Mr. Cynical. The manager isn't winning on any part of this deal." She rolled to her back and the hotel robe slipped, revealing more of her creamy, toned thigh. "I bet a couple's massage is a bigger investment than any of the fine dining options."

"No bet. You're probably right."

"Trust me. I'm one hundred percent right on this."

"Such an authority on decadence. Guess that means I'm not your first?"

She slanted him that sly look he found so intriguing. "First what?"

"Forget it," he said, hiding the truth of his question behind a lazy smile.

No point explaining he'd meant first husband. That wouldn't matter with Gin. Married or not, this was all temporary. With the help of his friend at Interpol, after they'd met in Colorado, he'd done enough digging to know Olin was her real name and that her cases had never intersected his. The recognition he'd sensed in Colorado last month had stemmed entirely from a long-distance surveillance photo taken when she happened to walk by a café his friend had had under surveillance.

To get his mind off of her tempting gaze and even more enticing bare leg, he reached for his phone and pulled up the police reports for the past few days. "What do you think they meant about other shootings in the area?"

"You're going to make me think, aren't you?"

"The guys didn't specifically warn against it."

"Maybe they should have," she muttered, sitting up.

For a moment he regretted the change of subject if only for the loss of scenery, but then she came over and sat down beside him and the soft scent of her washed over him.

"Might be easier if I get my laptop."

"Nah, that's too much effort right now." She waved a finger at the phone. "What's bugging you?"

"The shot at the pool." He pulled up a website that posted local crimes according to police reports. "You were obviously the target."

"Not so obvious."

"What do you mean?"

"Well, I've had some time to think it through. I know luck happens, and me suddenly reaching for your phone would have been unexpected, but why didn't he just bury the second shot in my brain since he was all lined up and everything?"

Jason's stomach bottomed out. She hadn't said anything he hadn't thought himself, but the finality, the harsh nature of her statement was somehow a thousand times worse when spoken. It shouldn't be this difficult to regain his objectivity. He studied the sculpted ceiling, hoping it would be easier if he didn't look at her.

Any way he looked at it she was right. "Not taking the kill shot doesn't fit. When we caught Wallace in the room, he was shocked to see you."

"I swear I've never met him."

"I believe you." But believing it didn't change the fact that Wallace had apparently expected her to be dead and had planted the ammunition to frame Jason for the kill. After studying the bastard in Europe, Jason understood Frost and had learned a little about how he accepted contracts. "I'm wondering if the other shootings they mentioned are simply to divide the local investigation focus."

"To lump my potential assassination in with other random lives cut short?"

"Maybe. Look." He tipped the phone so she could see the screen. "There was a shooting death last night around 3:00 a.m."

"Hmm." She scanned the article. "Doesn't say sniper." She leaned back, turning the water bottle around. "If there was a sniper in Vegas, why didn't the news report it?"

"They might have. You have to work pretty hard to get real news once you're in a casino."

"True, but it can be done. Due to the nature of my case, I've made the effort." She sipped at the water. "Our respective offices know we're here. If there was a sniper in the area, they would have told us."

"Maybe."

Her leg rubbed against his as she sat forward once more. She reached out and gently turned his chin her way so he had to meet her gaze.

"Explain."

"You said you didn't drug me. What if the person who did wanted me indisposed so I wouldn't have an alibi for your death today or the guy last night?"

"You'll notice news of my death is highly exaggerated."

He picked up his phone and showed her the other reports he'd tagged. "Yes, I'm making assumptions, but the first event that might be related happened within eight hours of my arrival in Las Vegas."

"Did you have orders to shoot me?"

He patted her knee. "No. My orders were to wait here in Caesar's for the compromised agent to contact me."

She turned the water bottle around again. "Like I told you this morning, I'm supposed to follow the virus vial. No backup required. It's my personal challenge to spot the buyer. My assignment isn't that complicated."

There was a little furrow between her brows that he was starting to learn meant she wasn't telling him all of it. "But you were desperate enough to haul me out and marry me last night after shooting at someone tailing you."

"You can let that go anytime. I promised you a quick divorce."

"Gin, last month my director was set up."

She nodded. "Bad news travels fast."

"I received a note at the wedding reception that said, *You're next.*"

"Is that some kind of joke? A male version of the catching the bridal bouquet?"

"No." He shook his head. "I didn't tell anyone in Mission Recovery about it."

"Why not?"

He didn't want to get into all of his reasons, especially because she'd been one of them. "I questioned the waiter who delivered it, had it tested by a friend in the lab and got nowhere. Wasn't much point in sending it up the line."

"But you think the note is related to what happened to your director."

"Yeah. Whoever rigged the setup nearly succeeded." Mission Recovery had suspects but hadn't moved on them yet. Jason wasn't privy to all the details and had assumed it was due to a lack of evidence. Now he wondered if there was a bigger problem. "What if my office hasn't mentioned an active sniper in Las Vegas because they believe *I am* the shooter?"

She rubbed a hand along his arm. "Relax. Even if the local police decide to announce a sniper is active in town, you have airtight alibis for last night and today."

"Not if the woman who drugged me had succeeded. That's my point. Whoever is setting me up didn't expect me to have an alibi."

She tugged at the sleeve of his robe. "But she didn't and you're welcome."

"Thanks, but whoever hired Frost wouldn't have expected your intervention."

"Which means we're in more danger than before?"

"It's a possibility we should consider." And the list of suspects who knew who he was, what he could do with a rifle and his general location last night was ridiculously short. "Who knows about your mission here?"

"You know I can't answer that, Jason."

"Fine. Let's go back to the question of who wants you dead."

"A great many people, I suppose." She shifted, crossed her legs. "I told you, none of them are here."

"What about Isely?"

"He's never seen my face. He has no reason to connect me with anything he's done or plans to do."

"And still he followed you last night."

"So the man has instincts." She bolted to her feet, but he caught her hand before she could stalk away from him. "Explains his longevity in a treacherous career as a black-market weapons dealer."

"It scared the hell out of me." It wasn't at all what he meant to say, wasn't at all professional. He was about to cross a line good agents stayed well clear of. "The bullet hole in that chair. The knife at your throat."

Her gaze softened and her lips parted. It reminded him of last night for some reason. He needed a new memory, something full of life to burn through the haze left by the drugs and to break the icy grip of nearly losing her at the pool. A new memory he wouldn't forget no matter which direction their careers took them from here.

"Is that the doting husband talking?"

He shook his head and gently pulled her down into his lap. Her sultry chuckle faded to a sweet silence full of promise and potential. Her gaze lingered on his mouth. He pushed the vibrant red silk of her hair behind her ear, then cupped her nape and drew her mouth closer to his.

Close enough to kiss. The first touch of lips, sweet and gentle, turned needy from one beat of his pulse to the next. Her mouth was still cool from the water she'd been drinking as directed. But that didn't last long. She grew hotter and hotter with each swipe of their dueling tongues.

He lost himself in her soft sigh of pleasure and when she shifted, straddling him, he tugged her hips closer, let her feel how much his body wanted hers. How much he needed the connection she'd offered from the moment she walked into that bar.

Her hands parted his robe, pushed it away from his shoulders. Her touch created such a craving inside him, a craving his body knew only she could satisfy.

With a soft scrape of her teeth on his lower lip, she leaned back, her hands hot on his shoulders, her breath coming in little pants as she rested her forehead on his. "Wait," she whispered.

Looked like the ground rules had just been demolished.

She sat back a little more and he fisted his hands at his sides because he wanted to hang on to her, to keep her close and never let go. His every instinct screamed it was the wrong move. Excuses, bargains, everything but an apology wanted to come spilling out of his mouth, but he bit back all of the words.

Nothing he said would do any good.

If he understood anything about this particular woman it was her ruthless independence. His physical desire was obvious enough. And mutual, he surmised based on her passionate response to him. Beyond that, what could he offer that she might accept?

She touched her lips with her fingertips, but he didn't think she meant the move provocatively. Her eyes were dark as she studied him. He felt a precious opportunity slipping through his hands and there was nothing he could do.

Not yet.

"I'm going to take a shower and dress for dinner."

He nodded.

"We should choose a restaurant. Not, um, room service."

He nodded again.

She walked out of his line of sight, her feet padding softly across the thick carpet. Then she stopped.

"I need to keep an eye on that vial. And we have to get a line on whoever is setting you up."

Business. It was the right answer, the safe topic. He didn't say anything, didn't need to. He heard her feet once more, but he waited until the sound of water running in the shower reached him before he got up from the sofa.

His damn imagination gave him an all-too-clear picture of what she would look like, hair slicked back from her face and soapy lather slipping over her curves.

Clinging to his willpower, he grabbed his shaving kit and suitcase from the room and headed for the bedroom suite on the other side of the penthouse.

Chapter Eight

Mission Recovery headquarters

In the wind.

Holt stared at the message on his monitor, still not quite able to comprehend how Grant had avoided the perfectly crafted noose. The man always followed orders, always found a way to succeed whether the assignment was tedious or overwhelming.

He'd put him in Las Vegas and told him to wait. What the hell had happened to the scheduled pickup? Painting the miscommunication as a failure, he'd ordered Grant out of the area, and now he was practically a missing person. *In the wind.* He was certain the contact wasn't implying Grant had actually boarded a plane.

Why in God's name had one of their top Specialists chosen this particular moment to buck a career-long pattern of obedience?

Feeling like it was *his* neck caught in the noose

Holt tugged on his tie and undid the button at his throat. He struggled for a deep breath and refused to give in to the hard knot in his chest.

Everything—*everything*—was riding on this. Grant might have unknowingly botched the latest battle, but Holt could still win the war.

The only good news was that local law enforcement hadn't gone public with the sniper theory and therefore Grant didn't have clues to develop a theory of his own.

Leaning against the wide window, he stared out at the dark landscape, not caring to see the stars or the moon or anything else beyond the dark haze of his own frustration.

He should have shifted Grant's role in this. He should have been clever enough to find a different method. But it was too late now and all the should-have-dones weren't going to get this resolved.

Like all the Specialists in Mission Recovery, Holt believed in success above all else. Setbacks were temporary, and a Specialist embraced by added motivation often overcame the obstacles that discouraged others.

He looked around his office, reminded himself what was on the line. It was all the motivation he needed to take the next step.

He buttoned his collar and straightened his tie before he opened his office door. Nadine sat at her desk, doing whatever she did to keep him organized and connected to Specialists deployed on various assignments.

"Has Specialist Grant arrived?"

"No, sir. Were you expecting him?"

Yes, actually. But he could hardly say that to Nadine. "At this morning's check-in I ordered him back to D.C. Has he booked a flight?"

Her monitor flashed with different logos and windows as she started her search. "Nothing on his corporate credit card. I'm checking airline manifests now."

"Thank you. Check his personal accounts and any aliases you know about."

"Yes, sir."

Nadine would have some leads, but Holt knew Grant had others. Every Specialist had alternate identification or knew how to create it quickly. Holt leaned against the doorjamb while he waited, the only sounds the soft instrumentals of the classical music Nadine preferred and her fingers on the keyboard.

"Anything?"

"Not so far. I can have the analysts dig deeper if you like."

Holt sighed. "We can give him some time." His personal cell phone started ringing. "Let me know when you get something," he said as he picked up the call and headed back into his office.

"Holt."

"Are you trying to renege?"

Isely. Holt wasn't surprised, though he knew how to fake it for the right effect. "Why are you calling me here?"

"Answer the question."

"I'll deliver as discussed."

"Ah, that is good. Things so often get messy when we improvise."

What the hell did that mean? "Patience pays off," Holt reminded him. The game wouldn't be out of balance for long and he sure as hell wouldn't be the first one to blink. "Your patsy is still in town."

"True. And with a lovely new wife who is complicating matters."

Holt barely restrained his shock. Grant was married? How did Isely know that before anyone here at Mission Recovery? "It's nothing," he said.

"It is out of character and off script," Isely bit out, his cold voice a clear indicator of his brutal intentions. "Do not cross me, *Deputy.*"

The call ended before Holt could reply. Damn the man and this whole twisted business. And damn Jason Grant for choosing the absolute worst time to mix romance with a mission.

Holt looked back at his screen. Who the hell

had he managed to exchange vows with if the woman who should have him contained had missed him?

"Sir?" Nadine's voice followed the beep of the office intercom.

"Yes?"

"I have something you should see."

"Bring it in."

Ignoring the bad feeling in his gut, he clicked on the small icon that appeared on his monitor as Nadine walked into the office. It was a certificate of marriage from one of the many chapels in Las Vegas, signifying the union of Jason Grant with Ginger Olin. "What do we know about her?"

"I'm working on that now."

"Good. What else?"

Nadine swiped something on her tablet and another document popped up. "I'm not sure how to interpret this, but the marriage isn't legal. The marriage license application was completed, but the official license has not been issued."

Maybe Grant hadn't lost all of his faculties after all. "See what you can do to sort it out."

"Shall I contact Specialist Grant?"

"Absolutely not. It could blow his cover with whatever angle he's working on." Considering he hadn't returned as Holt demanded, it was only reasonable that Grant was on to something else. But what? He couldn't possibly know about Isely.

"Yes, sir."

"Keep me posted."

With a nod, she exited his office and left him alone to sort out a mess she couldn't fathom.

His hands clenched around the leather-covered arms of his executive chair. He'd been working this for so long, he'd started to believe the light at the end of the tunnel was freedom, not a head-on collision with a train. If Grant screwed this up with an ill-timed and fake marriage or some off the wall rescue, Holt might just let him take the rap for the crimes about to occur in Nevada.

There was nothing he could do…but ride it out.

Chapter Nine

Caesar's Palace Penthouse

Gin washed away the sunblock and massage oil, all the while wishing she had the courage to invite Jason to help her. The hot spray of the waterfall showerhead drenched her body, and she trailed a finger over her lips, unable to put that kiss out of her mind.

Oh, who was she kidding? She didn't *want* to forget it. This time not even thoughts of a catastrophic epidemic could completely silence the part of her that wanted to explore what was happening between them.

She twisted the handle to cold, telling herself it was only to put more shine in her hair. Ha! Stepping out of the cavern of a shower and looking to the vanity, she realized his personal things were gone from the countertop.

Sneaky. Smart, but sneaky.

It couldn't be called cowardly—that had been

her, pulling back from that kiss and practically running away from the temptation of Jason.

She dried her hair and slipped into a black sheath that zipped up the side. Getting away from the seclusion of the penthouse had sounded like a good idea at the time, but now she realized the error. Dinner in public meant they would have to play the role as celebrity newlyweds, as Jason called it.

She paused, mascara wand halfway to her eye. They were just caught up in the moment, the atmosphere and the wild feel of the town. When he did that doting husband routine parts of her she didn't know existed just melted. But that wasn't a reflection of feelings as much as a commendation of his dedication to the job.

Except that kiss…

Her phone rang and Gin jumped. The number meant business, and she couldn't have been more grateful for the distraction. She set the mascara aside and picked up the phone.

"Yes."

"Our wiretap says the exchange happens tomorrow night."

"Understood."

She ended the call and resumed applying makeup, enormously settled by the thought of business. She swept her hair into a French twist and reached for the sexy black shoes.

Ready, she walked out of the bedroom, her strappy heels hanging from her finger and her clutch bag under her arm. She'd packed her lipstick, revolver and cell phone, which was set to vibrate. She wasn't worried about calls, but she needed to know if and when the virus was on the move.

It was a good thing the heels were in her hand because the sight of Jason made her knees buckle. He wore a navy suit with the crisp white shirt open at the throat. Freshly shaven, he looked so handsome and as sexy as hell. But it was the wedding band that made her wish this moment could be real...that he could be hers.

As much as she wanted to look at him as a tool, as simply a means to accomplishing her goal, she just couldn't do it. This was quickly becoming far too personal. She wasn't sure how to pull back to a professional distance.

It would have been easier if even the smallest part of her wanted to pull back.

"You look fantastic," she said with her brightest smile.

"Thanks, but I think I must only be a backdrop next to you."

She did a little turn for him and then leaned a hip against the sofa for balance as she slid into her heels. "According to the latest intel, the sale goes down tomorrow night."

"In the casino?"

"Maybe." She shrugged. "Could be anywhere in the resort."

"That leaves us plenty of options," he said. "Is there a time frame?"

"Not anything precise." She patted her clutch. "I've got the app open and working. We'll know when the virus moves, and we can follow it."

"Do you have orders to intervene?"

"Not necessarily, though I'd rather secure the vial than let it out into the world. Why?"

"Just debating how we ditch the protective detail if it comes to that."

She moistened her lips and wiggled her eyebrows. "We can always improvise."

"After we eat." He motioned her toward the door. "I called down to the restaurant and asked them to prepare a table."

"Great."

"Why make the sale here?"

She shrugged, looked up at him. "It wasn't my choice."

"I realize that, but I can't help wondering if this location has significance to the deal."

"That's doubtful. Probably just because it's a landmark with lots of tourists. An easy place to get lost."

"Sounds reasonable." With a flourish he opened the door and let her proceed.

But the question got her wondering. Maybe there was a clue to the buyer—or seller—that she'd overlooked.

Even expecting the security presence, it was a bit unnerving to step out into the vestibule and see the posted guard, but she recovered with a bright smile.

She cursed herself for choosing a sleeveless dress when Jason put his arm around her as they waited for the elevator. *For show,* she chanted in her head. The guards expected warm, familiar behavior from newlyweds and she had to play along.

The elevator arrived and another guard was waiting for them. It was a little much. Jason was right—the extra security would make her task more challenging. She'd worked in all kinds of conditions and under all sorts of security umbrellas, but having a private shadow hovering over them meant she'd have to get creative if she was going to catch this sale.

It was a relief to step out into the anonymous crowd and put some breathing room between them and the security detail.

"The Isely family was sidelined for five years when they tried to sell it last time," he murmured into her ear as they strolled toward the restaurant. "Seems a little brash to return to business here of all places."

She snorted, covering it with her clutch. "The initial deal for this product went sour, but they aren't the sort to let anything shy of the apocalypse stop them."

She shivered at her own words, recalling the fortuitous timing of seeing Jason at the bar when she needed to evade Isely. Unless. A terrible thought occurred to her. Maybe Isely had been tipped off about her and she'd been ushered toward Jason on purpose. Obviously someone knew Jason was here. That guy Wallace had planted incriminating evidence in his room. If that was the case, it was a newbie mistake to fall into a trap that resulted in more eyes on both of them. She couldn't have made that kind of mistake…could she?

Jason's warm breath brushed across the shell of her ear. "Smile, darling, or they'll think I'm useless in bed."

She complied immediately, feeling the heat of a blush on her face. The two kisses they'd shared were enough to convince her that the exact opposite would be true.

The maître d' escorted them to a table in the true Vegas paradox of implying privacy while managing to display their presence to anyone watching.

"Does the seller know you're here for the sale?"

"No. I've been in various disguises along the way. If they recognize me now—a highly doubtful scenario—our secret marriage and quick honeymoon are enough to chalk it up to coincidence."

He frowned at her. "You don't believe that?"

"Now who needs to smile?" She turned his hand over and stroked a slow path across his palm to his wrist. "We've seen each other around often enough to know it could happen. But, you're right. I'm having some second thoughts."

"That would be wise," he agreed. "Otherwise, why shoot at you?"

"Maybe I was wrong about that and it *was* you they were after in the bar last night."

"Anything is possible," he said with way too much innuendo.

"Possible but not likely." She couldn't believe neither of them had recognized such an obvious manipulation...if that's what it was. "You might not have noticed, being a slave to that newlywed glow, but I can get a little persistent and annoying at times."

He stared at her for a split second and then roared with laughter, causing heads to turn their way.

"Oh, stop." Was causing a scene part of his game? She leaned back, sipping her champagne and trying to catalog the faces aimed at them. "Stop it."

"I can't." He gulped in air. "Sorry. I just—just can't picture you a little bit of anything," he finished breathlessly.

"Should I be flattered?"

"Yes, please." He bobbed his head in the affirmative. "It was a compliment."

She gaped as the man actually wiped tears from his eyes. It didn't feel like a compliment. "Fine."

"Oh, no you don't." He reached across the table, lacing his fingers with hers. "We're not going to have our first argument in public."

"I see no reason to argue at all."

"So you're an anomaly?"

She frowned at him.

"I thought redheads liked drama." He scooted closer, nuzzling her neck. "And blondes are all about the fun."

Oh! It *was* a performance. He wouldn't have mentioned blondes without a reason. She tilted her head back, giving him better access and still managing to stay alert enough to scan the room. "I booked a facial for eleven o'clock," she said, indicating the direction she thought he meant.

"That's good. I'll use the time out on the driving range."

So they agreed about the woman waiting alone

a few tables away. Playing it to the hilt, Gin used her phone to get a picture of their wedding rings, managing to get the blonde in the frame. She wasn't sure where or who could analyze it for them, but that was a problem for later.

They parted long enough to listen to the evening's specials and place their respective orders. And while every touch and little whisper through each course looked like a devoted couple lost in each other, they continued to exchange information and theories.

Unfortunately it kept her body running hot. If they'd stayed in the room, she could have tried to reclaim the ground rules. Out here, being a couple in love—or at least enjoying the lust of a honeymoon—was eroding her ability to resist him.

Too bad staying in the room wouldn't get the primary job done. Well, she'd never been one to run from a challenge.

"We need to find out who she is," she murmured as she scraped off a tiny piece of the decadent chocolate torte they were sharing. "I don't like that neither of us knows her."

"You want to give her a chance to poison me again?"

"It's an option. I saved you once, and I can do it again."

"Hmm. Whatever helps you sleep at night," he said with a wink.

Her mind went back to last night, when they'd shared a bed, though not in the intimate way she'd staged it for him. It was an image guaranteed to keep her up tonight. And more than a few nights in the future.

She let another sliver of the rich cake dissolve on her tongue. "I was thinking we should go dancing, gamble a bit and see who is most surprised to see us."

"Other than Wallace?"

"He'd better be in custody," she grumbled. It had required a great deal of concealer to cover the scrape on her neck.

"Then maybe we can pay a visit to security and ask to review the tapes from the bar."

"I'm a tad overdressed for a visit to security. What happened to letting them handle it?"

"I don't know." He gazed at her cleavage then cleared his throat. "In that dress, we're likely to get everything they have on the pool and burglary investigations. A reporter and security expert would naturally be curious."

"Even a reporter would focus on her honeymoon. The hotel team said it was all in LVPD and FBI hands now."

"As if any man would resist you if you asked nicely. Besides, you must have connections."

She frowned at him. "Are you fishing? You know I don't have connections or any backup here aside from you." Reaching over, she brushed a crumb of chocolate cake from his lip. "What about you?"

"Not *here,* exactly."

She gasped when he caught her thumb with a nip of his teeth and soothed it with his tongue. Could the man be any sexier?

"I was thinking of—"

"Lucas Camp," she finished for him as the only possible answer dawned on her. Camp connected them both—loosely—due to his former position as the deputy director of Mission Recovery and his own alliances within covert agencies like her own CIA.

"There you go reading my mind."

"If we called him, what would you expect him to do?"

"The man has friends everywhere. He practically introduced us."

"True." And he was inherently trustworthy. Jason seemed to be reluctant to trust his own team.

"Maybe he has insight we're missing."

It was possible. She knew Jason hadn't told her everything about his reasons for keeping the note a secret. Now that she doubted her own anonymity where Isely was concerned, they probably needed someone on the outside they could trust.

She hadn't seen Isely so far tonight, but that

didn't mean much. Since his father had died five years ago, he had become militant about his personal security and those he let in on his plans to rebuild the family business. Micromanaging a deal like the virus transaction didn't fit the original profile she'd assembled on him, but people did strange things under duress.

Like get married.

Thoughts like that had to go—and quickly. She pulled out her phone.

"Is the virus moving?"

"Not yet. I'm just sending an email." She held the phone so Jason could read over her shoulder as she drafted a note, attached the photo of the blonde and sent it to the email address Mr. Camp had used to contact her last month.

"Thank you."

The sincerity in Jason's voice startled her. The urge to comfort him was automatic and she patted his knee. "We'll figure this out."

Though they had a better chance if he'd tell her everything he knew. But then that would mean she would have to tell all she knew.

Eventually, she supposed.

Chapter Ten

When they finally called it quits on that amazing chocolate cake, Jason signed the check and they headed into the casino. He did his best to relax and blend in, but without Gin by his side he would have stormed out after only a few minutes. No matter how posh, how clean or how many years had passed, when he entered a casino he smelled stale booze, cigarette smoke and the unmistakable stench of losing. His father's gambling addiction had destroyed his family and nearly broken his mom's spirit in the process.

He wondered—again—if Holt had sent him here on some wild-goose chase as a test of his willpower and ability to overcome the ghosts of his past. If so, despite the supposedly failed recovery, he intended to pass the test and restore his reputation.

Winding through the craps room they settled in to watch a gambler on a hot streak. Jason recognized the men in the shadows who kept a loose perimeter around every move he and Gin made. Having such an attentive audience went against his most ingrained instincts, but he couldn't argue with the precaution. Anything that kept her safe was fine with him.

He knew the manufactured background provided by Mission Recovery would hold up under scrutiny and Gin's rash move to marry only bolstered his reasons for being in Las Vegas, but he couldn't shake the feeling that everything was about to come crashing down.

No fewer than six pairs of eyes were on them at any given time. More, if you counted the electronic surveillance he knew watched from behind the discreet black bubbles dotting the ceilings.

It wasn't worth thinking about the cameras he couldn't see.

"Do you need a drink?" Her hand linked with his, she leaned in close. He was starting to like the habit. "You're twitchy."

He smiled down at her. "Blame the extra security."

"Aw. Got a case of performance anxiety?"

"Not even close." He kissed the smirk off her face. "But it is our honeymoon. Shouldn't we be upstairs, doing..." He didn't finish the thought, too pleased by the soft pink color staining her cheeks.

Maybe he wasn't the only one affected by this

happy couple role-playing gig. When they were tucked into that booth, the floral scent of her perfume had been more enticing than the perfectly prepared steak. It wasn't the smartest idea, but he was more than ready to toss the ground rules out the nearest window.

"You know I have a job to do."

"Any messages?"

She peered into her clutch. From his vantage point he could see the little tracking icon. The virus remained stationary. "Nope."

At least one of them had info that made sense because the deal was slated for tomorrow.

He leaned close to her ear as bets were placed on the next throw of the dice. "What do you think of making a side bet?"

She peered up at him from under her lashes. "Such as?"

He reeled in the request he wanted to make and opted for something less likely to scare her off. "A hard eight and we blow this pop stand and go dancing."

"Pop stand?" she chuckled.

"Bet or no?" He called as the dealer said much the same to the gamblers surrounding the table.

"Says the man who doesn't gamble."

"You're stalling."

Her wicked smirk lit up her face. "You're on."

He grinned back. To the rest of the world he

was amused by the player milking the moment for all it was worth before he sent the dice flying down the table. In reality, it was the anticipation of holding Gin close that put him in a good mood.

"Looks like I'm a lucky loser," she said when the dice stopped and the dealer raked away the two chips she'd placed on the table.

"Let's hope you still feel that way when we're dancing."

They made their way to the club, slipping through the crowd, the security team surrounding them but never crowding them.

"What do you think they'd do if we were attacked?" Gin asked.

"More than necessary considering what the two of us are capable of. If something does happen, we should probably let them take the lead."

"It would be the polite thing to do because it's their house."

"Well said."

Jason realized someone must have called ahead as they neared the club and a hostess appeared to escort them inside. "I could get used to this," he admitted.

Gin nodded her agreement, but conversation halted as he swept her out onto the dance floor.

Thanks to a required cotillion class as a kid, he was probably better equipped for the structure of a tango or waltz, but he could hold his own with the steady beat that currently had the dance floor jammed to capacity.

Gin moved well to the music, and for a few minutes it was a relief to just be a couple out on a date. He couldn't recall the last time that had happened.

He didn't resent his career or the hard choices he'd made along the way. The various challenges were what got him fired up until the mission was complete. He just didn't realize how long it had been since he'd had a different kind of fun.

When she fanned her face with her clutch and gestured to the bar, he nodded, ready for a cold beer. With his hand at her back they slipped through the crowd and when they reached the bar, he double-checked with her and ordered bottled beer for each of them. The bartender didn't bat an eye when Jason requested the bottles be opened in front of them.

Gin elbowed him. "Paranoid?"

He smiled. It was becoming a habit when she was around. "Doesn't mean they're not out to get us." He tapped his bottle to hers. "To paranoia."

"Cheers." She took a long drink, then patted the bottle like an ice pack along her low neckline and up over the place where Wallace had held the knife. "I haven't danced like that in years."

"Me either."

"Why do you hate casinos?"

"That's not an accurate statement."

"Bull."

He debated how much to share, knew it was better not to share anything that could be used against him later. The urge to tell her everything surprised him.

"Come on," she prodded. "I'm your wife."

He shook his head, still adjusting to the concept of wedded bliss. "My dad was a gambler. Always looking for the big score."

"So you had to be Mr. Dependable in the family?"

"Something like that."

She leaned forward, her hands on his knees, and he struggled not to stare at the sexy display of her breasts. Was that black lace under the dress?

"You're not making this easy, sweetheart."

"Well, you're distracting me." He dropped his gaze, just for a second, to her full breasts, then jerked his eyes back up to meet hers. He nudged her shoulders until she was sitting upright.

"Look, my past is over and done."

"But it made you who you are."

"*I* made me." He smiled to soften the contradiction. "With more than a little help from the U.S. Army." The music changed to the slower pace of a love song and he seized the opportunity. Standing, he held out his hand. "May I have this dance?"

She tilted her head, blatantly studying him, and the little furrow appeared between her auburn eyebrows.

"I'd love to," she replied, putting her hand in his.

When they were swaying to the music, he wasn't sure he'd ever felt anything more right than having Ginger in his arms. "Is this our first dance as husband and wife?"

She nodded and one corner of her mouth kicked up into half of her usual grin. "I'm sorry—"

"Shh." He didn't want to hear an apology right now. This marriage might not be destined to last, but he wanted to pretend, at least for tonight. "Then that makes this our song."

"Oh, that's not playing fair."

"Isn't it?"

"Not even close." But she laid her head on his shoulder.

Mesmerized by the play of light on her hair, he found the various colors from deep gold to auburn that gave her hair such a rich glossy hue.

He pressed his lips to her hair with all the affection he would show if they were meant to stay together. If he'd thought about it, he would have called it sappy. Then again, they were in public and that had been the game plan.

"Do you really have a facial tomorrow?"

She looked up at him. "With our access, I can book one easily enough. Are you implying I need some work done?"

"No." He ran his finger down the loose curl by her ear. "Do you golf?"

"Yes. Though it's been a long time." She gave a little sigh.

"Let's go play tomorrow. We could use the fresh air and sunshine."

She looked up at him, and he knew she saw more than he wanted her to see. "We can do that. The sale is an evening thing."

He dropped a kiss on her lips. "Thank you."

"Thank me later." She glanced around at the dance floor. "I wish I could just spot the buyer already."

A movement near the bar caught his eye. One of their tall, dark and stoic entourage was on the radio.

"We may have trouble," he murmured, turning as they danced so she could get a look.

"How do you want to play it?"

"I'd rather not aggravate the locals. We need to get access to the security videos."

"We can be casual. But it does look like something is up."

Definitely. Their protection approached the dance floor and signaled them toward the bar. Keeping her tucked to his side, they left as the song faded.

He exchanged a look with Gin as they followed the team behind the bar and through the kitchen.

"Hang on," Gin said, bringing the whole group to a stop. "What's going on?"

"Details are sketchy," the team leader said. "But someone just tried to break into the penthouse."

"That's ridiculous." Gin shook her head. "There's a guard posted in plain sight by the elevator."

"He's been drugged. The guard posted inside the door caught the burglar before any damage could be done."

"Inside?" Jason questioned.

"Just inside the vestibule, sir."

Jason waved it off. "I'm not trying to challenge your methods." He was more worried they'd see he'd taken up residence in the second bedroom and question the newlywed story. "Can we talk with him?" It had to be Frost trying to track down Gin. He reached for the inner pocket of his jacket, where he'd stashed the identification he'd brought along tonight.

"You're welcome to watch on a monitor, but I can't let you in the room with her."

"Her?" Jason and Gin said in unison.

The team leader shrugged a beefy shoulder. "Female burglars are more common than you think. Her method's a little different, but she's not nearly as bizarre as some we get around here."

"I bet," Gin muttered.

"Can you think of any reason you've been targeted?"

Gin looked up at him and gave an almost imperceptible shake of her head.

"No," Jason replied for them both. "We came here for a convention and got married." He put on his best besotted groom smile. "It's that simple and shouldn't matter to anyone but us."

"Well, come on then. But you're only invited as a professional courtesy."

"Thanks," Jason said. One step at a time. If they proved they could maintain their composure and just watch, maybe they could press the advantage and get a look at the security cameras.

They followed the team through the extensive network of halls and facilities that made everything run so smoothly for the guests and patrons of the hotel and casino.

There were plenty of cameras back here, too. Beside him, Jason knew Gin was also memorizing the route and prepared for the situation to change at any moment.

Mr. Latimore, chief of hotel security, met them at the door with a friendly introduction and ushered them into his office. The space looked more like a large living room with all the expected creature comforts than an office.

"I thought you'd be more comfortable watching from here." Latimore raised a remote toward the flat-panel monitor on the wall. "Have a seat. Would you like a drink?"

They declined the drink but sat together on the leather sofa, hands linked and balanced on his thigh. Just two normal people who'd inexplicably found themselves targets. If they got any better at this marriage and partnership thing, Jason might have to find a better-looking ring than the simple gold band she wore now.

He waited for the cold fear that should accompany such a thought, but it didn't come. Strange, but the thought of forever with this woman felt right. He'd have to figure it out later because he could see on the monitor that a blond-haired woman had entered the other room, a hotel security guard behind her.

Jason narrowed his gaze. It was the same woman they'd seen earlier in the restaurant, the one who'd tried to poison him in the bar last night.

"That's who tried to break in?" he asked.

"Yes, sir," Latimore replied.

She was seated at a small table, and the security officer across from her started his questioning.

Gin didn't twitch and her breathing didn't change, but somehow Jason knew something was wrong. They listened to the standard series of questions, but no one in either the interrogation room or here in the office was buying the answers.

"It was a dare. I just went up to look around." The blonde leaned forward. "Which celebrity is it? Come on," she wheedled. "I can't go back to my friends empty-handed."

"Discretion is part of our service."

"You're no fun."

The interrogator ignored that. "You aren't registered in our hotel."

"Does that mean you're about to be indiscreet with me?"

Jason recognized the dumb blonde routine, figured she'd ride it all the way to a misdemeanor charge—and a hefty fine—except for the poison thing.

"Do you know what she used on the guard?"

"Nothing lethal, just enough to knock him out. Probably a derivative of ketamine, based on his reactions. The guard inside heard voices near the elevator and assumed it was the other guard's girlfriend, but when he looked out, it was this woman."

"So she really didn't get past the vestibule?" Gin asked.

"No, ma'am."

She squeezed his hand, and when he met her gaze he saw tears welling in her eyes. He knew the tears were for show, but something had spooked her.

"Jason," she whispered. "This is ridiculous." She cleared her throat and turned to Latimore. "We appreciate all you've done, but maybe we should change hotels," Gin said.

"I'm not sure that would make any difference, honey," Jason argued gently. "Someone is determined to ruin our honeymoon."

"Our staff doesn't intend to let that happen. Our teams can keep you safe."

Jason knew it wasn't true. The woman was likely nothing more than a pawn in the bigger game. She probably didn't even know who really hired her to give them grief. "Does this woman have any ties to the person who opened fire at the pool?"

"Not that we've been able to connect, but we've just started investigating. I have teams going through all of the footage over the past several days, tracking her movements through our property."

"That doesn't eliminate the idea that she met with someone elsewhere."

"That's true." Latimore shook his head. "All of the casinos share information about this sort of risk." He turned down the volume on the monitor as the woman started weeping loudly.

Jason leaned forward, balancing his elbows on his knees. "This woman sent me a drugged drink at the bar last night."

"I haven't seen that report."

"We didn't file one."

Latimore leaned closer to his desk. "Would you like to?"

"No, thanks." Jason reached into his pocket for a business card. "We handled it. If you'd just keep us updated, please."

"I can do that. Standard procedure is to hand her over to LVPD. I can assure you she won't be allowed back on the premises."

"Thanks," Gin said. "That's the best news I've heard so far."

Now that Latimore had seen his business card, Jason ventured into deeper water. "What's the status of the incident at the pool?"

"The room he most likely used to stage the attack was clean. From what the police have told me, the shooter hasn't been caught, but he has not struck again."

"Thank you." To Gin, he said, "Shall we go?"

Gin nodded and they got to their feet.

"Please enjoy the rest of your evening. My team will make sure no one else can bother you." As they left, they were once more flanked by burly men in dark suits who escorted them back to the public areas of the hotel.

"Where to now?"

"The room," Gin replied. "I'm tired of these heels."

He didn't believe it. "We could rest your feet at a blackjack table for a bit. There's that line of credit with our name on it."

She shot him a look. "Maybe tomorrow."

"What about the sports betting room?" He couldn't risk being alone with her right now. That dance had him wanting something she wasn't offering. They were supposed to be platonic in private, but he wasn't sure he could manage that anymore. "A show maybe?"

She stopped short and went toe to toe with him. "What am I missing?"

Me, he thought but couldn't say it. "Have you spotted someone?"

"No." The defeat in her voice had him wanting to make all of this right for her.

The truth was, in a crowded place like this the

only way to find anyone was to become an easier target. She might be tracking the virus, but he wasn't convinced Frost had vacated the premises, which meant she was still in danger for reasons neither of them comprehended.

"Let's go upstairs." She pressed her body closer to his, whispering in his ear. "We need to talk."

Talk. If that was her plan, he needed time to cool off. "Thirty minutes." He'd spotted Frost playing blackjack before. Maybe he'd show up again. "I want to look around."

"Fine. But we leave when you're five hundred down."

Chapter Eleven

Gin couldn't believe Jason was up two grand after an hour of play. Her feet had never really been the problem, but the champagne she was sipping was starting to take a toll. It was enough to give her a sweet buzz but not so much that she couldn't keep an eye out for Isely or anyone who might be connected to him.

She had no idea what Jason might be looking for beyond the next card, the next bet. For a man who didn't care for casinos, he sure knew how to play with house money.

"That's it for me," he said, gathering his chips and pushing back from the table at last.

His hand was warm across her back, his palm resting lightly at her waist. Oh, she needed to find something else to think about. Casting her gaze over the faces in the crowded casino, she prayed for some sign of the seller or Isely to distract her from Jason's touch.

The second glass of champagne was clearly a mistake, making her all too eager to forget the thrill of the mission in favor of the sensual promise of the man at her side.

Upstairs he was supposed to stop touching her. That was good, though she was having a difficult time remembering why right now. If he kept touching her, she could keep touching him and she wouldn't have to tell him she recognized the blonde in the interrogation room. It should have been obvious last night, and she felt like a fool for not seeing it, not putting the pieces together.

"Can we take a turn through the shops, please?"

He gave her a dubious look. "I thought your feet hurt."

"They're rested." She needed a bit of time for the champagne to wear off before she was alone with him. The ground rules might have been her idea, but she'd broken them once with that kiss before dinner. And with this buzz, she'd lost her professional detachment where Jason was concerned.

He turned down the promenade, the security detail shifting along with them.

"Mrs. Grant?" One of them stepped closer.

"Yes?"

"This was just delivered for you."

She stared for a long moment at the note he

tried to hand her, finally accepting it and tucking it into her purse. "Thank you."

"You aren't going to open it?" Jason asked.

"Hadn't planned to."

"I think you should."

"It can wait until we're in the room."

He shook his head. "We're a team at this point. Secrets will only get us hurt. Open it."

Sexy and logical. She liked the combination a little too much.

"Fine." He led her to a bench and they sat down. She withdrew the note and opened it.

You can't protect him.

The letters were clipped from a glossy magazine and glued into the hotel stationery like a retro-style ransom note. It sent a chill down her spine and instantly cleared the champagne haze from her brain.

"We have to review the video from the front desk."

"Why?" He smiled at her like the note contained a sweet gift rather than a bold threat. "It won't do any good."

He was probably right, but she wasn't ready to give up. "It must be from the woman who's been bothering us."

"You know her?"

"I've been thinking about her the past few hours. I don't know her directly. She worked at a restaurant Isely favored in Germany. I saw her around. She was a brunette then."

"Now we just have to figure out why Isely wanted me out of commission."

"How can you be so calm?"

"A lesson I learned from you, perhaps? After all, you were the one being shot at poolside."

She glared at him.

"All right." He leaned back, spread his arms wide and all she could think was that he was inviting whoever was behind this to take their best shot. "This means we're making progress."

She exhaled, long and slow. "Maybe."

"Definitely. We just have to figure out in which direction."

"Yours apparently," she grumbled. "All is holding steady on my end."

"Except for the would-be burglars." His fingers teased her nape. "I was sent here to back up a human asset. No need to shoot at me or break into my rooms for that."

"No. But the sniper targeting me doesn't fit either. And they planted evidence in *your* room."

"Are you implying we're outmatched? Let's go upstairs and see if I can track down any news on other shootings or preliminary evidence on the ones that have already taken place."

As they started back toward the bank of elevators that served their penthouse, Gin had to know. "Are you telling me you're a hacker, too?"

"Not even close." He pressed the button for the elevator. "I'm just good at tracking down information." He scowled. "But I do have limitations."

Further discussion had to wait for privacy as two men from the security team boarded the elevator with them. The car surged up toward the penthouse level, but Gin's instincts prickled with warning. Jason sensed something, too; she could tell from the quick tap of his fingers against her lower back.

The guard to her left punched the button for the floor just below the penthouse then turned around, brandishing a knife. "Cooperate and no one gets hurt," he ordered.

Gin shifted closer to Jason. "I guess the manager doesn't know his staff as well as he thinks."

"Guess not," Jason agreed.

"I'm sure you have your orders," she said to the guard, "but please, we've been through enough. Can you put that away?"

"Shut up," the second guard barked, his deep voice resonating in the small space.

"Rude," Gin observed, offended and pretending this wasn't a life or death situation.

Feeling Jason tense beside her as the elevator slowed, she glanced at him. He winked and she understood he had a plan. He gave her a little nudge and she ducked. Jason spun, knocking away the knife.

With a bellow, guard two rushed them. Gin kicked and he went down with a shriek as his knee buckled in a way nature never intended. She then landed a blow to his larynx, cutting short his pained cries. She slammed the stop button on the elevator, hoping no one would override it and change the odds before they could wrap this up.

Behind her Jason exchanged blows with the other guard. He was holding his own, dodging and swerving, barely escaping a rib-crushing punch by sliding closer to the bigger man.

She wasn't counting on any help. If these two had been bought off by the enemy, chances were good they'd paid someone in the security room to look the other way during this attack.

The guard she'd dropped was struggling to get back in the mix, using the corners of the car to help get back on his feet. Gin laced her fingers for more power and took a swing like a batter hitting for the fence. The blow snapped the man's head back and he dropped to the floor, out cold.

"Best sedative I've found," she said, dusting off her hands while Jason pounded his opponent into a puddle on the floor.

"Nice work," she said. "Again." She reached

around and put the elevator into motion for the penthouse.

"Same goes for you. *Again*." He rubbed his jaw and cracked his neck, then smiled. "Have you checked for IDs?"

"Go ahead," she shrugged. "It can't matter. They're obviously hired help."

"They might know which one of us is the target."

"However it started, I'm pretty sure we both are now. Whoever hired these two obviously knows who we are and that we're working together."

The elevator chimed and the doors parted. Jason peered out first. "Looks clear."

"No surprise," Gin muttered. "They were probably told we didn't need them anymore." She grabbed the ankle of the man nearest her. "Help a girl out?"

Jason grabbed the other ankle and together they dragged him into the penthouse. "You get the other one. I'll get the old reliable duct tape."

Jason had the traitorous guards in a heap by the wet bar when she returned. They taped each of the men's wrists and ankles together, then taped them to the pipe under the small sink.

"That should buy us a few minutes."

Jason agreed. "I've got their phones. That

might give us something. And I sent the elevator back down so no one would come looking for it."

"Then we'd better hurry."

For the second time in hardly forty-eight hours, they packed in a rush. This time she knew they had to leave the hotel. Whoever was behind the problems plaguing them had enough money or leverage to get the cooperation they needed. Gin was done playing the game with a stacked deck.

She paused at the door to the penthouse. "Goodbye, best room ever." Couldn't blame a girl for enjoying a penthouse suite…even for just a little while.

"It was nice."

"*Nice?* That's the best you say about that glorious space?" She started for the stairs, but Jason led her in the other direction.

"Service access is safer."

"Hello? It was service guys who just tried to kill us."

"No, they were extras, hired on just to deal with us."

She didn't bother asking him how he knew this for certain. They started down the stairs, Jason carrying both suitcases while she had the computer bag. After half a flight, she slipped out of her heels. "Are we going the whole way like this?"

"I hope not. Do you still have your old room key?"

"Yeah."

"Which tower?"

"This one."

"Good."

"You can't be serious about staying here. Talk about long odds." Funny, last time he was the one who wanted to leave this hotel. A few more attempts on their lives were required to get her there, but she was squarely there now.

"We have to stay. All the players are here."

Duh. "And they know us now."

"Exactly."

"Jason." She stopped and forced him to do the same. "That doesn't make sense. Safety, regrouping—that makes sense."

"Only if you want to keep playing defense."

He winked at her and she sputtered, unable to think how to contradict him.

"How many more flights?" She was already getting dizzy from the fast pace. The man had a keen sense of balance as he somehow managed this with a suitcase in each hand. She, however, was likely dehydrated from the two glasses of champagne. And she was frustrated and flustered. She *never* got flustered. He did this to her. She was certain of it!

"Two more, then we'll try for an elevator."

"You know security is probably wondering what we're doing."

"They see plenty of weird stuff. By the time they catch up with us—if they even bother—we'll have a story together."

She hoped he was right. The etched treads of the cement steps bit into her feet, but as long as she wasn't leaving a trail of blood—she looked back to confirm—she would make it.

"Behind-the-scenes Vegas isn't so posh," she decided, suddenly feeling utterly disillusioned.

"It's a service stairwell, Gin. What did you expect?"

"I expected to stay on the pretty side of the hotel," she admitted.

"You've worked in grittier places."

"True." Which was only one more reason she appreciated the luxurious jobs.

She stopped when he did and held her breath while he opened and peered beyond the door. He listened for a few seconds then looked around the corner to see if the way was clear. Easing the door closed, he took a deep breath.

"We'll move out and to the left to the guest elevator. Take that to your floor."

She nodded.

He opened the door and she followed him,

grateful for the reprieve of the soft carpet under her feet. He pulled out both suitcase handles and rolled them along, like any other guests in search of their room.

"Keep your head down," he muttered when they reached the elevator.

She leaned against his shoulder, doing her best weary wife impersonation. He kissed her on the top of her head. How many times was that now? He was so good at this married thing, she wondered if he'd ever done it for real. What she'd dug up on him said no, but there had to be a serious relationship somewhere in his past. In her experience men didn't nurture women the way Jason had been doing it without prior on the job training.

She cultivated lust in her male targets because it blurred logic and served her better in the field. But there was an inherent kindness in Jason that had her longing for something different. Something more…personal. And no cultivation had been required with him. The lust came naturally.

For a moment she tried to imagine sharing so much with other men she'd used or targeted, and she couldn't see it happening. Neither could she see it working out with men she'd worked with inside the agency.

Only Jason.

Must be the kisses, she thought, pressing the number for the floor where her alternate identity was still checked in. When they reached her room, they'd review the ground rules again. She was a big girl and didn't need more tenderness from him. As for whatever that moment was in the penthouse before dinner, well…probably best if they avoided an encore performance of that, too.

"Do you have your keycard?"

"Hmm?" She looked up at him. "Oh, yes." She fished it out of her clutch. Because he was in front, she handed it to him to slide through the lock.

The do-not-disturb sign was still on the door and she hoped it meant no one had connected this room to Ginger Olin, CIA.

He pushed the door open and they stepped into the room. Nothing had been tossed or damaged. Everything was just as she'd left it.

"Wait here."

She stood by the door, humored by his gallant effort to clear the room of any threat. Hadn't she just proved she could be an asset in a conflict? For that matter, hadn't saving his reputation, if not his life, last night proved as much?

Of course he didn't remember that clearly, but she felt they needed to get a handle on it soon.

She couldn't let her rash decision to drag him into her case prevent her from accomplishing her task.

"Satisfied?"

"Almost." He turned on the television and tuned it to a music channel. Leaving the suitcases by the bed, he came back to join her at the door. His warm hands glided over her shoulders and down her back until he cupped her bottom and pulled her close to him. Oh, my, she thought, suddenly all too eager to toss out the ground rules. But when she met his gaze, she saw his eyes weren't full of desire but rather sharp and focused. He was in business mode.

"The room might be bugged," he whispered against her ear.

Why didn't she think of that? Because it was all she could do not to melt into his touch. "Okay," she murmured, nipping lightly at his earlobe. "Got any protection?"

"Always," he teased.

She gave a throaty laugh, though it was tough to tell where the game stopped and her real hunger for him began. "How should we proceed?"

"Careful and thorough or fast and hot." He trailed kisses down her neck. "Your choice."

"Mmm." She ran her bare foot up and down over his calf. "I like thorough." Reaching back,

she threw the dead bolt then twisted to push the swing lock into place.

"Me, too." He pulled a signal jammer from his pocket and turned it on.

Together they searched the room for listening devices and cameras. Even though finding a camera might alert the party on the other end, no way was she going to let anyone watch what probably wouldn't happen anyway.

Probably? Tempting as he was, taking this fake marriage to the next level of intimacy would be the worst possible thing to do.

Cases in the past had required the use of her every feminine skill. During some cases she'd met someone along the way and enjoyed a brief passionate affair. As much as her hormones shouted *do it,* her instincts declared he was a danger to her ability to focus and getting in deeper would change everything.

Done checking the vent near the bed, she hopped down to the floor and gave a soft cry at the hot bolt of pain shooting from her left foot to her knee.

"What is it?" Jason rushed to her side.

"Nothing. I bruised my foot in the fight and it's mad at me."

"I'll go for ice," he said.

She was going to protest, except she noticed the swelling along his cheekbone. "Good idea.

I think we could both use some. I'll find the aspirin."

"Deal."

Alone in the room, she looked around. What had seemed so fabulous when she checked in looked almost dingy compared to the penthouse they'd just escaped.

Maybe they should have locked themselves in up there and made a stand. Except they didn't have a clear lead on his enemy and she could hardly follow the virus vial if she was locked in a room.

The more she played it through her head, the more convinced she became that the personal attacks were about him. There might be a few international guests in town who would rather she were permanently out of their lives, but none of them knew her well enough to target her.

She changed the television station to the news network, but she turned the volume down. They didn't need all the local downers typical of news programs, but they did need to know if the local police had announced they were hunting a sniper.

Her foot was aching more as the adrenaline faded from her system. Adrenaline was more than a small factor in her attraction to Jason. Yes, he was gorgeous, and each time he was kind to her, every little touch that set her nerves reeling made it that much harder to remember this was temporary.

He returned with the full ice bucket topped with the liner bag full of more ice.

"It's not champagne, but it might feel as good."

"Probably better." She remembered the heady sensation as she'd watched him at the blackjack table. "I've had enough alcohol for now anyway." Vegas did enough to reduce the few inhibitions she still had.

He prepped an ice bag for both of them and smiled as she traded him two aspirin for one ice bag. He raised his bag in a toast. "To ease what ails you."

She chuckled and tapped her ice to his. "Hear, hear," she said, sinking onto the love seat while he took the chair.

JASON RELAXED AS the news anchor's voice droned quietly in the background and they sat in a comfortable silence. It was strange to be so at ease with a woman he barely knew. Maybe it was as simple as being with someone who understood the unique challenges of covert operations. When you had a chance to rest, you took it. It was a rare thing to meet a woman who knew how to live in the moment as well as he did.

A face popped up in the corner of the screen and Jason sat up, the idea of rest momentarily forgotten along with the throbbing in his cheek. He reached for the remote and dialed up the volume to listen to the report.

Bullet points appeared on the screen, giving a brief overview of the known facts. The body of James Redding, retired military expert who was in town for a security conference, had been found under the convention center monorail station early this morning. "Redding told friends he felt poorly and planned to go to his room to rest, according to a conference spokesperson. The apparent victim of a shooting, his body was found by monorail personnel early this morning. If you have any information relevant to this investigation, please call..."

Jason muted the volume but couldn't stop staring at the picture of Redding's face as he carefully leaned his cheek against the ice bag again.

"Jason?"

"Hmm."

"Did you know him?"

Jason nodded.

"Did you know he was here?"

"No."

"But isn't that conference your cover?"

"Yes, but I haven't bothered to do more than check in and occasionally walk by the vendor booths."

"Instead you've been waiting here to be contacted."

"Yes." He knew she was starting to draw the same conclusions about this being a setup. But only Holt knew he was here. Only Holt knew his orders and cover. The logical conclusion—that Holt was behind this—made him sick to his stomach.

She continued softly, "That shooting was supposed to look like your work." Her gaze locked on the television screen, where shots of the area where the body was found flashed in sequence.

"Agreed." Wasn't much point in arguing it and definitely not with the only person who knew he was innocent.

"Drugged, you wouldn't have had an alibi for that."

"Are you fishing for more gratitude? Because I have plenty, believe me." Jason rubbed the ice pack over his bruised knuckles, but it was Gin who shivered. "Were you trying to make a point?"

"Whoever wanted to pin that on you must know the blonde failed to contain you."

"You're saying all our recent fun is about killing me instead of framing me? The pool incident sure looked like it was all about you." Calling it a shooting rather than a mere "incident" made it too real.

"If Frost is as good as you say—"

"He is."

"—then you have to consider he missed me on purpose. Think about it. There were too many variables. You're the expert in the field—could any innocent bystander have moved into the shot?"

"Not from that angle," Jason argued.

"Exactly! He had no idea where we would sit, what we would do. But he had elevation and angle on his side."

"That's why he works with Wallace. To keep him informed, to stage the scene to misdirect the investigation."

"Wallace tailed me? Us? I don't think so. I would have noticed," she rebutted.

"Or not," Jason said with a shrug. "Makes sense. Whatever you're working on, someone wants to stop you."

"Then why not just kill me?" She gave an exasperated sigh. "Going way out on a theoretical limb here, even if he really was after me, he still missed me on purpose. It was either a scare tactic or part of a setup. Maybe both."

"Tell it to the lifeguard," he grumbled. He shifted the ice pack to his cheekbone, irritated he hadn't dodged the elbow strike more efficiently.

"She'll be back on the job in two to four weeks," Gin said dismissively.

"You can't really be that cold." In fact, he knew she wasn't that cold. She put on the master spy, cold, hard mask but underneath she was warm and soft.... *Stop, Jason.*

"I can be when we should be focused on who's out to get *you*."

He wasn't ready to go there just yet. "How's your foot?"

"Fine." She moved the melting ice bag back over the bruise, which was turning the side of her foot red and deep purple. "Don't try to distract me. I think you have a working theory about the sniper."

"Contrary to popular belief, snipers don't always stay in one place for days waiting for the shot." He shook his head, his mind in the past. During his stint with Interpol, he'd been ordered to line up a shot on a woman who'd ordered the assassination of a British spy. She enjoyed sunbathing topless on the French Riviera. He had the clear shot and his finger on the trigger when he'd been called off. He'd packed up his gun and spent the rest of the day flirting with a lovely brunette farther down the beach.

He could count on one hand the people who knew about his involvement with that operation and numerous others. The logical conclusion was about as illogical as anything could be. Holt hadn't reached his current position without being thoroughly vetted by more than one agency and undergoing extensive background checks and psych evaluations.

There had to be another answer. A mole in a nearby department somewhere. An undetected bug in Holt's office. There had to be an explanation that didn't involve his direct superior's plans to put the blame on him for murders in Las Vegas. "How many covert operations do you think go down in Vegas on an annual basis?"

"Not enough of mine," she groused.

"You like it here?"

"What's not to like? The food is fabulous, you can dress up or down, there's always something going on, and you can hide in plain sight."

"Or get married, if all else fails."

"I told you I was saving your butt. You'd remember that if your brain had been working properly." She limped over and perched on the side of his chair, pushed his hair back from his forehead. "Worried I'll take half of your assets in the divorce?"

"Nothing to take," he lied. "Government salary, government car."

"I don't believe you." She pulled the ice bag away from his cheek and brushed the spot with her lips. "Your ops are so black, there's no way they'd risk a typical government fleet contract. You shouldn't lie to your wife."

"Pot." He pointed to her, then to himself. "Kettle." He put the ice pack back on his cheek just to take away the heat that lingered from her touch. "Tell me more about your case. Any chance you're the operative I'm supposed to escort out of this town?"

"I answered that yesterday." She stood up and started to pace before her bruised foot stopped her. "CIA has no other assets here that I know of."

"Technically you shouldn't be working here."

She turned, her grin positively impish. It shouldn't amuse him, but it did. "Technically I'm not." Her grin faded. "Months ago, I was tasked with following the virus. I've found two of the four known vials, but the biologist who created it is still out there somewhere."

"Or dead."

"That tends to happen when people cross the Isely family." She slumped onto the couch.

He walked over and picked up her feet, propping them up with pillows to ease the potential swelling. Her level of pain made him worry she was nursing a hairline fracture. It was a common enough injury from the way she'd made the strike against the thug's knee.

"If the biologist is dead, that makes the product more valuable."

"Not necessarily," she countered. "Only the

wholesaler needs to know about the supplier or manufacturer. They can spread whatever lies work to their advantage to boost the market value of a product."

"So what is the wholesaler saying about the virus you're tracking?"

She frowned. "Nothing."

"Why not?" He returned to his chair, needing the distance to keep his hands off her.

"Well, until you started asking questions I assumed it was because the stuff is so new and relatively unproven."

"Relatively?"

Her eyebrows climbed toward her hairline, and he realized he didn't want to hear the answer. "Do you know the seller on sight?" he asked.

"Yes. But he isn't really my goal. I've been tracking GPS tags on the vials themselves."

"Can the seller identify you?"

"Highly unlikely." She sat up and tossed a small pillow at him. "Hey. You got me off topic. We were discussing the shooting and who's behind it. Talk to me. I'm a great listener."

"Except I don't need a great listener. I'm used to working alone." Irritated, he stood up and walked toward the bathroom, dumping the melting ice out of the bag and into the bathtub.

Talking about this wouldn't help. He needed some quiet to review the facts and crack the phones he'd taken off the thugs. Wouldn't it be ideal if he could get a look at the bullet that had ended Redding's life? How much could the cover story work to his advantage? A security conference offered a variety of suspects for this incident. Thanks to the media, most people liked to assume those in private security frequently went off the deep end. Whoever caught this case at the local level should know better, but stereotypes were hard to overcome.

His cover story closely mirrored his real story, including his military background, but not his sniper expertise. It was only a matter of time before the local law enforcement realized he had a potential connection to Redding. Along with his presence as a witness to the incident at the pool, this setup might catch him yet.

Without Gin—and her timely intervention at the bar—he might already be a person of interest in this case. He couldn't see any way that his involvement and possible detention benefitted Holt, but no one else knew he was here. There had to be another answer, or he had to accept a terrible truth about betrayal.

"Jason?"

She was right behind him. He'd felt her before she'd said a word. He met her gaze in the reflection of the mirror. "Yeah?"

"What can I do?"

He shook his head. He wasn't a fan of her tactics, but there was no doubt getting married offered him an incontrovertible alibi.

"Keep the marriage certificate close, I guess," he suggested.

"That's hardly a real answer."

True. He couldn't give her an answer while his mind wrestled with the best way to get a look at the crime scene and maybe the evidence in last night's murder. What the hell was going on here?

"Right." She slid down the zipper hidden in the side seam of her dress.

He'd wondered how she'd poured herself into the snug, black sheath.

She started peeling the dress from her body and he caught sight of sheer black lace against the pure ivory of her skin. He stilled her hand before he saw more than she intended to show. Married on paper didn't give him the right to ogle her. No matter what happened last night, no matter that he couldn't remember it, he'd been indisposed. He was in full control now and he refused to take advantage of her.

"What are you doing?" he asked.

"Changing clothes. You want to go out to the crime scene."

"Did I say that out loud?"

She smiled, and it was warm and kind without an ounce of smirk in her expression. She reached up but stopped short of touching him. Her hand fell away. "You didn't have to."

He stared as she pulled jeans and a sweater out of her suitcase then rooted around until she found socks and tennis shoes.

The woman had packed duct tape, so he shouldn't be surprised that she was prepped for any occasion.

"Are you going like that? Crime scenes usually aren't formal events." She kept herself covered with her dress, but it was clear that wouldn't last much longer.

He lurched into motion and headed for his own suitcase. "No." He couldn't figure out his sudden modesty. That had flown out the window this morning when she'd put him in the shower. But it was different now when he was completely aware of her and completely aware of his reactions to her. He swapped dress slacks for his own jeans and traded the shirt and tie for a polo shirt.

Before he could pull it over his head, he felt her staring at him.

He swiveled around. "What is it?"

"Admiring your tattoo. What does it symbolize?"

"A night of drunken stupidity." He pulled his shirt over his head and turned around before she could blink away the flash of pain in her eyes.

"Why are you pushing me away again?"

He bit back the truth. Letting her in only meant a bigger ache when this was over. They could hardly stay married, considering their divergent careers. "I'm not. I'm just thinking."

"So give me the short version."

"We were working a case in Dublin during my Interpol days. O'Marron convinced me a Celtic warrior dragon was the right choice."

"I'd agree." She looked at him. "It suits you." She tied her shoe with a bit too much enthusiasm, wincing when the laces cinched tightly across her injured foot.

"You could wait here."

"Not a chance." Her emerald eyes were snapping with ire and he regretted putting it there. "Whether or not you want to admit it, you need me. Especially at the crime scene."

"Okay." He wouldn't argue, afraid of revealing more emotion than she might be ready to take from him. He clipped his holster onto his belt and slid his sport coat over it. Tucking the wallet with his badge into the inner pocket, he looked at her. "How do you suggest we proceed?"

"Did you rent a car?"

"Yes."

"Great. Let's drive on out to the scene and then you can let me do the talking."

He found the key to the rental and confirmed she had a key for the room, and together they cautiously made their way out of the hotel to the valet stand.

Caution was the word of the day. They'd been lucky so far. Another run-in with trouble and their luck might just run out.

Chapter Twelve

When the valet returned with the car, a bright yellow Corvette, Gin had more cause to re-evaluate Mission Recovery's golden boy.

It would be easier if he'd open up to her, but he wasn't big on sharing. She could hardly fault him for that, but after what they'd recently survived she'd expected him to be more forthcoming.

Common sense and a basic understanding of investigative curiosity was enough to convince her he needed to visit the scene. Something about either the victim or the method of the shooting had tripped up Jason. Which meant there was no way she was letting him do this alone.

She recognized a setup and knew he did, too, and if he wouldn't share his theories, she'd develop her own.

The big engine purred as he pulled out on the Strip, and she couldn't help but admire the glitz of all the lights and stunning casino facades.

"When you were with Interpol, did you ever run across Isely or his family?"

"No."

"You're sure?"

"Yes. And you're fishing."

Like she had any choice but to fish for information when he was doing the strong, silent routine. At this rate he was as useful to her as one of the marble statues planted around Caesar's.

"Just trying to determine if my connection to you puts my own case at risk."

"Is that your way of asking for a divorce?"

"No." The question automatically drew her eye to the lights bouncing off his wedding band as he used his left hand to steer while his right rested lightly on the gear shift. Within reach if she chose to make personal contact.

Too bad he wasn't giving off any signal that said he'd be receptive to her touch right now. She might have teased him more when he'd reacted to the glimpse of her lacy bra, but when they did make love—and she decided they would—she wanted his undivided attention.

As they turned off Las Vegas Boulevard toward the crime scene at the monorail station, he cleared his throat. "Since you're doing the talking, why don't you give me a general idea of your approach?"

"I tend to wing it. Just play along."

"Great."

"It will be." She pulled a camera out of her tote. "And memorable. You can be my cameraman."

He turned toward her, one eyebrow arched. "We're still talking about the case, right?" He pulled to a stop behind a line of police cars and other official vehicles.

She handed him the camera. "Of course we are." She was out of the car, game face on, purpose in her stride as she sought out the lead investigator on the scene.

The news trucks were gone but the scene was plenty busy. Crime scene techs in their well-known jackets with cameras and evidence bags crawled over every inch of the site where Redding's body had been found.

Gin knew she probably should have pushed Jason for a few details about how he knew the man. Then again, winging it hadn't failed her yet.

"Wait," Jason stopped her with a hand on her arm. "Don't do this."

"You need a look at the scene and the evidence." She smiled at him. "Trust me."

She felt him at her back as she walked up to the yellow tape barrier and stepped into character. The one she chose was a familiar British role. "I need a minute with the lead investigator."

The police officer stared at her. "He's not available. I can give him a message."

"Thanks, but that doesn't always work out so well." She handed him a business card that showed her as a reporter from London. "I'm working a story and I have information that might help with his case."

"Really?" he asked, clearly unconvinced.

"Really." She grinned at him, turned on the charm, as she caught movement from the corner of her eye. Jason was moving toward the techs. "Would you give me a quote?"

"Can't do that."

"Not even off the record? We believe there's a vigilante on a world tour picking off criminals. And, personally, I believe it's the local cops on the ground like you who'll make all the difference." She made a face and shook her head. "Not the feds or Interpol."

She had the cop's interest now and she tweaked his curiosity. "Interpol says the bloke can make a long distance shot as cleanly as a small-caliber double-tap execution. But that's hardly relevant if this was a close-range sort of thing."

The cop leaned forward, his attention completely with Gin. "It wasn't." He glanced side to side and lowered his voice. "You can't quote me, but we're thinking sniper here, too."

"One shot?"

The cop shook his head. "Two."

She waited, leaned in just a smidge more.

"Head and heart. I heard one of the other guys say the bastard—pardon my French, ma'am—was showing off with the second shot."

She nodded as if this was familiar news. In reality, it scared the hell out of her.

"That's not all."

She gave him a wide-eyed, tell-me-more look. "We think this victim is related to a fatality on the highway a couple days ago."

"The big pileup I heard about?"

The cop nodded.

"But I thought that was just an accident."

"We don't want to cause panic, but between you and me, it was a bullet in the tire of the first car that started the whole thing."

More likely, the local team didn't want to have the FBI breathing down their necks and stealing the investigation. Which would happen if word got out they were dealing with a U.S. Army–trained sniper.

Jason's cover was just too close to the truth on this.

"Have they found where the shot came from?"

"That's the real mystery in this incident. We found the nest for the highway shooting but not this one yet."

"Hmm." She looked around, as if she could see

anything useful in the dark. "Please, please give my card to the lead detective on this. What we've gathered from other incidents might be helpful."

"Have you had any incidents in the past week?"

Gin winked at him. "There's a reason I'm here and not in the UK."

"Well, Vegas is a great place for a vacation."

Wasn't he well-trained to toe the tourism line even at a crime scene? Of course, she wasn't the typical tourist. "Quite true. I've found a wealth of diversions since my arrival." She wanted to glance at Jason but didn't want to break the spell she held over the cop.

He tapped her card against his palm. "If you need a guide, I could show you around when I'm off shift."

"That could be lovely." She used her left hand to smooth her hair back, flashing her wedding band. "Go ahead and make a note of my number there." Jason was striding her way, grim determination clear in the set of his jaw. "Thank you for your time," she said extending her hand to shake his. "We'll just get out of your way."

Back in the car Jason glared for a long moment before he put the key into the ignition.

"Problem, dear?"

"A flirty reporter? That was your big idea?"

"Flirty, British reporter," she corrected. "I left

my shiny fake badge in my other purse," she added.

"Right."

"What's the problem? I got useful information out of him."

"The poor sap thinks he's going to get something more than useful out of you."

"Are you jealous?"

"Of a Las Vegas rookie cop ogling my wife? No."

She watched the way he shielded his face as they rolled slowly by the personnel at the scene. "If not jealousy, what's crawled up your rear?"

"Do you even know you do that?"

"What?"

"Resort to a more colorful dialect when you're irritated."

She'd never been accused of doing it before. "I don't believe you," she said in a flat Midwestern accent. No way she'd admit the amount of concentration it took to pull it off.

"You're saying it's my influence, then?"

"No."

"My proximity?" He reached over and patted her leg, then left his big palm warm on her thigh.

With deliberate motions, like she was disposing of something unpleasant, she removed his hand from her leg and dropped it back on the gear shift between them. "Stop teasing me and just say what's on your mind."

"Now you're all business."

"I'm always all business." But she was watching his hands as he negotiated a turn and clicked the headlights to bright. "Where are we going?"

"To check out the nest for this hit."

"You figured that out?"

"We'll know in a few minutes."

"The cop said the pileup on the interstate started with a bullet to the left front tire rather than an accidental blowout."

"Sounds about right."

"Right for what?" She wanted to shake him. Why wouldn't he share the theory he was working on? She'd been open with him. More open than she'd ever been with anyone else—including her fellow agents within the CIA. Gin wasn't sure she wanted to evaluate that development any time soon. No matter what she did or thought, her emotions were fully engaged with this man. Whoever was after him shouldn't be her concern, but she couldn't maintain her professional distance. As much as she wanted to chalk it up to the close call at the pool, or Wallace's knife at her throat, lying to herself would only make it worse.

Her heart had skipped at the sight of Jason in that bar and it wanted to keep on skipping the longer they stayed together. An agent falling like this was never a pretty sight. She was in deep here.

Not just because she knew he'd help her; she had a variety of skills to coerce any red-blooded male into providing assistance when she needed it. It hadn't just been about seeing a friendly face, either. His initial greeting had been less than encouraging.

It had been him. No more, no less than the simple truth. Jason Grant had managed to ignite a spark of hope or happiness inside her she'd decided wasn't within her capacity to feel.

Good Lord, she wished the man would talk so she could stop thinking!

He pulled the car into a parking garage and drove up the ramps. "Let's just see if we find the nest."

"Okay." If he wouldn't share, she'd just have to figure it out. "The cop said the man was shot twice."

"Show off." Jason stopped on the top level and got out of the car, walking forward in the wash from the headlights.

"The local officials agree with you," she said, catching up to him. "The sniper put a bullet through his brain and then the heart as he went down just to prove he could."

Jason shook his head.

"Have you ever done that?"

"Only on a training dummy. I was the only one who could pull it off perfectly. Straight through the center of the heart before the victim—dummy, of course—slumped too far from the head shot that had already killed him."

"Something else in your closed file?"

He nodded.

A chill slid down her spine as potential connections bumped around in her mind. "So whoever is behind the rifle is trying to get your attention?"

"More likely he's trying to get me blamed. He just has to blow apart my cover story about why I'm in Vegas."

She patted him on the back. "No worries. I can arrange an exit strategy for you, Specialist Grant."

"Funny."

She was trying to lighten the mood, if only to prevent the unprecedented worry from choking her. Getting emotional was way, way out of character and entirely dangerous for all involved.

Jason stopped, stepping carefully using the glow of the headlights. "Here we are." He knelt down and used a flashlight to poke around the trash that had been blown against the low wall.

Gin looked down toward the crime scene to the big lights set up around the area. It appeared more than possible to her that a sniper had made the shots from here. "Why aren't the police up here?"

"Probably because the body was shifted so they would be looking at a different trajectory."

"Something else you learned in training?"

"No, that's something I heard about in the field."

When he didn't explain, she sighed. "Jason, darling, you simply must learn to keep some information to yourself. The way you go on and on it's a wonder you qualified for a security clearance."

"Unlike your new admirer down there, I know better than to talk with cute reporters."

"Cute?" She snorted. "No one's accused me of cute since I wore pigtails in grammar school."

"Ladies and gentlemen, may I present our Irish lass, Ginger Olin." He shot her a wink.

"You're a mixed-up sort of Yank," she said in her best Irish lilt. She punched him in the shoulder and set her voice to match the locals. "Keep it up and I'll have no choice but to seek revenge."

He looked up at her, his face an odd blend of humor and regret. "Let's hope you get the chance."

"What does that mean?" She dropped to her knees beside him, peering at an object he'd picked up. "Is that shell casing related to this case?"

"I believe so. There's another right over there."

"Sloppy to leave them lying around."

"Not if you want to get caught. Or rather, get *me* caught."

"No way." She frowned at the brass casing on the end of his pen. "Have you ever left a shell casing behind?"

"No."

"I didn't think so. I bet that detail is even a notation in your service record. Jason, you can't believe I'll let them so much as question you. I'm your alibi. Rock solid with a marriage certificate to prove it."

He stood and she followed suit, gazing up at his troubled face.

"Thanks. But doing that could blow your own mission here. You might be better off to hurry up with the divorce."

"Despite our whirlwind courtship, I'm not eager for the dubious honor of shortest marriage on record."

He laughed, just as she'd hoped, though it was painfully brief. "How do you want to deal with this?" He held the brass casing up between them.

"I say we leave them here." She planted her hands on her hips. "If we do the police work for them, it only raises more questions about how we knew where to look."

"How *I* knew where to look," he said.

"We. For better or worse, remember?"

His smile didn't reach his eyes. "No. I don't remember to be honest. But this is definitely one for the worse column."

She pushed his hand down until the brass shell slid off the pen and landed at their feet. He looked so desperately alone, she couldn't bear it. Taking his hand, she led him back to the car and opened the passenger door for him.

He slid in without protest—which worried her more. Before she could close the door, the window shattered, spilling safety glass across her shoes.

"Keys!" She scrambled around the back of the car, staying low even as she opened the door and adjusted the driver's seat.

Jason shoved the key in the ignition and she started the car and put it into reverse. They flew backward down the parking garage ramps, both cars. Keeping low in the seats as bullets peppered the windshield she prayed they wouldn't encounter a vehicle coming up.

"What the hell is this?" She wrestled with the steering wheel.

"A trap," he replied. "Small caliber. Go faster."

Judging the space wide enough, she executed

an impressively fast three-point turn and worked the high-performance engine until they were out of the garage and flying toward a main road. She heard the engine behind them closing in, swore when another bullet clipped her sideview mirror.

"Where's a cop when you need one?" she muttered.

Jason's hearty belly laugh made her jump. "At the crime scene with your new admirer."

"Funny." Grumbling, she turned away from the direction of the crime scene and headed south, determined to get back toward the famous glow of the Las Vegas strip. They needed a crowd and cops. Cops cruised the Strip 24/7. "Can you see anything back there?"

"Just headlights." He jerked and raised his hands to shield himself when the passenger-side mirror blew apart. "Head for the interstate."

She adjusted her course. "We'll be lucky to avoid a ticket for safety violations."

"That'll be the least of our worries if you can't lose them."

"The task would have been far easier if you'd rented a normal car."

"A normal car wouldn't have this engine."

"Mixed blessings," she allowed. Working through the gears, she edged away from their pursuers.

"Why didn't they shoot us while we were looking at the casing?"

"Guess they don't want us dead."

"Then it would be best to stop shooting in our general direction."

"Agreed. It's small-caliber fire." He dug a bullet out of the seat area near his shoulder.

She could tell he was mulling over this weird development, but discussion would have to wait as she navigated the increasing traffic.

"Slow down."

"You just told me to lose them."

"I know." He drew his own weapon, a semi-automatic nine millimeter. "Humor me."

She eased off the accelerator and downshifted, her palms damp on the leather-covered steering wheel as the other car closed the gap. "What's your plan?"

"I'm just going to wing it."

"Assuming we survive," Gin vowed, "I'm plotting a prolonged revenge at the earliest opportunity."

"That's just proof I'm the luckiest husband in Vegas," Jason said. He reclined the back of the seat, then tugged at the seat belt as he shifted and twisted around to get a better position.

"You shoot left-handed?"

"Only when I have to."

She was cruising now, exactly at the posted speed limit.

"If he's smart, he'll go for the tires," she muttered, mostly to herself. As if on cue, she caught the muzzle flash in her rearview mirror, and she braced to work with the spinout. Avoiding collateral damage out here was her first priority.

The first shot hit the car, and she heard the deep pop of Jason's gun as he returned fire.

Another flash and the left rear of the car lurched as the tire came apart.

Sparks of the wheel against the roadway reflected in the remaining shards of her side mirror. Gin didn't have time to appreciate the artistry of it as she struggled to maintain control of the Corvette. Steering into the spin, she said a prayer when the interstate median stopped the momentum with a sickening crunch as the front end crumpled.

Jason gave a victory whoop. When her stomach settled and the airbag deflated, she understood why.

The other car was stalled in the left lane, a few yards in front of them, the hood popped and smoke and steam pluming.

"You tagged the radiator?"

"Took me two tries."

"In the middle of a spin?"

"No, before that." He leaned over and planted a hard kiss on her mouth. "Listen."

She could only stare at him as the sounds of emergency sirens drew closer.

"Come on. Let's go make a citizen's arrest."

Jason bolted out of the car as the driver who'd been chasing them started limping away from the scene. She watched him go as she inventoried her situation. Her foot was more unhappy than ever and her lip was swelling from the airbag.

"The man is insane." This she knew with complete certainty.

Climbing out of the car became a problem. Her foot was caught between the clutch pedal and the crushed left front quarter panel. The painful bruise from the earlier fight would no longer be ignored. She could only watch as Jason ran down the other driver, tackling him to the pavement.

"Yay team," she muttered, leaning her head back against the headrest. Hopefully this would be the lead Jason was looking for. If she was really lucky, it would be the catalyst to get him talking about whatever he really thought was going on.

Wishing he'd come back to help her out of the car, she opened her eyes and screamed. Flames were licking at the hood and closing in on her. She scrabbled against the seat and pulled at her foot, but it wouldn't budge.

She refused to panic, told herself she'd been in worse situations and swore that later she'd laugh at the overwhelming urge to panic. Now, she had to think.

There was always a way out.

"Cover your head!"

She looked up into Jason's face at her window.

"Do it, Gin!"

She met his gaze and choked back the panicked scream. Flames at his back, he showed her a crowbar. She had no idea what he meant to do, only that any moment he could be in as much danger as she was.

"Get away! I'm stuck."

"Cover your head."

He didn't wait, and she turned her head as he smashed the window. What he might do against the crumpled door, she had no idea. Emergency crews were racing toward them. Over the sound of the fire and traffic, she heard Jason barking orders, and she saw shadows through the smoke and blue flashes of police lights.

Her thoughts disjointed and muddled by the swirling smoke, she vaguely wondered if she'd get ticketed for speeding.

Beneath her the car rocked and metal and fiberglass crunched with whatever they were doing. Then suddenly the pressure on her foot released and she scrambled back as white foam covered the car and doused the flames.

She wasn't ashamed to cling to Jason, was too relieved they were both alive as he carried her to the waiting paramedics.

"I'm fine," she began, but her protest was cut off by a fit of coughing. An oxygen mask landed on her face and she was urged to lie back and relax. An order that became more challenging when they pushed Jason out of reach and out of her sight.

Someone packed her foot in ice and propped it up, then covered her with a blanket while they measured her pulse and blood pressure. No surprise that both were slightly elevated.

They asked her several questions, which she remembered to answer as the British reporter. Hopefully Jason had grabbed her purse from the wrecked car. Aside from being a bit groggy and sore, she wasn't in terrible condition.

Another police officer stepped up beside her. Despite the oxygen mask she tried to smile when she recognized him from the murder scene.

"We should thank you."

She raised her eyebrows, her throat too raw and tender to speak much.

"You and your photographer found the sniper's nest for the Redding shooting. We were looking in a different area."

She nodded.

A warm hand landed on her shoulder, and she recognized Jason's touch. "Feeling better?"

She nodded again.

"They want to transport you for X-rays on that foot."

She shook her head. "Not broken," she rasped.

"You should make sure."

"I am," she said with a pointed look. Certainly he'd realize she had plenty of experience diagnosing and managing physical injuries. Her head clearing and her lungs feeling better, she nudged the oxygen mask out of the way. "Are you hurt?"

"Just a scratch."

He pointed to his head. It looked more like a gash to her, with four butterfly closures holding it together.

He smoothed a hand over her hair. "Neither of us is concussed and if you're sure about the foot, we're free to go."

Gin sat up, more than ready to get out of here. They needed to discuss this situation with the sniper and put a lid on it before it got any more out of control. Maybe her smoke-roughened throat was a good thing if it meant Jason had to do more of the talking.

What the hell were they going to do? That gorgeous car was destroyed. More important, where would they go? Sure they had a room, but returning to the hotel in this condition would raise eyebrows and suspicions.

Jason smiled down at her, smoothing her hair from her face. He couldn't seem to stop touching her, and she soaked up the comfort he offered.

"What now?"

"I'm not without resources. Trust me?"

She did, she realized, more than she'd ever trusted anyone else. "Lead on."

Chapter Thirteen

Emmett Holt's home,
11:15 p.m.

Holt's phone rang, interrupting his workout. He answered it when he saw the number from the Mission Recovery analyst department.

"Sir, our contact in Nevada wants to confirm a new requisition."

Holt stifled his first response. "Who is asking for what?"

"Specialist Grant requested a car, among other things."

Grant should have been out of the way by now, and "other things" covered a lot of gray area. "Approve it all and make sure I have a list on my desk in the morning."

He disconnected the call and dialed back his frustration. Intelligent, capable people were a boon when they were working with you. Having so many variables in play, so many people who could turn his plans inside out was a pain in the ass.

He threw a series of uppercuts into the heavy bag he'd been punching when Nadine had interrupted. As far as he could tell the woman never slept. Not that he could say anything. He rarely did himself.

What didn't kill him made him stronger. It would appear the same held true for Grant. Holt tried to be objective and find a way to turn this to his advantage.

The arrangements had been clear and specific; he didn't conduct business of this nature in any other fashion. He jabbed twice and came around with a left hook.

As his body worked out the combination, his mind flipped through the potential pitfalls like a slide show. Move one way, get result A. Move the other, result B.

His counterpart had dropped the ball, giving Holt a new opening. He just had to decide how to use it.

He drove his fists into the heavy bag then slumped against it, catching his breath. He checked the clock on the wall and knew he should get some of that sleep he more often than not denied himself.

Instead, he turned on the television in the corner and drained a bottle of water while he cruised the news stations.

Only a few more weeks. He could sleep for a month on a warm beach in a nonextradition country when this was over. Or he was dead. At this point he wasn't sure which outcome he preferred.

As long as it was done.

Chapter Fourteen

Nevada,
11:50 p.m.

Jason watched Gin's face as she tried to figure out what resources he might have called on, but now wasn't the time to explain it all. Right now he was just relieved she was alive. When the car had stopped spinning and the airbags deflated, he'd had one goal: catch the attacker and squeeze him for information before the cops pulled him out of reach.

Except Gin hadn't been beside him as he'd expected. He'd turned around just in time to see the fire catch, and his heart just stopped.

Looking at her now, he wondered when she had become so important to him. It couldn't be because of a piece of paper. Not when he couldn't even remember the wedding. He wanted to chalk it up to proximity and the camaraderie of working together, but he knew it went deeper than that.

She was gorgeous and he was thoroughly attracted, but there was more. Even knowing it would make her mad, he wanted to comfort and coddle. She could take care of herself and the paramedics had cleared her, but he couldn't shut down the instinct to protect her. To treasure her.

There probably wasn't an accurate term to define his degree of foolishness when her smoke-damaged voice only made her more appealing.

He could just imagine her laughter if she knew.

"Come on. Your new pal is giving us a lift to a truck stop."

She shot him a skeptical look.

"You said you'd trust me."

She smiled and when she put her hand in his, he felt like he'd won the jackpot at the Palace. In that habit she had, she rested her head on his shoulder and rubbed his arm with her free hand as she limped along to the patrol car.

He knew he was reading too much into it— they were in public after all—but something in her touch felt more sincere this time. A survivor's euphoria and definitely an adrenaline rush were going on here with both of them. Maintaining logic was critical to sorting out their respective missions and keeping their emotions in perspective.

They rode together in the back of the police car because he didn't want her out of reach.

"I'm okay," she whispered, but she kept her body pressed along his side for the duration of the twenty-minute ride.

"If you need anything, just give us a call," the officer said when they reached The King Truck Stop.

"Bet they try to call us first," Gin said as he pulled away, a tired smile on her lips.

Jason bent down and kissed her. "Probably. We should make the most of our time before that happens."

Those green eyes lit with a determined fire. He appreciated her enthusiasm, could only hope it lasted after she understood his theory and how he wanted to deal with it.

"Is your contact inside?"

"Should be." Jason nodded. "Lean on me," he offered when she started to limp. "If he's running late, we can ice that foot again."

"It's fine," she insisted.

"I could just carry you."

"In your dreams," she said, but the bravado wasn't as effective when she bit her lip with the exertion of the next step.

"Come on." He knelt in front of her. "Hop on."

"That's ridiculous."

He looked over his shoulder. "It'll be fun. You probably haven't had a piggyback ride since your *cute* days."

"Fine." She looped her bag across her body, then wrapped her arms around his neck and leaned onto his back. He reached around and, holding on to her thighs, stood up. He could have sworn she giggled, but she said, "You are impossible."

"Just what every husband wants to hear."

"Men are so easy," she whispered at his ear.

A trucker exiting the diner held the door open for them as they entered. Jason carried her to the counter and let her slide down onto one of the tall stools.

"I must look terrible." She pulled the barrette out of her hair and tried to smooth all the wayward strands back into place.

He shook his head. "Not as bad as you think."

"That doesn't make me feel one bit better." She pulled a face and rooted through her bag, holding up a small compact like a trophy. She took one look at her reflection and the color drained from her face. "I can't believe people aren't running away in terror."

Jason knew better than to protest while she tried to minimize the damage. "I can buy us a couple of T-shirts."

"Don't bother," she said, wiping mascara from under her eyes. "Who are we here to meet?"

Jason liked that *we* more than he should. "Just a contact." He didn't see anyone in the diner who fit the description in the Mission Recovery files. "He'll be here any minute. Are you hungry?"

"I could eat."

When they'd placed orders for bacon cheeseburgers, fries and milkshakes, she reached over and patted him on the knee. "You *are* going to talk to me."

He smiled, understanding it wasn't a question. "Not here."

"That's fair."

Her expression was ample warning that she wouldn't be distracted this time. Jason was surprised that didn't bother him. He clearly needed an ally—even though until this mission he'd preferred to work alone. He leaned close to her, his fingers tracing the fine bones of her hand. "Tell me something about you while we wait."

She sipped her water, and remembering her scorched throat, he felt like a jerk for making her talk.

"I was recruited at university," she said.

Of all the things she might have said, that one startled him, but he didn't show it. The timing of the recruiting wasn't the shock, but her accent and phrasing raised more questions. She had an enviable range of authentic-sounding accents.

"By whom?" She shook her head, her gaze locked on their joined hands. He reached over and gently tipped up her chin. "Tell me."

"IRA."

The Irish Republican Army was no easy group to get into. Or out of. It was hard to imagine the idealistic girl she must have been getting mixed up in the dangers of that world. He had a vivid image of her as a young girl in a school uniform jumper, red braids down her back and that pixie smile on her face. During his time with Interpol, he'd seen still photos of similar girls before and after the bombing they'd investigated.

"You weren't in deep." It wasn't a question. If she had been, she wouldn't be here now.

She shrugged. "Family connection."

That kind of background and hard-knock training would explain her indomitable spirit and headstrong methods in the field. She must have been turned into an informant for American interests somewhere along the way.

He wanted the whole story but not at the price of her pained voice. Whether physical or emotional, he could tell this conversation was taking a toll.

Rubbing her shoulder, he grinned at the waitress when their food arrived. "Dig in," he said trying to send her the signal that nothing in her past mattered to him. Definitely not tonight, when they should be celebrating being alive and generally uninjured. "Want to prop up your foot?"

She shook her head, her mouth full of burger.

He had just poured the last of his chocolate milkshake from the stainless cup into the tall classic serving glass when his contact finally walked in.

He slid onto the stool next to Jason, ordered coffee and a slice of cherry pie, and then placed a car key on the counter. "You're all set, man. I even gave her a fresh coat of wax."

"Thanks." Jason reached for the key and saw the man's eyes go wide when he spotted the shiny gold wedding band.

He leaned forward and gave Gin a long, appreciative look.

"Nicely done, man."

Jason cut him a sideways glance. "Keep your distance." The last thing he wanted was this guy sending details up the line to Mission Recovery before Jason had a chance to sort things out for himself. He'd never had to put an unplanned marriage on a mission report. He supposed he should be grateful she was CIA. At least their security clearances would match up.

"Dude." The guy shrugged a shoulder. "Whatever."

Gin elbowed Jason. "An introduction?"

Jason shook his head. "Not today." He pocketed the key and placed a couple of bills on the counter. "You ready?"

"I am." She showed off her to-go cup to prove it.

"Want a lift?" He patted his shoulder.

She shook her head. "I'll risk it this way."

He gave her as much support as she'd accept as they went out to the parking lot. The sedan gleamed in the glow of neon from the signs fronting the truck stop. Jason resisted the urge to check the merchandise before he got in. This was a trusted Mission Recovery asset. The rifle, ammunition, infrared scope and binoculars, along with another sidearm and ammunition, would be hidden in the trunk and back seat. It was a risk, but one he had to take. If he was right about the sniper, time was running out.

"Where's the virus?" he asked as they approached the Strip.

She checked her phone. "Not in the Palace

anymore. It's moving north." She pounded a fist into her knee. "Damn it. I've missed the deal."

He hit the accelerator. "Thought that was tomorrow night."

"That's what they told me."

"Maybe the seller got spooked. Or the buyer changed it up. Let's go see."

"Hurry."

He couldn't do much about the congestion. "You think someone has eyes on us and moved when you were out of range?"

She sneered at the screen in her palm. "Has to be it."

Who knew them both and had the resources to pull it off? Someone on the inside. Betrayal prickled along his skin like the pressure of a sharp knife between his shoulder blades. He shifted in the seat, trying to shake it off.

"What now?" Gin whispered into the silence.

"The car is clean. We talk." And try to find the point where her virus and his past intersected.

"We?"

"Well, you can listen."

She gestured for him to continue.

"You might be right about the miss at the pool. This guy seems to be re-creating some of my hits."

"You killed a woman at a pool?"

"No." He flexed his hands on the steering wheel. "I was called off killing a woman on a beach."

"Not the same."

"Close enough." It bothered him that his past had put her in danger and he struggled to push that back and stay focused on the primary issue.

He slowed down as they hit the thicker congestion of cars cruising up and down the glaring canyon of the strip. It wasn't fun, but it was relatively effective cover—for the moment.

"Movement?"

"No." She frowned. "Still holding north and east of Caesar's."

"I'm going to make a tour around the area, and let you confirm."

"Thanks." She kept her screen in her lap. "Continue."

She'd been serious about not being distracted this time. "My cover of being here for the security conference should hold up. Unless someone tips the local police department about who I am."

"What's your real-life connection to Redding?"

He nodded. "Way back he was one of my instructors."

She sipped at her milkshake. "Which makes you think your cover is about to blow wide open."

"Ironic, isn't it? Considering what I was sent to do."

"What you *thought* you were sent to do."

"Right." Although he appreciated her quick understanding, affirming his theory of betrayal didn't make it any more comfortable. And with every twist the inevitable conclusion loomed nearer. With Director Casey on his honeymoon and Holt the possible problem, Jason's back was against the wall and he didn't know which way to turn.

He could wave goodbye to his career and any hopes of moving up if he became a suspect in any of these events.

"Did you ever take anyone out by causing a traffic accident?"

"Other than tonight?"

"You didn't kill anyone tonight."

"Not for lack of trying." He hitched a shoulder. "You're thinking of that accident that happened on the interstate two days ago."

"Hours after you arrived, you said."

"Uh-huh."

"My cop buddy said the tire was shot out."

Jason cringed. "Yeah. I had a mission like that once."

"Hold that thought. The vial is moving again,"

Gin said. "I want eyes on this. We need to know if this is the buyer."

There was that *we* again. "Which direction?" He looked around, knowing he wouldn't be able to do much about it immediately. "We could walk faster than this."

"One of us could," she grumbled.

"True. Sorry."

"It's okay. Same side of the street." She pointed, her eyes still on the screen. "Are these places connected?"

He looked through the windshield. At the snail's pace, he had plenty of time to read the signs advertising various slots. "There are all kinds of marketing and security secrets in Las Vegas."

She snorted. "I've heard."

"Think either your seller or buyer likes slots?"

"Huh?" She glanced up and followed his gaze. "That would be lucky. Let's get in there."

"Thought our stench couldn't blend." They both looked pretty much like hell.

"It's slots. No one cares."

"If you say so."

"Which ID do you have with you?"

"Only the FBI one."

"We won't use it unless we have to."

"Planning to wing it again?" he asked, trying

not to sound jealous. The way men reacted to her made him crazy.

"No. Let's check in as the reporter and her strapping husband."

He shot her a look. She winked. "It's true enough. Then you can put me on a slot machine and herd the virus my way. Just for a visual."

"And checking in?"

"Gives us free parking."

"Is the CIA pinching pennies now?"

She nodded, then smacked his shoulder when he laughed. "Be thankful your division is under the budget radar."

"Duly noted." He maneuvered toward the next valet stand.

"Wait," she tapped his leg. "Do you have anything in here that could, umm…"

"Not that they can find."

"Good."

"What about our lack of luggage?"

"We'll worry about that after we find the virus."

"Got it." In other words she really was winging it again. Not that he could blame her—they were running out of options.

He pulled up to the valet stand of the Flamingo and handed over the key, then helped Gin inside to the registration desk. "We had a little mishap on the way from the airport," she said to the clerk. "We lost our luggage and had to wait for a replacement rental car."

"We can send fresh items to your room, if you'd like," the clerk offered.

Gin glanced up at him and he nodded, adding a tired shrug. "That would be wonderful."

He liked her British reporter accent a little too much, and reminding himself to focus on business, he scanned the lobby.

Gin provided a list of needed items to the clerk, accepted the keys and handed him one. Checking her phone, she looked him up and down and brushed at his jacket. "We're as good as it's going to get right now. Let's do this." She hobbled toward the end of a long row of slots.

He set her up with a stack of tokens and she handed him the phone, the tracking signal flashing like a beacon.

He wandered around the slot machines, flanking the signal until he spotted the likely candidate. No one he recognized. Checking faces in the vicinity, and relieved to come up empty, he started the process of herding the target in Gin's direction.

He hovered right behind the guy giving off the signal and pretended to talk on his phone. The guy looked to be in his early twenties and the poster child for nervous. His suit was black, and his skin looked as pale as the white shirt he wore. He moved to a different machine. A moment later Jason followed, pacing up and down the row, pausing at the end to drink a coffee a waitress brought him.

Looking annoyed and a little nervous, the guy sporting the signal moved toward Gin's row. For a second Jason thought he wouldn't have to show the badge or gun. Then his next visual sweep landed on the blonde who had drugged him at the bar and had tried to break into the penthouse. Who was bankrolling this woman to be the common denominator between Gin's walkabout virus and the sniper imitating him? And who was she informing about their actions?

He bent down, pretending to find a token on the floor, and hurried after the beacon on Gin's tracking app.

He tapped the shoulder of the guy giving off the signal and made a clumsy offer of the token that revealed the gold shield at his waist. "You dropped this," he said, holding it out.

"Not mine," his target grumbled.

"I saw it fall." Jason was earnest and sincere as he subtly nudged the guy back toward the row where Gin was waiting.

"You can keep it."

"No, I can't." Jason leaned close and confided

the truth. "I'm an officer of the court. Just here on a tip."

The ploy worked. The guy, who was basically a rookie kid, blanched and stutter-stepped backward. "I don't want to be involved with anything."

Jason caught Gin's sly expression over his shoulder as she trapped him.

"Oh, but you already are," she said with no discernible dialect.

"No." The kid looked around. "No. I'm just on vacation. I swear it."

Gin met his gaze and shook her head. "It takes all kinds. Come over here with us for a minute."

"I—I can't. I have to get out of here. You should get out of here."

His eyes were wide with panic now, and his gaze was darting all over the place.

"In just a few minutes," Jason amended. "We think you might know who we're looking for. We can do this here or at the bar."

"Here," Gin corrected with a glare.

The guy looked ready to burst into tears as she pushed him down onto the nearest stool and helped him play.

Gin fed the tokens and asked questions while Jason kept an eye out for the blonde or anyone with too much interest in the three of them.

"Are you the buyer?"

He shook his head.

"A courier for the buyer?"

"Look happy," Jason ordered as the machine paid out.

The resulting smile on the kid's face was closer to a grimace, but it was an admirable attempt.

"Keep playing. And relax," Jason suggested. "How'd you get the package?"

"Look, I'm just a bellhop at the Palace. A woman gave it to me. Told me to carry this thing—"

"What thing?"

"In my pocket."

Jason pulled it out, showed it to Gin and replaced it when she nodded.

"I was just supposed to carry it around for a few hours. Work my way down the Strip."

"And if you didn't agree?"

"If I don't make it to The Sahara by five o'clock this morning, they won't pay me. I need the money to get clear with my bookie."

Jason met Gin's gaze and knew they were thinking the same thing again. This had been another test to see how they'd respond. He was tired of getting jerked around by Isely and his crew.

Jason patted the guy on the shoulder. "Who's meeting you at five?"

"The woman who gave it to me said she'd be there."

"And she's been following you?"

"I think so."

"Stalking men—her favorite hobby," Gin said.

"When it's time to move on I'll get a text."

"Give my friend the package," Gin ordered.

Jason handed Gin the small case, which resembled an EpiPen a person might use for an allergic reaction, and then sent her a questioning look over the kid's shoulder. She ignored him.

"You just keep doing as she says."

"What about when I have to give it back?"

"Give her this."

Jason couldn't see what Gin dropped into the guy's pocket. He wasn't sure he wanted to know.

"Now go on and do your thing. When she pays you, settle your debt and then take a couple days off work."

All three of them played in silence for a few minutes before they told the kid to move on. Jason shifted to take the machine next to Gin's. "What did you give him?"

"A benign duplicate of the vial he is supposed to be carrying. No way to tell the difference until they go to use it. Or check the tracking tag."

"Why? Don't you want the buyer?"

"Not really. Other agencies can handle that. I

just needed to know where it is. Now the virus is with me and off the market."

"So you're done?" The realization landed like a sucker punch across his jaw. His ears were actually ringing and not just with the random bells and slot machine sound effects.

"Are you okay?"

"Yeah, sure." He stood up. "Just tired. It's been a hell of a day."

"You're right." But she fed another token into the machine and watched it play. It didn't win. She repeated the process.

"Do you want help up to your room?"

"My room? Not *our* room?"

Her expression was inscrutable. Any attempt to interpret it would only be skewed by his desire for her and what might have been if they were normal people.

The last thing he wanted was to leave her, yet...the best thing for her safety was for him to walk away. They'd been in more trouble together than either of them had been alone. Well, aside from the woman who'd drugged him. If he knew Gin was safely in her room, he could tail the woman and find out who hired her to get him out of the way.

"You want to go after her without me." Gin wasn't asking.

"No."

She drilled a finger into his chest. "Yes you do. I can see it all over your brooding face."

He trapped her hand against his chest. "You can't walk and you've got what you came for. Your best bet is to rest up and then get out of town."

"No one tells me what I can and can't do. I am perfectly capable of seeing this through."

Exasperated, he rolled his eyes. "Gin, you just said you were done."

"Assuming my precautions work, and they will, Isely can't track his product anymore. I am done." Her eyes flashed. "Which means I've got all kinds of time to help you with your problem."

"Not tonight, dear," he said through gritted teeth. He jerked his chin, trying to make her see the people staring at them.

"But we know where she'll be and when," Gin countered. "Her repeated involvement means something."

He shook his head. "Another hired hand."

"Come on. I'm just getting my second wind."

"Go to the room now or I'll toss you over my shoulder and tuck you into bed myself."

"Promises, promises." Her eyes locked with his, she deliberately dropped another token in the machine.

He wasn't sure what possessed him to do it,

but he couldn't let the dare in her eyes ride. Even as the payout began pouring from the machine, he scooped her into his arms.

"Wait! We won!"

"Looks that way."

"Just let me collect."

"Nope. Let someone else enjoy it. We have other things to do." She kicked her feet and squirmed, apparently all deals about how they'd behave in public forgotten. "Just married," he said with a wink for the closest group of people gawking at the scene they were making.

"Stop," he muttered close to her ear. "Or I'll drop you and you can't outrun me on that foot, which means when I catch you, you'll go over my shoulder."

She glared at him but went still, even wrapping an arm around his neck as he headed for the bank of elevators. It made carrying her easier, but he didn't think she was done fighting.

Not a problem. He wasn't ready to quit, either.

"Put me down," she said when they were alone in the elevator.

"No." He didn't trust her not to take a cheap shot.

"That scowl of yours doesn't scare me."

He kept his gaze on the screen showing the elevator's upward progress. "Maybe it should." He didn't know what he meant to do—only that he wanted her out of the casino, out of danger. It had been nothing but one problem on top of another since they started this married farce this morning and second wind or not, she needed rest.

It wasn't over. She wasn't walking away from this until he said so.

Chapter Fifteen

Gin tried to stay mad, but it was becoming more of a challenge with each passing second. Not even thinking of the coins she had left pouring from the slot machine squashed the excitement kicking through her bloodstream. The sexual energy was rolling off him like a cloud of steam. Her body was only too happy to respond in kind.

"This Neanderthal routine is not cute."

"No one's ever accused me of cute," he said without looking at her.

His refusal to make eye contact frustrated her. She wanted those rich brown eyes—and much, much more—on her. What started as a purely feminine appreciation when she'd undressed him last night had grown into a serious craving. The elevator rushed closer to their floor and her pulse rushed along with it. This close to him, the smooth, warm scent she recognized as all Jason teased her nose under the lingering bits of fire and hotel soap.

The doors parted and she nearly whimpered aloud when she felt the strength of his arms and abs flexing as he carried her to the room.

"Key."

She fished it out of his jacket pocket and pushed it into the lock. At the green light, she turned the handle and he kicked the door wide to carry her inside.

"That's becoming a habit," she teased when he set her gently on her feet.

"What do you mean?"

His confusion showed on his face and gave his frustration a target other than her. She should have been grateful for the reprieve. Should have been immune to the urge to soothe him. Nurture wasn't her strong suit.

"You insisted on doing the same thing last night after the wedding. Not all the way from the chapel—just when we reached the room," she explained. "You carried me over the threshold."

"I don't remember that."

"It was fun. *You* were fun."

"Fun." He grunted.

She nodded. She'd told some big fat lies in her career, but this one had to be the worst. Last night he'd been so loopy she worried he wouldn't pull out of his drug-induced haze.

"Have I wounded your pride?" She licked her lips, eager to see what he'd do about it.

He shoved his hands in his jacket pockets. "You should rest."

"That's why you brought me up here. To rest."

He jerked his chin affirmatively, but he refused to look at her, studying a spot just over her head.

"I told you I'm not tired."

"No. It's obvious you're wired from your success. You should sleep it off."

"We both know that's unlikely." She tugged on the zipper of his open jacket, running it up and back down again, the back of her hand brushing against his shirt. "If you won't let me help you track down the woman, you'll have to let me help with something else."

He twitched, not quite a flinch, when she tugged his shirt from his jeans and ran her fingertips along his warm skin just above his waistband. She wanted tonight to be something to take with her when this was over. She'd wanted it since spotting him last night at the bar.

Or maybe she'd wanted it since she ran into him in Colorado last month.

"We both could use a shower."

She shrugged out of her denim jacket and let it fall to the floor. His eyes tracked her movements as she unbuttoned her jeans and pushed the zipper down. Grateful for the smaller room, she hid the pain of her aching foot behind a smile as she walked backward toward the shower.

"Come on, Jason." *Why wouldn't he make a move?* She reached in and turned on the shower, then peeled off her sweater. "Come have some fun with your wife."

At the last word, his dark eyes flared and he advanced, stripping away his jacket and shirt as he rushed toward her.

She reached back to unhook her bra, but he caught her in that awkward position, arched her back a little more and bent his head to her breasts. His mouth, warm and wet, worked her nipple into stiff, needy peaks through the sheer fabric of her bra. She twisted a hand free and pushed her fingers through his thick sable hair, desperate for more.

He'd been tempting enough when he was incapacitated; she could hardly stand it now that he seemed ready to do all the things he thought they'd done last night.

She moaned a little as he shifted his attention to her other breast and she gripped his strong shoulders in an effort to keep her balance. Caught between the steam of the hot shower and the wall of heat Jason provided, her desire spiked to unprecedented levels. She pushed her jeans down over her hips then struggled to step out of them with her sore foot.

Jason knelt down and carefully resolved the problem, taking time to feather kisses over her midriff and thighs as he did. He slid a finger between her skin and the sheer fabric of her panties then slowly pulled them down and away.

Naked in front of him, she'd never felt more exposed or a more delicious anticipation. She experienced a sensory overload as he stood up, his rough jeans against her legs, his big hands trailing little fires over her skin.

His mouth closed over hers and she opened to him fully, her hands fumbling with his jeans. He nudged her back just so he could tug them off, then he nabbed a condom from his wallet. Watching him put it on was one of the sexiest things she'd ever watched.

He lifted her against his chest and stepped into the shower, the hot water cascading over their bodies.

He boosted her up and she wrapped her legs around his waist. He reached down and stroked her until she was rocking against his hand and using the last of her abused voice to beg him for more.

"Look at me," he said, his voice as hoarse as hers. She pushed her hair back and met his hungry gaze as he entered her slowly. She flexed her hips, so damned impatient for what she knew he could give her.

He obliged, thrusting inside her, and she rocked against him as he set the pace. She watched the water bead against his skin and she leaned forward, licking it away.

He nipped at her ear and whispered words she couldn't make out over the rush of water and the pounding of her blood through her veins. Her climax rolled through her and over him and she clung as he stroked into her twice more and then joined her in that place of pure sensation.

His breath sawing in and out of his lungs teased her breasts as his chest pressed against her. She sighed when he parted from her and lowered her legs to the shower floor, making sure she was steady.

Her knees were weak and her pulse didn't want to stop racing. She nudged him under the spray of the shower and indulged herself with washing his body. When they swapped places she discovered it was equally exciting to be on the receiving end of such tender treatment.

She never expected these feelings, never experienced this level of a connection with a lover. With a glance at the ring circling her finger, she wondered if the slim gold band was playing tricks on her mind. Tricks her heart was only too happy to fall for.

"Hey, where'd you go?" He traced the curve of her shoulder. "You'll give a guy a complex."

"Not you."

"You tired?"

She walked her fingers up his biceps. "Not even close."

"There's some good news." He grinned and kissed her as he reached around to shut off the faucet. She let him wrap her in one of the thick towels and was about to tease him when he kissed her so thoroughly she would have been hard pressed to remember her real name.

It was a heady sensation, to be swept away by the moment and the man guiding her through it. He lowered her to the bed without letting loose of the contact of their mouths.

"Jason."

"Hmm?"

She didn't know what to say, couldn't remember why speaking was important. She explored his stunning body as he touched hers, slowly stoking her passion and leading her up to another climax. Her entire world zeroed down to him. The concerns of the case—hers and his— fell away to a hazy place in the back of her mind and she forgot whatever she'd intended to say.

That had never happened to her, no matter the

personal involvement or isolation during an assignment. But right here, they were two normal people sharing something extraordinary.

When their bodies joined again, it was with a steady rhythm, less frantic, but just as intense and passionate. And when at last they parted, she curled next to his side, his heart beating strong under her hand as she let sleep claim her.

JASON, MORE THAN a little overwhelmed by what they'd just shared, let her sleep. Intoxicating didn't begin to describe her. He wanted to tell himself he should have resisted, but it would have been a waste of energy.

He was no stranger to temptation, but she'd been utterly irresistible. Already, his mind turned over the immediate and long-term options. They might be married, but would she want to stay that way?

It wasn't just the physical connection. Smoothing her hair back from her cheek, he kissed her, smiling as she snuggled closer. Had last night been this way for her? He wished like hell he could remember.

He also loved the way her mind worked, loved her dedication to the job.

Oh, Lord, it hit him like a fist to the gut. He loved *her*. Was there any way to actually make a marriage between them work?

Chapter Sixteen

Saturday, November 22, 9:30 a.m.

Gin awoke with a delicious contentment. She couldn't remember feeling quite this good. Ever. Warm and relaxed, with Jason's masculine scent surrounding her, she reached out. She wanted to indulge herself, to touch him when he wouldn't be awake enough to know how he fascinated her.

Her hand found only air and soft bedding. She sat up, confirmed the bed was empty, then grabbed the bedside clock. Half past nine already?

She pushed her hair behind her ears and, drawing the sheet up to cover herself, leaned against the headboard. He must have gone out to watch the blonde take back the vial.

A thousand dark thoughts and theories raced for dominance in her mind. The thought that wouldn't go away wasn't about the case at all, but rather about Jason.

The man had fooled her completely. Seducing her, lulling her into a deep sleep with his talented hands, then sneaking out to interfere with her case. Damn it!

"You would have done the same," she whispered to the empty room. She had, in fact, been considering it as a viable plan of action. Until somewhere along the way she'd gotten lost and let the fantasy become the reality. She buried her nose in the sheet, inhaling his lingering scent and remembering falling asleep in the perfect security of his embrace.

She swore. If she never saw the man again—and why would she—the past few hours had been worth it. Pragmatist that she was, it no longer mattered which of them was seducer and which one was fool because they'd both managed to win along the way.

Too late to go after him, she headed back to the shower to clean up. Her superiors would want that virus locked up in the lab as soon as possible so no one else could make a play for it.

She stopped, let the sheet fall as she rushed to the chair where she'd dropped her purse last night. It wasn't there. He couldn't have done it. Could he? Her breath stalled in her lungs and her hands fisted in her hair as she tried to think it through.

He wouldn't have done this—had no reason

to do this. But he obviously had. She looked everywhere in the room, but her purse—and the virus—were gone. He was a spy, like her, and sides were never as clear-cut as the lines of white picket fences of happily-ever-afters that had danced through her sappy love-blind dreams last night.

Choice words for Jason Grant rolled through her mind and were nearly out of her mouth when she heard the soft click of the electronic lock on the door.

Caught, she brazened it out, irrationally hoping it was Jason and her raw physical state would divert attention from her raw emotional state.

She enjoyed a fast, grim vision of attacking him for his sneaky betrayal, but it fizzled when he quietly backed into the room towing a hotel luggage cart loaded with everything they'd left behind at the Palace. As he turned to unload the cart, he saw her and almost dropped the white bag in his free hand.

"You're awake." He quickly closed the door behind him.

"I am." She'd gone from angry to shy to needy in such a short span she couldn't keep up with herself. Her head was spinning and her heart was pounding.

Feeling ridiculous modesty under his heated stare, considering all the things they'd done a few hours ago, she couldn't think. "Is that breakfast?" She forced herself to move forward, to smile, as she took the bag and set it on the table. "Smells good."

"I thought you might be hungry."

"In a minute. I was just about to hit the shower."

NOT WITHOUT ME, Jason thought, but he didn't say it. Faced with the stunning beauty of her body, it took him a little longer to process what he'd walked in on. His gut twisted at the reality of what the scene told him. "You thought I left."

She paused, tossed him a look over her shoulder, then turned to face him again. "You weren't here."

He wasn't buying the casual routine she was trying to sell. Trust didn't come easily to either one of them—for good reason. "Your purse is in the room safe."

Her face colored, along with the delectable column of her throat. "Thanks."

"I wanted to put as many layers as possible between that tag and any other tracking device. Especially since you were alone and asleep."

"I appreciate that." She turned on her heel and continued toward the bathroom, where she closed and locked the door.

Jason smiled to himself, more than a little

pleased he'd surprised her. She shouldn't be stuck expecting the worst from everyone she met—especially not from him.

He unloaded the luggage cart and pushed it back into the hallway, relieved beyond measure he'd told the bellhop he could manage on his own. He didn't want anyone else enjoying the view of Gin's amazing body. At least not while she was his wife.

"Fool," he muttered.

Maybe he should have left her a note, but he'd thought it would be a quick trip. As smoothly as the casinos managed people and details, he'd learned the hard way the streets were crowded no matter the hour. Getting sidetracked at the jewelry store hadn't helped his timing. The rings in his pocket would probably get returned when this was over, but he'd bought them anyway. Just in case what they'd shared felt as real to her as it did to him. Sure, the sex had been incredible and he'd be forever grateful for the memory if she did walk away. But the more time he spent with her, the more he realized he wanted whatever they'd started as part of her mission to go beyond that. Infinity might be enough time.

He'd recognized the calculating look in her green eyes when he'd returned. She most likely believed he'd stolen the virus and gone after the blonde.

To be fair, he'd thought about it for all of two seconds. The virus thing was her case, and he didn't need to interfere beyond the point the blonde intersected with his situation.

He carried Gin's suitcase to the bed and then returned to the table to start up his laptop. Getting into the protected systems of the hotel security offices might be a challenge, but he knew he could hack the email of at least one of the reporters covering the shootings.

He heard the bathroom door open and close, but he didn't turn around, didn't want to push her.

"Did you check me out?"

With a laugh, he shook his head, eyes still on the laptop. "Is that a trick question?"

She walked up behind him and gave his shoulders a rub. "I meant did you check me out of the other hotel room at Caesar's."

"No. I thought you might want access."

She bent down and kissed his ear. "You're a smart man."

"I try."

"What's this?" She peered over his shoulder at the screen.

"Grab a coffee and I'll tell you."

"*Mmm.* Okay."

Wrapped in the hotel robe, she pulled a chair around and propped her feet in his lap. He couldn't help but study the purplish bruise on her foot. He didn't touch it though. "Does it hurt?"

"It's not happy, but it'll be fine."

"Do you want ice?"

Her eyes twinkled with a smile over the rim of her coffee cup. "I want to hear what you've been up to."

God, he was starting to like that sly expression. Especially now that it felt like they were on the same side.

"I've been digging through the email accounts of local reporters on the police beat."

She arched an auburn eyebrow.

"Easier than hacking the hotel security feeds."

"If you say so."

"With Redding dead it's past time we find where Frost is hiding."

"And who's giving him the orders and targets."

"We'll get there." Jason nodded. "One step at a time."

She sipped her coffee. "How do the reporter emails help you?"

He sat back and ran a hand up and down her healthy foot as he explained. "I usually use a police scanner app when I'm working, just to get a pulse on the area. This time it was to keep an ear out for trouble that might involve the agent I was sent to assist."

"Not me."

"I think we both agree I've been sent on a wild-goose chase. By reviewing the incidents that caught my attention on the scanner app against the emails, I'm trying to sort out which events might be Frost."

"And…" she prompted.

He turned the laptop so she could see the incidents he'd highlighted. "Three so far."

"Including Redding, who you knew personally."

"Yes."

"There's more?"

"These three incidents loosely mirror my career strikes when I was with Interpol." The words seemed to drag at him. The memory of who he'd once been weighed heavy on his conscience—even if he'd been one of the good guys, so to speak.

She gasped and he was sure she'd recoil, but she only rubbed his arm in a soothing pattern. "You can't blame yourself for a job well done. You have a skill and you applied that skill to the service of your country and the world at large."

He smiled, but the weight of those lives he'd ended was heavier than it had ever been. "I used to think so."

"I know so. Trust me. You can't second-guess missions long over. Water under the bridge, right?"

"Clichés, Gin?"

"If they fit." She held his face close to hers, held his gaze. "We do what must be done, what others can't do. Believe that above all else, Jason, my love."

He knew those last two words weren't the thing to focus on, but he couldn't help it. It took a long moment for him to regain his composure. "With my service record, the Mission Recovery office should have notified me and asked me to look into it. The local media is talking *sniper* this morning. I heard the unofficial reports on several stations on the way back over here."

"If they haven't asked you to look into the rumors by now," she said, her voice somber, "they want you to take the fall."

He nodded, unable to say those words out loud himself. The betrayal stung too much. Of all he'd seen and survived through the military, Interpol and in Mission Recovery, this felt like the worst way to go out.

He shrugged. "I can disappear for a while."

"You can't believe your own office is picking off innocent people to get rid of you."

"I don't want to believe it, but not many people can access my full service record. Re-creating the beach strike at the pool..." He hated revisiting that scene because it filled him with irrational fear for Gin. He rubbed her foot. She was alive and well and they would get through this. "I think you should leave town now that your mission's accomplished."

She froze, her eyes wide. "Where is my phone?" She looked around.

"Must be in your purse. Why?"

She scrambled to her feet, sloshing coffee across the hotel robe in her rush to reach the safe. He was about to tell her the code when she typed in his birthday and the door swung open.

Too bad this wasn't the time to point out how in tune they were. "What's wrong?" he asked, coming up beside her.

"I haven't checked my email. But you're right. Those incidents would get attention, and any assets nearby would be called in to investigate. They'd never let local law enforcement try to handle you, I mean Frost, alone."

She pulled her purse from the safe and sat down right there in the closet doorway. "I don't have any new emails about a sniper or you in particular. Now that's weird. If the rumors of a sniper are making the media rounds, *they* have to know."

"What does that mean?"

"Only one thing I can think of," she said. "They must know we're together."

"But who would know that? Who told them?" He looked at her and they said it at the same time.

"The blonde."

"She dressed like me that night, and I don't think it was coincidence. We have to track her down and find out who hired her."

"She's a pawn." Jason shook his head. "I'm more concerned about who hired Frost and how they dug up my career history. If I'm right about mimicking the pattern, the next hit will take place somewhere at the Paris."

"What?"

"A club strike in Paris was my next mission after the Riviera."

"Same woman?"

"Still classified."

"My clearance is up-to-date and higher than yours, I bet."

"I'm not taking the bait."

"Then at least take my help."

"I don't want you to get hurt."

"Jason." She glared at him. "Having sex doesn't turn me into something fragile."

"I know that." He pushed a hand through his hair. "It's just—"

"Whatever it is, get over it. I'm not leaving you to deal with this alone. Call it jealousy if you like, but I'm not letting that bimbo get her claws into you."

He chuckled. "Jealous?"

She opened her mouth and quickly snapped

it shut. He could almost see the tirade ready to trip off her tongue.

He reached for her, but she dodged him. "Oh, no you don't." He faked one way and caught her when she fell for it. Bringing her up against his body ignited his senses. "You accused me of the same last night."

"And I believe you denied it."

"My mistake." Slowly he lowered his mouth to hers for a lingering kiss. Reluctantly, he eased back, pleased to see his own emotions reflected in the dazed green pools of hers. "No one but you is invited to get their claws in me." He wrapped her hair around his finger.

She swallowed. "Glad to hear it." She slipped her arms around his waist, linking her hands at his back. "Now, will you accept my assistance graciously, or will I be forced to coerce you?"

His curiosity piqued. "What methods of coercion are you considering?"

"That's for me to know and you to find out." She winked at him then stepped back. Her hands went to the tie of her robe and when he followed the movement, she laughed. "Get your mind back on the case, Specialist Grant. I'm going to dress while you tell me about Paris."

"Right." He would be sure to get even for that little bit of teasing later. "It was a night strike outside of a busy club. Night was the only thing that made it possible."

"The target?"

He returned to his computer. It was the only sane move. Watching her dress was far too distracting.

"Mid-level arms dealer."

He knew she'd stopped moving, knew she was thinking the same thing he'd thought at the time. The mid-level guys usually gave up their bosses for the right incentives.

"Can I borrow your computer?"

He nudged his laptop toward the chair she returned to. "Checking the local registry for arms dealers who like to gamble?"

"Close." Her fingertips flew across the keyboard. "You're not the only one with access to databases." She finished and leaned back in the chair. "So if you were tasked with replicating Jason Grant's biggest hits, how would you do that here?"

"If I'm not after anyone specific..." His voice trailed off as he put his hands on the keyboard. "I could ask the analyst at the office to check the registry at the resorts closest to monorail stops. There might be a bigger fish than Isely taking a holiday, and Frost would have to stay close in order to get in and out."

"True." She stopped him with a gentle touch

on his arm. "But let's hold off on that for a few minutes. Follow the nonspecific solution. What would you do in Frost's place?"

"Okay." He sighed, closed his eyes and put himself back in that world. "I'd perch on a rooftop at least a block away and take out the target while he was waiting in line. Chaotic, crowded, instant panic means I get away clean."

"So we can go clubbing at the Paris tonight."

He slanted her a look that warned he wasn't so sure that was such a good idea.

"Don't argue. I'll get dressed and then we can go over and poke around, study the skyline, do the tourist thing."

"You're forgetting I have a tee time at eleven and you were going to have a facial."

"So we cancel both. You might get lucky and stop Frost before he can get set up."

Jason checked the time. "We can walk through, but I have to get some fresh air and sunshine before I lose my mind."

"That's fine, sweetheart. We'll just pick up some golf clothes."

He eyed her suitcase.

"Don't judge me. I can hardly go out in that bikini you bought or any of the cocktail dresses I packed."

"That sparks a few interesting images. The club would have a fit." He held up his hands in surrender. "I get it." The image of her playing golf in that bikini danced through his head, making him smile. "The Paris has stores."

"You better believe it."

And, oddly enough, he was looking forward to spoiling her. While they searched for Frost's nest, of course.

Chapter Seventeen

Gin wasn't sure what was an act and what was real anymore. Especially since Jason had walked through that door with her luggage and breakfast and been kind enough not to alter her original reservation at the Palace.

Well, he was turning into a man her mother referred to as a keeper. Until Jason, she'd given up on the idea that men like him even existed anymore.

But here he was in the flesh, doting on his *wife* with the best of everything from golf gloves to shoes. The lingering glances and breathtaking kisses made the sales clerks swoon with envy.

She could get used to this.

Yesterday she might have thought it was all an act. Today she was all too aware of how real she wanted it to be.

Oh, she kept an eye out for Isely, the blonde woman or other faces she might recognize from either the criminal world or the spies who tried to counter their moves. Beside her, she knew he did the same.

Once they finished shopping, they strolled hand in hand through the resort, cruising by the inside entrance of the club. "He could set up in here just as easily," she observed, looking up at the elaborate architecture.

"I see that," he replied. "Let's go be tourists," he whispered at her ear.

"Right." She should be used to the tiny shivers created by his touch. With sunglasses on, they left the climate-controlled casino for the bright Nevada sunshine. "Wow," her eyes watered. "I either need more coffee or more sleep."

He squeezed her hand. "I vote for more coffee."

"You're greedy."

"For you, always."

The words shouldn't matter so much to her, but they did. She jerked her attention back to business. "Look." She turned their joined hands toward the club entrance.

"Yeah, I noticed." He raised his camera and took snapshots of the most famous rooflines and facades in the heart of the Strip.

She could tell by his tone it didn't make him happy. "There are a dozen places he could hide and reach anyone waiting in that line tonight."

"Uh-huh." Their reconnaissance complete, he

guided her back to their hotel to pick up the car and head out to the golf course.

"But you're thinking."

"Only about you, sweetheart."

"Not buying it," she said, leaning into him.

"I'm thinking about the course. It's a tough nine we're about to play." He handed over the valet ticket, and the young man went racing off to find their car.

"I'll probably double bogey everything." She knew he wanted to wait until they were in the car and couldn't be overheard. They chattered on about golf until they were safely in their vehicle and could speak freely.

"Weren't you nervous standing around outside? He might already be in his chosen nest."

Jason shook his head, and this time she didn't have to prompt him into talking. It was progress. "Frost has a routine. He'll be sleeping or gambling while he waits for nightfall."

"Where do you think he'll set up the nest?"

"Outside."

She snorted. "Obviously."

Jason turned off the Strip toward the golf club where he'd booked the tee time. "I'm thinking we find a way to close that inside access for the evening."

"You said the club strike was an outside deal."

"Yes, out of necessity." He patted her knee. "The real Paris isn't self-contained like the Paris"

"Low blow," she grumbled. "I'm quite familiar with the real Paris," she said in flawless French.

"Impressive."

"About time you noticed. Why, if Frost is mimicking you, would he take the shot inside?"

"This whole business feels rushed to me. Things are accelerating and none of it adds up. I understand who might win if I'm labeled a loose cannon, but who gained from the hit on Redding?"

"No one has to gain anything—the connection strengthens the case against you."

"Only if you don't know me."

She twisted in her seat. "Are you planning to shut me out again?"

"No." He scowled at the road ahead, clearly lost in thought. "There's nothing in my record that would indicate I'd go off the deep end this way."

"Except the stigma of being a successful sniper."

"Touché."

"Redding was at the convention for a reason. Last I heard he was with a defense contractor working on new technology."

"So?"

"So who loses if new tech helps the good guys?"

"In case you haven't noticed, the bad guys usually adapt faster than the good guys."

"Exactly."

"Jason, I'm not following your logic, if there is any here. Before we realized the pattern, you suggested Frost was here for me."

"That would be nice."

"What?"

"Relax." He reached across the seat and caught her hand. "I only meant that kind of mission would be cut and dried."

"Less than forty-eight hours and my husband already wants me dead."

"You know that's not what I meant."

She chuckled. "I do. But—wedded bliss aside—having been acquainted for such a short time, I'd think being framed for several sniper shots would put you on the offensive."

"This marriage thing rocks." He turned into the long drive leading to the low stone building of the golf club. "You know me far better than whoever is behind this. If the woman at the bar succeeded and the sniper succeeded, and my real name and history came up through the course of the investigation and I didn't have an alibi for Redding's death, I'd disappear, reverse engineer the shooting and call in a few favors to prove my innocence."

"Assuming the woman at the bar hadn't just killed you."

"Well, true. Then all of this speculation is moot. But if they wanted me dead, Frost had the shot at the pool. They want me alive to take the blame."

She nodded. It bothered her when she thought of that moment—not just the near miss for herself, but that the shooter might have simply put the bullet through Jason's head rather than through the deck chair.

Clearing her throat, she tried to keep it professional. "Aside from you being charged with crimes you didn't commit, who is the big loser in that scenario?"

"Mission Recovery." He pulled into a parking space a couple of rows back from the entrance. "After the rumors last month about the director, a rogue Specialist shooting up Las Vegas would be enough to shut us down."

Neither of them moved to get out of the car. "That opens the suspect pool again. Your department must have hundreds of enemies."

"But not all of them have access to my file."

"What are you thinking?"

"Worst case scenario?" He took a deep breath, poking at the key fob and watching it swing from the ignition. "This is an inside job. Someone in Mission Recovery is pulling the strings."

"Finally."

"Finally?"

She shook her head. "I thought you were never going to say it out loud, that you were going to give me some line about old enemies."

"You knew?"

"Not officially, and I was trying not to leap to conclusions. There might be an old enemy in your past."

"No, I don't have those. My missions were long distance, practically hands-off. All of them are still classified. Whoever is behind this has full access to my record. There's no other explanation for the replicated strikes." He slammed his fist against the steering wheel. "We shouldn't be golfing. We should be turning this over to the authorities."

"Later. First you have to stop Frost. You're the only one who can find him."

"That would be easier if we weren't in Las Vegas, land of a gazillion hotels and nearly guaranteed anonymity."

"Come on." She opened her door. "Let's see if some fresh air and sunshine help you sort this out before nightfall."

"All right. It's not like we have a lot of other

options." He twisted around and flipped up the back seat, withdrawing a pistol. "Let's go."

She grabbed the shopping bag. "All set. When was the last time you picked up a golf club?"

"Beginning of last month," he replied, taking her hand as they crossed the parking lot. "You?"

"Let's just say I'm probably better at shopping." As she'd hoped, her answer had them both smiling when they walked into the cool lobby of the club.

It was easy to be with Jason, and now that he was opening up and trusting her, being partners of a sort seemed like a natural progression. The whole situation made her long for something more permanent.

She was starting to think sentimental was going to be a way of life from here on out. Watching people was part of her job, one she enjoyed and excelled at. She imagined the same was true for Jason.

Is that why he was so good at playing the doting husband? According to that theory, she should be good at portraying an enamored wife. She knew better. Years ago, she'd nearly botched a married cover story because she was too stiff with the agent assigned to be her husband.

But this time, with Jason, they had everyone they encountered convinced of their mutual devotion. Which, she knew, meant she was becoming seriously attached to him.

Not such a bad thing…as long as she wasn't in this attachment thing alone.

Chapter Eighteen

Jason stopped the cart at the ninth tee, reluctant to move because it meant letting go of her hand. There were fewer people to judge the newly-weds out here, but by now they both knew he liked touching her.

If all went well tonight, they had a date with a divorce drive-through and he might never see her again. He didn't like way his stomach clutched at the thought.

"I should tell you something." She squeezed his hand. "Promise you won't interrupt?"

"Promise."

She took a deep breath. "There's two things. First, the morning after I saved you, I got an alert about a sniper in Vegas."

Jason kept his mouth shut—he'd promised to listen—but he pulled his hand from hers. He could tell he wasn't going to like whatever she was about to say.

"The police hadn't yet announced anything official about Redding and you were right there with me, so I knew it wasn't you."

He stepped out of the cart and walked back to get their drivers.

"Jason?"

"I'm listening." Except he wasn't. She'd done a fine job pretending she hadn't known anything about the sniper in Vegas. Acting was part of the job description for covert agents, but suddenly he didn't know if anything they'd shared had any meaning. She might as well have punched him in the gut.

How many ways could he screw up on this assignment? First he let a stranger drug him, then he let Elvis marry him, and now he'd let Gin put her life on the line.

She accepted the club he handed her. "Did you know he was in town?"

He stared at her. "Are you asking if I was tasked with removing him?"

"Is that what you call it?"

He sneered. "In polite company." He bent down to put his tee in the ground. "Why does it matter? We both know I didn't shoot him. You went through my belongings. Did you find a dossier or ammunition?"

"Lower your voice," she snapped in a whisper, glancing around. "You know I didn't."

The fact that she didn't deny performing the search made it worse somehow. As if being dragged to the altar while he was out of his mind on a drug wasn't enough of a problem.

He battled against the anger building inside him. Not because she'd lied—that was a frequent necessity—or even that she'd married him—apparently that was her best option at the time. No, he was furious because knowing there was a sniper in the area, she'd put herself in danger.

To protect him.

"You interfered—"

"They were setting you up!"

"—and willfully made yourself a target," he said over her justification.

She took a practice cut with the driver, then let the club swing from her hand. Her sunglasses hid her eyes, but it was a safe bet she was considering the appeal of bashing him over the head with it.

He couldn't blame her. Not for that anyway.

"Don't pretend it was about me." He told himself to shut up, but he just kept talking. "You like the rush of cheating death. Crave it."

"That's what you think of me?"

He jerked his chin in the affirmative. It wasn't even close. Professionally, operatives with that attitude didn't survive, and personally...he couldn't risk thinking personally right now.

She pursed her lips. "I see." She waved a hand toward the fairway. "Carry on or we'll soon be holding up the group behind us."

Though he heard the faint lilt in her voice that revealed how hard she was working to hold onto calm, Jason couldn't seem to stop himself. "What else are you keeping from me?"

"Oh, that's more than enough." She slammed her club to the ground. "I don't have to tolerate this." She started marching away toward the clubhouse.

He let her go. She had the right idea. They both needed to cool off, and some distance would give him a chance to get a grip on the irrational distraction about what would happen when they were done here.

So much for the happy couple cover, he thought as she stalked up the small rise. What was *wrong* with him? They couldn't afford to split up—not before he stopped Frost and they turned in the virus.

"Gin! Wait!"

She broke into a run.

Swearing a blue streak at his stupidity, he jumped into the golf cart and raced after her.

But the battery was fading and with a head

start fueled by temper, she was getting away even with an injured foot.

Hopping out of the useless cart, he chased after her. In the back of his mind he wondered if the casino had a couple's therapist on call. They had everything else.

He'd almost reached her when the turf flew up in front of him and just to her left. Bullet. Had to be. The breeze had carried it just wide of her.

"Down," he barked.

But she stood there, frozen in place, a perfect target even an average shooter could pick off. He didn't need to see her face to know it was blank with shock. A second bullet sent gravel spraying out of the landscaping to their left.

He couldn't be sure which of them was the real target, but it hardly mattered. They were out here with zilch for cover and he couldn't live on the hope that the next shot would miss. Whoever was behind the trigger was either impatient or new to the job. On his worst day, Frost would have tagged them both by now.

Of all the gambles in his career, all the hunches, everything that mattered was riding on this one. If they could make it to the clubhouse, or at least the deep sand trap, they had a chance.

Jason surged up behind Gin and forced her toward the sand trap and what he hoped was the better safety of the clubhouse beyond.

The sniper squeezed off two more shots before Jason shoved Gin deep into the bunker. It was a guess, based on the angle, but pressed against the carved-out edge, he thought they were out of harm's way.

For the moment.

He fumbled for his phone and dialed 911, reporting a shooting at the golf course as if he'd been a witness and not the potential target.

"Thank you," Gin said, tucked between him and the sand. "I can't believe I froze."

He looked down into her clear green gaze, grateful her sunglasses had been lost in the scramble. He kissed her lightly. "It happens."

"But it's not the first time I've been shot at. Not even this week."

"I'm aware of that," he said through gritted teeth.

She pulled him down for a more thorough kiss. "I am not an adrenaline junkie."

"I know. I was just so mad thinking you put yourself at risk for me on purpose."

"Don't flatter yourself."

"Hey. You married me."

"Well, sort of anyway."

"What's that mean?"

"I'll tell you later."

"Now is good."

She rolled her eyes and shoved at his shoulder, but when he raised himself up and off of her, she yanked him back down. "No. He might try again."

Jason smiled, understanding the depth of her concern completely. "Does that mean you don't want to be a widow?"

"Not today." Her smile was soft and full of an emotion he wasn't sure he wanted to decipher. "How do you think Frost got back on task so fast?" she asked.

"This wasn't him. He never works alone." He told her about his interpretation of the misses being impatience and poor timing. "Frost wouldn't make that mistake. Whoever just fired at us didn't allow for wind," he added. "And as far as I can tell, he doesn't care which one of us dies."

"That's new."

"Agreed." Sirens wailed in the distance. He wanted to get up and snag one of the bullets for closer inspection before the crime scene techs stashed them into evidence bags. "Maybe we're a two-for-one special because we're married." Hearing shouts from the clubhouse, he decided they were safe enough. "Come on."

"Jason." Her voice cracked on his name.

"What's wrong?" He reached down to help her up, but she held up bloodstained fingers.

"You're hit." Fear roared through him.

She shook her head. "No, it's you."

He felt fine, but she rolled to her feet and ripped open his shirt. "This kind of thing should wait until we're back in our room," he said.

She batted his hands away, clearly not amused, when she spotted the injury.

He shushed her when she gave a panicked shout for help. "It's just a scratch, Gin. I can't even feel it."

"Sit down."

"I'm not going to pass out." He walked out of the sand trap, buttoning his shirt as he went. "It's nothing." Now that she pointed it out, it had started to sting, but it wasn't a big deal. "We need a look at one of the rounds."

"Now who's the adrenaline junkie?"

"I would still vote for you," he said with a warm smile. He knelt by one of the furrows in the turf and used the pencil to dig the bullet out so he could look at it. "That's what I thought."

She crouched beside him. "Different ammo?"

"Definitely. This isn't the .338 Frost would use for a shot like this. I'm probably the only person other than Frost or Wallace who knows that. And Frost never works alone, remember? Last I checked no one had posted Wallace's bond on the burglary charge."

"Which means?"

"Whoever hired Frost has taken matters into his own hands."

"That implies a certain desperation. Why take the risk?"

"That's the million-dollar question, isn't it?"

He could tell from the look on her face that they were thinking the same thing. Only two men knew his past well enough to create such a viable and elaborate setup. One of them was on his honeymoon. The other had ordered him to sit in a Vegas casino and wait for a contact.

A contact that might have led to his incarceration, or even his death, if not for Gin's timely arrival at the bar.

Could Emmett Holt really be in league with Isely? Jason didn't want to believe it and refused to say it aloud. It would make it too real. Still, he had to get this information to the director. The way Washington politics operated, even in agencies that didn't officially exist, the rumor alone would be enough to crush Mission Recovery.

Why would Holt want to do that?

"Killing both of us expedites something we're not seeing. But we survived, which means Frost has to go through with the club strike tonight in order to finish the setup on me."

"Shh." She gave him a little shake. "The authorities are here. Let's give a bystander statement and get back to the room," she said, rubbing her hand over his shoulder. "I can clean you up as well as any paramedic."

"Sure." He pressed a hand to the wound. "One favor?"

"Anything."

"Update Camp about the inside job theory."

"Are you sure?"

Jason nodded. "Do it now. He'll tell Director Casey. And he's the only person I can trust right now."

"I'll take care of it," she promised.

They answered the questions for the police, and Jason relented when the paramedics insisted on treating him. He refused any painkillers or to be transported to the hospital. He just wanted to get back to the room and figure out which angle Frost would take for tonight's strike. That would require a clear head.

Chapter Nineteen

Flamingo resort,
8:52 p.m.

Jason and Gin had talked it through, analyzed the best intelligence offered from his friend in Interpol and her support team and developed a plan. Jason didn't like that she'd be in the mix—alone—her life as likely as any other for Frost to end, but it had to be done.

When he walked out of their room in a few minutes they might not meet again until the divorce. If he succeeded tonight—and he had to succeed—he'd be spending the night with the local police offering up evidence.

If she followed her standard procedure, she'd leave town to track the last of the virus vials and Isely. His new goal was to change her plan.

"So if I understand you," Jason said as he dressed for a night leaping rooftops, "sort of married means we've been living in sin these past few days?"

"Well, it is Sin City." Dressed for a night of clubbing, Gin sat back on the bed and he watched her twist the wedding band on her finger. Her foot was still a little swollen but she insisted on dressing the part. "Would it have been so bad if it was real?"

It would be the best thing that ever happened to him, Jason thought, but he didn't say the words. Studying her, he saw the price of asking was clear in her eyes. Nothing they'd faced in the past two days had put that vulnerability in her eyes. Only the possibility of his rejection.

Here was a woman he admired for her calm under fire and quick mind. A woman he trusted despite her tricks and the shadowy elements inherent to their line of work. Here was the woman he loved above all else.

For a man trained to work alone, it was a big change to admit he needed her. More than that, he wanted her. Now. Always.

He stepped close and reached out to trail a finger across her collarbone. He wanted to press a kiss to the spot he knew would raise goose bumps across her body, but he restrained himself. They had a lifetime ahead of them.

"Is that a proposal? It's not very romantic." He shrugged. "Just saying."

She cocked an eyebrow, clearly annoyed, and he almost cheered that he knew her every expression—or lack thereof—so well.

"Traditionally, proposing is the man's job."

"It's a little late for tradition in our case, don't you think?"

"Maybe," she admitted, the brief flare of bravado flickering back to vulnerable.

He almost relented and dropped to one knee, but she'd jerked him around so much at the start of all of this, he was due a little fun of his own.

If she was ready to make this official, he knew just what he had to do as soon as they captured Frost. He had tickets for an Alaskan cruise on hold along with an engagement ring and wedding bands engraved with Celtic warrior knots. He couldn't wait to see her face when he slipped it on her finger. He'd arranged to have them married by the ship's captain, but if she had something else in mind, he'd happily adjust his plan.

"Are you going to answer me?"

"Just as soon as you ask me the only question that matters."

Her tempestuous emerald gaze might well have killed him if such a thing were possible. He rocked back on his heels, smothering a laugh.

"Fine."

That one word, bearing a faint trace of her Irish blood, told him how much this meant to her. It was all he could do to keep from blurting out the question himself.

She took his left hand in both of hers and ran her thumb over the plain gold of the wedding band he already wore. When she looked up, her heart was shining in her eyes.

"Jason Grant, if you'll be my husband, meet me at this address tomorrow afternoon." She pressed a card into his palm, then a soft kiss to his lips, preventing him from answering. "Now let's go get this bastard."

Las Vegas Strip, 9:24 p.m.

IT SURPRISED HER to be nervous now, standing here in the club line as sniper bait, when she hadn't been nervous before in too many situations just like this to list. Not to mention she hadn't really been nervous when she'd proposed.

Oh God, she had.

Gin took a deep breath and reminded herself to focus. Jason was up there somewhere, ready to spring their trap on Frost. She trusted him completely to manage that before the notoriously accurate sniper ended her life for real this time. She had to believe Jason would prevail, couldn't bear the idea that she'd fallen in love only to die in the line of duty before she had a chance to enjoy it.

She had to believe she'd see him tomorrow.

Scanning the crowded line for a glimpse of Wallace, or whomever Frost might have been forced to help him misdirect the investigators who would be saddled with this crime, she was as surprised as everyone else when a neon sign across the street burst into a showy display of sparks.

People stared upward, but Gin sheltered her eyes and watched for anything out of place around her. She spotted the blond woman scurrying to catch a taxi across the street and smothered a shocked cry when she fell to the ground.

Had Jason taken that shot? *No.* He was a professional. But Gin knew the plan, knew Jason was on one of the rooftops on her side of the Strip taking aim at Frost—if he'd located him—who would be eyeing the crowd around her.

Police cars and emergency vehicles screamed to a stop in front of the Palace and fanned out. A helicopter lit up the rooftops on her side of the Strip with a roving spotlight until it found its target and held steady.

She sighed, moving with the crowd and squinting up at the lights and drama going on overhead. Of course, she realized it now. Jason had tricked her, and he'd done it so smoothly that she could only give him bonus points.

His assignment after the Riviera must not have

been Paris after all. By putting her here, he'd effectively put her out of Frost's reach while he'd gone hunting on his own. She didn't like it, but she had to admit he'd been damn clever about it.

A voice barked orders from the helicopter, but here on the ground with the clamoring crowd, the words were impossible to make out. She could only imagine what was going on up there on the rooftop.

Suddenly the spotlight went dark, thanks to a bullet from Frost no doubt, but she caught the two muzzle flashes from the rooftop of the casino just up the block from the Palace. Gin held her breath. Had Jason just put Frost out of commission? Likely with the same ammunition Wallace had tried to plant as evidence against him.

When nothing moved and no other shots were fired, she relaxed. Jason had done it. Wrapped his case with an elegant symmetry she appreciated despite her strong objection to his overprotective methods.

It was a detail they would have to work out. If he had the guts to show up and marry her tomorrow, it would prove his dedication and courage. He had to know that after pulling this stunt, she'd be hard pressed not to rough him up a little before the ceremony. The man had to learn to respect her ability to watch out for herself and handle things on her own.

"Your new husband's handiwork?"

Recognizing Isely's cultured voice, she turned to face him. She'd been so distracted, it wasn't a shock that he'd managed to sneak up on her. She ordered her heart rate to slow and slipped into operation mode. "I'm not married." *Yet.* She slid her clutch over her left hand. "What do *you* want?"

"Merely to say hello. You are a hard woman to track," he said his appreciative gaze sweeping her from head to toe. "I believe I prefer you as a blonde."

"Too bad."

"It is." The crowd shifted again as people tried to get a better look at the commotion across the street.

"Thanks for making my Vegas vacation so exciting," she said, daring to challenge him even as her nerves jangled.

"It was a pleasure. You have played a good game, my dear, but now I would like my product."

She laughed. "Sorry. It's long gone."

He gazed at her purse then leaned in close. "My intel suggests it's right here."

She muttered under her breath and Isely had the audacity to scold her for her foul language. "Fine. Here. You win." She shoved her glittery clutch into his chest. "It goes better with your tux anyway."

When the crowd shifted again, she slipped along with it, ignoring the persistent ache in her foot. Putting distance between her and Isely and the vial of hair gel she'd changed out for the real virus was essential. He might have back-tracked the tag, but she'd had one trick left.

She grinned. Just for him.

As much as she wanted to stay and take the guy down personally, it was better to let the casino authorities get the credit. "That man," she pointed in Isely's direction. "He stole my purse!"

And wouldn't they be thrilled by the card-counting app on the phone she'd dropped in his pocket. She watched a moment as security closed in on her nemesis, then she disappeared into the crowd and immediately turned her attention to more important, personal concerns.

Would Jason show up tomorrow or not?

Chapter Twenty

Holt settled into his first-class seat and watched the flight attendant open the small bottle of whiskey and pour it into the glass. "Thank you," he said with a curt nod.

A drink was his best hope of dulling the sharp pain behind his eyes and silencing the little voice in his head berating him for his mistakes. He'd flown in last night only to see the reports of a sniper in custody, but not the one he expected.

Hard to believe Jason Grant had not only slipped through an intricate web relatively unscathed, but come out the other side with a new bride. He checked his watch. They'd be toasting the happy union in just a few more hours.

He recognized the bulk of his irritation stemmed from the failed trip to Vegas. Oh, sure, Mission Recovery had captured a sniper and, with another vial of that dreaded virus off of the black market, the director would count it a victory—personally and professionally.

Any other time Holt would join the celebration, but not this time. He wanted Isely. He'd put every available resource into this operation, and leaving Vegas without a face-to-face meeting put him in the frustrating position of the underdog.

He knew his own team suspected him, was looking over his shoulder and waiting for him to slip up. He'd think less of them if they didn't, but he berated himself for letting things get to such a delicate impasse.

Having to evade both friends and foes made it hard to see which of the dwindling options was best as he moved forward.

"Looks like you dropped your phone, sir."

He frowned as another flight attendant handed him the device. It was a logical assumption because he was the only person in first class so far and the other passengers were boarding through a door behind him. "I would have missed this," he said with a self-deprecating smile. He waited until she walked away before checking the inner pocket of his suit coat where he'd stowed his phone after clearing security. His phone was right there, so what was this?

It vibrated in his hand and the screen showed

an envelope indicating a new text message, but the sender's number was blocked. Holt opened it.

We had a deal.

Furious, Holt started to reply when another message came in.

Last chance.

As if he didn't already know time was running out. Holt kept his cool, though he was tempted to stand up and search the plane until he found the sender. As much as he wanted to believe it was Isely, he knew better. Isely was cocky and determined, but he wasn't dumb enough to lock himself on a plane with Holt for four long hours.

He refused to reply and was about to take the phone apart when another message arrived. This time it was one word, *Beware,* with a picture of Cecelia Manning, Director Thomas Casey's sister.

Holt set the phone carefully on the armrest between the seats and sipped his drink. Whoever Isely sent to watch him would be disappointed. He refused to offer up any kind of reaction.

If Isely was still in the game, he'd soon discover Holt was more than eager to finish it.

He wasn't worried about Cecelia Manning or anyone else.

A smile stretched across his face. "To next time." He toasted the prospect of winning.

He hadn't lost...yet.

Chapter Twenty-One

Happily Ever After Wedding Chapel,
Sunday, November 23, 3:25 p.m.

Gin stood calmly in the waiting room of Happily Ever After wedding chapel, which was just outside the door to the chapel itself, keeping her eyes anywhere but on the front door. She would not be caught pining for him.

Why were the only clocks in Vegas in hotel rooms and wedding chapels? She didn't need a fancy one on the wall, with the hours marked by rosebuds, to know how many minutes had passed.

He was late.

She'd apparently been a fool to think this could work out. She'd compounded that foolishness with this dress and flowers.

Whatever she and Jason had shared over the past days, deception had been a big part of it on both sides. That was no foundation for a marriage, not even a marriage between spies. For a woman who knew how to control her nerves in all circumstances, a woman who'd cheated death a few times over these past days, she couldn't believe she was losing it over a wedding.

Her heart pounded harder with each passing tick of the clock. Her palms were damp and she knew no amount of training would compensate.

Love was the greatest joy and the worst pain she'd ever experienced. She peeked at the clock. Five minutes late. It might as well be a day.

He wasn't coming.

Chin high, she told herself to march over to the desk, take her name off the list and leave. *Just do it and don't think twice. Don't look back.* But her feet, in the shimmery heels she'd picked up last night stayed rooted to the small square of carpet she occupied.

Silly feet. He wasn't coming. He was getting even.

"Miss Olin?"

Oh. Her heart clutched. It was their turn and she had to either tell someone to go ahead of them or she had to just leave. Ridiculous emotions became tears, blurring her vision. She blinked rapidly. She would not leave this place with pathetic smears of mascara trailing down her face.

"Yes?" She managed to get the word past the lump in her throat.

"There's a call for you."

She forced her feet to move closer to the desk, knew it would take her by the wide front window. The jerk she loved probably arranged this so he could watch her misery through a sniper scope.

Deciding she'd use the time off she'd allotted for their honeymoon to track down Jason and make him pay, she accepted the call. "Yes?"

"You look stunning."

She spun toward the window, but her glare faded when she saw him on the other side of the glass. Right there on the sidewalk. Her heart, full of hope, pitched to her stomach in another moment of fear.

"Y-you are coming in?"

His cell phone to his ear, a smile spread slowly across his face and she realized her only foolish thoughts had been her doubts.

"Bet on it. I wouldn't miss this for anything. I was just afraid you'd given up on me and left."

He knew her so well. Her eyes on him, she didn't see the people in his wake until the small lobby was bursting with enthusiastic congratulations for both the mission and the wedding.

"We needed witnesses, right?" Jason introduced her to Director Thomas and his new wife,

Jo, and then she smiled as she recognized Lucas Camp and his wife, Victoria Colby-Camp.

When Jason leaned over the flowers she held in her shaking hands and kissed her, the chapel receptionist scolded him for doing things out of order.

Laughter filled the air as they entered the chapel for the ceremony. They exchanged vows, grinning as each said 'I do' and slid rings onto trembling fingers, all under the caring watch of friends. Gin had never felt more loved.

She truly was Mrs. Grant now. And she'd not only gained a husband, she'd also gained a big family with the Specialists and the Colbys.

* * * * *

LARGER-PRINT BOOKS!
GET 2 FREE LARGER-PRINT NOVELS PLUS
2 FREE GIFTS!

⊞ HARLEQUIN®

INTRIGUE®

BREATHTAKING ROMANTIC SUSPENSE

YES! Please send me 2 FREE LARGER-PRINT Harlequin Intrigue® novels and my 2 FREE gifts (gifts are worth about $10). After receiving them, if I don't wish to receive any more books, I can return the shipping statement marked "cancel." If I don't cancel, I will receive 6 brand-new novels every month and be billed just $5.49 per book in the U.S. or $5.99 per book in Canada. That's a saving of at least 13% off the cover price! It's quite a bargain! Shipping and handling is just 50¢ per book in the U.S. and 75¢ per book in Canada.* I understand that accepting the 2 free books and gifts places me under no obligation to buy anything. I can always return a shipment and cancel at any time. Even if I never buy another book, the two free books and gifts are mine to keep forever.

199/399 HDN F42Y

Name _____ (PLEASE PRINT) _____

Address _____ Apt. # _____

City _____ State/Prov. _____ Zip/Postal Code _____

Signature (if under 18, a parent or guardian must sign) _____

Mail to the Harlequin® Reader Service:
IN U.S.A.: P.O. Box 1867, Buffalo, NY 14240-1867
IN CANADA: P.O. Box 609, Fort Erie, Ontario L2A 5X3

**Are you a subscriber to Harlequin Intrigue books
and want to receive the larger-print edition?
Call 1-800-873-8635 today or visit www.ReaderService.com.**

* Terms and prices subject to change without notice. Prices do not include applicable taxes. Sales tax applicable in N.Y. Canadian residents will be charged applicable taxes. Offer not valid in Quebec. This offer is limited to one order per household. Not valid for current subscribers to Harlequin Intrigue Larger-Print books. All orders subject to credit approval. Credit or debit balances in a customer's account(s) may be offset by any other outstanding balance owed by or to the customer. Please allow 4 to 6 weeks for delivery. Offer available while quantities last.

Your Privacy—The Harlequin® Reader Service is committed to protecting your privacy. Our Privacy Policy is available online at www.ReaderService.com or upon request from the Harlequin Reader Service.

We make a portion of our mailing list available to reputable third parties that offer products we believe may interest you. If you prefer that we not exchange your name with third parties, or if you wish to clarify or modify your communication preferences, please visit us at www.ReaderService.com/consumerschoice or write to us at Harlequin Reader Service Preference Service, P.O. Box 9062, Buffalo, NY 14269. Include your complete name and address.

HILP13R